W9-AYF-382

Fodor's

ESSENTIAL
ITALY

3rd Edition

Fodor's Travel Publications   New York, Toronto, London, Sydney, Auckland
www.fodors.com

Excerpted from *Fodor's Italy*

Be a Fodor's Correspondent

Your opinion matters. It matters to us. It matters to your fellow Fodor's travelers, too. And we'd like to hear it. In fact, we need to hear it.

When you share your experiences and opinions, you become an active member of the Fodor's community. That means we'll not only use your feedback to make our books better, but we'll publish your names and comments whenever possible. Throughout our guides, look for "Word of Mouth," excerpts of your unvarnished feedback.

Here's how you can help improve Fodor's for all of us.

Tell us when we're right. We rely on local writers to give you an insider's perspective. But our writers and staff editors—who are the best in the business—depend on you. Your positive feedback is a vote to renew our recommendations for the next edition.

Tell us when we're wrong. We're proud that we update most of our guides every year. But we're not perfect. Things change. Hotels cut services. Museums change hours. Charming cafés lose charm. If our writer didn't quite capture the essence of a place, tell us how you'd do it differently. If any of our descriptions are inaccurate or inadequate, we'll incorporate your changes in the next edition and will correct factual errors at fodors.com immediately.

Tell us what to include. You probably have had fantastic travel experiences that aren't yet in Fodor's. Why not share them with a community of like-minded travelers? Maybe you chanced upon a beach or bistro or B&B that you don't want to keep to yourself. Tell us why we should include it. And share your discoveries and experiences with everyone directly at fodors.com. Your input may lead us to add a new listing or highlight a place we cover with a "Highly Recommended" star or with our highest rating, "Fodor's Choice."

Give us your opinion instantly at our feedback center at www.fodors.com/feedback. You may also e-mail editors£fodors.com with the subject line "Italy Editor." Or send your nominations, comments, and complaints by mail to Italy Editor, Fodor's, 1745 Broadway, New York NY 10019.

You and travelers like you are the heart of the Fodor's community. Make our community richer by sharing your experiences. Be a Fodor's correspondent.

Buon viaggio! (Or simply: Happy traveling!)

Tim Jarrell, Publisher

FODOR'S ESSENTIAL ITALY

Editor: Matthew Lombardi

Editorial Contributors: Linda Cabasin, Erica Duecy, Carolyn Galgano, Shannon Kelly, Jess Moss, Mark Sullivan
Writers: Lynda Albertson, Nicole Arriaga, Martin Wilmot Bennett, Peter Blackman, Erica Firpo, Dana Klitzberg, Bruce Leimsidor, Nan McElroy, Patricia Rucidlo, Jonathan Willcocks

Production Editor: Jennifer DePrima
Maps & Illustrations: David Lindroth and Mark Stroud, *cartographers;* Bob Blake, Rebecca Baer, *map editors;* William Wu, *information graphics*
Design: Fabrizio La Rocca, *creative director*; Guido Caroti, Siobhan O'Hare, *art directors*; Tina Malaney, Nora Rosansky, Chie Ushio, Jessica Walsh, Ann McBride, *designers*; Melanie Marin, *senior picture editor*
Cover Photo: (Gondolier hat, Venice): Peter Adams/The Image Bank/Getty. (Statue of David): carolgaranda/Shutterstock. (Colosseum, Rome): vichie81/Shutterstock. (Glass of red wine): Ford Photography/Shutterstock. (Spaghetti): Campania Tourism. (Shoe): hempuli/iStockphoto. (Coffee): Gustavo Fernandes/iStockphoto.
Production Manager: Angela L. McLean

3rd Edition

ISBN 978-1-4000-0488-1

ISSN 1934-5550

SPECIAL SALES

This book is available at special discounts for bulk purchases for sales promotions or premiums. Special editions, including personalized covers, excerpts of existing books, and corporate imprints, can be created in large quantities for special needs. For more information, write to Special Markets/Premium Sales, 1745 Broadway, MD 6-2, New York, New York 10019, or e-mail specialmarkets@randomhouse.com.

AN IMPORTANT TIP & AN INVITATION

Although all prices, opening times, and other details in this book are based on information supplied to us at press time, changes occur all the time in the travel world, and Fodor's cannot accept responsibility for facts that become outdated or for inadvertent errors or omissions. So **always confirm information when it matters**, especially if you're making a detour to visit a specific place. Your experiences—positive and negative— matter to us. If we have missed or misstated something, **please write to us.** We follow up on all suggestions. Contact the Essential Italy editor at editors@fodors.com or c/o Fodor's at 1745 Broadway, New York, NY 10019.

PRINTED IN SINGAPORE

10 9 8 7 6 5 4 3 2 1

CONTENTS

Fodor's Features

MAPS

ABOUT THIS BOOK

Our Ratings

Sometimes you find terrific travel experiences and sometimes they just find you. But usually the burden is on you to select the right combination of experiences. That's where our ratings come in.

As travelers we've all discovered a place so wonderful that its worthiness is obvious. And sometimes that place is so experiential that superlatives don't do it justice: you just have to be there to know. These sights, properties, and experiences get our highest rating, **Fodor's Choice**, indicated by orange stars throughout this book.

Black stars highlight sights and properties we deem **Highly Recommended**, places that our writers, editors, and readers praise again and again for consistency and excellence.

By default, there's another category: any place we include in this book is by definition worth your time, unless we say otherwise. And we will.

Disagree with any of our choices? Care to nominate a place or suggest that we rate one more highly? Visit our feedback center at www.fodors.com/feedback.

Budget Well

Hotel and restaurant price categories from ¢ to $$$$ are defined in the opening pages of each chapter. For attractions, we always give standard adult admission fees; reductions are usually available for children, students, and senior citizens. Want to pay with plastic? **AE, DC, MC, V** following restaurant and hotel listings indicate if American Express, Diners Club, MasterCard, and Visa are accepted.

Restaurants

Unless we state otherwise, restaurants are open for lunch and dinner daily. We mention dress only when there's a specific requirement and reservations only when they're essential or not accepted—it's always best to book ahead.

Hotels

Hotels have private bath, phone, TV, and air-conditioning. We indicate whether they operate on the European Plan (EP, meaning without meals), Breakfast Plan (BP, with a full breakfast), Modified American Plan (MAP, with breakfast and dinner) or American Plan (AP, including all meals). We always list facilities but not whether you'll be charged an extra fee to use them, so when pricing accommodations, find out what's included.

Listings
★	Fodor's Choice
★	Highly recommended
✉	Physical address
✛	Directions or Map coordinates
⌂	Mailing address
☎	Telephone
⊟	Fax
⊕	On the Web
✍	E-mail
☞	Admission fee
☉	Open/closed times
Ⓜ	Metro stations
▭	Credit cards

Hotels & Restaurants
☷	Hotel
↵	Number of rooms
☓	Facilities
⏀	Meal plans
✕	Restaurant
⌅	Reservations
⌂	Dress code
⌇	Smoking
⌸	BYOB

Outdoors
⚐	Golf
⛺	Camping

Other
♺	Family-friendly
⇨	See also
✉	Branch address
☞	Take note

Experience Italy

WHAT'S WHERE

Numbers correspond to the book's chapter numbers.

2 Rome. Italy's capital is one of the great cities of Europe. It's a large, busy metropolis that lives in the here and now, yet there's no other place on earth where you'll encounter such powerful evocations of a long and spectacular past, from the Colosseum to the dome of St. Peter's.

3 Between Rome and Florence. Umbria, north of Rome, is a region of beautiful rolling hills topped by attractive old towns. **Orvieto** sits atop a tufa plateau that gives a warm glow to its magnificent Duomo when seen from a distance. **Spoleto** is a quiet, elegant hill town, but each summer it brims with activity during the Festival dei Due Mondi. **Perugia** is Umbria's largest city, but it's far from overwhelming, and it has a well-preserved medieval core. In **Assisi,** birthplace of Saint Francis, the grand basilica draws millions of pilgrims annually. In **Tuscany, Siena,** once Florence's main rival, remains one of Italy's most appealing medieval towns. To its west, **San Gimignano** is famous for its 15th-century towers, and farther west still is **Volterra,** a town dating back to the Etruscans. The hills spreading south from Florence to Siena make up

Chianti, a region of sublime wine and fabulous views.

4 Florence. In the 15th century, Florence was at the center of the artistic revolution that would come to be known as the Renaissance. Today, the Renaissance remains the main reason people visit here—the abundance of art treasures is mind-boggling.

5 Between Florence and Venice. Many of Italy's signature foods come from the region of **Emilia–Romagna**—including Parmigiano-Reggiano cheese, prosciutto di Parma, and balsamic vinegar—and the pasta is considered Italy's finest. But there's more than food to draw you here. **Bologna** is a significant cultural center, and the mosaics of **Ravenna** are glittering Byzantine treasures. Farther north in the **Veneto** region, the plains stretching west of Venice hold three of northern Italy's most appealing midsize cities: **Padua, Vicenza,** and **Verona.**

6 Venice. One of the world's most novel cities, Venice has canals where the streets should be and an atmosphere of faded splendor that practically defines the word *decadent.*

ITALY PLANNER

Getting Here

The major gateways to Italy are Rome's Aeroporto Leonardo da Vinci (FCO), better known as Fiumicino, and Milan's Aeroporto Malpensa (MAL). There are some direct flights to secondary airports, primarily Venice and Pisa, but to fly into most other Italian cities you need to make connections at Fiumicino, Malpensa, or another European hub. You can also take the FS airport train to Rome's Termini station or a bus to Milan's central train station (Centrale) and catch a train to any other location in Italy. It will take about one hour to get from either Fiumicino or Malpensa to the train station.

Italy's airports are not known for being new or efficient. They all have restaurants and snack bars, and there is Internet access. Each airport has at least one nearby hotel. Ramped-up security measures may include random baggage inspection and bomb-detection dogs. In the case of Florence and Pisa, the city centers are only a 15-minute taxi ride away—so if you encounter a long delay, spend it in town.

For further information about getting where you want to go, see "Getting Here" at the beginning of each chapter of this book.

What to Pack

In summer, stick with light clothing, as things can get steamy in June, July, and August. But throw in a sweater in case of cool evenings, especially if you're headed for the mountains and/or islands. Sunglasses, a hat, and sunblock are essential. Brief summer afternoon thunderstorms are common in inland cities, so an umbrella will come in handy. In winter, bring a coat, gloves, hats, scarves, and boots. In winter, weather is generally milder than in the northern and central United States, but central heating may not be up to your standards, and interiors can be cold and damp; take wools or flannel rather than sheer fabrics. Bring sturdy shoes for winter and comfortable walking shoes in any season.

As a rule, Italians dress exceptionally well. They do not usually wear shorts. Men aren't required to wear ties or jackets anywhere, except in some of the grander hotel dining rooms and top-level restaurants, but are expected to look reasonably sharp—and they do. Formal wear is the exception rather than the rule at the opera nowadays, though people in expensive seats usually do get dressed up.

A certain modesty of dress (no bare shoulders or knees) is expected in churches, and strictly enforced in many.

For sightseeing, **pack a pair of binoculars**; they will help you get a good look at painted ceilings and domes. If you stay in budget hotels, **take your own soap.** Many such hotels do not provide it, or they give guests only one tiny bar per room. Washcloths, also, are rarely provided even in three- and four-star hotels.

1

Restaurants: The Basics

A full meal in Italy has traditionally consisted of five courses, and every menu you encounter will still be organized along some version of this five-course plan:

First up is the antipasto (appetizer), often consisting of cured meats or marinated vegetables. Next to appear is the primo, usually pasta or soup, and after that the secondo, a meat or fish course with, perhaps, a contorno (vegetable dish) on the side. A simple dolce (dessert) rounds out the meal.

This, you've probably noticed, is a lot of food. Italians have noticed as well—a full, five-course meal is an indulgence usually reserved for special occasions. Instead, restaurant meals are a mix-and-match affair: you might order a primo and a secondo, or an antipasto and a primo, or a secondo and a contorno.

The crucial rule of restaurant dining is that you should order at least two courses. It's a common mistake for tourists to order only a secondo, thinking they're getting a "main course" complete with side dishes. What they wind up with is one lonely piece of meat.

Hotels: The Basics

Hotels in Italy are usually well maintained (especially if they've earned our recommendation in this book), but in some respects they won't match what you find at comparably priced U.S. lodgings. Keep the following points in mind as you set your expectations, and you're likely to have a good experience:

■ First and foremost, rooms are usually smaller, particularly in cities. If you're truly cramped, ask for another room, but don't expect things to be spacious.

■ A "double bed" is commonly two singles pushed together.

■ In the bathroom, tubs are not a given—request one if it's essential. In budget places, showers sometimes use a drain in the middle of the bathroom floor. And washcloths are a rarity.

■ Most hotels have satellite TV, but there are fewer channels than in the United States, and only one or two will be in English.

■ Don't expect wall-to-wall carpeting. Particularly outside the cities, tile floors are the norm.

Speaking the Language

In most cities and many towns, you won't have a hard time finding locals who speak at least rudimentary English. Odds are if the person you want to talk with doesn't know English, there will be someone within earshot who can help translate. The farther south you travel, the fewer English speakers you'll encounter, but if nothing else someone at your hotel will know a few words. No matter where in Italy you're going, if you learn some common phrases in Italian, your effort will be appreciated.

Italy from Behind the Wheel

Americans tend to be well schooled in defensive-driving techniques. Many Italians are not. When you hit the road, don't be surprised to encounter tailgating and high-risk passing. Your best response is to take the same safety-first approach you use at home. On the upside, Italy's roads are very well maintained. Note that wearing a seat belt and having your lights on at all times are required by law. Bear in mind that a vehicle in Italian cities is almost always a liability, but outside the cities it's often crucial. An effective strategy is to start and end your Italian itinerary in major cities, car-free, and to pick up wheels for countryside touring in between.

ITALY TODAY

. . . is eating well

The old joke says that three-quarters of the food and wine served in Italy is good . . . and the rest is amazing. If that's true, the "good" 75% is getting even better.

Italy is home of one of the world's greatest cuisines, so it may seem disingenuous to claim that it's improving—but it clearly is. Ingredients that in the past were available only to the wealthy can now be found even in the remotest parts of the country at reasonable prices. Dishes originally conceived to make the most of inferior cuts of meat or the least flavorful part of vegetables are now made with the best.

The same is true of Italian wine. A generation ago, the omnipresent straw-basket Chianti was a mainstay of pizzerias around the world, but the wine inside was often watery and insipid. Today, through investment and experimentation, Italy's winemakers are figuring out how to get the most from their gorgeous vineyards. It's fair to say that Italy now produces more types of high-quality wine from more different grape varieties than any other country in the world.

Italian restaurateurs are keeping up with the changes. Though quaint family-run trattorias with checkered tablecloths, traditional dishes, and informal atmosphere are still common, there's no doubt that they are on the decline. And nearly every town has a newer eatery with matching flatware, a proper wine list, and an innovative menu.

. . . is passionate about soccer

Soccer stands without rival as the national sport of Italy, but recent years have seen some changes to the beautiful game. On the positive side, Italy won its fourth World Cup in 2006, giving the country more world titles than any other this side of Brazil. But since then, soccer lovers have digested a series of unwelcome developments involving alleged match fixing, backroom deals for television contracts, drug scandals among players, and a rising level of violence between rival fans.

Italian professional soccer leagues are trying to put those issues behind them and focus on on-the-field play, where the Italian leagues rank with England and Spain as the best in Europe. One emerging positive trend is geographic parity. After several years of the top *Serie A* league being dominated by northern teams, along with a handful from the central part of the country, success recently has been spread more evenly around, much to the joy of soccer-mad fans from the south.

. . . endures ongoing political upheaval

The political landscape in Italy is less stable than in any other industrialized nation. The country has endured a new government an average of about once a year since the end of World War II, and hopes are slim that the situation will change much in the near future.

This virtual turnstile outside the prime minister's office takes its toll on Italy: economic growth is slow in part because businesses are continually adapting to new government policies, and polls show that rank-and-file Italians are increasingly cynical about their political institutions. As a result, they're much less likely to trust in or depend on the government than neighbors elsewhere in Europe do.

. . . is getting older

Italy is the oldest country in Europe (worldwide, only Japan is older)—the result of its low birth rate, relatively strict immigration standards, and one of the highest life expectancy rates in the world.

As of 2010, the average Italian was 42.9 years old, and the number keeps rising.

The result is a remarkably stable population: the total number of Italian residents barely rises most years, and, according to the most recent estimates, is projected to start contracting by 2020. But the situation is putting a strain on the country's pension system and on families, since elderly family members are likely to live with their children or grandchildren in a country where nursing homes are rare.

The trend also has an impact on other areas, including politics (where older politicians are eager to promote policies aimed at older voters), the popular culture (where everything from fashion to television programming takes older consumers into consideration), and a kind of far-reaching nostalgia; thanks to a long collective memory, it's common to hear even younger Italians celebrate or rue something that happened 50 or 60 years earlier as if it had just taken place.

. . . lives with a black-market economy

Nobody knows how big Italy's black-market economy is, though experts all agree it's massive. Estimates place it at anywhere from a fourth to a half of the official, legal economy.

Put another way, if the highest estimates are correct, Italy's black market is about as large as the entire economy of Switzerland or Indonesia. If the estimated black-market figures were added to the official GDP, Italy would likely leapfrog France, the United Kingdom, and China to become the world's fourth-largest economy.

The presence of the black market isn't obvious to the casual observer, but whenever a customer is not given a printed receipt in a store or restaurant, tobacco without a tax seal is bought from a street seller, or a product or service is exchanged for another product or service, that means the transaction goes unrecorded, unreported, and untaxed.

. . . has a growing parks system

Italy boasts 25 national parks covering a total of around 1.5 million hectares (58,000 square mi), or about 5% of the entire surface area of the country—more than twice as much as 25 years ago. And a new park is added or an existing park is expanded every few months.

Part of the reason for the expansion has been a growing environmental movement in Italy, which has lobbied the government to annex undeveloped land for parks, thus protecting against development. But the trend is a boon for visitors and nature lovers, who can enjoy huge expanses of unspoiled territory.

. . . is staying home in August

Italy used to be the best example of Europe's famous August exodus—where city dwellers would spend most of the month at the seaside or in the mountains, leaving the cities nearly deserted. Today, the phenomenon continues but is much less prevalent, as economic pressures have forced companies to keep operating through August. As a result, vacations are more staggered and vacationers' plans are often more modest.

The loss of shared vacation time for Italian workers can be an advantage for visitors, both because in August there is more room at the seaside and in the mountains, and because cities have taken to promoting local events designed to appeal to residents who are staying put. These days, summers in Italy boast a plethora of outdoor concerts and plays; longer restaurant and museum hours; and food, wine, and culture fairs.

ITALY
TOP ATTRACTIONS

The Vatican

(A) The home of the Catholic Church, a tiny independent state tucked within central Rome, holds some of the city's most spectacular sights, including St. Peter's Basilica, the Vatican Museums, and Michelangelo's Sistine ceiling. (⇨ *Chapter 2.*)

Ancient Rome

(B) The Colosseum and the Roman Forum are remarkable ruins from Rome's ancient past. Sitting above it all is the Campidoglio, with a piazza designed by Michelangelo and museums containing Rome's finest collection of ancient art. (⇨ *Chapter 2.*)

Galleria Borghese, Rome

Only the best could only satisfy the aesthetic taste of Cardinal Scipione Borghese, and that means famed Bernini sculptures, great paintings by Titian and Raphael, and the most spectacular 17th-century palace in Rome. (⇨ *Chapter 2.*)

Basilica di San Francesco, Assisi

(C) The giant basilica—made up of two churches, one built on top of the other—honors St. Francis with its remarkable fresco cycles. (⇨ *Chapter 3.*)

Piazza del Campo, Siena

(D) Siena is Tuscany's classic medieval hill town, and its heart is the Piazza del Campo, the beautiful, one-of-a-kind town square. (⇨ *Chapter 3.*)

Galleria degli Uffizi, Florence

The Uffizi—Renaissance art's hall of fame—contains masterpieces by Leonardo, Michelangelo, Raphael, Botticelli, Caravaggio, and dozens of other luminaries. (⇨ Chapter 4.)

Duomo, Florence

(E) The massive dome of Florence's Cathedral of Santa Maria del Fiore (aka the Duomo) is one of the world's great feats of engineering. (⇨ *Chapter 4.*)

Ravenna's Mosaics

This small, out-of-the-way city houses perhaps the world's greatest treasure trove of early Christian art. The exquisite and surprisingly moving 5th- and 6th-century mosaics decorating several churches and other religious buildings still retain their startling brilliance. (⇨ *Chapter 5.*)

Giotto's Frescoes in the Scrovegni Chapel, Padua

(F) Dante's contemporary Giotto decorated this chapel with an eloquent and beautiful fresco cycle. Its convincing human dimension helped to change the course of Western art. (⇨ *Chapter 5.*)

Palladio's Villas and Palazzi

(G) The 16th-century genius Andrea Palladio is one of the most influential figures in the history of architecture. You can visit his creations in his hometown of Vicenza, in and around Venice, and outside Treviso. (⇨ *Chapter 5.*)

Venice's Piazza San Marco

The centerpiece of Venice's main square is the Basilica di San Marco, arguably the most beautiful Byzantine church in the West. Right next door is the Venetian Gothic Palazzo Ducale, which was so beloved by the Venetians that when it burnt down in the 16th century, they had their palace rebuilt *come era, dove era*—exactly how and where it was. (⇨ *Chapter 6.*)

Venice's Grand Canal

(H) No one ever forgets a first trip down the Grand Canal. The sight of its magnificent palaces, with the light reflected from the canal's waters shimmering across their facades, is one of Italy's great experiences. (⇨ *Chapter 6.*)

ITALY'S TOP EXPERIENCES

Hanging Out in Rome's Piazzas

For Italians young and old, la piazza serves as a *punto d'incontro*—a meeting place—for dinner plans, drinks, people-watching, catching up with friends and, as Romans would say, exchanging *due chiacchere* (two words). One of the most popular piazzas is Campo de' Fiori, right in the heart of the historic center. By day, the piazza is famous for its fresh food and flower market—no rival to Piazza Navona for sheer beauty, the market is nevertheless a favorite photo op, due to the *ombrelloni* (canvas umbrella) food stands. By night, the piazza turns into a popular hangout for Romans and foreigners lured by its pubs and street cafés, so much so that it has been dubbed "the American college campus of Rome." As dinner approaches at 9, the big question is: Are you "in" or "out" (inside or outside table)? No matter: the people-watching is unrivaled anywhere you sit.

Church Going

Few images are more identifiable with Italy than the country's great churches, amazing works of architecture that often took centuries to build. The name Duomo (derived from the Latin for "house," *domus*, and the root of the English "dome") is used to refer to the principal church of a town or city. Generally speaking, the bigger the city, the more splendid its duomo. Still, some impressive churches inhabit some unlikely places—in the Umbrian hill towns of **Assisi** and **Orvieto**, for example (⇨ *Chapter 3*).

In Venice, the Byzantine-influenced **Basilica di San Marco** (⇨ *Chapter 6*) is a testament to the city's East-meets-West character. **Milan's Duomo** (⇨ *Chapter 5*) is the largest, most imposing Gothic cathedral in Italy. The spectacular dome of **Florence's Duomo** (⇨ *Chapter 4*) is a work of engineering genius. The **Basilica di San Pietro** in Rome (⇨ *Chapter 2*) has all the grandeur you'd expect from the seat of the Catholic Church.

Hiking in the Footsteps of Saint Francis

Umbria, which bills itself as "Italy's Green Heart," is fantastic hiking country. Among the many options are two with a Franciscan twist: from the town of Cannara, 16 km (10 mi) south of Assisi, an easy half-hour walk leads to the fields of Pian d'Arca, where Saint Francis delivered his sermon to the birds. For slightly more demanding walks, you can follow the saint's path from Assisi to the *Ermeo delle Carceri* (Hermitage of Prisons), where Francis and his followers went to "imprison" themselves in prayer, and from here continue along the trails that crisscross Monte Subasio.

Wine-Tasting in Chianti

The gorgeous hills of the Chianti region, between Florence and Siena, produce exceptional wines, and they never taste better than when sampled on their home turf. Many Chianti vineyards are visitor-friendly, but the logistics of a visit are different from what you may have experienced in other wine regions. If you just drop in, you're likely to get a tasting, but for a tour you usually need to make an appointment several days ahead of time. The upside is, your tour may end up being a half day of full emersion—including extended conversation with the winemakers and even a meal.

Taking in the View from Florence's Piazzale Michelangelo

One of the best ways to introduce yourself to Florence is by walking up to this square on the hill south of the Arno. From

here you can take in the whole city, and much of the surrounding countryside, in one spectacular vista. To extend the experience, linger at one of the outdoor cafés, and for the finest view of all, time your visit to correspond with sunset.

Discovering the Cinque Terre

Along the Italian Riviera to the west of Lucca and Pisa are five tiny, remote fishing villages known collectively as the Cinque Terre. Tourism here was once limited to backpackers, but the beauty of the landscape—with steep, vine-covered hills pushing smack-dab against an azure sea—and the charm of the villages have turned the area into one of Italy's top destinations. The number-one activity is hiking the trails that run between the villages—the views are once-in-a-lifetime gorgeous—but if hiking isn't your thing, you can still have fun lounging about in cafés, admiring the water, and perhaps sticking a toe in it.

Eating in Bologna

Italians recognize the region of Emilia as the star of its culinary culture and Bologna as its epicenter. Many dishes native to Bologna, such as the slow-cooked meat-and-tomato sauce *sugo alla Bolognese*, have become so famous that they are widely available in all regions of Italy and abroad. But you owe it to yourself to try them in the city where they were born and are a subject of local pride. Take note, however: in Bologna a *sugo* (sauce) isn't served with spaghetti, but rather with an egg pasta in the form of tagliatelle, lasagne, or tortellini.

Picking Up Some Style in Milan

Italian clothing and furniture design are world famous, and the center of the Italian design industry is Milan. The best way to see what's happening in the world of fashion is to browse the designer showrooms and boutiques of the fabled *quadrilatero della moda (fashion quarter)*, along and around Via Montenapoleone. The central event in the world of furniture design is Milan's annual Salone Internazionale del Mobile, held at the Milan fairgrounds for a week in April. Admission is generally restricted to the trade, but the Salone is open to the general public for one day, generally on a Sunday, during the week of the show.

Going by Gondola in Venice

A ride down the Grand Canal by *vaporetto* (water bus) is a classic introduction to the unique character of Venice. But for a more intimate experience, there's nothing that can match a glide along one of the city's narrow side canals in a gondola— an escorted trip to nowhere in particular, watched over by Gothic palaces with delicately arched eyebrows.

Il Dolce Far Niente

"The sweetness of doing nothing" has long been an art form in Italy. This is a country in which life's pleasures are warmly celebrated, not guiltily indulged.

Of course, doing "nothing" doesn't really mean nothing. It means doing things differently: lingering over a glass of wine for the better part of an evening just to watch the sun slowly set; savoring a slow and flirtatious evening *passeggiata* (stroll) along the main street of a little town; and making a commitment—however temporary—to thinking that there is nowhere that you have to be next, that there is no other time than the magical present.

QUINTESSENTIAL ITALY

Il Caffè (Coffee)

The Italian day begins and ends with coffee, and more cups of coffee punctuate the time in between. To live as the Italians do, drink as they drink, standing at the counter or sitting at an outdoor table of the corner bar. (In Italy, a "bar" is a coffee bar.) A primer: *caffè* means coffee, and Italian standard issue is what Americans call espresso—short, strong, and usually taken very sweet. *Cappuccino* is a foamy half-and-half of espresso and steamed milk; cocoa powder *(cacao)* on top is acceptable, cinnamon is not. If you're thinking of having a cappuccino for dessert, think again—Italians drink only caffè or caffè *macchiato* (with a spot of steamed milk) after lunchtime. Confused? Homesick? Order caffè *americano* for a reasonable facsimile of good-old filtered joe. Note that you usually pay for your coffee first, then take your receipt to the counter and tell the barista your order.

Il Calcio (Soccer)

Imagine the most rabid American football fans—the ones who paint their faces on game day and sleep in pajamas emblazoned with the logo of their favorite team. Throw in a dose of melodrama along the lines of a tear-jerking soap opera. Ratchet up the intensity by a factor of 10, and you'll start to get a sense of how Italians feel about their national game, soccer—known in the mother tongue as *calcio*. On Sunday afternoons throughout the long September-to-May season, stadiums are packed throughout Italy. Those who don't get to games in person tend to congregate around television sets in restaurants and bars, rooting for the home team with a passion that feels like a last vestige of the days when the country was a series of warring medieval city-states. How calcio mania affects your stay in Italy depends on how eager you are to get involved. At the very least, you may notice an eerie

If you want to get a sense of contemporary Italian culture and indulge in some of its pleasures, start by familiarizing yourself with the rituals of daily life. These are a few highlights—things you can take part in with relative ease.

Sunday-afternoon quiet on the city streets, or erratic restaurant service around the same time, accompanied by cheers and groans from a neighboring room. If you want a memorable, truly Italian experience, attend a game yourself. Availability of tickets may depend on the current fortunes of the local team, but they often can be acquired with help from your hotel concierge.

Il Gelato (Ice Cream)

During warmer months, *gelato*—the Italian equivalent of ice cream—is a national obsession. It's considered a snack rather than a dessert, bought at stands and shops in piazzas and on street corners, and consumed on foot, usually at a leisurely stroll *(see La Passeggiata, below)*. Gelato is softer, less creamy, and more intensely flavored than its American counterpart. It comes in simple flavors that capture the essence of the main ingredient. (You won't find Chunky Monkey or Cookies 'n' Cream.) Standard choices include pistachio, *nocciola* (hazelnut), caffè, and numerous fresh-fruit varieties. Quality varies; the surest sign that you've hit on a good spot is a line at the counter.

La Passeggiata (Strolling)

A favorite Italian pastime is the *passeggiata* (literally, the promenade). In the late afternoon and early evening, especially on weekends, couples, families, and packs of teenagers stroll the main streets and piazzas of Italy's towns. It's a ritual of exchanged news and gossip, window-shopping, flirting, and gelato eating that adds up to a uniquely Italian experience. To join in, simply hit the streets for a bit of wandering. You may feel more like an observer than a participant, until you realize that observing is what la passeggiata is all about.

A GREAT ITINERARY

ROME, FLORENCE, VENICE, AND HIGHLIGHTS IN BETWEEN

This itinerary works like an accordion: it can expand or contract, depending on the amount of time you have and where your interests lie. If your top priority is seeing Italy's most famous sights, extend your visits to the great cities of Rome, Florence, and Venice. If you're more drawn by beautiful landscapes, exceptional food and wine, and the Italians' knack for living well, then devote a good part of your trip to the other stops along the way, where the pace of life is more relaxed.

Getting there: Rome and Milan have Italy's busiest international airports, but there are also direct flights between the United States and Venice. To follow the itinerary outlined here, look into "open-jaw" tickets, with which you fly into one city (in this case Rome) and out of another (Venice). You could also finish up your trip by making the three-hour train ride from Venice to Milan, where you'll have more return-flight options (and you can see yet another side of Italy). Or you could go back to Rome (one-way plane tickets for flights within Italy are surprisingly inexpensive; the train takes about five hours), and fly home from there. For transportation details, see Essentials at the end of this book.

Getting around: Your main decision is whether to rent a car or to use Italy's efficient, reasonably priced railway system. The smartest strategy may be to do some of both. Within the cities, a car is a liability: both driving and parking are generally worse in Italian cities than anything you'll find in the United States. Outside the cities, though, a car has its clear advantages:

it gives you the freedom and flexibility to go places not served (or poorly served) by public transit. Particularly in Tuscany, there are significant limits on what you'll be able to see and do without a car.

Stop 1: Rome (2–4 Days)

Rome is a large, bustling city that lives in the here and now, yet there's no other place on earth where you'll encounter such powerful evocations of a long and spectacular past. Take a few steps from Piazza del Campidoglio, designed by Michelangelo, and you're looking down upon the ruins of ancient Rome, smack-dab in the middle of the city. Exit a baroque church housing a masterpiece by Caravaggio, turn the corner, and find yourself face-to-face with the Pantheon. Such mind-bending juxtapositions are everywhere.

If you're arriving on an international flight, you'll settle into your hotel in the afternoon. Resist the temptation to nap; instead head outside and spend some time getting to know the surrounding neighborhood. In the evening, check out **Piazza Navona** and the **Trevi Fountain**—the energy of the city at night will perk you up like a shot of good espresso. For your first dinner, you can't miss with one of Rome's exceptional pizzerias.

In the morning, head to the Vatican to see **St. Peter's Basilica** and Michelangelo's glorious Sistine Chapel at the **Vatican Museums**. Have lunch back in Rome proper in the area around the Pantheon, then visit the **Pantheon** itself and spend the afternoon wandering the cobblestone streets of the neighborhood, taking time for a break at one the famous coffee shops in the area.

Begin the next day at **Campo de' Fiori**, where you'll find Rome's most colorful open-air market in full swing. Then head to the **Campidolgio**, and from there explore

the ruins of ancient Rome, topped off by a visit to the **Colosseum**. In the afternoon, hop across town to **Piazza di Spagna**, a good place to shop, lick gelato, and watch the sunset.

On further days here, follow the same basic strategy: devote mornings to significant sights (**Galleria Borghese** is a great choice; note that it requires a reservation) and afternoons to exploring neighborhoods (such as **Trastevere** and the **Jewish Ghetto**). In the evening, do as the Romans do: make a long, relaxed dinner the main event.

Extend your stay if: you're fascinated by Rome's mix of the ancient and the modern, and you love city life. You won't encounter such an intensely urban environment anywhere else on this trip.

Keep your visit short if: an urban environment is what you're on vacation to get away from.

Stop 2: Perugia (1–2 Days)
Perugia is about 2½ hours north of Rome by car or train, but consider a short detour along the way to **Orvieto**, a town with an impressive hilltop setting and one of Italy's great Gothic cathedrals. Both towns are in the largely rural **Umbria** region. The more relaxed pace of life makes a nice contrast to the energy of Rome.

Perugia is Umbria's largest city, but with a population of about 150,000 it's far from overwhelming, and it has a well-preserved medieval core. The pedestrian-only street through the heart of town, **Corso Vannucci**, is a classic place for a *passeggiata* (evening stroll), and there's a cluster of sights along the street that are worth checking out the next morning—particularly the **Collegio del Cambio**, a Renaissance guild hall frescoed by Perugia's greatest artist, Perugino.

Extend your stay if: you want to make a day trip to **Assisi**, the city of St. Francis, which is about half an hour (by car or train) east of Perugia.

Keep your visit short if: you're a thrill seeker. Umbria is a beautiful region, but it's not as likely to quicken your pulse as much as some of the other stops on the itinerary.

Stop 3: Chianti (1–2 Days)
To the northwest of Umbria is the region of **Tuscany**, which is rightly famous for having Italy's most gorgeous landscapes. Most beautiful of all is the Chianti district, between Florence and Siena, where vineyards and olive groves blanket rolling hills as far as the eye can see. To make the most of the experience, stay in the countryside at a converted villa or *agriturismo* (a farm taking overnight guests). Though

Chianti is Tuscany's most idyllic location, you can hardly go wrong in the surrounding districts as well—particularly outside Siena and in the hills to its west.

Siena itself is a magnificent hill town that shouldn't be missed. With the exception of Florence, it has more to see than anywhere else in Tuscany, and its **Piazza del Campo** is one of Italy's most appealing town squares. If you leave Perugia in the morning, you can make the 1½-hour drive west to Siena and spend the afternoon there. Tuscany is also a great place for winery tours; the **Strada Chiantigiana**, the beautiful road through the heart of Chianti, takes you past visitor-friendly vineyards and *enoteche* (wineshops).

Extend your stay if: *il dolce far niente* (the sweetness of doing nothing) is a concept you find appealing. Tuscany has some spectacular sights, but the greatest pleasure here is relaxing and unwinding.

Keep your visit short if: you're dead-set against driving. The only town south of Florence that's easily accessible by train is Arezzo, which is worth a visit but won't give you the full Tuscan experience.

Stop 4: Florence (2–4 Days)

It's hard to think of a place that's more closely linked to one specific historical period than Florence. In the 15th century the city was at the center of the artistic revolution that would come to be known as the Renaissance. Five hundred years later, the Renaissance remains the main reason people visit Florence—the abundance of art treasures is mind-boggling.

Begin your first day here at the heart of the city, the **Piazza del Duomo.** Check out Ghiberti's famous bronze doors on the **Battistero,** then climb the 463 steps to the top of Brunelleschi's splendid cathedral dome, from where you have an unbeatable view of the entire city and the hills beyond. Back on solid ground, take some time to visit the **Museo dell'Opera del Duomo,** which now holds much of the art that was once in the Duomo. Following lunch, spend the afternoon at the **Gallleria degli Uffizi** (reserve your ticket in advance), which houses one of the world's greatest art collections. When you're through there, step outside into the neighboring **Piazza della Signoria,** Florence's most impressive square. You'll find there a copy of Michelangelo's David, standing in the spot that was occupied by the original for centuries.

The following morning, visit the real David at his indoor home, the **Galleria dell'Accademia.** (Reserve your ticket here as well.) A few steps down the street are the works of another, completely different Renaissance master: the **Museo di San Marco,** a former convent, is decorated with simple, ethereal, occasionally bizarre frescoes of Fra Angelico. You can get another dose of Michelangelo before lunch a few blocks away at the **Capelle Medici.** After a day and a half of walking and art gazing, if a post-lunch nap appeals to you, don't resist. Later in the afternoon, use your revived energy to make the trip up to the **Piazzale Michelangelo,** high on a hill above Florence, from which you have a sweeping view of the city. Stick around for sunset, then head down to the Oltrarno neighborhood below and feast on a famed *bistecca alla fiorentina* (grilled T-bone steak with olive oil).

You'll have seen a lot by this point, but you've just scratched the surface here. Must-sees for additional days are the **Santa Croce** and **Santa Maria Novella** cathedrals and the **Bargello** sculpture museum. And Florence isn't exclusively about art;

some visitors come just for the shopping, from the food stalls of the **Mercato Centrale** to the showrooms of the exclusive boutiques along **Via Tournabuoni**.

Extend your stay if: you want to make a side trip to **Lucca, Pisa** (home of the leaning tower), or the gorgeous coastal villages of the **Cinque Terre**, all west of Florence.

Keep your visit short if: you put a premium on getting off the beaten path. After several hundred years of steady tourism, almost every path in Florence has been pretty well beaten.

Stop 5: Bologna (1–2 Days)

A one-hour trip by train north from Florence, or 1½ hours by car, brings you to Bologna, a city that doesn't have Florence's abundance of sights but will give you more of a taste of the pleasures of day-to-day life in Italy. With a population of about 375,000, Bologna is the largest city in **Emilia–Romagna**, a region famed for its cuisine. Many of Italy's signature food products originate here, including Parmigiano-Reggiano cheese (aka Parmesan), prosciutto di Parma, and balsamic vinegar. The pasta is considered Italy's finest—a reputation the region's chefs earn every day. If you're going to splurge on one over-the-top meal, this is the place to do it.

But a visit here is about more than food: Bologna is home to Europe's oldest university, making it a cultural and intellectual center, and it has rows of street arcades winding through grandiose towers. After you've settled into your hotel, take a walk around **Piazza Maggiore** at the heart of the city. Following dinner, you can check out some of northern Italy's best nightlife—one of the by-products of the university. The next day, continue your exploration of the city center, including a visit to the

basilica of **Santo Stefano** and a climb up Bologna's own leaning tower, the **Torre degli Asinelli**.

Extend your stay if: you're lured by a day trip east to see the glorious Byzantine mosaics in **Ravenna**.

Keep your visit short if: your priority is seeing Italy's most spectacular sights. Bologna's sights are impressive—they just don't rank with the treasures of Rome, Florence, and Venice.

Stop 6: Verona (1–2 Days)

North from Bologna (1½ hours by train, a little longer by car) is Verona, a charming midsize city with a distinctly northern Italian air. Standing alongside the fast-flowing River Adige, gazing at the rows of old palazzi along its banks and the rolling hills of cypress and beyond, it's easy to fall for this city of Romeo and Juliet. Spend your time here wandering the medieval piazzas; skip the touristy so-called House of Juliet, but don't miss the stunning ancient Roman **Arena**, the **Castelvecchio** (old castle), and **San Zeno Maggiore**, possibly Italy's finest Romanesque church.

Verona is often mentioned in the same breath with **Vicenza** and **Padua,** two other cities of similar size located in the **Veneto** region, on the green plains to the west of Venice. Vicenza is best known for its palaces designed by Andrea Palladio, one of history's most influential architects; Padua's star attraction is the **Cappella degli Scrovegni,** a chapel decorated with landmark Giotto frescoes. Both towns are well worth a visit as you make your way toward Venice.

Extend your stay if: you're here in the summer and have a chance to see an opera at Verona's Arena—a truly grand spectacle.

Keep your visit short if: you're impatient to see Venice.

Stop 7: Venice (2–4 Days)

Venice is one of the world's most novel cities, with canals where streets should be and an atmosphere of faded splendor that practically defines the word *decadent*. Once a great seafaring power, Venice now lives for tourism, prompting cynics to compare it to Disneyland. It's true that **Piazza San Marco**, the magnificent main square, is frequently packed with sightseers, and there are plenty of kitschy souvenirs for sale in the heavily trafficked area around the **Rialto Bridge**. But Venice is no Mickey Mouse affair: it has a rich history, it's packed with artistic treasures accumulated over a thousand years, and despite the crowds it remains inescapably romantic.

Allow yourself some time to get acclimated. If you have a rental car, return it to the offices on the city's western edge, then find your hotel (be sure to get directions in advance), and if all goes well, you'll have time left in the day for sightseeing. Rather than making a beeline for Piazza San Marco, check out some of the other spectacular attractions, such as the church of **Santa Maria Gloriosa dei Frari** and the **Scuola Grande di San Rocco**, or just spend a couple of hours getting lost in the city's back canals before finding your way to a seafood dinner. Afterward, consider a nightcap around the **Campo San Luca** or **Campo Santa Margarita**.

Begin the next morning *vaporetto* (water bus) cruise along the **Grand Canal**, then make your visit to **Piazza San Marco**, home to the Byzantine splendor of the **Basilica di San Marco** and the imposing **Palazzo Ducale**. After lunch, perhaps at a traditional Venetian *bacaro* (wine bar), take the Accademia footbridge across the Grand Canal and see the **Gallerie dell'Accademia**, Venice's most important art gallery. Wander through the **Dorsoduro** neighborhood, finishing up with a romantic sunset stroll along the **Zattere** boardwalk before proceeding to dinner.

On subsequent days, make your sightseeing priorities the **Rialto fish market** (a foodie highlight), **Ca' Rezzonico** and **Ca' d'Oro** (classic Venetian palaces), and **Santa Maria dei Miracoli** and **Santi Giovanni e Paolo** (two spectacular churches).

Extend your stay if: you want to discover Venice beyond the crowds. Exploring the neighborhoods east of Piazza San Marco and the quieter outer islands will take you to another world.

Keep your visit short if: you don't have a tolerance for getting lost. Navigating the streets of Venice can feel like working through a maze.

MAKING THE MOST OF YOUR EUROS

Below are suggestions for ways to save money on your trip, courtesy of the Travel Talk Forums at Fodors.com.

Transportation

"I take regional trains instead of the Eurostar trains. For example, Florence to Rome on Eurostar is 32.50 euros; the regional train is 15.80 euros. That's half the price; so what if it takes 15 minutes longer . . . big deal."   —JoanneH

"Instead of taking the Leonardo Express from Fiumicino to Termini in Rome, take the FR1 to whichever station is most convenient for you. The FR1 departs every 15 minutes (instead of every 30 minutes for the Express), costs only €5.50 (instead of €10.50 for the Express), and avoids the hullabaloo of Termini."   —Therese

Food and Drink

"Buy snacks and bottled water in bulk at a neighborhood supermarket at the beginning of your stay and keep them cool in your apartment or hotel fridge. Grab a bottle each when leaving in the am and that way avoid buying expensive water or snacks near tourist attractions, where prices are much higher. Save your euros for espresso or gelato."   —cruisinred

"Bars always have two different prices: If you have your coffee at the counter, it's cheaper than when a waiter serves it at a table (*servizio al tavolo*)."   —quokka

"Visit wine fill-up shops in Italy; get table wine from the cask for 2–3 euros a liter. In Rome we would get them filled at the Testaccio market . . . I will usually ask at the local bar where I go for my coffee."   —susanna

"If you aren't hungry, skip to *secondo*— the 'second course.' Rarely do Italians eat a *primo e secondo* when they go out."   —glittergirl

Sights

"The small cities can be less expensive but still fabulous. We were just in Assisi—all the sites were free, a delicious dinner for two with wine was 22 euros, and our hotel was reasonable at 65 euros per night."   —rosetravels

"For the art lover on a budget: Most of the art I saw in Rome is free. Where else can you see countless Caravaggios, two Michelangelos, and even more Berninis for the cost of the wear and tear on the soles of your shoes?"   —amyb

"One way to save on the expense of guided tours is to register online at Sound Guides (www.sound-guides.com) and download the various free self-guided tours to your Ipod or MP3 player."   —monicapileggi

Lodging

"Go off-season—March or November have better air prices and also accommodations, particularly if you stay in apartments, which you can rent for much less off-season (and plan some meals in-house—make the noon meal your biggest of the day, then have a small dinner in the apartment)."   —bobthenavigator

"Everyone talks about going in the off-season and mentions November or March. But in Florence at least, July is a shoulder season. I got a hotel room for half to a third the cost of the same room during the high season."   —isabel

"We try to book apartments whenever we can, and in Tuscany we rent farmhouses. Especially if you are traveling with more than two persons, these are usually much more reasonable."   —caroltis

FAQS

Is it okay to drink cappuccino after noon?
For most Italians, a frothy cappuccino is a morning thing: drinking milk later in the day is thought to be bad for digestion. So, if you order a cappuccino in the afternoon or evening, you'll give yourself away as a tourist, and you may encounter a hint of condescension from the barista. But unless you're trying to pass as a local, there's no reason not to order whatever suits your fancy.

Are Italian drivers as crazy as I've heard?
Yes—at least some of them are. Americans tend to be well schooled in defensive-driving techniques, but many Italians are not. When you hit the road, don't be surprised to encounter tailgating and high-risk passing.

Your best response is to take the same safety-first approach you use at home; on the road is one place where you don't want to be mistaken for a local. On the up side, Italy's roads are for the most part very well maintained. Note that wearing a seat belt and having your lights on at all times are required by law.

Is the Cinque Terre a viable day trip from Florence? Technically it's doable, but we don't recommend it. You'll spend about five hours on the train round-trip, or something close to that if you go by car. And if it's summer and you want to hike the trails (which most people do), you're better off getting started early in the morning so you can beat the heat.

The Cinque Terre is a beautiful, one-of-a-kind destination, and it deserves an overnight. If you're set on a day trip, you're better off starting from Pisa or Lucca.

What's crime like in Italy? By and large, the cities of central and northern Italy are remarkably crime free. An exception, unfortunately, are the tourist-focused crimes of purse snatching and pickpocketing. It would be an overstatement to say these crimes are rampant, but they do happen on a regular basis, particularly around train stations and major tourist attractions. They're commonly perpetrated by groups of street kids and by well-dressed professionals cruising for easy targets.

A little common sense goes a long way toward keeping yourself safe: if children approach you, don't be reluctant to shoo them away firmly; don't keep your wallet in your back pocket; carry a purse with a shoulder strap, and wear it across your chest, so it can't be separated from you with a simple tug.

On restaurant bills, does "coperto" mean tip, and if it doesn't, what does it mean? "Coperto" means cover, and it's a mandatory surcharge intended to cover the cost of tableware, linens, and the bread in the obligatory breadbasket. It's an inescapable charge that comes with the territory—it's neither a tip nor a scam markup perpetrated on tourists.

So how do I tip, then? Italians typically don't tip. This doesn't mean that you shouldn't, though. Always check your bill to see if service is included automatically (usually 10%). If it is, leave no more. If not, tip no more than 10%, remembering that Italian waitstaff are paid a living wage.

Rome

WORD OF MOUTH

"Once we got our 'Rome legs,' we loved the place. My philosophy is 'don't try to do Rome, let Rome do you.'"

—SallyJo

"Eat a lot of gelati. Eat more gelati. Have I mentioned gelati?"

—DWeller

WELCOME TO ROME

TOP REASONS TO GO

★ **The Pantheon:** Of ancient Rome's remains, this is the best preserved and most impressive.

★ **St.** Peter's Square and Basilica: The primary church of the Catholic faith is truly awe-inspiring.

★ **Galleria Borghese:** With a setting as exquisite as its collection, this small, elegant museum showcases some of the finest baroque and Renaissance art in Italy.

★ **A morning walk through Campo de' Fiori:** The city comes alive in this bustling market square.

★ **Roman pizza:** Maybe it's the ovens, maybe the crust, maybe the cheese, but they just don't make it like this back home.

1 **Ancient Rome.** Backstopped by the stupendous Colosseum, the Roman Forum and Palatine Hill were once the hub of Western civilization.

2 **Navona and Campo.** At the heart of Rome's historic quarter, these districts revolve around the ancient Pantheon, Campo de' Fiori, and spectacular Piazza Navona.

3 **Corso and Spagna.** Rome's "Broadway," Via del Corso, begins at Piazza Venezia and neatly divides the city center in two. A few blocks east is Piazza de Spagna, a classic area for people-watching and sophisticated shopping.

4 **Repubblica and Quirinale.** A largely 19th-century district, Repubblica lets art lovers go for baroque with a bevy of Bernini works. To the south looms the Quirinale hill, crowned by Italy's presidential palace.

5 **Villa Borghese and Piazza del Popolo.** Rome's largest park is home to the treasure-packed Galleria Borghese. Neighboring Piazza del Popolo is one of the city's main squares.

6 **The Vatican.** Hundreds of thousands of pilgrims and artlovers come here to see St. Peter's Basilica, the Vatican Museums, and the Sistine Chapel.

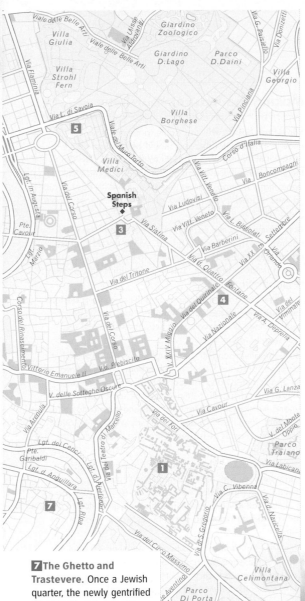

2

GETTING ORIENTED

Rome is a sprawling city, but you'll likely spend most of your time in and around the historic center. The area is split by the River Tiber (*Tevere* in Italian). To its west are the Vatican and the Trastevere neighborhood. To its east is everything else you've come to see: the Colosseum, the Spanish Steps, and scores of other exceptional sights, not to mention piazzas, fountains, shops, and restaurants. This is one of the most culturally rich plots of land in the world.

7 The Ghetto and Trastevere. Once a Jewish quarter, the newly gentrified Ghetto still preserves the flavor of Old Rome. Across the Tiber, Trastevere is a neighborhood of mom-and-pop trattorias and medieval alleyways.

ROME PLANNER

Reservations Required

You should reserve tickets for the following sights. See the listings within the chapter for contact information:

Galleria Borghese requires reservations. Visitors are admitted in two-hour shifts, and prime time slots can sell out days in advance, so it pays to plan ahead. You can reserve by phone or through the gallery's Web site.

In the ancient Rome archaeological area, reservations for the Colosseum save you from standing in a ticket line that sometimes takes upward of an hour. You can reserve by phone or on the Web.

At the Vatican, you need to reserve several days in advance to see the gardens, and several weeks in advance to see the necropolis. For information about attending a papal audience, see the Close Up box "A Morning with the Pope" several pages into this chapter.

Making the Most of Your Time

Roma, non basta una vita ("Rome, a lifetime is not enough"): this famous saying should be stamped on the passport of every first-time visitor to the Eternal City. On the other hand, it's a warning: Rome is so packed with sights that it is impossible to take them all in; it's easy to run yourself ragged trying to check off the items on your "Santa Claus" list.

At the same time, the saying is a celebration of the city's abundance. There's so much here, you're bound to make discoveries you hadn't anticipated. To conquer Rome, strike a balance between visits to major sights and leisurely neighborhood strolls.

In the first category, the Vatican and the remains of ancient Rome loom the largest. Both require at least half a day; a good strategy is to devote your first morning to one and your second to the other.

Leave the afternoons for exploring the neighborhoods that comprise "Baroque Rome" and the shopping district around the Spanish Steps and Via Condotti. If you have more days at your disposal, continue with the same approach. Among the sights, Galleria Borghese and the multilayered church of San Clemente are particularly worthwhile, and the neighborhoods of Trastevere and the Ghetto make for great roaming.

Since there's a lot of ground to cover in Rome, it's wise to plan your busy sightseeing schedule with possible savings in mind, and purchasing the Roma Pass (⊕ *www.romapass.it*) allows you to do just that. The three-day pass costs €20 and is good for unlimited use of buses, trams, and the metro.

It includes free admission to two of more than 40 participating museums or archaeological sites, including the Colosseum (and bumps you to the head of the long line there, to boot!), the Ara Pacis museum, the Musei Capitolini, and Galleria Borghese, plus discounted tickets to many other museums. The Roma Pass can be purchased at tourist information booths across the city, at Termini Station, or at Terminal C of the International Arrivals section of Fiumicino Airport.

When to Go

Not surprisingly, spring and fall are the best times to visit, with mild temperatures and many sunny days; the famous Roman sunsets are also at their best. Summers are often sweltering. In July and August, come if you like, but learn to do as the Romans do—get up and out early, seek refuge from the afternoon heat, resume activities in early evening, and stay up late to enjoy the nighttime breeze. Come August, many shops and restaurants close as locals head out for vacation. Remember that air-conditioning is still a relatively rare phenomenon in this city. Roman winters are relatively mild, with persistent rainy spells.

Hop-On, Hop-Off

Rome has its own "hop-on, hop-off" sightseeing buses. The Trambus Open Roma 110 bus leaves with 10-minute frequencies from Piazza dei Cinquecento (at the main Termini railway station), with a two-hour loop including the Quirinale, the Colosseum, Piazza Navona, St. Peter's, the Trevi Fountain, and Via Veneto. Tickets are €16 (kids 6–12, €7). A variant is the Archeobus, which departs every 20 minutes from the Piazza dei Cinquecento and heads on out to the Via Appia Antica, including stops at the Colosseum, Baths of Caracalla, and the Catacombs. Tickets are €13 (kids 6–12, €6). The Web site for both is ⊕ www.trambusopen.com.

Roman Hours

Virtually the entire city shuts down on Sundays, although museums, pastry shops, and most restaurants are closed Mondays. However, most stores in the *centro storico* area, the part of town that caters to tourists, remain open. Shop hours generally run from 10 AM to 1 PM, then reopen around 4 PM until 7:30 or 8 PM. Unless advertised as having *orario continuato* (open all day), most businesses close from 1 to 4 PM for lunch, or *riposo*. On Mondays, shops usually don't open until around 3 or 4 PM. Pharmacies tend to have the same hours of operation as stores unless they advertise *orario notturno* (night hours); two can be found at Piazza Barberini and Piazza Risorgimento (near St. Peter's Square). As for churches, most open at 8 or 9 in the morning, close from noon to 3 or 4, then reopen until 6:30 or 7. St. Peter's, however, is open 7 AM to 7 PM (6 in the fall and winter).

Information, Please

Rome's main APT (Azienda Per Turismo) Tourist Information Office is at Via Parigi 5–11 (☎ 06/488991 ⊕ www.romaturismo.it), near the main Termini rail station.

In addition, green APT information kiosks with multilingual personnel are situated near the most important sights and squares, as well as at Termini Station and Leonardo da Vinci Airport. These kiosks, called Tourist Information Sites (Punti Informativi Turistici, or PIT) can be found at:

PIT Castel S. Angelo, Lungotevere Vaticano; open 9:30–7 PM

PIT Cinque Lune, Piazza delle Cinque Lune (Piazza Navona); open 9:30–7 PM

PIT Fiumicino, Aeroporto Leonardo Da Vinci–Arrivi Internazionali Terminal C; open 9–7:30 PM

PIT Minghetti, Via Marco Minghetti (corner of Via del Corso); open 9:30–7 PM

PIT Nazionale, Via Nazionale (Palazzo delle Esposizioni); open 9:30–7 PM

PIT Santa Maria Maggiore, at Via dell'Olmata; open 9:30–7 PM

PIT Termini, Stazione Termini, at Via Giovanni Giolitti 34; open 8–8 PM

PIT Trastevere, on Piazza Sidney Sonnino; open 9:30–7 PM

GETTING HERE AND AROUND

Getting Here by Car

The main access routes from the north are A1 (Autostrada del Sole) from Milan and Florence and the A12-E80 highway from Genoa. The principal route to or from points south, including Naples, is the A2. All highways connect with the Grande Raccordo Anulare Ring Road (GRA), which channels traffic into the city center. For driving directions, check out ⊕ *www.tuttocitta.it.* Note: private cars not belonging to residents aren't allowed in the entire historic center during the day (weekdays 8–6; Saturday 2 PM–6 PM). Parking in Rome can be a nightmare.

Getting Here by Train

Rome is a major hub for Trenitalia (☎ *892/2021 within Italy, 06/68475475 from abroad* ⊕ *www.trenitalia.it*), which has service throughout Italy. The main station in Rome is Termini, but there is also significant traffic through the Tiburtina, Ostiense, and Trastevere stations. On longer routes (to Florence and Venice, for instance), you can either travel by the cheap but slow *diretto* trains, or the fast but more expensive Intercity or Eurostar.

Getting Here by Air

Rome's principal airport is Leonardo da Vinci Airport/Fiumicino (☎ *06/65951* ⊕ *www.adr.it*) commonly known as Fiumicino (FCO). It's 30 km (19 mi) southwest of the city but has a direct train link with downtown Rome. Rome's other airport, with no direct train link, is Ciampino (☎ *06/794941* ⊕ *www.adr.it*) or CIA, 15 km (9 mi) south of downtown and used mostly by low-cost airlines.

Two trains link downtown Rome with Fiumicino. Inquire at the APT tourist information counter in the International Arrivals hall (Terminal B) or train information counter near the tracks to determine which takes you closest to your destination in Rome. The 30-minute nonstop Airport-Termini express (called the Leonardo Express) goes directly to Track 25 at Termini Station, Rome's main train station; tickets cost €11. The FM1 train stops in Trastevere. Always stamp your tickets in the little machines near the track before you board.

For Ciampino, COTRAL buses connect to trains that go to the city.

Getting Here by Bus

Bus lines cover all of Rome's surrounding Lazio region and are operated by the Compagnia Trasporti Laziali, or COTRAL (☎ *800/150008* ⊕ *www.cotralspa.it*). These bus routes terminate either near Tiburtina Station or at outlying Metro stops, such as Rebibbia and Ponte Mammolo (Line B) and Anagnina (Line A).

COTRAL and buses run by SENA (☎ *800/930960* ⊕ *www.sena.it*) are good options for taking short day trips from Rome, such as those that leave daily from Rome's Ponte Mammolo (Line B) metro station for the town of Tivoli, where Hadrian's Villa and Villa D'Este are located.

Rome Public Transit

Rome's integrated transportation system is ATAC (☎ *06/46952027 or 800/431784* ⊕ *www.atac.roma.it*), which includes the Metropolitana subway, city buses, and municipal trams. A ticket (BIT) valid for 75 minutes on any combination of buses and trams and one entrance to the Metro costs €1. Day passes can be purchased for €4, and weekly passes for €16. Tickets (singly or in quantity—it's a good idea to have a few tickets handy so you don't have to hunt for a vendor when you need one) are sold at tobacconists, newsstands, some coffee bars, automatic ticket machines in Metro stations, some bus stops, and ATAC and COTRAL ticket booths. Time-stamp tickets at Metro turnstiles and in little yellow machines on buses and trams when boarding the first vehicle, and stamp it again when boarding for the last time within 75 minutes.

Getting Around by Bus and Tram

ATAC city buses and trams are orange, gray-and-red, or blue-and-orange. You board at the rear and to exit at the middle; you must buy your ticket before boarding, and stamp it in a machine as soon as you enter.

Buses and trams run from 5:30 AM to midnight, plus there's an extensive network of night (*notturno*) buses. ATAC has a Web site (⊕ *www.atac.roma.it*) that can help you plan your route. To navigate the site, look for *"Muoversi a Roma"* and then click on *"Calcola il percorso"* to get to another page that changes the site into English.

Be aware that *festivi* buses run only on Sundays and holidays; regular buses will either be marked *feriali* (daily) or won't be labeled. Free Metro Routes maps are available at tourist info booths.

Getting Around by Metropolitana

The Metropolitana (or Metro) is the easiest and fastest way to get around Rome. The Metro A line—known as the *linea turistica* (tourist line) will take you to a chunk of the main attractions in Rome: Piazza di Spagna (Spagna stop), Piazza del Popolo (Flaminio), St. Peter's Square and the Vatican Museums (Cipro-Musei Vaticani), and the Trevi Fountain (Barberini). The B line will take you to the Coliseum (Colosseo stop) and Circus Maximus (Ostiense Station), and also lead you to the heart of Testaccio, Rome's nightlife district. The two lines intersect at Rome's main station, Termini. Street entrances are marked with red "M" signs. The Metro opens at 5:30 AM, and the last trains leave the last station at either end at 11:30 PM (12:30 AM on Friday and Saturday nights).

Getting Around by Taxi

Taxis in Rome do not cruise, but if free they will stop if you flag them down. They wait at stands but can also be called by phone (☎ *06/6645, 06/3570, 06/4994, 06/5551, or 06/4157*). Always ask for a receipt (*ricevuta*) to make sure the driver charges you the correct amount. Use only licensed cabs with a plaque next to the license plate reading *"Servizio Pubblico."*

EATING AND DRINKING WELL IN ROME

In Rome, traditional cuisine reigns supreme. Most chefs follow the mantra of freshness over fuss, simplicity of flavor and preparation over complex cooking methods.

So when Romans continue ordering the standbys, it's easy to understand why. And we're talking about *very* old standbys: some restaurants re-create dishes that come from ancient recipes of Apicius, probably the first celebrity chef (to Emperor Tiberius) and cookbook author of the Western world. Today, Rome's cooks excel at what has taken hundreds, or thousands, of years to perfect.

Still, if you're hunting for newer-than-now developments, things are slowly changing. Talented young chefs are exploring new culinary frontiers, with results that tingle the taste buds: potato gnocchi with sea urchin sauce, artichoke strudel, and oysters with red-onion foam are just a few recent examples. Of course, there's grumbling about the number of chefs who, in a clumsy effort to be *nuovo*, end up with collision rather than fusion. That noted, Rome *is* the capital city, and the influx of residents from other regions of the country allows for many variations on the Italian theme.

FOODIE FINDS

Via Cola di Rienzo is home to two of Rome's best specialty shops: **Castroni** (⊠ *Via Cola di Rienzo 200, Prati* ☎ *06/6874651*), pictured above, a gastro-shop that sells high-quality cured meats, Italian cheeses, wines, pastas, and fresh truffles. Next door, **Franchi** (⊠ *Via Cola di Rienzo 196, Prati* ☎ *06/68743382*) is well known among expats for its imported foreign foods from the United States, Great Britain, Japan, India, and Mexico, as well as its impressive selection of candies, preserves, olive oils, and balsamic vinegars. Franchi is a great place to stop in for caffé and a cornetto (an Italian croissant).

2

ARTICHOKES

If there's one vegetable Rome is known for, it's the artichoke, or *carciofo*. The classic Roman preparation, *carciofo alla romana,* is a large, globe-shaped artichoke stuffed with wild mint and garlic, then braised. It's available at restaurants throughout the city in spring, when artichokes are in season. For the excellent Roman-Jewish version, *carciofo alla giudia*—a younger artichoke deep-fried until crisp and brown—head to any restaurant in the Ghetto.

BUCATINI ALLA MATRICIANA

What may appear to the naked eye as spaghetti with red sauce is actually *bucatini alla matriciana*—a spicy, rich, and complex dish that owes its flavor to an important ingredient: *guanciale,* or cured pig's cheek. Once you taste a meaty, guanciale-flavored dish, you'll understand why Romans swear by it. Along with guanciale, the simple sauce features crushed tomatoes and red pepper flakes. It is served over *bucatini*, a hollow, spaghetti-like pasta, and topped with grated pecorino romano cheese.

CODA ALLA VACCINARA

Rome's largest slaughterhouse in the 1800s was housed in the Testaccio neighborhood. That's where you'll find dishes like *coda alla vaccinara,* or "oxtail in the style of the slaughterhouse." This dish is made from oxtails stewed with tomatoes and wine, and seasoned with

garlic, cinnamon, pancetta, and myriad other flavorings. The stew cooks for a day or two, then is finished with the sweet-and-sour element—often raisins or bittersweet chocolate—and served over polenta or pasta.

GELATO

For many travelers, the first taste of *gelato* is one of the most memorable moments of their Italian trip. Almost a cross between regular American ice cream and soft serve, gelato's texture is dense but softer than hard ice cream because of the process by which it's whipped when freezing. Gelato is extremely flavorful, and often made daily. In Rome, a few common flavors are *stracciatella* (chocolate chip), *caffè* (coffee), *nocciola* (hazelnut), *fragola* (strawberry), and *cioccolato* (chocolate).

PIZZA

Roman pizza comes in two types: *pizza rustica* and *pizza al taglio* (by the slice), which has a thicker focaccialike crust and is cut into squares. These slices are sold by weight and are available all day. The other type, *pizza tonda* (whole rounds), has a very thin crust. *Pizza tonda* is cooked in wood-burning ovens that reach extremely high temperatures. Since they're so hot, the ovens are usually fired up only in the evenings, which is why Roman pizzerias are only open for dinner.

Updated by
Martin Wilmot
Bennett, Dana
Klitzberg,
Nicole
Arriaga,
Erica Firpo,
and Lynda
Albertson

COMING OFF THE AUTOSTRADA at Roma Nord or Roma Sud, you know by the convergence of heavily trafficked routes that you are entering a grand nexus: All roads lead to Rome. And then the interminable suburbs, the railroad crossings, the intersections—no wonder they call it the Eternal City. As you enter the city proper, features that match your expectations begin to take shape: a bridge with heroic statues along its parapets; a towering cake of frothy marble decorated with allegorical figures in extravagant poses; a piazza and an obelisk under an umbrella of pine trees. Then you spot what looks like a multistory parking lot; with a gasp, you realize it's the Colosseum.

You have arrived. You're in the city's heart. You step down from your excursion bus onto the broad girdle of tarmac that encircles the great stone arena of the Roman emperors, and scurry out of the way of the passing Fiats—the motorists behind the wheels seem to display the panache of so many Ben-Hurs. The excitement of arriving here jolts the senses and sharpens expectations.

The timeless city to which all roads lead, Mamma Roma, enthralls visitors today as she has since time immemorial. More than Florence, more than Venice, this is Italy's treasure storehouse. Here, the ancient Romans made us heirs-in-law to what we call Western civilization; where centuries later Michelangelo painted the Sistine Chapel; where Gian Lorenzo Bernini's baroque nymphs and naiads still dance in their marble fountains; and where, at Cinecittà Studios, Fellini filmed *La Dolce Vita* and *8½*. Today, the city remains a veritable Grand Canyon of culture: Ancient Rome rubs shoulders with the medieval, the modern runs into the Renaissance, and the result is like nothing so much as an open-air museum.

Little wonder Rome's enduring popularity feeds a gluttonous tourism industry that can feel more like *National Lampoon's European Vacation* than *Roman Holiday*. As tour buses belch black smoke and the line at the Vatican Museums stretches on into eternity, even the steeliest of sightseers have been known to wonder, why am I here? The answer, with apologies to Dorothy, is: There's no place like Rome. Yesterday's Grand Tourists thronged the city for the same reason today's Expedians do. Majestic, complicated, enthralling, romantic, chaotic, monumental Rome is one of the world's great cities—past, present, and, probably, future.

But always remember: *Quando a Roma vai, fai come vedrai* ("When in Rome, do as the Romans do"). Don't feel intimidated by the press of art and culture. Instead, contemplate the grandeur from a table at a sun-drenched café on Piazza della Rotonda; let Rome's colorful life flow around you without feeling guilty because you haven't seen everything. It can't be done, anyway. There's just so much here that you will have to come back again, so be sure to throw a coin in the Trevi Fountain. It works.

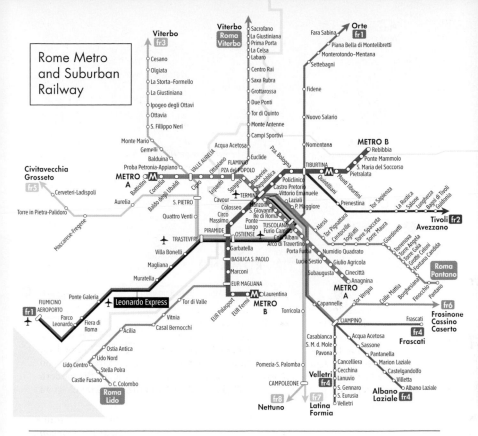

EXPLORING ROME

Updated by
Martin Wilmot
Bennett

Most everyone begins by discovering the grandeur that was Rome: the Colosseum, the Forum, and the Pantheon. Then many move on to the Vatican, the closest thing to heaven on Earth for some.

The historical pageant continues with the 1,001 splendors of the baroque era: glittering palaces, jewel-studded churches, and Caravaggio masterpieces. Arrive refreshed—with the help of a shot of espresso—at the foot of the Spanish Steps, where the picturesque world of the classic Grand Tour (peopled by such spirits as John Keats and Tosca) awaits you.

Thankfully, Rome provides delightful ways to catch your historic breath along the way: a walk through the cobblestone valleys of Trastevere or an hour stolen alongside a splashing Bernini fountain. Keep in mind that an uncharted ramble through the heart of the old city can be just as satisfying as the contemplation of a chapel or a trek through marbled museum corridors. No matter which aspect of Rome you end up enjoying the most, a visit to the Eternal City will live up to its name in memory.

Continued on page 50

ADMISSION

Roma Pass*	€25
Arco di Constantino	Free
Circo Massimo	Free
Mercato di Traiano	€6.50
Colosseo, Colle Palatino & Foro Romano	€12
Domus Aurea	€4.50
Musei Capitolini	€6.50
Piazza del Campidoglio	Free
Santa Maria d'Aracoeli	Free
Terme di Caracalla	€6

* Includes access to two sites or museums (including the Colosseum and Musei Capitolini) and a three-day public transport pass.

CAPITOLINE HILL: The ancient Romans built their most important temples here, and it's been the seat of city government since the Middle Ages. It now holds the Capitoline Museums, chock-full of the treasures of antiquity.

ROMAN FORUM: Downtown Ancient Rome. People from all corners of the empire crowded into the Forum to do business, to hear the latest news, and to worship.

PALATINE HILL: Home of the empire's rich and famous. Luxurious villas lined Palatine Hill; emperors held court on its heights and vied with their predecessors for lasting renown.

CAMPIDOGLIO   FORO ROMANO   COLLE PALATINO

ANCIENT ROME
GLORIES OF
THE CAESARS

Time has reduced ancient Rome to fields of silent ruins, but the powerful impact of what happened here, of the genius and power that made Rome the center of the Western world, echoes across the millennia.

In this one compact area of the city, you can step back into the Rome of Cicero, Julius Caesar, and Virgil. Walk along the streets they knew, cool off in the shade of the Colosseum that loomed over the city, and see the sculptures poised above their piazzas. At the end of a day of exploring, climb one of the famous hills and watch the sun set over what was once the heart of the civilized world.

Today, this part of Rome, more than any other, is a perfect example of that layering of historic eras, the overlapping of ages, of religions, of a past that is very much a part of the present. Christian churches rise from the foundations of ancient pagan temples. An immense marble monument to a 19th-century king shares a square with a Renaissance palace built by a pope. Still, the history and memory of ancient Rome dominate the area. It's fitting that in the aftermath of centuries of such pageantry Percy Bysshe Shelley and Edward Gibbon reflected here on the meaning of *sic transit gloria mundi* (so passes away the glory of the world).

COLOSSEUM: Gladiators fought for the chance to live another day on the floor of the Colosseum, iconic symbol of ancient Rome.

CAMPIDOGLIO

The Capitoline Museums are closed on Monday. Late evening is an option for this area. Though the Santa Maria d'Aracoeli church is closed, the museums are open until 8 PM, and the views of the city lights and the illuminated Altare della Patria (aka the Victor Emmanuel II monument) and the Foro Romano are striking.

CLIMB MICHELANGELO'S DRAMATIC RAMP TO THE SUMMIT of one of Rome's famous hills, the Campidoglio (also known as Capitoline Hill), for views across the rooftops of modern Rome in one direction and across the ruins of ancient Rome in the other. Check out the stellar Musei Capitolini, crammed with a collection of masterpieces rivaled only by the Vatican museums.

★ **Piazza del Campidoglio.** In Michelangelo's piazza at the top of the Campidoglio stands a bronze equestrian statue of Marcus Aurelius (AD 121–180). A legend foretells that some day the statue's original gold surface will return, heralding the end of the world. Pending the arrival of that day, the original 2nd century statue was moved inside the Musei Capitolini; a copy sits on the piazza. Stand with your back to it to survey central Rome.

The Campidoglio, the site of the Roman Republic's first and holiest temples, had fallen into ruin by the Middle Ages and was called *Monte Caprino* (Goat Hill). In 1536 Pope Paul III (1468–1549) decided to restore its grandeur for the triumphal entry into the city of Charles V (1500–1558), the Holy Roman Emperor. He called upon Michelangelo to create the staircase ramp, the buildings and facades

on the square, the pavement decoration, and the pedestal for the bronze statue.

The two buildings that make up the **Musei Capitolini** are on the piazza, flanking the **Palazzo Senatorio**. The Campidoglio has long been the seat of Rome's government; its Latin name is the root for the word capitol. Today, Rome's city hall occupies the Palazzo Senatorio. Head to the vantage points in the belvederes on the sides of the palazzo for great views of the ruins of ancient Rome.

★ **Musei Capitolini** (Capitoline Museums). Housed in the twin Palazzo Nuovo and Palazzo dei Conservatori buildings, this is a greatest hits collection of Roman art through the ages, from the ancients to the baroque.

The **Palazzo Nuovo** contains hundreds of Roman busts of philosophers and

---

AN EMPEROR CHEAT SHEET

OCTAVIAN/AUGUSTUS (27 BC–AD 14)
After the death of Julius Caesar, Octavian gained control of Rome following a decade-long civil war that ended with the defeat of Antony and Cleopatra at Actium. Later known as Caesar Augustus, he was Rome's first emperor. His rule began a 200-year period of peace known as the Pax Romana.
Colle Palatino

CALIGULA (AD 37–41)
Caligula was tremendously popular when he came to power at the age of 25, but he very soon became infamous for his excessive cruelty, immorality, and erratic behavior. His contemporaries universally considered him to be insane. He was murdered by his own guard within four years.

emperors—a fascinating Who's Who of the ancient world. A dozen Roman emperors are represented. Unlike the Greeks, whose portraits are idealized, the Romans preferred a more realistic representation. Other notable sculptures include the poignant *Dying Gaul* and the regal *Capitoline Venus*. In the Capitolino courtyard is a gigantic, reclining sculpture of Oceanus, found in the Roman Forum and later dubbed *Marforio*. This was one of Rome's "talking statues" to which citizens from the 1500s to the 1900s affixed anonymous satirical verses and notes of political protest. Opened in 2006, the Esedra di Marco Aurelio displays the famous bronze equestrian statue of emperor Marcus Aurelius (180 AD).

Lining the courtyard of the **Palazzo dei Conservatori** are the colossal fragments of a head, leg, foot, and hand—all that remains of the famous statue of the emperor Constantine. These immense effigies were much in vogue throughout the Roman Empire. The renowned symbol of Rome, the *Capitoline Wolf*, a medieval bronze (long thought to be Etruscan), holds a place of honor in the museum; the suckling twins were added during the Renaissance to adapt the statue to the legend of Romulus and Remus. The Palazzo also contains some of baroque painting's great masterpieces, including Caravaggio's *La Buona Ventura* (1595) and *San Giovanni Battista* (1602), Peter Paul Rubens's *Romulus and Remus* (1614), and Pietro da Cortona's sumptuous portrait of Pope Urban VIII (1627). When museum fatigue sets in, enjoy the view and refreshments on a large open terrace in the Palazzo dei Conservatoria. ☎ *06/39967800* ⊕ *www.museicapitolini. org* ⊘ *Tues.–Sun. 9–8.*

Santa Maria in Aracoeli. Seemingly endless, steep stairs climb from Piazza Venezia to the Santa Maria. There are 15th-century frescoes by Pinturicchio (1454–1513) in the first chapel on the right. ⊠ *Piazza d'Aracoeli* ⊘ *Daily, 9–12:30, 3–6:30.*

NERO (AD 54–68)

Nero is infamous as a violent persecutor of Christians. He also murdered his wife, his mother, and countless others. Although it's certain he didn't actually fiddle as Rome burned in AD 64, he was well known as a singer and a composer of music.

Domus Aurea

DOMITIAN (AD 81–96)

The first emperor to declare himself "Dominus et Deus" (Lord and God), he stripped away power from the Senate. After his death, the Senate retaliated by declaring him "Damnatio Memoriae" (his name and image were erased from all public records).

Colle Palatino

FORO ROMANO
⏱ **TIMING TIPS**

It takes about an hour to explore the Roman Forum. There are entrances on the Via dei Fori Imperiali and Piazza del Colosseo. A 30-minute walk will cover the Imperial Fora. You can reserve tickets online or by phone—operators speak English. If you are buying tickets in person, remember there are shorter lines here than at the Colosseum and the ticket is good for both sights.

EXPERIENCE THE ENDURING ROMANCE OF THE FORUM. Wander among its lonely columns and great, broken fragments of sculpted marble and stone—once temples, law courts, and shops crowded with people from all corners of the known world. This was the heart of ancient Rome and a symbol of the values that inspired Rome's conquest of an empire.

★ **Foro Romano** (Roman Forum). Built in a marshy valley between the Capitoline and Palatine hills, the Forum was the civic core of Republican Rome, the austere era that preceded the hedonism of the emperors. The Forum was the political, commercial, and religious center of Roman life. Hundreds of years of plunder and the tendency of later Romans to carry off what was left of the better building materials reduced it to the series of ruins you see today. Archaeological digs continue to uncover more about the sight; bear in mind that what you see are the ruins not of one period but of almost 900 years, from about 500 BC to AD 400.

The **Basilica Giulia**, which owes its name to Julius Caesar who had it built, was where the Centumviri, the hundred-or-so judges forming the civil court, met to hear cases. The open space before it was the core of the forum proper and prototype of Italy's famous piazzas. Let your imagination dwell on Mark Antony (circa 81 BC–30 BC), who delivered the funeral address in Julius Caesar's honor from the rostrum left of the **Arco di Settimio Severo**. This arch, one of the grandest of all antiquity, was built several hundred years later in AD 203 to celebrate the victory of the emperor Severus (AD 146–211) over the Parthians, and was topped by a bronze equestrian statuary group with four horses. You can explore the reconstruction of the large brick senate hall, the **Curia**; three Corinthian columns (a favorite of 19th-century poets) are all that remains of the **Tempio di Vespasiano**. In the **Tempio di Vesta**, six highly privileged vestal virgins kept the sacred fire, a tradition that dated back to the very earliest days of Rome, when guarding the community's precious fire was essential to its well-being. The cleaned and restored **Arco di Tito**, which stands in a slightly

AN EMPEROR CHEAT SHEET

TRAJAN (AD 98–117)

Trajan, from Southern Spain, was the first Roman emperor not born in Italy. He enlarged the empire's boundaries to include modern-day Romania, Armenia, and Upper Mesopotamia.

Colonna di Traiano, Foro di Traiano, Mercato di Traiano

HADRIAN (AD 117–138)

He expanded the empire in Asia and the Middle East. He's best known for rebuilding the Pantheon, constructing a majestic villa at Tivoli, and initiating myriad other constructions across the empire, including the famed wall across Britain.

Pantheon, in Baroque Rome

elevated position on a spur of the Palatine Hill, was erected in AD 81 to honor the recently dead Emperor Titus. It depicts the sacking of Jerusalem 10 years earlier, after the great Jewish revolt. A famous relief shows the captured contents of Herod's Temple—including its huge seven-branched menorah—being carried in triumph down Rome's Via Sacra. Making sense of the ruins isn't always easy; consider renting an audio guide (€4) or buying a booklet that superimposes an image of the Forum in its heyday over a picture of it today. Guided tours in English usually begin at 10:30 AM. ☎ 06/39967700 ⊕ www.pierreci.it ☉ Daily, Jan.–Feb. 15 and last Sun. in Oct.–Dec., 8:30–4:30; Feb. 16–Mar. 15, 8:30–5; Mar. 16–28, 8:30–5:30; Mar. 29–Aug., 8:30–7:15; Sept., 8:30–7; Oct.1– last Sat. in Oct., 8:30–6:30.

THE OTHER FORA

Fori Imperiali (Imperial Fora). These five grandly conceived squares flanked with columnades and temples were built by Caesar, Augustus, Vespasian, Nerva, and Trajan. The original Roman Forum, built up over 500 years of Republican Rome, had grown crowded, and Julius Caesar was the first to attempt to rival it. He built the **Foro di Cesare** (Forum of Caesar), including a temple dedicated to the goddess Venus. Four later emperors followed his lead, creating their own fora. The grandest was the **Foro di Traiano** (Forum of Trajan) a veritable city unto itself built by Trajan (AD 53–117). Here you find the 100-ft Colonna di Traiano (Trajan's Column, AD 110), carved with 2,600 reliefs. In the 20th century, Benito Mussolini built the Via dei Fori Imperiali directly through the Imperial Fora area. Marble and limestone maps on the wall along the avenue portray the extent of the Roman Republic and Empire, and many of the remains of the Imperial Fora lay buried beneath its surface.

Mercati di Traiano (Trajan's Markets). This huge multilevel brick complex of 120 shops was one of the marvels of the ancient world. Reopened to the public in 2007, it provides a glimpse into Roman daily life and offers a stellar view from the belvedere at its top. ☎ 06/820771 ⊕ www.mercatiditraiano.it ☉ Tues.–Sun., 9–7.

MARCUS AURELIUS (AD 161–180)

Remembered as a humanitarian emperor, Marcus Aurelius was a Stoic philosopher and his *Meditations* are still read today. Nonetheless, he was an aggressive leader devoted to expanding the empire.

Piazza del Campidoglio

CONSTANTINE I (AD 306–337)

Constantine changed the course of history by legalizing Christianity. He legitimized the once-banned religion and paved the way for the papacy in Rome. Constantine also founded Constantinople, an Imperial capital in the East.

Arco di Constantino

COLLE PALATINO

A stroll on the Palatino, with a visit to the Museo Palatino, takes about two hours. The hill was once home to several major imperial palaces. Domitian's 1st-century AD palace is the best preserved. The Colle Palatino entrances are in the Roman Forum and at Via S. Gregorio 30.

IT ALL BEGAN HERE. ACCORDING TO LEGEND, ROMULUS, THE FOUNDER OF ROME, lived on the Colle Palatino (Palatine Hill). It was an exclusive address in ancient Rome, where emperors built palaces upon the slopes. Tour the Palatine's hidden corners and shady lanes, take a welcome break from the heat in its peaceful gardens, and enjoy a view of the Circo Massimo fit for an emperor.

★ **Colle Palatino** (Palatine Hill). A lane known as the Clivus Palatinus, paved with worn stones that were once trod by emperors and their slaves, climbs from the Forum area to a site that historians identify as one of Rome's earliest settlements. The legend goes that the infant twins Romulus and Remus were nursed by a she-wolf on the banks of the Tiber and adopted by a shepherd. Encouraged by the gods to build a city, Romulus chose this site in 753 BC. Remus preferred the Aventine. The argument that ensued left Remus dead and Romulus Rome's first king.

During the Republican era the hill was an important religious center, housing the Temple of Cybele and the Temple of Victory, as well as an exclusive residential area. Cicero, Catiline, Crassus, and Agrippa all had homes here. Augustus was born on the hill, and as he rose in power, he built libraries, halls, and temples here; the **House of Augustus**, opened in 2008, preserves exquisite 1st-century BC frescoes. Emperor Tiberius was the next to build a palace here; others followed. The structures most visible today date back to the late 1st century AD, when the Palatine experienced an extensive remodeling under Emperor Domitian. During the Renaissance, the powerful Farnese family built gardens in the only area overlooking the ruins of the Forum. Known as the **Orti Farnesiani**, they were Europe's first botanical gardens. The **Museo Palatino** charts the history of the hill. Splendid sculptures, frescoes, and mosaic intarsia from various imperial buildings are on display. ☎ *06/39967700* ⊕ *www.pierreci.it* ⊙ *Daily, 8:30–1 hour before sunset.*

THE RISE AND FALL OF ANCIENT ROME

218 BC

ca. 800 BC	Rise of Etruscan city-states.
510	Foundation of the Roman republic; expulsion of Etruscans from Roman territory.
343	Roman conquest of Greek colonies in Campania.
264–241	First Punic War (with Carthage): increased naval power helps Rome gain control of southern Italy and then Sicily.
218–200	Second Punic War: Hannibal's attempted conquest of Italy, using elephants, is eventually crushed.

NEAR THE COLLE PALATINO

Circo Massimo (Circus Maximus). Ancient Rome's oldest and largest racetrack lies in the natural hollow between Palatine and Aventine hills. From the imperial box in the palace on Palatine Hill, emperors could look out over the oval course. Stretching about 650 yards from end to end, the Circus Maximus could hold more than 200,000 spectators. On certain occasions there were as many as 100 chariot races a day, and competitions could last for 15 days. The central ridge was framed by two Egyptian obelisks. Check out the panoramic views of the Circus Maximus from the Palatine Hill's Belvedere. You can also see the green slopes of the Aventine and Celian hills, as well as the bell tower of Santa Maria in Cosmedin.

Terme di Caracalla (Baths of Caracalla). For the Romans, public baths were much more than places to wash. The baths also had recital halls, art galleries, libraries, massage rooms, sports grounds, and gardens. Even the smallest public baths had at least some of these amenities, and in the capital of the Roman Empire, they were provided on a lavish scale. Ancient Rome's most beautiful and luxurious public baths were opened by the emperor Caracalla in AD 217 and were used until the 6th century.

Taking a bath was a long process, and a social activity first and foremost. You began by sweating in the *sudatoria*, small rooms resembling saunas. From these you moved on to the *calidarium* for the actual business of washing, using an olive-oil-and-sand exfoliant, then removing it with a *strigil* (scraper). Next was the *tepidarium*, where you gradually cooled down. Finally, you splashed around in the *frigidarium*, in essence a cold–water swimming pool. There was a nominal admission fee, often waived by officials and emperors wishing to curry favor with the plebeians. The baths' functioning depended on the slaves who cared for the clients and stoked the fires that heated the water. ☎ 06/39967700 ⊕ *www.pier-reci.it* ⊗ *Tues.–Sun., Jan.–Feb. 15 and last Sun. in Oct.–Dec., 9–4:30; Feb. 16–Mar. 15, 9–5; Mar. 16–last Sat. in Mar., 9–5:30; last Sun. in Mar.–Aug., 9–7:15; Sept., 9–7; Oct. 1–last Sat. in Oct., 9–6:30. For all Mondays, 9–2.*

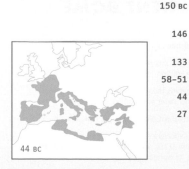

44 BC

150 BC	Roman Forum begins to take shape as the principal civic center in Italy.
146	Third Punic War: Rome razes city of Carthage and emerges as the dominant Mediterranean force.
133	Rome rules entire Mediterranean Basin except Egypt.
58–51	Julius Caesar conquers Gaul.
44	Julius Caesar is assassinated.
27	Rome's Imperial Age begins; Octavian (now named Augustus) becomes the first emperor and is later deified. The Augustan Age is celebrated in the works of Virgil (70 BC–AD 19), Ovid (43 BC–AD 17), Livy (59 BC–AD 17), and Horace (65–8 BC).

COLOSSEO

⊙ **TIMING TIPS**

You can give the Colosseum a cursory look in about 30 minutes, but it deserves at least an hour. Make reservations by phone (there are English-speaking operators) or online at least a day in advance to avoid long lines. Or buy your ticket at the Roman Forum or Palatine Hill, where the lines are usually shorter.

LEGEND HAS IT THAT AS LONG AS THE COLOSSEUM STANDS, ROME WILL STAND; and when Rome falls, so will the world. No visit to Rome is complete without a trip to the obstinate oval that has been the iconic symbol of the city for centuries.

★ **Colosseo.** A program of games and shows lasting 100 days celebrated the opening of the massive and majestic Colosseum in AD 80. On the opening day Romans claimed that 5,000 wild beasts perished. More than 50,000 spectators could sit within the arena's 573-yard circumference, which had limestone facing, hundreds of statues for decoration, and a *velarium*—an ingenious system of sail-like awnings rigged on ropes manned by imperial sailors—to protect the audience from the sun and rain. Before the imperial box, gladiators would salute the emperor and cry, "*Ave, imperator, morituri te salutant*" ("Hail, emperor, men soon to die salute you"); it is said that when one day they heard the emperor Claudius respond, "Or maybe not," they were so offended that they called a strike.

Originally known as the Flavian Amphitheater, it took the name Colosseum after a truly colossal gilt bronze statue of Nero that stood nearby. Gladiator combat ended by the 5th century and staged animal hunts by the 6th. The arena later served as a quarry from which materials were looted to build Renaissance churches and palaces, including St. Peter's Basilica. Finally, it was declared sacred by the Vatican in memory of the many Christians believed martyred here. (Scholars now maintain that Christians met their death elsewhere.) During the 19th century, romantic poets lauded the glories of the ruins when viewed by moonlight. Now its arches glow at night with mellow golden spotlights.

Expect long lines at the entrance and actors dressed as gladiators who charge a hefty fee to pose for pictures. (Agree on a price in advance if you want a photo.) Once inside you can walk around about half of the outer ring of the structure and look down into the exposed passages under what was once the arena floor, now represented by a small stage at one end. Climb the steep stairs for panoramic views

THE RISE AND FALL OF ANCIENT ROME

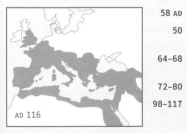

AD 116

58 AD	Rome invades Britain.
50	Rome is the largest city in the world, with a population of a million.
64–68	Emperor Nero begins the persecution of Christians in the Empire; Saints Peter and Paul are executed.
72–80	Vespasian begins the Colosseum; Titus completes it.
98–117	Trajan's military successes are celebrated with his Baths (98), Forum (110), and Column (113); the Roman Empire reaches its apogee.

in the Colosseum and out to the Forum and Arch of Constantine. A museum space on the upper floor holds temporary archaeological exhibits. ☎ 06/39967700 ⊕ *www.pierreci.it* ☉ *Daily, 8:30–1 hour before sunset.*

Arco di Costantino. The largest (69 feet high, 85 feet long, 23 feet wide) and the best preserved of Rome's triumphal arches was erected in AD 315 to celebrate the victory of the emperor Constantine (280–337) over co-emperor Maxentius (died 312). It was just before this battle that Constantine, the emperor who legalized Christianity, had a vision of a cross in the heavens and heard the words "In this sign, thou shalt conquer."

NEAR THE COLOSSEO

Domus Aurea. Nero's "Golden House"was undergoing renovation at press time. The site gives a good sense of the excesses of Imperial Rome. After fire destroyed much of the city in AD 64, Nero took advantage of the resulting open space to construct a lavish palace so large that it spread over a third of the city. It had a facade of marble, seawater piped into the baths, gilded vaults, decorations of mother-of-pearl, and vast gardens. Not much of this ornamentation has survived; a good portion of the building and grounds was buried under the public works with which subsequent emperors sought to make reparation to the Roman people for Nero's phenomenal greed. As a result, the site of the Domus Aurea itself remained unknown for many centuries. A few of Nero's original halls were discovered underground at the end of the 15th century. Raphael (1483–1520) was one of the artists who had themselves lowered into the rubble-filled rooms, which resembled grottoes. The artists copied the original painted Roman decorations, barely visible by torchlight, and scratched their names on the ceilings. Raphael later used these models—known as *grotesques* because they were found in the so-called grottoes—in his decorative motifs for the Loggia of Julius II in the Vatican. The palace remains impressive in scale, even if a lot of imagination is required to envision the original. ✉ *Via della Domus Aurea* ☎ 06/39967700 ⊕ *www.pierreci.it* 🎟 €4.50 ☉ *Temporarily closed for renovation at press time.*

AD 450

238 AD	The first wave of Germanic invasions penetrates Italy.
293	Diocletian reorganizes the Empire into West and East.
330	Constantine founds a new Imperial capital (Constantinople) in the East.
410	Rome is sacked by Visigoths.
476	The last Roman emperor, Romulus Augustus, is deposed. The Roman Empire falls.

NAVONA AND CAMPO: BAROQUE ROME

Long called Vecchia Roma (Old Rome), this time-burnished district is the city's most beautiful neighborhood. Set between the Via del Corso and the Tiber bend, it is filled with narrow streets bearing curious names, airy piazzas, and half-hidden courtyards. Some of Rome's most coveted residential addresses are nestled here. So, too, are the ancient Pantheon and the Renaissance square of Campo de' Fiori, but the spectacular, over-the-top baroque monuments of the 16th and 17th centuries predominate.

The hub of the district is the queen of squares, Piazza Navona—a cityscape adorned with the most eye-knocking fountain by Gian Lorenzo Bernini, father of the baroque. Streets running off the square lead to many historic must-sees, including noble churches by Borromini and Caravaggio's greatest paintings at San Luigi dei Francesi. This district has been an integral part of the city since ancient times, and its position between the Vatican and Lateran palaces, both seats of papal rule, put it in the mainstream of Rome's development from the Middle Ages onward. Craftsmen, shopkeepers, and famed artists toiled in the shadow of the huge palaces built to consolidate the power of leading figures in the papal court. Artisans and artists still live here, but their numbers are diminishing as the district becomes increasingly posh and—so critics say—"Disneyfied." But three of the liveliest piazzas in Rome—Piazza Navona, Piazza della Rotonda, and Campo de' Fiori— are lodestars in a constellation of some of Rome's most authentic cafés, stores, and wine bars.

GETTING HERE   To bus it from Termini rail station or the Vatican, take the No. 40 Express or the No. 64 and get off at Corso Vittorio Emanuele II, a five-minute stroll to either Campo de' Fiori or Piazza Navona, or take little electric No. 116 from Via Veneto past the Spanish Steps to Campo de' Fiori. Buses Nos. 87 and 571 link the area to the Forum and Colosseum. Tram No. 8 runs from Largo Argentina to Trastevere.

TOP ATTRACTIONS

⑧ **★** **Campo de' Fiori.** Home to Rome's oldest (since 1869) outdoor produce market, open Monday through Saturday, this bustling square was originally used for public executions, making its name—Field of Flowers—a bit sardonic. In fact, the central statue commemorates the philosopher Giordano Bruno, who was burned at the stake here in 1600 by the Inquisition. Today, he frowns down upon food vendors galore, who, by early afternoon, are all gone, giving way to the square's cafés and bars that attract throngs of Rome's hip, young professionals as the hours wend their way into evening. ⊠ *Campo de' Fiori, near Piazza Navona.*

QUICK
BITES

Some of Rome's best pizza comes out of the ovens of **Forno di Campo de' Fiori** (⊠ *Campo de' Fiori 22* ☎ *06/68806662*). Choose *pizza bianca,* topped with salt and olive oil, or *rossa,* with tomato sauce. Move to the annex across the alley to have your warm pizza filled with prosciutto and figs in September, or other mouthwatering combinations year-round.

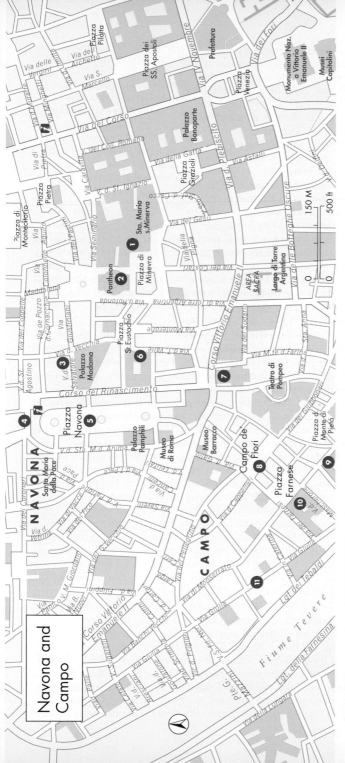

Navona and Campo

4 **Palazzo Altemps.** Containing some of the finest ancient Roman statues in the world, this collection formerly formed the core of the Museo Nazionale Romano. As of 1995, it was moved to these new, suitably grander digs. The palace's sober exterior belies a magnificence that appears as soon as you walk into the majestic courtyard. Set within some gorgeously frescoed, 16th-century rooms is an array of noted antiquities. Look for two works from the famed Ludovisi collection: the *Ludovisi Throne*, a sensual rendering of the birth of Venus (as the goddess is pulled from the water, garments cling to her body in a way that leaves little to the imagination), and *Galata suicida*, a poignant work portraying a barbarian warrior who chooses death for himself and his wife rather than humiliation by the enemy. ⊠ *Piazza Sant'Apollinare 46, near Piazza Navona* ☎ *06/6872719* 🕾 *€7* ☉ *Tues.–Sun. 9–6:45.*

10 **Palazzo Farnese.** The most beautiful Renaissance palace in Rome, the Palazzo Farnese is noted for the grandeur of its rooms, notably the Galleria Carracci, whose ceiling is to the baroque age what the Sistine ceiling is to the Renaissance. The Farnese family rose to great power and wealth during the Renaissance, culminating in the election of Alessandro Farnese as Pope Paul III in 1534. The uppermost frieze decorations and main window overlooking the piazza are the work of Michelangelo, who also designed part of the courtyard, as well as the graceful arch over Via Giulia at the back. The showpiece of the palace is the **Galleria Carracci** vault painted by Annibale Carracci between 1597 and 1607, depicting the loves of the pagan gods in a swirling style that announced the birth of the baroque style. Also eye-popping is the **Salon of Hercules,** with its massive replica of the ancient Farnese Hercules. Now housing the French Embassy, the historic salons can be seen on free tours (in French and Italian only) on Monday and Thursday. You'll need to send a letter or e-mail to reserve tickets, one to four months in advance (depending on peak-season visit or not), specifying the number in your party, when you wish to visit, and a local phone number, for confirmation a few days before the visit. ⊠ *French Embassy, Servizio Culturale, Piazza Farnese 67, i, near Campo de' Fiori* ☎ *06/686011* ✐ *visitefarnese£france-italia.it* 🕾 *Free* ☉ *(Tours by appointment only) on Mon. and Thurs. at 3, 4, and 5 PM. Closed July 24 to Sept. 7.*

9 **Palazzo Spada.** An impressive stuccoed facade on Piazza Capo di Ferro, southeast of Piazza Farnese, fronts an equally magnificent inner courtyard. On the southeast side of the inner courtyard, the gallery designed by Borromini creates an elaborate optical illusion, appearing to be much longer than it really is. On the second floor there are paintings and sculptures that belonged to Cardinale Bernardino Spada, an art connoisseur who collected works by Italian and Flemish masters. Note that the palazzo occasionally closes in the afternoon because of staff shortages. ✉ *Piazza Capo di Ferro 13, near Campo de' Fiori* ☎ *06/6832409* ⊕ *www.galleriaborghese.it/spada/en/einfo.htm* 💶 *€5* ⊙ *Tues.–Sun. 8:30–7:30.*

② **Pantheon.** One of Rome's most impressive and best-preserved ancient **Fodor's Choice** monuments, the Pantheon is particularly close to the hearts of Romans. **★** The emperor Hadrian had it built around AD 120 on the site of an earlier temple that had been damaged by fire. Although the sheer size of the Pantheon is impressive (it is still the largest unreinforced concrete dome ever built), what's most striking is its tangible sense of harmony. In large part this feeling is the result of the building's symmetrical design: at 43.3 meters (142 feet), the height of the dome is equal to the diameter of the circular interior. The "eye of heaven" oculus, or hole in the dome, is open to the skies, illuminating the heavy stone dome. Originally, the dome was covered in bronze plates that would have reflected beams of sunlight, creating a celestial glow. Centuries of plunder by emperors and popes have stripped most of the bronze ornamentation, though the original bronze doors have survived more than 1,800 years. Art lovers can pay homage to the tomb of Raphael, who is buried in an ancient sarcophagus under the altar of Madonna del Sasso. ✉ *Piazza della Rotonda, Navona* ☎ *06/68300230* 💶 *Free* ⊙ *Mon.–Sat. 8:30– 7:30, Sun. 9–6.*

⑤ **Piazza Navona.** With its carefree air of the days when it was the scene **☾** of Roman circus games, medieval jousts, and 17th-century carnivals, **★** the spectacularly beautiful Piazza Navona today often attracts fashion photographers on shoots and Romans out for their *passeggiata* (evening stroll). Bernini's splashing **Fontana dei Quattro Fiumi** (Fountain of the Four Rivers), with an enormous rock squared off by statues representing the four corners of the world, makes a fitting centerpiece. Behind the fountain is the church of **Sant'Agnese in Agone,** an outstanding example of baroque architecture built by the Pamphilj pope Innocent X. The facade—a wonderfully rich mélange of bell towers, concave spaces, and dovetailed stone and marble—is by Borromini, a contemporary and rival of Bernini, and by Carlo Rainaldi (1611–91). One story has it that the Bernini statue nearest the church, which represents the River Plate, has its hand up before its eye because it can't bear the sight of the Borromini facade. Though often repeated, the story is fiction: the facade was built after the fountain. From December 8 through January 6, a Christmas market fills the square with games, Nativity scenes (some well crafted, many not), and multiple versions of the Befana, the ugly but good witch who brings candy and toys to Italian children on the Epiphany. (Her name is a corruption of the Italian word for "epiphany," *Epifania*.) ✉ *Junction of Via della Cuccagna, Corsia Agonale, Via di Sant'Agnese, and Via Agonale, Navona.*

③ **San Luigi dei Francesi.** The official church of Rome's French community **★** and a pilgrimage spot for art lovers everywhere, San Luigi is home to the **Cappella Contarelli,** adorned with three stunningly dramatic works by Caravaggio (1571–1610). Set in the last chapel in the left aisle, they were commissioned by Cardinal Matthieu Cointrel (in Italian, Contarelli) and perfectly embody the baroque master's heightened approach to light and dark. The inevitable coin machine will light up his *Calling*

Going Baroque

Flagrantly emotional, heavily expressive, and visually sensuous, the 17th-century artistic movement known as baroque was born in Rome. It was the creation of three geniuses: the sculptor and architect Gianlorenzo Bernini (1598–1680), the painter and architect Pietro da Cortona (1596–1669), and the architect and sculptor Francesco Borromini (1599–1667). From the drama found in the artists' paintings to the jewel-laden, gold-on-gold detail of 17th-century Roman palaces, baroque style was intended both to shock and delight by upsetting the placid, "correct" rules of proportion and scale in the Renaissance. If a building looks theatrical—like a stage or a theater, especially with curtains being drawn back—it is usually baroque. Look for over-the-top, curvaceous marble work, trompe l'oeil, allusions to other art, and high drama to identify the style. Baroque's appeal to the emotions made it a powerful weapon in the hands of the Counter-Reformation.

of St. Matthew, *Matthew and the Angel*, and *Matthew's Martyrdom*, seen from left to right, and Caravaggio's mastery of light and shadow takes it from there. When painted, they caused considerable consternation to the clergy of San Luigi, who thought the artist's dramatically realistic approach was scandalously disrespectful. But these paintings did to 17th-century art what Picasso's *Demoiselles d'Avignon* did to the 20th century. ⊠ *Piazza San Luigi dei Francesi 5, Navona* ☎ 06/688271 ⊑ *Free* ⊘ *Fri.–Wed. 10–12:30 and 4–7.*

❶ **Santa Maria sopra Minerva.** Michelangelo's *Christ the Redeemer* and the tomb of the gentle 15th-century artist Fra Angelico are two noted sights in the only Gothic-style church in Rome. Have some coins handy to light up the **Cappella Carafa** in the right transept, where exquisite 15th-century frescoes by Filippino Lippi (circa 1457–1504) are well worth the small investment. Historians believe that Botticelli apprenticed under Lippi during this time. In front of the church is one of Rome's best photo ops, Bernini's charming elephant bearing an Egyptian obelisk; an inscription on the memorial's base states that it takes a strong mind to sustain solid wisdom. ⊠ *Piazza della Minerva 42, Pantheon* ☎ 06/6793926 ⊘ *Mon.–Sun. 9–7.*

⓫ **Via Giulia.** Named after Pope Julius II and serving for more than five centuries as the "salon of Rome," this street—running between Piazza Farnese and the Tiber—is still the address of choice for Roman aristocrats and rich foreigners. Built with funds garnered by taxing prostitutes, the street is lined with elegant palaces, including the Palazzo Falconieri, old churches (one, San Eligio, reputedly designed by Raphael himself), and, in springtime, glorious hanging wisteria. The area around Via Giulia is a wonderful place to wander in to get the feeling of daily life as carried on in a centuries-old setting—an experience enhanced by the dozens of antiques shops in the neighborhood. ⊠ *1 block east of the Tiber River, Campo de' Fiori.*

WORTH NOTING

❼ Sant'Andrea della Valle. Topped by the second-tallest dome in Rome, this huge 17th-century church looms mightily over a busy intersection. Puccini set the first act of his opera *Tosca* here; fans have been known to hire a horse-drawn carriage at night to trace the course of the opera from Sant'Andrea up Via Giulia to Palazzo Farnese—Scarpia's headquarters—to the locale of the opera's climax, Castel Sant'Angelo. Inside, above the apse, are striking frescoes depicting scenes from Saint Andrew's life by the Bolognese painter Domenichino (1581–1641). ✉ *Corso Vittorio Emanuele II, Navona* ☎ *06/6861339* ☉ *Daily 7:30–noon and 4:30–7:30.*

❻ Sant'Ivo alla Sapienza. Borromini's eccentric 17th-century church has what must surely be Rome's most unusual dome—topped by a softly molded spiral said to have been inspired by a bee's stinger. Visit during the limited opening hours for a glimpse of Borromini's manic genius, an undulating white stucco interior bathed in gleaming daylight. ✉ *Corso Rinascimento 40, Navona* ☎ *06/3612562* ☉ *Sun. 9–noon.*

CORSO AND SPAGNA: PIAZZA VENEZIA TO THE SPANISH STEPS

In spirit, and in fact, this section of the city is its most grandiose. The overblown Vittoriano monument, the labyrinthine treasure-chest palaces of Rome's surviving aristocracy, even the diamond-draped denizens of Via Condotti's shops—all embody the exuberant ego of a city at the center of its own universe. Here's where you'll see ladies in furs gobbling pastries at café tables, and walk through a thousand snapshots as you climb the famous Spanish Steps, admired by generations from Byron to Versace. Cultural treasures abound around here: gilded 17th-century churches, glittering palaces, and the greatest example of portraiture in Rome: Velázquez's incomparable *Innocent X* at the Galleria Doria Pamphilj. Have your camera ready—along with a coin or two—for that most beloved of Rome's landmarks, the Trevi Fountain.

GETTING HERE   One of Rome's handiest subway stations, the Spagna Metro station is tucked just to the left of the Spanish Steps. Buses No. 117 (from the Colosseum area) and No. 119 (from Largo Argentina) hum through the neighborhood.

TOP ATTRACTIONS

❶ Altare della Patria. Also known as the Monumento Vittorio Emanuele II or the Vittoriano, this vast marble monument was erected in the late 19th century to honor Italy's first king, Vittorio Emanuele II (1820–78), and the unification of Italy. Aesthetically minded Romans have derided the oversize structure, visible from many parts of the city, calling it "the typewriter" and "the wedding cake." Whatever you think of its design, the views from the top are memorable. Here also is the **Tomb of the Unknown Soldier** with its eternal flame. A side entrance in the monument leads to the rather somber **Museo del Risorgimento** (entrance to the right as you face the monument), which charts Italy's struggle for nationhood. For those not interested or able to climb the many stairs, there's now an elevator to the roof (use museum entrance). Before you head up, stop at the museum information kiosk to get a pamphlet identifying the sculpture groups on the monument itself and the landmarks you will be able to see once at the top. ⊠ *Piazza Vene-zia, Corso* ☎ *06/6991718* ⊕ *www.*

ambienterm.arti.beniculturali.it/ vittoriano/index.html ▤ *Monument free, museum free, elevator €7* ◎ *Mon.–Thurs. 9:30–6:30, Fri.–Sun. 9:30–7:30.*

❼ Fontana di Trevi *(Trevi Fountain).* The huge fountain designed by Nicola ★ Salvi (1697–1751) is a whimsical rendition of mythical sea creatures amid cascades of splashing water. The fountain is the world's most spectacular wishing well: legend has it that you can ensure your return to Rome by tossing a coin into the fountain. It was featured in the 1954 film *Three Coins in the Fountain* and was the scene of Anita Ekberg's aquatic frolic in Fellini's *La Dolce Vita.* By day this is one of the most crowded sites in town; at night the spotlighted piazza feels especially festive. ⊠ *Piazza di Trevi, off Via del Tritone, Corso.*

❿ Palazzetto Zuccari. The real treasure at the top of the Spanish Steps is not
Fodor'sChoice the somewhat dull church of Trinità dei Monti, but to the right on Via
★ Gregoriana, the street that leads off to the right of the obelisk. Shaped to form a monster's face, this Mannerist-era house was designed in 1592 by noted painter Federico Zuccari (1540–1609). Typical of the outré style of the period, the eyes are the house's windows; the entrance portal is through the monster's mouth (this is a great photo op—have someone photograph you standing in front of the door with your own mouth gaping wide). Via Gregoriana is a real charmer and has long been one of Rome's most elegant addresses, with residents ranging from French 19th-century painters Ingres and David to famed couturier Valentino. Today the Palazzetto houses the Bibliotheca Hertziana, an important library for art historians. ⊠ *Via Gregoriana 28, Spagna.*

❹ Palazzo Colonna. Inside the fabulous, private Palazzo Colonna, the 17th-century **Sala Grande**—more than 300 feet long, with bedazzling chandeliers, colored marble, and enormous paintings—is best known as the site where Audrey Hepburn met the press in *Roman Holiday.* The entrance to the picture gallery, the **Galleria Colonna,** hides behind a plain, inconspicuous door. The private palace is open to the public Saturday only; reserve ahead to get a free guided tour in English. ⊠ *Via della Pilotta 17, Corso, near Piazza di Trevi* ☎ *06/6784350* ⊕ *www.galleriacolonna. it* ▤ *€7* ◎ *Sept.–July, Sat. 9–1.*

❺ Palazzo Doria Pamphilj. This bona fide patrician palace is still home to a
★ princely family, which rents out many of its 1,000 rooms. You can visit the remarkably well-preserved **Galleria Doria Pamphilj** (pronounced pam-*fee*-lee), a picture-and-sculpture gallery that gives you a sense of the sumptuous living quarters. ◼**TIP➔** Numbered paintings (the bookshop's museum catalog comes in handy) are packed onto every available

Corso and Spagna

SPANISH STEPS

M Spagna

SS. Trinità dei Monti

Piazza di Spagna

9

8

SPAGNA

10

Barberini **M**

Mausoleo di Augusto

SS. Carlo e Ambrogio

Palazzo Borghese

Palazzo Fiano

Piazza Parlamento

Palazzo Parlamento

Piazza S. Silvestro

Palazzo Poli

Piazza di Montecitorio

Galleria Colonna

Piazza Accad. di S. Luca

Piazza Colonna

7

Piazza Fontana di Trevi

Piazza Pietra

i

Pantheon

Piazza St. Eustachio

6

Piazza Pilotta

Piazza di Minevra

5

SS. Apostoli

Villa Colonna

Piazza dei SS. Apostoli

4

MONTE QUIRINALE

Giardino del Quirinale

Piazza Grazioli

Palazzo Bonaparte

Prefettura

AREA SACRA

3

2

Piazza Venezia

1

| 0 | 150 M |
| 0 | 500 ft |

KEY

M Metro Stop

i Tourist information

inch of wall space. The first large salon is nearly wallpapered with paintings, and not just any paintings: on one wall, you'll find no fewer than three works by Caravaggio, including his *Penitent Magdalen* and his breathtaking early *Rest on the Flight to Egypt.* Off the gilded **Galleria degli Specchi** (Gallery of Mirrors)—reminiscent of Versailles—are the famous Velázquez portrait and the Bernini bust of the Pamphilj pope Innocent X. The free audio guide by Jonathan Doria Pamphilj, the current heir, provides an intimate family history well worth listening to. ⊠ *Piazza del Collegio Romano 2, near Piazza Venezia, Corso* ☎ *06/6797323* ⊕ *www.doriapamphilj.it* ⊠ €9 ⊗ *Daily 10–5.*

❻ **Sant'Ignazio.** Rome's largest Jesuit church, this 17th-century landmark
★ harbors some of the most magnificent illusions typical of the baroque style. Capping the 17th-century nave is the trompe l'oeil ceiling painted by Andrea Pozzo (1642–1709), frescoed with flying angels and heavenly dignitaries, including Saint Ignatius himself, who floats about in what appears to be a rosy sky above. The crowning jewel, however, is an illusionistic oddity—a cupola that is completely flat yet, from most vantage points, appears convincingly three-dimensional. The Jesuits resorted to this optical illusion when funds to build a real dome dried up. The church also contains some of Rome's most splendid, gilt-encrusted altars. If you're lucky, you might catch an evening concert performed here (check the posters). Step outside the church to look at it from Filippo Raguzzini's 18th-century piazza, where the buildings, as in much baroque art, are arranged resembling a stage set. ⊠ *Piazza Sant'Ignazio, Corso* ☎ *06/6794560* ⊗ *Daily 7:30–12:15 and 3–7:15.*

❾ **Spanish Steps.** That icon of postcard Rome, the Spanish Steps—called
★ the Scalinata di Spagna in Italian—and the Piazza di Spagna from which they ascend both get their names from the Spanish Embassy to the Vatican on the piazza, opposite the American Express office—in spite of the fact that the staircase was built with French funds in 1723. In an allusion to the church of Trinità dei Monti at the top of the hill, the staircase is divided by three landings (beautifully banked with azaleas from mid-April to mid-May). For centuries, La Scalinata ("staircase," as natives refer to the Spanish Steps) has always welcomed tourists: 18th-century dukes and duchesses on their grand tour, 19th-century artists and writers in search of inspiration—among them Stendhal, Honoré de Balzac, William Makepeace Thackeray, and Byron—and today's enthusiastic hordes. The **Fontana della Barcaccia** (Fountain of the Unfortunate Boat) at the base of the steps is by Pietro Bernini, father of the famous Gianlorenzo. ⊠ *Piazza di Spagna, at head of Via Condotti.*

WORTH NOTING

❸ **Il Gesù.** Grandmother of all baroque churches, this huge structure was designed by the architect Vignola (1507–73) to be the tangible symbol of the Jesuits, a major force in the Counter-Reformation in Europe. It remained unadorned for about 100 years, but when it finally was decorated, no expense was spared: the interior drips with lapis lazuli, precious marbles, gold, and more gold. A fantastically painted ceiling by Baciccia (1639–1709) seems to merge with the painted stucco figures at its base. Saint Ignatius's apartments, reached from the side entrance of the church, are also worth a visit (afternoons only) for the

DID YOU KNOW?

Andrea Pozzo's eye-popping Sant'Ignazio 1694 ceiling fresco set the standard for trompe l'oeil aerial perspective and made it all the rage in Europe.

trompe l'oeil frescoes and relics of the saint. ⊠ *Piazza del Gesù, near Piazza Venezia, Corso* ☏ *06/697001* ⊕ *www.chiesadelgesu.org* ⊙ *Daily 6:45–12:30 and 4–7:30.*

❽ Keats-Shelley Memorial House. English Romantic poet John Keats (1795–1821), famed for "Ode to a Nightingale" and "She Walks in Beauty," once lived in what is now a (very small) museum dedicated to him and his great contemporary and friend Percy Bysshe Shelley (1792–1822). You can visit his tiny rooms, at the foot of the Spanish Steps, preserved as they were when he died here. Just across the steps is Babington's Tea Shops, a relic from the 19th-century grand tour era and still a favorite for Rome's grande dames. ⊠ *Piazza di Spagna 26* ☏ *06/6784235* ⊕ *www.keats-shelley-house.org* ⊠ *€4* ⊙ *Weekdays 10–1 and 2–6, Sat. 11–2 and 3–6.*

❷ Palazzo Venezia. A Roman landmark on the city's busiest square, this palace is best known for the balcony over the main portal, from which Mussolini gave public addresses to crowds in Piazza Venezia during the dark days of fascism. Today it's home to a haphazard collection of mostly early-Renaissance weapons, ivories, and paintings in its grand salons; the palace also hosts touring art exhibits. ⊠ *Via del Plebescito 118 Piazza Venezia, Corso* ☏ *06/699941* ⊕ *www.galleriaborghese.it/nuove/evenezia.htm* ⊠ *€4* ⊙ *Tues.–Sun. 8:30–7:30.*

PIAZZA DELLA REPUBBLICA TO QUIRINALE

This sector of Rome stretches down from the 19th-century district built up around the Piazza della Repubblica—originally laid out to serve as a monumental foyer between the Termini rail station and the rest of the city—and on to Il Quirinale. The highest of ancient Rome's famed seven hills, it is crowned by the massive Palazzo Quirinale, home to the popes until 1870 and now Italy's presidential palace. Along the way, you can see ancient Roman sculptures, Early Christian churches, and highlights from the 16th and 17th centuries, when Rome was conquered by the baroque—and by Bernini.

Although Bernini's work feels omnipresent in much of the city center, the Renaissance-man range of his work is particularly notable here. The artist as architect considered the church of Sant'Andrea al Quirinale one of his best; Bernini the urban designer and water worker is responsible for the muscle-bound sea gods who wrestle so provocatively in the fountain at the center of whirling Piazza Barberini. And Bernini the master gives religious passion a joltingly corporeal treatment in what is perhaps his greatest work, the *Ecstasy of St. Theresa*, in the church of Santa Maria della Vittoria.

GETTING HERE   Bus No. 40 will get you from Termini station to the Quirinale in two stops; from the Vatican take bus No. 64 or Line A to the very busy and convenient Repubblica Metro stop on the piazza of the same name. Bus No. 62 and the Metro also run from the Vatican to Piazza Barberini, near the Quirinale.

TOP ATTRACTIONS

9 **Il Quirinale.** The highest of ancient Rome's famed seven hills, this is where ancient senators, and later popes, built their residences in order to escape the deadly miasmas and malaria of the low-lying area around the Forum and Pantheon. Framing the hilltop vista, the fountain in the square has gigantic ancient statues of Castor and Pollux reining in their unruly steeds. The **Palazzo del Quirinale** passed from the popes to Italy's kings in the late 19th century; it's now the official residence of the nation's president. There is a daily ceremony of the changing of the guard at the portal, including a miniparade complete with band (June–September, 6 PM; October–May, 3:15 PM). ⊠ *Piazza del Quirinale, near Piazza di Trevi* ☎ *06/46991* ⊕ *www.quirinale.it* 🎫 *€5* ⊙ *Sept.–June, Sun. 8:30–noon.*

Directly opposite the main entrance of the Palazzo del Quirinale sits the **Scuderie del Quirinale**, the former papal stables. Designed by Alessandro Specchi (1668–1729) in 1722, it was among the major achievements of baroque Rome. Now remodeled by eminent architect Gae Aulenti, they serve as a venue for touring art exhibitions. ⊠ *Via XXIV Maggio 16, Quirinale* ☎ *06/39967500* ⊕ *www.scuderiequirinale.it* 🎫 *€10* ⊙ *Sun.–Thurs. 10–8, Fri. and Sat. 10–10:30.*

6 **Palazzo Barberini.** Along with architect Carlo Maderno (1556–1629), Borromini helped make the splendid 17th-century Palazzo Barberini a residence worthy of Rome's leading art patron, Pope Urban VIII, who began the palace for his family in 1625. Inside, the **Galleria Nazionale d'Arte Antica** has some fine works by Caravaggio and Raphael, including the latter's portrait of his lover, *La Fornarina*. Rome's biggest ballroom is here; its ceiling, painted by Pietro da Cortona, depicts Immortality bestowing a crown upon Divine Providence escorted by a "bomber squadron"—to quote Sir Michael Levey—of mutant bees (bees adorn the family's heraldic crest). The museum expanded its exhibition space in late 2006, opening eight newly refurbished rooms. ⊠ *Via delle Quattro Fontane 13, Quirinale* ☎ *06/4824184* ⊕ *www. galleriaborghese.it/barberini/it* 🎫 *€6* ⊙ *Tues.–Sun. 8:30–7:30.*

1 **Palazzo Massimo alle Terme.** This 19th-century palace in neobaroque style holds part of the collections of antiquities belonging to the Museo Nazionale Romano (also exhibited in the Palazzo Altemps). Here you can see extraordinary examples of the fine mosaics and masterful frescoes that decorated ancient Rome's palaces and villas. Don't miss the fresco depicting a lush garden in bloom that came from the villa that Livia shared with her husband Emperor Augustus in Primaporta outside Rome. ⊠ *Largo di Villa Peretti 1, Repubblica* ☎ *06/480201* ⊕ *www. pierreci.it* 🎫 *€9* ⊙ *Tues.–Sun. 9–7:30.*

10 **San Clemente.** Worth the long detour, this extraordinary church–cum–
★ archaeological site lies a good 20 blocks southeast of Piazza della Repubblica, nestled between the Celian Hill and the Colle Oppio park and just a few blocks east of the Colosseum. This ancient reference point is apropos because San Clemente is a 12th-century church built over a 4th-century church, which in turn was constructed over 1st- and 2nd-century Roman buildings, including a sanctuary dedicated

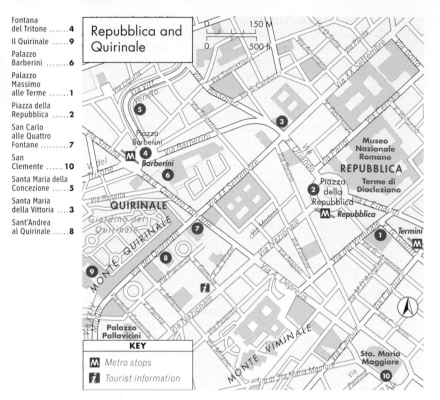

Repubblica and Quirinale

KEY

Ⓜ *Metro stops*

🛈 *Tourist information*

to the Persian god Mithras. The upper church holds a beautiful early-12th-century mosaic showing a crucifixion on a gold background, surrounded by swirling green acanthus leaves teeming with little scenes of everyday life. From the right aisle, a door leads to the excavations ticket office. From there, there are stairs leading down to the remains of the 4th-century church—the former portico is decorated with marble fragments found during the excavations, and in the nave are colorful 11th-century frescoes of the life of Saint Clement. Another level down is the famous **Mithraeum,** a shrine dedicated to the god Mithras, whose cult spread from Persia to Rome in the 1st century BC and went on to gain a major hold in the 2nd and 3rd centuries. Farther up the Esquiline Hill are two other churches fabled for their Early Christian mosaics, Santa Prassede (Via di Santa Prassede 9/a) and Santa Pudenziana (Via Urbana 160). ✉ *Via San Giovanni in Laterano 108, Colosseo* ☎ *06/7740021* ⊕ *www.basilicasanclemente.com* 🎫 *€5 (archaeological area)* ⊙ *Mon.–Sat. 9–12:30 and 3–6, Sun. noon–6.*

⑤ **Santa Maria della Concezione.** In the crypt under the main Capuchin
Ⓒ church, the bones of some 4,000 dead Capuchin monks are arranged in peculiar decorative designs around the skeletons of their kinsmen, a macabre reminder of the impermanence of earthly life. Signs declare WHAT YOU ARE, WE ONCE WERE; WHAT WE ARE, YOU SOMEDAY WILL BE.

Although not for the easily spooked, the crypt is oddly beautiful. ⌱ *Via Veneto 27, Quirinale* ☎ *06/4871185* ⊕ *www.cappucciniviaveneto.it Donation expected* ⊘ *Fri.–Wed. 9–noon and 3–6.*

❸ **Santa Maria della Vittoria.** The most famous feature here is Bernini's triumph of baroque decoration of the **Cappella Cornaro,** an exceptional fusion of architecture, relief, and sculpture. *The Ecstasy of St. Theresa,* an example of Counter-Reformation art at its most alluring, is the focal point. Bernini's audacious conceit was to model the chapel after a theater: members of the Cornaro family—sculpted in white marble— watch from theater boxes as, center stage, Saint Theresa, in the throes of mystical rapture, is pierced by an angel's gilded arrow. To quote one 18th-century observer, President de Brosses: "If this is divine love, I know it well." ⌱ *Via XX Settembre 17, Repubblica* ☎ *06/42740571* ⊘ *Mon.–Sat. 9–noon and 3–6, Sun. 3–6.*

Fodor's Choice
★

WORTH NOTING

❹ **Fontana del Tritone** *(Triton Fountain).* The centerpiece of busy Piazza Barberini is Bernini's graceful fountain designed in 1642 for the sculptor's patron, Pope Urban VIII. The pope's Barberini family coat of arms, featuring bees, is at the base of the large shell. Close by, at the beginning of the Via Veneto, is the **Fontana delle Api** (Fountain of the Bees), the last fountain designed by Bernini. ⌱ *Piazza Barberini, Repubblica.*

❷ **Piazza della Repubblica.** Smog-blackened porticoes, a subway station, and a McDonald's can make this grand piazza feel a bit derelict. The racy **Fontana delle Naiadi** *(*Fountain of the Naiads*),* however, is anything but. An 1888–1901 addition to the square, the fountain depicts voluptuous bronze ladies wrestling happily with marine monsters. In ancient times, the Piazza della Repubblica served as the entrance to the immense Terme di Diocleziano *(*Baths of Diocletian*),* an archaeological site today. Built in the early 4th century AD, these were among the largest and most impressive of the baths of ancient Rome, with vast halls, pools, and gardens that could accommodate up to 6,000 people at a time. Centerpiece of the **Museo della Terme di Diocleziano** is the *aula ottagonale* (octagonal hall), which holds a sampling of the sculptures excavated from ancient bathing complexes throughout the city. ⌱ *Viale E. De Nicola 79, near Termini* ☎ *06/39967700* ▦ *€5* ⊘ *Tues.– Sun. 9–7:30.*

The curving ancient Roman brick facade on one side of the Piazza della Repubblica marks the church of **Santa Maria degli Angeli,** adapted by Michelangelo from the vast central chamber of the colossal baths. Look for the sundial inlaid in the floor. ⌱ *Piazza della Repubblica* ☎ *064880812* ⊕ *www.santamariadegliangeliroma.it* ⊘ *Mon.–Sat. 7–6:30, Sun. 7* AM*–7:30* PM*.*

❼ **San Carlo alle Quattro Fontane.** In a church no larger than the base of one of the piers of St. Peter's, Borromini attained geometric architectural perfection. Characteristically, he chose a subdued white stucco for the interior decoration, so as not to distract from the form of the amazing honeycombed cupola. Don't miss the cloister, which you reach through the door to the right of the altar. The exterior of the church is Borromini at his bizarre best, all curves and rippling movement. (Keep an eye out for cars whipping around the corner as you're looking.) Outside the *Quattro Fontane* (four fountains) frame views in four directions. ✉ *Via del Quirinale 23* 🕾 *06/4883261* ⊕ *www.sancarlino-borromoni. it* ⊙ *Weekdays 10–1 and 3–6, Sat. 10–1, Sun. noon–1.*

❽ Sant'Andrea al Quirinale. This small but imposing baroque church was designed and decorated by Bernini, Borromini's rival, who considered it one of his finest works. Unfortunately, various cracks appeared as a collateral effect of the April 2009 Aquila earthquake; at this writing, the church was closed to the public and awaiting restoration work. ✉ *Via del Quirinale 29* 🕾 *06/4740807* ⊙ *Wed.–Mon. 8–noon and 4–7.*

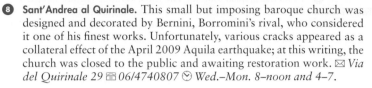

VILLA BORGHESE AND PIAZZA DEL POPOLO

Touring Rome's artistic masterpieces while staying clear of its hustle and bustle can be, quite literally, a walk in the park. Some of the city's finest sights are tucked away in or next to green lawns and pedestrian piazzas, offering a breath of fresh air for weary sightseers, especially in the Villa Borghese park. One of Rome's largest, this park can alleviate gallery gout by offering an oasis in which to cool off under the ilex, oak, and umbrella pine trees. If you feel like a picnic, have an *alimentari* (food shop) make you some *panini* (sandwiches) before you go; food carts within the park are overpriced.

GETTING HERE   Electric bus No. 119 does a loop that connects Largo Argentina, Piazza Venezia, Piazza di Spagna, and Piazza del Popolo. The No. 117 connects Piazza del Popolo to Piazza Venezia and the Colosseum. The No. 116 motors through the Villa Borghese to the museum and connects the area with Piazza Navona, Campo de' Fiori, and the Pantheon. Piazza del Popolo has a Metro stop called Flaminio.

TOP ATTRACTIONS

❹ Ara Pacis *(Altar of Peace).* This magnificent classical monument, with ★ an exquisitely detailed frieze, was erected in 13 BC to celebrate Emperor Augustus's triumphant return from military conflicts in Gaul and Spain. It's housed in one of Rome's newest landmarks, a glass-and-travertine structure designed by American architect Richard Meier. The building was opened in 2006 after 10 years of delays and heated controversy concerning the architect's appointment and design. Overlooking the Tiber on one side and the ruins of the dilapidated Mausoleo di Augusto (Mausoleum of Augustus) on the other, the result is a luminous oasis in the center of Rome. ✉ *Lungotevere in Augusta, near Piazza di Popolo* 🕾 *06/82059127* ⊕ *www.arapacis.it* 🎫 *€6.50* ⊙ *Tues.–Sun. 9–7.*

❸ Galleria Borghese. It's a real toss-up which is more magnificent—the
 villa built for Cardinal Scipione Borghese in 1615 or the collection of ★ 17th- and 18th-century art that lies within. The luxury-loving cardinal built Rome's most splendiferous palace as a showcase for his antiquities collection. The interiors are a monument to 18th-century Roman interior decoration at its most luxurious, dripping with colored porphyry and alabaster, and they are a fitting showcase for the statues of various deities, including one officially known as *Venus Victrix*. There has never been any doubt, however, as to the statue's real subject: Pauline

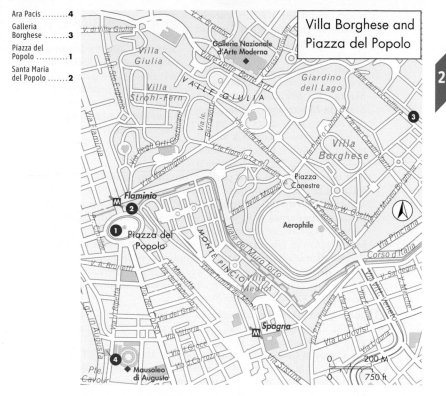

Villa Borghese and
Piazza del Popolo

2

Bonaparte, Napoléon's sister, who married Prince Camillo Borghese in one of the storied matches of the 19th century. Sculpted by Canova (1757–1822), the princess reclines on a chaise, bare-breasted, her hips swathed in classical drapery, the very model of haughty detachment and sly come-hither. Pauline is known to have been shocked that her husband took pleasure in showing off the work to his guests. This coyness seems curious given the reply she is supposed to have made to a lady who asked her how she could have posed for the work: "Oh, but the studio was heated." Other rooms hold important sculptures by Bernini, including *David* and the breathtaking *Apollo and Daphne.* The picture collection has splendid works by Titian, Caravaggio, and Raphael, among others. Entrance is every two hours, and reservations are required. Make sure to book online or by phone at least a few days in advance. ⊠ *Piazza Scipione Borghese 5, off Via Pinciana, Villa Borghese* ☎ *06/8413979 information, 06/32810 reservations* ⊕ *www. galleriaborghese.it* ⊠ *€10.50 (including €2 reservation fee), audio guide or English tour €6* ⊙ *Tues.–Sun. 9–7, with sessions on the hr every 2 hrs (9, 11, 1, 3, 5) Bus 910 from Piazza della Repubblica or Tram 19 or 3 from Policlinico (near Piazza del Popolo).*

❶ **Piazza del Popolo.** Designed by neoclassical architect Giuseppe Valadier (1762–1839) in the early 1800s, this piazza is one of the largest in

Rome, and it has a 3,200-year-old obelisk in the middle. A favorite spot for café-sitting and people-watching, the pedestrians-only piazza is landmarked by its two bookend baroque churches, **Santa Maria dei Miracoli** and **Santa Maria in Montesanto**. On the piazza's eastern side, stairs lead uphill to Villa Borghese's **Pincio**, a formal garden that was highly fashionable in 19th-century Rome. Here you'll

WORD OF MOUTH

"Something about the Borghese reminded me of the Frick in New York; although the space is grand, it feels easily accessible to the visitor.... The interiors alone, even if the rooms had been empty, are worth the price of admission."
—ekscrunchy

find the magnificent park pavilion restaurant known as the **Casino Valadier** (⊠ *Piazza Bucarest, Pincio Gardens* ☎ *06/69922090* ⊕ *www.casinavaladier.it*). First designed in 1814, it has always attracted celebrities like King Farouk of Egypt, Richard Strauss, Gandhi, and Mussolini, all who came to see the lavish Empire-style salons and, of course, to be seen. At the north end of the piazza is the 400-year-old **Porta del Popolo,** Rome's northern city gate, and next to it the church of Santa Maria del Popolo. The city gate was designed by Bernini to welcome the Catholic convert Queen Christina of Sweden to Rome in 1605. ⊠ *At head of the Corso, near Villa Borghese.*

❷ ★ Santa Maria del Popolo. This church next to the Porta del Popolo goes almost unnoticed, but it has one of the richest art collections of any church in Rome. Here is Raphael's High Renaissance masterpiece the **Cappella Chigi** (which has found new fame as one of the "Altars of Science" in Dan Brown's *Angels & Demons* novel and the 2009 Tom Hanks film), as well as two stunning Caravaggios in the **Cappella Cerasi.** Each December an exhibit of Christmas Nativity scenes is held in the adjacent building. ⊠ *Piazza del Popolo, near Villa Borghese* ☎ *06/3610836* ⊗ *Mon.–Sat. 7–noon and 4–7, Sun. 8–1:30 and 4:30–7:30* Ⓜ *Flaminio.*

WORTH NOTING

MAXXI—Museo Nazionale delle Arti del XXI Secolo (National Museum of 21st-Century Arts). Billed as a cultural space for the art of the 21st century, the museum—opened May 2010 and walkable from the Parco della Musica complex—contains 350 works from Warhol to tomorrow's hottest artists. Arguably the most impressive exhibit of all is the hyperdramatic building designed by architect Zaha Hadid. Get to this museum by taking Line A of the Metro to Flaminio (near Piazza del Popolo), then taking Tram 2 to the Apollodoro stop. From there, the museum is about 200 yards to the left. ⊠ *Via Guido Reni 4A, near Villa Borghese* ☎ *06/3201829* ⊗ *www.maxxi.darc.beniculturali.it* ⊠ *€11* ⊗ *Tues., Wed., and Fri.–Sun. 11–7; Thurs. 11–10* Ⓜ *Flaminio.*

THE VATICAN: ROME OF THE POPES

Capital of the Catholic Church, this tiny walled city-state is a place where some people go to find a work of art—Michelangelo's frescoes, rare ancient Roman marbles, or Bernini's statues. Others go to find their soul. Whatever the reason, thanks to being the seat of world Catholicism and also address to the most overwhelming architectural achievement of the 16th century—St. Peter's Basilica—the Vatican attracts millions of travelers every year. In addition, the Vatican Museums are famed for magnificent rooms decorated by Raphael, sculptures such as the *Apollo Belvedere* and the *Laocoön,* frescoes by Fra Angelico, paintings by Giotto and Melozzo da Forlì, and the celebrated ceiling of the Sistine Chapel. The Church power that emerged as the Rome of the emperors declined gave impetus to a profusion of artistic expression and shaped the destiny of the city for a thousand years. Allow yourself an hour to see St. Peter's Basilica, at least two hours for the museums, an hour for Castel Sant'Angelo, and an hour to climb to the top of the dome. Note that ushers at the entrance of St. Peter's Basilica and the Vatican Museums bar entry to people with "inappropriate" clothing—which means no bare knees or shoulders.

GETTING HERE   From Termini station, hop on the No. 40 Express or the No. 64 to be delivered to Piazza San Pietro. Metro stops Cipro or Ottaviano will get you within about a 10-minute walk of the entrance to the Vatican Museums.

TOP ATTRACTIONS

② **Basilica di San Pietro.** The largest church of Christendom, St. Peter's
★ Basilica covers about 18,100 square yards, extends 212 yards in length, and carries a dome that rises 435 feet and measures 138 feet across its base. Its history is equally impressive: No fewer than five of Italy's greatest architects—Bramante, Raphael, Peruzzi, Antonio Sangallo the Younger, and Michelangelo—died while striving to erect this "new" St. Peter's. In fact, the church's history dates back to the year AD 319, when the emperor Constantine built a basilica over the site believed to be the tomb of Saint Peter (died circa AD 68). This early church stood for more than 1,000 years, undergoing a number of restorations, until it was on the verge of collapse.

In 1506 Pope Julius II (1443–1513) commissioned the architect Bramante to build a new and greater basilica, but construction would take more than 120 years. In 1546 Michelangelo was persuaded to take over the job, but the magnificent cupola he designed was finally completed after his death at age 89 by Giacomo della Porta (circa 1537–1602) and Domenico Fontana (1543–1607). The new church wasn't dedicated until 1626; by that time Renaissance had given way to baroque, and many of the plan's original elements had gone the way of their designers. Off the entry portico, architect and sculptor Gianlorenzo Bernini's famous *Scala Regia,* the ceremonial entry to the Apostolic Palace—and originally the way to the Sistine Chapel—is one of the most magnificent staircases in the world and is graced with Bernini's dramatic statue of Constantine the Great.

Entering the sanctuary, take a moment to adjust to the enormity of the space stretching in front of you. The cherubs over the holy-water fonts have feet as long as the distance from your fingertips to your elbow. It is because the proportions are in such perfect harmony that the vastness may escape you at first. The megascale was inspired by the size of the ancient Roman ruins.

Over an altar in a side chapel to the right of the entrance is Michelangelo's *Pietà*, a sculpture of Mary holding her son Jesus' body after crucifixion—the star attraction here other than the basilica itself. Legend has it that the artist, only 24 at the time the work was completed, overheard other artists being given credit for his design. It's said that his offense at the implication was why he crept back that night and signed the piece—in big letters, on a ribbon falling from the Virgin's left shoulder across her breast.

At the crossing of the transept four massive piers support the dome, and the mighty Bernini **baldacchino** (canopy) rises high above the papal altar, where the pope celebrates mass. The bronze throne behind the main altar in the apse, the *Cathedra Petri* (Chair of Saint Peter), is Bernini's work (1656), and it covers a wooden-and-ivory chair that Saint Peter himself is said to have used. However, scholars contend that this throne probably dates only from the Middle Ages. See how the adoration of a million caresses has completely worn down the bronze on the left foot of the statue of Saint Peter in front of the near-right pillar in the transept. Free one-hour English-language tours of the basilica depart Monday–Saturday at 10 and 3, Sunday at 2:30 (sign up at the little desk under the portico). St. Peter's is closed during ceremonies in the piazza. ⊠ *Piazza San Pietro* ☎ *06/6982* ⊕ *www.vatican.va* ⊙ *Daily 8–6* Ⓜ *Cipro-Musei Vaticani.*

The **Grotte Vaticane** *(Vatican Grottoes)* directly beneath the basilica contain the tombs of many popes, including John Paul II. The entrance is beside the cupola entrance, outside the basilica. The only exit leads outside the church, so don't go down until you're finished elsewhere. 🕮 *Free* ⊙ *Apr.–Sept., daily 7–6; Oct.–Mar., daily 7–5.*

The **roof** of St. Peter's Basilica, reached by elevator or stairs, provides a view among a landscape of domes and towers. An interior staircase (170 steps) leads to the base of the dome for a dove's-eye look at the interior of St. Peter's. Only if you are stout of heart and sound of lung should you attempt the taxing and claustrophobic climb up the remaining 370 steps to the balcony of the lantern, where the view embraces the Vatican Gardens and all of Rome. The up and down staircases are one way; once you commit to climbing, there's no turning back. 🕮 *Elevator €7, stairs €5* ⊙ *Daily 8–5 (12:30–5 on Wed. if the pope has audience in Piazza San Pietro).*

❺ **Castel Sant'Angelo.** For hundreds of years this fortress guarded the Vatican, to which it is linked by the **Passetto,** an arcaded passageway (the secret "lair of the Illuminati," according to Dan Brown's *Angels & Demons*, the Rome-based prequel to *The Da Vinci Code*). According to legend, Castel Sant'Angelo got its name during the plague of 590, when Pope Gregory the Great (circa 540–604), passing by in a religious procession, had a vision of an angel sheathing its sword atop the stone ramparts. Though it may look like a stronghold, Castel Sant'Angelo was in fact built as a tomb for the emperor Hadrian (76–138) in AD 135. By the 6th century it had been transformed into a fortress, and it remained a refuge for the popes for almost 1,000 years. It has dungeons, battlements, cannon and cannonballs, and a collection of antique weaponry

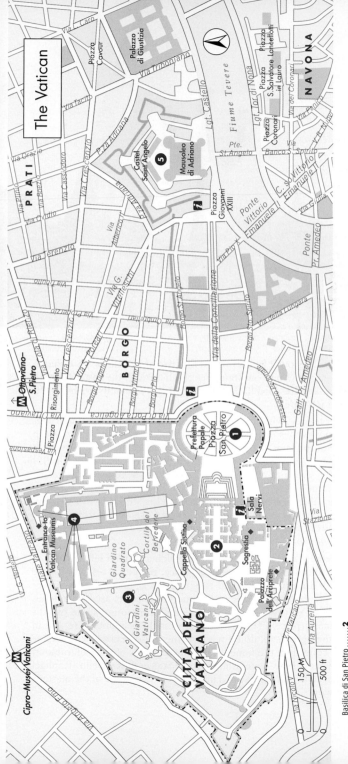

The Vatican

PRATI

BORGO

CITTÀ DEL VATICANO

NAVONA

Ⓜ Ottaviano–S. Pietro

Ⓜ Cipro–Musei Vaticani

Fiume Tevere

Castel Saint'Angelo

Mausoleo di Adriano ⑤

Palazzo di Giustizia

Piazza Cavour

Piazza Giovanni XXIII

Ponte Vittorio Emanuele

Pte. St. Angelo

Piazza Coronari

Piazza S. Salvatore Lancellotti in Lauro

Prefettura Papale

Piazza San Pietro ①

Sala Nervi

Cappella Sistina ②

Sagrestia

Palazzo dell'Arciprete

Entrance to Vatican Museums ④

Giardino Quadrato

Cortile del Belvedere

Giardini Vaticani ③

150 M

500 ft

Via Ottaviano

Via Germanico

Via Cola di Rienzo

Via Crescenzio

Via Terenzio

Via G. Vitelleschi

Via della Conciliazione

Borgo S. Angelo

Borgo Pio

Borgo Vittorio

Borgo S. Spirito

Via di Porta Angelica

Via di Porta Cavalleggeri

Viale Vaticano

Lgt. Castello

For St. Peter's, Michelangelo originally designed a dome much higher than the one ultimately built and designed by his follower, Giacomo della Porta.

and armor. The lower levels formed the base of Hadrian's mausoleum; ancient ramps and narrow staircases climb through the castle's core to courtyards and frescoed halls, where temporary exhibits are held. Off the loggia is a café.

The upper terrace, with the massive angel statue commemorating Gregory's vision, evokes memories of Tosca, Puccini's poignant heroine in the opera of the same name, who threw herself off these ramparts with the cry, *"Scarpia, avanti a Dio!"* ("Scarpia, we meet before God!") On summer evenings exhibits and concerts are held inside the castle. One of Rome's most beautiful pedestrian bridges, **Ponte Sant'Angelo** spans the Tiber in front of the fortress and is studded with graceful angels designed by Bernini. ⊠ *Lungotevere Castello 50, near Vatican* ☎ *06/6819111* ⊕ *www.castelsantangelo.com* ☒ *€5* ☉ *Tues.–Sun. 8:30–7:30* Ⓜ *Ottaviano.*

❹ Musei Vaticani *(Vatican Museums).* The building on your left as you exit St. Peter's Basilica is the Apostolic Palace, the papal residence since 1870, with an estimated 1,400 rooms, chapels, and galleries. Other than the pope and his court, the primary occupants are the galleries of the Musei Vaticani (Vatican Museums), containing some of art's greatest masterpieces. The Sistine Chapel is the headliner here, but in your haste to get there, don't overlook the Museo Egizio, with its fine Egyptian collection; the famed classical sculptures of the Chiaramonti and the Museo Pio Clementino; and the Stanze di Raffaello (Raphael Rooms), a suite of halls covered floor-to-ceiling in some of the master's greatest works.

FodorsChoice
★

CLOSE UP

A Morning with the Pope

The pope holds audiences in a large, modern hall (or in St. Peter's Square in summer) on Wednesday morning at 10. To attend, you must get tickets; apply in writing at least 10 days in advance to the **Papal Prefecture** (*Prefettura della Casa Pontificia* ☏ *Vatican City* ☎ *06/69884857* 🖶 *06/69885863* ⊕ *www.vatican.va*), indicating the full name of attendants, the date you prefer, your language, and your hotel's contact information. Or go to the prefecture, through the Porta di Bronzo, the bronze door at the end of the colonnade on the right side of the piazza; the office is open Monday–Saturday 9–1, and last-minute tickets may be available.

You can also arrange to pick up free tickets on Tuesday from 5 to 6:30 at the **Santa Susanna American Church** (✉ *Via XX Settembre 15, near Piazza della Repubblica* ☎ *06/42014554* ⊕ *www. santasusanna.org*) ; call first. For a fee, travel agencies make arrangements that include transportation. Arrive early, as security is tight and the best places fill up fast.

On a first visit to the Vatican Museums, you may just want to see the highlights—even that will take several hours and a good, long walk. ■ **TIP→** In peak tourist season, be prepared for at least an hour's wait to get into the museums and large crowds once inside. The best time to avoid lines and crowds is not first thing in the morning but during lunch hour and the Wednesday papal audiences. The collection is divided among different galleries, halls, and wings connected end to end. Pick up a leaflet at the main entrance to the museums to see the overall layout. The Sistine Chapel is at the far end of the complex, and the leaflet charts two abbreviated itineraries through other collections to reach it. An audio guide (€6, about 90 minutes) for the Sistine Chapel, the Stanze di Raffaello, and 350 other works and locations is worth the added expense. Phone or e-mail at least a week in advance (a month for peak season) to book a guided tour (€30) through the Vatican Museums. The main entrance to the museums, on Viale Vaticano, is a long walk from Piazza San Pietro along a busy thoroughfare. Some city buses stop near the main entrance: Bus 49 from Piazza Cavour stops right in front; buses 81 and 492 and Tram 19 stop at Piazza Risorgimento, halfway between St. Peter's and the museums. The Ottaviano–San Pietro and the Cipro–Musei Vaticani stops on Line A also are in the vicinity. Entry is free the last Sunday of the month, and the museum is closed on Catholic holidays, of which there are many. Last admission is two hours before closing.

Besides the galleries mentioned here, there are many other wings along your way—full of maps, tapestries, classical sculpture, Egyptian mummies, Etruscan statues, and even Aztec treasures. From the main entrance of the Vatican Museums take the escalator up to the glass atrium. Follow the hall to the right to the **Pinacoteca** (Picture Gallery). This is a self-contained section, and it's worth visiting first for works by such artists as Leonardo (1452–1520), Giotto (circa 1266–1337),

Continued on page 80

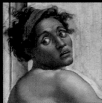

AGONY AND ECSTASY:
THE SISTINE CEILING

Forming lines that are probably longer than those waiting to pass through the Pearly Gates, hordes of visitors arrive at the Sistine Chapel daily to view what may be the world's most sublime example of artistry:

Michelangelo: *The Creation of Adam*, Sistine Chapel, The Vatican, circa 1511.

Michelangelo's Sistine Ceiling. To paint this 12,000-square-foot barrel vault, it took four years, 343 frescoed figures, and a titanic battle of wits between the artist and Pope Julius II. While in its typical fashion, Hollywood focused on the element of agony, not ecstasy, involved in the saga of creation, a recently completed restoration of the ceiling has revolutionized our appreciation of the masterpiece of masterpieces.

By Martin Wilmot Bennett

MICHELANGELO'S
MISSION IMPOSSIBLE

Designed to match the proportions of Solomon's Temple described in the Old Testament, the Sistine Chapel is named after Pope Sixtus VI, who commissioned it as a place of worship for himself and as the venue where new popes could be elected. Before Michelangelo, the barrel-vaulted ceiling was an expanse of azure fretted with golden stars. Then, in 1504, an ugly crack appeared. Bramante, the architect, managed do some patchwork using iron rods, but when signs of a fissure remained, the new Pope Julius II summoned Michelangelo to cover it with a fresco 135 feet long and 44 feet wide.

Taking in the entire span of the ceiling, the theme connecting the various participants in this painted universe could be said to be mankind's anguished waiting. The majestic panel depicting the Creation of Adam leads, through the stages of the Fall and the expulsion from Eden, to the tragedy of Noah found naked and mocked by his own sons; throughout all runs the underlying need for man's redemption. Witnessing all from the side and end walls, a chorus of ancient Prophets and Sibyls peer anxiously forward, awaiting the Redeemer who will come to save both the Jews and the Gentiles.

APOCALYPSE NOW

The sweetness and pathos of his Pietà, carved by Michelangelo only ten years earlier, have been left behind. The new work foretells an apocalypse, its congregation of doomed sinners facing the wrath of heaven through hanging, beheading, crucifixion, flood, and plague. Michelangelo, by nature a misanthrope, was already filled with visions of doom thanks to the fiery orations of Savonarola, whose thunderous preachments he had heard before leaving his hometown of Florence. Vasari, the 16th-century art historian, coined the word "terribilità" to describe Michelangelo's tension-ridden style, a rare case of a single word being worth a thousand pictures.

Michelangelo wound up using a *Reader's Digest* condensed version of the stories from Genesis, with the dramatis personae overseen by a punitive and terrifying God. In real life, poor Michelangelo answered to a flesh-and-blood taskmaster who was almost as vengeful: Pope Julius II. Less vicar of Christ than latter-day Caesar, he was intent on uniting Italy under the power of the Vatican, and was eager to do so by any means, including riding into pitched battle. Yet this "warrior pope" considered his most formidable adversary to be Michelangelo. Applying a form of blackmail, Julius threatened to wage war on Michelangelo's Florence, to which the artist had fled after Julius canceled a commission for a grand papal tomb unless Michelangelo agreed to return to Rome and take up the task of painting the Sistine Chapel ceiling.

MICHELANGELO, SCULPTOR

A sculptor first and foremost, however, Michelangelo considered painting an inferior genre— "for rascals and sissies" as he put it. Second, there was the sheer scope of the task, leading Michelangelo to suspect he'd been set up by a rival, Bramante, chief architect of the new St. Peter's Basilica. As Michelangelo was also a master architect, he regarded this fresco commission as a Renaissance mission-impossible. Pope Julius's powerful will prevailed—and six years later the work of the Sistine Ceiling was complete. Irving Stone's famous novel *The Agony and the Ecstasy*—and the granitic 1965 film that followed—chart this epic battle between artist and pope.

THINGS ARE LOOKING UP

To enhance your viewing of the ceiling, bring along opera-glasses, binoculars, or just a mirror (to prevent your neck from becoming bent like Michelangelo's). Note that no photos are permitted. Insiders know the only time to get the chapel to yourself is during the papal blessings and public audiences held in St. Peter's Square. Failing that, get there during lunch hour. Admission and entry to the Sistine Chapel is only through the Musei Vaticani (Vatican Museums).

SCHEMATIC OF THE SISTINE CEILING

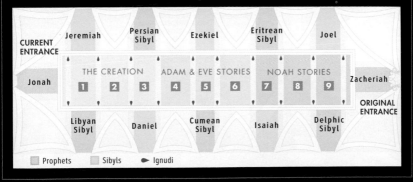

HEAVEN'S ABOVE

The ceiling's biblical symbols were ideated by three Vatican theologians, Cardinal Alidosi, Egidio da Viterbo, and Giovanni Rafanelli, along with Michelangelo. As for the ceiling's painted "framework," this *quadratura* alludes to Roman triumphal arches because Pope Julius II was fond of mounting "triumphal entries" into his conquered cities (in imitation of Christ's procession into Jerusalem on Palm Sunday).

THE CENTER PANELS

Prophet turned art-critic or, perhaps doubling as ourselves, the ideal viewer, Jonah the prophet (painted at the altar end) gazes up at the

Creation, or Michelangelo's version of it.

1 The first of three scenes taken from the Book of Genesis: God separates Light from Darkness.

2 God creates the sun and a craterless pre-Galilean moon while the panel's other half offers an unprecedented rear view of the Almighty creating the vegetable world.

3 In the panel showing God separating the Waters from the Heavens, the Creator tumbles towards us as in a self-made whirlwind.

4 Pausing for breath, next admire probably Western Art's most famous image—God giving life to Adam.

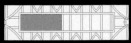

5 The Creation of Eve from Adam's rib leads to the sixth panel.

6 In a sort of diptych divided by the trunk of the Tree of Knowledge of Good and Evil, Michelangelo retells the Temptation and the Fall.

7 Illustrating Man's fallen nature, the last three panels narrate, in un-chronological order, the Flood. In the first Noah offers a pre-Flood sacrifice of thanks.

8 Damaged by an explosion in 1794, next comes Michelangelo's version of Flood itself.

9 Finally, above the monumental Jonah, you can just make out the small, wretched figure of Noah, lying drunk—in pose, the shrunken anti-type of the majestic Adam five panels down the wall.

THE CREATION OF ADAM

Michelangelo's Adam was partly inspired by the Creation scenes Michelangelo had studied in the sculpted doors of Jacopo della Quercia in Bologna and Lorenzo Ghiberti's Doors of Paradise in Florence. Yet in Michelangelo's version Adam's hand hangs limp, waiting God's touch to impart the spark of life. Facing his Creation, the Creator—looking a bit like the pagan god Jupiter—is for the first time ever depicted as horizontal, mirroring the Biblical "in his own likeness." Decades after its completion, a crack began to appear, amputating Adam's fingertips. Believe it or not, the most famous fingers in Western art are the handiwork, at least in part, of one Domenico Carnevale.

9

Fra Angelico (1387–1455), and Filippo Lippi (circa 1406–69), and the exceptional *Transfiguration, Coronation,* and *Foligno Madonna* by Raphael (1483–1520).

The **Cortile Ottagonale** (Octagonal Courtyard) of the Vatican Museums displays some of sculpture's most famous works, including the 1st century AD Roman copy of the 4th century BC Greek *Apollo Belvedere* (and Canova's 1801 *Perseus,* heavily influenced by it) and the 1st-century *Laocoön*.

The **Stanze di Raffaello** (Raphael Rooms) are second only to the Sistine Chapel in artistic interest—and draw crowds comparable. In 1508 Pope Julius II employed Raphael, on the recommendation of Bramante, to decorate the rooms with allegories, scenes of papal history, and biblical scenes. The result is a Renaissance tour de force. Of the four rooms, the second and third were decorated mainly by Raphael. The others were decorated by Giulio Romano (circa 1499–1546) and other assistants of Raphael, based on his designs.

The frescoed **Stanza della Segnatura** (Room of the Signature), where papal bulls were signed, is one of Raphael's finest works; indeed, they are thought by many to be some of the finest frescoes in the history of Western art. This was Julius's private library, and the room's use is reflected in the frescoes' themes, philosophy, and enlightenment. A paradigm of High Renaissance painting, the works demonstrate the revolutionary ideals of naturalism (Raphael's figures lack the awkwardness of those painted only a few years earlier); humanism (the idea that human beings are the noblest and most admirable of God's creations); and a profound interest in the ancient world, the result of the 15th-century rediscovery of classical antiquity. The *School of Athens* glorifies some of philosophy's greats, including Plato (pointing to Heaven) and Aristotle (pointing to Earth) at the fresco's center. The pensive figure on the stairs is thought to be modeled after Michelangelo, who was painting the Sistine ceiling at the same time Raphael was working here. Look for a confident Raphael, dressed in a red cloak, on the far right, beside his white-clad friend Il Sodoma, the artist who frescoed the ceiling.

In 1508, just before Raphael started work on his rooms, the redoubtable Pope Julius II commissioned Michelangelo to paint single-handedly the more-than-10,000-square-foot ceiling of the **Cappella Sistina** (Sistine Chapel). For an in-depth look at Michelangelo's masterpiece, see our photo feature, "Agony and Ecstasy: The Sistine Ceiling." ⊠ *Main museum entrance, Viale Vaticano 100; guided visit office, Piazza San Pietro* ☎ *06/69884947* ⊕ *www.vatican.va* ⊠ *€14* ⊘ *Mon.–Sat. 9–6 (last entrance at 4); closed Sun., except for last Sun. of month (9–12:30), when admission is free; other dates of closure include Jan. 1 and 6; Feb. 11; May 1 and 21; June 11 and 29; Aug. 15; Dec. 25 and 26* ☞ *Note: ushers at entrance of St. Peter's and Vatican Museums will bar entry to people with bare knees or bare shoulders* Ⓜ *Cipro-Musei Vaticani or Ottaviano-San Pietro.*

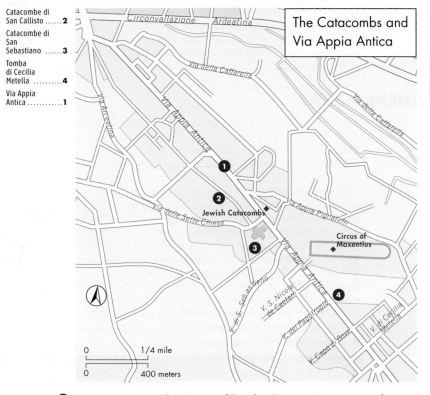

The Catacombs and Via Appia Antica

2

❶ **Via Appia Antica.** This Queen of Roads, (*Regina Viarium*), was the most
★ important of the extensive network of roads that traversed the Roman
☺ Empire, a masterful feat of engineering that made possible Roman control of a vast area by allowing for the efficient transport of armies and
commercial goods. Begun in 312 BC by Appius Claudius, the road was
ancient Europe's first highway. The first part reached as far as Capua
near Naples, ultimately being extended in 191 BC to Brindisi 584 km
(365 mi) southeast of Rome on the Adriatic Coast. The ancient roadway
begins at Porta San Sebastiano, southeast of the Circus Maximus, passing through grassy fields and shady groves and by the villas of movie
stars (Marcello Mastroianni and Gina Lollobrigida had homes here).
The area of primary interest lies between the second and third milestones
and is still paved with the ancient *basoli* (basalt stones) over which the
Romans drove their carriages—look for the wheel ruts. Pick a sunny day
for your visit, wear comfortable shoes, and bring a bottle of water. The
Appia Antica is best reached with public transport (there are no sidewalks along the road); see Getting Here, *above*. For more information,
or bike rentals for exploring the Via Appia, visit the **Information Point** at
(✉ *Via Appia Antica 58/60* ☎ *06/5135316* ☉ *Daily 9:30–5:30* ⊕ *www.
parcoappiaantica.it* ✉ *Exit Via Cristoforo Colombo at Circonvallazione
Ardeatina, follow signs to Appia Antica parking lot.*

WORTH NOTING

❷ Catacombe di San Callisto (Catacombs of St. Calixte). A friar will guide you through the crypts and galleries of the well-preserved San Callisto catacombs. ☒ *Via Appia Antica 110* ☎ *06/51301580* ⊕ *www.catacombe.roma.it* ☜ *€6* ☉ *Mar.–Jan., Thurs.–Tues. 9–noon and 2–5.*

WHERE TO EAT

Updated by
Dana Klitzberg

Rome has been known since ancient times for its great feasts and banquets, and though the days of the triclinium and the Saturnalia are long past, dining out is still the Romans' favorite pastime. The city is distinguished more by its good attitude toward eating out than by a multitude of world-class restaurants; simple, traditional cuisine reigns, although things are slowly changing as talented young chefs explore new culinary frontiers. Many of the city's restaurants cater to a clientele of regulars, and atmosphere and attitude are usually friendly and informal. The flip side is that in Rome the customer is not always right—the chef and waiters are in charge, and no one will beg forgiveness if you wanted *skim* milk in that cappuccino. Be flexible and you're sure to *mangiar bene* (eat well). Lunch is served from approximately 12:30 to 2:30 and dinner from 7:30 or 8 until about 11, though some restaurants stay open later, especially in summer, when patrons linger at sidewalk tables to enjoy the parade of people and the *ponentino* (evening breeze).

Use the coordinate (✛ B2) at the end of each listing to locate a site on the Where to Eat in Rome map.

WHAT IT COSTS IN EUROS					
	¢	$	$$	$$$	$$$$
AT DINNER	under €20	€20–€30	€30–€45	€45–€65	over €65

Prices are for first course (primo), second course (secondo), and dessert (dolce).

PANTHEON AND NAVONA

PANTHEON

$$

MODERN ITALIAN

✕ **Il Bacaro.** With a handful of choice tables set outside against an ivy-draped wall, this tiny candlelit spot not far from the Pantheon makes for an ideal evening, equally suited for a romantic twosome or close friends and convivial conversation. Pastas—like *orecchiette* (little ear-shaped pasta) with broccoli and sausage, a dish that lip-smacks of Puglia—are star players. As a bonus, the kitchen keeps its clients from picking at each other's plates by offering side dishes of all the pastas ordered among those at the table. The choice main courses are mostly meat—the beef fillet with balsamic vinegar or London broil–style marinated in olive oil and rosemary are winners. ☒ *Via degli Spagnoli 27, Pantheon* ☎ *06/6872554* ⊕ *www.ilbacaro.com* ⚛ *Reservations essential* ▭ *DC, MC, V* ☉ *Closed Sun. and 1 wk in Aug. No lunch Sat.* ✛ *E3.*

BEST BETS FOR ROME DINING

With hundreds of restaurants to choose from, how will you decide where to eat? Fodor's writers and editors have selected their favorite restaurants by price, cuisine, and experience in the Best Bets lists below. In the first column, Fodor's Choice properties represent the "best of the best" in every price category.

Fodor'sChoice ★

Agata e Romeo, $$$$, p. 98

Alle Fratte di Trastevere, $$, p. 100

Cul de Sac, ¢–$, p. 90

Da Baffetto, ¢–$, p. 90

Etablì, $$, p. 90

Filetti di Baccalà, ¢, p. 92

Il Convivio, $$$$, p. 90

Il Sanlorenzo, $$$$, p. 93

La Pergola, $$$$, p. 99

Taverna Angelica, $$, p. 99

Trattoria Monti, $$, p. 97

Uno e Bino, $$, p. 98

Best by Price

¢

Filetti di Baccalà, p. 92

$

Cul de Sac, p. 90

Da Baffetto, p. 90

Dar Poeta, p. 100

Remo, p. 101

$$

Alle Fratte di Trastevere, p. 100

Etablì, p. 90

Ōbikā, p. 91

Taverna Angelica, p. 99

Trattoria Monti, p. 97

$$$

Al Pompiere, p. 93

Il Palazzetto, p. 96

La Veranda dell'Hotel Columbus, p. 98

Uno e Bino, p. 98

$$$$

Agata e Romeo, p. 98

Il Convivio, p. 90

Il Sanlorenzo, p. 93

La Pergola, p. 99

San Teodoro, p. 96

Best by Cuisine

MODERN ITALIAN

Agata e Romeo, $$$$, p. 98

Il Bacaro, $$, p. 88

Il Convivio, $$$$, p. 90

La Pergola, $$$$, p. 99

Taverna Angelica, $$, p. 99

Uno e Bino, $$$, p. 98

PIZZA

Da Baffetto, ¢–$, p. 90

Dar Poeta, ¢–$, p. 100

Remo, ¢–$, p. 101

ROMAN

Alle Fratte di Trastevere, $$, p. 100

Al Pompiere, $$$, p. 93

Checchino dal 1887, $$$–$$$$, p. 100

Da Sergio, $$, p. 92

La Veranda dell'Hotel Columbus, $$$, p. 98

Maccheroni, $$, p. 90

WINE BAR

Cul de Sac, ¢–$, p. 90

Roscioli, $$–$$$, p. 92

Trimani Il Winebar, $$, p. 97

Best by Experience

OUTDOOR DINING

Alle Fratte di Trastevere, $$, p. 100

Dal Bolognese, $$$$, p. 96

Il Bacaro, $$, p. 88

La Veranda dell'Hotel Columbus, $$$, p. 98

Maccheroni, $$, p. 90

GORGEOUS SETTING

Il Convivio, $$$$, p. 90

Il Palazzetto, $$$, p. 96

La Pergola, $$$$, p. 99

La Veranda dell'Hotel Columbus, $$$, p. 98

LOTS OF LOCALS

Dar Poeta, ¢–$, p. 100

'Gusto-Osteria, $$, p. 96

Trattoria Monti, $$, p. 97

2

$$ ✕**Maccheroni.** This boisterous, convivial trattoria north of the Pantheon
ROMAN   makes for a fun evening out. The decor is basic: white walls with wooden
shelves lined with wine bottles, blocky wooden tables covered in white
butcher paper—but there's an "open" kitchen (with even the dishwash-
ers in plain view of the diners) and an airy feel that attracts a young
clientele as well as visiting celebrities. The menu sticks to Roman basics
such as simple pasta with fresh tomatoes and basil, or rigatoni *alla gri-
cia* (with bacon, sheep's-milk cheese, and black pepper). The specialty
pasta, *trofie* (short pasta twists) with a black truffle sauce, inspires you
to lick your plate. Probably the best choice on the menu is the *tagliata
con rughetta,* a juicy, two-inch-thick steak sliced thinly and served on
arugula. ✉ *Piazza delle Coppelle 44, Pantheon* ☎ *06/68307895* ⊕ *www.
ristorantemaccheroni.com* ▭ *AE, MC, V* ✦ *E3.*

NAVONA
¢–$ ✕**Cul de Sac.** This popular wine bar near Piazza Navona is among the
WINE BAR   city's oldest enoteche and offers a book-length selection of wines from
Fodor'sChoice   Italy, France, the Americas, and elsewhere. Food is eclectic, ranging
★   from a huge assortment of Italian meats and cheeses (try the delicious
lonza, cured pork loin, or *speck,* a northern Italian smoked prosciutto)
to various Mediterranean dishes, including delicious baba ghanoush,
a tasty Greek salad, and a spectacular wild boar pâté. Outside tables
get crowded fast, so arrive early, or come late, as they serve until about
1 AM. ✉ *Piazza Pasquino 73, Piazza Navona* ☎ *06/68801094* ▭ *AE,
MC, V* ⊙ *Closed 2 wks in Aug.* ✦ *D4.*

¢–$ ✕**Da Baffetto.** Down a cobblestone street not far from Piazza Navona,
PIZZA   this is Rome's most popular pizzeria and a summer favorite for street-
Fodor'sChoice   side dining. The plain interior is mostly given over to the ovens, but
★   there's another room with more paper-covered tables. Outdoor tables
(enclosed and heated in winter) provide much-needed additional seat-
ing. Turnover is fast and lingering is not encouraged. ✉ *Via del Governo
Vecchio 114, Navona* ☎ *06/6861617* ▭ *No credit cards* ⊙ *Closed Aug.
No lunch* ✦ *D4.*

$$ ✕**Etablì.** On a narrow vicolo off beloved Piazza del Fico, this mul-
MEDITERRANEAN   tidimensional locale serves as a lounge-bar, and becomes a hot spot
Fodor'sChoice   by aperitivo hour. Beautifully finished with vaulted wood beam ceil-
★   ings, wrought-iron touches, plush leather sofas, and chandeliers, it's
all modern Italian farmhouse chic. In the restaurant section (the place
is sprawling), it's minimalist Provençal hip (*etabli* is French for the
regionally typical tables within). And the food is clean and Mediterranean, with touches of Asia in the raw fish appetizers. Pastas are more
traditional Italian, and the *secondi* run the gamut from land to sea.
Arrive early as the place fills up by dinnertime and it's a popular post-
dining spot for sipping and posing. ✉ *Vicolo delle Vacche 9/a, Navona*
☎ *06/6871499* ⊕ *www.etabli.it* ▭ *MC, V* ⊙ *Closed Sun. in summer,
Mon. in winter* ✦ *D3.*

$$$$ ✕**Il Convivio.** In a tiny, nondescript vicolo north of Piazza Navona, the
MODERN ITALIAN   three Troiani brothers—Angelo in the kitchen, and brothers Giuseppe
Fodor'sChoice   and Massimo presiding over the dining room and wine cellar—have
★   quietly been redefining the experience of Italian eclectic *alta cucina* for
many years. Antipasti include a "roast beef" of tuna fillet lacquered

The Piazza del Pantheon is a striking restaurant location—though you'll find better food elsewhere in the neighborhood.

with chestnut honey, rosemary, red peppercorns, and ginger served with a green apple salad, while a squid ink risotto with baby cuttlefish, sea asparagus, lemongrass, and basil sates the appetites of those with dreams of *fantasia*. Main courses include a fabulous version of a cold-weather pigeon dish for which Il Convivio is famous. Service is attentive without being overbearing, and the wine list is exceptional. It is definitely a splurge spot. ⊠ *Vicolo dei Soldati 31, Navona* ☎ *06/6869432* ⚛ *Reservations essential* ▭ *AE, DC, MC, V* ☉ *Closed Sun., 1 wk in Jan., and 2 wks in Aug. No lunch* ✛ *D3.*

$$
ITALIAN
✕ **Ōbikā.** If you've ever wanted to take in a "mozzarella bar," here's your chance. Mozzarella is featured here much like sushi bars showcase fresh fish—even the decor is modern Japanese minimalism–meets–ancient Roman grandeur. The cheese, in all its varieties, is the focus of the dishes: there's the familiar cow's milk, the delectable water buffalo milk varieties from the Campagnia region, and the sinfully rich *burrata* from Puglia (a fresh cow's milk mozzarella encasing a creamy center of unspun mozzarella curds and fresh cream). They're all served with various accompanying cured meats, vegetables, sauces, and breads. An outdoor deck is a great spot for dining alfresco. Also visit the new, supercentral smaller location in Campo de' Fiori. The concept has been such a success that other locations recently opened in Florence and midtown Manhattan. ⊠ *Piazza di Firenze 26, Navona* ⊕ *www.obika.it* ☎ *06/6832630* ▭ *AE, DC, MC, V* ✛ *E3.*

CAMPO DE' FIORI AND GHETTO

CAMPO DE' FIORI

$$ ✗ **Da Sergio.** Every neighborhood has at least one "old-school" Roman
ROMAN trattoria, and for the Campo de' Fiori area Da Sergio is it.
Once you're seated (there's usually a wait), the red-and-white-check paper table-covering, bright lights, '50s kitsch, and the stuffed boar's head on the wall remind you that you're smack in the middle of the genuine article. Go for the delicious version of pasta *all'amatriciana*, or the generous helping of gnocchi with a tomato sauce and lots of Parmesan cheese, served, as tradition dictates, on Thursday. ⊠ *Vicolo delle Grotte 27* 🕾 *06/6864293* ▭ *DC, MC, V* ☺ *Closed Sun. and 2 wks in Aug.* ✛ *D5.*

¢ ✗ **Dar Filettaro a Santa Barbara (Filetti di Baccalà).** For years, Filetti di
ITALIAN Baccalà has been serving just that—battered, deep-fried fillets of salt
Fodor'sChoice cod—and not much else. You'll find no-frills starters such as *bruschette*
★ *al pomodoro* (garlic-rubbed toast topped with fresh tomatoes and olive oil), sautéed zucchini, and, in winter months, the cod is served alongside *puntarelle*, chicory stems topped with a delicious anchovy-garlic-lemon vinaigrette. The location, down the street from Campo de' Fiori in a little piazza in front of the beautiful Santa Barbara church, begs you to eat at one of the outdoor tables, weather permitting. Long operating hours allow those still on U.S. time to eat as early (how gauche!) as 6 PM. ⊠ *Largo dei Librari 88, Campo de' Fiori* 🕾 *06/6864018* ▭ *No credit cards* ☺ *Closed Sun. and Aug. No lunch* ✛ *D5.*

$$ ✗ **Ditirambo.** Don't let the country-kitchen ambience fool you. At this
ITALIAN little spot off Campo de' Fiori, the constantly changing selection of offbeat takes on Italian classics is a step beyond ordinary Roman fare. The place is usually packed with diners who appreciate the adventuresome kitchen, though you may overhear complaints about the brusque service. Antipasti can be delicious and unexpected, like Gorgonzola-pear soufflé drizzled with aged balsamic vinegar, or a mille-feuille of eggplant, wild fennel, and anchovies. But people really love this place for rustic dishes like osso buco, Calabrian eggplant "meatballs," and hearty pasta with rabbit ragù. Vegetarians will adore the cheesy potato gratin with truffle shavings. Desserts can be skipped in favor of a *digestivo.* ⊠ *Piazza della Cancelleria 74, Campo de' Fiori* 🕾 *06/6871626* ⊕ *www.ristoranteditirambo.it* ▭ *AE, MC, V* ☺ *Closed Aug. No lunch Mon.* ✛ *D4.*

$$–$$$ ✗ **Roscioli.** This food shop and wine bar is dark and decadent, more
WINE BAR like a Caravaggio painting than a place of business. The shop in front beckons with top-quality comestibles: wild Alaskan smoked salmon, more than 300 cheeses, and a dizzying array of wines. Venture farther inside to be seated in a wine cavelike room where you'll be served artisanal cheeses and salumi, as well as an extensive selection of unusual menu choices and interesting takes on classics. Try the Caprese salad with DOC buffalo milk mozzarella, fresh and roasted tomatoes with bread crumbs and pistachios, or go for pasta with *bottarga* (dried mullet roe). The menu is further divided among meats, seafood (including a nice selection of tartars and other *crudi* (raw-fish preparations), and vegetarian-friendly items. ∎TIP➔ Book ahead to reserve a table in the cozy wine cellar beneath the dining room. And afterward head around the

corner to their bakery for rightfully famous breads and sweets. ⊠ *Via dei Giubbonari 21/22, Campo de' Fiori* ☎ *06/6875287* ⊕ ▤ *AE, DC, MC, V* ☉ *Closed Sun.* ✢ *D5.*

$$
ITALIAN

✕ **Trattoria Moderna.** The space is as the name implies—modern, with high ceilings, and done in shades of beige and gray—and an oversize chalkboard displays daily specials, such as a delicious chickpea and *baccalà* (salt cod) soup. The food runs toward the traditional but with a twist, like a pasta *all'amatriciana* with kosher beef instead of the requisite *guanciale* (cured pork jowl). Main courses are more creative, as well as more hit-or-miss. The jumbo shrimp in a cognac sauce with couscous was tasty, but the scant four shrimp a drawback. The trattoria gets an "A" for effort, with its friendly serving staff and very reasonable prices. An extra bonus is the outdoor seating—a few tables surrounded by greenery, off the lovely cobblestone street. ⊠ *Vicolo dei Chiodaroli 16, Campo de' Fiori* ☎ *06/68803423* ▤ *AE, DC, MC, V* ✢ *E4.*

GHETTO

$$$
ROMAN

✕ **Al Pompiere.** The entrance on a narrow side street leads you up a charming staircase and into the main dining room of this neighborhood favorite. Its Roman Jewish dishes, such as fried zucchini flowers, battered salt cod, and gnocchi, are all consistently good and served without fanfare on white dishes with a simple border. There are also some nice, historical touches like a beef-and-citron stew that comes from an ancient Roman recipe of Apicius. And if you come across the traditional Roman *porchetta* (roasted suckling pig) special, make sure to order it before it runs out—it is truly divine. In 2004, there was a terrible fire in a shop below the restaurant, but the kitchen was soon back in business, though the irony here is as thick as the chef's tomato sauce: *Al Pompiere* means "the fireman." ⊠ *Via Santa Maria dei Calderari 38, Ghetto* ☎ *06/6868377* ▤ *AE, MC, V* ☉ *Closed Sun. and Aug.* ✢ *E5.*

$$$
ROMAN JEWISH

✕ **Ba' Ghetto.** This new hot spot is a welcome addition to the main drag in the Jewish ghetto. The kitchen is kosher (many places featuring Roman Jewish fare are not), and not only do they feature an assortment of Roman Jewish dishes, they also offer a variety of Mediterranean–Middle Eastern Jewish fare. Enjoy starters like phyllo "cigars" stuffed with ground meat and spices, or the *brik*—egg and tomato wrapped in phyllo triangles and briefly fried. There's a nice assortment of pasta dishes, but we advise going for main plates like the assortment of couscous dishes (the spicy seafood is delicious) or baccalà with raisins and pine nuts. Interesting sides like chicory with *bottarga* (cured mullet roe) round out the meal. Kosher wines are on offer as well. Beware the strictly adhered-to hours: Saturday night, the restaurant posts post-Sabbath/sundown opening times to the minute on a blackboard out front. ⊠ *Via del Portico d'Ottavia 57, Ghetto* ☎ *06/68892868* ⊕ *www.kosherinrome.com* ▤ *AE, MC, V* ☉ *No dinner Fri. No lunch Sat.* ✢ *E5.*

$$$$
SEAFOOD
Fodor's Choice
★

✕ **Il Sanlorenzo.** This revamped, gorgeous space—think chandeliers and soaring original brickwork ceilings—houses one of the better seafood spots in the eternal city. Tempting tasting menus are on offer, as well as à la carte items like a wonderful series of small plates in their *crudo* (raw fish) appetizer, which can include a perfectly seasoned fish tartare trio, sweet *scampi* (local langoustines), and a wispy-thin carpaccio of

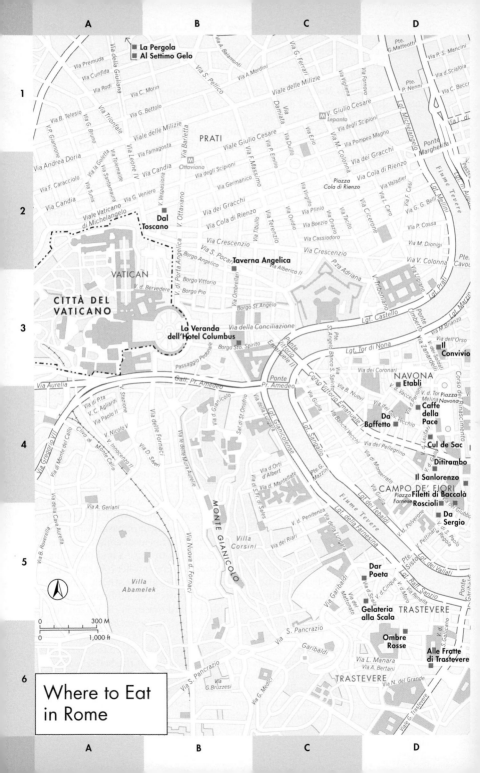

Where to Eat in Rome

La Pergola
Al Settimo Gelo

Via A. Baiamonti
Via G. Ferrari
Via G. Mancini
Via P. S. Mancini
Via Premuda
Pte. G. Matteotti
Via della Giulana
Via S. Pellico
Via A.Mordini
Viale delle Milizie
Via Vigliena
Pte. P. Nenni
Via d. Scialoia
Via Cunfida
Via C. Morin
Via Formovo
Via C. Beccr
Via Rodi
Via Damiata
V. Giulio Cesare
Via T. di
Via B. Telesio
Via G. Bettolo
Lepanto
Via degli Scipioni
Viale delle Milizie
PRATI
Via Giulio Cesare
Via P. Emilio
Via M. Colonna
Via Pompeo Magno
Ponte Margherita
Via V.P. Giannone
Via G. Bruno
Via Trionfale
Via Leone IV
Via F. Massimo
Via dei Gracchi
Via Andrea Doria
Via A. Goletta
Via Santamaura
Via Candia
Via G. Veniero
Via Germanico
Via P. Duillo
Via Ezio
Via Cola di Rienzo
Via Valadier
Piazza Cola di Rienzo
Fiume Tevere
Via F. Caracciolo
Via Tunis
Ottaviano
Via degli Scipioni
Via Virgilio
Via Plinio
Via Boezio
Via Cicerone
Via L. Caro
Via G. G. Belli
Via Mellini
Via Candia
Viale Vaticano di Michelangelo
V. Ottaviano
Via dei Gracchi
Via Cola di Rienzo
Via Terenzio
Via Tibullo
Via Orazio
Via Tacito
Via P. Cossa
Dal Toscano
Via Crescenzio
Via M. Dionigi
Pte. Cavou
VATICAN
Via S. Pocar
Taverna Angelica
Via V. Colonna
V. d. Belvedere
V. di Porta Angelica
Borgo Angelico
Via Alberico II
Via Crescenzio
Lgt. Prati
CITTÀ DEL VATICANO
Borgo Vittorio
Pza Adriana
Lgt. Castello
Via M. Brianzo
Borgo Pio
Via V. Uliano
Via dell'Orso
Il Convivio
La Veranda dell'Hotel Columbus
Via della Conciliazione
Borgo St.Angelo
Ponte Umberto I
Lgt. Tor di Nona
V. d. Soldati
Borgo Sto. Spirito
Lgt. Castello
Via dei Coronari
NAVONA
Via Aurelia
Passaggio Pedone
Galt. Pr. Amedeo
Ponte Vittorio Emanuele II
Corso Vittorio Emanuele
Via B. Nuovi
Etabli
Via del Banco S. Spirito
V. d. Tor Melina
Piazza Navona
Ponte Pr. Amedeo
Via Giulia
Via dei Banchi Vecchi
Caffe della Pace
Via di Pta
V.C. Agliardi
V. Paolo II
Via Monte del Gallo
Clivo di
Monte del Gallo
Via Innocenzo II
V. Nicolo V
Via dei Bresci Vecchio
Da Baffetto
Via dei Pellegrino
Cul de Sac
V. Gregorio VII
Via delle Fornaci
Via delle Mura Aurelie
Via del Monserrato
Ditirambo
MONTE GIANICOLO
Via Garibaldi
Il Sanlorenzo
CAMPO DE' FIORI
Piazza Farnese
Filetti di Baccalà
Roscioli
Via A. Gerlani
Via d'Orti d'Albert
Via d.S.Fr. di Sales
Via d. Mantellate
Pte G. Mazzini
Via del Pettinari
Da Sergio
Via B. Rovorella
Via della Cava Aurelia
Fiume Tevere
Lgt. dei Tebaldi
Lgt. della Farnesina
Lgt. Sanzio
Via Nuova d. Fornaci
Villa Corsini
Via d. Penitenza
Via dei Riari
Villa Abamelek
Dar Poeta
Via della Scala
Via di Cinque
Via d. Moro
Via Renella
TRASTEVERE
Gelateria alla Scala
S. Pancrazio
Via di S.
Ombre Rosse
Alle Fratte di Trastevere
Garibaldi
Via L. Manara
Via A. Bertani
TRASTEVERE
Via N. del Grande
Viale G. Trastevere
Via S. Pancrazio
Via G. Bruzzesi
Via G. Medici
S. Pancrazio

0   300 M
0   1,000 ft

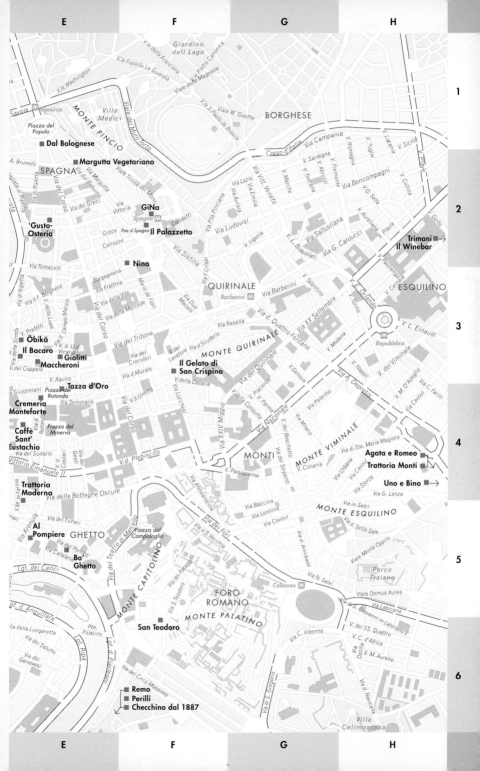

red shrimp. The restaurant's version of spaghetti with lobster is an exquisite example of how this dish should look and taste (the secret is cooking the pasta in a lobster stock!). Try a main course of a freshly caught seasonal fish prepared to order. Menu items often change based on the chef's whim and the catch of the day. A subterranean lounge and wine room offer refuge for those who seek private dining. ☒ *Via dei Chiavari 4/5, Campo de' Fiori* ☎ *06/6865097* ⊕ *www.ilsanlorenzo. it* ▭ *AE, DC, MC, V* ☻ *No lunch Sat.–Mon.* ✛ *D4.*

$$$$ ✕ **San Teodoro.** The atmosphere: far removed from the madding crowds.
SEAFOOD The setting: a pair of enclosed piazzas, walls covered in ivy, nestled by the Roman Forum and the Campidoglio. The specialty: refined Roman cuisine, featuring tastes of Roman Jewish fare and specializing in seafood. In spring and summer there's a lovely outdoor dining deck, and in cooler months, the bright rooms decorated with contemporary art offer pleasant surroundings. The menu includes classic fried artichokes (among the best in the city), homemade ravioli *con cipolla di Tropea* (filled with red onion and tossed in balsamic vinegar), and favorite local fish turbot, barely adorned with perfectly roasted potatoes and extra-virgin olive oil. Everything down to the last bite (make your dessert choice the chocolate medley) is a pleasure, even if it doesn't come cheaply. ☒ *Via dei Fienili 50-51, Ghetto* ☎ *06/6780933* ▭ *AE, DC, MC, V* ☻ *Closed Sun.* ✛ *F6.*

SPAGNA

$$$$ ✕ **Dal Bolognese.** The darling of the media, film, and fashion communities,
EMILIAN this classic restaurant on Piazza del Popolo is not only an "in-crowd" dinner destination but makes a convenient shopping-spree lunch spot. As the name promises, the cooking adheres to the hearty tradition of Bologna. Start with a plate of sweet San Daniele prosciutto with melon, then move on to the traditional egg pastas of Emilia-Romagna. Second plates include the famous Bolognese *bollito misto,* a steaming tray of an assortment of boiled meats (some recognizable, some indecipherable) served with its classic accompaniment, a tangy, herby *salsa verde* (green sauce). ☒ *Piazza del Popolo 1, Spagna* ☎ *06/3222799* ▭ *AE, DC, MC, V* ☻ *Closed Mon. and 3 wks in Aug.* ✛ *E1.*

$$ ✕ **'Gusto-Osteria.** You can get regular osteria fare and service at this
ITALIAN member of the 'Gusto restaurant empire, but why would you? The beauty of this spot is what makes it *different*: its adaptation of the idea of *cichetti,* a sort of Italian tapas that originated in the venerable bars of Venice. Head to the bar area here (the only place this service is available) and, for between €2 and €4, sample pretty much anything on the regular menu in a snack-size portion. Many will want to begin by choosing from the incredible selection of 400 cheeses in the basement cellar, then from the various *fritti* (fried items), moving onto pastas such as sheep's milk and pepper spaghetti. Even enjoy mini desserts: the portions make you feel as if you're behaving! ☒ *Via della Frezza 16, Spagna* ☎ *06/32111482* ⊕ *www.gusto.it* ▭ *AE, DC, MC, V* ✛ *E2.*

$$$ ✕ **Il Palazzetto.** This small restaurant near the Piazza di Spagna is part of
MODERN ITALIAN the International Wine Academy of Rome. Chef Antonio Martucci creates seasonal menus using traditional Roman ingredients, to which he

gives a unique twist in preparation and flavor pairings. Stuffed calamari on an eggplant puree with sautéed baby peppers is a study in contrasting flavor and texture; homemade ricotta-filled gnocchi with sausage and asparagus hits all the right notes. It's wise to call in advance, both for reservations and to find out about regular prix-fixe dinners, sometimes with guest chefs, focusing on wine-food pairings. ⊠ *Vicolo del Bottino 8, Spagna* ☎ *06/6993400* ⊟ *AE, DC, MC, V* ✢ *F2.*

$–$$
VEGETARIAN

✗ **Margutta Vegetariano.** Parallel to posh Via del Babuino, Via Margutta has long been known as *the* street where artists have their studios in Rome. How fitting, then, that the rare Italian vegetarian restaurant, with changing displays of modern art, sits on the far end of this gallery-lined street closest to Piazza del Popolo. Here it takes on a chic and cosmopolitan air, where you'll find meat-free versions of classic Mediterranean dishes as well as more daring tofu concoctions. Lunch is essentially a pasta/salad bar to which you help yourself, while dinner offers à la carte and prix-fixe options. ⊠ *Via Margutta 118, Spagna* ☎ *06/32650577* ⊟ *AE, DC, MC, V* ✢ *E2.*

$$
ITALIAN

✗ **Nino.** Tom Cruise and Katie Holmes had their celeb-studded rehearsal dinner here, a testament that this dressed-up trattoria has been a favorite among international journalists and the rich and famous for decades. Nino sticks to the classics, in food and decor, as well as in its waiters. Much of what you find on the menu here are Roman staples with a Tuscan slant. To start, try a selection from the fine antipasto spread, or go for the cured meats or warm *crostini* (toasts) spread with liver pâté. Move on to pappardelle *al lepre* (a rich hare sauce) or the juicy grilled beef. One warning: if you're not Italian, or a regular, or a celebrity, the chance of brusque service multiplies—so insist on good service and you'll win the waiters' respect (and probably their attention). ⊠ *Via Borgognona 11, Spagna* ☎ *06/6786752* ⊟ *AE, DC, MC, V* ☉ *Closed Sun. and Aug.* ✢ *F2.*

MONTI, REPUBBLICA, AND SAN LORENZO

MONTI

$$
CENTRAL ITALIAN
Fodor's Choice
★

✗ **Trattoria Monti.** Not far from Santa Maria Maggiore, Monti is one of the most dependable, moderately priced trattorias in the city, featuring the cuisine of the Marches, an area to the northeast of Rome. There are surprisingly few places specializing in this humble fare considering there are more people hailing from Le Marche in Rome than in the whole region of Le Marche. The fare served up by the Camerucci family is hearty and simple, represented by various roasted meats and game, and a selection of generally vegetarian timbales and soufflés that change seasonally. The region's rabbit dishes are much loved, and here the *timballo di coniglio con patate* (rabbit casserole with potatoes) is no exception. ⊠ *Via di San Vito 13, Monti* ☎ *06/4466573* ⊟ *AE, DC, MC, V* ☉ *Closed Aug., 2 wks at Easter, and 10 days at Christmas* ✢ *H4.*

REPUBBLICA

$$
WINE BAR

✗ **Trimani Il Winebar.** Trimani operates nonstop from 11 AM to 12:30 AM and serves hot food at lunch and dinner. Decor is minimalist, and the second floor provides a subdued, candlelit space to sip wine. There's always a choice of a soup and pasta plates, as well as second courses and *torte salate* (savory tarts). Around the corner is a wineshop, one of the oldest in Rome, of the same name. Call about wine tastings and classes (in Italian). ✉ *Via Cernaia 37/b, Repubblica* ☎ *06/4469630* ⊟ *AE, DC, MC, V* ۞ *Closed Sun. and 2 wks in Aug.* ✛ *H2.*

SAN LORENZO

$$$$ ✕ **Agata e Romeo.** For the perfect marriage of fine dining, creative cui-
MODERN ITALIAN sine, and rustic Roman tradition, the husband-and-wife team of Agata
FodorsChoice Parisella and Romeo Caraccio is the top. Romeo presides over the din-
★ ing room and delights in the selection of wine-food pairings. And Chef
Agata was perhaps the first in the capital city to put a gourmet spin on
Roman ingredients and preparations, elevating dishes of the common
folk to new levels, wherein familiar staples like *cacao e pepe* are trans-
formed with the addition of even richer Sicilian aged cheese and saffron.
From antipasti (try the seafood crudo tasting: it's so artfully presented,
it's actually served on a glass plate resembling a painter's palette) to
desserts, many dishes are the best versions of classics you can get. The
prices here are steep, but for those who appreciate extremely high-
quality ingredients, an incredible wine cellar, and warm service, dining
here is a real treat. ✉ *Via Carlo Alberto 45, Termini* ☎ *06/4466115*
⊟ *AE, DC, MC, V* ۞ *Closed weekends, 2 wks in July, and 2 wks in
Aug.* ✛ *H4.*

$$$ ✕ **Uno e Bino.** The setting is simple: wooden tables and chairs on a stone
MODERN ITALIAN floor with little more than a few shelves of wine bottles lining the walls
FodorsChoice for decor. Giampaolo Gravina's restaurant in this artsy corner of the
★ San Lorenzo neighborhood is popular with foodies and locals alike, as
the kitchen turns out inventive cuisine inspired by the family's Umbrian
and Sicilian roots. Dishes like octopus salad with asparagus and carrots,
and spaghetti with swordfish, tomatoes, and capers are specialties. The
Parmesan soufflé is a study in light, silky, salty, and absolute perfection.
Delicious and simple, yet upscale, desserts cap off the dinner, making
this small establishment one of the top dining deals—and pleasurable
meals—in Rome. ✉ *Via degli Equi 58, San Lorenzo* ☎ *06/4460702*
⊟ *MC, V* ۞ *Closed Mon. and Aug. No lunch* ✛ *H4.*

VATICAN, BORGO, PRATI, AND NORTHWEST ROME

BORGO

$$$ ✕ **La Veranda dell'Hotel Columbus.** Deciding where to sit at La Veranda is
ROMAN not easy, since both the shady courtyard, torch-lit at night, and the fres-
coed dining room are among Rome's most spectacular settings. While
La Veranda has classic Roman cuisine on tap, the kitchen offers nice,
refreshing twists on the familiar with an innovative use of flavor com-
binations. Try the unusual duck-leg confit starter, stuffed with raisins
and pine nuts with an onion compote and plum sorbet. Or go for the
grilled tuna bites with anchovy-caper dumplings and an eggplant torta.
Even the pastas are unexpected: saffron fettucine with cuttlefish and
zucchini flowers is subtle and elegant—much like the surroundings. Call
ahead, especially on Saturday, because the hotel often hosts weddings,
which close the restaurant, and you don't want to miss passing a few

hours of your Roman holiday in these environs. ⊠ *Borgo Santo Spirito 73, Borgo* ☎ *06/6872973* ⊕ *www.hotelcolumbus.net* ⌖ *Reservations essential* ☰ *AE, DC, MC, V* ✛ *B3.*

$$ ✗ **Taverna Angelica.** The area surrounding St. Peter's Basilica isn't known
MODERN ITALIAN for culinary excellence, but Taverna Angelica is an exception. Its tiny
Fodor'sChoice size allows the chef to concentrate on each individual dish, and the
★ menu is creative without being pretentious. Dishes such as warm octopus salad on a bed of mashed potatoes with a basil-parsley pesto drizzle are more about taste than presentation. The lentil soup with pigeon breast brought hunter's cuisine to a new level. And the breast of duck in balsamic vinegar was exquisitely executed. It may be difficult to find, on a section of the street that's set back and almost subterranean, but it's worth searching out. ⊠ *Piazza A. Capponi 6, Borgo* ☎ *06/6874514* ⊕ *www.tavernaangelica.it* ⌖ *Reservations essential* ☰ *AE, V* ✛ *B3.*

PRATI

$$ ✗ **Dal Toscano.** An open wood-fired grill and classic dishes such as *ribol-*
TUSCAN *lita* (a thick bread and vegetable soup) and *pici* (fresh, thick pasta with wild hare sauce) are the draw at this great family-run Tuscan trattoria near the Vatican. The cuts of beef visible at the entrance tell you right away that the house special is the prized *bistecca alla fiorentina*—a thick grilled steak left rare in the middle and seared on the outside, with its rub of gutsy Tuscan olive oil and sea salt forming a delicious crust to keep in the natural juices of the beef. Seating outside on the sidewalk in warm weather is a nice touch. ⊠ *Via Germanico 58/60, Prati* ☎ *06/39723373* ⊕ *www.ristorantedaltoscano.it* ☰ *AE, DC, MC, V* ☻ *Closed Mon., 3 wks in Aug., and 1 wk in Jan.* ✛ *B2.*

NORTHWEST ROME

$$$$ ✗ **La Pergola.** La Pergola's rooftop location offers a commanding view
MODERN ITALIAN of the city, and as you're seated in your plush chair, you know you're
Fodor'sChoice in for a three–Michelin star experience. First, your waiter will present
★ you with menus—food, wine, and water (you read correctly). Then you must choose between the German Wunder-chef Heinz Beck's *alta cucina* specialties, though most everything will prove to be the best version of the dish you've ever tasted. Lobster is oh-so-lightly poached, and melt-in-your-mouth lamb is deceptively simple but earthy and perfect. Each course comes with a flourish of sauces or extra touches that makes it an event in its own right, while the cheese cart is well explained by knowledgeable servers. The dessert course is extravagant, including tiny petits fours and treats tucked away in small drawers that make up the serving "cabinet." The wine list is as thrilling as one might expect with the financial backing of the Hilton and their investment in one of the top wine cellars in Italy. ⊠ *Cavalieri Hilton, Via Cadlolo 101, Monte Mario, Northwest Rome* ☎ *06/3509221* ⊕ *www. romecavalieri.com/lapergola.php* ⌖ *Reservations essential. Jacket and tie* ☰ *AE, DC, MC, V* ☻ *Closed Sun. and Mon., and 2 wks in Dec. No lunch* ✛ *A1.*

TRASTEVERE

$$
ROMAN
☺
Fodor'sChoice
★

✕ **Alle Fratte di Trastevere.** Here you can find staple Roman trattoria fare as well as dishes with a southern slant. This means that *spaghetti alla carbonara* (with pancetta, eggs, and cheese) shares the menu with the likes of penne *alla Sorrentina* (with tomato, basil, and fresh mozzarella). For starters, the bruschette here are exemplary, as is the pressed octopus carpaccio on a bed of arugula. As for secondi, you can again look south and to the sea for a mixed seafood pasta or a grilled sea bass with oven-roasted potatoes, or go for the meat with a fillet *al pepe verde* (green peppercorns in a brandy cream sauce). Service is always with a smile, as the owners and their trusted waitstaff make you feel at home. ⊠ *Via delle Fratte di Trastevere 49/50* ☎ *06/5835775* ⊕ *www. allefratteditrastevere.com* ⊟ *AE, DC, MC, V* ۞ *Closed Wed. and 2 wks in Aug.* ✛ *D6.*

¢–$
PIZZA

✕ **Dar Poeta.** Romans drive across town for great pizza from this neighborhood institution on a small street in Trastevere. Maybe it's the dough—it's made from a secret blend of flours that's reputed to be easier to digest than the competition. They offer both thin-crust pizza and a thick-crust (*alta*) Neapolitan-style pizza with any of the given toppings. For dessert, there's a ridiculously good calzone with Nutella chocolate-hazelnut spread and ricotta cheese, so save some room. Service from the owners and friendly waitstaff is smile inducing. ⊠ *Vicolo del Bologna 45, Trastevere* ☎ *06/5880516* ⊟ *AE, MC, V* ✛ *D5.*

¢–$
ITALIAN

✕ **Ombre Rosse.** Set on lovely Piazza Sant'Egidio in the heart of Trastevere, this open-day-and-night spot is a great place to pass the time. You can have a morning cappuccino and read one of their international newspapers; have a light lunch (soups and salads are fresh and delicious) while taking in some sun; enjoy an aperitivo and nibbles at an outdoor table; or finish off an evening with friends at the bar. Ombre Rosse bustles with regulars and expats who know the value of a well-made cocktail and an ever-lively atmosphere. ⊠ *Piazza Sant'Egidio 12, Trastevere* ☎ *06/5884155* ⊟ *AE, MC, V* ۞ *No lunch Sun.* ✛ *D6.*

TESTACCIO

$$$–$$$$
ROMAN

✕ **Checchino dal 1887.** Literally carved out of a hill of ancient shards of amphorae, Checchino remains an example of a classic, family-run Roman restaurant, with one of the best wine cellars in the region. Though the slaughterhouses of Testaccio are long gone, an echo of their past existence lives on in the restaurant's soul food—mostly offal and other less–appealing cuts like *trippa* (tripe), *pajata* (intestine with the mother's milk still inside), and *coratella* (sweetbreads and heart of beef) are all still on the menu for die-hard Roman purists. For the less adventuresome, house specialties include braised milk-fed lamb with seasonal vegetables. Head here for a taste of old Rome, but note that Checchino is really beginning to show its age. ⊠ *Via di Monte Testaccio 30* ☎ *06/5746318* ⊟ *AE, DC, MC, V* ۞ *Closed Sun., Mon., Aug, and 1 wk at Christmas* ✛ *F6.*

$$
ITALIAN

✕ **Perilli.** In this restaurant dating from 1911, the old Testaccio remains, and it has the decor to prove it. A seasonal antipasto table starts things

Dining al fresco in Trastevere

off, offering Roman specialties like stewed Roman artichokes and *puntarelle* (curled chicory stems in a garlicky vinaigrette based on lots of lemon and anchovy). The waiters wear crooked bow ties and are just a little bit too hurried—until, that is, you order classics like pasta all'amatriciana and carbonara, which they relish tossing in a big bowl tableside. This is also the place to try rigatoni *con pajata* (with calves' intestines)—if you're into that sort of thing. Secondi plates are for carnivores only, and the house wine is a golden enamel-remover from the Castelli Romani. ✉ *Via Marmorata 39, Testaccio* ☎ *06/5742415* ▭ *AE, DC, MC, V* ⏲ *Closed Wed.* ✣ *F6.*

¢–$ PIZZA ✕ **Remo.** Expect a wait at this perennial favorite in Testaccio frequented by students and locals. You won't find tablecloths or other nonessentials, just classic Roman pizza and boisterous conversation. ✉ *Piazza Santa Maria Liberatrice 44, Testaccio* ☎ *06/5746270* ▭ *No credit cards* ⏲ *Closed Sun., Aug., and Christmas wk. No lunch* ✣ *F6.*

CAFÉS

Café sitting is a popular leisure-time activity in Rome, practiced by all and involving nothing more strenuous than gesturing to catch the waiter's eye. Part of the pleasure is resting your tired feet; you won't be rushed, even when the cafés are most crowded, just before lunch and dinner. (Be aware, though, that you pay for your seat—prices are higher at tables than at the counter.) Nearly every corner in Rome holds a faster-paced coffee bar, where locals stop for a quick caffeine hit at the counter. You can get coffee drinks, fruit juices, pastries, sandwiches, liquor, and beer there, too.

With its sidewalk tables taking in Santa Maria della Pace's adorable piazza, **Caffè della Pace** (✉ *Via della Pace 3, Navona* ☎ *06/6861216* ✛ *D4*) has long been the haunt of Rome's *beau monde*. Set on a quiet street near Piazza Navona, it also has two rooms filled with old-world personality.

Caffè Sant'Eustachio (✉ *P. Sant'Eustachio 82, Pantheon* ☎ *06/68802048* ✛ *E4*), traditionally frequented by Rome's literati, has what is generally considered Rome's best cup of coffee. Servers are hidden behind a huge espresso machine, vigorously mixing the sugar and coffee to protect their "secret method" for the perfectly prepared cup. (If you want your *caffè* without sugar here, ask for it *amaro*.

Fodor'sChoice
★ **Tazza d'Oro** (✉ *Via degli Orfani, Pantheon* ☎ *06/6789792* ✛ *E3*) has many admirers who contend it serves the city's best cup of coffee. The hot chocolate in winter, all thick and gooey goodness, is a treat. And in warm weather, the coffee granita is the perfect cooling alternative to a regular espresso.

GELATO

Along with the listings here, you can find a number of gelaterias in Via di Tor Millina, a street off the west side of Piazza Navona.

Fodor'sChoice
★ **Il Gelato di San Crispino** (✉ *Via della Panetteria 54, Piazza di Trevi* ☎ *06/6793924* ⊙ *Closed Tues.* ✛ *F3*) makes perhaps the most celebrated gelato in all of Italy, without artificial colors or flavors. It's worth crossing town for—nobody else creates flavors this pure. To preserve the "integrity" of the flavor, the ice cream is served only in paper cups. For years **Giolitti** (✉ *Via degli Uffici del Vicario 40, Pantheon* ☎ *06/6991243* ✛ *E3*) was considered the best gelateria in Rome, and it's still worth a stop if you're near the Pantheon. Immediately beside the Pantheon is **Cremeria Monteforte** (✉ *Via della Rotonda 22, Pantheon* ☎ *06/6867720* ✛ *E4*), which has won several awards for its flavors. Also worth trying is its chocolate sorbetto—it's an icier version of the gelato without the dairy. **Gelateria alla Scala** (✉ *Via della Scala 51, Trastevere* ☎ *06/5813174* ⊙ *Closed Dec. and Jan.* ✛ *D5*) is a tiny place, but don't let the size fool you. It does a good business offering artisanal gelato prepared in small batches, so when one flavor runs out on any given day, it's finished. **Al Settimo Gelo** (✉ *Via Vodice 21/a, Prati* ☎ *06/3725567* ✛ *A1*), in Prati, has been getting rave reviews for both classic flavors and newfangled inventions such as cardamom and chestnut, wowing locals and gelato fans from all over Rome.

WHERE TO STAY

Updated by Nicole Arriaga

There are more luxury lodgings, bed-and-breakfasts, and designer boutique hotels in Rome than ever before, but if you prefer more modest accommodations (because really, who comes to Rome to hang out in the hotel room?), you still have plenty of options. There are many midrange and budget hotels and *pensioni* (small, family-run lodgings) available. You may also consider staying at a monastery or convent, a hostel, or an apartment.

If fancy is what you're looking for, you're bound to find it on the Via Veneto and the Spanish Steps area. On the flip side, many of the city's cheapest and modest accommodations are scattered near the Stazione Termini. But for the most authentic Roman experience, stay in or near the *centro storico* (the historic center).

Use the coordinate (⊕ B2) at the end of each listing to locate a site on the Where to Stay in Rome map.

2

WHAT IT COSTS IN EUROS				
¢	$	$$	$$$	$$$$
FOR TWO PEOPLE	under €75	€75–€125	€125–€200	€200–€300	over €300

Prices are for a standard double room in high season.

PANTHEON, NAVONA, AND TREVI

PANTHEON

$$$ ⚏ **Albergo Santa Chiara.** The Santa Chiara, which has been in the fam-
Fodor's Choice ily for some 200 years, is situated just behind the Pantheon and near
★ Michelangelo's obelisk in Piazza della Minerva. The hotel lobby is *alla Romana*—an all-white affair, elegantly accented with a Venetian chandelier, a stucco statue, a gilded baroque mirror, and a walnut concierge desk. Upstairs, the pricier rooms are slightly swankier with stylish, yet comfortable furniture. Each room has built-in oak headboards, a marble-top desk, and a travertine bath. Double-glaze windows keep out the noise, especially for those rooms facing the piazza. There are also three apartments, for two to five people, with full kitchens. **Pros:** great location in the historical center behind the Pantheon; most of the rooms are spacious; the staff is both polite and helpful. **Cons:** layout is mazelike (you must take two elevators to some of the rooms); rooms don't get a lot of light. ⊠ *Via Santa Chiara 21, Pantheon* ☎ *06/6872979* ⊕ *www.albergosantachiara.com* ⇱ *96 rooms, 3 suites, 3 apartments* ♿ *In-room: safe, kitchen (some), refrigerator. In-hotel: room service, bar, Wi-Fi, laundry service* ▤ *AE, DC, MC, V* ⦿I *CP* ⊕ *E4.*

$$$–$$$$ ⚏ **Pantheon.** The Pantheon is a superb place to stay right next door to the grand monument of the same name. The lobby is the very epitome of a Roman hotel lobby—a warm, cozy, yet opulent setting that comes replete with stained glass, sumptuous wood paneling, a Renaissance beamed ceiling, and a massive and glorious chandelier. A print of one of Rome's obelisks on the door welcomes you to your room, where you'll find antique walnut furniture, fresh flowers, and more wood-beam ceilings. **Pros:** proximity to the Pantheon; big, clean bathrooms; friendly staff. **Cons:** rooms are in need of some upgrading; the lighting is low and the carpets are worn; the breakfast lacks variety. ⊠ *Via dei Pastini 131, Pantheon* ☎ *06/6787746* ⊕ *www.hotelpantheon.com* ⇱ *13 rooms, 1 suite* ♿ *In-room: safe, refrigerator, Wi-Fi. In-hotel: room service, bar, laundry service, public Wi-Fi, no-smoking rooms* ▤ *AE, DC, MC, V* ⦿I *CP* ⊕ *E4.*

BEST BETS FOR ROME LODGING

Fodor's offers a selective listing of quality lodgings at every price range, from the city's best budget motel to its most sophisticated luxury hotel. Here, we've compiled our top picks by price and experience. The best properties—those that provide a particularly remarkable experience in their price range—are designated in the listings with the Fodor's Choice logo.

CHILD-FRIENDLY

Cavalieri Hilton, $$$$, p. 117

Hassler, $$$$, p. 110

Hotel Lancelot, $$–$$$, p. 120

Hotel Ponte Sisto, $$$$, p. 106

Hotel de Russie, $$$$, p. 111

Mascagni, $$$–$$$$, p. 115 *(JIM + LINDA)*

Fodor's Choice ★

Albergo Santa Chiara, $$$, p. 103

Aleph, $$$$, p. 107

The Beehive, ¢–$, p. 113

Casa di Santa Brigida, $$, p. 105

Daphne Veneto, $$–$$$, p. 107

Eden, $$$$, p. 110

Hassler, $$$$, p. 110

Hotel San Pietrino, ¢–$, p. 117

Relais Le Clarisse, $$$, p. 118

Scalinata di Spagna, $$$–$$$$, p. 112

Yes Hotel, $$, p. 115

By Price

¢

The Beehive, p. 113

Hotel San Pietrino, p. 117

Italia, p. 112

$

Hotel Trastevere, p. 118

Panda, p. 112

$$

Casa di Santa Brigida, p. 105

Daphne Veneto, p. 107

Hotel Campo de' Fiori, p. 106

Hotel Santa Maria, p. 117

Yes Hotel, p. 115

$$$

Albergo Santa Chiara, p. 103

Pantheon, p. 103

Relais Le Clarisse, p. 118

Scalinata di Spagna, p. 112

$$$$

Aleph, p. 107

Eden, p. 110

Hassler, p. 110

Hotel Ponte Sisto, p. 106

Hotel de Russie, p. 111

Best by Experience

B&BS

Daphne Veneto, $$–$$$, p. 107

Relais Le Clarisse, $$$, p. 118

BUSINESS TRAVEL

Cavalieri Hilton, $$$$, p. 117

Exedra, $$$$, p. 113

CONCIERGE

The Beehive, ¢–$, p. 113

Daphne Veneto, $$–$$$, p. 107

Hotel Lancelot, $$–$$$, p. 120

Scalinata di Spagna, $$$–$$$$, p. 112

DESIGN

Capo d'Africa, $$$$, p. 119

Cavalieri Hilton, $$$$, p. 117

Exedra, $$$$, p. 113

GREAT VIEWS

Cavalieri Hilton, $$$$, p. 117

Eden, $$$$, p. 110

Genio, $$–$$$, p. 105

Hassler, $$$$, p. 110

Hotel Campo de' Fiori, $$, p. 106

HIDDEN OASES

Capo d'Africa, $$$$, p. 119

Domus Aventina, $$$, p. 118

Hotel Lancelot, $$–$$$, p. 120

Hotel Santa Maria, $$–$$$, p. 117

MOST ROMANTIC

Daphne Veneto, $$–$$$, p. 107

Relais Le Clarisse, $$$, p. 118

NAVONA

$$-$$$ ▦ **Genio.** If this hotel were any closer to Piazza Navona, you'd actually be in the fountain. This medium-size hotel offers top-floor rooms with terraces and citywide views. There's also a roof terrace for all, where you can eat your breakfast. Modeled along classic Roman lines, the lobby and public areas are cozy. Rooms are decorated in warm colors and have parquet floors and a harmonious mix of modern and antique reproduction furnishings. **Pros:** you can sip wine on the rooftop and take in the view; rooms are a decent size for a Roman hotel; the bathrooms have been designed especially well. **Cons:** Genio is on a busy street so there is often traffic noise; you might hear your neighbors through the walls; both the decor and the carpet have seen better days. ⊠ *Via G. Zanardelli 28, Navona* ☎ *06/6832191* ⊕ *www.hotelgenioroma.it* ↩ *60 rooms* ☉ *In-room: refrigerator. In-hotel: room service, bar, laundry service, Wi-Fi (paid), Internet terminal (paid), parking (paid), safe* ▭ *AE, DC, MC, V* ⦿*CP* ✛ *D3.*

TREVI

$$ ▦ **Trevi.** Location, location, location: this delightful place is tucked away down one of Old Rome's quaintest alleys near the Trevi Fountain. The smallish rooms are bright and clean, and a few of the larger ones have antique furniture and wooden ceilings with massive beams. There's also an arborlike roof-garden restaurant where you can eat marvelous pasta as you peer out at the city below. **Pros:** pass the Trevi Fountain each day as you come and go; comfortable rooms; roof-garden restaurant. **Cons:** breakfast room is cramped; staff is brusque. ⊠ *Vicolo del Babbuccio 20/21, Piazza di Trevi* ☎ *06/6789563* ⊕ *www.hoteltrevirome.com* ↩ *29 rooms* ☉ *In-room: safe, refrigerator, Internet. In-hotel: restaurant, room service, laundry service, parking (paid), no-smoking rooms, pets allowed (some)* ▭ *AE, DC, MC, V* ⦿*CP* ✛ *F3.*

CAMPO DE' FIORI AND GHETTO

CAMPO DE' FIORI

$$ ▦ **Casa di Santa Brigida.** One of the nicest convents to stay in is run by
Fodor's Choice the friendly sisters of Santa Brigida. The convent overlooks the Piazza
★ Farnese (where one of Michelangelo's buildings surveys all), and a most enviable location in the heart of Old Baroque Rome. It's also conveniently close to Campo de' Fiori. But you have to remember this is part of the Convent of St. Bridget, so guest rooms are simple (and serene—no TV), the nuns don't bend over backward to get you ice for your soda (presumably they have more important things on their minds) and the breakfast is served after they've finished their prayers. Still, the atmosphere is redolent. There's a lovely roof terrace overlooking the Palazzo Farnese, as well as a fine chapel and library. The Brigidine sisters wear a distinctive habit and veil with a caplike headband, and they are known for their gentle manner. Sometimes, the sisters also offer their guests insider tickets to the papal audience. It's hard to book a room here, so try to reserve well in advance. If you're interested in eating at the Casa, inquire about meal plans when you book. Note that the address is that of the church of Santa Brigida, but the guesthouse entrance is around

the corner at Via Monserrato 54. **Pros:** no curfew in this historic convent; insider papal tickets; location in the Piazza Farnese. **Cons:** weak a/c; no TVs in the rooms (though there is a common TV room); mediocre breakfast. ✉ *Piazza Farnese 96, Campo de' Fiori* 🕾 *06/68892497* ⊕ *www.brigidine.org* ⤳ *2 rooms* ♿ *In-room: no TV, Internet. In-hotel: no-smoking rooms* ▤ *AE, DC, MC, V* ❢❂❢ *CP* ✛ *D4.*

\$\$ ▦ **Hotel Campo de' Fiori.** Frescoes, exposed brickwork, and picturesque effects throughout this little hotel could well be the work of a set designer, but a recent renovation attributes the charming ambience to interior designer Dario di Blasi. Each room is entirely unique in its colors, furniture, and refined feel. The hotel underwent a complete renovation in 2006, retaining its old-world charm but modernizing with soundproofing, air-conditioning, flat-screen TVs, DSL, and Wi-Fi in all the rooms. There is also a marvelous view from the roof terrace. If you desire more extensive accommodations, Hotel Campo de' Fiori offers an additional selection of 14 different apartments in the area that can accommodate two to five guests. **Pros:** newly renovated; superb location; modern amenities that many Roman hotels haven't caught up with yet; rooftop terrace. **Cons:** some of the rooms are very small; breakfast works on a voucher system with a nearby café; the staff can be a bit rude and don't necessarily go out of their way to help you settle in. ✉ *Via del Biscione 6, Campo de' Fiori* 🕾 *06/68806865* ⊕ *www. hotelcampodefiori.it* ⤳ *23 rooms* ♿ *In-room: safe, refrigerator, Internet, Wi-Fi. In-hotel: no-smoking rooms* ▤ *MC, V* ❢❂❢ *CP* ✛ *D4.*

\$\$\$\$ ▦ **Hotel Ponte Sisto.** With one of the prettiest patio-courtyards in Rome,
☾ this hotel offers its own blissful definition of *Pax Romana.* Peace, indeed, will be yours sitting in this enchanting spot, shadowed by palm trees, set with tables, and adorned with pink and white flowers, all surrounded by the ochre walls of the hotel, which was renovated in 2001 from a palazzo built by the noble Venetian Palottini family. Some rooms overlook the garden of the historic Palazzo Spada. Inside, the sleek decor, replete with cherry wood accents, recessed lighting, and luminous marble floors, also gives a calming effect. Guest rooms are refined—suites come with Jacuzzis and furnished balconies or terraces, bathrooms can be lavishly modern, and there's also a bar and restaurant. The location is an award winner—just off the Ponte Sisto, the pedestrian bridge that connects the Campo de' Fiori area with Trastevere (whose trattorias and bars are thus just a quick jaunt away), and a second from Via Giulia, Rome's prettiest street. **Pros:** staff is friendly; rooms with views (and some with balconies and terraces); luxury bathrooms; beautiful courtyard garden. **Cons:** street-side rooms can be a bit noisy; some rooms are on the small side; restaurant doesn't serve lunch or dinner. ✉ *Via dei Pettinari 64, Campo de' Fiori* 🕾 *06/686310* ⊕ *www. hotelpontesisto.it* ⤳ *103 rooms, 4 suites* ♿ *In-room: safe, refrigerator, Internet. In-hotel: restaurant, room service, bar, laundry service, Internet terminal, parking (paid), some pets allowed, no-smoking rooms* ▤ *AE, DC, MC, V* ❢❂❢ *BP* ✛ *D5.*

2

GHETTO

$ ⊡ **Arenula.** Standing on an age-worn byway off central Via Arenula, this hotel is a superb bargain by Rome standards. With an imposingly elegant stone exterior, this hotel welcomes you with a luminous and cheerful all-white interior. Guest rooms are simple in decor but have pale-wood furnishings and gleaming bathrooms, as well as double-glaze windows and air-conditioning (in summer only; ask when you reserve). Two of the rooms accommodate four beds. Of course, you can't have everything, so that the graceful oval staircase of white marble and wrought iron in the lobby cues you that there is no elevator. Those guests with rooms on the fourth floor had better be in good shape! **Pros:** it's a real bargain; conveniently located in the Ghetto (close to Campo de' Fiori and Trastevere), and it's spotless. **Cons:** totally no-frills accommodations; four floors and no elevator; traffic and tram noise can be heard throughout the night despite the double-glazing. ⊠ *Via Santa Maria dei Calderari 47, off Via Arenula, Ghetto* ☎ *06/6879454* ⊕ *www.hotelarenula.com* ⤴ *50 rooms* ⅋ *In-room: Wi-Fi. In-hotel: public Wi-Fi, Internet terminal* ▭ *AE, DC, MC, V* ⦿ *CP* ✛ *E5.*

VENETO AND SPAGNA

VENETO

$$$$ ⊡ **Aleph.** Wondering where the beautiful people are? Look no farther
Fodor'sChoice than the Aleph, the most unfalteringly fashionable of Rome's design
★ hotels. The just-this-side-of-kitsch theme here is Dante's Divine Comedy, and you can walk the line between heaven and hell through the Angelo bar, the red-red-red Sin restaurant, and Paradise spa. The shiny blood-red-and-black color scheme looks great, but guest rooms are thankfully less threatening, in subdued neutral tones with wood furniture, made galleryesque by giant black-and-white photos of Rome. As many will guess, this hotel was überdesigned by Adam Tihany (who also did the honors at Rome's Exedra). His relentless, in-your-face decors throw everything into the mix, from Shogun suits to his signature red twigs to shirred silk lamps. Fortunately, he likes to poke fun at himself (clothes hooks shaped like devil's horns; tiny TVs set in the bathroom floors in front of your toilet), and earnestly cool staff notwithstanding, the Aleph doesn't take itself as seriously as might be feared. When Old Rome feels, well, old—this is something new. **Pros:** award-winning design; the invitation to test the temptations of heaven and hell; the sauna, Turkish bath, and thermal swimming pool at Paradise spa. **Cons:** rooms are too petite for the price; cocktails are expensive; Internet is costly, too. ⊠ *Via San Basilio 15, Veneto* ☎ *06/422901* ⊕ *www.boscolohotels.com* ⤴ *96 rooms, 6 suites* ⅋ *In-room: safe, refrigerator, Internet (paid). In-hotel: restaurant, room service, bars, gym, spa, laundry service, Wi-Fi (paid), Internet terminal, parking (paid), no-smoking rooms* ▭ *AE, DC, MC, V* ⦿ *EP* ✛ *G2.*

$$–$$$ ⊡ **Daphne Veneto.** Inspired by baroque artist Gianlorenzo Bernini's
Fodor'sChoice exquisite Apollo and Daphne sculpture at the Borghese Gallery, the
★ Daphne Inn at Via Veneto is an "urban B&B" run by people who love Rome and who will do their best to make sure you love it, too. This boutique hotel offers an intimate lodging experience, elegantly designed

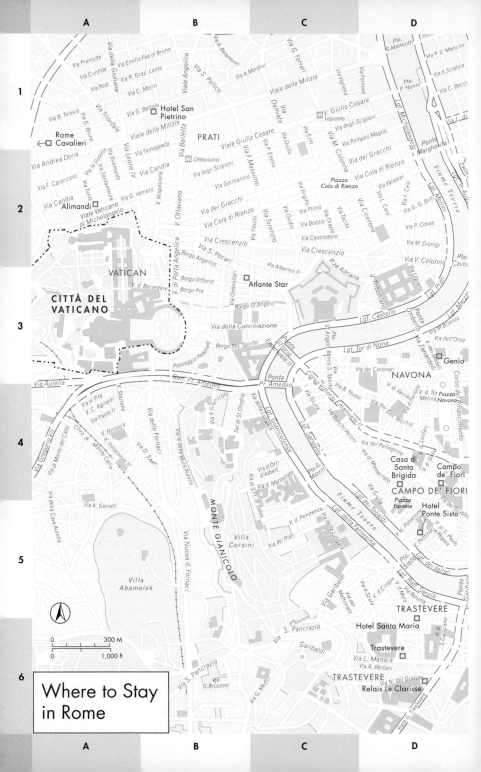

Where to Stay
in Rome

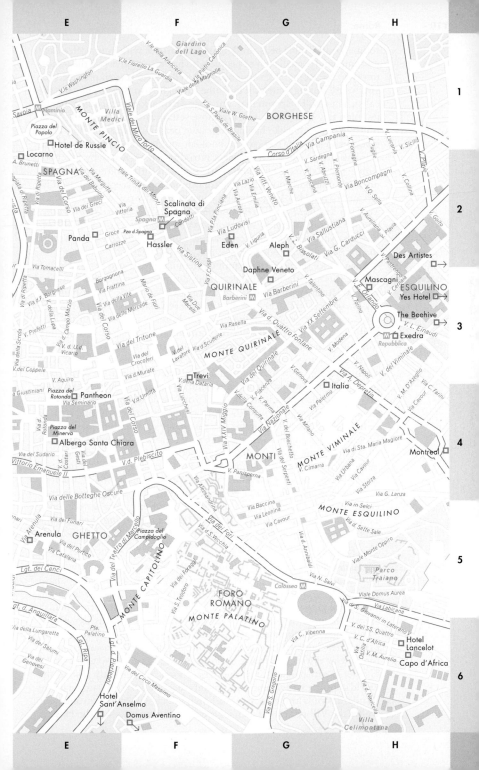

rooms, comfortable beds, fresh fruit and pastries with your coffee each morning, and a small staff of people who promise to give you the opportunity to see Rome "like an insider." A cell phone is even provided for you to use during your stay in Rome (though, you have to pay for the calls). They will help you map out your destinations, schedule itineraries, plan day trips, book tours, choose restaurants, and organize your transportation. It's like having your own personal travel planner. **Pros:** if rooms at Daphne Veneto are booked, inquire about its sister hotel, Daphne Trevi; you get a priceless introduction to Rome by lovers of Rome; the beds have Simmons mattresses and fluffy comforters. **Cons:** no TVs; some bathrooms are shared; Daphne only accepts Visa or MasterCard to hold bookings (though you can actually pay with an AmEx). ⊠ *Via di San Basilio 55, Veneto* ☎ *06/87450087* ⊕ *www.daphne-rome. com* ⤳ *7 rooms, 2 suites* ⚴ *In-room: safe, refrigerator, no TV, Wi-Fi. In-hotel: bicycles, laundry service, Internet terminal, public Wi-Fi, parking (paid), no-smoking rooms* ▤ *AE, MC, V* �📧 *CP* ✛ *G3.*

$$$$
Fodor's Choice
★

🛏 **Eden.** Once the preferred haunt of Hemingway, Ingrid Bergman, and Fellini, this superlative hotel combines dashing elegance and stunning vistas of Rome with the warmth of Italian hospitality. Set atop an oh-my-weary-feet hill near the Villa Borghese (and a bit out of the historic center for serious sightseers), this hotel was opened in the late 19th century and quickly became famous for its balcony views and Roman splendor. After an extensive restoration in the 1990s by Lord Forte, you'll now dive deep here into the whoooooossh of luxury, with antiques, sumptuous Italian fabrics, linen sheets, and marble baths competing for your attention. Even the most basic room here is elegantly designed (which is as it should be if your basic double room goes for some €700). Banquette window seats, rich mahogany furniture, soaring ceilings, Napoléon-Trois sofas are just some of the allurements here. **Pros:** gorgeous panoramic view from roof terrace; you could be rubbing elbows with the stars; 24-hour room service. **Cons:** expensive (unless money is no object for you); no Wi-Fi in the rooms; some say the staff can be hit-or-miss. ⊠ *Via Ludovisi 49, Veneto* ☎ *06/478121* ⊕ *www. lemeridien.com/eden* ⤳ *121 rooms, 13 suites* ⚴ *In-room: safe, refrigerator, DVD (some), Internet. In-hotel: restaurant, room service, bars, gym, Wi-Fi, laundry service, Internet terminal, parking (paid), some pets allowed, no-smoking rooms* ▤ *AE, DC, MC, V* �📧 *EP* ✛ *G2.*

SPAGNA

$$$$
Fodor's Choice
★
☺

🛏 **Hassler.** When it comes to million-dollar views, this exclusive hotel has the best seats in the house. Which is why movie stars, money shakers, and the *nouveau riche* are all willing to pay top dollar (or top euro, shall we say) to stay at the best address in Rome, just atop the Spanish Steps. The hotel is owned by the Wirth family, a famous dynasty of Swiss hoteliers who also own Il Palazzetto—a small yet stylish boutique hotel—and the International Wine Academy (also nearby), which offers wine tastings and wine appreciation courses. The exterior of the Hassler is rather bland, but the guest rooms are certainly among the world's most extravagant and lavishly decorated. You can get more standard rooms at the back of the hotel, which will spare you and your wallet the VIP prices. Of course, even the lowest prices at the Hassler can't compare with what you could find somewhere else. The recently renovated penthouse boasts the largest terrace in Rome. The rooftop restaurant, the Imàgo (which guests use for the breakfast buffet), is world-famous for its view, if not for its food; and the Palm Court garden, which becomes the hotel bar in summer, is overflowing with flowers. **Pros:** charming old-world feel; prime location and panoramic views at the top of the Spanish Steps; just "steps" away from some of the best shopping in the world. **Cons:** VIP prices; many think the staff is too standoffish; some say the cuisine at the rooftop restaurant isn't worth the gourmet price tag. ✉ *Piazza Trinità dei Monti 6, Spagna* ☎ *06/699340* ⊕ *www.lhw.com* ⚲ *85 rooms, 13 suites* ⚙ *In-room: safe, refrigerator, Internet. In-hotel: restaurant, room service, bar, gym, spa, laundry service, public Wi-Fi, parking (paid), no-smoking rooms* ☰ *AE, DC, MC, V* ⍩ *EP* ✛ *F2.*

$$$$ ⌖ **Hotel de Russie.** A ritzy retreat for government big wigs and Holly-
⟲ wood high rollers, de Russie raises the bar on lavish lodging. The hotel lies just steps away from the famed Piazza del Popolo and is set in a 19th-century historic hotel once boasting a clientele that included royalty. Famed hotelier Sir Rocco Forte decided to give de Russie a major makeover in 2002 and transformed it into one of the swankiest hotels in Eternal City. The furnishings are Donghia-style, the colors scream gloomy glamour, and the bathrooms have Roman mosaic motifs. The hotel's most prized possessions are the spectacular glimpse of the garden courtyard from many (but not all) of the rooms and its sharp Le Jardin de Russie restaurant. When not lounging outside on their plushy terrace, VIPs can be found at the world-class spa facility or sipping on a *prosecco* poolside. **Pros:** big potential for celebrity sightings; special activities for children; extensive gardens (including a butterfly reserve); first-rate luxury spa. **Cons:** hotel is a bit worn around the edges; decor is a little generic; breakfast is nothing special. ✉ *Via del Babuino 9, Spagna* ☎ *06/328881* ⊕ *www.rfhotels.com* ⚲ *122 rooms, 33 suites* ⚙ *In-room: safe, refrigerator, Internet. In-hotel: restaurant, room service, bar, pool, gym, spa, children's programs (ages toddler–12), public Wi-Fi, parking (paid), no-smoking rooms* ☰ *AE, DC, MC, V* ⍩ *BP* ✛ *E1.*

$$$–$$$$ ⌖ **Locarno.** The sort of place that inspired a movie (Bernard Weber's 1978 *Hotel Locarno*, to be exact), this has been a longtime choice for art aficionados and people in the cinema. But everyone will appreciate this hotel's fin de siècle charm, intimate feel, and central location off Piazza del Popolo. Exquisite wallpaper and fabric prints are coordinated in the rooms, and some rooms are decorated with antiques—the grandest room looks like an art director's take on a Medici bedroom. Everything is lovingly supervised by the owners, a mother-daughter duo. The buffet breakfast is ample, there's bar service on the panoramic roof garden, and complimentary bicycles are available if you feel like braving the traffic. A newly renovated annex is done in art deco style. **Pros:** luxurious feel (it may even seem like you're in a movie); spacious rooms (even by American standards); free bicycles for exploring Rome. **Cons:** some of the rooms are dark; the annex doesn't compare to the main hotel; the regular staff probably won't go out of their way to help you. ✉ *Via della Penna 22, Spagna* ☎ *06/3610841* ⊕ *www.hotellocarno.com*

↩ *64 rooms, 2 suites* ♿ *In-room: safe, refrigerator, Wi-Fi. In-hotel: restaurant, bar, bicycles, laundry service, Internet terminal, public Wi-Fi, no-smoking rooms* ▤ *AE, DC, MC, V* ⍩ *BP* ✛ *E2.*

$ ⊞ **Panda.** You couldn't possibly find a better deal in Rome than here at the Panda, especially given its key location just behind the Spanish Steps. The small hotel is situated on one of the poshest shopping streets in the centro, Via della Croce. Guest rooms are outfitted in terra-cotta, wrought iron, and very simple furnishings; they're on the small-side, spotlessly clean, and quiet, thanks to double-glaze windows. Pay even less by sharing a bath—in low season, you may have it to yourself anyway. **Pros:** discount if you pay cash; free Wi-Fi; located on a quiet street but still close to the Spanish Steps. **Cons:** some say the Wi-Fi signal is weak; not all rooms have private bathrooms; no elevator; no TVs in the rooms. ⊠ *Via della Croce 35, Spagna* ☎ *06/6780179* ⊕ *www. hotelpanda.it* ↩ *20 rooms, 14 with bath* ♿ *In-room: no a/c (some), no TV, Wi-Fi. In-hotel: laundry service, public Wi-Fi* ▤ *AE, DC, MC, V* ⍩ *CP* ✛ *E2.*

$$$-$$$$ ⊞ **Scalinata di Spagna.** A longtime favorite of hopeless romantics, it's
Fodor's Choice   often hard to snag a room at this tiny hotel as it's often booked up for
★   months, even years at a time. And it's not hard to guess why. For starters, its prime location at the top of the Spanish Steps, inconspicuous little entrance, and quiet, sunny charm all add to the character that guests fall in love with over and over again. Rooms were renovated in a stylish manner, focusing on accentuated floral fabrics and Empire-style sofas. Rooms that overlook the Spanish Steps are the first to go. But don't fret it you don't snatch up the room of your choice. You can always escape to the hotel's extravagant rooftop garden and gaze over ancient Rome as you nibble on your *cornetto* and sip on your *cappuccino.* Amenities, such as breakfast service until noon and in-room Internet access, are a nice touch. **Pros:** friendly and helpful concierge; fresh fruit in the rooms; free Wi-Fi throughout the Scalinata. **Cons:** it's a hike up the hill to the hotel; no porter and no elevator; service can be hit-or-miss. ⊠ *Piazza Trinità dei Monti 17, Spagna* ☎ *06/6793006* ⊕ *www.hotelscalinata. com* ↩ *16 rooms* ♿ *In-room: safe, refrigerator, Wi-Fi. In-hotel: room service, laundry service, Internet terminal, public Wi-Fi, parking (paid), no-smoking rooms* ▤ *AE, D, MC, V* ⍩ *BP* ✛ *F2.*

MONTI, REPUBBLICA, AND SAN LORENZO

MONTI

¢–$ ⊞ **Italia.** It looks and feels like a classic pensione: low-budget with a lot of heart. A block off the very trafficky Via Nazionale, this friendly, family-run hotel offers inexpensive rooms with big windows, desks, parquet floors, and baths with faux-marble tiles, but the rooms aren't really the point. The price is, and it's made all the more tempting by a generous buffet breakfast and thoughtful touches like an ice machine and free wireless Internet access. Ask for even lower midsummer rates. **Pros:** free Wi-Fi and Internet access in the rooms and lobby; great price; individual attention and personal care. **Cons:** it's sometimes noisy; a/c is an extra €10. ⊠ *Via Venezia 18, Monti* ☎ *06/4828355* ⊕ *www.hotelitaliaroma.*

com ↝ *31 rooms, 1 apartment* �&ch; *In-room: safe, Wi-Fi. In-hotel: bar, Internet terminal, public Wi-Fi, parking (paid), no-smoking rooms* ☰ *AE, DC, MC, V* ⫟◎⫠ *CP* ✛ *G3.*

$ ☷ **Montreal.** A good choice for budget travelers, this hotel is on a central avenue across the square from Santa Maria Maggiore, three blocks from Stazione Termini, Rome's main transportation hub. The modest Montreal occupies three floors of an older building and has been totally renovated and offers bright, fresh-looking, though small, rooms. The owner-managers are pleasant and helpful, and the neighborhood has plenty of reasonably priced restaurants. **Pros:** informative staff provides maps and good recommendations; bathrooms are spacious; hotel has a cozy feel. **Cons:** location can be noisy at night; it's either a bus, metro, or long walk to most historic sights. ⊠ *Via Carlo Alberto 4, Monti* ☎ *06/4457797* ⊕ *www.hotelmontrealroma.com* ↝ *27 rooms* �&ch; *In-room: safe, refrigerator. In-hotel: room service, bar, Internet terminal, parking (paid), no-smoking rooms* ☰ *AE, DC, MC, V* ⫟◎⫠ *CP* ✛ *H4.*

REPUBBLICA

¢–$

Fodor's Choice

★

☷ **The Beehive.** You won't feel like you're in Rome once you step foot into this hip alternative budget hotel. Rather, one might mistake it for a cross between a holistic center and a place that holds yoga classes. Started by a Los Angeles couple following their dream in 1999, the Beehive might be the most unique budget hotel in Rome in that it also offers hostel accommodations, a vegetarian café, a yoga space and art gallery with a garden, a reading lounge, and a few off-site apartments. It offers a respite from Rome's chaos, but is conveniently located only a few blocks from Termini. All the rooms come with shared bathrooms (where, along with the facilities, you'll find handmade vegetable-based soaps and recycled toilet paper). There is a lovely little garden with fruit trees, herbs, and flowers. The Beehive offers complimentary Wi-Fi, but no TVs or air-conditioning (though rooms do have ceiling fans). If you would prefer your own self-catering apartment (with a kitchen and private bathroom) for your group or family, or if you'd just like an individual room in an apartment, the Beehive also has three apartments in the neighborhood that can be rented. **Pros:** yoga, massage, and other therapies offered on-site; no set price for meals served at the vegetarian café—it's left entirely up to the guest to decide how much he/she thinks the meal is worth. **Cons:** no TV, a/c, baggage storage, or private bathroom; breakfast is not included in the room rate. ⊠ *Via Marghera 8, Repubblica* ☎ *06/44704553* ⊕ *www. the-beehive.com* ↝ *8 rooms, 1 dormitory, 3 apartments* �&ch; *In-room: no a/c, kitchen (some), no TV, Wi-Fi. In-hotel: public Wi-Fi, no-smoking rooms* ☰ *MC, V* ⫟◎⫠ *EP* ✛ *H3.*

$$$$ ☷ **Exedra.** If Rome's semistodgy hotel scene has an It-Girl, it's the Exedra. High rollers love to host splashy parties here and magazines love to rave about them; this luxury hotel is, indeed, hard to top. Unlike its naughty younger brother the Aleph, the Exedra is a model of neoclassical respectability, all gilt-framed mirrors and fresh flowers, but there's a glint of cutting edge in the paparazzi-inspired (and inspiring) Tazio brasserie. Rooms are predictably luscious in an uptown way, with silky linens and handsome nouveau-colonial bedsteads, and many face the spectacular fountain in the piazza outside. Why stay here rather

Fodor's Choice ★

Hassler

Scalinata di Spagna

Eden

Relais Le Clarisse

Daphne Veneto

Yes Hotel

than at the umpteen other expensively elegant hotels in central Rome? You can think about it while you lounge by the rooftop swimming pool. **Pros:** spacious and attractive rooms; great spa and pool; terrace with cocktail service; close to Termini station. **Cons:** food and beverages are expensive; beyond the immediate vicinity, parts of the neighborhood seem unsavory. ✉ *Piazza della Repubblica 47, Repubblica* ☎ *06/489381* ⊕ *www.boscolohotels.com* ↝ *240 rooms, 18 suites* ⛄ *In-room: safe, refrigerator, Wi-Fi. In-hotel: 3 restaurants, room service, bars, pool, gym, spa, laundry service, Internet terminal, public Wi-Fi, parking (paid), some pets allowed, no-smoking rooms* ▭ *AE, DC, MC, V* ⑩*CP* ⊹ *H3.*

$$$–$$$$ ⚏ **Mascagni.** Situated on one of Rome's busiest streets and close to one of Rome's most impressive piazzas (Piazza della Repubblica), sits the hotel Mascagni. The public spaces of the hotel have been cleverly styled with contemporary art pieces, and the bedrooms feature black and white photographs of Rome. The intimate lounges and charming bar—very cozy and attractive with its floral fabric and wood bar—follow the same decorating scheme, as does the breakfast room, where a generous buffet is laid in the morning, complete with free newspapers. The friendly, creative management is always coming up with new offers, including the "Family Perfect" room, which includes a PlayStation, a DVD player with Disney movies, and wooden blocks for small children to play with. **Pros:** staff is friendly and attentive with good advice; evening lounge that serves up cold cuts or light pasta dishes; bathrooms are spacious and they come with nice toiletries; great for families with kids. **Cons:** small lobby; weak a/c; slow Internet. ✉ *Via Vittorio Emanuele Orlando 90, Repubblica* ☎ *06/48904040* ⊕ *www.hotelmascagni. com* ↝ *40 rooms* ⛄ *In-room: safe, refrigerator, DVD (some), Internet. In-hotel: bar, laundry service, Internet terminal, parking (paid), no-smoking rooms* ▭ *AE, DC, MC, V* ⑩*BP* ⊹ *H3.*

SAN LORENZO

$–$$ ⚏ **Des Artistes.** The three personable Riccioni brothers have transformed their hotel into the best in the neighborhood in its price range. It's bedecked with paintings and handsome furnishings in mahogany, and rooms are decorated in attractive fabrics. Marble baths are smallish but luxurious for this price, and they're stocked with hair dryers and towel warmers. Des Artistes hasn't forgotten its roots, though: there's also a "hostel" floor with 11 simpler rooms for travelers on a budget. Book well ahead. As for location, this is somewhat on the fringe, being several blocks (in the wrong direction) from Stazione Termini. **Pros:** good value; decent-size rooms; relaxing roof garden. **Cons:** breakfast area is overcrowded; reception is on the fifth floor. ✉ *Via Villafranca 20, San Lorenzo* ☎ *06/4454365* ⊕ *www.hoteldesartistes.com* ↝ *40 rooms, 27 with bath* ⛄ *In-room: no a/c (some), safe, refrigerator, Wi-Fi. In-hotel: bar, parking (paid), public Wi-Fi, no-smoking rooms* ▭ *AE, DC, MC, V* ⑩*BP* ⊹ *H2.*

$$ ⚏ **Yes Hotel.** Don't let the contemporary coolness of this hotel fool you. **Fodor's**Choice It is a budget hotel. A newcomer to the scene, the Yes was opened ★ in April 2007 by the owners of the Hotel Des Artistes. It's situated just near Stazione Termini, which is key for moving around, and also has plenty of dining options in the area. Yes also offers the kind of amenities that are usually found in more expensive hotels, including mahogany furniture, decorative art, electronic safes, flat-screen TVs, and air-conditioning. Wireless Internet access is available in the rooms and throughout the hotel for an extra free. **Pros:** flat-screen TVs with satellite TV; it doesn't feel like a budget hotel, but it is; discount if you pay cash; great value. **Cons:** rooms are small; no individual climate control or refrigerators in the rooms. ⊠ *Via Magenta 15, San Lorenzo* ☎ *06/44363836* ⊕ *www.yeshotelrome.com* ↘ *29 rooms, 1 suite* △ *In-room: safe, Wi-Fi (paid). In-hotel: parking (paid) Wi-Fi (paid), no-smoking rooms* ▭ *MC, V* ⑩ *CP* ✛ *H3.*

VATICAN, BORGO, PRATI, AND NORTHWEST ROME

VATICAN

$$ ⊡ **Alimandi.** Just behind the Vatican Museums, this family-run hotel is a real bargain considering the location and service. A spiffy lobby, spacious lounges, a tavern, terraces, and roof gardens are some of the perks, as is a recreation room with a billiard and an exercise room equipped with step machines and a treadmill. Rooms are spacious and well furnished; many can accommodate extra beds. Needless to say, the location here is quite far away from Rome's historic center. However, a few stops on the metro (there's a stop nearby) and you're there. If requested, the hotel will also arrange for a shuttle to pick you up from the airport at an extra cost of €5 per person for all flights that arrive before 2 PM. **Pros:** nice family-owned hotel with a friendly staff, a terrace, a gym and reasonably priced restaurants and shops in the area. **Cons:** breakfast is a good spread but it goes quickly; rooms are small; not close to much of interest other than the Vatican. ⊠ *Via Tunisi 8, Vatican* ☎ *06/39723948* ⊕ *www.alimandi.it* ↘ *35 rooms* △ *In-room: safe, refrigerator (some), Wi-Fi. In-hotel: bar, gym, Wi-Fi, Internet terminal, parking (paid), no-smoking rooms* ▭ *AE, DC, MC, V* ⑩ *BP* ✛ *A2.*

BORGO

$$$–$$$$ ⊡ **Atlante Star.** The lush rooftop-terrace garden café with probably the best views of St. Peter's Basilica and the rest of Rome is one of the prime reasons why guests book their stay here. Other reasons include close proximity to the Vatican, top-notch service, and superb shopping all at your fingertips. In a distinguished 19th-century building, the guest rooms are attractively decorated with striped silks and prints for an old-world atmosphere; many bathrooms have hot tubs. The friendly family management is attentive to guests' needs and takes pride in offering extra-virgin olive oil from their own trees in the country. A sister hotel, the **Atlante Garden,** just around the corner, has larger rooms at slightly lower rates. If requested, the Atlante Star will pick you up at Fiumicino airport for free. **Pros:** close to St. Peter's; impressive view from the restaurant and some of the rooms. **Cons:** some rooms are nicer than others (and some aren't as pretty as the ones on the Web site); the area can be overrun with tourists; it's not close to Rome's other attractions. ⊠ *Via Vitelleschi 34, Borgo* ☎ *06/6873233* ⊕ *www. atlantehotels.com* ↘ *65 rooms, 10 suites* △ *In-room: safe, refrigerator,*

Internet. In-hotel: restaurant, room service, bar, laundry service, Internet terminal, public Wi-Fi, parking (paid), no-smoking rooms = AE, DC, MC, V ¶◎∣ BP ♣ B3.

2

PRATI

¢–$

Fodor's Choice

★

🔲 **Hotel San Pietrino.** How this simple, but cute hotel within close proximity to the Vatican manages to keep its bargain prices is definitely a mystery. It's located on the third floor of a 19th-century palazzo that's only a five-minute walk to St. Peter's Square. In addition to clean, simple rooms, San Pietrino offers air-conditioning, TVs with DVD players, and high-speed Internet to guests. There is no breakfast included and no bar in the hotel, but not to worry—with all the local cafés and bars, you won't have any trouble finding yourself a *cornetto* and cappuccino in the morning or a prosecco for aperitivo in the evening. **Pros:** heavenly prices near the Vatican; TVs with DVD players; high speed Internet; close to Rome's famous farmers' market, Mercato Trionfale. **Cons:** a couple of metro stops away from the center of Rome; no breakfast; no bar. ⊠ *Via Giovanni Bettolo 43, Prati* 🕿 *06/3700132* ⊕ *www. sanpietrino.it* ⤴ *12 rooms* ⚭ *In-room: DVD (some), Internet, Wi-Fi. In-hotel: Internet terminal, public Wi-Fi* = *MC, V* ¶◎∣ *EP* ♣ *B1.*

NORTHWEST ROME

$$$$

☾

🔲 **Cavalieri Hilton.** Though the Cavalieri is outside the city center, distance has its advantages, one of them being the magnificent view over Rome (ask for a room facing the city), and another, that elusive element of more central Roman hotels: space. Occupying a vast area atop modern Rome's highest hill, this oasis of good taste often feels more like a resort than a city hotel. Central to its appeal, particularly in summer, is a terraced garden that spreads out from an Olympic-size pool and smart poolside restaurant and café; legions of white-clothed cushioned lounge chairs are scattered throughout the greenery, so there's always a place to sun yourself. Inside, spacious rooms, often with large balconies, are done up in striped damask, puffy armchairs, and Hiltonesque amenities, such as a "pillow menu." If you can tear yourself away, the city center is just a 15-minute complimentary shuttle-bus ride away. The strawberry on top: La Pergola restaurant is renowned as one of Rome's very best. **Pros:** beautiful bird's-eye view of Rome; shuttle to the city center; three-Michelin-star dining. **Cons:** you definitely pay for the luxury of staying here—everything is expensive; outside the city center; not all rooms have the view. ⊠ *Via Cadlolo 101, Monte Mario* 🕿 *06/35091* ⊕ *www.cavalieri-hilton.com* ⤴ *357 rooms, 17 suites* ⚭ *In-room: safe, refrigerator, DVD (some), Internet. In-hotel: 2 restaurants, bars, tennis court, pools, gym, spa, laundry service, Internet terminal, no-smoking rooms* = *AE, DC, MC, V* ¶◎∣ *CP* ♣ *A1.*

TRASTEVERE

$$–$$$

🔲 **Hotel Santa Maria.** A Trastevere treasure, this hotel has a pedigree going back four centuries. This ivy-covered, mansard-roofed, rosy-brick-red, erstwhile Renaissance-era convent has been transformed by Paolo and Valentina Vetere into a true charmer. Surrounded by towering tenements, the complex is centered on a monastic porticoed courtyard, lined with orange trees—a lovely place for breakfast. The guest rooms are sweet and simple: a mix of brick walls, "cotto" tile floors, modern oak furniture, and stylishly floral bedspreads and curtains. Best of all, the location is *buonissimo*—just a few blocks from the Tiber and its *isola*. **Pros:** a quaint and pretty oasis in a chaotic city; relaxing court-yard; stocked wine bar. **Cons:** it might be tricky to find; some of the showers drain slowly; it's not always easy finding a cab in Trastevere. ⊠ *Vicolo del Piede 2, Trastevere* ☎ *06/5894626* ⊕ *www.htlsantamaria. com* ⤳ *18 rooms, 2 suites* ⚒ *In-room: safe, refrigerator. In-hotel: bar, bicycles, laundry service, Internet terminal, no-smoking rooms* ▭ *AE, DC, MC, V* ⵁ *BP* ⊹ *D6.*

$ ⊞ **Hotel Trastevere.** This tiny hotel captures the villagelike charm of the Trastevere district. The entrance hall features a mural of the famous Piazza di Santa Maria, a few blocks away, and hand-painted art nouveau wall designs add a touch of graciousness throughout. Open medieval brickwork and a few antiques here and there complete the mood. Most rooms face Piazza San Cosimato, where there's an outdoor food market every morning except Sunday. **Pros:** cheap with a good location; convenient to transportation; friendly staff. **Cons:** no frills; few amenities. ⊠ *Via Luciano Manara 24–25, Trastevere* ☎ *06/5814713* ⊕ *www. hoteltrastevere.net* ⤳ *20 rooms, 3 apartments* ⚒ *In-room: safe (some), Wi-Fi. In-hotel: no-smoking rooms* ▭ *AE, DC, MC, V* ⵁ *CP* ⊹ *D6.*

$$$ ⊞ **Relais Le Clarisse.** In one of Rome's most popular neighborhoods, this
Fodor's Choice charming little oasis features five simple, but classically styled accom-
★ modations (two doubles and three suites) with terra-cotta-tiled floors, wrought-iron bed frames, and oak furnishings. Each room opens up onto a bright courtyard surrounded by a Mediterranean garden of grapevines and olive and lemon trees. Though Le Clarisse is set on the former cloister grounds of the Santa Chiara order, its rooms are equipped with the most modern technologies, including individual climate control, flat-screen TVs, air-conditioning, high-speed Internet and Wi-Fi, as well as Jacuzzi showers and tubs. Travelers feel more like personal guests at a friend's villa rather than at a hotel, thanks to the comfortable size of the accommodations and the personal touches and service extended by the staff. Le Clarisse is also located across the street from the Alcazar movie theater, which shows original language films (as opposed to versions that have been dubbed into Italian) on Monday nights. **Pros:** spacious rooms with comfy beds; high-tech showers/tubs with good water pressure; staff is multilingual, friendly, and at your service. **Cons:** this part of Trastevere can be noisy at night; the rooms here fill up quickly; they serve only American coffee. ⊠ *Via Cardinale Merry del Val 20, Trastevere* ☎ *06/58334437* ⊕ *www.leclarisse.com* ⤳ *5 rooms, 3 suites* ⚒ *In-room: safe, refrigerator, Internet. In-hotel: room service, laundry service, Internet terminal, public Wi-Fi, parking (paid), no-smoking rooms* ▭ *AE, MC, V* ⵁ *CP* ⊹ *D6.*

AVENTINO

$$$ ⊞ **Domus Aventina.** The best part of this quaint, friendly hotel is that it's situated between two of Rome's loveliest gardens: a municipal rose garden and Rome's famous Orange Garden, where you can often catch

2

a glimpse of brides and grooms taking their wedding pictures. The Domus Aventina is located in the *cuore* (heart) of the historic Aventine district not far from the Temple to Mithras and the House of Aquila and Priscilla (where St. Peter touched down). The 17th-century facade has been restored so it almost looks modern—ditto for the inside, where guest rooms have standard modern decor. Half of the rooms also have balconies. **Pros:** quiet location; walking distance to tourist attractions; complimentary Wi-Fi in rooms and public spaces. **Cons:** no elevator in the hotel; small showers; no tubs. ⊠ *Via di Santa Prisca 11/b, Aventino* ☎ *06/5746135* ⊕ *www.domus-aventina.com* ⤳ *26 rooms* ♿ *In-room: safe, refrigerator, Wi-Fi. In-hotel: bar, laundry service, public Wi-Fi, parking (paid)* ▤ *AE, DC, MC, V* ¶◯¶ *CP* ✛ *F6.*

$$$ 🖳 **Hotel San Anselmo.** Birdsongs add to the mood and charm of this already romantic retreat. The Hotel San Anselmo is far from the bustle of the city center, perched on top of the Aventine Hill in a residential neighborhood. This full-scale 19th-century villa was completely refurbished in 2006 and given a sleek metropolitan feel. The new look blends bits of baroque antique-flair such as the chandelier from the 800s mixed with contemporary pieces such as the sharp stainless-steel fireplace in the public spaces. Others will find the best features here are the verdant garden and terrace bar. Guest rooms are each carefully designed to follow a particular theme. Among the favorites are "Room of Poems," which feature poems beautifully scrawled onto the walls, and the "Room of Kisses," which has a big canopy bed with romantic and suggestive drapes. All in all, the San Anselmo is *molto* charming. **Pros:** historic building with artful decor; great showers with jets; a garden where you can enjoy your breakfast. **Cons:** some consider it a bit of a hike to sights; limited public transportation; the wireless is pricey. ⊠ *Piazza San Anselmo 2, Aventino* ☎ *06/570057* ⊕ *www. aventinohotels.com* ⤳ *45 rooms* ♿ *In-room: safe, refrigerator, Internet. In-hotel: room service, bar, laundry service, public Wi-Fi (paid), parking (paid), no-smoking rooms* ▤ *AE, DC, MC, V* ¶◯¶ *BP* ✛ *E6.*

COLOSSEO AREA

$$$$ 🖳 **Capo d'Africa.** Many find the modern look and feel of Capo d'Africa— not to mention its plush beds and deep bathtubs—refreshing after a long day's journey through ancient Rome. Each room is decorated in warm, muted color tones with sleek furniture, stylish accents, and contemporary art. The hotel features a nonsmoking floor, fitness center, and solarium. It sits on a quiet street near the Colosseum, Palatine, and Forum, and it's not far from the metro. A delicious breakfast is served on the rooftop terrace, where you can also enjoy an *aperitivo* overlooking Rome at the end of your day. And if you're not too tuckered out, you can take a spin at the gym before bed. **Pros:** quiet, comfortable rooms; fitness center. **Cons:** despite proximity to the Colosseum, there isn't a great view of it from the hotel; far from the other Roman sites and the rest of the city scene; not a lot of restaurants in the immediate neighborhood. ⊠ *Via Capo d'Africa 54, Colosseo* ☎ *06/772801* ⊕ *www. hotelcapodafrica.com* ⤳ *64 rooms, 1 suite* ♿ *In-room: safe, refrigerator,*

DVD (some), Wi-Fi. In-hotel: room service, bar, gym, Wi-Fi, parking (paid), no-smoking rooms ▭ *AE, DC, MC, V* ⦿⦀ *CP* ✛ *H6.*

$$–$$$ 🌐 **Hotel Lancelot.** This home away from home close to the Colosseum
ⓒ   has been run by the same family since 1970 and is quite popular thanks
to its carefully and courteously attentive staff who go the extra mile for
their guests. Located in a quiet residential area, rooms at Hotel Lancelot
tend to have big windows, so they're bright and airy, and some have
terraces or balconies as well. Over the years, the hotel has undergone
a number of renovations. They most recently updated the rooms with
air-conditioning, en-suite bathrooms, TVs, and Wi-Fi. In the restaurant,
where hearty breakfasts and dinners are served, guests sit at Lancelot's
"round tables"—partly a play on the knight's tale and partly an effort
to encourage communal dining among guests from around the world.
And these round tables seem to be a big hit, since Hotel Lancelot boasts
that most of their guests are either return visitors or new guests recommended by others who've spent vacations here. **Pros:** hospitable
staff; secluded and quiet; very family-friendly. **Cons:** some of the bathrooms are on the small side; no refrigerators in the rooms; room walls
are a bit thin, which means you can sometimes hear your neighbors
next door. ⊠ *Via Capo d'Africa 47, Colosseo* ☎ *06/70450615* ⦿ *www.
lancelothotel.com* ⇥ *60 rooms* ⚲ *In-room: safe, Wi-Fi. In-hotel: restaurant, room service, bar, laundry service, Internet terminal, public Wi-Fi,
parking (paid), no-smoking rooms* ▭ *AE, DC, MC, V* ⦿⦀ *CP* ✛ *H6.*

NIGHTLIFE AND THE ARTS

THE ARTS

Updated by
Erica Firpo

Rome is finally au courant with advance publication and promotion of
cultural events. Begin with the city's official Web site (⦿ *www.comune.
roma.it*). Likewise, events listings can be found in the *Cronaca* and
Cultura section of Italian newspapers, as well as in *Metro* (the free
newspaper). The most comprehensive listings are in the weekly *roma
c'è* booklet, which comes out every Wednesday. Flip to the back for the
brief yet very detailed English-language section. Check out the events
site ⦿ *inromenow.com*, in English, as well as the monthly updated
Time Out: Rome (⦿ *www.timeout.com/travel/rome*) and *The American* (⦿ *www.theamericanmag.com*). In addition, consult the monthly
English-language periodical (with accompanying Web site), *Wanted in
Rome* (⦿ *www.wantedinrome.com*), available at many newsstands.

VENUES

★   Rome used to be a performing arts backwater until 2002, when it
opened its state-of-the-art **Auditorium-Parco della Musica** (⊠ *Via de Coubertin 15, Flaminio* ☎ *06/80241; 06/68801044 information and tickets*
⦿ *www.auditorium.com*), a 10-minute tram ride (north) from Piazza
del Popolo. Three futuristic concert halls designed by famed architect
Renzo Piano have excellent acoustics and a large courtyard used for
concerts and other events—everything from chamber music to jazz to
big-name pop, even film screenings, art exhibits, fashion shows, and

"philosophy festivals." To get to the Auditorium from Rome's Termini train station, take Bus No. 910, which drops you off directly in front of the complex. Just behind Piazza del Popolo in Piazzale Flaminio, hop on the No. 2 tram for six stops to the Auditorium area. Using the Metro, take Line A to Flaminio, then switch to No. 2 tram for six stops to the Auditorium.

Teatro Argentina (⌧ *Largo Argentina 52* ☎ *06/6840001* ⊕ *www. teatrodiroma.net*), built in 1732 by the architect Theoldi, has been the home of the Teatro Sabile theater company since 1994. The theater is a beautiful, ornate structure, with velvet seats and chandeliers, and plays host to many plays, classical music performances, operas, and dance performances. Both the city's ballet and opera companies, as well as visiting international performers, appear at the **Teatro dell'Opera** (⌧ *Piazza Beniamino Gigli 8, Repubblica* ☎ *06/481601, 06/48160255 tickets* ⊕ *www.operaroma.it*). **Teatro Olimpico** (⌧ *Piazza Gentile da Fabriano 17, Flaminio* ☎ *06/3265991* ⊕ *www.teatroolimpico.it*) hosts both concerts and dance performances.

Teatro Valle (⌧ *Via del Teatro Valle 23A, Navona* ☎ *06/68803794* ⊕ *www.teatrovalle.it*) hosts dramatic performances of the same caliber as its neighbor, Teatro Argentina, but often with a more experimental bent, particularly in fall. Dance and classical music are also presented here. The ancient **Terme di Caracalla** (⌧ *Via delle Terme di Caracalla 52, Aventino* ☎ *06/48160255* ⊕ *www.operaroma.it*) has one of the most spectacular and enchanting outdoor stages in the world, often hosting performances presented by Rome's opera company ranging from *Aida* (with elephants) to avant-garde.

TICKETS

Tickets for major events can be bought online at **Ticket One** (⊕ *www. ticketone.it*). Tickets for larger musical performances as well as many cultural events can usually be found at **Hello Ticket** (⊕ *www.helloticket. it*), which lists all cultural events and the many *punta di vendita*, ticket sellers, in Rome. Or go in person to **Orbis** (⌧ *Piazza Esquilino 37, Repubblica* ☎ *06/4744776*) or to **Mondadori** (⌧ *Via del Corso 472, Spagna* ☎ *06/684401*), a huge and central store that sells music, DVDs, books, and concert tickets.

CONCERTS

Christmastime is an especially busy classical concert season in Rome. Many small classical concert groups perform in cultural centers and churches year-round; all performances in Catholic churches are religious music and are free. Look for posters outside the churches. Pop, jazz, and world music concerts are frequent, especially in summer, although they may not be well advertised. Many of the bigger-name acts perform outside the center, so it's worth asking about transportation *before* you buy your tickets (about €10–€40).

CLASSICAL

A year-round classical concert series, often showcasing the famed Orchestra dell'Accademia di Santa Cecilia, is organized by the **Accademia di Santa Cecilia** (*Concert hall and box office* ⌧ *Via Pietro de Coubertin 34, Flaminio* ☎ *06/8082058* ⊕ *www.santacecilia.it*). The **Accademia**

Filarmonica Romana (⊠ *Via Flaminia 118, Flaminio* ☎*06/3201752, 06/3265991 tickets* ⊕ *www.filarmonicaromana.org*) has concerts at the Teatro Olimpico. The Renaissance-era **Chiostro del Bramante** (⊠ *Vicolo della Pace 2, Navona* ☎ *06/68809098* ⊕ *www.chiostrodelbramante. it*) has a summer concert series. **Il Tempietto** (☎*06/87131590* ⊕*www. tempietto.it*) organizes classical music concerts indoors in winter and in otherwise inaccessible sites in summer. The internationally respected **Oratorio del Gonfalone series** (⊠ *Via del Gonfalone 32/a, Campo de' Fiori* ☎ *06/6875952* ⊕ *www.oratoriogonfalone.it*) focuses on baroque music. The **Orto Botanico** (⊠ *Largo Cristina di Svezia 23/a, Trastevere* ☎ *06/6868441*), off Via della Lungara in Trastevere, has a summer concert series with a beautiful, verdant backdrop. The church of **Sant'Ignazio** (⊠ *Piazza Sant'Ignazio, near Pantheon* ☎ *06/6889951*) often hosts classical concerts in its spectacularly frescoed setting.

DANCE

Modern dance and classical ballet companies from Russia, the United States, and Europe sporadically visit Rome; performances are at the Teatro dell'Opera, Teatro Olimpico, or one of the open-air venues in summer. Small dance companies from Italy and abroad perform in numerous venues.

The **Rome Opera Ballet** (☎*06/481601, 06/48160255 tickets* ⊕*www. operaroma.it*) performs at the Teatro dell'Opera, often with international guest stars.

FILM

Movie tickets range in price from €4.50 for matinees and some weeknights up to €10 for reserved seats on weekend evenings; all films, unless noted "V.O." in the listing, which means *versione originale* (original version or original language), are shown in Italian. Check listings in *Roma C'è* or ⊕ *www.inromenow.com* for reviews of all English-language films currently playing, or visit ⊕ *www.mymovies.it* for a list of current features. The **Metropolitan** (⊠ *Via del Corso 7, Popolo* ☎*06/32600500*) has four screens, one dedicated to English-language films, September–June. The five-screen **Warner Village Moderno** (⊠ *Piazza della Repubblica 45–46* ☎ *06/47779202* ⊕ *www.warnervillage.it*), close to the train station, usually has one theater with an English-language film.

OPERA

The season for the **Opera Theater of Rome** (☎*06/481601, 06/48160255 tickets* ⊕ *www.operaroma.it*) runs from November or December to May. Main performances are staged at the Teatro dell'Opera, on Piazza Beniamino Gigli, in cooler weather, and at outdoor locations, such as Piazza del Popolo and the spectacular Terme di Caracalla (Baths of Caracalla), in summer.

NIGHTLIFE

Rome's nightlife is decidedly more happening for locals and insiders who know whose palms to grease and when to go where. The "flavor of the month" factor is at work here, and many places fade into oblivion after their 15 minutes of fame. Smoking has been banned in all public

Entertainment Alfresco

Roman nightlife moves outdoors in summertime, and that goes not only for pubs and discos but for higher culture as well. Open-air opera in particular is a venerable Italian tradition; competing companies commandeer church courtyards, ancient villas, and soccer stadiums for performances that range from student-run mom-and-poperas to full-scale extravaganzas. The same goes for dance and for concerts covering the spectrum of pop, classical, and jazz. Look for performances at the Baths of Caracalla, site of the famous televised "Three Tenors"

concert; regardless of the production quality, it's a breathtaking setting. In general, though, you can count on performances being quite good, even if small productions often resort to school-play scenery and folding chairs to cut costs. Tickets run about €15–€50. The more-sophisticated productions may be listed in newspapers and magazines such as *Roma C'è*, but your best sources for information are old-fashioned posters plastered all over the city, advertising classics such as *Tosca* and *La Traviata*.

---

areas in Italy (that's right, it actually happened); Roman aversion to clean air has meant a decrease in crowds at bars and clubs. The best sources for an up-to-date list of nightspots are the *Roma C'è* and *Time Out Roma* magazines. Trastevere and the area around Piazza Navona are both filled with bars, restaurants, and, after dark, people. In summer, discos and many bars close to beat the heat (although some simply relocate to the beach, where many Romans spend their summer nights). The city-sponsored *Estate Romana* (Rome Summer) festival takes over, lighting up hot city nights with open-air concerts, bars, and discos. Pick up the event guide at newsstands.

CAFÉS AND WINE BARS

Ai Tre Scalini (⊠ *Via Panisperna 251, Monti* ☎ *06/48907495* ⊕ *www. aitrescalini.org*) is a rustic local hangout with a wooden bar in Monti, one of the new boho sections of Rome. It serves delicious antipasti and light entrées.

★ Celebrities and literati hang out at the coveted outdoor tables of **Antico Caffè della Pace** (⊠ *Via della Pace 5, Navona* ☎ *06/6861216*), set on the enchanting *piazzatina* (tiny piazza) of Santa Maria della Pace. The only drawbacks: overpriced table service and distracted waiters. **Fluid** (⊠ *Via del Governo Vecchio 46/47, Navona* ☎ *06/6832361* ⊕ *www. fluideventi.com*), with its slick design and Zen waterfall, is all about the scene, especially with its looking-glass front window where pretty young things primp on ice cube–shaped chairs. For the cocktail crowd, Fluid's many variations on the traditional martini are quite laudable. **Freni e Frizioni** (⊠ *Via de Politeama 4–6, Trastevere* ☎ *06/58334210* ⊕ *www.frenifrizioni.com*) is one of Rome's latest artsy hangouts—it spills out onto its Trastevere piazza and down the stairs, filling the area around Piazza Trilussa with an attractive crowd of local mojito-sippers. The wood-paneled walls of **L'Angolo Divino** (⊠ *Via dei Balestrari 12, Campo de' Fiori* ☎ *06/6864413*) are racked with more than 700 bottles of wine. A quiet enoteca in a back alley behind Campo, L'Angolo Divino allows you to sidestep the crowds while enjoying homemade pastas with a vintage bottle. **Enoteca Antica** (⊠ *Via della Croce 76/b, Spagna* ☏ *06/6790896* ⊕ *www.anticaenoteca.com*) is Piazza di Spagna's most celebrated wine bar, occupying a prime people-watching corner just below the piazza. In addition to a vast selection of wine (also available for takeout), Enoteca Antica has delectable antipasti, perfect for a snack or a light lunch.

Fodor'sChoice ★ **Shaki** (⊠ *Via Mario de Fiori 29a, Spagna* ☏ *06/6791694* ⊕ *www.shakiroma.com*, Piazza di Spagna's mod wine bar and restaurant (think Los Angeles meets Rome) is perfect for aperitivi, after-dinner drinks, and just being seen.

Vineria Reggio (⊠ *Campo de' Fiori 15, Campo* ☏ *06/68803268*), or "Vineria" as those in-the-know call it, is the quintessential local Roma wine bar where the crowd ranges from grandfathers to glitterati.

ROOFTOP TERRACES AND UPSCALE BARS

Crudo (⊠ *Via Degli Specchi 6, Campo de' Fiori* ☏ *06/6838989*) is a spacious, modern, New York–style lounge serving well-made cocktails and *crudo* (raw) nibbles such as sushi and carpaccio. With a large lounge decked out in mod design and hued in gray, white, and red, Crudo also doubles as art space.

★ For a dip into La Dolce Vita, the **Jardin de Hotel de Russie** (⊠ *Via del Babuino 9, Popolo* ☏ *06/328881* ⊕ *www.hotelderussie.it*)is the location for every Hollywood VIP, as well as up-and-coming starlets. Mixed drinks are well above par, as are the prices.

Fodor'sChoice ★ **Rosé Terrazzo at the St. George Hotel** (⊠ *Via Giulia 62, Campo de' Fiori* ☏ *06/686611* ⊕ *www.stgeorgehotel.it*) is the latest front-runner in Rome's ever-growing list of rooftop sweet spots. With a delicious oyster selection headlining its seafood-only menu, the Rosé Terrazzo's dizzying drink selection includes cocktails, wine, and many rosés—from pink champagnes to Italian *rosati*. This option, on Rome's classiest street, is open only in the summer months.

Sitting in front of a 2nd-century temple, **Salotto 42** (⊠ *Piazza di Pietra 42, Pantheon* ☏ *06/6785804* ⊕ *www.salotto42.it*) holds court from morning until late in the evening. The cozy-sleek room (high-back velvet chairs, zebra-print rugs, chandeliers) is a smorgasbord of the owners' Roman–New York–Swedish pedigree. The den, complete with art books, local sophisticates, and models moonlighting as waitresses, is the fashionista's favorite choice for late-night drinks.

★ **Tazio** (⊠ *Hotel Exedra, Piazza della Repubblica 47* ☏ *06/489381*), named after the original Italian paparazzo (celebrity photographer), is an Adam Tihany–designed champagne bar. The red, black, and white lacquered interior, with crystal chandeliers, has a distinct '80s feel (think Robert Palmer, *Addicted to Love*). In summer, the hotel's rooftop bar **Sensus** is the place to be, with its infinity pool and terrace view overlooking downtown.

Terrace Bar of the Hotel Raphael (⊠ *Largo Febo 2, Navona* ☏ *06/682831* ⊕ *www.raphaelhotel.com*) is noted for its bird's-eye view of the

The Spanish Steps by night

campaniles and palazzi of the Piazza Navona. High up in the moonlit sky, the Terrace Bar tends to be the choice place for a romantic evening.

NIGHTCLUBS AND DISCOS

Most dance clubs open about 10:30 PM and charge an entrance fee of about €20, which may include the first drink (subsequent drinks cost about €10). Clubs are usually closed Monday, and all those listed here close in summer, some opening instead at the beaches of Ostia or Fregene. The liveliest areas for clubs with a younger clientele are the grittier working-class districts of Testaccio and Ostiense. Any of the clubs lining Via Galvani, leading up to Monte Testaccio, are fair game for a trendy, crowded dance-floor experience—names and ownership of clubs change frequently, but the overall scene has shown exciting staying power, growing into a DJ "Disneyland."

Behind the Vatican Museums, **Alexanderplatz** (⊠ *Via Ostia 9, Vaticano* ☎ *06/39742171* ⊕ *www.alexanderplatz.it*), Rome's most famous jazz and blues club, has a bar and a restaurant. Local and internationally known musicians play nightly. In trendy Testaccio, **Caffè Latino** (⊠ *Via Monte Testaccio 96* ☎ *06/57288556* ⊕ *www.caffelatinoroma.com*) is a vibrant Roman locale that has live music (mainly Latin) almost every night, followed by recorded soul, funk, and '70s and '80s revival; it's closed Monday. **Gilda** (⊠ *Via Mario de' Fiori 97, Spagna* ☎ *06/6784838* ⊕ *www.gildabar.it*) used to be the place to spot famous Italian actors and politicians. Now it is host to B-actors and leftover politniks. This nightspot near the Spanish Steps has a piano bar as well as a restaurant and dance floors with live and disco music. Jackets are required. **Hulala** (⊠ *Via dei Conciatori 7, Ostiense* ☎ *06/57300429* ⊕ *www.desamis.it*)

is home to Rome's fashionistas. Mod films are projected on the walls, and champagne is drunk through straws.

★ Housed in a medieval palazzo is **La Cabala** (✉ *Via dei Soldati 23, Navona* ☎ *06/68301192* ⊕ *www.hdo.it*), Rome's version of a supper club. This three-level space has a piano bar, restaurant, and club, and often has a very dressy crowd vying to get past the velvet rope.

★ Lounge fever is all over Rome, with **La Maison** (✉ *Vicolo dei Granari 4, Navona* ☎ *06/6833312* ⊕ *www.lamaisonroma.it*) one of the best. Bedecked in purple velvet and crystal chandeliers, the club has two distinct spaces, a VIP area and a dance floor, with a DJ dishing up the latest dance tunes. Head straight to the back room and grab a couch. **Qube** (✉ *Via di Portonaccio 212, San Lorenzo* ☎ *06/4385445*), open only Thursday through Saturday, is Rome's biggest underground disco, where bodies mix and mingle like a rugby game. Friday night hosts the **Muccassassina** (⊕ *www.muccassassina.com*), Rome's most popular gay event. It has paid a price for its fame, and is now more straight than gay.

SHOPPING

Updated by Lynda Albertson

They say when in Rome to do as the Romans do—and the Romans love to shop. After all, this is the city that gave us the Gucci "moccasin" loafer, the Fendi bag, and the Valentino dress that Jackie O wore when she became Mrs. Onassis. Stores are generally open from 10 to 1 and from 3:30 or 4 to 7 or 7:30. There's a tendency for shops in central districts to stay open all day, and hours are becoming more flexible throughout the city. Many places close Monday morning and all day Sunday, though this is changing, too, especially in the city center. Some stores also close Saturday afternoon from mid-June through August.

You can stretch your euros by taking advantage of the Tax-Free for Tourists V.A.T. tax refunds, available at most large stores for purchases over €155. Or hit Rome in January and early February or in late July and August, when stores clean house with the justly famous biannual sales. There are so many hole-in-the-wall boutiques selling top-quality merchandise in Rome's center that even just wandering you're sure to find something that catches your eye.

SHOPPING DISTRICTS

The city's most famous shopping district, **Piazza di Spagna,** is conveniently compact, fanning out at the foot of the Spanish Steps in a galaxy of boutiques selling gorgeous wares with glamorous labels. Here you can ricochet from Gucci to Prada to Valentino to Versace with less effort than it takes to pull out your credit card. If your budget is designed for lower altitudes, you also can find great clothes and accessories at less-extravagant prices. But here, buying is not necessarily the point— window displays can be works of art, and dreaming may be satisfaction enough. Via dei Condotti is the neighborhood's central axis, but there are shops on every street in the area bordered by Piazza di Spagna on the east, Via del Corso on the west, between Piazza San Silvestro and

Via della Croce, and extending along Via del Babuino to Piazza del Popolo. **Via Margutta,** a few blocks north of the Spanish Steps, is a haven for contemporary art galleries.

Shops along **Via Campo Marzio,** and adjoining Piazza San Lorenzo in Lucina, stock eclectic, high-quality clothes and accessories—both big names (Bottega Veneta, Louis Vuitton) and smaller European designers—at slightly lower prices. Running from Piazza Venezia to Piazza del Popolo lies **Via del Corso,** a main shopping avenue that has more than a mile of clothing, shoes, leather goods, and home furnishings from classic to cutting-edge. Running west from Piazza Navona, **Via del Governo Vecchio** has numerous women's boutiques and secondhand-clothing stores.

Via Cola di Rienzo, across the Tiber from Piazza del Popolo and extending to the Vatican, is block after block of boutiques, shoe stores, department stores, and midlevel chain shops, as well as street stalls and upscale food shops. **Via dei Coronari,** across the Tiber from Castel Sant'Angelo, has quirky antiques and home furnishings. **Via Giulia** and other surrounding streets are good bets for decorative arts. Should your gift list include religious souvenirs, look for everything from rosaries to Vatican golf balls at the shops between Piazza San Pietro and **Borgo Pio.** Liturgical vestments and statues of saints make for good window-shopping on **Via dei Cestari,** near the Pantheon.

Via Nazionale is a good bet for affordable stores of the Benetton ilk, and for shoes, bags, and gloves. The **Termini** train station has become a good one-stop place for many shopping needs. Its 60-plus shops are open until 10 PM and include a Nike store, the Body Shop, Sephora, Mango (women's clothes), a UPIM department store, a grocery store, and a three-story bookstore with selections in English. Local designers and smaller designer boutiques also pepper the trendy shopping districts of **Monti** near the Forum and **Trastevere** across the Tiber from the historical center.

MARKETS

Outdoor markets are open Monday–Saturday from early morning to about 1 PM (a bit later on Saturday), but get there early for the best selection. Remember to keep an eye on your wallet—the money changing hands draws Rome's most skillful pickpockets. And don't go if you can't stand crowds. Rome's most central outdoor food market is at **Campo de' Fiori,** south of Piazza Navona, though for a more authentic feel head to **Testaccio,** where the covered market is far less touristy. The renovated **Trionfale market** (✉ *Via Andrea Doria, near Vatican*) is big and bustling with more than 270 stalls; it's about a five-minute walk north of the entrance to the Vatican Museums with access from Via Tunisi and Via Santamaura. There's room for bargaining at the Sunday-morning flea market at **Porta Portese** (✉ *Piazza Ippolito Nievo, Trastevere*). Seemingly endless rows of merchandise include new and secondhand clothing, bootleg CDs, old furniture, car stereos of suspicious origin, and all manner of old junk and hidden treasures.

SPECIALTY STORES

DESIGNER CLOTHING

All of Italy's top fashion houses and many international designers have stores near Piazza di Spagna. Buying clothes can be a bit tricky for American women, as sizes tend to be cut for a petite Italian frame. A size 12 (European 46) is not always easy to find, but the more-expensive stores should carry it. Target less-expensive stores for accessories if this is an issue.

D&G (⊠ *Piazza di Spagna 94* ☎ *06/69924999*), a spin-off of the top-of-the-line Dolce&Gabbana, shows trendy casual wear and accessories for men and women. The flagship store for **Fendi** (⊠ *Largo Carlo Goldoni 419-421, near Piazza di Spagna* ☎ *06/334501*) is in the former Palazzo Boncompagni, renamed "Palazzo Fendi." It overlooks the intersection of famed Via dei Condotti and Via del Corso, and it's the quintessential Roman fashion house, presided over by the Fendi sisters. Their signature baguette bags, furs, accessories, and sexy separates are all found here. The **Giorgio Armani** (⊠ *Via dei Condotti 77, near Piazza di Spagna* ☎ *06/6991460*) shop is as understated and elegant as its designs. **Gucci** (⊠ *Via dei Condotti 8, near Piazza di Spagna* ☎ *06/6790405*) often has lines out the door of its two-story shop, testament to the continuing popularity of its colorful bags, wallets, and shoes in rich leathers. Edgy clothes designs are also available. There is another Gucci boutique nearby on Via Borgognona. Sleek, vaguely futuristic **Prada** (⊠ *Via dei Condotti 92-95, near Piazza di Spagna* ☎ *06/6790897*) has two entrances: the one for the men's boutique is to the left of the women's. Rome's immortal fashion superstar, **Valentino** (*Valentino Donna* ⊠ *Via dei Condotti 15, near Piazza di Spagna* ☎ *06/6739420 Valentino Uomo* ⊠ *Via Bocca di Leone 15, near Piazza di Spagna* ☎ *06/36001906*), is recognized the world over by the "V" logo. The now-retired couturier has new designers manning his shops for the *donna* (woman) and the *uomo* (man) not far from his headquarters in Piazza Mignanelli beside the Spanish Steps. **Versace** (⊠ *Via Bocca di Leone 26-27, near Piazza di Spagna* ☎ *06/6780521*) sells the rock-star styles that made the house's name.

MEN'S CLOTHING

Brioni (⊠ *Via dei Condotti 21, near Piazza di Spagna* ☎ *06/6783428* ⊠ *Via Barberini 79, near Piazza Barberini* ☎ *06/485855*) has a well-deserved reputation as one of Italy's top tailors. There are ready-to-wear garments in addition to impeccable custom-made apparel. **Davide Cenci** (⊠ *Via Campo Marzio 1-7, near Piazza della Rotonda [Pantheon]* ☎ *06/6990681*), Rome's answer to a high-end department store, is famed for conservative clothing of exquisite craftsmanship. **Ermenegildo Zegna** (⊠ *Via Borgognona 7/e, near Piazza di Spagna* ☎ *06/6789143*) has the finest in men's elegant styles and accessories. **Il Portone** (⊠ *Via delle Carrozze 73, near Piazza di Spagna* ☎ *06/6793355*) embodies a tradition in custom shirtmaking.

WOMEN'S CLOTHING

38 Leopardo (✉ *Vicolo del Leopardo 38, Trastevere* ☎ *06/45435476*) American designer Jessica Harris's shop in Trastevere, evokes the image of a large-scale dollhouse where her one-of-a-kind collections are displayed alongside dresses, separates, and accessories by other local designers. Her clothes are delicately constructed by hand from the finest materials.

Fodor's Choice
★ **L'Anatra all'Arancia** (✉ *Via Tiburtina 105, San Lorenzo* ☎ *06/4456293*) has the locals in this bustling working-class district agog at its window displays of flowing innovative designer clothes, teeny-weeny bikinis, and zany underwear. Owner Donatella Baroni believes in fashion being fun. The men's shop is across the road at No. 130, where style-conscious hipsters can find pure linen shirts and trousers in unusual colors. The clientele includes Italian TV and stage personalities who live in the trendy area.

★ **Maga Morgana** (✉ *Via del Governo Vecchio 27, near Piazza Navona* ☎ *06/6879995* ✉ *Via del Governo Vecchio 98, Navona* ☎ *06/6878085*) is a family-run business where everyone's nimble fingers contribute to producing the highly original clothes and accessories. From hippie chick to bridal chic, designer Luciana Iannace creates lavishly ornate clothes that are as inventive as they are distinguishing.

Save the Queen (✉ Via del Babuino 49, *Spagna* ☎ *06/36003039*) is a hot Florentine design house with pieces with artistic and renaissance frills, cutouts, and textures. The silhouettes are youthful chic and not the least bit discreet.

Victory (✉ *Via S. Francesco a Ripa 19, Trastevere* ☎ *06/5812437*) spotlights youthful, lighthearted styles created by lesser-known stylists, such as Rose D, Nina, Alessandrini, and Marithé et François Girbaud. Victory's clothing is made for flaunting. A menswear version of the store is located at Piazza San Calisto 10 in Trastevere.

JEWELRY

Fodor's Choice
★ **Gioielli in Movimento** (✉ *Via della Stelletta 23, near Piazza Navona* ☎ *06/6867431*) draws celebrity customers hooked on Carlo Cardena's ingenious designs. Carlo's "Twice as Nice" earrings, which can be transformed from fan-shape clips into elegant drops, were Uno Erre's best-selling earrings between 1990 and 1998, and his "Up and Down" pendant, which can be worn two different ways, is another hit. **Quattrocolo** (✉ *Via della Scrofa 54, near Piazza Navona* ☎ *06/68801367*) has been specializing in antique micromosaic jewelry and baubles from centuries past since 1938.

SHOES AND LEATHER ACCESSORIES

For gloves as pretty as Holly Golightly's, shop at **Sermoneta** (✉ *Piazza di Spagna 61* ☎ *06/6791960*). Any color or style one might desire, from elbow-length black leather to scallop-edged lace-cut lilac suede, is available at this glove institution. **Furla** (✉ *Piazza di Spagna 22* ☎ *06/69200363*) has 14 franchises in Rome alone. At its flagship store, to the left of the Spanish Steps, be prepared for crowds of passionate shoppers, all anxious to possess one of the delectable bags, wallets, or watch straps in ice-cream colors. **Salvatore Ferragamo** (✉ *Via dei*

Condotti 65, near Piazza di Spagna ☎ *06/6781130* ✉ *Via dei Condotti 73/74, near Piazza di Spagna* ☎ *06/6791565*) is one of the top-10 most-wanted men's footwear brands in the world and for years has been providing Hollywood glitterati and discerning clients with unique hand-made designs. The Florentine design house also specializes in handbags, small leather goods, men's and women's ready-to-wear, and scarves and ties. Men's styles are found at Via dei Condotti 64, women's at 73/74. **Di Cori** (✉ *Piazza di Spagna 53* ☎ *06/6784439*) has gloves in every color of the spectrum. **Bruno Magli** (✉ *Via dei Condotti 6, near Piazza di Spagna* ☎ *06/69292121*) has classy shoes with simple, elegant lines—for men and women—that have character without compromising comfort.

Fodor's Choice
★

Tod's (✉ *Via Fontanella di Borghese 56a/57, near Via del Corso* ☎ *06/68210066*) has become hyperfashionable again due in large part to owner Diego Della Valle's ownership of Florence's soccer team. The brand is known for its sporty flats and comfortable, casual styling. Tod's occupies the ground floor in the celebrated 16th-century Palazzo Ruspoli. **Fausto Santini** (✉ *Via Frattina 120, near Piazza di Spagna* ☎ *06/6784114*) gives a hint of extravagance in minimally decorated, all-white show windows displaying surprising shoes that fashion mavens love. Santini's footwear for men and women is bright, colorful, and trendy, sporting unusual forms, especially in heels. Coordinated bags and wallets add to the fun.

Between Rome and Florence

HIGHLIGHTS OF UMBRIA AND TUSCANY

WORD OF MOUTH

"If I could only return to one town in Umbria, it would be Assisi. Loved the setting, the history, the evening ambiance. But Perugia would be a very close second choice for many of the above reasons."

—galelstorm

WELCOME TO UMBRIA AND TUSCANY

TOP REASONS TO GO

★ **Assisi, shrine to St. Francis:** Recharge your soul in this rose-color hill town with a visit to the gentle saint's majestic basilica.

★ **Orvieto's Duomo:** Arresting visions of heaven and hell on the facade and brilliant frescoes within make this Gothic cathedral a dazzler.

★ **Piazza del Campo, Siena:** Sip a cappuccino, lick some gelato, and take in this spectacular piazza.

★ **Piero della Francesca's** *True Cross* **frescoes, Arezzo:** If your holy grail is great Renaissance art, seek out these 12 silently enigmatic scenes.

★ **Sunset, San Gimignano:** Grab a spot on the steps of the Collegiata church as flocks of swallows swoop in and out of the famous medieval towers.

★ **Wine tasting in Chianti:** Sample the fruits of the region's gorgeous vineyards, at either the wineries themselves or the towns' wine bars.

1 **Southern Umbria.** The town of Orvieto is famed for its cathedral, its dry white wines, and its spectacular hilltop location. Further east, Spoleto offers Filippo Lippi frescoes, a massive castle towering over the town, and one of the world's great summer music festivals.

2 **Northern Umbria.** Assisi—sanctified by St. Francis—doubles as a beautiful medieval village and a major pilgrimage site. Umbria's largest town, Perugia, is home to some of Perugino's great frescoes and a hilltop *centro storico.* It's also beloved by choco-holics: hazelnut Baci candies were born here.

3 **Central Tuscany.** The privileged hilltop site that helped Siena flourish in the Middle Ages keeps it one of Italy's most enchanting medieval towns today. To the west, San Gimignano, bristles with 15th-century stone towers. To the north, the hills of the Chianti district present a rolling pageant of ageless vineyards and villas.

4 **Eastern Tuscany.** The ancient stone town of Cortona sits high above the perfectly flat Valdichiana valley, offering great views of beautiful countryside. Arezzo, to the north, is best known for its sublime frescoes by Piero della Francesca.

GETTING ORIENTED

3

The path between Rome and Florence runs along the Apennine mountain range through the hilly regions of Tuscany and Umbria. A mix of forests, vineyards, olive groves, and poppy fields adds up to the Italian countryside at its most beautiful. The hillside towns, many dating from the days of ancient Rome, wear their history on their sleeves: you'll encounter towering Gothic cathedrals, glowing Renaissance frescoes, and cobblestone streets worn smooth by a thousand years of strollers. When people close their eyes and dream of Italy, this is what they see.

Duomo, Orvieto

[map of central Italy showing Arezzo, Sansepolcro, Cortona, Perugia, Assisi, Foligno, Todi, Spoleto, Orvieto, Rieti, Terni, Tivoli, Rome, Tarquinia, Lido di Ostia, with regions UMBRIA and LAZIO]

UMBRIA AND TUSCANY PLANNER

Making the Most of Your Time

The best strategy for visiting Umbria and Tuscany is to choose one town as a base for several nights and then take day trips through the surrounding region. The beauty of this plan is that it's virtually impossible to choose the wrong base: every town listed in this chapter has countless adherents who have fallen in love with it. Even places with heavy tourist traffic—Assisi, Siena, San Gimignano—seem to breathe a sigh and relax in the evening after the day-trippers have departed.

Wherever you settle, keep in mind that this isn't the place for a jam-packed itinerary. One of the great pleasures here is indulging in rustic hedonism, marked by long lunches and showstopping sunsets.

Typical Travel Times	
Hours by Car/Train	
Rome–Florence	3:00/1:35
Rome–Orvieto	1:30/1:10
Rome–Assisi	2:15/2:00
Rome–Siena	2:45/3:30
Florence–Assisi	1:45/2:30
Florence–Siena	1:00/1:30
Florence–Arezzo	1:00/0:30

Getting Around

A crucial thing to know when you're traveling through the hilly terrain of Umbria and Tuscany is that the valleys primarily run north–south. That means you can move in a north–south direction, following a valley, with relative ease, but when you're going east–west, you're climbing over hills, which involves slow, winding roads.

By Car: The major highway through the regions is the north–south A1 superstrada, which runs a 277-km (172-mi) course between Rome and Florence. It passes through western Umbria, skirting the hill town of Orvieto, and eastern Tuscany, passing close to Arezzo.

For more than a fleeting glance at these two regions, you need to get off the superstrada. Fortunately, the quality of the secondary roads is good, and driving them is a pleasure in itself. In Umbria, a loop of highway (made up of road nos. 204, 3, and 75) takes you off A1 to Spoleto, Assisi, and Perugia. In Tuscany, the A14 is the major highway between Siena and Florence, whereas road no. 222, known as the Strada Chiantigiana, is the slower, more picturesque alternative.

By Train: Like the main highway, the direct train line from Rome to Florence runs through Orvieto and Arezzo. Other towns in Umbria are accessible by regional trains, but in Tuscany, the towns of the Chianti region aren't; there's train service to Siena, but the station isn't near the center of the old city—you need to take a taxi between the two.

Getting Here

Most flights to Tuscany originating in the United States stop either in Rome, London, Paris, or Frankfurt, and then connect to Florence's small **Aeroporto A. Vespucci** (commonly called **Peretola**), or to Pisa's **Aeroporto Galileo Galilei**. The only exception at this writing is Delta's New York/JFK flight going directly into Pisa.

There are several other alternatives for getting into the region. If you want to start your trip in Umbria, it works to fly into Rome's **Aeroporto Leonardo da Vinci** (commonly called Fiumincino); from Rome it's an hour by train or an hour and a half by car to reach the lovely town of Orvieto. Another option is to fly to Milan and pick up a connecting flight to Pisa, Florence, or Perugia.

Finding a Place to Stay

It's a common practice in Umbria and Tuscany to convert old villas, farms, and monasteries into first-class hotels. The natural beauty of the countryside more than compensates for being located outside town—provided you have a car. Hotels in towns tend to be simpler than their country cousins, with a few notable exceptions.

Though it's tempting to think of this as an area where you can wander the hills and then stumble upon a charming little hotel at the end of the day, you're better off not testing your luck. Reservations are the way to go.

WHAT IT COSTS (IN EUROS)

	¢	$	$$	$$$	$$$$
Restaurants	under €20	€20–€30	€30–€45	€45–€65	over €65
Hotels	under €75	€75–€125	€125–€200	€200–€300	over €300

Restaurant prices are for a first course (*primo*), second course (*secondo*), and dessert (*dolce*). Hotel prices are for two people in a standard double room in high season, including tax and service.

When to Go

Throughout Tuscany and Umbria, the best times to visit are spring and fall. Days are warm, nights are cool, and though there are still tourists, the crowds are smaller. In the countryside the scenery is gorgeous, with abundant greenery and flowers in spring, and burnished leaves in autumn.

July and August are the most popular times to visit. Note, though, that the heat is often oppressive and mosquitoes are prevalent. Try to start your days early and visit major sights first to beat the crowds and the midday sun.

November through March, you might wonder who invented the term "sunny Italy." The panoramas are still beautiful, even with overcast skies, frequent rain, and occasional snow. In smaller towns and in the countryside, many hotels and restaurants close for the season.

Gubbio

UMBRIA

Updated
by Jonathan
Willcocks

UMBRIA CONTAINS A SERIES OF CHARACTER-RICH HILL TOWNS, all within an hour or two drive of one another; you can choose one as your base, then explore the others, and the countryside and forest in between, on day trips. No single town here has the extravagant wealth of art and architecture of Florence, Rome, or Venice, but this can work in their favor: the towns feel knowable, not overwhelming. And there's plenty to admire: Orvieto's cathedral and Assisi's basilica are two of the most important sights in Italy, while Perugia and Spoleto are rich in art and architecture. While you're here, keep an eye out for remnants of ancient Rome, which crop up all over—expect to see Roman villas, aqueducts, theaters, walls, and temples.

ORVIETO

The natural defenses of an enormous plateau rising 1,000 feet above the flat valley proved very attractive to settlers in central Italy as far back as the Bronze Age, making Orvieto among the oldest cities in the region. The Etruscans developed the town considerably, carving a network of 1,200 wells and storage caves out of the soft tufa (volcanic stone) of the mountain on which the city was built. By 283 BC the Romans had attacked, sacked, and destroyed the city, by then known as Volsinii Veteres. Perhaps they were attracted by the golden Orvieto Classico made from grapes grown in the rich volcanic soil of the valley below—a wine the town is still famous for today.

Charlemagne (742–814) changed the name to Urbs Vetus, from which the modern name derives. The town rose steadily as an independent commune in the late Middle Ages. When the Guelphs won decisively over the Ghibellines in the 14th century, Orvieto passed under the control of the papacy, and was subsequently used by the popes as a refuge from enemies or the summer heat of Rome.

In addition to wine and some of the best restaurants in the region, Orvieto has much to offer: the celebrated Duomo, with Italy's finest Gothic facade, is alone worth the trip. Inside are masterly frescoes by Luca Signorelli (circa 1450–1523)—stunningly restored—perhaps the most underrated in the entire country. A couple of good museums and some excavations round out the sights.

The festival highlight of the year is the Festa della Palombella on Pentecost Sunday (the seventh Sunday after Easter). In this unique take on a fireworks show, a tabernacle with images of the Madonna and the Apostles is set up on the steps in front of the central doorway of the Duomo. A white dove attached to a cable strung across the piazza slides down and ignites the fireworks.

A more traditional celebration is the Festa del Corpus Domini (the ninth Sunday after Easter), begun by Pope Urban IV in 1264, which may have its origin in the Miracle at Bolsena. Each year Bolsena's miraculous, bloodstained *corporale* (square linen cloth) is taken out of the chapel and led around town in a solemn procession, preceded by a rich court in sumptuous period costumes. Between Christmas and the first days of January, the Umbria Jazz Festival comes to Orvieto. Plan on big crowds, high-season rates in the hotels, and plenty of music flowing through the streets.

GETTING HERE

Orvieto is well connected by train to Rome, Florence, and Perugia. It's also adjacent to the A1 Superstrada that runs between Florence and Rome. Parking areas in the upper town tend to be crowded. A better idea is to follow the signs for the Porta Orvetiana parking lot, then take the free funicular that carries people up the hill.

VISITOR INFORMATION

Orvieto tourism office (✉ *Piazza del Duomo 24* ☎ *0763/341772* ⊕ *www. orvieto.umbria2000.it*).

EXPLORING ORVIETO

If you are arriving by train, take the funicular that runs from the train station up the side of the hill and through the fortress to Piazzale Cahen. It runs every 20 minutes, daily 7:15 AM–8:30 PM, and costs €1. Although the workings have been modernized, there are a few pictures in each station of the old cog railcars, which were once run hydraulically. Keep your funicular ticket, as it will get you a discount on admission to the Museo Claudio Faina. Bus 1 makes the same trip from 8 AM to 11 PM. From Piazzale Cahen, Bus A runs to Piazza del Duomo in the town center.

A *Carta Orvieto Unica* (single ticket) is expensive, but a great deal if you want to visit everything; for €18 you get admission to the four major sights in town—Cappella di San Brizio (at the Duomo), Museo Claudio Faina, Torre del Moro, and Orvieto Underground—plus a combination bus–funicular pass or five hours of free parking.

TOP ATTRACTIONS

⑤ Fodor's Choice ★

Duomo. Orvieto's Duomo is, quite simply, stunning. The church was built to commemorate the Miracle at Bolsena. In 1263 a young priest who questioned the miracle of transubstantiation (in which the Communion bread and wine become the flesh and blood of Christ) was saying mass at nearby Lago di Bolsena. His doubts were put to rest, however, when a wafer he had just blessed suddenly started to drip blood, staining the linen covering the altar. The cloth and the host were taken to the pope, who proclaimed a miracle and a year later provided for a new religious holiday—the Feast of Corpus Domini. Thirty years later, construction began on a *duomo* to celebrate the miracle and house the stained altar cloth.

It is thought that Arnolfo di Cambio (circa 1245–1302), the famous builder of the Duomo in Florence, was given the initial commission for the Duomo, but the project was soon taken over by Lorenzo Maitani

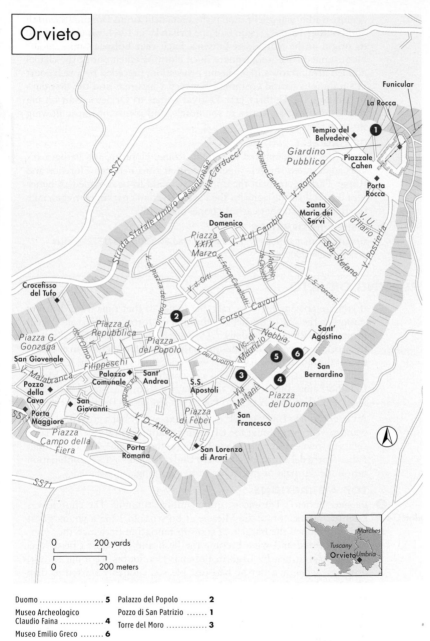

Orvieto

Funicular
La Rocca
Tempio del Belvedere
1
Giardino Pubblico
Piazzale Cahen
Porta Rocca
Santa Maria dei Servi
San Domenico
Piazza XXIX Marzo
Crocefisso del Tufo
Corso Cavour
2
Sant' Agostino
Piazza d. Repubblica
Piazza del Popolo
Piazza G. Gonzaga
San Giovenale
V. Filippeschi
Palazzo Comunale
Sant' Andrea
Pozzo della Cava
San Giovanni
Porta Maggiore
Piazza Campo della Fiera
Porta Romana
Piazza di Febei
San Francesco
San Lorenzo di Arari
S.S. Apostoli
5 **6**
San Bernardino
3 **4**
Piazza del Duomo

Via Maitani

V. di Prazza del Popolo
del Olmo
V. Malabranca
SS71
V. D. Alberici
Strada Statale Umbro Casentinese
SS71
Via Carducci
V. Quattro Cantone
V. Roma
V. A di Cambio
V. di Orti
V. Felice Cavallotti
V. Angelo da Orvieto
V. S. Porcari
V. U. d'Itario
Sta. Stefano
V. Postierla
V.C. Nebbia
Vic. di Maurizio
V. del Duomo

0 ——— 200 yards
0 ——— 200 meters

Marches
Tuscany
Orvieto
Umbria

(circa 1275–1330), who consolidated the structure and designed the monumental facade. Maitani also made the bas-relief panels between the doorways, which graphically tell the story of the Creation (on the left) and the Last Judgment (on the right). The lower registers, now protected by Plexiglas, succeed in conveying the horrors of hell as few other works of art manage to do, an effect made all the more powerful by the worn gray marble. Above, gold mosaics are framed by finely detailed Gothic decoration.

Inside, the cathedral is rather vast and empty; the major works are in the transepts. To the left is the **Cappella del Corporale,** where the square linen cloth (*corporale*) is kept in a golden reliquary that's modeled on the cathedral and inlaid with enamel scenes of the miracle. The cloth is removed for public viewing on Easter and on Corpus Domini (the ninth Sunday after Easter). In the right transept is the **Cappella di San Brizio,** or Cappella Nuova. In this chapel is one of Italy's greatest fresco cycles, notable for its influence on Michelangelo's *Last Judgment,* as well as for the extraordinary beauty of the figuration. In these works, a few by Fra Angelico and the majority by Luca Signorelli, the damned fall to hell, demons breathe fire and blood, and Christians are martyred. Some scenes are heavily influenced by the imagery in Dante's (1265–1321) *Divine Comedy.* ⊠ *Piazza del Duomo* ☎ *0763/342477* 🖾 *Cappella Nuova €5* ☉ *Nov.–Feb., daily 7:30–12:45 and 2:30–5:15; Mar. and Oct., daily 7:30–12:45 and 2:30–6:15; Apr.–Sept., daily 7:30–12:45 and 2:30–7:15.*

QUICK BITES

Orvieto has plenty of spots to grab a quick bite—a boon in off-hours, when restaurants are closed and sightseers get peckish. **Gastronomia Carraro** (⊠ *Corso Cavour 101* ☎ *0763/342870*) has an excellent selection of local sausages and cheeses. (Try the different kinds of pecorino.) It also has delicious pickled olives and tomatoes, perfect on a roll if the sightseeing has made you hungry. Alas, it's closed Sunday. For a snack or coffee at tables outside, check out **Bar Sant'Andrea** (⊠ *Piazza della Repubblica* ☎ *0763/343285*). You can get simple, cheap food here, and in summer sit on the small terrace. The service is quick and friendly, and if conversation is lacking you can always contemplate the rather odd-looking 12-sided bell tower of the church of Sant'Andrea across the piazza. Wonderful gelato in large scoops is to be had at ivy-shaded alfresco tables at **Pasqualetti** (⊠ *Piazza del Duomo 14* ☎ *0763/341034*). Try the delicately flavored pistachio and coconut ice cream while you admire the facade of the Duomo. It's closed mid-December through February.

❹ **Museo Archeologico Claudio Faina.** This superb private collection, beautifully arranged and presented, goes far beyond the usual museum offerings of a scattering of local remains. The collection is particularly rich in Greek- and Etruscan-era pottery, from large Attic amphorae (6th–4th century BC) to Attic black- and red-figure pieces to Etruscan *bucchero* (dark, reddish clay) vases. Other interesting pieces in the collection include a 6th-century sarcophagus and a substantial display of Roman-era coins. ⊠ *Piazza del Duomo 29* ☎ *0763/341511* ⊕ *www. museofaina.it* ✉ *€4.50* ⊙ *Oct.– Mar., Tues.–Sun. 10–5; Apr.–Sept., daily 9:30–6.*

6 Museo Emilio Greco. Another medieval building built by a pope on leave here from Rome, the 13th-century Palazzo Soliano was for many years the location of the Museo dell'Opera del Duomo, a fine collection that includes works by Signorelli and other notable names like

WORD OF MOUTH

"Orvieto makes a nice day or overnight stop. Lots of great shoe shops. The nearby hilltop village of Civita makes a great side trip—you have to park your vehicle and walk across a suspension bridge to get there, but when you arrive, you'll find a quaint and cute village." —DOCK

Simone Martini and Arnolfo di Cambio. But the art treasures have been locked away during an interminable restoration. Meanwhile, the ground floor has been made into the Museo Emilio Greco, a good-looking space filled with sculpture and sketches from the prolific Sicilian artist Emilio Greco (born 1913)—who also made the doors for the Duomo in the 1960s. ⊠ *Piazza del Duomo, Palazzo Soliano* ☎ *0763/344605* ✉ *€6.50, includes admission to Capella di San Brizio* ⊙ *Oct.–Mar., weekdays 10:30–1, 2:00–5: Apr.–Sept., weekdays 10:30–1, 2–6:30.*

Orvieto Underground. More than just about any other town, Orvieto has grown from its own foundations—if one were to remove from present-day Orvieto all the building materials that were dug up from below, there would hardly be a building left standing. The Etruscans, the Romans, and those who followed dug into the tufa (the same soft volcanic rock from which catacombs were made), and over the centuries created more than 1,000 separate cisterns, caves, secret passages, storage areas, and production areas for wine and olive oil. Some of the tufa removed was used as building blocks for the city that exists today, and some was partly ground into *pozzolana,* which was made into mortar. The most thorough **Orvieto Underground tour** (⊠ *Orvieto tourism office, Piazza del Duomo 24* ☎ *0763/341772*) is run daily at 11, 12:15, 4, and 5:15. (In February tours are given only on weekends.) Admission for the hour-long English tour is €5.50. If you are short on time but still want a look at what it was like down there, head for the **Pozzo della Cava** (⊠ *Via della Cava 28* ☎ *0763/342373*), an Etruscan well for spring water. It's open Tuesday through Friday from 9 to 8, and costs €3.

WORTH NOTING

2 Palazzo del Popolo. Built in tufa and basaltic rock, this was once the town hall. Restoration work in the late 1980s revealed the remains of an Etruscan temple underneath, and it now holds the state archives. There are no tours of the interior. ⊠ *Piazza del Popolo*

1 Pozzo di San Patrizio *(St. Patrick's Well).* When Pope Clement VII (1478–1534) took shelter in Orvieto during the Sack of Rome in 1527, he had to ensure a safe water supply should Orvieto come under siege. Many wells and cisterns were built, and the pope commissioned one of the great architects of the day, Antonio da Sangallo the Younger

(1493–1546), to build the well adjacent to the Rocca. After nearly a decade of digging, water was found at a depth of 203 feet. Two one-way spiral stairways allowed donkey-driven carts to descend and return without running into one another. Windows open onto the shaft, providing natural light in the stairwells. There are 248 steps down to the bottom, but you'll probably get the idea after just a few. The well was once compared to St. Patrick's Well in Ireland. The name stuck, and "pozzo di San Patrizio" has come to represent an inexhaustible source of wealth. ⊠ *Viale Sangallo, off Piazzale Cahen* 🕾 *0763/343768* 🖾*€4.50* ⊙ *Oct.–Mar., daily 10–5:45; Apr.–Sept., daily 10–6:45.*

3 **Torre del Moro.** It's hard to imagine a simpler, duller affair than this tower in the center of town. It took on a little more character in the 19th century, when the large, white-face clock was added along with the fine 14th-century bell, marked with the symbols of the 24 arts and craft guilds then operating in the city. The views, however, are worth the climb. ⊠ *Corso Cavour at Via del Duomo* 🕾 *0763/344567* 🖾*€2.80* ⊙ *May–Aug., daily 10–7; Mar., Apr., Sept., and Oct., daily 10–7; Nov.–Feb., daily 103 and 2:30–7.*

OFF THE BEATEN PATH

Crocefisso del Tufo. This 6th-century BC Etruscan necropolis, about 2 km (1 mi) down Viale Crispi, doesn't have the frescoes that other Etruscan tombs are famous for, and the relics that were buried within have long since been taken away (mostly to the Museo Claudio Faino). But the walk here is pleasant, and it can be interesting to see the type of site from which nearly all our knowledge of Etruscans comes. Names of the deceased are carved into the stone architraves above tomb chambers. ✛ *2 km (1 mi) from Piazzale Cahen, down Viale F. Crispi (SS71)* 🕾 *0763/343611* 🖾*€3* ⊙ *Daily 9–7.*

WHERE TO EAT

The streets around the Duomo are lined with all types of bars and restaurants where you can eat simple or elaborate food and try the wines by the glass.

$$$
UMBRIAN
Fodor's Choice
★

✕ **Il Giglio D'Oro.** A great view of the Duomo is coupled with superb food. Eggplant is transformed into an elegant custard with black truffles in the *sformatino di melenzane con vellutata al tartuffo nero.* Pastas, like *ombrichelli al pesto umbro,* are traditional, but perhaps with a new twist like fresh coriander leaves instead of the usual basil. Lamb roasted in a crust of bread is delicately seasoned with a tomato cream sauce. The wine cellar includes some rare vintages. ⊠ *Piazza Duomo 8* 🕾 *0763/341903* 🖃 *AE, MC, V* ⊙ *Closed Wed.*

$$$
UMBRIAN

✕ **Le Grotte del Funaro.** If you can't do the official hour tour of Underground Orvieto, dine here instead, inside tufa caves under central Orvieto, where the two windows have splendid views of the hilly countryside during the day. The traditional Umbrian food is average, but with good, simple grilled meats and vegetables and pizzas. Oddly, the food is outclassed by an extensive wine list, with top local and Italian labels and quite a few rare vintages. ⊠ *Via Ripa Serancia 41* 🕾 *0763/343276* ⌕ *Reservations essential* 🖃 *AE, DC, MC, V* ⊙ *Closed Mon. and 1 wk in July.*

$$
UMBRIAN
★

✕ **Trattoria La Grotta.** The owner has been in this location for more than 20 years, and locals are still fond of him. He has attracted a steady American clientele without losing his touch with homemade pasta, perhaps with a duck or wild-boar sauce. Roast lamb, veal, and pork are all good, and the desserts are homemade. Franco knows the local wines well, and has a carefully selected list, including some from smaller but excellent wineries, so ask about them. ⊠ *Via Luca Signorelli 5* ☎ *0763/341348* ⊟ *AE, DC, MC, V* ☺ *Closed Tues.*

WHERE TO STAY

Orvieto has a wide choice of lodging options, so if you haven't reserved a hotel in advance, take the time to wander around and choose your favorite.

$

⊞ **Gran Hotel Reale.** The best feature of this hotel is its location in the center of Orvieto, across a square that hosts a lively market. Facing the impressive Gothic–Romanesque Palazzo del Popolo, rooms are spacious and adequately furnished, with a traditional accent. **Pros:** good budget option; friendly staff. **Cons:** can be noisy; very basic rooms. ⊠ *Piazza del Popolo 27* ☎ *0763/341247* ⤴ *31 rooms* ♿ *In-room: a/c (some). In-hotel: bar* ⊟ *MC, V* ☺ *Closed Jan. and Feb.*⊺⊙⫽ *BP.*

$$$
★

⊞ **Hotel La Badia.** One of the region's best-known country hotels occupies a 12th-century monastery. Vaulted ceilings and exposed stone walls establish the rustic elegance in the guest rooms, which have beamed ceilings and polished terra-cotta floors covered with rugs. The rolling park around the hotel provides wonderful views of the valley. It's 4 km (2½ mi) south of Orvieto. **Pros:** elegant atmosphere; fine views. **Cons:** slightly overpriced; need a car to get around. ⊠ *Località La Badia, Orvieto Scalo* ☎ *0763/301959* ⊕ *www.labadiahotel.it* ⤴ *18 rooms, 9 suites* ♿ *In-room: a/c, refrigerator. In-hotel: restaurant, bar, tennis courts, pool, parking (free)* ⊟ *AE, MC, V* ☺ *Closed Jan. and Feb.* ⊺⊙⫽ *BP.*

$$

⊞ **Hotel Palazzo Piccolomini.** This hotel is often preferred by local wine makers and other professionals for its updated look with inviting lobby areas and a convenient location near the church of San Giovanni. From here it's a lovely short walk past Piazza della Repubblica to the Duomo. **Pros:** peaceful atmosphere; efficient staff, good location. **Cons:** unattractive building; slightly overpriced. ⊠ *Piazza Ranieri 36* ☎ *0763/341743* ⊕ *www.hotelpiccolomini.it* ⤴ *28 rooms, 3 suites* ♿ *In-room: a/c, refrigerator, Internet. In-hotel: bar, laundry service, parking (paid)* ⊟ *AE, MC* ⊺⊙⫽ *BP.*

WINE BARS

Orvieto has been known for white wine since its beginnings. There is evidence that the Etruscans grew grapes in the rich volcanic soil in the valley below and then fermented their wine in the cool caverns dug out of the tufa atop the hill. The Romans made special efforts to bring the local wine, which they blended with water and spices, back to Rome with them. Things had not changed by the early 16th century, when Signorelli was paid in part with wine for his work on the Cappella di San Brizio.

UMBRIA THROUGH THE AGES

The earliest inhabitants of Umbria, the Umbri, were thought by the Romans to be the most ancient inhabitants of Italy. Little is known about them; with the coming of Etruscan culture the tribe fled into the mountains in the eastern portion of the region. The Etruscans, who founded some of the great cities of Umbria, were in turn supplanted by the Romans. Unlike Tuscany and other regions of central Italy, Umbria had few powerful medieval families to exert control over the cities in the Middle Ages—its proximity to Rome ensured that it would always be more or less under papal domination.

In the center of the country, Umbria has for much of its history been a battlefield where armies from north and south clashed. Hannibal destroyed a Roman army on the shores of Lake Trasimeno, and the bloody course of the interminable Guelph-Ghibelline conflict of the Middle Ages was played out here. Dante considered Umbria the most violent place in Italy. Trophies of war still decorate the Palazzo dei Priori in Perugia, and the little town of Gubbio continues a warlike rivalry begun in the Middle Ages—every year it challenges the Tuscan town of Sansepolcro to a crossbow tournament. Today the bowmen shoot at targets, but neither side has forgotten that 500 years ago its ancestors shot at each other. In spite of—or perhaps because of—this bloodshed, Umbria has produced more than its share of Christian saints. The most famous is St. Francis, the decidedly pacifist saint whose life shaped the Church of his time. His great shrine at Assisi is visited by hundreds of thousands of pilgrims each year. St. Clare, his devoted follower, was Umbria-born, as were St. Benedict, St. Rita of Cascia, and the patron saint of lovers, St. Valentine.

Although Orvieto Classico is the best-known wine in the region, it is no longer one of Italy's best. However, it is pleasantly drinkable and light. You will also have the chance to taste different types of Orvieto, from the well-known dry Orvieto Classico to the less-commercialized *abboccato* (semisweet) and the intensely flavored, sweeter *muffato*.

Begin your tastings at these *enoteche* (wine bars), *cantine* (wineshops), and *vinerie* (wineries).

At **Cantina Foresi** (✉ *Piazza del Duomo 2* ☎ 0763/341611), a light lunch of cheese, salami, bread, and salad is hard to beat. Hundreds of bottles are stored in the cool earth of the cellar, which was built in 1290 and is worthy of a visit. The few outdoor tables are a great place for a light snack while sipping.

At **La Bottega del Buon Vino** (✉ *Via della Cava 26* ☎ 0763/342373), a window in the floor looks down into the caves. It's closed Monday.

Many area wine producers create excellent variations of the standard Orvieto Classico wine. Close to town and highly recommended is **Azienda Agricola Palazzone** (✉ *Località Rocca Ripesana* ✛ *5 km [3 mi] from Orvieto* ☎ 0763/344921), where you can sample Muffa Nobile—a warm, golden, sweet wine with a rich taste caused by the fungus that is cultivated—Grechetto, and Orvieto Classico Superior that has been

Continued on page 146

EATING AND DRINKING WELL IN UMBRIA

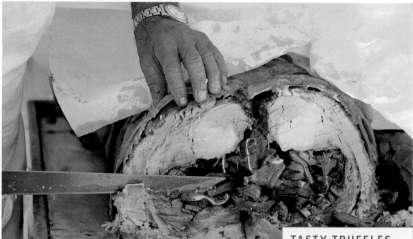

Central Italy is mountainous, and its food is hearty and straightforward, with a stick-to-the-ribs quality that sees hardworking farmers and artisans through a long day's work and helps them make the steep climb home at night.

In restaurants here, as in much of Italy, you're rewarded for seeking out the local cuisines, and you'll often find better, and cheaper, food if you're willing to stray a few hundred yards from the main sights. Spoleto is noted for its good food and service, probably a result of high expectations from the international arts crowd. For gourmets, however, it's hard to beat Spello, which has both excellent restaurants and first-rate wine merchants.

A rule of thumb for eating well throughout Umbria is to order what's in season; the trick is to stroll through local markets to see what's for sale. A number of restaurants in the region offer *degustazione* (tasting) menus, which give you a chance to try different local specialties without breaking the bank.

TASTY TRUFFLES

More truffles are found in Umbria than anywhere else in Italy. Spoleto and Norcia are prime territory for the *tartufo nero* (reddish-black interior and fine white veins), pictured below right, prized for its extravagant flavor and intense aroma.

The mild summer truffle, *scorzone estivo* (black outside and beige inside), is in season from May through December. The *scorzone autunnale* (burnt brown color and visible veins inside) is found from October through December. Truffles can be shaved into omelets or over pasta, pounded into sauces, or chopped and mixed with oil.

OLIVE OIL

Nearly everywhere you look in Umbria, olive trees grace the hillsides. The soil of the Apennines allows the olives to ripen slowly, guaranteeing low acidity, a cardinal virtue of fine oil. Look for restaurants that proudly display their own oil, often a sign that they care about their food.

Umbria's finest oil is found in Trevi, where the local product is intensely green and fruity. You can sample it in the town's wine bars, which often do double duty, offering olive-oil tastings.

PORK PRODUCTS

Much of traditional Umbrian cuisine revolves around pork. It can be cooked in wood-fire stoves, sometimes basted with a rich sauce made from innards and red wine. The roasted pork known as *porchetta*, pictured at left, is grilled on a spit and flavored with fennel and herbs, leaving a crisp outer sheen.

The art of pork processing has been handed down through generations in Norcia, so much so that charcuterie producers throughout Italy are often known as *norcini*. Don't miss *prosciutto di Norcia*, which is aged for two years.

LENTILS AND SOUPS

The town of Castelluccio di Norcia is particularly known for its lentils and its *farro* (an ancient grain used by the Romans, similar to wheat), and a variety

of beans used in soups. Throughout Umbria, look for *imbrecciata*, a soup of beans and grain, delicately flavored with local herbs. Other ingredients that find their way into thick Umbrian soups are wild beet, sorrel, mushrooms, spelt, chickpeas, and the elusive, fragrant saffron, grown in nearby Cascia.

WINE

Sagrantino grapes are the star in Umbria's most notable red wines. For centuries they've been used in Sagrantino *passito*, a semisweet wine made by leaving the grapes to dry for a period after picking in order to intensify their sugar content. In recent decades, the *secco* (dry) Sagrantino has occupied the front stage. Both passito and secco have a deep red-ruby color, with a full body and rich flavor.

In the past few years the phenomenon of the *enoteca* (wineshop and wine bar) has taken off, making it easier to arrange wine tastings. Many also let you sample different olive oils on toasted bread, known as *bruschetta*. Some wine information centers, such as La Strada del Sagrantino in the town of Montefalco, will help set up appointments for tastings.

aged longer than most and has a richer taste than the mass-produced Orvietos. This vintner has also won awards for his Armaleo, a rich ruby red.

Castello della Sala (✛ *20 km [12 mi] north of Orvieto, Località Sala* ☎ *0763/86051*), owned by the Antinori group, produces white wines of high quality. Housed in a 14th-century castle, this is an especially interesting place to try out some of Orvieto's new-style wines—Cervaro della Sala, Grechetto, and chardonnay—all aged in oak barrels.

SHOPPING

Orvieto has a few shops selling Orvietan-style pottery, bright-white vessels with hand-painted motifs. **La Torreta** (✉ *Corso Cavour 283* ☎ *0763/340248*) has a kiln right in the shop, and will custom paint something for you on the spot. For copies of ancient Etruscan and Greek ceramics, try **L'Arte del Vasaio** (✉ *Via Pedota 3* ☎ *0763/342022*).

Established in 1907 to provide work for impoverished women, the tradition of lace-making, or *ars wetana*, has flourished in Orvieto. Using designs inspired by the reliefs on the facade of the Duomo, the patterns of Orvietan lace are unique and distinctive.

Specializing in *merletto* (lace) products, **Duranti** (✉ *Corso Cavour 107* ☎ *0763/342124*) maintains the high standards set by one of the sustainers of the tradition during the last century, Eleonora Duranti.

Orvieto is a center for woodworking, particularly fine inlays and veneers. Corso Cavour is lined with a number of artisan woodworking shops, the best known being the **Michelangeli Family Studio** (✉ *Via Michelangeli 3, at Corso Cavour* ☎ *0763/342660*). The imaginatively designed objects range in size from a giant *armadio* (wardrobe) to a simple wooden spoon. If all those Michelangeli flourishes don't quite suit you, head over to **Patris** (✉ *Via dei Magioni, 11* ☎ *0763/341936*), who has a shop full of imaginative items that he has made, from crafts for children to trompe-l'oeil intarsia windows in wood.

SPOLETO

GETTING HERE

Spoleto is an hour's drive from Perugia. From the E45 highway, take the exit toward Assisi and Foligno, then merge onto the SS75 until you reach the Foligno Est exit. Merge onto the SS3, which leads to Spoleto. There are regular trains on the Perugia-Foligno line. From the train station it's a 15-minute uphill walk to the center, so you'll probably want to take a taxi.

VISITOR INFORMATION

Spoleto tourism office (✉ *Piazza della Libertà 7* ☎ *0743/238921* ⊕ *www. spoleto.umbria2000.it*).

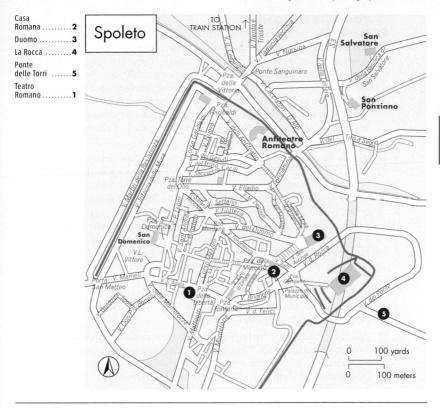

EXPLORING SPOLETO

The walled city is set on a slanting hillside, with the most interesting sections clustered toward the upper portion. Parking options inside the walls include Piazza Campello (just below the Rocca) on the southeast end, Via del Trivio to the north, and Piazza San Domenico on the west end. You can also park at Piazza della Vittoria farther north, just outside the walls. There are also several well-marked lots near the train station. If you arrive by train, you can walk 1 km (½ mi) from the station to the entrance to the lower town. Regular bus connections are every 15 to 30 minutes. You can also use the *trenino,* as locals call the shuttle service, from the train station to Piazza della Libertà, near the upper part of the old town, where you'll find the tourist office.

Like most other towns with narrow, winding streets, Spoleto is best explored on foot. Bear in mind that much of the city is on a steep slope, so there are lots of stairs and steep inclines. The well-worn stones can be slippery even when dry; wear rubber-sole shoes for good traction. Several pedestrian walkways cut across Corso Mazzini, which zigzags up the hill. A €12 combination ticket purchased at the tourist office allows you entry to all the town's museums and galleries.

TOP ATTRACTIONS

❸ **Duomo.** The cathedral's 12th-century Romanesque facade received a
★ Renaissance face-lift with the addition of a loggia in a rosy pink stone.
A stunning contrast in styles, the Duomo is one of the finest cathedrals
in the region. The eight rose windows are especially dazzling in the late
afternoon sun. Look under the largest rose window and you see two
figures that appear to be holding up the structure; in the corners of
the square surrounding the window, the four Evangelists are sculpted.
Inside, the original tile floor dates from an earlier church that was
destroyed by Frederick I (circa 1123–90).

Above the church's entrance is Bernini's bust of Pope Urban VIII (1568–
1644), who had the rest of the church redecorated in 17th-century
baroque; fortunately he didn't touch the 15th-century frescoes painted
in the apse by Fra Filippo Lippi (circa 1406–69) between 1466 and
1469. These immaculately restored masterpieces—the *Annunciation,
Nativity,* and *Dormition*—tell the story of the life of the Virgin. The
Coronation of the Virgin, adorning the half dome, is the literal and
figurative high point. Portraits of Lippi and his assistants are on the
right side of the central panel. The Florentine artist priest WHOSE COLORS
EXPRESSED GOD'S VOICE (the words inscribed on his tomb) died shortly
after completing the work. His tomb, which you can see in the right
transept (note the artist's brushes and tools), was designed by his son,
Filippino Lippi (circa 1457–1504).

Another fresco cycle, including work by Pinturicchio, is in the Cappella
Eroli, off the right aisle. Note the grotesques in the ornamentation, then
very much in vogue with the rediscovery of ancient Roman paintings.
The bounty of Umbria is displayed in vivid colors in the abundance of
leaves, fruits, and vegetables that adorn the center seams of the cross
vault. In the left nave, not far from the entrance, is the well-restored
12th-century crucifix by Alberto Sozio, the earliest known example of
this kind of work, with a painting on parchment attached to a wood
cross. To the right of the presbytery is the Cappella della Santissima
Icona (Chapel of the Most Holy Icon), which contains a small Byzantine
painting of a Madonna given to the town by Frederick Barbarossa as a
peace offering in 1185, following his destruction of the cathedral and
town three decades earlier. ⊠ *Piazza del Duomo* ☎ *0743/44307* ☉ *Mar.–
Oct., daily 8:30–12:30 and 3:30–6; Nov.–Feb., daily 8:30–12:20 and
3:30–6.*

❺ **Ponte delle Torri** *(Bridge of the Towers).* Standing massive and graceful
★ through the deep gorge that separates Spoleto from Monteluco, this
14th-century bridge is one of Umbria's most photographed monuments,
and justifiably so. Built over the foundations of a Roman-era aqueduct,
it soars 262 feet above the forested gorge—higher than the dome of St.
Peter's in Rome. Sweeping views over the valley and a pleasant sense of
vertigo make a walk across the bridge a must, particularly on a starry
night. ⊠ *Via del Ponte.*

A fresco by Fra Filippo Lippi in Spoleto's Duomo

WORTH NOTING

2 **Casa Romana.** Spoleto became a Roman colony in the 3rd century BC, but the best excavated remains date from the 1st century AD. Excavated in the late 9th century, the Casa Romana was not a typical Roman residence. According to an inscription, it belonged to Vespasia Polla, the mother of Emperor Vespasian (one of the builders of the Colosseum and perhaps better known by the Romans for taxing them to install public toilets, later called "vespasians"). The rooms, arranged around a large central atrium built over an *impluvium* (rain cistern), are decorated with black-and-white geometric mosaics. ⊠ *Palazzo del Municipio, Via Visiale 9* ☎ *0743/224656* ⌲ *€2.50, €6 combination ticket (includes Pinacoteca Comunale and Galleria d'Arte Moderna)* ⊙ *Oct. 15–March 15, daily 10–5; March 16–Oct. 14, daily 10–7.*

4 **La Rocca.** Built in the mid-14th century for Cardinal Egidio Albornoz, this massive fortress served as a seat for the local pontifical governors, a tangible sign of the restoration of the Church's power in the area when the pope was ruling from Avignon. Several popes spent time here, and one of them, Alexander VI, in 1499 sent his capable teenage daughter Lucrezia Borgia (1480–1519) to serve as governor for three months. The Gubbio-born architect Gattapone (14th century) used the ruins of a Roman acropolis as a foundation and took materials from many Roman-era sites, including the Teatro Romano. La Rocca's plan is long and rectangular, with six towers and two grand courtyards, an upper loggia, and inside some grand reception rooms. In the largest tower, Torre Maestà, you can visit an apartment with some interesting frescoes. A small shuttle bus gives you that last boost up the hill from the ticket booth to the entrance of the fortress. If you phone in advance, you may be able to secure an English-speaking guide. ⊠ *Via del Ponte* ☎ *0743/223055* ⚟ *€7.50* ⊘ *Mid-Mar.–early June and mid-Sept.–Oct., weekdays 10–noon and 3–6:45, weekends 10–7; early June–mid-Sept., daily 10–7; Nov.–mid-Mar., weekdays 10–noon and 3–5, weekends 10–5.*

① Teatro Romano. The Romans who had colonized the city in 241 BC constructed this small theater in the 1st century AD; for centuries afterward it was used as a quarry for building materials. The most intact portion is the hallway that passes under the *cavea* (stands). The rest was heavily restored in the early 1950s and serves as a venue for Spoleto's Festival dei Due Mondi. The theater was the site of a gruesome episode in Spoleto's history: during the medieval struggle between Guelph (papal) and Ghibelline (imperial) forces, Spoleto took the side of the Holy Roman Emperor. Afterward, 400 Guelph supporters were massacred in the theater, their bodies burned in an enormous pyre. In the end, the Guelphs were triumphant, and Spoleto was incorporated into the states of the Church in 1354. Through a door in the west portico of the adjoining building is the **Museo Archeologico,** with assorted artifacts found in excavations primarily around Spoleto and Norcia. The collection contains Bronze Age and Iron Age artifacts from Umbrian and pre-Roman eras. Another section contains black-glaze vases from the Hellenistic period excavated from the necropolis of Saint Scolastica in Norcia. The highlight is the stone tablet inscribed on both sides with the Lex Spoletina (Spoleto Law). Dating from 315 BC, this legal document prohibited the desecration of the woods on the slopes of nearby Monteluco. ⊠ *Piazza della Libertà* ☎ *0743/223277* ⚟ *€4* ⊘ *Daily 8:30–7:30.*

WHERE TO EAT

$$ ✕ **Apollinare.** Low wooden ceilings and flickering candlelight make this
UMBRIAN monastery from the 10th and 11th centuries Spoleto's most romantic spot. The kitchen serves sophisticated, innovative variations on local dishes. Sauces of cherry tomatoes, mint, and a touch of red pepper, or of porcini mushrooms, top the long, slender strangozzi. The *caramella* (light puff-pastry cylinders filled with local cheese and served with a creamy Parmesan sauce) is popular. In warm weather you can dine under a canopy on the piazza across from the archaeological museum. ⊠ *Via Sant'Agata 14* ☎ *0743/223256* ▭ *AE, D, MC, V* ⊘ *Closed Tues.*

$$ ✕ **Il Tartufo.** As the name indicates, dishes prepared with truffles are the
UMBRIAN specialty here—don't miss the *risotto al tartufo*. But there are also dishes not perfumed with this expensive delicacy. Incorporating the ruins of a Roman villa, the restaurant's decor is rustic on the ground floor and more modern upstairs. In summer, tables appear outdoors and the traditional fare is spiced up to appeal to the cosmopolitan crowd attending

Hiking the Umbrian Hills

Magnificent scenery makes the heart of Italy excellent walking, hiking, and mountaineering country. In Umbria, the area around Spoleto is particularly good; several pleasant, easy, and well-signed trails begin at the far end of the Ponte alle Torri bridge over Monteluco. From Cannara an easy half-hour walk leads to the fields of Pian d'Arca, the site of Saint Francis's sermon to the birds. For slightly more arduous walks, you can follow the saint's path, uphill from Assisi to the Eremo delle Carceri, and then continue along the trails that crisscross Monte Subasio. At 4,250 feet, the Subasio's treeless summit affords views of Assisi, Perugia, far-off Gubbio, and the distant mountain ranges of Abruzzo.

For even more challenging hiking, the northern reaches of the Valnerina are exceptional; the mountains around Norcia should not be missed. Throughout Umbria and the Marches, you'll find that most recognized walking and hiking trails are marked with the distinctive red-and-white blazes of the Club Alpino Italiano. Tourist offices are a good source for walking and climbing itineraries to suit all ages and levels of ability, while bookstores, *tabacchi* (tobacconists), and *edicole* (newsstands) often have maps and hiking guides that detail the best routes in their area. Depending on the length and location of your walk, it can be important that you have comfortable walking shoes or boots, appropriate attire, and plenty of water to drink.

(or performing in) the Festival dei Due Mondi. ⊠ *Piazza Garibaldi 24* ☎ *0743/40236* ⌖ *Reservations essential* ▭ *AE, DC, MC, V* ☾ *Closed Mon. and last 2 wks in July. No dinner Sun.*

$ ✕ **Osteria del Trivio.** At this friendly trattoria everything is made on the
UMBRIAN   premises. The menu changes daily, depending on what's in season. Dishes might include stuffed artichokes, pasta with local mushrooms, or chicken with artichokes. For dessert, try the homemade biscotti, made for dunking in sweet wine. There is a printed menu, but the owner can explain the dishes in a number of languages. A complete meal from appetizer to dessert with house wine is likely to cost no more than €25. ⊠ *Via del Trivio 16* ☎ *0743/44349* ▭ *AE, DC, MC, V* ☾ *Closed Tues.*

$$ ✕ **Ristorante Panciolle.** In the heart of Spoleto's medieval quarter, this
UMBRIAN   restaurant has one of the most appealing settings you could wish for: a
★   small garden filled with lemon trees. Dishes change throughout the year, and may include pastas served with asparagus or mushrooms, as well as grilled meats. More expensive dishes prepared with fresh truffles are also available in season. ⊠ *Via Duomo 3/5* ☎ *0743/221241* ⌖ *Reservations essential* ▭ *DC, MC, V* ☾ *Closed Wed.*

WHERE TO STAY

$$$ 🔛 **Cavaliere Palace Hotel.** An arched passageway off one of the city's
★   busy shopping streets leads to an elegant world through a quiet courtyard. Built in the 17th century for an influential cardinal, the rooms, particularly those on the second floor, retain their sumptuous frescoed

ceilings; care has been taken to retain a sense of Old World comfort throughout. In warm weather enjoy breakfast on the terrace or in the peaceful garden at the back of the hotel. **Pros:** quiet elegance; central position. **Cons:** finding parking can be a problem; crowded in summer. ⊠ *Corso Garibaldi 49* ☏ *0743/220350* ⊕ *www.hotelcavaliere.eu* ⟿ *29 rooms, 2 suites* ⚭ *In-room: a/c, safe, refrigerator. In-hotel: restaurant, bar* ☰ *AE, DC, MC, V* ⦿ *BP.*

$ ⊡ **Hotel Clitunno.** A renovated 18th-century building in the center of town houses this pleasant hotel. Cozy guest rooms and intimate public rooms, some with timbered ceilings, have the sense of a traditional Umbrian home—albeit one with a good restaurant. The staff is glad to light the fireplace in Room 212 in advance of winter arrivals. Upper-floor rooms look over Spoleto's rooftops. The "older style" rooms, which have wood ceilings, iron beds, and nicer textiles, are more attractive. **Pros:** friendly staff; good restaurant. **Cons:** difficult to find a parking space; some small rooms. ⊠ *Piazza Sordini 6* ☏ *0743/223340* ⊕ *www. hotelclitunno.com* ⟿ *45 rooms* ⚭ *In-room: a/c. hotel: restaurant, bar-* ☰ *AE, DC, MC, V* ⦿ *BP.*

$$ ⊡ **Hotel San Luca.** The elegant San Luca is one of Spoleto's finest hotels,
Fodor'sChoice   thanks to its commendable attention to detail, such as the hand-painted
★   friezes that decorate the walls of the spacious guest rooms and the generous selection of up-to-date magazines for your reading pleasure. The service is very gracious, and the prices are surprisingly modest. Enjoy an ample breakfast buffet, including homemade cakes, served in a cheerful room facing the central courtyard. You can sip afternoon tea in oversize armchairs by the fireplace, or take a walk in the hotel's sweet-smelling rose garden. The staff will give you route maps or help you book a guided bicycle tour. **Pros:** very helpful staff; peaceful location. **Cons:** outside the town center; a long walk to the main sights. ⊠ *Via Interna delle Mura 19* ☏ *0743/223399* ⊕ *www.hotelsanluca. com* ⟿ *33 rooms, 2 suites* ⚭ *In-room: a/c, safe, refrigerator, Internet. In-hotel: restaurant, laundry service, Internet terminal, parking (paid)* ☰ *AE, DC, MC, V* ⦿ *BP.*

THE ARTS

Fodor'sChoice   In 1958, composer Gian Carlo Menotti chose Spoleto for the first
★   **Festival dei Due Mondi** (*Festival of Two Worlds* ⊠ *Piazza Duomo 8* ☏ *0743/220320 or 800/565600* ⊕ *www.spoletofestival.it*), a gathering of artists, performers, and musicians intended to bring together the "new" and "old" worlds of America and Europe. (A corresponding festival in South Carolina is no longer connected to this festival.) The annual event, held in late June and early July, is one of the most important cultural happenings in Europe, attracting big names in all branches of the arts, particularly music, opera, and theater.

ASSISI

The small town of Assisi is one of the Christian world's most important pilgrimage sites and home of the Basilica di San Francesco—built to honor Saint Francis (1182–1226) and erected in swift order after his death. The peace and serenity of the town is a welcome respite after the hustle and bustle of some of Italy's major cities.

Like most other towns in the region, Assisi began as an Umbri settlement in the 7th century BC and was conquered by the Romans 400 years later. The town was Christianized by Saint Rufino, its patron saint, in the 3rd century, but it is the spirit of Saint Francis, a patron saint of Italy and founder of the Franciscan monastic order, that is felt throughout its narrow medieval streets. The famous 13th-century basilica was decorated by the greatest artists of the period.

GETTING HERE

Assisi lies on the Terontola–Foligno rail line, with almost hourly connections to Perugia and direct trains to Rome and Florence several times a day. The Stazione Centrale is 4 km (2½ mi) from town, with a bus service about every half hour. Assisi is easily reached from the A1 Motorway (Rome–Florence) and the S75b highway. The walled town is closed to traffic, so cars must be left in the parking lots at Porta San Pietro, near Porta Nuova, or beneath Piazza Matteotti. Pay your parking fee at the *cassa* (ticket booth) before you return to your car to get a ticket to insert in the machine that will allow you to exit. It's a short but sometimes steep walk into the center of town; frequent minibuses (buy tickets from a newsstand or tobacco shop near where you park your car) make the rounds for weary pilgrims.

VISITOR INFORMATION

Assisi tourism office (✉ *Piazza del Commune 22* ☎ *075/812534* ⊕ *www.assisi. umbria2000.it*).

EXPLORING ASSISI

Assisi is pristinely medieval in architecture and appearance, owing in large part to relative neglect from the 16th century until 1926, when the celebration of the 700th anniversary of Saint Francis's death brought more than 2 million visitors. Since then, pilgrims have flocked here in droves, and today several million arrive each year to pay homage. But not even the constant flood of visitors to this town of just 3,000 residents can spoil the singular beauty of this significant religious center, the home of some of the Western tradition's most important works of art. The hill on which Assisi sits rises dramatically from the flat plain, and the town is dominated by a medieval castle at the very top.

Even though Assisi can become besieged with sightseers disgorged by tour buses, who clamor to visit the famous basilica, it's difficult not to be charmed by the tranquility of the town and its medieval architecture. Once you've seen the basilica, stroll through the town's narrow winding streets to see beautiful vistas of the nearby hills and valleys peeking through openings between the buildings.

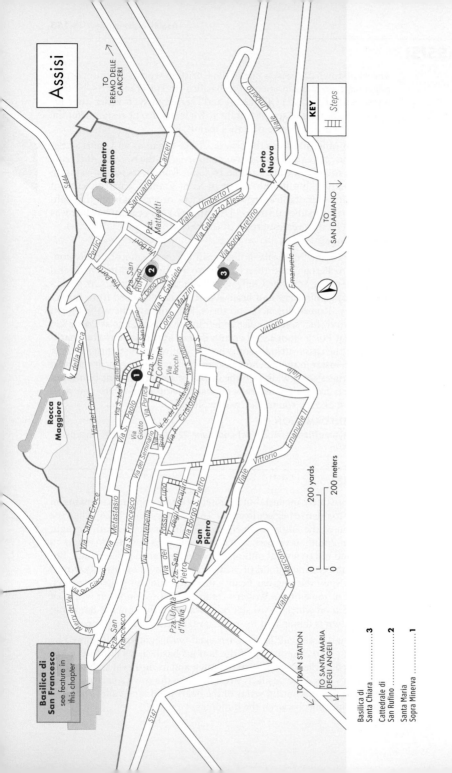

Assisi

Basilica di San Francesco
see feature in this chapter

Rocca Maggiore

Anfiteatro Romano

TO EREMO DELLE CARCERI →

Porto Nuova

TO SAN DAMIANO →

San Pietro

KEY

Steps

TO TRAIN STATION

TO SANTA MARIA DEGLI ANGELI

0   200 yards
0   200 meters

Via Metri del Val
Via S. Giacomo
Via San Francesco
Pza. San Francesco
Via Santa Croce
Via Metastasio
Via S. Francesco
Via Fontebella
Via del Fosso
Pza.-San Pietro
Via degli Anciaiari
Via Borgo S. Pietro
Pza. Unità d'Italia
Viale G. Marconi
Viale Vittorio Emanuele II
Via Metri del Val
Via del Corte
Via S. Maria delle Rose
Via S. Paolo
Via Giotto
Via del Seminario
Pza. del Comune
Via Portica
Vic. B. del Comune
Via del Comune
Via A. Cristofani
Via Rocchi
Via S. Antonio
Via B. di Perlici
Via della Rocca
Via della Rocca
Via Portica
Via S. Rufino
Via di San Rufino
Pza. San Rufino
Via Dono Doni
Via Dono Doni
Pza. Mattigotti
Via Dovi
V. Santuario d. Carceri
Via S. Gabriele
Corso Mazzini
Via del Paese
Viale Umberto I
Via Galeazzo Alessi
Via Borgo Aretino
Viale Vittorio Emanuele II
Viale Umberto I
S444
S444

TOP ATTRACTIONS

3 Basilica di Santa Chiara. The lovely, wide piazza in front of this church is reason enough to visit. The red-and-white-striped facade of the church frames the piazza's panoramic view over the Umbrian plains. Santa Chiara is dedicated to Saint Clare, one of the earliest and most fervent of Saint Francis's followers and the founder of the order of the Poor Ladies—or Poor Clares—which was based on the Franciscan monastic order. The church contains Clare's body, and in the **Cappella del Crocifisso** (on the right) is the cross that spoke to Saint Francis. A heavily veiled nun of the Poor Clares order is usually stationed before the cross in adoration of the image. ⊠ *Piazza Santa Chiara* ☎ *075/812282* ⊘ *Nov.–mid-Mar., daily 6:30–noon and 2–6; mid-Mar.–Oct., daily 6:30–noon and 2–7.*

WORD OF MOUTH

"Assisi is surrounded by gorgeous walks. The side road from the basilica around to the Rocca is absolutely wonderful. The same can be said for a walk out to the Eremo delle Carceri, and further into the woods past the Eremo."

—tuscanlifeedit

3

2 Cattedrale di San Rufino. Saint Francis and Saint Clare were among those baptized in Assisi's Cattedrale, which was the principal church in town until the 12th century. The baptismal font has since been redecorated, but it is possible to see the crypt of Saint Rufino, the bishop who brought Christianity to Assisi and was martyred on August 11, 238 (or 236 by some accounts). Admission to the crypt includes the small **Museo Capitolare,** with its detached frescoes and artifacts. ⊠ *Piazza San Rufino* ☎ *075/812283* ⊕ *www.sistemamuseo.it* ⌨ *Crypt and Museo Capitolare €2.50* ⊘ *Cattedrale: daily 7–noon and 2–6; crypt and Museo Capitolare: mid-Mar.–mid-Oct., daily 10–1 and 3–6; mid-Oct.–mid-Mar., daily 10–1 and 2:30–5:30.*

WORTH NOTING

1 Santa Maria Sopra Minerva. Dating from the time of the Emperor Augustus (27 BC–AD 14), this structure was originally dedicated to the Roman goddess of wisdom, in later times used as a monastery and prison before being converted into a church in the 16th century. The expectations raised by the perfect classical facade are not met by the interior, which was subjected to a thorough baroque transformation in the 17th century. ⊠ *Piazza del Comune* ☎ *075/812268* ⊘ *Daily 8–7.*

OFF THE BEATEN PATH

Eremo delle Carceri. About 4 km (2½ mi) east of Assisi is a monastery set in a dense wood against Monte Subasio. The "Hermitage of Prisons" was the place where Saint Francis and his followers went to "imprison" themselves in prayer. The only site in Assisi that remains essentially unchanged since Saint Francis's time, the church and monastery are the kinds of tranquil places that Saint Francis would have appreciated. The walk out from town is very pleasant, and many trails lead from here across the wooded hillside of Monte Subasio (now a protected forest), with beautiful vistas across the Umbrian countryside. True to their Franciscan heritage, the friars here are entirely dependent on alms from visitors. ⊠ *Via Santuario delle Carceri* ♦ *4 km (2½ mi) east of Assisi*

☎ *075/812301* ⊕ *www.eremocarceri.it* ✉ *Donations accepted* ☉ *Nov.–Mar., daily 6:30–6; Apr.–Oct., daily 6:30* AM*–7:15* PM.

WHERE TO EAT

Assisi is not a late-night town, so don't plan on any midnight snacks. What you can count on is the ubiquitous *strangozzi* (thick spaghetti), as well as the local specialty *piccione all'assisana* (roasted pigeon with olives and liver). The locals eat *torta al testo* (a dense flatbread, often stuffed with vegetables or cheese) with their meals.

$ ✗ **Buca di San Francesco.** In summer, dine in a cool green garden; in
UMBRIAN winter, under the low brick arches of the restaurant's cozy cellars. The unique settings and the first-rate fare make this central restaurant Assisi's busiest. Try homemade spaghetti *alla buca,* served with a roasted mushroom sauce. ⊠ *Via Eugenio Brizi 1* ☎ *075/812204* ☰ *AE, DC, MC, V* ☉ *Closed Mon. and July 20–30.*

$ ✗ **La Pallotta.** At this homey, family-run trattoria with a crackling fire-
UMBRIAN place and stone walls, the women do the cooking and the men serve the
Fodor's Choice food. Try the strangozzi *alla pallotta* (with a pesto of olives and mush-
★ rooms). Connected to the restaurant is an inn whose eight rooms have firm beds and some views across the rooftops of town. Hotel guests get a discount if they dine here. ⊠ *Vicolo della Volta Pinta* ☎ *075/812649* ☰ *AE, DC, MC, V* ☉ *Closed Tues. and 2 wks in Jan. or Feb.*

$$ ✗ **Osteria Piazzetta dell'Erba.** Hip service and sophisticated presentations
UMBRIAN attract locals to this trattoria. The owners carefully select wine at local
★ vineyards, buy it in bulk, and then bottle it themselves, resulting in high quality and reasonable prices. Choose from the wide selection of appetizers, including smoked goose breast, and from four or five types of pasta, plus various salads and a good selection of torta al testo fillings. For dessert, try the homemade biscuits, which you dunk in sweet wine. Outdoor seating is available. ⊠ *Via San Gabriele dell'Addolorata 15b* ☎ *075/815352* ☰ *AE, V* ☉ *Closed Mon. and a few wks in Jan. or Feb.*

$$$ ✗ **San Francesco.** An excellent view of the Basilica di San Francesco is
UMBRIAN the primary reason to come here. Locals consider this the best restaurant in town, where creative Umbrian dishes are made with aromatic locally grown herbs. The seasonal menu might include gnocchi topped with a sauce of wild herbs and *oca stufata di finocchio selvaggio* (goose stuffed with wild fennel). Appetizers and desserts are especially good. ⊠ *Via di San Francesco 52* ☎ *075/812329* ☰ *AE, DC, MC, V* ☉ *Closed Wed. and July 15–30.*

WHERE TO STAY

Advance reservations are essential at Assisi's hotels between Easter and October and over Christmas. Latecomers are often forced to stay in the modern town of Santa Maria degli Angeli, 8 km (5 mi) away. As a last-minute option, you can always inquire at restaurants to see if they are renting out rooms.

Until the early 1980s, pilgrim hostels outnumbered ordinary hotels in Assisi, and they present an intriguing and economical alternative

Continued on page 163

ASSISI'S BASILICA DI SAN FRANCESCO

The legacy of St. Francis, founder of the Franciscan monastic order, pervades Assisi. Each year the town hosts several million pilgrims, but the steady flow of visitors does nothing to diminish the singular beauty of one of Italy's most important religious centers. The pilgrims' ultimate destination is the massive Basilica di San Francesco, which sits halfway up Assisi's hill, supported by graceful arches.

The basilica is not one church but two. The Romanesque **Lower Church** came first; construction began in 1228, just two years after St. Francis's death, and was completed within a few years. The low ceilings and candlelit interior make an appropriately solemn setting for St. Francis's tomb, found in the crypt below the main altar. The Gothic **Upper Church,** built only half a century later, sits on top of the lower one, and is strikingly different, with soaring arches and tall stained-glass windows (the first in Italy). Inside, both churches are covered floor to ceiling with some of Europe's finest frescoes: the Lower Church is dim and full of candlelit shadows, and the Upper Church is bright and airy.

VISITING THE BASILICA

THE LOWER CHURCH

The most evocative way to experience the basilica is to begin with the dark Lower Church. As you enter, give your eyes a moment to adjust. Keep in mind that the artists at work here were conscious of the shadowy environment—they knew this was how their frescoes would be seen.

In the first chapel to the left, a superb fresco cycle by Simone Martini depicts scenes from the life of St. Martin. As you approach the main altar, the vaulting above you is decorated with the *Three Virtues of St. Francis* (poverty, chastity, and obedience) and *St. Francis's Triumph*, frescoes attributed to Giotto's followers. In the transept to your left, Pietro Lorenzetti's *Madonna and Child with St. Francis and St. John* sparkles when the sun hits it. Notice Mary's thumb; legend has it Jesus is asking which saint to bless, and Mary is pointing to Francis. Across the way in the right transept, Cimabue's *Madonna Enthroned Among Angels and St. Francis* is a famous portrait of the saint. Surrounding the portrait are painted scenes from the childhood of Christ, done by the assistants of Giotto.

Nearby is a painting of the crucifixion attributed to Giotto himself.

You reach the crypt via stairs midway along the nave—on the crypt's altar, a stone coffin holds the saint's body. Steps up from the transepts lead to the cloister, where there's a gift shop, and the treasury, which contains holy objects.

THE UPPER CHURCH

The St. Francis fresco cycle is the highlight of the Upper Church. (See facing page.) Also worth special note is the 16th-century choir, with its remarkably delicate inlaid wood. When a 1997 earthquake rocked the basilica, the St. Francis cycle sustained little damage, but portions of the ceiling above the entrance and altar collapsed, reducing their frescoes (attributed to Cimabue and Giotto) to rubble. The painstaking restoration is ongoing. ⚠ The dress code is strictly enforced—no bare shoulders or bare knees. Piazza di San Francesco, 075/819001, Lower Church Easter–Oct., Mon.–Sat. 6 AM–6:45 PM, Sun. 6:30 AM–7:15 PM; Nov.–Easter, daily 6:30–6. Upper Church Easter–Oct., Mon.–Sat. 8:30–6:45, Sun. 8:30–7:15; Nov.–Easter, daily 8:30–6.

FRANCIS, ITALY'S PATRON SAINT

PREGANDO ASPETTERO CHE TORNI

St. Francis was born in Assisi in 1181, the son of a noblewoman and a well-to-do merchant. His troubled youth included a year in prison. He planned a military career, but after a long illness Francis heard the voice of God, renounced his father's wealth, and began a life of austerity. His mystical embrace of poverty, asceticism, and the beauty of man and nature struck a responsive chord in the medieval mind; he quickly attracted a vast number of followers. Francis was the first saint to receive the stigmata (wounds in his hands, feet, and side corresponding to those of Christ on the cross). He died on October 4, 1226, in the Porziuncola, the secluded chapel in the woods where he had first preached the virtue of poverty to his disciples. St. Francis was declared patron saint of Italy in 1939, and today the Franciscans make up the largest of the Catholic orders.

THE UPPER CHURCH'S ST. FRANCIS FRESCO CYCLE

The 28 frescoes in the Upper Church depicting the life of St. Francis are the most admired works in the entire basilica. They're also the subject of one of art history's biggest controversies. For centuries they thought to be by Giotto (1267-1337), the great early Renaissance innovator, but inconsistencies in style, both within this series and in comparison to later Giotto works, have thrown their origin into question. Some scholars now say Giotto was the brains behind the cycle, but that assistants helped with the execution; others claim he couldn't have been involved at all.

Two things are certain. First, the style is revolutionary—which argues for Giotto's in-

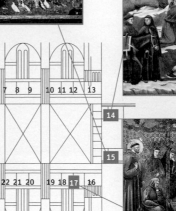

volvement. The tangible weight of the figures, the emotion they show, and the use of perspective all look familiar to modern eyes, but in the art of the time there was nothing like it. Second, these images have played a major part in shaping how the world sees St. Francis. In that respect, who painted them hardly matters.

Starting in the transept, the frescoes circle the church, showing events in the saint's life (and afterlife). Some of the best are grouped near the church's entrance—look for the nativity at Greccio, the miracle of the spring, the death of the knight at Celano, and, most famously, the sermon to the birds.

3

IN FOCUS ASSISI'S BASILICA DI SAN FRANCISCO

```
  1 2 3   4 5 6   7 8 9   10 11 12  13
                                          14
                                          15
  28 27 26  25 24  22 21 20  19 18 17  16
```

The St. Francis fresco cycle

1. Homage of a simple man	10. Chasing devils from Arezzo	20. Death of St. Francis
2. Giving cloak to a poor man	11. Before the sultan	21. Apparition before Bishop
3. Dream of the palace	12. Ecstasy of St. Francis	Guido and Fra Agostino
4. Hearing the voice of God	13. Nativity at Greccio	22. Verification of the stigmata
5. Rejection of worldly goods	14. Miracle of the spring	23. Mourning of St. Clare
6. Dream of Innocent III	15. Sermon to the birds	24. Canonization
7. Confirmation of the rules	16. Death of knight at Celano	25. Apparition before Gregory IX
8. Vision of flaming chariot	17. Preaching to Honorius III	26. Healing of a devotee
9. Vision of celestial thrones	18. Apparition at Arles	27. Confession of a woman
	19. Receiving the stigmata	28. Repentant heretic freed

DID YOU KNOW?

Assisi's Basilica di San Francesco consists of two churches built on top of each other; the Lower Church was done in Romanesque style, the Upper in Gothic.

FODOR'S FIRST PERSON

Sister Marcellina,
Order of St. Bridget

Sister Marcellina of the Order of St. Bridget talks about her life in Assisi, where she and 11 other sisters live in a convent and guesthouse on the outskirts of the town:

"Before coming to Assisi, I lived in various countries. I've lived in India, and in England, and been to Holland, to Sweden, and to Finland, as well as lived in Rome. But Assisi is the place that I would never want to change for any other. I don't know, I think there is something very special about this place. I've been here 13 years now, and each year I pray that I won't be sent somewhere else. I'm very happy here.

"I like the atmosphere of Assisi, it's very friendly, and of course with St. Francis and St. Claire, but especially St. Francis, there is a simplicity to life that I like very much. Even though I'm in the Order of St. Bridget, living here I feel very much a part of Franciscan spirituality. There is also a very strong ecumenical feeling to Assisi and this is very nice. There are over 60 different religious communities, with people from all over the world. And even though they come from different religious backgrounds they still feel a part of Assisi. Living here, you don't see the people of Assisi, you see people who have come from all over the world.

"There is something you feel when you come to Assisi, something you feel in your heart that makes you want to come back. And people do return! They feel the peacefulness and tranquility. Not that there aren't other aspects, like the commercialism—but these things happen. People return for the simplicity of this place. People feel attracted to Assisi. There's always something that people feel when they come here—even the hard-hearted ones!"

Asked if she thinks Assisi is changing, Sister Marcellina answers, with laughter in her voice, "When they wanted to make all the changes in the year 2000, the Jubilee Year, our Lord said, 'I must stop everything.' They had lots of projects to build new accommodations to house the people coming for the Jubilee Year, but the Lord said, 'No!'"

to conventional lodgings. They are usually called *conventi* or *ostelli* ("convents" or "hostels") because they're run by convents, churches, or other Catholic organizations. Rooms are spartan but peaceful. Check with the tourist office for a list.

$$ ☑ **Castello di Petrata.** Built as a fortress in the 14th century, the Castello

Fodor'sChoice di Petrata rightfully dominates the area, with Monte Subasio, Assisi, and

★ the distant hills and valleys of Perugia all in view. Every room is different from the last: wood beams and sections of exposed medieval stonework add character, and comfortable couches turn each room into a delightful retreat. **Pros:** great views of Assisi hills, gardens, and walks. **Cons:** slightly isolated; far from Assisi town center. ☒ *Via Petrata 25, Località Petrata* ☎ *075/815451* ⊕ *www.castellopetrata.com* ↝ *16 rooms, 7 suites* ⚇ *In-room: no a/c, Internet. In-hotel: restaurant, bar, pool, some pets allowed* ⊟ *AE, DC, MC, V* ⊘ *Closed Jan.–Mar.* �{○} *BP.*

$$ ☑ **Hotel Subasio.** The converted monastery close to the Basilica di San Francesco is well past its prime, when guests included celebrities like Marlene Dietrich and Charlie Chaplin. If you can get past the kitschy hangings on the walls, you'll notice such vestiges of glamour as Venetian chandeliers. The hotel does have splendid views, comfortable sitting rooms, and flower-decked terraces, and it's a stone's throw from all those Giotto frescoes. Some rooms are grand in size and overlook the valley, whereas others are small and rough around the edges. The restaurant has a nice view, but the food could be better. **Pros:** perfect location; views of the Assisi plain. **Cons:** lobby a bit drab; some small rooms; service can be spotty. ☒ *Via Frate Elia 2* ☎ *075/812206* ⊕ *www. hotelsubasioassisi.com* ↝ *54 rooms, 8 suites* ⚇ *In-room: no a/c. In-hotel: restaurant, bar, parking (paid)* ⊟ *AE, DC, MC, V* �{○} *BP.*

$ ☑ **Hotel Umbra.** A 16th-century town house is the setting for this charming hotel near Piazza del Comune. Ask for an upper room with a view over the Assisi rooftops to the valley below. The restaurant, closed for lunch on Tuesday and Wednesday, has a charming vine-covered terrace leading to a secluded garden. **Pros:** friendly welcome; pleasant small garden. **Cons:** difficult parking; some small rooms. ☒ *Via degli Archi 6* ☎ *075/812240* ⊕ *www.hotelumbra.it* ↝ *6 suites, 19 rooms* ⚇ *In-room: a/c. In-hotel: restaurant, bar* ⊟ *AE, DC, MC, V* ⊘ *Closed mid-Jan.–mid-Mar.* �{○} *BP.*

$$ ☑ **San Francesco.** You can't beat the location—the roof terrace and some of the rooms look out onto the Basilica di San Francesco, which is opposite the hotel. Rooms and facilities range from simple to dreary, but you may be reminded that looks aren't everything by the nice touches like slippers, a good-night piece of chocolate, and soundproofing. Fruit, homemade tarts, and fresh ricotta make for a first-rate breakfast. **Pros:** excellent location; great views. **Cons:** simple rooms; sometimes noisy in peak season. ☒ *Via San Francesco 48* ☎ *075/812281* ⊕ *www. hotelsanfrancescoassisi.it* ↝ *44 rooms* ⚇ *In-room: a/c, refrigerator, Internet. In-hotel: restaurant, bar, Wi-Fi, some pets allowed* ⊟ *AE, DC, MC, V* �{○} *BP.*

3

PERUGIA

Perugia is a majestic, handsome, wealthy city, and with its trendy boutiques, refined cafés, and grandiose architecture, it doesn't try to hide its affluence. A student population of more than 30,000 means that the city is abuzz with activity throughout the year. Umbria Jazz, one of the region's most important music festivals, attracts music lovers from around the world, and Eurochocolate, the international chocolate festival, is an irresistible draw for anyone with a sweet tooth.

GETTING HERE

The best approach to the city is by train. The area around the station doesn't attest to the rest of Perugia's elegance, but buses running from the station to Piazza d'Italia, the heart of the old town, are frequent. If you're in a hurry, take the new *minimetro*, a one-line subway, to Stazione della Cupa. If you are driving to Perugia and your hotel doesn't have parking facilities, leave your car in one of the lots close to the center. Electronic signs indicate the location of lots and the number of spaces free. If you park in the Piazza Partigiani, take the escalators that pass through the fascinating subterranean excavations of the Roman foundations of the city and lead to the town center.

VISITOR INFORMATION

Umbria's regional tourism office (✉ *Piazza Matteotti 18* ☎ *075/5736458* ⊕ *www.perugia.umbria2000.it*) is in Perugia. The staff is well informed about the area and can give you a wide selection of leaflets and maps to assist you during your trip. It's open Monday to Saturday 8:30 to 1:30 and 3 to 6:30, and Sunday 8:30 to 1.

EXPLORING PERUGIA

Thanks to Perugia's hilltop position, the medieval city remains almost completely intact. It is the best-preserved hill town of its size, and few other places in Italy better illustrate the model of the self-contained city-state that so shaped the course of Italian history.

TOP ATTRACTIONS

❹ **Collegio del Cambio** *(Bankers' Guild Hall)*. These elaborate rooms, on
★ the ground floor of the **Palazzo dei Priori,** served as the meeting hall and chapel of the guild of bankers and moneychangers. Most of the frescoes were completed by the most important Perugian painter of the Renaissance, Pietro Vannucci, better known as Perugino. He included a remarkably honest self-portrait on one of the pilasters. The iconography includes common religious themes, such as the Nativity and the Transfiguration seen on the end walls. On the left wall are female figures representing the virtues, beneath them the heroes and sages of antiquity. On the right wall are figures presumed to have been painted in part by Perugino's most famous pupil, Raphael. (His hand, experts say, is most apparent in the figure of Fortitude.) The *cappella* (chapel) of San Giovanni Battista has frescoes painted by Giannicola di Paolo, another student of Perugino's. ✉ *Corso Vannucci 25* ☎ *075/5728599* 🎫 *€4.50, €5.50 with Collegio della Mercanzia* ⊙ *Mon.–Sat. 9–12:30 and 2:30–5:30, Sun. 9–1.*

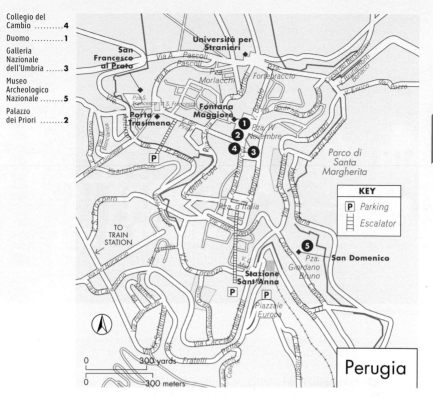

Perugia

KEY

P Parking

Escalator

Corso Vannucci. A string of elegantly connected palazzi expresses the artistic nature of this city center, the heart of which is concentrated along Corso Vannucci. Stately and broad, this pedestrians-only street runs from Piazza d'Italia to Piazza IV Novembre. Along the way, the entrances to many of Perugia's side streets might tempt you to wander off and explore. But don't stray too far as evening falls, when Corso Vannucci fills with Perugians out for their evening *passeggiata,* a pleasant pre-dinner stroll that may include a pause for an aperitif at one of the many bars that line the street.

③ **Galleria Nazionale dell'Umbria.** The region's most comprehensive art gal-

Fodor's Choice   lery is housed on the fourth floor of the **Palazzo dei Priori.** Enhanced
★   by skillfully lit displays and computers that allow you to focus on the works' details and background information, the collection includes work by native artists—most notably Pintoricchio (1454–1513) and Perugino (circa 1450–1523)—and others of the Umbrian and Tuscan schools, among them Gentile da Fabriano (1370–1427), Duccio (circa 1255–1318), Fra Angelico (1387–1455), Fiorenzo di Lorenzo (1445–1525), and Piero della Francesca (1420–92). In addition to paintings, the gallery has frescoes, sculptures, and some superb examples of crucifixes from the 13th and 14th centuries. Some rooms are dedicated to Perugia itself, showing how the medieval city evolved.

Perugia's Fontana Maggiore by night

✉ *Corso Vannucci 19, Piazza IV Novembre* ☎ *075/5721009* ⊕ *www. gallerianazionaleumbria.it* 🎟 *€6.50* ⊙ *Tues.–Sun. 8:30–7:30; last admission ½ hr before closing.*

 Palazzo dei Priori *(Palace of Priors).* A series of elegant connected buildings, the palazzo serves as Perugia's city hall and houses three of the city's museums. The buildings string along Corso Vannucci and wrap around the Piazza IV Novembre, where the original entrance is located. The steps here lead to the **Sala dei Notari** (Notaries' Hall). Other entrances lead to the **Galleria Nazionale dell'Umbria,** the **Collegio del Cambio,** and the **Collegio della Mercanzia.** The Sala dei Notari, which dates back to the 13th century and was the original meeting place of the town merchants, had become the seat of the notaries by the second half of the 15th century. Wood beams and an interesting array of frescoes attributed to Maestro di Farneto embellish the room. Coats of arms and crests line the back and right lateral walls; you can spot some famous figures from Aesop's *Fables* on the left wall. The palazzo facade is adorned with symbols of Perugia's pride and past power: the griffin is the city symbol, and the lion denotes Perugia's allegiance to the Guelph (or papal) cause. ✉ *Piazza IV Novembre* 🎟 *Free* ⊙ *June–Sept., Tues.–Sun. 9–1 and 3–7.*

Rocca Paolina. A labyrinth of little streets, alleys, and arches, this underground city was originally part of a fortress. It was built at the behest of Pope Paul III between 1540 and 1543 to confirm papal dominion over the city. Parts of it were destroyed after the end of papal rule, but much still remains. Begin your visit by taking the escalators from Piazza

Italia and Via Masi. In the summer this is the coolest place in the city. ⊙ *Daily 8–7.*

WORTH NOTING

❶ **Duomo.** Severe yet mystical, the Duomo, also called the Cathedral of San Lorenzo, is most famous for being the home of the wedding ring of the Virgin Mary, stolen by the Perugians in 1488 from the nearby town of Chiusi. The ring, kept high up in a red-curtained vault in the chapel immediately to the left of the entrance, is kept under lock—15 locks, to be precise— and key most

of the year. It's shown to the public on July 30 (the day it was brought to Perugia) and the second-to-last Sunday in January (Mary's wedding anniversary). The cathedral itself dates from the Middle Ages, and has many additions from the 15th and 16th centuries. The most visually interesting element is the altar to the Madonna of Grace; an elegant fresco on a column at the right of the entrance of the altar depicts *La Madonna delle Grazie* and is surrounded by prayer benches decorated with handwritten notes to the Holy Mother. Around the column are small amulets—symbols of gratitude from those whose prayers were answered. There are also elaborately carved choir stalls, executed by Giovanni Battista Bastone in 1520. The altarpiece (1484), an early masterpiece by Luca Signorelli (circa 1441–1523), shows the Madonna with Saint John the Baptist, Saint Onophrius, and Saint Lawrence. Sections of the church may be closed to visitors during religious services.

The **Museo Capitolare** displays a large array of precious objects associated with the cathedral, including vestments, vessels, and manuscripts. Outside the Duomo is the elaborate **Fontana Maggiore,** which dates from 1278. It is adorned with zodiac figures and symbols of the seven arts. ⊠ *Piazza IV Novembre* ☎ *075/5724853* 🎟 *Museum €3.50* ⊙ *Duomo: Mon.–Sat. 7–12:30 and 4–6:45, Sun. 8–12:30 and 4–6:45; museum: daily 10–1 and 2:30–5:30; last admission ½ hr before closing.*

❺ **Museo Archeologico Nazionale.** The museum, next to the imposing church of San Domenico, contains an excellent collection of Etruscan artifacts from throughout the region. Perugia was a flourishing Etruscan city long before it fell under Roman domination in 310 BC. Little else remains of Perugia's mysterious ancestors, although the Arco di Augusto, in Piazza Fortebraccio, the northern entrance to the city, is of Etruscan origin. ⊠ *Piazza G. Bruno 10* ☎ *075/5727141* ⊕ *www.archeopg.arti. beniculturali.it* 🎟 *€4* ⊙ *Mon. 2:30–7:30, Tues.–Sun. 8:30–7:30.*

WHERE TO EAT

$$$

UMBRIAN

✕ **Antica Trattoria San Lorenzo.** Brick vaults are not the only distinguishing feature of this small restaurant next to the Duomo, as both the food and the service are outstanding. Particular attention is paid to adapting traditional Umbrian cuisine to the modern palate. There is also a nice variety of seafood dishes on the menu. The *trenette alla farina di noce con pesce di mare* (flat noodles made with walnut flour topped with fresh fish) is a real treat. ✉ *Piazza Danti 19-A* ☎ *075/5721956* ⊟ *AE, D, MC, V* ⊘ *Closed Sun.*

¢   ✕ **Dal Mi' Cocco.** A great favorite with Perugia's university students, this

UMBRIAN   place is fun, crowded, and inexpensive. You may find yourself seated

★   at a long table with other diners, but some language help from your neighbors could come in handy—the menu is in pure Perugian dialect. The fixed-price meals change with the season, and each day of the week brings some new creation *dal cocco* (from the "coconut," or head) of the chef. ✉ *Corso Garibaldi 12* ☎ *075/5732511* ⊟ *Reservations essential* ⊟ *No credit cards* ⊘ *Closed late July–mid-Aug.*

$ ✕ **Il Falchetto.** Exceptional food at reasonable prices makes this Peru-

UMBRIAN   gia's best bargain. Service is smart but relaxed in the two medieval dining rooms that put the chef on view. The house specialty is *falchetti* (homemade gnocchi with spinach and ricotta cheese). ✉ *Via Bartolo 20* ☎ *075/5731775* ⊟ *AE, DC, MC, V* ⊘ *Closed Mon. and last 2 wks in Jan.*

$$ ✕ **La Rosetta.** The restaurant, in the hotel of the same name, is a peaceful,

ITALIAN   elegant spot. In winter you dine inside under medieval vaults; in summer, in the cool courtyard. The food is simple but reliable, and flawlessly served. The restaurant caters to travelers seeking to get away from the bustle of central Perugia. The delightful courtyard is 10 meters off the Corso Vannucci. ✉ *Piazza d'Italia 19* ☎ *075/5720841* ⊟ *Reservations essential* ⊟ *AE, DC, MC, V.*

$$ ✕ **La Taverna.** Medieval steps lead to a rustic two-story restaurant where

UMBRIAN   wine bottles and artful clutter decorate the walls. Good choices from the regional menu include *caramelle al gorgonzola* (pasta rolls filled with red cabbage and mozzarella and topped with a Gorgonzola sauce) and grilled meat dishes, such as the *medaglioni di vitello al tartuffo* (grilled veal with truffles). ✉ *Via delle Streghe 8, off Corso Vannucci* ☎ *075/5724128* ⊟ *AE, DC, MC, V* ⊘ *Closed Mon.*

WHERE TO STAY

$$$ ⌂ **Castello dell'Oscano.** A splendid neo-Gothic castle, a late-19th-century

villa, and a converted farmhouse hidden in the tranquil hills north of Perugia offer a wide range of accommodations. Step back in time in the castle, where spacious suites and junior suites, all with high oak-beam ceilings, and some with panoramic views of the surrounding country, are decorated with 18th- and 19th-century antiques. The sweeping wooden staircase of the main lounge, and the wood-panel reading rooms and restaurant are particularly elegant. Rooms in the villa are smaller and more modern, and the apartments of the farmhouse, in the valley below the castle, have their own kitchens. The complex is in Cenerente, 5 km (3 mi) north of Perugia. **Pros:** quiet elegance; fine gardens; Umbrian wine list. **Cons:** distance from Perugia; not easy to find. ✉ *Strada della Forcella 32, Cenerente* ☎ *075/584371* ⊕ *www.oscano.it* ⟿ *24 rooms, 8 suites, 13 apartments* ⚛ *In-room: no a/c (some), Internet. In-hotel: restaurant, bar, pool, gym, bicycles* ⊟ *AE, D, V* ¶⊙¶ *BP.*

$$ ⊞ **Hotel Fortuna.** The elegant decor in the large rooms of this friendly hotel complements the frescoes, which date from the 1700s. Some rooms have balconies. The building itself, just out of sight of Corso Vannucci, dates to the 1300s. **Pros:** central but quiet; homely atmosphere. **Cons:** some small rooms; no restaurant. ⊠ *Via Bonazzi 19, Corso Vannucci* ☎ *075/5722845* ⊕ *www.hotelfortunaperugia.com* ⟿ *51 rooms* ⚴ *a/c, safe. In-hotel: restaurant, bar, parking (paid)* ⊟ *AE, DC, MC, V* ⎜⎝ *BP.*

$$ ⊞ **Il Cantico della Natura.** Don't let the rustic appearance of the buildings fool you—this is one of the plushest agriturismi in Umbria. The rooms are furnished in varying ethnic styles, with nice little extras thrown in such as bedside kettles and an array of teas and herbal infusions. The owners also organize a series of outdoor activities. **Pros:** views of Lake Trasimeno and the surrounding countryside. **Cons:** not easy to find; road poor in winter. ⊠ *Vocabolo Penna, Montesperello di Magione* ☎ *075/841699* ⊕ *www.ilcanticodellanatura.it* ⟿ *12 rooms* ⚴ *In-room: a/c, safe. In-hotel: restaurant, gym, bicycles* ⊟ *AE, DC, MC, V* ⎜⎝ *BP.*

$$ ⊞ **Locanda della Posta.** In the city's old district, this lodging is in an 18th-century palazzo. Renovations have left the lobby and other public areas rather bland, but the rooms are soothingly decorated in muted colors. Although facing busy Corso Vannucci and supposedly soundproof, they're still a bit noisy. Those on the upper floors at the back of the building are quieter and have great views. **Pros:** some fine views; central position. **Cons:** uninspiring lobby; some small rooms, no restaurant. ⊠ *Corso Vannucci 97* ☎ *075/5728925* ⟿ *38 rooms, 1 suite* ⚴ *In-room: a/c, safe. In-hotel: bar, parking (paid)* ⊟ *AE, DC, MC, V* ⎜⎝ *BP.*

NIGHTLIFE AND THE ARTS

With its large student population, the city has plenty to offer in the way of bars and clubs. The best ones are around the city center, off Corso Vanucci. *Viva Perugia* is a good source of information about nightlife. The monthly, sold at newsstands, has a section in English.

MUSIC FESTIVALS

Summer sees two music festivals in Perugia. **Umbria Jazz** (☎ *075/5732432* ⊕ *www.umbriajazz.com*) is held for 10 days in July. Tickets are available starting at the end of April. The **Sagra Musicale Umbra** (☎ *075/5721374* ⊕ *www.perugiamusicaclassica.com*), held from mid-August to mid-September, celebrates sacred music.

SHOPPING

Take a stroll down any of Perugia's main streets, including Corso Vannucci, Via dei Priori, Via Oberdan, and Via Sant'Ercolano, and you'll see many well-known designer boutiques and specialty shops.

The most typical thing to buy in Perugia is some Perugina chocolate, which you can find almost anywhere. The best-known chocolates made by Perugina are the chocolate-and-hazelnut-filled nibbles called Baci (literally, "kisses"). They're wrapped in silver paper that includes a sliver of paper, like the fortune in a fortune cookie, with multilingual romantic sentiments or sayings.

TUSCANY

There's a magic about Tuscany: the right elements have all fallen into place here. The art and the culture, the food and the wine, are justly famous. The gorgeous countryside and the picture-book towns take on a certain glow in the late afternoon sun. And the people mix warmth, modesty, and pride in a way that honors their glorious past without bowing down to it.

Tuscany isn't the place for a jam-packed itinerary. One of the great pleasures here is indulging in rustic hedonism, marked by long lunches and show-stopping sunsets. Whether by car, bike, or foot, you'll want to get out into the glorious landscape, but it's smart to keep your plans modest. Set a church or a hill town or an out-of-the-way restaurant as your destination, knowing that half the pleasure is in getting there—admiring as you go the stately palazzos, the tidy geometry of row upon row of grape vines, the fields vibrant with red poppies and yellow broom.

You'll need to devise a Siena strategy. The town shouldn't be missed; it's compact enough that you can see the major sights on a day trip, and that's exactly what most people do. Spend the night, and you'll get to witness the town breath a sigh and relax upon the day-trippers' departure. The flip side is, your favorite place to stay in Tuscany is more likely to be out in the country than in town.

SIENA

With its narrow streets and steep alleys, a stunning Gothic duomo, a bounty of early Renaissance art, and the glorious Palazzo Pubblico overlooking its magnificent Campo, Siena is often described as Italy's best-preserved medieval city. Victory over Florence in 1260 at Montaperti marked the beginning of Siena's golden age. During the following decades Siena erected its greatest buildings (including the Duomo); established a model city government presided over by the Council of Nine; and became a great art, textile, and trade center. Siena succumbed to Florentine rule in the mid-16th century, when a yearlong siege virtually eliminated the native population. Ironically, it was precisely this decline that, along with the steadfast pride of the Sienese, prevented further development, to which we owe the city's marvelous medieval condition today.

Although much looks as it did in the early 14th century, Siena is no museum. Walk through the streets and you can see that the medieval *contrade,* 17 neighborhoods into which the city has been historically divided, are a vibrant part of modern life. You may see symbols of the *contrada*—Tartuca (turtle), Oca (goose), Istrice (porcupine), Torre (tower)—emblazoned on banners and engraved on building walls. The Sienese still strongly identify themselves by the contrada where they were born and raised; loyalty and rivalry run deep. At no time is this more visible than during the centuries-old Palio, a twice-yearly horse race held in the Piazza del Campo, but you need not visit during the wild festival to come to know the rich culture and enchanting pleasures of Siena; those are evident at every step.

GETTING HERE

From Florence, the quickest way to Siena is via the Florence–Siena Superstrada. Otherwise, take the Via Cassia (SR2), for a scenic route. Coming from Rome, leave the A1 at Valdichiana, and follow the Siena–Bettole Superstrada. SITA provides excellent bus service between Florence and Siena. Because buses are direct and speedy, they are preferable to the train, which sometimes involves a change in Empoli.

VISITOR INFORMATION

Siena tourism office (⊠ *Piazza del Campo 56* ☎ *0577/280551* ⊕ *www.comune.siena.it*).

EXPLORING SIENA

If you come by car, you're better off leaving it in one of the parking lots around the perimeter of town. Driving is difficult or impossible in most parts of the city center. Practically unchanged since medieval times, Siena is laid out in a "Y" over the slopes of several hills, dividing the city into *terzi* (thirds). Although the most-interesting sites are in a fairly compact area around the Campo at the center of town in the neighborhoods of Città, Camollìa, and San Martino, be sure to leave some time to wander into the narrow streets that rise and fall steeply from the main thoroughfares, giving yourself at least two days to really explore the town. At the top on the list of things to see is the Piazza del Campo, considered by many to be the finest public square in Italy. The Palazzo Pubblico sits at the lower end of the square and is well worth a visit. The Duomo is a must-see, as is the nearby Cripta.

Tra-In (☎ *0577/204111* ⊕ *www.trainspa.it*) buses also run frequently within and around Siena, including through the centro storico. Tickets cost €0.95 and should be bought in advance at tobacconists or newsstands. Routes are marked with signposts.

The **Association of Official Tour Guides** (⊠ *Piazza del Campo 56* ☎ *0577/288084* ⊕ *www.terredisiena.it*) offers a two-hour walking tour that takes in most of the major sights, such as the Duomo, the Campo, and the exterior of Palazzo Pubblico. You can arrange for English-speaking guides.

TIMING It's a joy to walk in Siena—hills notwithstanding—as it's a rare opportunity to stroll through a medieval city rather than just a town. (There is quite a lot to explore, in contrast to tiny hill towns that can be crossed in minutes.) The walk can be done in as little as a day, with minimal stops at the sights. But stay longer and take time to tour the church building and museums, and to enjoy the streetscapes themselves. Several of the sites have reduced hours on Sunday afternoon and Monday.

TUSCANY THROUGH THE AGES

Etruscans and Romans. Tuscany was populated, at least by the 7th century BC, by the Etruscans, a mysterious lot who chose to live on hills—the better to see the approaching enemy—in such places as present-day Arezzo, Chiusi, Cortona, Fiesole, and Volterra. Some 500 years later, the Romans came, saw, and conquered; by 241 BC they had built the Aurelia, a road from Rome to Pisa that is still in use today. The crumbling of the Roman Empire and subsequent invasions by marauding Lombards, Byzantines, and Holy Roman Emperors meant centuries of turmoil. By the 12th century city-states were being formed throughout Tuscany in part, perhaps, because it was unclear exactly who was in charge.

Guelphs and Ghibellines. The two groups vying for power were the Guelphs and the Ghibellines, champions of the pope and the Holy Roman Emperor, respectively. They jostled for control of individual cities and of the region as a whole. Florence was more or less Guelph, and Siena more often than not Ghibelline. This led to bloody battles, most notably the 1260 battle of Montaperti, in which the Ghibellines roundly defeated the Guelphs.

Eventually—by the 14th century—the Guelphs became the dominant force. But this did not mean that the warring Tuscan cities settled down to a period of relative peace and tranquillity. The age in which Dante wrote his *Divine Comedy* and Giotto and Piero della Francesca created their incomparable frescoes was one of internecine strife.

Florentines and Sienese. Florence was the power to be reckoned with; it coveted its main rival, Siena, which it conquered, lost, and reconquered during the 15th and 16th centuries. Finally, in 1555, following in the footsteps of Volterra, Pisa, Prato, and Arezzo, Siena fell for good. They were all united under Florence to form the grand duchy of Tuscany. The only city to escape Florence's dominion was Lucca, which remained fiercely independent until the arrival of Napoléon. Eventually, however, even Florence's influence waned, and the 17th and 18th centuries saw the decline of the entire region as various armies swept across it.

TOP ATTRACTIONS

❸ **Cripta.** After it had lain unseen for possibly 700 years, a crypt was
Fodor'sChoice rediscovered under the grand *pavimento* (floor) of the Duomo dur-
★ ing routine excavation work and was opened to the public in 2003. An unknown master executed the breathtaking frescoes here sometime between 1270 and 1280; they retain their original colors and pack an emotional punch even with sporadic damage. The *Deposition/Lamentation* gives strong evidence that the Sienese school could paint emotion just as well as the Florentine school—and did it some 20 years before Giotto. Guided tours in English take place more or less every half hour and are limited to no more than 35 persons. ⊠ *Piazza del Duomo, Città* ☎ *0577/283048* 🎫 *€6; €10 combined ticket includes the Duomo, Battistero, and Museo dell'Opera Metropolitana* ☉ *June–Aug., daily 9:30–8; Sept.–May, daily 9:30–7.*

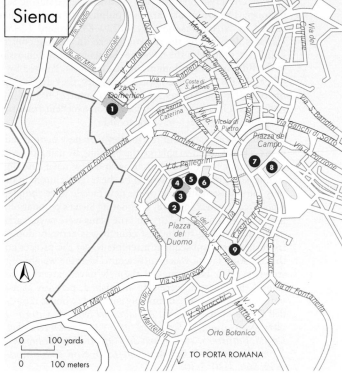

Siena

❹ **Duomo.** Siena's Duomo is beyond question one of the finest Gothic
Fodor's Choice cathedrals in Italy. The multicolored marbles and painted decoration
★ are typical of the Italian approach to Gothic architecture—lighter and
much less austere than the French. The amazingly detailed façade has
few rivals in the region, although it's quite similar to the Duomo in
Orvieto. It was completed in two brief phases at the end of the 13th
and 14th centuries. The statues and decorative work were designed
by Niccolo and Giovanni Pisano, although most of what we see today
are copies, the originals having been removed to the nearby Museo
dell'Opera Metropolitana. The gold mosaics are 18th-century restorations. The Campanile (no entry) is among central Italy's finest, the
number of windows increasing with each level.

The Duomo's interior, with its black-and-white striping throughout
and finely coffered and gilded dome, is simply striking. Step in and
look back up at Duccio's (circa 1255–1319) panels of stained glass
that fill the circular window. Finished in 1288, it's the oldest example
of stained glass in Italy. The Duomo is most famous for its unique
and magnificent inlaid-marble floors, which took almost 200 years to
complete; more than 40 artists contributed to the work, made up of
56 separate compositions depicting biblical scenes, allegories, religious
symbols, and civic emblems. The floors are covered for most of the

year for conservation purposes, but are unveiled during September and October. The Duomo's carousel pulpit, also much appreciated, was carved by Nicola Pisano (circa 1220–84) around 1265; the *Life of Christ* is depicted on the rostrum frieze. In striking contrast to all the Gothic decoration in the nave are the magnificent Renaissance frescoes in the **Biblioteca Piccolomini,** off the left aisle. Painted by Pinturicchio (circa 1454–1513) and completed in 1509, they depict events from the life of native son Aeneas Sylvius Piccolomini (1405–64), who became Pope Pius II in 1458. The frescoes are in excellent condition, and have a freshness rarely seen in work so old.

The Duomo is grand, but the medieval Sienese people had even bigger plans. They wanted to enlarge the building by using the existing church as a transept for a new church, with a new nave running toward the southeast, to make what would be the largest church in the world. But only the side wall and part of the new facade were completed when the Black Death struck in 1348, decimating Siena's population. The city fell into decline, funds dried up, and the plans were never carried out. (The dream of building the biggest church was actually doomed to failure from the start—subsequent attempts to get the project going revealed that the foundation was insufficient to bear the weight of the proposed structure.) The beginnings of the new nave, extending from the right side of the Duomo, were left unfinished, perhaps as a testament to unfulfilled dreams, and ultimately enclosed to house the adjacent **Museo dell'Opera Metropolitana.** ⊠ *Piazza del Duomo, Città* ☎ *0577/283048* ⌨ *€3 Nov.–Aug.; €5 Sept. and Oct.; €10 combined ticket includes the Cripta, Battistero, and Museo dell'Opera Metropolitana* ☉ *Mar.–Oct., Mon.–Sat. 10:30–7:30, Sun. 1:30–6:30; Nov.–Feb., Mon.–Sat. 10:30–6:30, Sun. 1:30–5:30.*

WORTH NOTING

❺ Battistero. The Duomo's 14th-century Gothic Baptistery was built to prop up one side of the Duomo. There are frescoes throughout, but the highlight is a large bronze 15th-century baptismal font designed by Jacopo della Quercia (1374–1438). It's adorned with bas-reliefs by various artists, including two by Renaissance masters: the *Baptism of Christ* by Lorenzo Ghiberti (1378–1455) and the *Feast of Herod* by Donatello. ⊠ *Entrance on Piazza San Giovanni* ☎ *0577/283048* ⌨ *€3; €10 combined ticket includes the Duomo, Cripta, and Museo dell'Opera del Duomo* ☉ *June–Aug., daily 9:30–8; Sept.–May, daily 9:30–7.*

❻ Museo dell'Opera Metropolitana. Part of the unfinished nave of what was to have been a new cathedral, the museum contains the Duomo's treasury and some of the original decoration from its facade and interior. The first room on the ground floor displays weather-beaten 13th-century sculptures by Giovanni Pisano (circa 1245–1318) that were brought inside for protection and replaced by copies, as was a tondo of the *Madonna and Child* (now attributed to Donatello) that once hung on the door to the south transept. The masterpiece is unquestionably Duccio's *Maestà,* one side with 26 panels depicting episodes from the Passion, the other side with a *Madonna and Child Enthroned.* Painted between 1308 and 1311 as the altarpiece for the Duomo (where it remained until 1505), its realistic elements, such as the lively depiction of the Christ child and the treatment of interior space, proved an enormous influence on later painters. The second floor is divided between the treasury, with a crucifix by Giovanni Pisano and several statues and busts of biblical characters and classical philosophers, and La Sala della Madonna degli Occhi Grossi (the Room of the Madonna with the Big Eyes), named after the namesake painting it displays by the Maestro di Tressa, who painted in the early 13th century. The work originally decorated the Duomo's high altar, before being displaced by Duccio's *Maestà*. There is a fine view from the tower inside the museum. ✉ *Piazza del Duomo 8, Città* ☎ *0577/283048* 🎫*€6; €10 combined ticket includes the Duomo, Cripta, and Battistero* ⊙ *Mar.–May and Sept. and Oct., daily 9:30–7; June–Aug., daily 9:30* AM*–10* PM*; Nov.–Feb., daily 10–5.*

❾ Pinacoteca Nazionale. The superb collection of five centuries of local painting in Siena's national picture gallery can easily convince you that the Renaissance was by no means just a Florentine thing—Siena was arguably just as important a center of art and innovation as its rival to the north, especially in the mid-13th century. Accordingly, the most interesting section of the collection, chronologically arranged, has several important "firsts." Room 1 contains a painting of the *Stories of the True Cross* (1215) by the so-called Master of Tressa, the earliest identified work by a painter of the Sienese school, and is followed in Room 2 by late-13th-century artist Guido da Siena's *Stories from the Life of Christ,* one of the first paintings ever made on canvas (earlier painters used wood panels). Rooms 3 and 4 are dedicated to Duccio, a student of Cimabue (circa 1240–1302) and considered to be the last of the proto-Renaissance painters. Ambrogio Lorenzetti's landscapes in Room 8 are the first truly secular paintings in Western art. Among later works in the rooms on the floor above, keep an eye out for the preparatory sketches used by Domenico Beccafumi (1486–1551) for the 35 etched marble panels he made for the floor of the Duomo. ✉ *Via San Pietro 29, Città* ☎*0577/281161* 🎫*€4* ⊙ *Tues.–Sat. 8:15–7:15; Sun. 8:15–1:15; Mon. 8:30–1:30; last entrance ½ hr before closing.*

❶ San Domenico. Although the Duomo is celebrated as a triumph of 13th-century Gothic architecture, this church, built at about the same time, turned out to be an oversize, hulking brick box that never merited a finishing coat in marble, let alone a graceful facade. Named for the founder of the Dominican order, the church is now more closely associated with Saint Catherine of Siena. Just to the right of the entrance is the chapel in which she received the stigmata. On the wall is the only known contemporary portrait of the saint, made in the late 14th century by Andrea Vanni (circa 1332–1414). Farther down is the famous **Cappella di Santa Caterina,** the church's official shrine. Catherine, or bits and pieces of her, was literally spread all over the country—a foot is in Venice, most of her body is in Rome, and only her head and finger are here (kept in a reliquary on the altar). She was revered throughout the country long before she was officially named a patron saint of Italy in 1939. On either side of the chapel are well-known frescoes by Sodoma (aka Giovanni Antonio Bazzi, 1477–1549) of *St. Catherine in Ecstasy.* Don't miss the view of the Duomo and town center from the apse-side terrace. ✉ *Costa di Sant'Antonio, Camollìa* ☎ *0577/280893*

Continued on page 180

Climbing the 400 narrow steps of the **Torre del Mangia** rewards you with unparalleled views of Siena's rooftops and the countryside beyond.

The **Palazzo Pubblico**, Siena's town hall since the 14th century.

Something about the fan-shaped, sloping design of **Il Campo** encourages people to sit and relax (except during the Palio, when they stand and scream). The communal atmosphere here is unlike that of any other Italian piazza.

PIAZZA DEL CAMPO

Fodor'sChoice ★

❼ The fan-shaped **Piazza del Campo,** known simply as il Campo (The Field), is one of the finest squares in Italy. Constructed toward the end of the 12th century on a market area unclaimed by any contrada, it's still the heart of town. The bricks of the Campo are patterned in nine different sections—representing each member of the medieval Government of Nine. At the top of the Campo is a copy of the **Fonte Gaia,** decorated in the early 15th century by Siena's greatest sculptor, Jacopo della Quercia, with 13 sculpted reliefs of biblical events and virtues. Those lining the rectangular fountain are 19th-century copies; the originals are in the Spedale di Santa Maria della Scala. On Palio horse race days (July 2 and August 16), the Campo and all its surrounding buildings are packed with cheering, frenzied locals and tourists craning their necks to take it all in.

❽ The Gothic **Palazzo Pubblico,** the focal point of the Piazza del Campo, has served as Siena's town hall since the 1300s. It now also contains the **Museo Civico,** with walls covered in early Renaissance frescoes. The nine governors of Siena once met in the Sala della Pace, famous for Ambrogio Lorenzetti's frescoes called *Allegories of Good and Bad Government,* painted in the late 1330s to demonstrate the dangers of tyranny. The good government side depicts utopia, showing first the virtuous ruling council surrounded by angels and then scenes of a perfectly running city and countryside. Conversely, the bad government fresco tells a tale straight out of Dante. The evil ruler and his advisers have horns and fondle strange animals, and the town scene depicts the seven mortal sins in action. Interestingly, the bad government fresco is severely damaged, and the good government fresco is in terrific condition. The **Torre del Mangia,** the palazzo's famous bell tower, is named after one of its first bell ringers, Giovanni di Duccio (called Mangiaguadagni, or earnings eater). The climb up to the top is long and steep, but the view makes it worth every step. ⊠ *Piazza del Campo 1, Città* ☎ *0577/41169* ⊠ *Museo €7, Torre €6, combined ticket €10* ☉ *Museo Nov.–Mar. 15, daily 10–6:30; Mar. 16–Oct., daily 10–7. Torre Nov.–Mar. 15, daily 10–4; Mar. 16–Oct., daily 10–7.*

Map labels:
Via Banchi di Sopra
Banchi di Sotto
Palazzo Sansedoni
Fonte Gaia
Palazzo Piccolomini
Via
Via di Fontebranda
Il Campo
Torre del Mangia
Via del Porrione
Palazzo d'Elci
Via di Città
Sinagoga
Palazzo Pubblico
Via Giov. Duprè
Via di Salicotto
Piazza del Mercato
Palazzo Patrizi
Via Casato di Sotto
0   50 yards
0   50 meters

THE PALIO

The three laps around a makeshift racetrack in Piazza del Campo are over in less than two minutes, but the spirit of Siena's Palio— a horse race held every July 2 and August 16—lives all year long.

The Palio is contested between Siena's contrade, the 17 neighborhoods that have divided the city since the Middle Ages. Loyalties are fiercely felt. At any time of year you'll see on the streets contrada symbols—Tartuca (turtle), Oca (goose), Istrice (porcupine), Torre (tower)—emblazoned on banners and engraved on building walls. At Palio time, simmering rivalries come to a boil.

It's been that way since at least August 16, 1310, the date of the first recorded running of the Palio. At that time, and for centuries to follow, the race went through the streets of the city. The additional July 2 running was instituted in 1649; soon thereafter the location was moved to the Campo and the current system for selecting the race entrants established. Ten of the contrade are chosen at random to run in the July Palio. The August race is then contested between the 7 contrade left out in July, plus 3 of the 10 July participants, again chosen at random. Although the races are in theory of equal importance, Sienese will tell you that it's better to win the second and have bragging rights for the rest of the year.

The race itself has a raw and arbitrary character—it's no Kentucky Derby. There's barely room for the 10 horses on the makeshift Campo course, so falls and collisions are inevitable. Horses are chosen at random three days before the race, and jockeys (who ride bareback) are mercenaries hired from surrounding towns. Almost no tactic is considered too underhanded. Bribery, secret plots, and betrayal are commonplace—so much so that the word for "jockey," *fantino*, has come to mean "untrustworthy" in Siena. There have been incidents of drugging (the horses) and kidnapping (the jockeys); only sabotaging a horse's reins remains taboo.

Above: The tension of the starting line. Top left: The frenzy of the race. Bottom left: A solemn flag bearer follows in the footsteps of his ancestors.

AQUILA	BRUCO	CHIOCCIOLA

17 MEDIEVAL CONTRADE

Festivities kick off three days prior to the Palio, with the selection and blessing of the horses, trial runs, ceremonial banquets, betting, and late-night celebrations. Residents don their contrada's colors and march through the streets in medieval costumes. The Campo is transformed into a racetrack lined with a thick layer of sand. On race day, each horse is brought to the church of the contrada for which it will run, where it's blessed and told, "Go little horse and return a winner." The Campo fills through the afternoon, with spectators crowding into every available space until bells ring and the piazza is sealed off. Processions of flag wavers in traditional dress march to the beat of tambourines and drums and the roar of the crowds. The *palio* itself—a banner for which the race is named, dedicated to the Virgin Mary—makes an appearance, followed by the horses and their jockeys.

The race begins when one horse, chosen to ride up from behind the rest of the field, crosses the starting line. There are always false starts, adding to the frenzied mood. Once underway, the race is over in a matter of minutes. The victorious rider is carried off through the streets of the winning contrada (where in the past tradition dictated he was entitled to the local girl of his choice), while winning and losing sides use television replay to analyze the race from every possible angle. The winning contrada will celebrate into the night, at long tables piled high with food and drink. The champion horse is guest of honor.

Reserved seating in the stands is sold out months in advance of the races; contact the Siena Tourist Office (✉ Piazza del Campo 56 ☎ 0577/280551) to find out about availability, and ask your hotel if it can procure you a seat. The entire area in the center is free and unreserved, but you need to show up early in order to get a prime spot against the barriers.

CIVETTA	DRAGO
GIRAFFA	ISTRICE
LEOCORNO	LUPA
NICCHIO	OCA
ONDA	PANTERA
SELVA	TARTUCA
TORRE	VALDIMONTONE

⊙ *Mid-Mar.–Oct., daily 7–1 and 2:30–6:30; Nov.–mid-Mar., daily 9–1 and 3–6.*

❷ **Spedale di Santa Maria della Scala.** For more than a thousand years, this complex across from the Duomo was home to Siena's hospital, but now it serves as a museum to display some terrific frescoes and other Sienese Renaissance treasures.

Restored 15th-century frescoes in the Sala del Pellegrinaio (once the emergency room) tell the history of the hospital, which was created to give refuge to passing pilgrims and to those in need, and to distribute charity to the poor. Incorporated into the complex is the church of the Santissima Annunziata, with a celebrated *Risen Christ* by Vecchietta (also known as Lorenzo di Pietro, circa 1412–80). Down in the dark Cappella di Santa Caterina della Notte is where Saint Catherine went to pray at night. The subterranean archaeological museum contained within the *ospedale* (hospital) is worth seeing even if you're not particularly taken with Etruscan objects: the interior design is sheer brilliance—it's beautifully lighted, eerily quiet, and an oasis of cool on hot summer days. The displays—including the *bucchero* (dark, reddish clay) ceramics, Roman coins, and tomb furnishings—are clearly marked and can serve as a good introduction to the history of regional excavations. Don't miss della Quercia's original sculpted reliefs from the Fonte Gaia. Although the fountain has been faithfully copied for the Campo, there's something incomparably beautiful about the real thing. ✉ *Piazza del Duomo, Città* ☎ *0577/224811* 🎫 *€6* ⊙ *Mar. 16–Jan. 9, daily 10:30–6:30; Jan. 10–Mar. 15, daily 10:30–4:30.*

WHERE TO EAT

$$$ ✕ **Antica Trattoria Botteganova.** Along the road that leads to Chianti is
TUSCAN   arguably the best restaurant in Siena. Chef Michele Sorrentino's cooking
★   is all about clean flavors, balanced combinations, and inviting presentation. Look for inspiring dishes such as spaghetti *alla chitarra in salsa di astice piccante* (with a spicy lobster sauce), or ravioli *di ricotta con ragù d'agnello* (with sheep's-milk cheese and lamb sauce). The interior, with high vaulting, is relaxed yet elegant, and the service is first-rate. ✉ *Strada per Montevarchi 29* ✛ *2 km (1 mi) northeast of Siena* ☎ *0577/284230* ⊕ *www.anticatrattoriabotteganova.it* 🍽 *Reservations essential* ▭ *AE, DC, MC, V* ⊙ *Closed Sun.*

$$ ✕ **Le Logge.** Bright flowers provide a dash of color at this classic Tuscan
TUSCAN   dining room, and stenciled designs on the ceilings add some whimsy. The wooden cupboards (now filled with wine bottles) lining the walls recall its past as a turn-of-the-19th-century grocery store. The menu, with four or five *primi* (first courses) and *secondi* (second courses), changes regularly, but almost always includes their classic *malfatti all'osteria* (ricotta and spinach dumplings in a cream sauce). Desserts such as *coni con mousse al cioccolato e gelato allo zafferano* (two diminutive ice-cream

cones with chocolate mousse and saffron ice cream) provide an inventive ending to the meal. When not vying for one of the outdoor tables, make sure to ask for one in the main downstairs room. ⊠ *Via del Porrione 33, San Martino* ☎ *0577/48013* ⊕ *www.osterialogge.it* ⚐ *Reservations essential* ⊟ *AE, DC, MC, V* ⊘ *Closed Sun. and 3 wks in Jan.*

¢ ✕**Osteria Il Grattacielo.** Wiped out from too much sightseeing? Con-
TUSCAN sider a meal at this hole-in-the-wall restaurant where locals congre-
gate for a simple lunch over a glass of wine. There's a collection of *verdure sott'olio* (marinated vegetables), a wide selection of *affettati misti* (cured meats), and various types of frittatas. All of this can be washed down with the cheap, yet eminently drinkable, house red. A couple of bench tables provide outdoor seating in summer. Don't be put off by the absence of a written menu. All the food is displayed at the counter, so you can point if you need to. ⊠ *Via Pontani 8, Camollìa* ☎ *0577/289326* ⊟ *No credit cards* ⊘ *Closed Sun.*

$ ✕**Trattoria Papei.** The menu hasn't changed for years, and why should
TUSCAN it? The *pici al cardinale* (handmade spaghetti with a duck and bacon
★ sauce) is wonderful, and all the other typically Sienese dishes are equally delicious. Tucked away behind the Palazzo Pubblico in a square that serves as a parking lot for most of the day, the restaurant's location isn't great, but the food is. ⊠ *Piazza del Mercato 6, Città* ☎ *0577/280894* ⊟ *MC, V* ⊘ *Closed Mon.*

WHERE TO STAY

$ ⌂**Antica Torre.** The cordial Landolfo family has carefully evoked a pri-
vate home with their eight guest rooms inside a restored 16th-century tower. Simple but tastefully furnished rooms have ornate wrought-iron headboards, usually atop twin beds. The old stone staircase, large wooden beams, wood shutters, and original brick vaults here and there are reminders of the building's great age. Antica Torre is in a southeast corner of Siena, a 10-minute walk from Piazza del Campo. **Pros:** near the town center; charming atmosphere. **Cons:** narrow stairway up to the rooms; low ceilings; cramped bathrooms. ⊠ *Via Fieravecchia 7, San Martino* ☎ *0577/222255* ⊕ *www.anticatorresiena.it* ⇆ *8 rooms* ⚐ *In-hotel: Internet terminal* ⊟ *AE, DC, MC, V* ⓘⓞⓛ *BP.*

$$ ⌂**Borgo Pretale.** A small hamlet hidden in the hills to the south of Siena
★ has been converted into this delightful hotel. Surrounded by open fields and rolling woodlands, Borgo Pretale is an amazingly tranquil place to stay, but close enough to Siena to be a base of exploration. Rooms vary in size, but all are filled with elegant furnishings, including some canopy beds. One room of the restaurant (closed Monday) has a wall of windows looking out into the countryside. **Pros:** bucolic location; lots of walking trails; lovely rooms. **Cons:** few restaurant options nearby; need a car to get around. ⊠ *Località Pretale* ✛ *11 km (7 mi) east of Siena Sovicille* ☎ *0577/345401* 🖷 *0577/345625* ⊕ *www.borgopretale.it* ⇆ *27 rooms, 7 suites* ⚐ *In-hotel: restaurant, bar, tennis court, pool, gym, bicycles, Internet terminal* ⊟ *AE, D, MC, V* ⊘ *Closed Nov.–Easter* ⓘⓞⓛ *BP.*

$$ ⌂**Hotel Santa Caterina.** Manager Lorenza Capannelli and her fine staff
★ are welcoming, hospitable, enthusiastic, and go out of their way to ensure a fine stay. Dark, straight-lined wood furniture stands next to

Continued on page 184

EATING AND DRINKING WELL IN TUSCANY

The influence of the ancient Etruscans—who favored the use of fresh herbs—is still felt in Tuscan cuisine three millennia later. Simple and earthy, Tuscan food celebrates the seasons with fresh vegetable dishes, wonderful bread-based soups, and meats perfumed with sage, rosemary, and thyme.

Throughout Tuscany there are excellent upscale restaurants that serve elaborate dishes, but to get a real taste of the flavors of the region, head for the family-run trattorias found in every town. The service and setting are often basic, but the food can be memorable.

Few places serve lighter fare at midday, so expect substantial meals at lunch and dinner, especially in out-of-the-way towns. Dining hours are fairly standard: lunch between 12:30 and 2, dinner between 7:30 and 10.

HOLD THE SALT

Tuscan bread is famous for what it's missing: it's made without salt. That's because it's intended to pick up seasoning from the food it accompanies; it's not meant to be eaten alone or dipped in a bowl of oil (which is a custom developed by American restaurants—it's not standard practice in Italian ones).

That doesn't mean Tuscans don't like to start a meal with bread, but usually it's prepared in some way. It can be grilled and drizzled with olive oil *(fettunta)*, covered with chicken liver spread *(crostino nero)*, or rubbed with garlic and topped with tomatoes *(bruschetta)*.

AFFETTATI MISTI

The name, roughly translated, means "mixed cold cuts," pictured left, and it's something Tuscans do exceptionally well. A platter of cured meats, served as an antipasto, is sure to include *prosciutto crudo* (ham, cut paper thin) and *salame* (dry sausage, prepared in dozens of ways—some spicy, some sweet). The most distinctly Tuscan affettati are made from *cinta senese* (a once nearly extinct pig found only in the heart of the region) and *cinghiale* (wild boar, which roam all over central Italy). You can eat these delicious slices unadorned or layered on a piece of bread.

PASTA

Restaurants throughout Tuscany serve dishes similar to those in Florence, but they also have their own local specialties. Many recipes are from the *nonna* (grandmother) of the restaurant's owner, handed down through time but never written down.

Look in particular for pasta creations made with *pici* (a long, thick, hand-rolled spaghetti), pictured below. *Pappardelle* (a long, flat pasta noodle, pictured upper right), is frequently paired with sauces made with game, such as *lepre* (hare) or cinghiale. In the northwest, a specialty of Lucca is *tordelli di carne al ragù* (meat-stuffed pasta with a meat sauce).

MEAT

Bistecca all fiorentina (a thick T-bone steak, grilled rare) is the classic meat dish of Tuscany, but there are other specialties as well. Many menus will include *tagliata di manzo* (thinly sliced, roasted beef, drizzled with olive oil), *arista di maiale* (roast pork with sage and rosemary), and *salsiccia e fagioli* (pork sausage and beans). In the southern part of the region, don't be surprised to find *piccione* (pigeon), which can be roasted, stuffed, or baked.

WINE

Grape cultivation here also dates from Etruscan times, and, particularly in Chianti, vineyards are abundant. The resulting medium-body red wine is a staple on most tables; however, you can select from a multitude of other varieties, including such reds as Brunello di Montalcino and Vino Nobile di Montepulciano and such whites as Vermentino and Vernaccia.

Super Tuscans (a fanciful name given to a group of wines by American journalists) now command attention as some of the best produced in Italy; they have great depth and complexity. The dessert wine *vin santo* is made throughout the region and is often sipped with *biscotti* (twice-baked almond cookies), perfect for dunking.

beds with floral spreads; some have upholstered headboards. Rooms in the back look out onto the garden or the countryside in the distance. When it's warm, breakfast is served in the flower-filled garden with a view of the Siena countryside, providing a gorgeous start to the day. The well-run hotel is outside Porta Romana—a 15-minute walk south of Piazza del Campo. **Pros:** friendly staff; a short walk to center of town, breakfast in the garden. **Cons:** on a busy intersection; outside city walls. ✉ *Via Piccolomini 7, San Martino* ☎ *0577/221105* ⊕ *www. hscsiena.it* ⤳ *22 rooms* ⚭ *In-room: Internet. In-hotel: concierge, laundry service, Internet terminal, parking (fee), some pets allowed* ⊟ *AE, DC, MC, V* ⑂❘ *BP.*

$$ 🖳 **Palazzo Ravizza.** This romantic palazzo exudes a sense of genteel shab-

★ biness. Rooms have high ceilings, antique furnishings, and bathrooms decorated with hand-painted tiles. The location is key: from here it's just a 10-minute walk to the Duomo. Il Capriccio ($$–$$$), ably run by chef Fabio Tozzi, specializes in traditional Tuscan fare. In warm weather, enjoy your meal in the garden with a trickling fountain. "We have only positive things to say about Palazzo Ravizza. From the amazing Tuscan view, to the proximity to Il Campo this hotel was by far the best one we stayed at throughout our Italy vacation," says one traveler on Fodors. com. **Pros:** 10-minute walk to the center of town; pleasant garden with a view beyond the city walls; professional staff. **Cons:** not all rooms have views; some rooms are a little cramped. ✉ *Pian dei Mantellini 34, Città* ☎ *0577/280462* ⊕ *www.palazzoravizza.it* ⤳ *38 rooms, 4 suites* ⚭ *In-room: safe, Wi-Fi (some). In-hotel: restaurant, bar, concierge, laundry service, Internet terminal, Wi-Fi, parking (no fee), some pets allowed* ⊟ *AE, DC, MC, V* ⑂❘ *BP.*

AREZZO AND CORTONA

The hill towns of Arezzo and Cortona carry on age-old local traditions—in June and September, for example, Arezzo's Romanesque and Gothic churches are enlivened by the Giostra del Saracino, a costumed medieval joust. Arezzo has been home to important artists since ancient times, when Etruscan potters produced their fiery-red vessels here. Fine examples of the work of Luca Signorelli are preserved in Cortona, his hometown.

AREZZO

63 km (39 mi) northeast of Siena, 81 km (50 mi) southeast of Florence.

GETTING HERE

Arezzo is easily reached by car from the A1 (Autostrada del Sole), the main highway running between Florence and Rome. Direct trains connect Arezzo with Rome (2½ hours) and Florence (1 hour). Direct bus service is available from Florence, but not from Rome.

VISITOR INFORMATION

Arezzo tourism office (✉ *Piazza della Repubblica 28* ☎ *0575/377678* ⊕ *www. apt.arezzo.it).*

EXPLORING

The birthplace of the poet Petrarch (1304–74) and the Renaissance artist and art historian Giorgio Vasari, Arezzo is today best known for the magnificent Piero della Francesca frescoes in the church of San Francesco. The city dates from pre-Etruscan times and thrived as an Etruscan capital from the 7th to the 4th century BC. During the Middle Ages it was fully embroiled in the conflict between the Ghibellines (pro–Holy Roman Emperor) and the Guelphs (pro-pope), losing its independence to Florence at the end of the 14th century after many decades of doing battle.

Urban sprawl testifies to the fact that Arezzo (population 90,000) is the third-largest city in Tuscany (after Florence and Pisa). But the old town, set on a low hill, is relatively small, and almost completely closed to traffic. Look for parking along the roads that circle the lower part of town, near the train station, and walk into town from there. You can explore the most interesting sights in a few hours, adding time to linger for some window-shopping at Arezzo's many antiques shops.

Fodor's Choice ★ The remarkable frescoes by Piero della Francesca (circa 1420–92) in the **Basilica di San Francesco** were painted between 1452 and 1466. They depict scenes from the *Legend of the True Cross* on three walls of the Capella Bacci, a chapel behind the high altar. What Sir Kenneth Clark called "the most perfect morning light in all Renaissance painting" may be seen in the lowest section of the right wall, where the troops of the emperor Maxentius fled before the sign of the cross. A 15-year project restored the works to their original brilliance. A distant but free view of the frescoes is to be had from the main body of the church. For a closer look, make reservations at the ticket office in Piazza San Francesco, two doors down from the church. ⊠ *Piazza San Francesco* ☎ *0575/20630 church, 0575/352757 Capella Bacci reservations* ⊕ *www.pierodellafrancesca.it* ⊠ *Capella Bacci €6* ☉ *Church: daily 8:30–6:30. Capella Bacci: Apr.–Oct., weekdays 9–6:30, Sat. 9–5:30, Sun. 1–5:30; Nov.–Mar., weekdays 9–5:30, Sat. 9–5, Sun. 1–5.*

Some historians maintain that Arezzo's oddly shaped, sloping **Piazza Grande** was once the site of an ancient Roman forum. Now it hosts a first-Sunday-of-the-month antiques fair as well as the **Giostra del Saracino** (Joust of the Saracen), featuring medieval costumes and competition, held here in the middle of June and on the first Sunday of September. Check out the 16th-century loggia designed by native son Giorgio Vasari on the northeast side of the piazza.

The curving, tiered apse on Piazza Grande belongs to **Santa Maria della Pieve**, one of Tuscany's finest Romanesque churches, built in the 12th century. Don't miss the Portale Maggiore (great door) with its remarkably vibrant polychrome figures representing the months. ⊠ *Corso Italia 7* ☎ *0575/22629* ☉ *May–Sept., daily 8–1 and 3–7; Oct.–Apr., daily 8–noon and 3–6.*

Arezzo's medieval **Duomo** (at the top of the hill) contains a fresco of a somber *Magdalen* by Piero della Francesca; look for it next to the large marble tomb near the organ. ⊠ *Piazza del Duomo 1* ☎ *0575/23991* ☉ *Daily 6:30–12:30 and 3–6:30.*

WHERE TO EAT AND STAY

$ ✕**Antica Trattoria da Guido.** Owned by a southern Italian, this small trattoria serves tasty adaptations of Calabrian dishes, such as home-made pasta served with *salsa ai pomodori secchi* (a spicy sauce of sun-dried tomatoes, capers, and red peppers). The display of homemade pastries makes decisions difficult at the end of the meal. The dining room is a pleasant mix of rustic and modern, and the service is friendly. ⊠ *Via di San Francesco 1* ☎ *0575/23760* ⊕ *www.anticatrattoriadaguido. it* ⊟ *MC, V* ⊘ *Closed Sun. and 2 wks in mid-Aug.*

SOUTHERN
ITALIAN

> ## WORD OF MOUTH
>
> "Arezzo holds a huge antiques fair the first weekend of each month that takes over the streets in the historical center of town. You may want to check your dates, either to avoid or take advantage of it."
>
> —shellio

$ ✕**La Torre di Gnicche.** Wine lovers shouldn't miss this wine bar/eatery with more than 700 labels on the list, just off Piazza Grande. Seasonal dishes of traditional fare, such as *acquacotta del casentino* (porcini mushroom soup) and *baccalà in umido* (salt-cod stew), are served in the simply decorated, vaulted dining room. You can accompany your meal with one, or more, of the almost 30 wines that are available by the glass. Limited outdoor seating is available in warm weather. ⊠ *Piaggia San Martino 8* ☎ *0575/352035* ⊕ *www.latorredignicche.it* ⊟ *AE, MC, V* ⊘ *Closed Wed., Jan., and 2 wks in July.*

ITALIAN

$$ 🏠**Castello di Gargonza.** Enchantment reigns at this tiny 13th-century countryside hamlet, part of the fiefdom of the aristocratic Florentine Guicciardini. The modern Count Roberto Guicciardini reinvented the place as an agriturismo to rescue a dying village. A castle, church, and cobbled streets set the stage. Guest rooms vary in style; some are decidedly more basic than others. However, high wood-beam ceilings, terra-cotta floors, and modern bathrooms are the rule throughout. Apartments have three to eight rooms each, sleeping as many as 10 people, and have as many as four baths. A minimum three-night stay is required for most rooms; a minimum one-week stay for the apartments. **Pros:** romantic, one-of-a-kind accommodation in a medieval castle; peaceful, isolated setting. **Cons:** standard rooms are extremely basic; a little out of the way for exploring the region; private transportation is a necessity. ⊠ *SR73* ✛ *28 km (17 mi) southwest of Arezzo, Monte San Savino* ☎ *0575/847021* 🖶 *0575/847054* ⊕ *www.gargonza.it* 🗭 *37 rooms, 8 apartments* ⚎ *In-room: no a/c, kitchen (some), refrigerator, no TV. In-hotel: restaurant, bar, pool, Internet terminal, Wi-Fi* ⊟ *AE, DC, MC, V* ⊘ *Closed last 3 wks in Jan. and Feb.* ⊺◎⊺ *BP.*

$$ 🏠**Cavaliere Palace Hotel.** On a quiet backstreet in the old town, the Cavaliere is moments away from the main sights. The carpeted rooms in the restored 19th-century town house are small but comfy, with contemporary furnishings. **Pros:** location, location, location. **Cons:** some complain of noise from nearby disco; very plain decor. ⊠ *Via Madonna del Prato 83, Arezzo* ☎ *0575/26836* ⊕ *www.cavalierehotels.com* 🗭 *27 rooms* ⚎ *In-room: Wi-Fi. In-hotel: Wi-Fi, Internet terminal, parking (fee)* ⊟ *AE, MC, V* ⊺◎⊺ *CP.*

SHOPPING

Ever since Etruscan goldsmiths set up their shops here more than 2,000 years ago, Arezzo has been famous for its jewelry. Today the town lays claim to being one of the world's capitals of jewelry design and manufacture, and you can find an impressive display of big-time baubles in the town center's shops.

Arezzo is also famous, at least in Italy, for its antiques dealers. The first weekend of every month, between 8:30 and 5:30 each day, Piazza Grande, a colorful flea market selling antiques and not-so-antiques takes place here in the town's main square.

3

CORTONA

29 km (18 mi) south of Arezzo, 79 km (44 mi) east of Siena, 117 km (73 mi) southeast of Florence.

GETTING HERE

Cortona is easily reached by car from the A1 (Autostrada del Sole): take the Valdichiana exit toward Perugia, then follow signs for Cortona. Regular bus service, provided by Etruria Mobilità, is available between Arezzo and Cortona (1 hour). Train service to Cortona is made inconvenient by the location of the train station, in the valley 3 km (2 mi) steeply below the town itself. From there, you have to rely on bus or taxi service to get up to Cortona.

VISITOR INFORMATION

Cortona tourism office (⊠ *Via Nazionale 42* ☎ *0575/630352* ⊕ *www.apt. arezzo.it*).

EXPLORING

With olive trees and vineyards creeping up to its walls, pretty Cortona—popularized by Frances Mayes's glowing descriptions in *Under the Tuscan Sun*—commands sweeping views over Lake Trasimeno and the plain of the Valdichiana. Its two galleries and churches are rarely visited; its delightful medieval streets are a pleasure to wander for their own sake. The heart of town is formed by Piazza della Repubblica and the adjacent Piazza Signorelli; both contain pleasant shops to browse in.

The **Museo Diocesano** *(Diocesan Museum)* houses an impressive number of large and splendid paintings by native son Luca Signorelli, as well as a stunning *Annunciation* by Fra Angelico, a delightful surprise in this small town. ⊠ *Piazza Duomo* ☎ *0575/62830* 💶*€5* 🕙 *Apr.–Oct., Tues.–Sun. 10–7; Nov.–Mar., Tues.–Sun. 10–5.*

★ Legend has it that **Santa Maria del Calcinaio** was built between 1485 and 1513 after the image of the Madonna appeared on a wall of the medieval *calcinaio* (lime pit used for curing leather) that had occupied the site. The linear gray-and-white interior recalls Florence's Duomo. Sienese architect Francesco di Giorgio (1439–1502) most likely designed the sanctuary: the church is a terrific example of Renaissance architectural principles. ⊠ *Località Il Calcinaio 227* ⊕ *3 km (2 mi) southeast of Cortona's center on Via Guelph* ☎ *0575/604830* 🕙 *Mon.–Sat. 3:30–6, Sun. 10–12:30.*

WHERE TO EAT AND STAY

$$$$ ✕ **Osteria del Teatro.** Photographs from theatrical productions spanning
TUSCAN many years line the walls of this tavern off Cortona's large Piazza del
★ Teatro. The food is simply delicious—try the *filetto al lardo di colon-nata e prugne* (beef cooked with bacon and prunes); service is warm and friendly. ✉ *Via Maffei 2* ☎ *0575/630556* ⊕ *www.osteria-del-teatro. it* ▭ *AE, DC, MC, V* ⊙ *Closed Wed. and 2 wks in Nov. and in Feb.*

$$$$ ▦ **Il Falconiere.** Choose here from rooms in an 18th-century villa, suites
★ in the *chiesetta* (chapel, or little church), or for more seclusion, Le Vigne del Falco suites at the far end of the property. Husband-and-wife team Riccardo and Silvia Baracchi run the show, serving an almost exclusively American and British clientele. Their restaurant's ($$$$) inventive seasonal menu includes *pici alla carbonara con lo zafferano di Centoia e pancetta croccante* (homemade thick spaghetti with carbonara sauce), over which, if your heart desires, you can add shaved white truffles. Cooking classes and guided wine tastings are available, and a small shop sells estate-produced olive oil and wine. **Pros:** attractive setting in the valley beneath Cortona; excellent service; elegant, but relaxed. **Cons:** a car is a must; some find rooms in main villa a little noisy. ✉ *Località San Martino 370* ✛ *3 km (1½ mi) north of Cortona* ☎ *0575/612679* 🖨 *0575/612927* ⊕ *www.ilfalconiere.com* ⤏ *13 rooms, 7 suites* ৬ *In-room: safe, refrigerator, Internet. In-hotel: restaurant, room service, bar, pools, spa, concierge, laundry service, Wi-Fi, Internet terminal, parking (no fee), some pets allowed (fee)* ▭ *AE, MC, V* ⊙ *No lunch in restaurant Tues. Nov.–Mar. Hotel closed last 3 wks in Jan.–mid-Feb.* ❙⊙❙ *BP.*

HILL TOWNS WEST OF SIENA

Submit to the draw of Tuscany's enchanting fortified cities that crown the hills west of Siena, many dating to the Etruscan period. San Gimignano, known as the "medieval Manhattan" because of its forest of stout medieval towers built by rival families, is the most heavily visited. This onetime Roman outpost, with its tilted cobbled streets and ancient buildings, can make the days of Guelph-Ghibelline conflicts palpable. Rising from a series of bleak gullied hills and valleys, Volterra has always been popular for its minerals and stones, particularly alabaster, which was used by the Etruscans for many implements. Examples are now displayed in the exceptional and unwieldy Museo Etrusco Guarnacci.

VOLTERRA

48 km (30 mi) south of San Miniato, 75 km (47 mi) southwest of Florence.

GETTING HERE

By car, the best route from San Gimignano follows the SP1 south to Castel San Gimignano and then the SS68 all the way to Volterra. Coming from the west, take the SS1, a coastal road to Cecina, then follow the SS68 to Volterra. Either way, there's a long, winding climb at the end of your trip. Getting here by bus or train is complicated; avoid it if possible. From Florence or Siena, the journey is best made by bus and involves a change in Colle di Val d'Elsa.

VISITOR INFORMATION

Volterra tourism office (⊠ *Piazza dei Priori 20* ☎ *0588/87257* ⊕ *www. volterratur.it*).

EXPLORING

Unlike other Tuscan hill towns rising above sprawling vineyards and rolling fields of green, Volterra is surrounded by desolate terrain marred with industry and mining equipment. D. H. Lawrence described it as "somber and chilly alone on her rock" in his *Etruscan Places*. The fortress, walls, and gates still stand mightily over Le Balze, a distinctive series of gullied hills and valleys to the west that were formed by irregular erosion. The town has long been known for its alabaster, which has been mined since Etruscan times; today the Volterrans use it to make ornaments and souvenirs sold all over town.

Volterra has some of Italy's best small museums. The extraordinarily large and unique collection of Etruscan artifacts at the **Museo Etrusco Guarnacci** is a treasure in the region. (Many of the other Etruscan finds from the area have been shipped off to state museums or the Vatican.) If only a curator had thought to cull the best of the 700 funerary urns rather than to display every last one of them. ⊠ *Via Don Minzoni 15* ☎ *0588/86347* ⊕ *www.comune.volterra.pi.it* ⊠ *€8, includes admission to Museo Diocesano di Arte Sacra and Pinoteca* ☉ *Mid-Mar.–early Nov., daily 9–6:45; early Nov.–mid-Mar., daily 9–1:15.*

The **Pinacoteca e Museo Civico** houses a highly acclaimed collection of religious art, including a *Madonna and Child with Saints* by Luca Signorelli (1445/50–1523) and a *Deposition* by Rosso Fiorentino (1494–1541). These alone are reason enough to visit Volterra. ⊠ *Via dei Sarti 1* ☎ *0588/87580* ⊕ *www.comune.volterra.pi.it* ⊠ *€8, includes admission to Museo Etrusco Guarnacci and Museo Diocesano di Arte Sacra* ☉ *Mid-Mar.–early Nov., daily 9–7; early Nov.–mid-Mar., daily 9–1:45.*

Next to the altar in the town's unfinished **Duomo** is a magnificent 13th-century carved-wood *Deposition*. Note the fresco by Benozzo Gozzoli in the Cappella della Addolorata. Along the left wall of the nave you can see the arrival of the Magi. ⊠ *Piazza San Giovanni* ☎ *0588/86192* ☉ *Daily 7–7.*

Among Volterra's best-preserved ancient remains is the Etruscan **Porta all'Arco**, an arch dating from the 4th century BC now incorporated into the city walls.

The ruins of the 1st-century BC **Teatro Romano**, a beautifully preserved Roman theater, are worth a visit. Adjacent to the theater are the remains of the *terme* (baths). The complex is outside the town walls past Porta Fiorentina. ⊠ *Viale Francesco Ferrucci* ☎ *0586/260837* ⊠ *€2* ☉ *Mar.– May and Sept.–Nov., daily 10–1 and 2–4; June–Aug., daily 10–6:45; Dec.–Feb., weekends 10–1 and 2–4.*

WHERE TO EAT AND STAY

$$ **✕ Il Sacco Fiorentino.** Start with the *antipasti del Sacco Fiorentino*—a
TUSCAN medley of sautéed chicken liver, porcini mushrooms, and polenta driz-
★ zled with balsamic vinegar. The meal just gets better when you move on
to the *tagliatelle del Sacco Fiorentino,* a riot of curried spaghetti with
chicken and roasted red peppers. The wine list is a marvel, as it's long
and very well priced. White walls, tile floors, and red tablecloths create
an understated tone that is unremarkable, but once the food starts arriv-
ing, it's easy to forgive the lack of decoration. ✉ *Piazza XX Settembre
18* ☎ *0588/88537* ⊟ *AE, DC, MC, V* ☾ *Closed Wed.*

$ 🛏 **Etruria.** Giuseppina and Lisa, owners of this simple yet tasteful hotel,
go out of their way to make your visit memorable. The rooms are mod-
est and the bathrooms are out of date, but the central location, the
ample buffet breakfast, and the modest rates make the Etruria ideal for
those on a budget. A quiet terraced garden, overlooking the rooftops of
town, is a definite plus during the hot summer months. **Pros:** on a pedes-
trian street; helpful staff; tranquil garden. **Cons:** rooms can be noisy
during the day; steps to climb; bathrooms old-fashioned and small.
✉ *Via Matteotti 32* ☎ *0588/87377* ⊕ *www.albergoetruria.it* ⤴ *21* ♿ *In-
room: no a/c. In-hotel: Internet terminal, Wi-Fi* ⊟ *AE, DC, MC, V.*

$ 🛏 **San Lino.** Within the town's medieval walls, this convent-turned-hotel
has wood-beam ceilings, graceful archways, and terra-cotta floors in
public spaces. The furnishings are contemporary wood laminate and
straight-line ironwork. Sip a beverage or write a postcard on the small
terrace filled with potted geraniums; the pool area is framed on one
side by a church with a stained-glass window of the Last Supper. The
restaurant ($–$$) serves Tuscan classics and local specialties such as
zuppa alla volterrana, a thick vegetable soup. Half-board is available.
Pros: steps away from center of town; friendly and helpful staff; convenient parking. **Cons:** a little run-down; elevators are noisy; breakfast is adequate, but nothing to write home about. ✉ *Via San Lino 26*
☎ *0588/85250* 🖨 *0588/80620* ⊕ *www.hotelsanlino.com* ⤴ *43 rooms*
♿ *In-room: refrigerator, dial-up. In-hotel: restaurant, bar, pool, concierge, laundry service, public Internet, parking (fee), some pets allowed*
⊟ *AE, DC, MC, V* ☾ *Closed Nov.–Jan.* ⦿*BP.*

SAN GIMIGNANO

27 km (17 mi) east of Volterra, 57 km (35 mi) southwest of Florence.

GETTING HERE

You can reach San Gimignano by car from the Florence–Siena Superstrada. Exit at Poggibonsi Nord and follow signs for San Gimignano.
Although it involves changing buses in Poggibonsi, getting to San
Gimignano by bus is a relatively straightforward affair. SITA operates
the service between Siena or Florence and Poggibonsi, while Tra-In
takes care of the Poggibonsi to San Gimignano route. You cannot reach
San Gimignano by train.

VISITOR INFORMATION

San Gimignano tourism office (✉ *Piazza Duomo 1* ☎ *0577/940008* ⊕ *www.
sangimignano.com*).

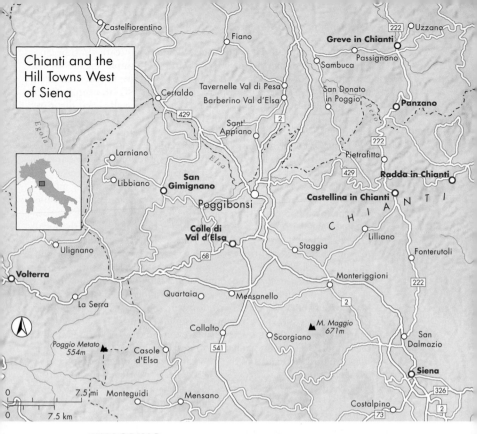

Chianti and the
Hill Towns West
of Siena

Castelfiorentino
Fiano
222 Uzzano
Greve in Chianti
Passignano
Sambuca
Tavernelle Val di Pesa
San Donato
in Poggio
Panzano
Certaldo
Barberino Val d'Elsa
429
2
Sant'
Appiano
222
Pietrafitta
Larniano
Elsa
429
Radda in Chianti
Libbiano
San
Gimignano
Castellina in Chianti
N T I
Poggibonsi
C H I A
Colle di
Val d'Elsa
Lilliano
68
Staggia
Fonterutoli
Ulignano
Monteriggioni
Quartaia
Mensanello
222
Volterra
2
La Serra
M. Maggio
671m
Collalto
San
Dalmazio
Poggio Metato
554m
Casole
d'Elsa
541
Scorgiano
Siena
Monteguidi
Mensano
Costalpino
326
0   7.5 mi
0   7.5 km
73
2

Egola
Peso
Elsa

EXPLORING

When you're on a hilltop surrounded by soaring medieval towers sil-houetted against the sky, it's difficult not to fall under the spell of San Gimignano. Its tall walls and narrow streets are typical of Tuscan hill towns, but it's the medieval "skyscrapers" that set the town apart from its neighbors. Today 14 towers remain, but at the height of the Guelph–Ghibelline conflict there was a forest of more than 70, and it was pos-sible to cross the town by rooftop rather than by road. The towers were built partly for defensive purposes—they were a safe refuge and useful for pouring boiling oil on attacking enemies—and partly for bolster-ing the egos of their owners, who competed with deadly seriousness to build the highest tower in town.

Today San Gimignano isn't much more than a gentrified walled city, touristy but still very much worth exploring because, despite the pro-fusion of cheesy souvenir shops lining the main drag, there's some serious Renaissance art to be seen here. Tour groups arrive early and clog the wine-tasting rooms—San Gimignano is famous for its light white Vernaccia—and art galleries for much of the day, but most sights stay open through late afternoon, when all the tour groups have long since departed.

The town's main church is not officially a *duomo* (cathedral) because San Gimignano has no bishop. Behind the simple facade of the Romanesque **Collegiata** lies a treasure trove of fine frescoes, covering nearly every part of the interior. Bartolo di Fredi's 14th-century fresco cycle of Old Testament scenes extends along one wall. Their distinctly medieval feel, with misshapen bodies, buckets of spurting blood, and lack of perspective, contrasts with the much more reserved scenes from the *Life of Christ* (attributed to 14th-century artist Lippo Memmi), painted on the opposite wall just 14 years later. Taddeo di Bartolo's otherworldly *Last Judgment* (late 14th century), with its distorted and suffering nudes, reveals the great influence of Dante's horrifying imagery in *The Inferno* and was surely an inspiration for later painters. Proof that the town had more than one protector, Benozzo Gozzoli's arrow-riddled *St. Sebastian* was commissioned in gratitude after the locals prayed to the saint for relief from plague. The Renaissance **Cappella di Santa Fina** is decorated with a fresco cycle by Domenico Ghirlandaio illustrating the life of Saint Fina. A small girl who suffered from a terminal disease, Fina repented for her sins—among them having accepted an orange from a boy—and in penance lived out the rest of her short life on a wooden board, tormented by rats. The scenes depict the arrival of Saint Gregory, who appeared to assure her that death was near; the flowers that miraculously grew from the wooden plank; and the miracles that accompanied her funeral, including the healing of her nurse's paralyzed hand and the restoration of a blind choirboy's vision. ✉ *Piazza Duomo* 🖀 *0577/940316* 🖃 *€3.50; €5.50 includes the Museo d'Arte Sacra* ☉ *Apr.–Oct., weekdays 9:30–7:10, Sat. 9:30–5:10, Sun. 12:30–5:10; Nov. 1–15, Dec. 1–Jan. 15, and Feb. 1–Mar., Mon.–Sat. 9:30–4:40, Sun. 12:30–5:10. Closed Nov. 16–30 and Jan. 16–31.*

★   The impressive **Museo Civico** occupies what was the "new" Palazzo del Popolo; the Torre Grossa is adjacent. Dante visited San Gimignano for only one day as a Guelph ambassador from Florence to ask the locals to join the Florentines in supporting the pope—just long enough to get the main council chamber, which now holds a 14th-century *Maestà* by Lippo Memmi, named after him. Off the stairway is a small room containing the racy frescoes by Memmo di Filippuccio (active 1288–1324) depicting the courtship, shared bath, and wedding of a young, androgynous-looking couple. That the space could have been a private room for the commune's chief magistrate may have something to do with the work's highly charged eroticism.

Upstairs, paintings by famous Renaissance artists Pinturicchio (*Madonna Enthroned*), Benozzo Gozzoli (*Madonna and Child*), and two large *tondi* (circular paintings) by Filippino Lippi (circa 1457–1504) attest to the importance and wealth of San Gimignano. Also worth seeing are Taddeo di Bartolo's *Life of San Gimignano*, with the saint holding a model of the town as it once appeared; Lorenzo di Niccolò's gruesome martyrdom scene in the *Life of St. Bartholomew* (1401); and scenes from the *Life of St. Fina* on a tabernacle that was designed to hold her head. Admission includes the steep climb to the top of the Torre Grossa, which on a clear day has spectacular views. ✉ *Piazza Duomo*

DID YOU KNOW?

San Gimignano, sometimes called "the medieval Manhattan," once had more than 70 towers. Today, 14 remain standing.

2 ☎ 0577/990312 ☜ €5 ⊙ Mar.–
Oct., daily 9:30–7; Nov.–Feb., daily
10–5:30.

★ Make a beeline for Benozzo Gozzoli's superlative frescoes inside
the church of **Sant'Agostino**. This
Romanesque–Gothic church contains Benozzo's stunning 15th-cen-
tury fresco cycle depicting scenes
from the life of Saint Augustine.
The saint's work was essential to
the early development of church

doctrine. As thoroughly discussed in his autobiographical *Confessions*
(an acute dialogue with God), Augustine, like many saints, sinned considerably in his youth before finding God. But unlike the lives of other
saints, where the story continues through a litany of deprivations, peni-
tence, and often martyrdom, Augustine's life and work focused on philosophy and the reconciliation of faith and thought. Benozzo's 17 scenes
on the choir wall depict Augustine as a man who traveled and taught
extensively in the 4th and 5th centuries. The 15th-century altarpiece by
Piero del Pollaiolo (1443–96) depicts *The Coronation of the Virgin* and
the various protectors of the city. On your way out of Sant'Agostino,
stop in at the **Cappella di San Bartolo**, with a sumptuously elaborate
tomb by Benedetto da Maiano (1442–97). ⊠ *Piazza Sant'Agostino, off
Via San Matteo* ☎ *0577/907012* ☜ *Free* ⊙ *Apr.–Oct., daily 7–noon and
3–7; Nov. and Dec. and Mar., daily 7–noon and 3–6; Jan. and Feb.,
Mon. 3–6, Tues.–Sun. 10–noon and 3–6.*

WHERE TO EAT AND STAY

The **Cooperativa Hotels Promotion** (⊠ *Via di San Giovanni 125*
☎ *0577/940809* ⊕ *www.hotelsiena.com*) provides commission-free
booking for local hotels and farmhouses.

$ ✕ **La Mangiatoia.** Multicolor gingham tablecloths provide an interesting
TUSCAN   juxtaposition with rib-vaulted ceilings dating from the 13th century.
The lighthearted touch might be explained by the influence of chef
Susi Cuomo, who has been presiding over the kitchen for more than
20 years. The menu is seasonal—in autumn, don't miss her *sacottino
di pecorino al tartufo* (little packages of pasta stuffed with pecorino
and seasoned with truffles). In summer, eat lighter fare on the intimate,
flower-bedecked terrace in the back. ⊠ *Via Mainardi 5, off Via San
Matteo* ☎ *0577/941528* ⊕ *www.ristorantelamangiatoia.it* ☐ MC, V
⊙ *Closed Tues., 3 wks in Nov., and 1 wk in Jan.*

$–$$ ⊡ **Pescille.** A rambling farmhouse has been transformed into a hand-
some hotel with understated contemporary furniture in the bedrooms
and country-classic motifs such as farm implements hanging on the
walls in the bar. From this charming spot you get a splendid view
of San Gimignano's towers. **Pros:** splendid views; quiet atmosphere;
10-minute walk to town. **Cons:** furnishings a bit austere; there's an
elevator for luggage but not for guests. ⊠ *Strada Provinciale Castel San
Gimignano, Località Pescille* ✛ *4 km (2½ mi) south of San Gimignano*

town center ☏ *0577/940186* ⊕ *www.pescille.it* ⤳ *38 rooms, 12 suites* ♿ *In-room: Wi-Fi. In-hotel: bar, tennis court, pool, gym, no elevator, Internet terminal, Wi-Fi, parking (no fee)* ⊟ *AE, DC, MC, V* ☉ *Closed Nov.–Mar.* ⵊⵔ *BP.*

COLLE DI VAL D'ELSA

15 km (9 mi) southeast of San Gimignano, 50 km (31 mi) southwest of Florence.

GETTING HERE

You can reach Colle di Val d'Elsa by car on either the SR2 from Siena or the Florence–Siena Superstrada. Bus service to and from Siena and Florence is frequent.

VISITOR INFORMATION

Colle di Val d'Elsa Tourism Office (✉ *Via Campana 43* ☏ *0577/922791*).

EXPLORING

Most people pass through on their way to and from popular tourist destinations Volterra and San Gimignano—a shame, since Colle di Val d'Elsa has a lot to offer. It's another town on the Via Francigena that benefited from trade along the pilgrimage route to Rome. Colle got an extra boost in the late 16th century when it was given a bishopric, probably related to an increase in trade when nearby San Gimignano was cut off from the well-traveled road. The town is arranged on two levels, and from the 12th century onward the flat lower portion was given over to a flourishing papermaking industry; today the area is mostly modern, and efforts have shifted toward the production of fine glass and crystal.

WHERE TO EAT AND STAY

$$$$ ✕ **Ristorante Arnolfo.** Food lovers should not miss Arnolfo, one of Tusca-
MODERN ITALIAN ny's most highly regarded restaurants. Chef Gaetano Trovato sets high
Fodor'sChoice standards of creativity; his dishes daringly ride the line between innova-
★ tion and tradition, almost always with spectacular results. The menu changes frequently and has a fixed-price option, but you are always sure to find fish and lots of fresh vegetables in the summer. You're in for a special treat if the specials include *carrè di agnello al vino rosso e sella alle olive* (rack of lamb in a red wine sauce and lamb saddle with olives). ✉ *Piazza XX Settembre 52* ☏ *0577/920549* ⊕ *www.arnolfo. com* ⊟ *AE, DC, MC, V* ☉ *Closed Tues. and Wed., last wk in Jan. and Feb., and last wk in Aug.*

$$$$ ⵊ **La Suvera.** Pope Julius II once owned this luxurious estate in the valley
★ of the River Elsa. The papal villa and an adjacent building have magnificently furnished guest rooms and suites appointed with antiques. A wall-size tapestry depicting the Roman army hangs beside a red canopy bed in the Angels Room. La Suvera's first-rate facilities include drawing rooms, a library, an Italian garden, a park, and the Oliviera restaurant (serving organic estate wines). **Pros:** luxurious accommodations; historic setting; far from the madding crowd. **Cons:** out-of-the-way location; showing its age; some bristle at the extremely formal service. ✉ *Off SS541* ⊹ *15 km (9 mi) south of Colle di Val d'Elsa, Pievescola* ☏ *0577/960300* ⊕ *www.lasuvera.it* ⤳ *36 rooms, 12 suites* ♿ *In-room:*

safe. In-hotel: restaurant, room service, bar, tennis court, pool, bicycles, concierge, laundry service, Internet terminal, no kids under 12 ☰ *AE, DC, MC, V* ☺ *Closed Nov.–Easter* ⑩| *BP.*

CHIANTI

Chianti, directly south of Florence, is one of Italy's most famous wine-producing areas; its hill towns, olive groves, and vineyards are quintessential Tuscany. Many British and northern Europeans have relocated here, drawn by the unhurried life, balmy climate, and charming villages; there are so many Britons, in fact, that the area has been nicknamed Chiantishire. Still, it remains strongly Tuscan in character, with drop-dead views of vine-quilted hills and elegantly elongated cypress trees.

The sinuous SR222 highway, known as the Strada Chiantigiana, runs from Florence through the heart of Chianti. Its most scenic section connects Strada in Chianti, 16 km (10 mi) south of Florence, and Greve in Chianti, whose triangular central piazza is surrounded by restaurants and vintners offering *degustazioni* (wine tastings), 11 km (7 mi) farther south.

GREVE IN CHIANTI

40 km (25 mi) northeast of Colle Val d'Elsa, 27 km (17 mi) south of Florence.

GETTING HERE

Driving from Florence or Siena, Greve is easily reached via the Strada Chiantigiana (SR222). SITA buses travel frequently between Florence and Greve. Tra-In and SITA buses connect Siena and Greve, but a direct trip is virtually impossible. There is no train service to Greve.

VISITOR INFORMATION

Greve in Chianti tourism offices (⊠ *Via Giovanni da Verrazzano 59* ☏ *055/8546287*).

EXPLORING

If there is a capital of Chianti, it is Greve, a friendly market town with no shortage of cafés, *enoteche* (wine bars), and crafts shops lining its streets. The gently sloping, asymmetrical **Piazza Matteotti** is an attractive arcade whose center holds a statue of the discoverer of New York harbor, Giovanni da Verrazano (circa 1480–1527). Check out the lively market held here on Saturday morning.

The church of **Santa Croce** has a triptych by Bicci di Lorenzo (1373–1452) and an Annunciation painted by an anonymous Florentine master that dates from the 14th century. ⊠ *Piazza Santa Croce 1* ☏ *055/853085* ☺ *Daily 9–1 and 3–7.*

About 2 km (1 mi) west of Greve in Chianti is the tiny hilltop hamlet of **Montefioralle.** This is the ancestral home of Amerigo Vespucci (1454–1512), the mapmaker, navigator, and explorer who named America. (His niece Simonetta may have been the inspiration for Sandro Botticelli's *Birth of Venus,* painted sometime in the 1480s.)

WHERE TO EAT

$ ✕ **Enoteca Fuoripiazza.** Detour off Greve's flower-strewn main square for
TUSCAN   food that relies heavily on local ingredients (especially those produced
by nearby makers of cheese and salami). The lengthy wine list provides a
bewildering array of choices to pair with *affettati misti* (a plate of cured
meats) or one of their primi—the *pici* (a thick, short noodle) is deftly
prepared here. All the dishes are made with great care. ⊠ *Via I Maggio
2, Piazza Trenta* ☎ *055/8546313* ⊟ *AE, DC, MC, V* ⊗ *Closed Mon.*

$$$$ ✕ **Osteria di Passignano.** In an ancient wine cellar owned by the Antinori
ITALIAN   family (who own much of what you see in these parts) is a sophisticated
★   restaurant ably run by chef Marcello Crini and his attentive staff. The
menu changes seasonally; traditional Tuscan cuisine is given a delightful
twist through the use of unexpected herbs. Particularly tantalizing is the
filetto di vitello alle spezie (spiced veal fillet), served with roast tomatoes and beans flavored with sage. The extensive wine list includes both
local and international labels. Daylong cooking courses are available.
⊠ *Via Passignano 33,Località Badia a Passignano* ✛ *15 km (9 mi) east
of Greve in Chianti* ☎ *055/8071278* ⊕ *www.osteriadipassignano.com*
⊟ *AE, D, MC, V* ⊗ *Closed Sun., 3 wks in Jan., and 1 wk in Aug.*

$$ ✕ **Ristoro di Lamole.** Although off the beaten path, this place is worth
TUSCAN   the effort to find—up a winding hill road lined with olive trees and
★   vineyards. The view from the outdoor terrace is divine, as is the simple,
exquisitely prepared Tuscan cuisine. Start with the bruschetta drizzled
with olive oil or the sublime *verdure sott'olio* (marinated vegetables)
before moving on to any of the fine secondi. The kitchen has a way
with *coniglio* (rabbit); don't pass it up if it's on the menu. ⊠ *Via di
Lamole 6, Località Lamole in Chianti* ☎ *055/8547050* ⊟ *AE, DC, MC,
V* ⊗ *Closed Wed. and Nov.–Apr.*

WHERE TO STAY

$ 🏠 **Albergo del Chianti.** At a corner of the Piazza Matteotti, the Albergo
del Chianti has rooms with views of the square or out over the tile roof-
tops toward the surrounding hills. Plain modern cabinets and wardrobes
stand near wrought-iron beds. The swimming pool, sunny terrace, and
grassy lawn behind the hotel are a nice surprise. **Pros:** central location;
best value in Greve. **Cons:** rooms facing the piazza can be noisy; lobby
is run-down; small bathrooms. ⊠ *Piazza Matteotti 86* ☎ *055/853763*
⊕ *www.albergodelchianti.it* ⇨ *16 rooms* ♿ *In-room: refrigerator. In-
hotel: restaurant, bar, pool, Wi-Fi* ⊟ *MC, V* ⊗ *Closed Jan.* ⦶ *BP.*

$$$ 🏠 **Villa Bordoni.** David and Catherine Gardner, Scottish expats, have
Fodor'sChoice   transformed a 16th-century villa into a stunning little hotel nestled
★   in the hills above Greve. Much care has been taken in decorating the
rooms, no two of which are alike. All have stenciled walls; some have
four-poster beds, others small mezzanines. Bathrooms are a riot of color,
with tiles from Vietri. The sitting room, with a cozy fireplace, is the
perfect place for a cup of tea or a glass of wine. The hotel's restaurant
has a talented young chef who gives cooking lessons in the modern
kitchen. **Pros:** splendidly isolated; beautiful decor; wonderful hosts.
Cons: on a long and bumpy dirt road. ⊠ *Via San Cresci 31/32, Località Mezzuola* ☎ *055/8547453* ⊕ *www.villabordoni.com* ⇨ *8 rooms,
3 suites* ♿ *In-room: safe, Wi-Fi. In-hotel: restaurant, pool, bicycles,*

laundry service, Wi-Fi, parking (no fee) ⊟ *AE, DC, MC, V* ⊘ *Closed 3 wks in Jan. and Feb.* ⎮◎⎮ *BP.*

$$ 🖭 **Villa Il Poggiale.** A 16th-century villa with renaissance gardens, beau-
Fodor's Choice   tiful rooms with high ceilings and elegant furnishings, a panoramic
★   pool, and expert staff all make a stay here memorable. A short walk
outside the small town of San Casciano Val di Pesa—with bus service
to Florence—Il Poggiale sits on a ridge with spectacular views of the
Chianti hills. An excellent breakfast is served on an outdoor terrace
in fine weather, and the hotel's restaurant provides a fixed-price buf-
fet (€28) for guests in the evening. The numerous public sitting rooms
are intimate and cozy; a small spa, with a sauna, massage room, and
Jacuzzi complete the picture. **Pros:** Beautiful gardens and panoramic
setting; exceptionally professional staff. **Cons:** A little isolated; some
rooms face a country road and may be noisy during the day. ⊠ *Via
Empolese 69, 20 km (12 mi) northwest of Greve, San Casciano Val
di Pesa* 🕾 *055/828311* ⊕ *www.villailpoggiale.it* ⇒ *20 rooms, 4 suites*
⌂ *In-room: Wi-Fi. In-hotel: restaurant, bar, tennis court, pool, Internet
terminal* ⊟ *AE, MC, V* ⊘ *Closed Nov.–Easter* ⎮◎⎮ *BP.*

PANZANO

7 km (4½ mi) south of Greve, 29 km (18 mi) south of Florence.

GETTING HERE

From Florence or Siena, Panzano is easily reached by car along the
Strada Chiantigiana (SR222). SITA buses travel frequently between
Florence and Panzano. From Siena, the journey by bus is extremely
difficult because SITA and Tra-In do not coordinate their schedules.
There is no train service to Panzano.

EXPLORING

The magnificent views of the valleys of the Pesa and Greve rivers eas-
ily make Panzano one of the prettiest stops in Chianti. The triangular
Piazza Bucciarelli is the heart of the new town. A short stroll along Via
Giovanni da Verrazzano brings you up to the old town, Panzano Alto,
which is still partly surrounded by medieval walls. The town's 13th-
century castle is now almost completely absorbed by later buildings (its
central tower is now a private home).

An ancient church even by Chianti standards, the hilltop **San Leolino**
probably dates from the 10th century, but it was completely rebuilt
in the Romanesque style sometime in the 13th century. It has a 14th-
century cloister worth seeing. The 16th-century terra-cotta tabernacles
are attributed to Giovanni della Robbia, and there's also a remarkable
triptych (attributed to the Master of Panzano) that was executed some-
time in the mid-14th century. Open days and hours are unpredictable;
check with the tourist office in Greve in Chianti for the latest. ✛ *3 km
(2 mi) south of Panzano, Località San Leolino* 🕾 *No phone.*

WHERE TO EAT AND STAY

$$ ✗ **Solociccia.** "Abandon all hope, ye who enter here," announces the menu,
TUSCAN   "you're in the hands of a butcher." Indeed you are, for this restaurant
is the creation of Dario Cecchini, Panzano's local merchant of meat.
Served at communal tables, the set meal consists of no less than six meat

courses, chosen at Dario's discretion. They are accompanied by seasonal vegetables, white beans with olive oil, and focaccia bread. Though Cecchini emphasizes that steak is never on the menu, this lively, crowded place is definitely not for vegetarians. The entrance is on Via XX Luglio. ⊠ *Via Chiantigiana 5* ☎ *055/852727* ⊕ *www.solociccia.it* ⚞ *Reservations essential* ⊟ *AE, DC, MC, V* ⊘ *Closed Mon.–Wed. No dinner Sun.*

$$$$ ▒ **Villa Le Barone.** Once the home of the Viviani della Robbia family,
Fodor's Choice   this 16th-century villa in a grove of ancient cypress trees retains many
★   aspects of a private country dwelling. It feels like a "second home," according to some Fodors.com users. The honor bar allows you to enjoy an *aperitivo* on the terrace while admiring the views of the pool to the rose gardens, across the hills to the town. Guest rooms have white-plaster walls, timber ceilings, and some tile floors. The restaurant uses fresh produce from the owner's farm in western Tuscany. Though the hotel staff may recommend it, the full, three-meal plan is not mandatory. **Pros:** beautiful location; wonderful restaurant; great base for exploring the region. **Cons:** noisy a/c; 20-minute walk to nearest town. ⊠ *Via San Leolino 19* ☎ *055/852621* ⊕ *www.villalebarone.it* ⇝ *30 rooms* ⚘ *In-room: no a/c (some), no TV. In-hotel: restaurant, bar, tennis court, pool, concierge, laundry service, Internet terminal* ⊟ *AE, MC, V* ⊘ *Closed Nov.–Easter* ⎮◎⎮ *BP.*

RADDA IN CHIANTI

26 km (15 mi) south of Panzano, 52 km (32 mi) south of Florence.

GETTING HERE

Radda can be reached by car from either Siena or Florence along the SR222 (Strada Chiantigiana), and from the A1 highway. Three Tra-In buses make their way from Siena to Radda. One morning SITA bus travels from Florence to Radda. There is no train service convenient to Radda.

VISITOR INFORMATION

Radda in Chianti tourism office (⊠ *Piazza Ferrucci 1* ☎ *0577/738494*).

EXPLORING

Radda in Chianti sits on a hill separating two valleys, Val di Pesa and Val d'Arbia. It's one of many tiny Chianti villages that invite you to stroll their steep streets; follow the signs pointing you toward the *camminamento,* a covered medieval passageway circling part of the city inside the walls.

★   If you have time for only one castle, visit the stunning **Castello di Brolio.** At the end of the 12th century, when Florence conquered southern Chianti, Brolio became Florence's southernmost outpost, and it was often said, "When Brolio growls, all Siena trembles." Brolio was built about AD 1000 and owned by the monks of the Badia Fiorentina; the "new" owners, the Ricasoli family, have been in possession since 1141. Bettino Ricasoli (1809–80), the so-called Iron Baron, was one of the founders of modern Italy, and is said to have invented the original formula for Chianti wine. Brolio, one of Chianti's best-known labels, is still justifiably famous. Its cellars may be toured by appointment. The grounds are worth visiting, even though the 19th-century manor house is not open to the public. (The current baron is very much in residence.) There are two apartments here available for rent by the week. ✉ *Località Brolio* ✚ *2 km (1 mi) southeast of Gaiole* ☎ *0577/730227* 🖅 *€5* ⊙ *Mar.–Nov., daily 10–5:30; first 3 wks of Dec. daily 10–4.*

North of Gaiole a turnoff leads to the **Badia a Coltibuono** *(Abbey of the Good Harvest),* which has been owned by Lorenza de' Medici's family for more than a century and a half (the family isn't closely related to the Renaissance-era Medici). Wine has been produced here since the abbey was founded by Vallombrosan monks in the 11th century. Today the family continues the tradition, making Chianti Classico and other wines, along with cold-pressed olive oil and various flavored vinegars and floral honeys. A small Romanesque church with campanile is surrounded by 2,000 acres of oak, fir, and chestnut woods threaded with walking paths—open to all—that pass two small lakes. Though the abbey itself, built between the 11th and 18th centuries, serves as the family's home, parts are open for tours (in English, German, or Italian). Visit the jasmine-draped main courtyard, the inner cloister with its antique well, the musty old aging cellars, and the Renaissance-style garden redolent of lavender, lemons, and roses. In the shop, **L'Osteria,** you can taste wine and honey, as well as pick up other items like homemade beeswax hand lotion in little ceramic dishes. The Badia is closed on public holidays. ✉ *Località Badia a Coltibuono* ✚ *4 km (2½ mi) north of Gaiole* ☎ *0577/749498 for tours, 0577/749479 for shop* 🖅 *0577/749235* ⊕ *www.coltibuono.com* 🖅 *Abbey €5* ⊙ *Tours: May–Oct., weekdays at 2, 3, 4, and 5; shop: Mar.–mid-Jan., daily 9–1 and 2–7.*

WHERE TO EAT AND STAY

$ · TUSCAN · Fodor's Choice · ★ ✕ **Osteria Le Panzanelle.** Silvia Bonechi's experience in the kitchen—and a few precious recipes handed down from her grandmother—is one of the reasons for the success of this small restaurant. The other is the front-room hospitality of Nada Michelassi. These two *panzanelle* (women from Panzano) serve a short menu of tasty and authentic dishes at what the locals refer to as *prezzi giusti* (the right prices). Both the *pappa al pomodoro* (tomato soup) and the *peposo* (peppery beef stew) are exceptional. Whether you are eating inside or under large umbrellas on the terrace near a tiny stream, the experience is always congenial. "The best food we had in Tuscany," writes one user of Fodors.com. Reservations are essential in July and August. ✉ *Località Lucarelli 29* ✚ *8 km (5 mi) northwest of Radda on road to Panzano* ☎ *0577/733511* ⊕ *www.osteria.lepanzanelle.it* ▭ *MC, V* ⊙ *Closed Mon. and Jan. and Feb.*

¢ 🖭 **La Bottega di Giovannino.** The name is actually that of the wine bar run by Giovannino Bernardoni and his daughter Monica, who also rent rooms in the house next door. This is a fantastic place for the budget-conscious traveler, as rooms are immaculate. Most have a stunning view of the surrounding hills. All have their own bath, though most of them necessitate taking a short trip outside one's room. **Pros:** great location in the center of town; close to restaurants and shops; super value. **Cons:** some rooms are small; some bathrooms are down the hall; basic decor. ✉ *Via Roma 6–8* ☎ *0577/738056* ⊕ *www.labottegadigiovannino. it* ⇥ *10 rooms, 2 apartments* ⚘ *In-room: no a/c, no phone. In-hotel: bar* ▭ *AE, MC, V* 🍽 *EP.*

Continued on page 207

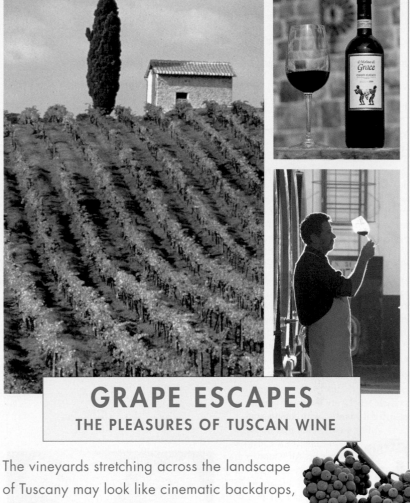

GRAPE ESCAPES
THE PLEASURES OF TUSCAN WINE

The vineyards stretching across the landscape of Tuscany may look like cinematic backdrops, but in fact they're working farms, and they produce some of Italy's best wines. No matter whether you're a wine novice or a connoisseur, there's great pleasure to be had from exploring this lush terrain, visiting the vineyards, and uncorking a bottle for yourself.

GETTING TO KNOW TUSCAN WINE

Most of the wine produced in Tuscany is red (though there are some notable whites as well), and most Tuscan reds are made primarily from one type of grape, sangiovese. That doesn't mean, however, that all wines here are the same. God (in this case Bacchus) is in the details: differences in climate, soil, and methods of production result in wines with several distinct personalities.

Chianti

Chianti is the most famous name in Tuscan wine, but what exactly the name means is a little tricky. It once identified wines produced in the region extending from just south of Florence to just north of Siena. In the mid-20th century, the official Chianti zone was expanded to include a large portion of central Tuscany. That area is divided into eight subregions. **Chianti Classico** is the name given to the original zone, which makes up 17,000 of the 42,000 acres of Chianti-producing vineyards.

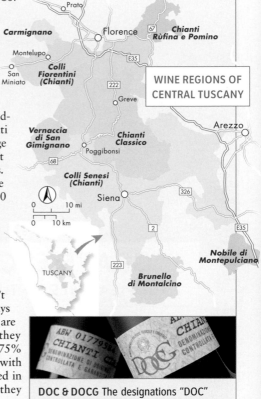

WINE REGIONS OF CENTRAL TUSCANY

Classico wines, which bear the *gallo nero* (black rooster) logo on their labels, are the most highly regarded Chiantis (with **Rùfina** running second), but that doesn't mean Classicos are always superior. All Chiantis are strictly regulated (they must be a minimum 75% to 80% sangiovese, with other varieties blended in to add nuance), and they share a strong, woodsy character that's well suited to Tuscan food. It's a good strategy to drink the local product—**Colli Senesi Chianti** when in Siena, for example. The most noticeable, and costly, difference comes when a Chianti is from *riserva* (reserve) stock, meaning it's been aged for at least two years.

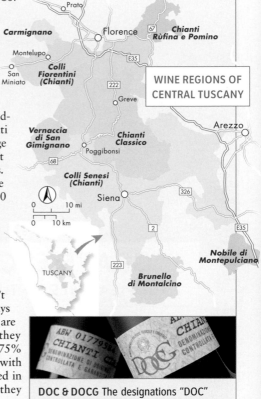

DOC & DOCG The designations "DOC" and "DOCG"—Denominazione di Origine Controllata (e Garantita)—mean a wine comes from an established region and adheres to rigorous standards of production. Ironically, the esteemed Super Tuscans are labeled *vini da tavola* (table wines), the least prestigious designation, because they don't use traditional grape blends.

Brunello di Montalcino

The area surrounding the hill town of Montalcino, to the south of Siena, is drier and warmer than the Chianti regions, and it produces the most powerful of the sangiovese-based wines. Regulations stipulate that Brunello di Montalcino be made entirely from sangiovese grapes (no blending) and aged at least four years. **Rosso di Montalcino** is a younger, less complex, less expensive Brunello.

The Super Tuscans

Beginning in the 1970s, some winemakers, chafing at the regulations imposed on established Tuscan wine varieties, began blending and aging wines in innovative ways. Thus were born the so-called Super Tuscans. These pricey, French oak–aged wines are admired for their high quality, led by such star performers as **Sassicaia**, from the Maremma region, and **Tignanello**, produced at the Tenuta Marchesi Antinori near Badia a Passignano. Purists, however, lament the loss of local identity resulting from the Super Tuscans' use of nonnative grape varieties such as cabernet sauvignon and merlot.

Vino Nobile di Montepulciano

East of Montalcino is Montepulciano, the town at the heart of the third, and smallest, of Tuscany's top wine districts.

Blending regulations aren't as strict for Vino Nobile as for Chianti and Brunello, and as a result it has a wider range of characteristics. Broadly speaking, though, Vino Nobile is a cross between Chianti and Brunello—less acidic than the former and softer than the latter. It also has a less pricey sibling, **Rosso di Montepulciano**.

The Whites

Most whites from Tuscany are made from **trebbiano** grapes, which produce a wine that's light and refreshing but not particularly aromatic or flavorful—it may hit the spot on a hot afternoon, but it doesn't excite connoisseurs.

Golden-hewed **Vernaccia di San Gimignano** is a local variety with more limited production but greater personality—it's the star of Tuscan whites. Winemakers have also brought chardonnay and sauvignon grapes to the region, resulting in wines that, like some Super Tuscans, are pleasant to drink but short on local character.

TOURING & TASTING IN TUSCAN WINE COUNTRY

Strade del Vino di Toscana

Tuscany has visitor-friendly wineries, but the way you go about visiting is a bit different here from what it is in California or France. Many wineries welcome drop-ins for a tasting, but for a tour you usually need to make an appointment a few days in advance. There are several approaches you can take, depending on how much time you have and how serious you are about wine:

PLAN 1: FULL IMMERSION. Make an appointment to tour one of the top wineries (see our recommendations on the next page), and you'll get the complete experience: half a day of strolling through vineyards, talking grape varieties, and tasting wine, often accompanied by food. Groups are small; in spring and fall, it may be just you and the winemaker. The cost is usually €10 to €15 per person, but can go up to €40 if a meal is included. Remember to specify a tour in English.

PLAN 2: SEMI-ORGANIZED. If you want to spend a few hours going from vineyard to vineyard, make your first stop one of the local tourist information offices—they're great resources for maps, tasting itineraries, and personalized advice about where to visit. The offices in **Greve, Montalcino,** and **Montepulciano** are the best equipped. **Enoteche** (for more about them, turn the page) can also be good places to pick up tips about where to go for tastings.

PLAN 3: SPONTANEOUS. Along Tuscany's country roads you'll see signs for wineries offering **vendita diretta** (direct sales) and **degustazioni** (tastings). For a taste of the local product with some atmosphere thrown in, a spontaneous visit is a perfectly viable approach. You may wind up in a simple shop or an elaborate tasting room; either way, there's a fair chance you'll sample something good. Expect a small fee for a three-glass tasting.

THE PICK OF THE VINEYARDS

Within the Chianti Classico region, these wineries should be at the top of your to-visit list, whether you're dropping in for a taste or making a full tour. (Tours require reservations unless otherwise indicated.)

CHIANTI CLASSICO

Badia a Coltibuono

(✉ Gaiole in Chianti ☎ 0577/749498 ⊕ www.coltibuono. com). Along with an extensive prelunch tour and tasting, there are shorter afternoon tours, no reservation required, starting on the hour from 2 to 5. (See "Radda in Chianti" in this chapter.)

Castello di Fonterutoli

(✉ Castellina in Chianti ☎ 0577/73571 ⊕ www. fonterutoli.it). Hour-long tours include a walk through the neighboring village.

Castello di Volpaia

(✉ Radda in Chianti ☎ 0577/738066 ⊕ www. volpaia.com). The castle is part of the tiny town of Volpaia, perched above Radda.

Castello di Verrazzano

(✉ Via S. Martino in Valle 12, Greve in Chianti ☎ 055/854243 ⊕ www. verrazzano.com). Tours here take you down to the cellars, through the gardens, and into the woods in search of wild boar.

Villa Vignamaggio (✉ Via Petriolo 5, Greve in Chianti ☎ 055/854661 ⊕ www. vignamaggio.com). Along with a wine tour, you can spend the night at this villa where Mona Lisa is believed to have been born. (See "Where to Stay" under "Greve in Chianti" in this chapter.)

Rocca delle Màcie

(✉ Località Le Macìe 45, Castellina in Chianti ☎ 0577/732236 ⊕ www.rocca dellemacie.com). A full lunch or dinner can be incorporated into your tasting here.

Castello di Brolio

(✉ Gaiole in Chianti ☎ 0577/730220 ⊕ www.ricasoli.it). One of Tuscany's most impressive castles also has a centuries-old winemaking tradition. (See "Radda in Chianti" in this chapter.)

REMEMBER

Always have a designated driver when you're touring and tasting. Vineyards are usually located off narrow, curving roads. Full sobriety is a must behind the wheel.

3

IN FOCUS GRAPE ESCAPES

MORE TUSCAN WINE RESOURCES

Enoteche: Wine Shops

The word *enoteca* in Italian can mean "wine store," "wine bar," or both. In any event, *enoteche* (the plural, pronounced "ay-no-*tek*-ay") are excellent places to sample and buy Tuscan wines, and they're also good sources of information about local wineries. There are scores to choose from. These are a few of the best:

Enoteca Italiana, Siena (Fortezza Medicea, Viale Maccari ☎ 0577/288497 ⊕ www. enoteca-italiana.it). The only one of its kind, this *enoteca* represents all the producers of DOC and DOCG wines in Italy and stocks over 400 labels. Wine by the glass and snacks are available.

Enoteca Osticcio, Montalcino (✉ Via Matteotti 23 ☎ 0577/848271 ⊕ www. osticcio.com). There are more than one thousand labels in stock. With one of the best views in Montalcino, it is also a very pleasant place to sit and meditate over a glass of Brunello.

Enoteca del Gallo Nero, Greve in Chianti (✉ Piazzetta S. Croce 8 ☎ 055/853297). This is one of the best stocked *enoteche* in the Chianti region.

La Dolce Vita, Montepulciano (Via di Voltaia nel Corso 80/82 ☎ 0578/757872). An elegantly restored monastery is home to the excellent enoteca in the upper part of Montepulciano, which has a wide selction of wines by the glass.

Wine on the Web

Tuscan wine country is well represented on the Internet. A good place for an overview is ⊕ www.terreditoscana.-regione.toscana.it. (Click on "Le Strade del Vino"; the page that opens next will give you the option of choosing an English-language version.) This site shows 14 *strade del vino* (wine roads) that have been mapped out by consortiums representing major wine districts (unfortunately, Chianti Classico isn't included), along with recommended itineraries. You'll also find links to the consortium Web sites, where you can dig up more detailed information on touring. The Chianti Classico consortium's site is ⊕ www.chianticlassico.com. The Vino Nobile di Montepulciano site is ⊕ www.vinonobiledimontepulciano.it, and Brunello di Montalcino is ⊕ www. consorziobrunellodimontalcino.it. All have English versions.

The Tuscan countryside in early autumn

$$$$ ☉ **Relais Fattoria Vignale.** On the outside, it's a rather plain manor house
Fodor'sChoice   with an annex across the street. Inside, it's a refined and comfortable
★   country house with numerous sitting rooms that have terra-cotta floors
and nice stonework. Guest rooms have exposed-brick walls and wood
beams, and are filled with simple wooden furnishings and handwoven
rugs. The grounds, flanked by vineyards and olive trees, are equally
inviting, with lawns, terraces, and a pool. The sophisticated Ristorante
Vignale ($–$$$) serves excellent wines and local specialties like *cinghiale
in umido con nepitella e vin cotto* (wild boar stew flavored with catmint
and wine). **Pros:** intimate public spaces; excellent restaurant; helpful and
friendly staff. **Cons:** north-facing rooms blocked by tall cypress trees;
single rooms are small; annex across a busy road. ⊠ *Via Pianigiani 9*
☎ *0577/738300 hotel, 0577/738094 restaurant, 0577/738012 enoteca*
⊕ *www.vignale.it* ⤶ *37 rooms, 5 suites* ⚄ *In-room: safe. In-hotel: res-*
taurant, bar, pool, concierge, laundry service, Internet terminal ▭ *AE,*
DC, MC, V ☾ *Closed Nov.–Mar. 15* ⑩*BP.*

CASTELLINA IN CHIANTI

14 km (8 mi) west of Radda, 59 km (35 mi) south of Florence.

GETTING HERE

As with all the towns along the Strada Chiantigiana (SR222), Castellina
is an easy drive from either Siena or Florence. From Siena, Castellina is
well served by the local Tra-In bus company. However, only one bus a
day travels here from Florence. The closest train station is at Castellina
Scalo, some 15 km (9 mi) away.

VISITOR INFORMATION

Castellina tourism office (⊠ *Piazza del Comune 1* ☎ *0577/741392*).

EXPLORING

Castellina in Chianti, or simply Castellina, is on a ridge above the Val di Pesa, Val d'Arbia, and Val d'Elsa, with beautiful panoramas in every direction. The imposing 14th-century tower in the central piazza hints at the history of this village, which was an outpost during the continuing wars between Florence and Siena.

WHERE TO EAT AND STAY

$$$

TUSCAN

✕ **Albergaccio.** The fact that the dining room can seat only 35 guests makes a meal here an intimate experience. The ever-changing menu mixes traditional and creative dishes. In late September and October *zuppa di funghi e castagne* (mushroom and chestnut soup) is a treat; grilled meats and seafood are on the list throughout the year. There's also an excellent wine list. When the weather is warm, make sure you dine on the terrace. ⊠ *Via Fiorentina 25* ☎ *0577/741042* ⊕ *www. albergacciocast.com* ⚐ *Reservations essential* ▭ *No credit cards* ☺ *Closed Sun. No lunch Wed. and Thurs.*

$

TUSCAN

✕ **Ristorante Le Tre Porte.** The specialty of the house, a thick slab of beef called *bistecca alla fiorentina*, is usually served very rare. Paired with grilled fresh porcini mushrooms when in season (in spring and fall), it's a heady dish. The main floor of the restaurant has a small dining room serving full-course meals. In the evening a second room is opened downstairs where you can order pizzas from the wood-burning oven. Reservations are essential in July and August. ⊠ *Via Trento e Trieste 4* ☎ *0577/741163* ▭ *AE, DC, MC, V* ☺ *Closed Tues.*

$–$$

Fodor's Choice

★

🏨 **Palazzo Squarcialupi.** In the center of Castellina, this 15th-century palace is a tranquil place to stay. Rooms are spacious, with high ceilings, tile floors, and 18th-century furnishings; bathrooms are tiled in local stone. Many of the rooms have views of the valley below, some look toward the town's main pedestrian street. Common areas are elegant, with deep, plush couches that invite you to recline. There's an ample breakfast buffet throughout the year, and you can arrange for a light lunch in the warmer months. The multilingual staff goes out of its way to be helpful. Users of Fodors.com praised the "lovely room, fantastic views," and "friendly staff." **Pros:** great location; elegant public spaces. **Cons:** on a street with no car access; across from a noisy restaurant. ⊠ *Via Ferruccio 22* ☎ *0577/741186* 🖷 *0577/740386* ⊕ *www. palazzosquarcialupi.com* ⤴ *17 rooms* ⚲ *In-hotel: bar, pool, laundry service, Wi-Fi, some pets allowed* ▭ *AE, DC, MC, V* ☺ *Closed Nov.– Mar.* ⊚| *BP.*

Florence

WORD OF MOUTH

"The city that made me fall in love with Italy was Florence, when I visited for the first time in the mid 1990s. I have been back four times, and we have enjoyed it each and every time. Yes, it is crowded, but so are Rome and Venice. If you like history and art, there is plenty to see."

—maitaitom

WELCOME TO FLORENCE

TOP REASONS TO GO

★ **Galleria degli Uffizi:** Italian Renaissance art doesn't get much better than this vast collection bequeathed to the city by the last Medici, Anna Maria Luisa.

★ **The dome of the Duomo:** Brunelleschi's work of engineering genius is the city's undisputed centerpiece.

★ **Michelangelo's** *David*: One look and you'll know why this is the Western world's most famous sculpture.

★ **The view from Piazzale Michelangelo:** From this perch the city is laid out before you. The colors at sunset heighten the experience.

★ **Piazza Santa Croce:** After you've had your fill of Renaissance masterpieces, hang out here and watch the world go by.

1 The Duomo to the Ponte Vecchio. You're in the heart of Florence here. Among the numerous highlights are the city's greatest museum (the Uffizi) and its most impressive square (Piazza della Signoria).

2 San Lorenzo to the Accademia. The blocks from the church of San Lorenzo to the Accademia museum bear the imprints of the Medici and of Michelangelo, culminating in his masterful *David*. Just to the north, the former convent of San Marco is an oasis decorated with ethereal frescoes.

3 Santa Maria Novella to the Arno. This part of town includes the train station, 15th-century palaces, and the city's chicest shopping street, Via Tornabuoni.

4 Santa Croce. The district centers on its namesake basilica, filled with the tombs of Renaissance luminaries. The area is also known for its leather shops, some of which have been in operation since the 16th century.

5 The Oltrarno. Across the Arno you encounter the massive Palazzo Pitti and the narrow streets of the Santo Spirito district, which is filled with artisans' workshops. A climb to Piazzale Michelangelo gives you a spectacular view of the city.

Piazza del Duomo

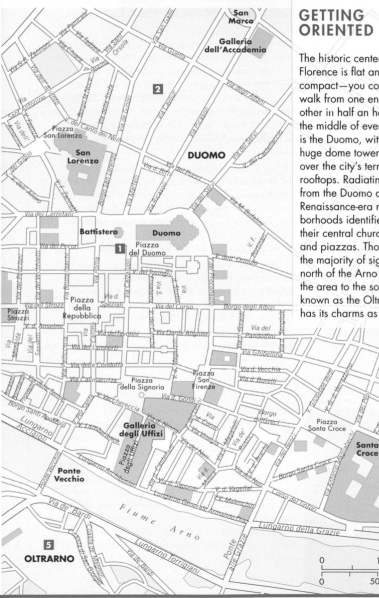

San Marco

Galleria dell'Accademia

2

Piazza San Lorenzo

San Lorenzo

DUOMO

Battistero   **Duomo**

1 Piazza del Duomo

Piazza della Repubblica

Piazza Strozzi

Piazza della Signoria

Piazza San Firenze

Galleria degli Uffizi

Ponte Vecchio

Piazza Santa Croce

Santa Croce

4 SANTA CROCE

Fiume Arno

5
OLTRARNO

| 0 | | 150 M |
| 0 | | 500 ft |

GETTING ORIENTED

The historic center of Florence is flat and compact—you could walk from one end to the other in half an hour. In the middle of everything is the Duomo, with its huge dome towering over the city's terra-cotta rooftops. Radiating out from the Duomo are Renaissance-era neighborhoods identified by their central churches and piazzas. Though the majority of sights are north of the Arno River, the area to the south, known as the Oltrarno, has its charms as well.

4

FLORENCE PLANNER

Avoiding an Art Hangover

Even for the most dedicated art enthusiast, trying to take in Florence's abundance of masterpieces can turn into a headache—there's just too much to see.

Especially if you don't count yourself as an art lover, remember to pace yourself. Allow time to wander and follow your whims, and ignore any pangs of guilt if you'd rather relax in a café and watch the world go by than trudge on sore feet through another breathtaking palace or church.

Florence isn't a city that can be "done." It's a place you can return to again and again, confident there will always be more treasures to discover.

Making the Most of Your Time

With some planning, you can see Florence's most famous sights in a couple of days. Start off at the city's most awe-inspiring work of architecture, the **Duomo,** climbing to the top of the dome if you have the stamina. On the same piazza, check out Ghiberti's bronze doors at the **Battistero.** (They're actually high-quality copies; the Museo dell'Opera del Duomo has the originals.) Set aside the afternoon for the **Galleria degli Uffizi,** making sure to reserve tickets in advance.

On Day 2, visit Michelangelo's *David* in the **Galleria dell'Accademia**—reserve tickets here, too. Linger in **Piazza della Signoria,** Florence's central square, where a copy of *David* stands in the spot the original occupied for centuries, then head east a couple of blocks to **Santa Croce,** the city's most artistically rich church. Double back and walk across Florence's landmark bridge, the **Ponte Vecchio.**

Do all that, and you'll have seen some great art, but you've just scratched the surface. If you have more time, put the **Bargello,** the **Museo di San Marco,** and the **Cappelle Medicee** at the top of your list. When you're ready for an art break, stroll through the **Boboli Gardens** or explore Florence's lively shopping scene, from the food stalls of the **Mercato Centrale** to the chic boutiques of **Via Tornabuoni.**

Tourist Offices

The Florence tourist office, known as the **APT** (☎ *055/290832* ⊕ *www.firenze.turismo.toscana.it*), has branches next to the Palazzo Medici-Riccardi, across the street from Stazione di Santa Maria Novella (the main train station) and around the corner from the Basilica di Santa Croce. The offices are generally open from 9 in the morning until 7 in the evening. The multilingual staff will give you directions (but usually not free maps) and the latest on happenings in the city. It's particularly worth a stop if you're interested in finding out about performing-arts events. The APT Web site provides information in both Italian and English.

Piazza della Signoria

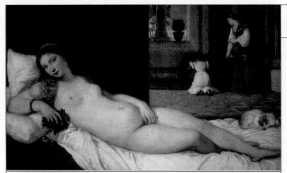

Florentine Hours

Titian's *Venus of Urbino*

Florence's sights keep tricky hours. Some are closed on Wednesday, some on Monday, some on every other Monday. Quite a few shut their doors each day (or on most days) by 2 in the afternoon. Things get even more confusing on weekends. Make it a general rule to check the hours closely for any place you're planning to visit; if it's someplace you have your heart set on seeing, it's worthwhile to call to confirm.

Here's a selection of major sights that might not be open when you'd expect—consult the sight listings within this chapter for the full details. And be aware that, as always, hours can and do change.

The **Uffizi** and the **Accademia** are both closed Monday. All but a few of the galleries at Palazzo Pitti are closed Monday as well.

The **Duomo** closes at 3:30 on Thursday (as opposed to 5:30 on other weekdays, 4:45 on weekends). The dome of the Duomo is closed on Sunday.

The **Battistero** is open from noon until 7, Monday through Saturday, and on Sunday from 8:30 to 2.

The **Bargello** closes at 1:50 PM, and is closed entirely on alternating Sundays and Mondays.

The **Cappelle Medicee** are closed on alternating Sundays and Mondays.

Museo di San Marco closes at 1:50 on weekdays but stays open until 7 on weekends—except for alternating Sundays and Mondays, when it's closed entirely.

Palazzo Medici-Riccardi is closed Wednesday.

With Reservations

At most times of day you'll see a line of people snaking around the Uffizi. They're waiting to buy tickets, and you don't want to be one of them. Instead, call ahead for a reservation (☎ 055/294883; reservationists speak English). You'll be given a reservation number and a time of admission—the further in advance you call, the more time slots you'll have to choose from. Go to the museum's reservation door at the appointed hour, give the clerk your number, pick up your ticket, and go inside. You'll pay €4 for this privilege, but it's money well spent. You can also book tickets online through the Web site ⊕ *www.polomuseale.firenze. it*; the booking process takes some patience, but it works.

Use the same reservation service to book tickets for the Galleria dell'Accademia, where lines rival those of the Uffizi. (Reservations can also be made for the Palazzo Pitti, the Bargello, and several other sights, but they usually aren't needed.) An alternative strategy is to check with your hotel—many will handle reservations.

Top Passeggiata

Via dei Calzaiuoli, between Piazza del Duomo and Piazza della Signoria, is where Florence comes out for its evening stroll.

4

GETTING HERE AND AROUND

Getting Here by Car

Florence is connected to the north and south of Italy by the Autostrada del Sole (A1). It takes about an hour and a half of driving on scenic roads to get to Bologna (although heavy truck traffic over the Apennines often makes for slower going), about three hours to Rome, and three to 3½ hours to Milan. The Tyrrhenian Coast is an hour west on the A11.

Getting Here by Bus

Long-distance buses provide inexpensive if somewhat claustrophobic service between Florence and other cities in Italy and Europe. **Lazzi Eurolines** (✉ *Via Mercadante 2, Santa Maria Novella* ☎ *055/363041* ⊕ *www.lazzi.it*) and **SITA** (✉ *Via Santa Caterina da Siena 17/r, Santa Maria Novella* ☎ *055/47821* ⊕ *www.sita-on-line.it*) are the major lines; they have neatly divided up their routes, so there's little overlap.

Getting Here by Air

Florence's small **Aeroporto A. Vespucci** (✈ *10 km [6 mi] northwest of Florence* ☎ *055/30615* ⊕ *www.aeroporto. firenze.it*) commonly called **Peretola,** is just outside of town and receives flights from Milan, Rome, London, and Paris. To get into the city center from the airport by car, take the autostrada A11. A Sita bus will take you directly from the airport to the center of town. Tickets may be purchased on the bus.

Pisa's **Aeroporto Galileo Galilei** (✈ *12 km [7 mi] south of Pisa and 80 km [50 mi] west of Florence* ☎ *050/849300* ⊕ *www.pisa-airport.com*) is the closest landing point with significant international service, including a few direct flights from New York each week on Delta. It's a straight shot down the SS67 to Florence. A train service connects Pisa's airport station with Santa Maria Novella, roughly a 1½-hour trip. Trains start running about 7 AM from the airport, 6 AM from Florence, and continue service every hour until about 7 PM from the airport, 4 PM from Florence.

For flight information, call the airport or **Florence Air Terminal** (✉ *Stazione Centrale di Santa Maria Novella* ☎ *055/216073*)—which, despite the misleading name, is simply an office at the Santa Maria Novella train station, around the corner from train tracks 1 and 2.

Getting Here by Train

Florence is on the principal Italian train route between most European capitals and Rome, and within Italy it is served frequently from Milan, Venice, and Rome by Intercity (IC) and nonstop Eurostar trains. **Stazione Centrale di Santa Maria Novella** (☎ *892021* ⊕ *www.trenitalia.com*) is the main station and is in the center of town. Avoid trains that stop only at the Campo di Marte or Rifredi stations, which are not convenient to the city center.

Neptune Fountain,
Piazza della Signoria

Getting Around by Bus

Florence's flat, compact city center is made for walking, but when your feet get weary you can use the efficient bus system, which includes small electric buses making the rounds in the center. Buses also climb to Piazzale Michelangelo and San Miniato south of the Arno.

Maps and timetables for local bus service are available for a small fee at the ATAF (Azienda Trasporti Area Fiorentina) booth next to the train station, or for free at visitor information offices. Tickets must be bought in advance from tobacco shops, newsstands, automatic ticket machines near main stops, or ATAF booths. The ticket must be canceled in the small validation machine immediately upon boarding.

You have several ticket options, all valid for one or more rides on all lines. A €1.20 ticket is good for one hour from the time it is first canceled. A multiple ticket—four tickets, each valid for 70 minutes—costs €4.50. A 24-hour tourist ticket costs €5. Two-, three-, and seven-day passes are also available.

Getting Around by Taxi

Taxis usually wait at stands throughout the city (in front of the train station and in Piazza della Repubblica, for example), or you can call for one (☎ *055/4390 or 055/4798*). The meter starts at €3.20, with extra charges at night, on Sunday, for radio dispatch, and for luggage. Women out on the town after midnight seeking taxis are entitled to a 10% discount on the fare; you must, however, request it.

Getting Around by Bike and Moped

Brave souls (cycling in Florence is difficult at best) may rent bicycles at easy-to-spot locations at Fortezza da Basso, the Stazione Centrale di Santa Maria Novella, and Piazza Pitti. Otherwise try **Alinari** (✉ *Via San Zanobi 38/r, San Marco* ☎ *055/280500* ⊕ *www. alinarirental.com*). You'll be up against hordes of tourists and those pesky *motorini* (mopeds). (For a safer ride, try Le Cascine, a former Medici hunting ground turned into a large public park with paved pathways.) The historic center can be circumnavigated via bike paths lining the *viali*, the ring road surrounding the area. If you want to go native and rent a noisy Vespa (Italian for "wasp") or other make of motorcycle or *motorino*, you may do so at **Maxirent** (✉ *Borgo Ognissanti 133/r, Santa Maria Novella* ☎ *055/265420* ⊕ *www. maxirent.com*) or **Massimo** (✉ *Via Campo d'Arrigo 16/r* ☎ *055/573689*).

Getting Around by Car

An automobile in Florence is a major liability. If your itinerary includes parts of Italy where you'll want a car (such as Tuscany), pick the vehicle up on your way out of town.

EATING AND DRINKING WELL IN FLORENCE

In Florence simply prepared meats, grilled or roasted, are the culinary stars, usually paired with seasonal vegetables such as artichokes or porcini. Bistecca's big, but there's plenty more that tastes great off the grill.

Traditionalists go for their gustatory pleasures in trattorie and osterie, places where decor is unimportant, place-mats are mere paper, and service is often perfunctory. Culinary innovation comes slowly in this town, though some cutting-edge restaurants have been appearing, usually with young chefs who have worked outside Italy. Though some of these places lack charm (many have an international, you-could-be-anywhere feel), their menus offer exciting, updated versions of Tuscan classics.

By American standards, Florentines eat late: 1:30 or 2 is typical for lunch and 9 for dinner. Consuming a primo, secondo, and dolce is largely a thing of the past, and no one looks askance if you don't order the whole nine yards. For lunch, many Florentines simply grab a panino and a glass of wine at a bar. Those opting for a simple trattoria lunch often order a plate of pasta and dessert.

STALE AND STELLAR

Florence lacks signature pasta and rice dishes, perhaps because it has raised frugality with bread to culinary craft. Stale bread is the basis for three classic Florentine primi: *pappa al pomodoro, ribollita,* and *panzanella.* "Pappa" is made with either fresh or canned tomatoes and that stale bread. Ribollita is a vegetable soup fortified with *cavolo nero* (sometimes called Tuscan kale), cannellini beans, and thickened with bread. Panzanella, a summertime dish, is reconstituted Tuscan bread combined with tomatoes, cucumber, and basil. They all are greatly enhanced with a generous application of fragrant Tuscan olive oil.

A CLASSIC ANTIPASTO: CROSTINI DI FEGATINI

This beloved dish consists of a chicken-liver spread, served warm or at room temperature, on toasted, garlic-rubbed bread. It can be served smooth, like a pâté, or in a rougher spread. It's made by sautéeing chicken livers with finely diced carrot and onion, enlivened with the addition of wine, broth, or Marsala reductions, and mashed anchovies and capers.

A CLASSIC SECONDO: BISTECCA FIORENTINA

The town's culinary pride and joy is a thick slab of beef, resembling a T-bone steak, from large white oxen called *Chianina*. The meat's slapped on the grill and served rare, sometimes with a pinch of salt.

It's always seared on both sides, and just barely cooked inside (experts say five minutes per side, and then 15 minutes with the bone sitting perpendicularly on the grill). To ask for it more well done is to incur disdain; some restaurants simply won't serve it any other way but rare.

A CLASSIC CONTORNO: CANNELLINI BEANS

Simply boiled, they provide the perfect accompaniment to bistecca. The small white beans are best when they go straight from the garden into the pot.

They should be annointed with a generous outpouring of Tuscan olive oil; the combination is oddly felicitous, and it goes a long way toward explaining why Tuscans are referred to as *mangiafagioli* (bean eaters) by other Italians.

A CLASSIC DOLCE: BISCOTTI DI PRATO

These are sometimes the only dessert on offer, and are more or less an afterthought to the glories that have preceded them. *Biscotti* means twice-cooked (or, in this case, twice baked). They are hard almond cookies that soften considerably when dipped languidly into *vin santo* ("holy wine"), a sweet dessert wine, or into a simple *caffè*.

A CLASSIC WINE: CHIANTI CLASSICO

This blend from the region just south of Florence relies mainly on the local, hardy Sangiovese grape; it's aged for at least one year before hitting the market. (*Riserve*—reserves—are aged at least an additional six months.)

Chianti is usually the libation of choice for Florentines, and it pairs magnificently with grilled foods and seasonal vegetables. Traditionalists opt for the younger, fruitier (and usually less expensive) versions often served in straw flasks. You can sample *Chianti classico* all over town, and buy it in local *salumerie, enoteche,* and supermarkets.

4

Updated
by Patricia
Rucidlo

FLORENCE, THE CITY OF THE LILY, gave birth to the Renaissance and changed the way we see the world. For centuries it has captured the imagination of travelers, who have come seeking rooms with views and phenomenal art. Florence's is a subtle beauty—its staid, unprepossessing palaces built in local stone are not showy. They take on a certain magnificence when day breaks and when the sun sets; their muted colors glow in this light. A walk along the Arno offers views that don't quit and haven't much changed in 700 years; navigating Piazza Signoria, almost always packed with tourists and locals alike, requires patience. There's a reason why everyone seems to be here, however. It's the heart of the city, and home to the Uffizi—arguably the world's finest repository of Renaissance art.

Florence was "discovered" in the 1700s by upper-class northerners making the grand tour. It became a mecca for travelers, particularly the Romantics, who were inspired by the elegance of its palazzi and its artistic wealth. Today millions of modern visitors follow in their footsteps. When the sun sets over the Arno and, as Mark Twain described it, "overwhelms Florence with tides of color that make all the sharp lines dim and faint and turn the solid city to a city of dreams," it's hard not to fall under the city's spell.

THE DUOMO TO THE PONTE VECCHIO

The heart of Florence, stretching from the Piazza del Duomo south to the Arno, is dense with artistic treasures. The churches, medieval towers, Renaissance palaces, and world-class museums and galleries contain some of the most outstanding aesthetic achievements of Western history.

Much of the *centro storico* (historic center) is closed to automobile traffic, but you still must dodge mopeds, cyclists, and masses of fellow tourists as you walk the narrow streets, especially in the area bounded by the Duomo, Piazza della Signoria, Galleria degli Uffizi, and Ponte Vecchio.

TOP ATTRACTIONS

⑤ ★ Bargello. This building started out as the headquarters for the Capitano del Popolo (chief of police) during the Middle Ages and was later used as a prison. The exterior served as a "most wanted" billboard: effigies of notorious criminals and Medici enemies were painted on its walls. Today it houses the **Museo Nazionale,** home to what is probably the finest collection of Renaissance sculpture in Italy. The concentration of masterworks by Michelangelo (1475–1564), Donatello (circa 1386–1466), and Benvenuto Cellini (1500–71) is remarkable; the works are distributed among an eclectic collection of arms, ceramics, and miniature bronzes, among other things. For Renaissance art lovers, the Bargello is to sculpture what the Uffizi is to painting.

In 1401 Filippo Brunelleschi (1377–1446) and Lorenzo Ghiberti (circa 1378–1455) competed to earn the most prestigious commission of the day: the decoration of the north doors of the Baptistery in Piazza

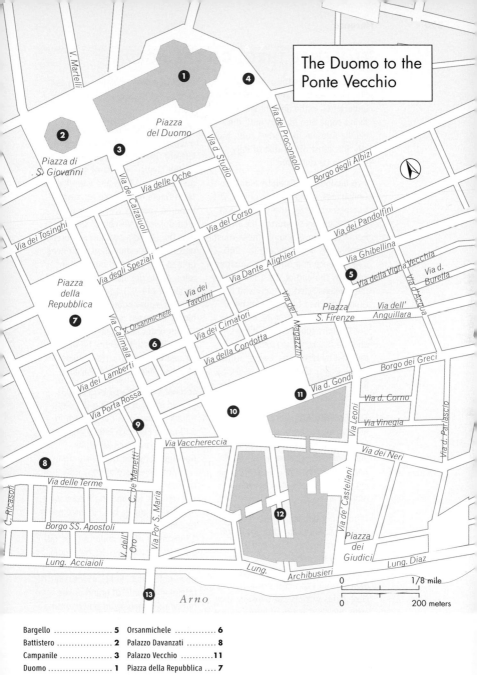

The Duomo to the Ponte Vecchio

Piazza del Duomo

Piazza di S. Giovanni

V. Martelli

Via d. Studio

Via del Proconsolo

Borgo degli Albizi

Via delle Oche

Via dei Calzaiuoli

Via del Corso

Via dei Pandolfini

Via dei Tosinghi

Via degli Speziali

Via Dante Alighieri

Via Ghibellina

Via della Vigna Vecchia

Via d. Burella

Piazza della Repubblica

V. Orsanmichele

Via dei Tavolini

Via dei Cimatori

Piazza S. Firenze

Via dell' Anguillara

Via d. Arcqua

Via dei Magazzini

Via Calimala

Via della Condotta

Borgo dei Greci

Via dei Lamberti

Via d. Gondi

Via d. Corno

Via Porta Rossa

Via Leoni

Via Vinegia

Via d. Pat.lascio

Via delle Terme

C.d. Manetti

Via Vacchereccia

Via dei Neri

Via de' Castellani

C. Ricasoli

Borgo SS. Apostoli

V. dell' Oro

Via Por S. Maria

Piazza dei Giudici

Lung. Acciaioli

Lung. Archibusieri

Lung. Diaz

Arno

Bargello	5	Orsanmichele	6
Battistero	2	Palazzo Davanzati	8
Campanile	3	Palazzo Vecchio	11
Duomo	1	Piazza della Repubblica	7
Galleria degli Uffizi	12	Piazza della Signoria	10
Mercato Nuovo	9	Ponte Vecchio	13
Museo dell'Opera del Duomo	4		

0   1/8 mile

0   200 meters

FLORENCE THROUGH THE AGES

Guelph vs. Ghibelline. Though Florence can lay claim to a modest importance in the ancient world, it didn't come into its own until the Middle Ages. In the early 1200s, the city, like most of the rest of Italy, was rent by civic unrest.

Two factions, the Guelphs and the Ghibellines, competed for power. The Guelphs supported the papacy, and the Ghibellines supported the Holy Roman Empire. Bloody battles—most notably one at Montaperti in 1260—tore Florence and other Italian cities apart. By the end of the 13th century the Guelphs ruled securely and the Ghibellines had been vanquished. This didn't end civic strife, however: the Guelphs split into the Whites and the Blacks for reasons still debated by historians. Dante, author of the *Divine Comedy*, was banished from Florence in 1301 because he was a White.

The Guilded Age. Local merchants had organized themselves into guilds by 1250. In that year they proclaimed themselves the *primo popolo* (literally, "first people"), making a landmark attempt at elective, republican rule.

Though the episode lasted only 10 years, it constituted a breakthrough in Western history. Such a daring stance by the merchant class was a by-product of Florence's emergence as an economic powerhouse. Florentines were papal bankers; they instituted the system of international letters of credit; and the gold florin became the international standard of currency. With this economic strength came a building boom. Palaces and basilicas were erected, enlarged, or restructured. Sculptors such as Donatello and Ghiberti decorated them; painters such as Giotto and Botticelli frescoed their walls.

Mighty Medici. Though ostensibly a republic, Florence was blessed (or cursed) with one very powerful family, the Medici, who came to prominence in the 1430s and were the de facto rulers of Florence for several hundred years. It was under patriarch Cosimo il Vecchio (1389–1464) that the Medici's position in Florence was securely established. Florence's golden age occurred during the reign of his grandson Lorenzo de' Medici (1449–92). Lorenzo was not only an astute politician but also a highly educated man and a great patron of the arts. Called "Il Magnifico" (the Magnificent), he gathered around him poets, artists, philosophers, architects, and musicians.

Lorenzo's son, Piero (1471–1503), proved inept at handling the city's affairs. He was run out of town in 1494, and Florence briefly enjoyed its status as a republic while dominated by the Dominican friar Girolamo Savonarola (1452–98). After a decade of internal unrest, the republic fell and the Medici were recalled to power, but Florence never regained its former prestige. By the 1530s most of the major artistic talent had left the city—Michelangelo, for one, had settled in Rome. The now-ineffectual Medici, eventually attaining the title of grand dukes, remained nominally in power until the line died out in 1737, after which time Florence passed from the Austrians to the French and back again until the unification of Italy (1865–70), when it briefly became the capital under King Vittorio Emanuele II.

del Duomo. For the contest, each designed a bronze bas-relief panel depicting the sacrifice of Isaac; the panels are displayed together in the room devoted to the sculpture of Donatello, on the upper floor. The judges chose Ghiberti for the commission; see if you agree with their choice. ⊠ *Via del Proconsolo 4, Bargello* ☎ *055/294883* ⊕ *www.polomuseale.firenze.it* ✉ *€4* ☺ *Daily 8:15–1:50; closed 2nd and 4th Mon. of month and 1st, 3rd, and 5th Sun. of month.*

4

❷ **Battistero** *(Baptistery).* The octagonal Baptistery is one of the supreme monuments of the Italian Romanesque style and one of Florence's oldest structures. Local legend has it that it was once a Roman temple dedicated to Mars; modern excavations, however, suggest that its foundations date from the 1st century A.D. The round Romanesque arches on the exterior date from the 11th century. The interior dome mosaics from the beginning of the 14th century are justly renowned, but—glittering beauties though they are—they could never outshine the building's famed bronze Renaissance doors decorated with panels crafted by Lorenzo Ghiberti. The doors—or at least copies of them—on which Ghiberti worked most of his adult life (1403–52) are on the north and east sides of the Baptistery, and the Gothic panels on the south door were designed by Andrea Pisano (circa 1290–1348) in 1330. The original Ghiberti doors were removed to protect them from the effects of pollution and acid rain and have been beautifully restored; they are now on display in the Museo dell'Opera del Duomo.

Ghiberti's north doors depict scenes from the life of Christ; his later east doors (dating from 1425–52), facing the Duomo facade, render scenes from the Old Testament. Both merit close examination, for they are very different in style and illustrate the artistic changes that marked the beginning of the Renaissance. Look at the far right panel of the middle row on the earlier (1403–24) north doors (*Jesus Calming the Waters*). Ghiberti here captured the chaos of a storm at sea with great skill and economy, but the artistic conventions he used are basically pre-Renaissance: Jesus is the most important figure, so he is the largest; the disciples are next in size, being next in importance; the ship on which they founder looks like a mere toy.

The exquisitely rendered panels on the east doors are larger, more expansive, more sweeping—and more convincing. The middle panel on the left-hand door tells the story of Jacob and Esau, and the various episodes of the story—the selling of the birthright, Isaac ordering Esau to go hunting, the blessing of Jacob, and so forth—have been merged into a single beautifully realized street scene. Ghiberti's use of perspective suggests depth: the background architecture looks far more credible than on the north-door panels, the figures in the foreground are grouped realistically, and the naturalism and grace of the poses (look at Esau's left leg and the dog next to him) have nothing to do with the sacred message being conveyed. Although the religious content remains, the figures and their place in the natural world are given new prominence, and are portrayed with a realism not seen in art since the fall of the Roman Empire nearly a thousand years before.

As a footnote to Ghiberti's panels, one small detail of the east doors is worth a special look. To the lower left of the Jacob and Esau panel, Ghiberti placed a tiny self-portrait bust. From either side, the portrait is extremely appealing—Ghiberti looks like everyone's favorite uncle—but the bust is carefully placed so that you can make direct eye contact with the tiny head from a single spot. When that contact is made, the impression of intelligent life—of *modern* intelligent life—is astonishing. It's no wonder that these doors received one of the most famous compliments in the history of art from an artist known to be notoriously stingy with praise: Michelangelo declared them so beautiful that they could serve as the Gates of Paradise. ⊠ *Piazza del Duomo* ☎ *055/2302885* ⊕ *www.operaduomo.firenze.it* ✉ *€6* ⊙ *Mon.–Sat. 9–7:30, Sun. 9–1:30; 1st Sat. of month 8:30–2.*

⑫ **Galleria degli Uffizi.** The venerable Uffizi Gallery occupies the top floor
Fodor's Choice of the U-shaped **Palazzo degli Uffizi** fronting the Arno, designed by
★ Giorgio Vasari (1511–74) in 1560 to hold the *uffizi* (administrative offices) of the Medici grand duke Cosimo I (1519–74). Later, the Medici installed their art collections here, creating what was Europe's first modern museum, open to the public (at first only by request) since 1591.

Among the highlights are Paolo Uccello's *Battle of San Romano,* its brutal chaos of lances one of the finest visual metaphors for warfare ever captured in paint; the *Madonna and Child with Two Angels,* by Fra Filippo Lippi (1406–69), in which the impudent eye contact established by the angel would have been unthinkable prior to the Renaissance; the *Birth of Venus* and *Primavera* by Sandro Botticelli (1445–1510), the goddess of the former seeming to float on air and the fairy-tale charm of the latter exhibiting the painter's idiosyncratic genius at its zenith; the portraits of the Renaissance duke Federico da Montefeltro and his wife Battista Sforza, by Piero della Francesca (circa 1420–92); the *Madonna of the Goldfinch* by Raphael (1483–1520), which underwent a stunning years-long restoration, completed in 2009 (check out the brilliant blues that decorate the sky, as well as the eye contact between mother and child, both clearly anticipating the painful future; Michelangelo's *Doni Tondo*; the *Venus of Urbino* by Titian (circa 1488/90–1576); and the splendid *Bacchus* by Caravaggio (circa 1571/72–1610). In the last two works, the approaches to myth and sexuality are diametrically opposed, to put it mildly. Six additional exhibition rooms opened in 2004, convoluting the way you exit the museum. Many of the more than 400 works now displayed would have been better left in storage, though a couple of Caravaggios at the very end of your hike out are well worth a look.

Late in the afternoon is the least crowded time to visit. For a €4 fee advance tickets can be reserved by phone, online, or, once in Florence, at the Uffizi reservation booth at least one day in advance of your visit. Keep the confirmation number and take it with you to the door at

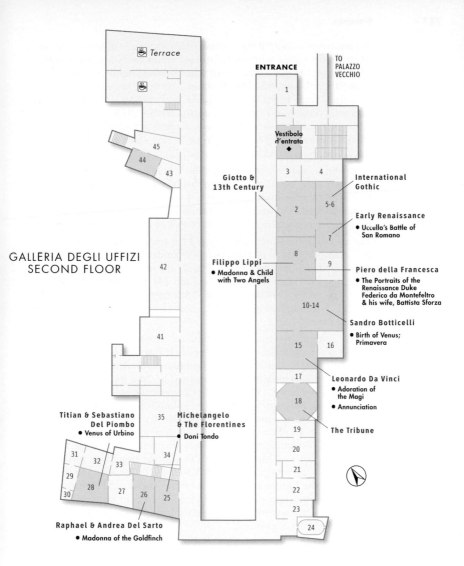

Terrace

ENTRANCE

TO PALAZZO VECCHIO

1

Vestibolo d'entrata ◆

45

44

43

3   4

Giotto & 13th Century

International Gothic

2

5-6

Early Renaissance
● Uccello's Battle of San Romano

7

GALLERIA DEGLI UFFIZI SECOND FLOOR

42

8

Filippo Lippi
● Madonna & Child with Two Angels

9

Piero della Francesca
● The Portraits of the Renaissance Duke Federico da Montefeltro & his wife, Battista Sforza

41

10-14

Sandro Botticelli
● Birth of Venus; Primavera

15   16

17

Leonardo Da Vinci
● Adoration of the Magi
● Annunciation

18

The Tribune

Titian & Sebastiano Del Piombo
● Venus of Urbino

35

Michelangelo & The Florentines
● Doni Tondo

19

20

31

32

33

34

29

28

27

26   25

21

30

22

23

Raphael & Andrea Del Sarto
● Madonna of the Goldfinch

24

the museum marked "Reservations." Usually you're ushered in almost immediately. Come with cash, because credit cards are not accepted (though you can use a credit card when booking online). When there's a special exhibit on, which is often, the base ticket price goes up to €10. ✉ *Piazzale degli Uffizi 6, Piazza della Signoria* ☎ *055/23885 advance tickets* ✉ *Consorzio ITA, Piazza Pitti 1* ☎ *055/294883* ⊕ *www.uffizi. firenze.it; reservations www.polomuseale.firenze.it* ✍ €6.50, €10 *during special exhibitions; reservation fee €4* ⊗ *Tues.–Sun. 8:15–6:50.*

⑩ Piazza della Signoria. This is by far the most striking square in Florence.
★ It was here, in 1497, that the famous "bonfire of the vanities" took place, when the fanatical friar Savonarola induced his followers to hurl their worldly goods into the flames; it was also here, a year later, that he was hanged as a heretic and, ironically, burned. A bronze plaque in the piazza pavement marks the exact spot of his execution.

The statues in the square and in the 14th-century **Loggia dei Lanzi** on the south side vary in quality. Cellini's famous bronze *Perseus* holding the severed head of Medusa is certainly the most important sculpture in the loggia. Other works here include *The Rape of the Sabine* and *Hercules and the Centaur,* both late-16th-century works by Giambologna (1529–1608), and in the back, a row of sober matrons dating from Roman times.

In the square, the Neptune Fountain, created between 1550 and 1575, takes something of a booby prize. It was created by Bartolomeo Ammannati, who considered it a failure himself. The Florentines call it *il Biancone,* which may be translated as "the big white man" or "the big white lump." Giambologna's equestrian statue, to the left of the fountain, portrays Grand Duke Cosimo I. Occupying the steps of the Palazzo Vecchio are a copy of Donatello's proud heraldic lion of Florence, the *Marzocco* (the original is now in the Bargello), a copy of Donatello's *Judith and Holofernes* (the original is in the Palazzo Vecchio), a copy of Michelangelo's *David* (the original is in the Galleria dell'Accademia), and Baccio Bandinelli's *Hercules* (1534). The Marzocco, the Judith, and the David were symbols of Florentine civic pride—the latter two subjects had stood up to their oppressors. They provided apt metaphors for the republic-loving Florentines, who often chafed at Medici hegemony.

⑬ Ponte Vecchio *(Old Bridge).* This charmingly simple bridge was built in
★ 1345 to replace an earlier bridge swept away by flood. Its shops first housed butchers, then grocers, blacksmiths, and other merchants. But in 1593 the Medici grand duke Ferdinand I (1549–1609), whose private corridor linking the Medici palace (Palazzo Pitti) with the Medici offices (the Uffizi) crossed the bridge atop the shops, decided that all this plebeian commerce under his feet was unseemly. So he threw out the butchers and blacksmiths and installed 41 goldsmiths and eight jewelers. The bridge has been devoted solely to these two trades ever since.

The **Corridoio Vasariano** (✉ *Piazzale degli Uffizi 6, Piazza della Signoria* ☎ *055/23885 or 055/294883*), the private Medici corridor, was built by Vasari in 1565. Though the ostensible reason for its construction was one of security, it was more likely designed so that the Medici family wouldn't have to walk amid the commoners. The corridor is notoriously fickle with its operating hours; at this writing, it was temporarily closed, but it can often be visited by prior special arrangement. Call for the most up-to-date details. Take a moment to study the Ponte Santa Trinita, the next bridge downriver, from either the bridge or the corridor. It was designed by Bartolomeo Ammannati in 1567 (probably from sketches by Michelangelo), blown up by the retreating Germans during World War II, and painstakingly reconstructed after the war. The view from the Ponte Santa Trinita is beautiful, which might explain why so many young lovers seem to hang out there.

WORTH NOTING

❸ Campanile. The Gothic bell tower designed by Giotto (circa 1266–1337) is a soaring structure of multicolor marble originally decorated with sculptures by Donatello and reliefs by Giotto, Andrea Pisano, and others (which are now in the Museo dell'Opera del Duomo). A climb of 414 steps rewards you with a close-up of Brunelleschi's cupola on the Duomo next door and a sweeping view of the city. ⊠ *Piazza del Duomo* ☎ *055/2302885* ⊕ *www.operaduomo.firenze.it* 🎟 *€6* ⊘ *Daily 8:30–7:30.*

❾ Mercato Nuovo *(New Market).* The open-air loggia, built in 1551, teems with souvenir stands, but the real attraction is a copy of Pietro Tacca's bronze *Porcellino* (which translates as "little pig" despite the fact the animal is, in fact, a wild boar). The *Porcellino* is Florence's equivalent of the Trevi Fountain: put a coin in his mouth, and if it falls through the grate below (according to one interpretation), it means you'll return to Florence someday. The statue dates from around 1612, but the original version, in the Museo Bardini, is an ancient Greek work. ⊠ *Corner of Via Por Santa Maria and Via Porta Rossa, Piazza della Repubblica* ⊘ *Market: Tues.–Sat. 8–7, Mon. 1–7.*

❹ Museo dell'Opera del Duomo *(Cathedral Museum).* Ghiberti's original Baptistery door panels and the *cantorie* (choir loft) reliefs by Donatello and Luca della Robbia (1400–82) keep company with Donatello's *Mary Magdalene* and Michelangelo's *Pietà* (not to be confused with his more famous *Pietà* in St. Peter's in Rome). Renaissance sculpture is in part defined by its revolutionary realism, but in its palpable suffering Donatello's *Magdalene* goes beyond realism. Michelangelo's heart-wrenching *Pietà* was unfinished at his death; the female figure supporting the body of Christ on the left was added by Tiberio Calcagni (1532–65), and never has the difference between competence and genius been manifested so clearly. ⊠ *Piazza del Duomo 9* ☎ *055/2302885* ⊕ *www. operaduomo.firenze.it* 🎟 *€6* ⊘ *Mon.–Sat. 9–7:30, Sun. 9–1:45.*

❻ Orsanmichele. This multipurpose structure began as an 8th-century oratory and then in 1290 was turned into an open-air loggia for selling grain. Destroyed by fire in 1304, it was rebuilt as a loggia-market. Between 1367 and 1380 the arcades were closed and two stories were added above; finally, at century's end it was turned into a church. Inside is a beautifully detailed 14th-century Gothic tabernacle by Andrea Orcagna (1308–68). The exterior niches contain sculptures, now mostly copies of the originals by Donatello and Verrocchio (1435–88), among

Continued on page 231

THE DUOMO
FLORENCE'S BIGGEST MASTERPIECE

For all its monumental art and architecture, Florence has one undisputed centerpiece: the Cathedral of Santa Maria del Fiore, better known as the Duomo. Its cupola dominates the skyline, presiding over the city's rooftops like a red hen over her brood. Little wonder that when Florentines feel homesick, they say they have *"nostalgia del cupolone."*

The Duomo's construction began in 1296, following the design of Arnolfo da Cambio, Florence's greatest architect of the time. By modern standards, construction was slow and haphazard—it continued through the 14th and into the 15th century, with some dozen architects having a hand in the project.

In 1366 Neri di Fioravante created a model for the hugely ambitious cupola: it was to be the largest dome in the world, surpassing Rome's Pantheon. But when the time finally came to build the dome in 1418, no one was sure how—or even if—it could be done. Florence was faced with a 143-ft hole in the roof of its cathedral, and one of the greatest challenges in the history of architecture.

Fortunately, local genius Filippo Brunelleschi was just the man for the job. Brunelleschi won the 1418 competition to design the dome, and for the next 18 years he oversaw its construction. The enormity of his achievement can hardly be overstated. Working on such a large scale (the dome weighs 37,000 tons and uses 4 million bricks) required him to invent hoists and cranes that were engineering marvels. A "dome within a dome" design and a novel herringbone bricklaying pattern were just two of the innovations used to establish structural integrity. Perhaps most remarkably, he executed the construction without a supporting wooden framework, which had previously been thought indispensable.

Brunelleschi designed the lantern atop the dome, but he died soon after its first stone was laid in 1446; it wouldn't be completed until 1461. Another 400 years passed before the Duomo received its façade, a 19th-century neo-Gothic creation.

DUOMO TIMELINE

1296 Work begins, following design by Arnolfo di Cambio.

1302 Arnolfo dies; work continues, with sporadic interruptions.

1331 Management of construction taken over by the Wool Merchants guild.

1334 Giotto appointed project overseer, designs campanile.

1337 Giotto dies; Andrea Pisano takes leadership role.

1348 The Black Plague; all work ceases.

1366 Vaulting on nave completed; Neri di Fioravante makes model for dome.

1417 Drum for dome completed.

1418 Competition is held to design the dome.

1420 Brunelleschi begins work on the dome.

1436 Dome completed.

1446 Construction of lantern begins; Brunelleschi dies.

1461 Antonio Manetti, a student of Brunelleschi, completes lantern.

1469 Gilt copper ball and cross added by Verrocchio.

1587 Original façade is torn down by Medici court.

1871 Emilio de Fabris wins competition to design new façade.

1887 Façade completed.

WHAT TO LOOK FOR INSIDE THE DUOMO

The interior of the Duomo is a fine example of Florentine Gothic with a beautiful marble floor, but the space feels strangely barren—a result of its great size and the fact that some of the best art has been moved to the nearby **Museo dell'Opera del Duomo.**

Notable among the works that remain are two towering equestrian frescoes of famous mercenaries: *Niccolò da Tolentino* (1456), by Andrea del Castagno, and *Sir John Hawkwood* (1436), by Paolo Uccello. There's also fine terra-cotta work by Luca della Robbia. Ghiberti,

Brunelleschi's great rival, is responsible for much of the stained glass, as well as a reliquary urn with gorgeous reliefs. A vast fresco of the Last Judgment, painted by Vasari and Zuccari, covers the dome's interior. Brunelleschi had wanted mosaics to go there; it's a pity he didn't get his wish.

In the crypt beneath the cathedral, you can explore excavations of a Roman wall and mosaic fragments from the late sixth century; entry is near the first pier on the right. On the way down you pass Brunelleschi's modest tomb.

1. Entrance; stained glass by Ghiberti
2. Fresco of Niccolò da Tolentino by Andrea del Castagno
3. Fresco of John Hawkwood by Paolo Uccello
4. *Dante and the Divine Comedy* by Domenico di Michelino
5. Lunette: *Ascension* by Luca della Robbia
6. Above altar: two angels by Luca della Robbia. Below the altar: reliquary of St. Zenobius by Ghiberti.
7. Lunette: *Resurrection* by Luca della Robbia
8. Entrance to dome
9. Bust of Brunelleschi by Buggiano
10. Stairs to crypt
11. Campanile

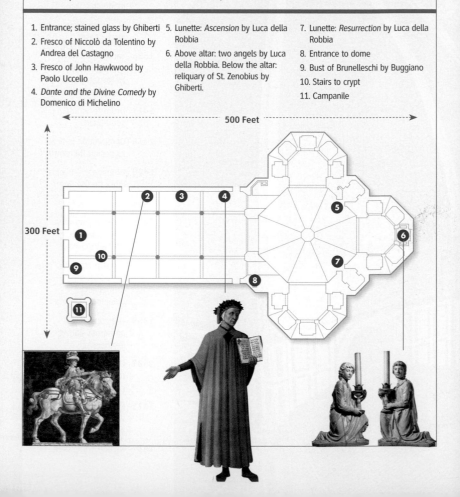

MAKING THE CLIMB

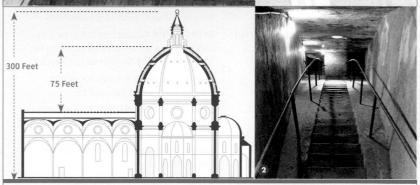

Climbing the 463 steps to the top of the dome is not for the faint of heart—or for the claustrophobic—but those who do it will be awarded a smashing view of Florence ❶. Keep in mind that the way up is also the way down, which means that while you're huffing and puffing in the ascent, people very close to you in a narrow staircase are making their way down ❷.

300 Feet

75 Feet

DUOMO BASICS

- Even first thing in the morning during high season (May through September), a line is likely to have formed to climb the dome. Expect an hour wait.

- For an alternative to the dome, consider climbing the less trafficked campanile, which gives you a view from on high of the dome itself.

- Dress code essentials: covered shoulders, no short shorts, and hats off upon entering.

✉ Piazza del Duomo
☎ 055/2302885
🌐 www.operaduomo.firenze.it
💶 Free, crypt €3, cupola €6
🕓 Crypt: Mon.–Wed., Fri., Sun. 10–5; Thurs. 10–4:30; Sat. 10–5:45; first Sat. of month 10–3:30. Cupola: Weekdays 8:30–7, Sat. 8:30–5:40, 1st Sat. of month 8:30–4. Duomo: Mon.–Wed. and Fri. 10–5, Thurs. 10–4:30, Sat., 10–4:45, Sun 1:30–4:45, 1st Sat. of month 10–3:30.

BRUNELLESCHI vs. GHIBERTI
The Rivalry of Two Renaissance Geniuses

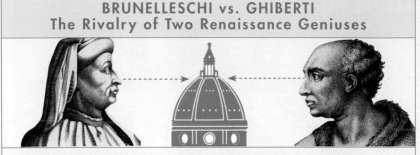

In Renaissance Florence, painters, sculptors, and architects competed for major commissions, with the winner earning the right to undertake a project that might occupy him (and keep him paid) for a decade or more. Stakes were high, and the resulting rivalries fierce—none more so than that between Filippo Brunelleschi and Lorenzo Ghiberti.

The two first clashed in 1401, for the commission to create the bronze doors of the Baptistery. When Ghiberti won, Brunelleschi took it hard, fleeing to Rome, where he would remain for 15 years. Their rematch came in 1418, over the design of the Duomo's cupola, with Brunelleschi triumphant. For the remainder of their lives, the two would miss no opportunity to belittle each other's work.

FILIPPO BRUNELLESCHI (1377–1446)

MASTERPIECE: The dome of Santa Maria del Fiore.

BEST FRIENDS: Donatello, whom he stayed with in Rome after losing the Baptistery doors competition; the Medici family, who rescued him from bankruptcy.

SIGNATURE TRAITS: Paranoid, secretive, bad tempered, practical joker, inept businessman.

SAVVIEST POLITICAL MOVE: Feigned sickness and left for Rome after his dome plans were publicly criticized by Ghiberti, who was second-in-command. The project proved too much for Ghiberti to manage on his own, and Brunelleschi returned triumphant.

MOST EMBARRASSING MOMENT: In 1434 he was imprisoned for two weeks for failure to pay a small guild fee. The humiliation might have been orchestrated by Ghiberti.

OTHER CAREER: Shipbuilder. He built a huge vessel, *Il Badalone*, to transport marble for the dome up the Arno. It sank on its first voyage.

INSPIRED: The dome of St. Peter's in Rome.

LORENZO GHIBERTI (1378–1455)

MASTERPIECE: *The Gates of Paradise*, the ten-paneled east doors of the Baptistery.

BEST FRIEND: Giovanni da Prato, an underling who wrote diatribes attacking the dome's design and Brunelleschi's character.

SIGNATURE TRAITS: Instigator, egoist, know-it-all, shrewd businessman.

SAVVIEST POLITICAL MOVE: During the Baptistery doors competition, he had an open studio and welcomed opinions on his work, while Brunelleschi labored behind closed doors.

OTHER CAREER: Collector of classical artifacts, historian.

INSPIRED: *The Gates of Hell* by Auguste Rodin.

The Gates of Paradise detail

others, dating from the early 1400s to the early 1600s and paid for by the guilds. Although it is a copy, Verrocchio's *Doubting Thomas* (circa 1470) is particularly deserving of attention. Here you see Christ, like the building's other figures, entirely framed within the niche, and St. Thomas standing on its bottom ledge, with his right foot outside the niche frame. This one detail, the positioning of a single foot, brings the whole composition to life. It's possible to see nearly all of the original sculptures at the **Museo di Orsanmichele**, which is open Monday. The museum entrance is on Via Arte della Lana. ⊠ *Via dei Calzaiuoli, Piazza della Repubblica* ☎ *055/284944* ◷ *Closed for restoration; museum Mon. 10–5.*

4

⑧ **Palazzo Davanzati.** The prestigious Davanzati family owned this 14th-century palace in one of Florence's swankiest medieval neighborhoods. It reopened in May 2005 after a 10-year restoration. The place is a delight, as you can wander through the surprisingly light-filled courtyard, and climb the steep stairs to the *piano nobile,* where the family did most of its living. The beautiful *Sala dei Pappagalli* (Parrot Room) is adorned with trompe-l'oeil tapestries and gaily painted birds. Though some claim that these date from the 14th century, many art historians are much less sure. ⊠ *Piazza Davanzati 13, Piazza della Repubblica* ☎ *055/2388610* ⊡ *Free* ◷ *Daily 8:15–1:50. Closed 1st, 3rd, and 5th Sun. of month; closed 2nd and 4th Mon. of month.*

⑪ **Palazzo Vecchio** *(Old Palace).* Florence's forbidding, fortresslike city hall was begun in 1299, presumably designed by Arnolfo di Cambio, and its massive bulk and towering campanile dominate Piazza della Signoria. It was built as a meeting place for the heads of the seven major guilds governing the city at the time; over the centuries it has served lesser purposes, but today it is once again city hall. The interior courtyard is a good deal less severe, having been remodeled by Michelozzo (1396–1472) in 1453; a copy of Verrocchio's bronze *puttino* (cherub), topping the central fountain, softens the space. (The original is upstairs.)

The main attraction is on the second floor: two adjoining rooms that supply one of the most startling contrasts in Florence. The first is the vast **Sala dei Cinquecento** (Room of the Five Hundred), named for the 500-member Great Council, the people's assembly established after the death of Lorenzo the Magnificent, that met here. Giorgio Vasari and others decorated the room, around 1563–65, with gargantuan frescoes celebrating Florentine history; depictions of battles with nearby cities predominate. Continuing the martial theme, the room also contains Michelangelo's *Victory,* intended for the never-completed tomb of Pope Julius II (1443–1513), plus other sculptures of decidedly lesser quality.

The second room is the little **Studiolo,** to the right of the Sala dei Cinquecento's entrance. Here the melancholy Francesco I (1541–87), son of Cosimo I, stored his priceless treasures and conducted scientific experiments. Designed by Vasari, it was decorated by him, Giambologna, and many others. ✉ *Piazza della Signoria* ☎ *055/2768465* ☑ *€6* ◷ *Mon.–Wed. and Fri.–Sun. 9–7, Thurs. 9–2.*

❼ Piazza della Repubblica. The square marks the site of the ancient forum that was the core of the original Roman settlement. The street plan around the piazza still reflects the carefully plotted Roman military encampment. The Mercato Vecchio (Old Market), which had been here since the Middle Ages, was demolished and the current piazza was constructed between 1885 and 1895 as a neoclassical showpiece. The piazza is lined with outdoor cafés, affording an excellent opportunity for people-watching.

SAN LORENZO TO THE ACCADEMIA

A sculptor, painter, architect, and a poet, Florentine native son Michelangelo was a consummate genius, and some of his finest creations remain in his hometown. A key to understanding Michelangelo's genius can be found in the magnificent Cappelle Medicee, where both his sculptural and architectural prowess can be clearly seen. Planned frescoes were never completed, sadly, for they would have shown in one space the artistic triple threat that he certainly was. The towering yet graceful *David,* his most famous work, resides in the Galleria dell'Accademia.

After visiting San Lorenzo, resist the temptation to explore the market that surrounds the church. You can always come back later, after the churches and museums have closed; the market is open until 7 PM. Note that the Museo di San Marco closes at 1:50 on weekdays.

TOP ATTRACTIONS

❷ ★ Cappelle Medicee *(Medici Chapels).* This magnificent complex includes the **Cappella dei Principi,** the Medici chapel and mausoleum that was begun in 1605 and kept marble workers busy for several hundred years, and the **Sagrestia Nuova** (New Sacristy), designed by Michelangelo and so called to distinguish it from Brunelleschi's Sagrestia Vecchia (Old Sacristy) in San Lorenzo.

Michelangelo received the commission for the New Sacristy in 1520 from Cardinal Giulio de' Medici (1478–1534), who later became Pope Clement VII. The cardinal wanted a new burial chapel for his cousins Giuliano, Duke of Nemours (1478–1534), and Lorenzo, Duke of Urbino (1492–1519), and he also wanted to honor his father, also named Giuliano, and his uncle, Lorenzo il Magnifico. The result was a tour de force of architecture and sculpture. Architecturally, Michelangelo was as original and inventive here as ever, but it is, quite properly, the powerfully sculpted tombs that dominate the room. The scheme is allegorical: on the tomb on the right are figures representing Day and Night, and on the tomb to the left are figures representing Dawn and Dusk; above them are idealized sculptures of the two men, usually interpreted to represent the active life and the contemplative life. But the allegorical meanings are secondary; what is most important is the intense presence of the sculptural figures and the force with which they hit the viewer. Ticket prices jump to €9 when special exhibitions are on—which is frequently. ✉ *Piazza di Madonna degli Aldobrandini, San Lorenzo* ☎ *055/294883 reservations* ✉ *€4* ⊘ *Mar.–Nov., daily 8:15– 4:50; Dec.–Feb., daily 8:15–1:50. Closed 1st, 3rd, and 5th Mon. and 2nd and 4th Sun. of month.*

➐ **Galleria dell'Accademia** *(Accademia Gallery).* The collection of Florentine
☯ paintings, dating from the 13th to the 18th centuries, is largely unre-
★ markable, but the sculptures by Michelangelo are worth the price of admission. The unfinished *Slaves,* fighting their way out of their marble prisons, were meant for the tomb of Michelangelo's overly demanding patron Pope Julius II (1443–1513). But the focal point is the original *David,* moved here from Piazza della Signoria in 1873. *David* was com- missioned in 1501 by the Opera del Duomo (Cathedral Works Com- mittee), which gave the 26-year-old sculptor a leftover block of marble that had been ruined forty years earlier by another artist. Michelangelo's success with the block was so dramatic that the city showered him with honors, and the Opera del Duomo voted to build him a house and a studio in which to live and work.

Today *David* is beset not by Goliath but by tourists, and seeing the statue at all—much less really studying it—can be a trial. Save yourself a long wait in line by reserving tickets in advance. A Plexiglas barrier surrounds the sculpture, following a 1991 attack on it by a hammer- wielding artist who, luckily, inflicted only a few minor nicks on the toes. The statue is not quite what it seems. It is so poised and graceful and alert—so miraculously alive—that it is often considered the definitive sculptural embodiment of the High Renaissance perfection. But its true place in the history of art is a bit more complicated.

As Michelangelo well knew, the Renaissance painting and sculpture that preceded his work were deeply concerned with ideal form. Perfection of proportion was the ever-sought holy grail; during the Renaissance, ideal proportion was equated with ideal beauty, and ideal beauty was equated with spiritual perfection. But *David,* despite its supremely calm and dignified pose, departs from these ideals. Michelangelo didn't give the statue perfect proportions. The head is slightly too large for the body, the arms are too large for the torso, and the hands are dramatically large for the arms. The work was originally commissioned to adorn the exterior of the Duomo and was intended to be seen from a distance and on high. Michelangelo knew exactly what he was doing, calculating that the perspective of the viewer would be such that, in order for the statue to appear proportioned, the upper body, head, and arms would have to be bigger, as they are farther away from the viewer. But he also did it to express and embody, as powerfully as possible in a single fig- ure, an entire biblical story. *David*'s hands *are* big, but so was Goliath,

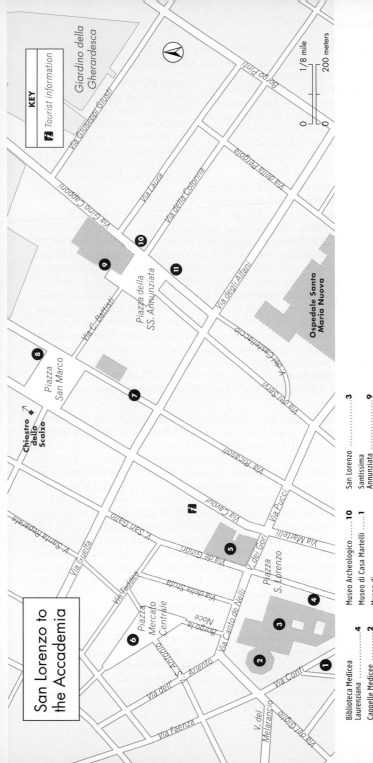

San Lorenzo to the Accademia

Giardino della Gherardesca

Via Giuseppe Giusti

Via Laura

Via della Colonna

Via degli Alfani

Borgo Pinti

Piazza della SS. Annunziata

V. della Pergola

Ospedale Santa Maria Nuova

V. dei Castellaccio

Via dei Servi

0   1/8 mile

0   200 meters

Piazza San Marco

Via C. Battisti

Chiostro dello Scalzo

Via Ricasoli

Via de Ginori

Via S. Gallo

Via Guelfa

Via A. Santa Reparata

Piazza Mercato Centrale

Borgo la Noce

Via della Stufa

Via Taddea

Via dell'Ariento

Via S. Antonino

Via Canto de Nelli

Via Panicale

Via Faenza

V. del Melarancio

V. del Giglio

Via Conti

Via Cavour

Via Pucci

Via Martelli

Via del Gori

Piazza S. Lorenzo

ℹ️

and these are the hands that slew him. Music lovers might want to check out the Museo degli Instrumenti Musicali contained within the Accademia; its Stradivarius is the main attraction. ⊠ *Via Ricasoli 60, San Marco* ☎ *055/294883 reservations, 055/2388609 gallery* 🖱 *€6.50, reservation fee €4* ☉ *Tues.–Sun. 8:15–6:50.*

8 Museo di San Marco. A Dominican convent adjacent to the church of San Marco now houses this museum, which contains many stunning works by Fra Angelico (circa 1400–55), the Dominican friar famous for his piety as well as for his painting. When the friars' cells were restructured between 1439 and 1444, he decorated many of them with frescoes meant to spur religious contemplation. His unostentatious and direct paintings exalt the simple beauties of the contemplative life. Fra Angelico's works are everywhere, from the friars' cells to the superb panel paintings on view in the museum. Don't miss the famous *Annunciation*, on the upper floor, and the works in the gallery off the cloister as you enter. Here you can see his beautiful *Last Judgment*; as usual, the tortures of the damned are far more inventive and interesting than the pleasures of the redeemed. ⊠ *Piazza San Marco 1* ☎ *055/2388608* 🖱 *€4* ☉ *Weekdays 8:15–1:50, weekends 8:15–6:50. Closed 1st, 3rd, and 5th Sun., and 2nd and 4th Mon. of month.*

3 San Lorenzo. Filippo Brunelleschi designed this basilica, as well as that of Santo Spirito in the Oltrarno, in the 15th century. He never lived to see either finished. The two interiors are similar in design and effect. San Lorenzo, however, has a grid of dark, inlaid marble lines on the floor, which considerably heightens the dramatic effect. The grid makes the rigorous geometry of the interior immediately visible, and is an illuminating lesson on the laws of perspective. If you stand in the middle of the nave at the church entrance, on the line that stretches to the high altar, every element in the church—the grid, the nave columns, the side aisles, the coffered nave ceiling—seems to march inexorably toward a hypothetical vanishing point beyond the high altar, exactly as in a single-point-perspective painting. Brunelleschi's **Sagrestia Vecchia** (Old Sacristy) has stucco decorations by Donatello; it's at the end of the left transept. ⊠ *Piazza San Lorenzo* ☎ *055/2645144* 🖱 *€2.50* ☉ *Mon.–Sat. 10–5; Mar.–Oct., Sun. 1:30–5. Closed Sun. Nov.–Feb.*

WORTH NOTING

4 Biblioteca Medicea Laurenziana *(Laurentian Library)*. Michelangelo the architect was every bit as original as Michelangelo the sculptor. Unlike Brunelleschi (the architect of the Spedale degli Innocenti), however, he wasn't obsessed with proportion and perfect geometry. He was interested in experimentation and invention and in the expression of a personal vision at times highly idiosyncratic.

Florence's Trial by Fire

One of the most striking figures of Renaissance Florence was Girolamo Savonarola, a Dominican friar who, for a moment, captured the conscience of the city. In 1491 he became prior of the convent of San Marco, where he adopted a life of austerity and delivered sermons condemning Florence's excesses and the immorality of his fellow clergy. Following the death of Lorenzo de' Medici, Savonarola was instrumental in the formation of the republic of Florence, ruled by a representative council with Christ enthroned as monarch. In one of his most memorable acts, he urged Florentines to toss worldly possessions—from frilly dresses to Botticelli paintings—onto a "bonfire of the vanities" in Piazza della Signoria. Savonarola's antagonism toward church hierarchy led to his undoing: he was excommunicated in 1497, and the following year was hanged and burned on charges of heresy. Today, at the Museo di San Marco, you can visit Savonarola's cell and see his arresting portrait.

4

It was never more idiosyncratic than in the Laurentian Library, begun in 1524 and finished in 1568 by Bartolomeo Ammannati. Its famous **vestibolo,** a strangely shaped anteroom, has had scholars scratching their heads for centuries. In a space more than two stories high, why did Michelangelo limit his use of columns and pilasters to the upper two-thirds of the wall? Why didn't he rest them on strong pedestals instead of on huge, decorative curlicue scrolls, which rob them of all visual support? Why did he recess them into the wall, which makes them look weaker still? The architectural elements here do not stand firm and strong and tall, as inside San Lorenzo, next door; instead, they seem to be pressed into the wall as if into putty, giving the room a soft, rubbery look that is one of the strangest effects ever achieved by classical architecture. It's almost as if Michelangelo intentionally flouted the conventions of the High Renaissance to see what kind of bizarre, mannered effect might result. His innovations were tremendously influential, and produced a period of architectural experimentation. As his contemporary Giorgio Vasari put it, "Artisans have been infinitely and perpetually indebted to him because he broke the bonds and chains of a way of working that had become habitual by common usage."

The anteroom's staircase (best viewed straight on), which emerges from the library with the visual force of an unstoppable lava flow, has been exempted from the criticism, however. In its highly sculptural conception and execution, it is quite simply one of the most original and fluid staircases in the world. ⊠ *Piazza San Lorenzo 9, entrance to left of San Lorenzo* ☎ *055/210760* ⊕ *www.bml.firenze.sbn.it* ▢ *Special exhibitions €5, museum €3* ☉ *Sun.–Fri. 9–1.*

❻ **Mercato Centrale.** Some of the food at this huge, two-story market hall is remarkably exotic. The ground floor contains meat and cheese stalls, as well as some very good bars serving *panini* (sandwiches), and the second floor teems with vegetable stands. ⊠ *Piazza del Mercato Centrale, San Lorenzo* ☎ *No phone* ☉ *Mon.–Sat. 7–2.*

🔟 Museo Archeologico *(Archaeological Museum).* Of the Etruscan, Egyptian, and Greco-Roman antiquities here, the Etruscan collection is particularly notable—one of the most important in Italy (the other being in Turin). The famous bronze *Chimera* was discovered (without the tail, which is a 16th-century reconstruction by Cellini). If you're traveling with kids, they might par-

ticularly enjoy the small mummy collection. Those with a fondness for gardens should visit on Saturday morning, when the tiny but eminently pleasurable garden is open for tours. ⊠ *Via della Colonna 38, Santissima Annunziata* ☎ *055/23575* ⊕ *www.comune.firenze.it/soggetti/sat/didattica/museo.html* ⊠ *€4* ⊗ *Mon. 2–7, Tues. and Thurs. 8:30–7, Wed. and Fri.–Sun. 8:30–2.*

❶ Museo di Casa Martelli. The wealthy Martelli family, long associated with the all-powerful Medici, lived, from the 16th century, in this palace on a quiet street near the basilica of San Lorenzo. The last Martelli died in 1986, and in October 2009 the casa-museo (house-museum) opened to the public. It's the only nonreconstructed example of such a house in all of Florence, and for that reason alone it's worth a visit. The family collected art, and while most of the stuff is B-list, a couple of gems by Beccafumi, Salvatore Rosa, and Piero di Cosimo adorn the walls. Reservations are essential, and you will be shown the glories of this place by well-informed, English-speaking guides. ⊠ *Via Zanetti 8, San Lorenzo* ☎ *055/294883* ⊕ *www.polomuseale.firenze.it* ⊠ *€3* ⊗ *Guided tours Thurs. noon, 3:30, and 5; Sat. 9, 10:30, and noon.*

❺ Palazzo Medici-Riccardi. The main attraction of this palace, begun in 1444 by Michelozzo for Cosimo de' Medici, is the interior chapel, the so-called **Cappella dei Magi** on the *piano nobile* (second) floor. Painted on its walls is Benozzo Gozzoli's famous *Procession of the Magi*, finished in 1460 and celebrating both the birth of Christ and the greatness of the Medici family. Gozzoli wasn't a revolutionary painter, and today is considered by some not quite first-rate because of his technique, which was old-fashioned even for his day. Gozzoli's gift, however, was for entrancing the eye, not challenging the mind, and on those terms his success here is beyond question. Entering the chapel is like walking into the middle of a magnificently illustrated children's storybook, and this beauty makes it one of the most enjoyable rooms in the city. ⊠ *Via Cavour 1, San Lorenzo* ☎ *055/2760340* ⊠ *€6* ⊗ *Thurs.–Tues. 9–7.*

❾ Santissima Annunziata. Dating from the mid-13th century, this church was restructured in 1447 by Michelozzo, who gave it an uncommon (and lovely) entrance cloister with frescoes by Andrea del Sarto (1486–1530), Pontormo (1494–1556), and Rosso Fiorentino (1494–1540). The interior is a rarity for Florence: an overwhelming example of the baroque. But it's not really a fair example, because it's merely 17th-century baroque decoration applied willy-nilly to an earlier structure—exactly the sort of violent remodeling exercise that has given the baroque a bad name. The **Cappella dell'Annunziata,** immediately inside the entrance to the left, illustrates the point. The lower half, with its stately Corinthian columns and carved frieze bearing the Medici arms, was commissioned by Piero de' Medici in 1447; the upper half, with its erupting curves and impish sculpted cherubs, was added 200 years later. Fifteenth-century-fresco enthusiasts should also note the very fine *Holy Trinity with St. Jerome* in the second chapel on the left. Done by Andrea del Castagno (circa 1421–57), it shows a wiry and emaciated St. Jerome with Paula and Eustochium, two of his closest followers. ⊠ *Piazza di Santissima Annunziata* ☎ *055/266186* ⊘ *Daily 7–12:30 and 4–6:30.*

⓫ **Spedale degli Innocenti.** Built by Brunelleschi in 1419 to serve as an orphanage, it takes the historical prize as the very first Renaissance building. Brunelleschi designed its portico with his usual rigor, building it out of the two shapes he considered mathematically (and therefore philosophically and aesthetically) perfect: the square and the circle. Below the level of the arches, the portico encloses a row of perfect cubes; above the level of the arches, the portico encloses a row of intersecting hemispheres. The entire geometric scheme is articulated with Corinthian columns, capitals, and arches borrowed directly from antiquity. At the time he designed the portico, Brunelleschi was also designing the interior of San Lorenzo, using the same basic ideas. But because the portico was finished before San Lorenzo, the Spedale degli Innocenti can claim the honor of ushering in Renaissance architecture. The 10 ceramic medallions depicting swaddled infants that decorate the portico are by Andrea della Robbia (1435–1525/28), done in about 1487.

Within the Spedale degli Innocenti is a small museum, or **Pinacoteca** (⊡ €4 ⊘ *Thurs.–Tues. 8:30–2*). Most of the objects are minor works by major artists, but well worth a look is Domenico Ghirlandaio's (1449–94) *Adorazione dei Magi (Adoration of the Magi),* executed in 1488. His use of color, and his eye for flora and fauna, shows that art from north of the Alps made a great impression on him. ⊠ *Piazza di Santissima Annunziata 12* ☎ *055/20371* ⊡ *€4* ⊘ *Mon.–Sat. 8:30–7, Sun. 8:30–2.*

SANTA MARIA NOVELLA TO THE ARNO

Piazza Santa Maria Novella, near the train station, has been restored to its former glory thanks to a years-long project completed in 2009. The streets in and around the piazza have their share of architectural treasures, including some of Florence's most tasteful palaces. Between Santa Maria Novella and the Arno is Via Tornabuoni, Florence's finest shopping street.

TOP ATTRACTIONS

❶ **Santa Maria Novella.** The facade of this church looks distinctly clumsy by later Renaissance standards, and with good reason: it is an architectural hybrid. The lower half was completed mostly in the 14th century; its pointed-arch niches and decorative marble patterns reflect the Gothic style of the day. About 100 years later (around 1456), architect Leon Battista Alberti was called in to complete the job. The marble decoration of his upper story clearly defers to the already existing work below, but the architectural motifs he added evince an entirely different style. The central doorway, the four ground-floor half-columns with Corinthian capitals, the triangular pediment atop the second story, the inscribed frieze immediately below the pediment—these are borrowings from antiquity, and they reflect the new Renaissance style in architecture, born some 35 years earlier at the Spedale degli Innocenti. Alberti's most important addition, however, the S-curve scrolls that surmount the decorative circles on either side of the upper story, had no precedent whatever in antiquity. The problem was to soften the abrupt transition between wide ground floor and narrow upper story. Alberti's solution turned out to be definitive. Once you start to look for them, you will find scrolls such as these (or sculptural variations of them) on churches all over Italy, and every one of them derives from Alberti's example here.

The architecture of the interior is, like that of the Duomo, a dignified but somber example of Florentine Gothic. Exploration is essential, however, because the church's store of art treasures is remarkable. Highlights include the 14th-century stained-glass rose window depicting the *Coronation of the Virgin* (above the central entrance); the Cappella Filippo Strozzi (to the right of the altar), containing late-15th-century frescoes and stained glass by Filippino Lippi; the *cappella maggiore* (the area around the high altar), displaying frescoes by Ghirlandaio; and the Cappella Gondi (to the left of the altar), containing Filippo Brunelleschi's famous wood crucifix, carved around 1410 and said to have so stunned the great Donatello when he first saw it that he dropped a basket of eggs.

Of special interest for its great historical importance and beauty is Masaccio's *Trinity,* on the left-hand wall, almost halfway down the nave. Painted around 1426–27 (at the same time he was working on his frescoes in Santa Maria del Carmine), it unequivocally announced the arrival of the Renaissance. The realism of the figure of Christ was revolutionary in itself, but what was probably even more startling to contemporary Florentines was the barrel vault in the background. The mathematical rules for employing perspective in painting had just been discovered (probably by Brunelleschi), and this was one of the first works of art to employ them with utterly convincing success.

In the cloisters of the **Museo di Santa Maria Novella,** to the left of Santa Maria Novella, is a faded fresco cycle by Paolo Uccello depicting tales from Genesis, with a dramatic vision of the Deluge. Earlier and better-preserved frescoes painted in 1348–55 by Andrea da Firenze are in the chapter house, or the **Cappellone degli Spagnoli** (Spanish Chapel), off the cloister. ⊠ *Piazza Santa Maria Novella 19* ☎ *055/210113, museo 005/282187* ☜ *church free, museum and chapel €2.70* ☉ *Mon.–Thurs. 9–5, Fri. and Sun. 9–1.*

❸ **Santa Trinita.** Started in the 11th century by Vallombrosian monks and originally Romanesque in style, the church underwent a Gothic remodeling during the 14th century. (Remains of the Romanesque construction are visible on the interior front wall.) Its major works are the

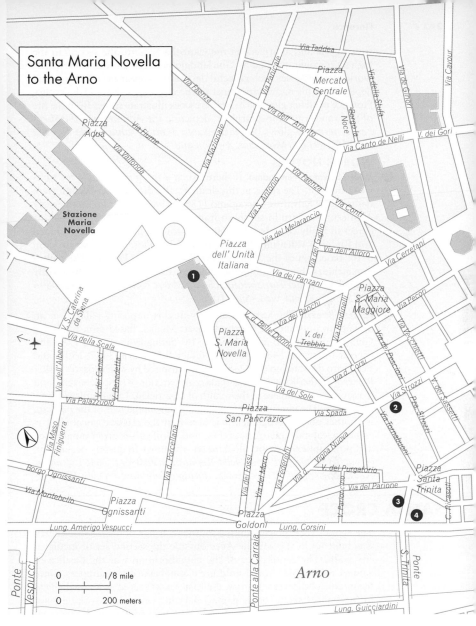

Santa Maria Novella
to the Arno

Via Taddea

Piazza
Mercato
Centrale

Via del Ginori

Via Cavour

Via Faenza

Via Panicale

Via della Stufa

Piazza
Adua

Via Fiume

Via dell'Ariento

Bertolla

Via Nazionale

Via Vallonda

Noce

Via Canto de Nelli

V. dei Gori

Stazione
Maria
Novella

Via S. Antonio

Via Faenza

Via Conti

Via del Melarancio

Via dei Giglio

Via dell'Alloro

Via Cerretani

Piazza
dell' Unità
Italiana

1

Via dei Panzani

Piazza
S. Maria
Maggiore

Via Pecori

V. S. Caterina
da Siena

Via dei Banchi

V. Rondinelli

V. d. Belle Donne

V. del
Trebbio

V. de Pescioni

Via della Scala

Piazza
S. Maria
Novella

Via d. Corsi

Via Strozzi

V. dei Sassetti

Via dell'Albero

V. dei Canacci

V. Benedetta

Via Palazzuolo

Via del Sole

Piazza
San Pancrazio

Via Spada

2

Prg. Strozzi

Via Maso Finiguerra

Via d. Porcellana

Vigna Nuova

V. Tornabuoni

Piazza
Santa
Trinita

Borgo Ognissanti

Via dei Fossi

Via del Moro

Via Federighi

V. del Purgatorio

Via del Parione

3

Via Montebello

Piazza
Ognissanti

Piazza
Goldoni

V. Parioncino

C. Ricasoli

4

Lung. Amerigo Vespucci

Lung. Corsini

Ponte Vespucci

Ponte alla Carraia

Arno

S. Trinita

Ponte
S. Trinita

0   1/8 mile

0   200 meters

Lung. Guicciardini

fresco cycle and altarpiece in the Cappella Sassetti, the second to the high altar's right, painted by Ghirlandaio between 1480 and 1485. His work here possesses such graceful decorative appeal as well as a proud depiction of his native city (most of the cityscapes show 15th-century Florence in all her glory). The wall frescoes illustrate scenes from the life of St. Francis, and the altarpiece, depicting the *Adoration of the Shepherds,* veritably glows. ⊠ *Piazza Santa Trinita, Santa Maria Novella* ☎ *055/216912* ⏱ *Mon.–Sat. 8–noon and 4–6.*

WORTH NOTING

④ Museo Salvatore Ferragamo. If there's such a thing as a temple for footwear, this is it. The shoes in this dramatically displayed collection were designed by Salvatore Ferragamo (1898–1960) beginning in the early 20th century. Born in southern Italy, the late master jump-started his career in Hollywood by creating shoes for the likes of Mary Pickford and Rudolph Valentino. He then returned to Florence and set up shop in the basement of the 13th-century Palazzo Spini Ferroni. The collection includes about 16,000 shoes, and those on exhibition are frequently rotated. ⊠ *Via dei Tornabuoni 2, Santa Maria Novella* ☎ *055/3360846* 🎟 *€5* ⏱ *Mon. and Wed.–Sun. 10–6.*

② Palazzo Strozzi. The Strozzi family built this imposing palazzo in an attempt to outshine the nearby Palazzo Medici. Based on a model by Giuliano da Sangallo (circa 1452–1516) dating from around 1489 and executed between 1489 and 1504 under Il Cronaca (1457–1508) and Benedetto da Maiaino (1442–97), it was inspired by Michelozzo's earlier Palazzo Medici-Riccardi. The palazzo's exterior is simple, severe, and massive: it's a testament to the wealth of a patrician, 15th-century Florentine family. The interior courtyard, entered from the rear of the palazzo, is another matter altogether. It is here that the classical vocabulary—columns, capitals, pilasters, arches, and cornices—is given uninhibited and powerful expression. Blockbuster art shows frequently occur here. ⊠ *Via Tornabuoni, Piazza della Repubblica* ☎ *055/2776461* ⊕ *www. palazzostrozzi.org* 🎟 *Free, except during exhibitions* ⏱ *Daily 10–7.*

SANTA CROCE

The Santa Croce quarter, on the southeast fringe of the historic center, was built up in the Middle Ages outside the second set of medieval city walls. The centerpiece of the neighborhood was the basilica of Santa Croce, which could hold great numbers of worshippers. Since the middle of the 16th century, the vast piazza served as a playing field for no-holds-barred soccer games. A center of leather working since the Middle Ages, the neighborhood is still packed with leatherworkers and leather shops.

TOP ATTRACTIONS

② Piazza Santa Croce. Originally outside the city's 12th-century walls, this piazza grew with the Franciscans, who used the large square for public preaching. During the Renaissance it was used for *giostre* (jousts), including one sponsored by Lorenzo de' Medici. "Bonfires of the vanities" occurred here, as well as soccer matches in the 16th century. Lined

Meet the Medici

The Medici were the dominant family of Renaissance Florence, wielding political power and financing some of the world's greatest art. You'll see their names at every turn around the city. These are some of the clan's more notable members:

Cosimo il Vecchio (1389–1464), incredibly wealthy banker to the popes, was the first in the family line to act as de facto ruler of Florence. He was a great patron of the arts and architecture; he was the moving force behind the family palace and the Dominican complex of San Marco.

Lorenzo il Magnifico (1449–92), grandson of Cosimo il Vecchio, presided over a Florence largely at peace with her neighbors. A collector of cameos, a writer of sonnets, and lover of ancient texts, he was the preeminent Renaissance man.

Leo X (1475–1521), also known as Giovanni de' Medici, became the first Medici pope, helping extend the family power base to include Rome and the Papal States. His reign was characterized by a host of problems, the biggest one being a former friar named Martin Luther.

Catherine de' Medici (1519–89) was married by her cousin Pope Clement VII to Henry of Valois, who later became Henry II of France. Wife of one king and mother of three, she was the first Medici to marry into European royalty. Lorenzo il Magnifico, her great-grandfather, would have been thrilled.

Cosimo I (1519–74), the first grand duke of Tuscany, should not be confused with his ancestor Cosimo il Vecchio.

4

---

with many palazzi dating from the 15th century, it remains one of Florence's loveliest piazze and is a great place to people-watch.

① **Santa Croce.** Like the Duomo, this church is Gothic, but, also like the
Fodor'sChoice Duomo, its facade dates from the 19th century. As a burial place, the
★ church probably contains more skeletons of Renaissance celebrities than any other in Italy. The tomb of Michelangelo is on the right at the front of the basilica; he is said to have chosen this spot so that the first thing he would see on Judgment Day, when the graves of the dead fly open, would be Brunelleschi's dome through Santa Croce's open doors. The tomb of Galileo Galilei (1564–1642) is on the left wall; he was not granted a Christian burial until 100 years after his death because of his controversial contention that Earth is not the center of the universe. The tomb of Niccolò Machiavelli (1469–1527), the political theoretician whose brutally pragmatic philosophy so influenced the Medici, is halfway down the nave on the right. The grave of Lorenzo Ghiberti, creator of the Baptistery doors, is halfway down the nave on the left. Composer Gioacchino Rossini (1792–1868) is buried at the end of the nave on the right. The monument to Dante Alighieri (1265–1321), Italy's greatest poet, is a memorial rather than a tomb (he is buried in Ravenna); it's on the right wall near the tomb of Michelangelo.

The collection of art within the complex is by far the most important of any church in Florence. The most famous works are probably the

Giotto frescoes in the two chapels immediately to the right of the high altar. They illustrate scenes from the lives of Saint John the Evangelist and Saint John the Baptist (in the right-hand chapel) and scenes from the life of Saint Francis (in the left-hand chapel). Time has not been kind to these frescoes; through the centuries, wall tombs were placed in the middle of them, they were whitewashed and plastered over, and in the 19th century they suffered a clumsy restoration. But the reality that Giotto introduced into painting can still be seen. He did not paint beautifully stylized religious icons, as the Byzantine style that preceded him prescribed; he instead painted drama—Saint Francis surrounded by grieving friars at the very moment of his death. This was a radical shift in emphasis: before Giotto, painting's role was to symbolize the attributes of God; after him, it was to imitate life. His work is indeed primitive compared with later painting, but in the early 14th century it caused a sensation that was not equaled for another 100 years. He was, for his time, the equal of both Masaccio and Michelangelo.

Among the church's other highlights are Donatello's *Annunciation,* a moving expression of surprise (on the right wall two-thirds of the way down the nave); 14th-century frescoes by Taddeo Gaddi (circa 1300–66) illustrating scenes from the life of the Virgin Mary, clearly showing the influence of Giotto (in the chapel at the end of the right transept); and Donatello's *Crucifix,* criticized by Brunelleschi for making Christ look like a peasant (in the chapel at the end of the left transept). Outside the church proper, in the **Museo dell'Opera di Santa Croce** off the cloister, is the 13th-century *Triumphal Cross* by Cimabue (circa 1240–1302), badly damaged by the flood of 1966. A model of architectural geometry, the Cappella Pazzi, at the end of the cloister, was designed by Brunelleschi, who did not live to see it finished. ⊠ *Piazza Santa Croce 16* ☎ *055/2466105* ☜ *Church and museum €5* ☉ *Mon.– Sat. 9:30–5:30, Sun. 1–5.*

❹ **Sinagoga.** Jews were well settled in Florence by 1396, when the first money-lending operations became officially sanctioned. Medici patronage helped Jewish banking houses to flourish, but by 1570 Jews were required to live within the large "ghetto," near today's Piazza della Repubblica, by decree of Cosimo I, who had cut a deal with Pope Pius V (1504–72): in exchange for ghettoizing the Jews, he would receive the title Grand Duke of Tuscany.

Construction of the modern Moorish-style synagogue began in 1874 as a bequest of David Levi, who wished to endow a synagogue "worthy of the city." Falcini, Micheli, and Treves designed the building on a domed Greek cross plan with galleries in the transept and a roofline bearing three distinctive copper cupolas visible from all over Florence. The exterior has alternating bands of tan travertine and pink granite, reflecting an Islamic style repeated in Giovanni Panti's ornate interior. Of particular interest are the cast-iron gates by Pasquale Franci, the eternal light by Francesco Morini, and the Murano glass mosaics by Giacomo dal Medico. The gilded doors of the Moorish ark, which fronts the pulpit and is flanked by extravagant candelabra, are decorated with symbols of the ancient Temple of Jerusalem and bear bayonet marks from vandals. The synagogue was used as a garage by the Nazis, who

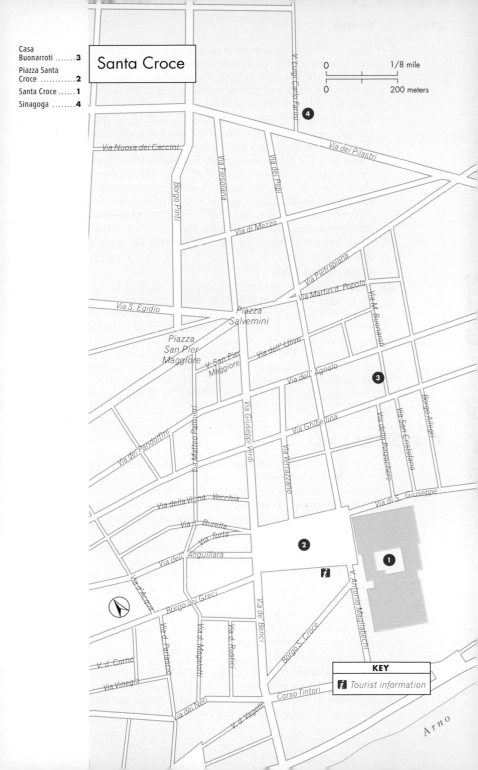

Santa Croce

0   1/8 mile

0   200 meters

V. Luigi Carlo Farini

4

Via Nuova dei Caccini

Via dei Pilastri

Via Fiesolana

Via dei Pepi

Borgo Pinti

Via di Mezzo

Via Pietrapiana

Via Martiri d. Popolo

Via S. Egidio

Piazza
Salvemini

Via dell' Ulivo

Via M. Buonarroti

Piazza
San Pier
Maggiore

V. San Pier
Maggiore

Via dell' Agnolo

3

Via dei Pandolfini

Via Giuseppe Verdi

Via delle Conce

Via Ghibellina

Via delle Pinzochere

Via San Cristofano

Borgo Allegri

Via Verrazzano

Via della Vigna Vecchia

Via di Burella

Via di S. Giuseppe

Via Torta

Via dell' Anguillara

2

1

Via dell'Acqua

Borgo dei Greci

Via de' Benci

V. Antonio Magliabechi

V. d. Corno

Via Pandrosso

Via d. Magalotti

Via d. Rustici

Borgo S. Croce

Via Vinegia

Via dei Neri

V. d. Vagelli

Corso Tintori

Arno

failed to inflict much damage in spite of an attempt to blow up the place with dynamite. Only the columns on the left side were destroyed, and even then, the Women's Balcony above did not collapse. Note the Star of David in black and yellow marble inlaid in the floor. The original capitals can be seen in the garden.

Some of the oldest and most beautiful Jewish ritual artifacts in all of Europe are displayed upstairs in the small **Museo Ebraico.** Exhibits document the Florentine Jewish community and the building of the synagogue. The donated objects all belonged to local families and date from as early as the late 16th century. Take special note of the exquisite needlework and silver pieces. A small but well-stocked gift shop is downstairs. ✉ *Via Farini 4, Santa Croce* ☎ *055/2346654* ✉ *Synagogue and museum €5* ⊙ *Apr., May, Sept., and Oct., Sun.–Thurs. 10–5, Fri. 10–2; June–Aug., Sun.–Thurs. 10–6, Fri. 10–2; Nov.–Mar., Sun.–Thurs. 10–3, Fri. 10–2. English guided tours: 10:10, 11, noon, 1, 2 (no tour at 2 on Fri.).*

WORTH NOTING

❸ Casa Buonarroti. If you are really enjoying walking in the footsteps of the great genius, you may want to complete the picture by visiting the Buonarroti family home. Michelangelo lived here from 1516 to 1525, and later gave it to his nephew, whose son, called Michelangelo il Giovane (Michelangelo the Younger) turned it into a gallery dedicated to his great-uncle. The artist's descendants filled it with art treasures, some by Michelangelo himself. Two early marble works—the *Madonna of the Steps* and the *Battle of the Centaurs*—hint at the marvels to come. ✉ *Via Ghibellina 70, Santa Croce* ☎ *055/241752* ⊕ *www.casabuonarroti.it* ✉ *€6.50* ⊙ *Fri.–Wed. 9:30–2.*

THE OLTRARNO

A walk through the Oltrarno (literally "the other side of the Arno") takes in two very different aspects of Florence: the splendor of the Medici, manifest in the riches of the mammoth Palazzo Pitti and the gracious Giardino di Boboli; and the charm of the Oltrarno, a slightly gentrified but still fiercely proud working-class neighborhood with artisans' and antiques shops.

Farther east across the Arno, a series of ramps and stairs climbs to Piazzale Michelangelo, where the city lies before you in all its glory (skip this trip if it's a hazy day). You can avoid the long walk by taking Bus 12 or 13 at the west end of Ponte alle Grazie and getting off at Piazzale Michelangelo; you still have to climb the monumental stairs to and from San Miniato, but you can then take the bus from Piazzale Michelangelo back to the center of town. If you decide to take a bus, remember to buy your ticket before you board.

TOP ATTRACTIONS

❺ Giardino di Boboli *(Boboli Gardens).* The main entrance to these landscaped gardens is from the right side of the courtyard of **Palazzo Pitti.** The gardens began to take shape in 1549, when the Pitti family sold the palazzo to Eleanor of Toledo, wife of the Medici grand duke

Continued on page 253

WHO'S WHO IN RENAISSANCE ART

Michelangelo. Leonardo da Vinci. Raphael. This heady triumvirate of the Italian Renaissance is synonymous with artistic genius. Yet they are only three of the remarkable cast of characters whose work defines the Renaissance, that extraordinary flourishing of art and culture in Italy, especially in Florence, as the Middle Ages drew to a close. The artists were visionaries, who redefined painting, sculpture, architecture, and even what it means to be an artist.

THE PIONEER. In the mid-14th century, a few artists began to move away the flat, two-dimensional painting of the Middle Ages. **Giotto**, who painted seemingly three-dimensional figures who show emotion, had a major impact on the artists of the next century.

THE GROUNDBREAKERS. The generations of **Brunelleschi** and **Botticelli** took center stage in the 15th century. **Ghiberti**, **Masaccio**, **Donatello**, **Uccello**, **Fra Angelico**, and **Filippo Lippi** were other major players. Part of the Renaissance (or "re-birth") was a renewed interest in classical sources—the texts, monuments, and sculpture of Ancient Greece and Rome. Perspective and the illusion of three-dimensional space in painting was another discovery of this era, known as the Early Renaissance. Suddenly the art appearing on the walls looked real, or more realistic than it used to be.

Roman ruins were not the only thing to inspire these artists. There was an incredible exchange of ideas going on. In Santa Maria del Carmine, Filippo Lippi was inspired by the work of Masaccio, who in turn was a friend of Brunelleschi. Young artists also learned from the masters via the apprentice system. Ghiberti's workshop (*bottega* in Italian) included, at one time or another, Donatello, Masaccio, and Uccello. Botticelli was apprenticed to Filippo Lippi.

THE BIG THREE. The mathematical rationality and precision of 15th-century art gave way to what is known as the High Renaissance. **Leonardo, Michelangelo**, and **Raphael** were much more concerned with portraying the body in all its glory and with achieving harmony and grandeur in their work. Oil paint, used infrequently up until this time, became more widely employed: as a result, Leonardo's colors are deeper, more sensual, more alive. For one brief period, all three were in Florence at the same time. Michelangelo and Leonardo surely knew one another, as they were simultaneously working on frescoes (never completed) inside Palazzo Vecchio.

When Michelangelo left Florence for Rome in 1508, he began the slow drain of artistic exodus from Florence, which never really recovered her previous glory.

A RENAISSANCE TIMELINE

IN THE WORLD

Black Death in Europe kills one third of the population, 1347-50.

Joan of Arc burned at the stake, 1431.

IN FLORENCE

Dante, a native of Florence, writes *The Divine Comedy*, 1302-21.

Founding of the Medici bank, 1397.

Medici family made official papal bankers.

1434, Cosimo il Vecchio becomes de facto ruler of Florence. The Medici family will dominate the city until 1494.

1300

1400

IN ART

EARLY RENAISSANCE

Masaccio and Masolino fresco Santa Maria del Carmine, 1424-28.

GIOTTO (ca. 1267-1337)

BRUNELLESCHI (1377-1446)

Giotto fresoes in Santa Croce, 1320-25.

LORENZO GHIBERTI (ca. 1381-1455)

DONATELLO (ca. 1386-1466)

PAOLO UCCELLO (1397-1475)

1334, 67-year-old Giotto is appointed chief architect of Santa Maria del Fiore, Florence's Duomo (below). He begins to work on the Campanile, which will be completed in 1359, after his death.

FRA ANGELICO (ca. 1400-1455)

MASACCIO (1401-1428)

FILIPPO LIPPI (ca. 1406-1469)

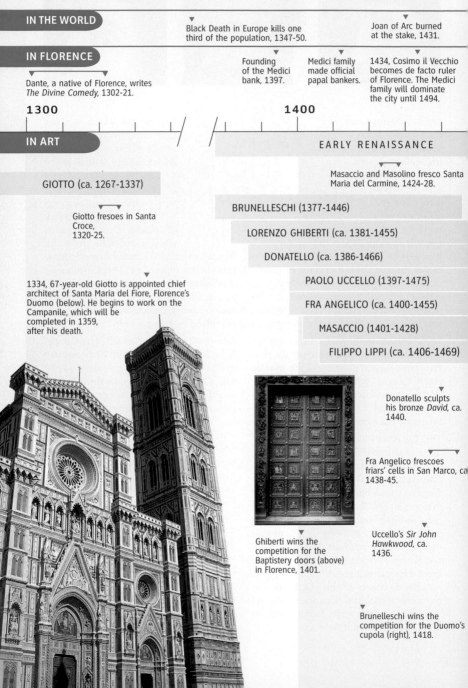

Donatello sculpts his bronze *David*, ca. 1440.

Fra Angelico frescoes friars' cells in San Marco, ca. 1438-45.

Uccello's *Sir John Hawkwood*, ca. 1436.

Ghiberti wins the competition for the Baptistery doors (above) in Florence, 1401.

Brunelleschi wins the competition for the Duomo's cupola (right), 1418.

Gutenberg Bible is printed, 1455.

Columbus discovers America, 1492.

Martin Luther posts his 95 theses on the door at Wittenberg, kicking off the Protestant Reformation, 1517.

Constantinople falls to the Turks, 1453.

Machiavelli's *Prince* appears, 1513.

Copernicus proves that the earth is not the center of the universe, 1530-43.

Lorenzo "il Magnifico" (right), the Medici patron of the arts, rules in Florence, 1449-92.

Two Medici popes Leo X (1513-21) and Clement VII (1523-34) in Rome.

Catherine de'Medici becomes Queen of France, 1547.

1450   **1500**   **1550**

4

HIGH RENAISSANCE   MANNERISM

Fra Filippo Lippi's *Madonna and Child*, ca. 1452.

1508, Raphael begins work on the chambers in the Vatican, Rome.

Giorgio Vasari publishes his first edition of *Lives of the Artists*, 1550.

1504, Michelangelo's *David* is put on display in Piazza della Signoria, where it remains until 1873.

Botticelli paints the *Birth of Venus*, ca. 1482.

Michelangelo begins to fresco the Sistine Chapel ceiling, 1508.

BOTTICELLI (ca. 1444-1510)

LEONARDO DA VINCI (1452-1519)

RAPHAEL (1483-1520)

MICHELANGELO (1475-1564)

Leonardo paints *The Last Supper* in Milan, 1495-98.

IN FOCUS WHO'S WHO IN RENAISSANCE ART

Giotto's *Nativity*   Donatello's *St. John the Baptist*   Ghiberti's *Gates of Paradise*

GIOTTO (CA. 1267-1337)
Painter/architect from a small town north of Florence.
He unequivocally set Italian painting on the course that led to the triumphs of the Renaissance masters. Unlike the rather flat, two-dimensional forms found in then prevailing Byzantine art, Giotto's figures have a fresh, life-like quality. The people in his paintings have bulk, and they show emotion, which you can see on their faces and in their gestures. This was something new in the late Middle Ages. Without Giotto, there wouldn't have been a Raphael.
In Florence: **Santa Croce; Uffizi; Campanile; Santa Maria Novella**
Elsewhere in Italy: **Scrovegni Chapel, Padua; Vatican Museums, Rome**

FILIPPO BRUNELLESCHI (1377-1446)
Architect/engineer from Florence.
If Brunelleschi had beaten Ghiberti in the Baptistery doors competition in Florence, the city's Duomo most likely would not have the striking appearance and authority that it has today. After his loss, he sulked off to Rome, where he studied the ancient Roman structures first-hand. Brunelleschi figured out how to vault the Duomo's dome, a structure unprecedented in its colossal size and great height. His Ospedale degli Innocenti employs classical elements in the creation of a stunning, new architectural statement; it is the first truly Renaissance structure.
In Florence: **Duomo; Ospedale degli Innocenti; San Lorenzo; Santo Spirito; Baptistery Doors Competition Entry, Bargello; Santa Croce**

LORENZO GHIBERTI (CA. 1381-1455)
Sculptor from Florence.
Ghiberti won a competition—besting his chief rival, Brunelleschi—to cast the gilded bronze North Doors of the Baptistery in Florence. These doors, and the East Doors that he subsequently executed, took up the next 50 years of his life. He created intricately worked figures that are more true-to-life than any since antiquity, and he was one of the first Renaissance sculptors to work in bronze. Ghiberti taught the next generation of artists; Donatello, Uccello, and Masaccio all passed through his studio.
In Florence: **Door Copies, Baptistery; Original Doors, Museo dell'Opera del Duomo; Baptistry Door Competition Entry, Bargello; Orsanmichele**

DONATELLO (CA. 1386-1466)
Sculptor from Florence.
Donatello was an innovator who, like his good friend Brunelleschi, spent most of his long life in Florence. Consumed with the science of optics, he used light and shadow to create the effects of nearness and distance. He made an essentially flat slab look like a three- dimensional scene. His bronze *David* is probably the first free-standing male nude since antiquity. Not only technically brilliant, his work is also emotionally resonant; few sculptors are as expressive.
In Florence: ***David*, Bargello; *St. Mark*, Orsanmichele; Palazzo Vecchio; Museo dell'Opera del Duomo; San Lorenzo; Santa Croce**
Elsewhere in Italy: **Padua; Prato; Venice**

Fra Angelico's *The Deposition*   Masaccio's *Trinity*   Filippo Lippi's *Madonna and Child*

PAOLO UCCELLO (1397-1475)
Painter from Florence.
Renaissance chronicler Vasari once observed that had Uccello not been so obsessed with the mathematical problems posed by perspective, he would have been a very good painter. The struggle to master single-point perspective and to render motion in two dimensions is nowhere more apparent than in his battle scenes. His first major commission in Florence was the gargantuan fresco of the English mercenary Sir John Hawkwood (the Italians called him Giovanni Acuto) in Florence's Duomo.
In Florence: *Sir John Hawkwood*, Duomo; *Battle of San Romano*, Uffizi; Santa Maria Novella
Elsewhere in Italy: Urbino

FRA ANGELICO (CA. 1400-1455)
Painter from a small town north of Florence.
A Dominican friar, who eventually made his way to the convent of San Marco, Fra Angelico and his assistants painted frescoes for aid in prayer and meditation. He was known for his piety; Vasari wrote that Fra Angelico could never paint a crucifix without a tear running down his face. Perhaps no other painter so successfully translated the mysteries of faith and the sacred into painting. And yet his figures emote, his command of perspective is superb, and his use of color startles even today.
In Florence: Museo di San Marco; Uffizi
Elsewhere in Italy: Vatican Museums, Rome; Fiesole; Cortona; Perugia; Orvieto

MASACCIO (1401-1428)
Painter from San Giovanni Valdarno, southeast of Florence.
Masaccio and Masolino, a frequent collaborator, worked most famously together at Santa Maria del Carmine. Their frescoes of the life of St. Peter use light to mold figures in the painting by imitating the way light falls on figures in real life. Masaccio also pioneered the use of single-point perspective, masterfully rendered in his *Trinity*. His friend Brunelleschi probably introduced him to the technique, yet another step forward in rendering things the way the eye sees them. Masaccio died young and under mysterious circumstances.
In Florence: Santa Maria del Carmine; *Trinity*, Santa Maria Novella

FILIPPO LIPPI (CA. 1406-1469)
Painter from Prato.
At a young age, Filippo Lippi entered the friary of Santa Maria del Carmine, where he was highly influenced by Masaccio and Masolino's frescoes. His religious vows appear to have made less of an impact; his affair with a young nun produced a son, Filippino (Little Philip, who later apprenticed with Botticelli), and a daughter. His religious paintings often have a playful, humorous note; some of his angels are downright impish and look directly out at the viewer. Lippi links the earlier painters of the 15th century with those who follow; Botticelli apprenticed with him.
In Florence: Uffizi; Palazzo Medici Riccardi; San Lorenzo; Palazzo Pitti
Elsewhere in Italy: Prato

Botticelli's *Primavera* Leonardo's *Portrait of a Young Woman* Raphael's *Madonna on the Meadow*

BOTTICELLI (CA. 1444-1510)
Painter from Florence.
Botticelli's work is characterized by stunning, elongated blondes, cherubic angels (something he undoubtedly learned from his time with Filippo Lippi), and tender Christs. Though he did many religious paintings, he also painted monumental, nonreligious panels—his *Birth of Venus* and *Primavera* being the two most famous of these. A brief sojourn took him to Rome, where he and a number of other artists frescoed the Sistine Chapel walls.
In Florence: **Birth of Venus, Primavera, Uffizi; Palazzo Pitti**
Elsewhere in Italy: **Vatican Museums, Rome**

LEONARDO DA VINCI (1452-1519)
Painter/sculptor/engineer from Anchiano, a small town outside Vinci.
Leonardo never lingered long in any place; his restless nature and his international reputation led to commissions throughout Italy, and took him to Milan, Vigevano, Pavia, Rome, and, ultimately, France. Though he is most famous for his mysterious *Mona Lisa* (at the Louvre in Paris), he painted other penetrating, psychological portraits in addition to his scientific experiments: his design for a flying machine (never built) predates Kitty Hawk by nearly 500 years. The greatest collection of Leonardo's work in Italy can be seen on one wall in the Uffizi.
In Florence: **Adoration of the Magi, Uffizi**
Elsewhere in Italy: **Last Supper, Santa Maria delle Grazie, Milan**

RAPHAEL (1483-1520)
Painter/architect from Urbino.
Raphael spent only four highly productive years of his short life in Florence, where he turned out made-to-order panel paintings of the Madonna and Child for a hungry public; he also executed a number of portraits of Florentine aristocrats. Perhaps no other artist had such a fine command of line and color, and could render it, seemingly effortlessly, in paint. His painting acquired new authority after he came up against Michelangelo toiling away on the Sistine ceiling. Raphael worked nearly next door in the Vatican, where his figures take on an epic, Michelangelesque scale.
In Florence: **Uffizi; Palazzo Pitti**
Elsewhere in Italy: **Vatican Museums, Rome**

MICHELANGELO (1475-1564)
Painter/sculptor/architect from Caprese.
Although Florentine and proud of it (he famously signed his St. Peter's *Pietà* to avoid confusion about where he was from), he spent most of his 90 years outside his native city. He painted and sculpted the male body on an epic scale and glorified it while doing so. Though he complained throughout the proceedings that he was really a sculptor, Michelangelo's Sistine Chapel ceiling is arguably the greatest fresco cycle ever painted (and the massive figures owe no small debt to Giotto).
In Florence: **David, Galleria dell'Accademia; Uffizi; Casa Buonarroti; Bargello**
Elsewhere in Italy: **St. Peter's Basilica, Vatican Museums, and Piazza del Campidoglio in Rome**

Cosimo I. The initial landscaping plans were laid out by Niccolò Tribolo (1500–50). After his death, work was continued by Ammannati, Giambologna, Bernardo Buontalenti (circa 1536–1608), and Giulio (1571–1635) and Alfonso Parigi (1606–56), among others. Italian landscaping is less formal than French, but still full of sweeping drama. A copy of the famous *Morgante,* Cosimo I's favorite dwarf astride a particularly unhappy tortoise, is near the exit. Sculpted by Valerio Cioli (circa 1529–99), the work seems to illustrate the perils of culinary overindulgence. A visit here can be disappointing, because the gardens are somewhat underplanted and undercared for, but it's still a great walk with some terrific views. ✉ *Enter through Palazzo Pitti* ☎ *055/294883* ⊕ *www.polomuseale.firenze.it* 🎟 *€10, combined ticket with Museo degli Argenti, Museo delle Porcellane, Villa Bardini, and Giardino Bardini* ☉ *Jan., Feb., Nov., and Dec., daily 8:15–4:30; Mar., daily 8:15–5:30; Apr., May, Sept., and Oct., daily 8:15–6:30; June–Aug., daily 8:15–7:30. Closed 2nd and 3rd Mon. of month.*

❽ Piazzale Michelangelo. From this lookout you have a marvelous view of Florence and the hills around it, rivaling the vista from the Forte di Belvedere. It has a copy of Michelangelo's *David* and outdoor cafés packed with tourists during the day and with Florentines in the evening. In May the **Giardino dell'Iris** (Iris Garden) off the piazza is abloom with more than 2,500 varieties of the flower. The **Giardino delle Rose** (Rose Garden) on the terraces below the piazza is also in full bloom in May and June.

❹ Palazzo Pitti. This enormous palace is one of Florence's largest architectural set pieces. The original palazzo, built for the Pitti family around 1460, comprised only the main entrance and the three windows on either side. In 1549 the property was sold to the Medici, and Bartolomeo Ammannati was called in to make substantial additions. Although he apparently operated on the principle that more is better, he succeeded only in producing proof that more is just that: more.

Today the palace houses several museums: The **Museo degli Argenti** displays a vast collection of Medici treasures, including exquisite antique vases belonging to Lorenzo the Magnificent. The **Galleria del Costume** showcases fashions from the past 300 years. The **Galleria d'Arte Moderna** holds a collection of 19th- and 20th-century paintings, mostly Tuscan. Most famous of the Pitti galleries is the **Galleria Palatina,** which contains a broad collection of paintings from the 15th to 17th centuries. The rooms of the Galleria Palatina remain much as the Lorena, the rulers who took over after the last Medici died in 1737, left them. Their floor-to-ceiling paintings are considered by some to be Italy's most egregious exercise in conspicuous consumption, aesthetic overkill, and trumpery. Still, the collection possesses high points, including a number of portraits by Titian and an unparalleled collection of paintings by Raphael, notably the double portraits of Angelo Doni and his wife, the sullen Maddalena Strozzi. The price of admission to the Galleria Palatina also allows you to explore the former **Appartamenti Reali,** containing furnishings from a remodeling done in the 19th century. ✉ *Piazza Pitti* ☎ *055/210323* 🎟 *Galleria Palatina and Galleria d'Arte Moderna, combined ticket €12; Galleria del Costume, Giardino*

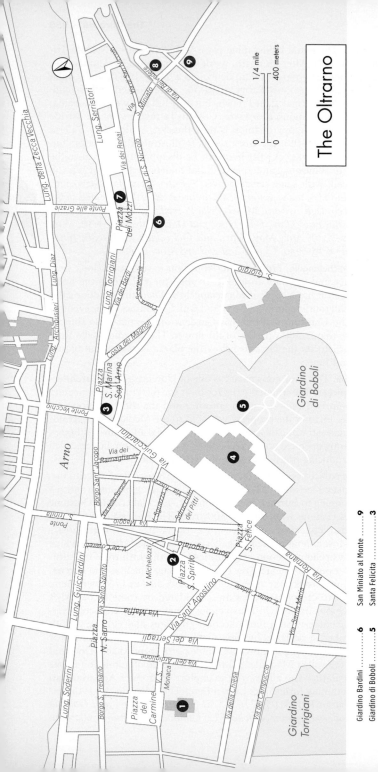

The Oltrarno

0   1/4 mile

0   400 meters

Bardini, Giardino di Boboli, Museo degli Argenti, and Museo Porcel-leane, combined ticket €10 ⓧ Tues.–Sun. 8:15–6:50.

❾ San Miniato al Monte. This church, like the Baptistery, is a fine example of Romanesque architecture and is one of the oldest churches in Florence, dating from the 11th century. A 12th-century mosaic topped by a gilt bronze eagle, emblem of San Miniato's sponsors, the *Calimala* (cloth merchants' guild) crowns the lovely green-and-white marble facade. Inside are a 13th-century inlaid-marble floor and apse mosaic. Artist Spinello Aretino (1350–1410) covered the walls of the **Sagrestia** with frescoes depicting scenes from the life of St. Benedict. The **Cappella del Cardinale del Portogallo** (Chapel of the Portuguese Cardinal) is one of the richest 15th-century Renaissance works in Florence. It contains the tomb of a young Portuguese cardinal, Prince James of Lusitania, who died in Florence in 1459. Its glorious ceiling is by Luca della Robbia, and the sculpted tomb by Antonio Rossellino (1427–79). ⊠ *Viale Galileo Galilei, Piazzale Michelangelo, Lungarno Sud* ☎ *055/2342731* ⓧ *Apr.–Oct., daily 8–7; Nov.–Mar., Mon.–Sat. 8–1 and 2:30–6, Sun. 3–5.*

❶ Santa Maria del Carmine. The **Cappella Brancacci**, at the end of the right transept of this church, houses a masterpiece of Renaissance paint-ing: a fresco cycle that changed the course of Western art. Fire almost destroyed the church in the 18th century; miraculously, the Brancacci Chapel survived nearly intact. The cycle is the work of three artists: Masaccio and Masolino (1383–circa 1447), who began it around 1424, and Filippino Lippi, who finished it some 50 years later, after a long interruption during which the sponsoring Brancacci family was exiled. It was Masaccio's work that opened a new frontier for painting, as he was among the first artists to employ single-point perspective; tragi-cally, he died in 1428 at the age of 27, so he didn't live to experience the revolution his innovations caused.

Masaccio collaborated with Masolino on several of the frescoes, but his style predomintates in the *Tribute Money,* on the upper-left wall; *St. Peter Baptizing,* on the upper altar wall; the *Distribution of Goods,* on the lower altar wall; and the *Expulsion of Adam and Eve,* on the chapel's upper-left entrance pier. If you look closely at the last painting and compare it with some of the chapel's other works, you should see a pronounced difference. The figures of Adam and Eve possess a startling presence primarily thanks to the dramatic way in which their bodies seem to reflect light. Masaccio here shaded his figures consistently, so as to suggest a single, strong source of light within the world of the paint-ing but outside its frame. In so doing, he succeeded in imitating with paint the real-world effect of light on mass, and he thereby imparted to his figures a sculptural reality unprecedented in his day.

These matters have to do with technique, but with the *Expulsion of Adam and Eve* his skill went beyond mere technical innovation. In the faces of Adam and Eve, you see more than finely modeled figures; you see terrible shame and suffering depicted with a humanity rarely achieved in art. Reservations to see the chapel are mandatory but can be booked on the same day. Your time inside is limited to 15 minutes—a frustration that's only partly mitigated by a highly informative 40-minute DVD about the history of the chapel you can watch either before or after your visit. ⊠ *Piazza del Carmine, Santo Spirito* ☎ *055/2768224 reservations* 💶 *€4* ⊙ *Mon. and Wed.–Sat. 10–5, Sun. 1–5.*

WORTH NOTING

❻ **Giardino Bardini.** Garden lovers, those who crave a view, and those who enjoy a nice hike should visit this lovely villa and garden, whose history spans centuries. The villa had a walled garden as early as the 14th century; the "Grand Stairs"—a zigzag ascent well worth scaling—has been around since the 16th. The garden is filled with irises, roses, and heirloom flowers, and includes a Japanese garden and statuary. A very pretty walk (all for the same admission ticket) takes you through the Giardino di Boboli and past the Forte Belvedere to the upper entrance to the giardino. ⊠ *Via de'Bardini, San Niccolò* ☎ *005/294883* 💶 *€10, combined ticket with Galleria Costume, Giardino di Boboli, Museo Argenti, Museo Porcellane* ⊙ *Jan., Feb., Nov., and Dec., daily 8:15– 4:30; Mar., daily 8:15–5:30; Apr., May, Sept., and Oct., daily 8:15–6:30; June–Aug., daily 8:15–7:30. Closed 1st and last Mon. of month.*

❼ **Museo Bardini.** The 19th-century collector and antiquarian Stefano Bardini turned his palace into his own private museum. Upon his death, the collection was turned over to the state. It includes an interesting assortment of Etruscan pieces, sculpture, paintings, and furniture that dates mostly from the Renaissance and the baroque. ⊠ *Piazza de' Mozzi 1* ☎ *055/2342427* 💶 *€3.10* ⊙ *Thurs.–Tues. 9–2.*

❸ **Santa Felicita.** This late-baroque church (its facade was remodeled between 1736 and 1739) contains the mannerist Jacopo Pontormo's *Deposition,* the centerpiece of the Cappella Capponi (executed 1525– 28) and a masterpiece of 16th-century Florentine art. The remote figures, which transcend the realm of Renaissance classical form, are portrayed in tangled shapes and intense pastel colors (well preserved because of the low lights in the church), in a space and depth that defy reality. Note, too, the exquisitely frescoed *Annunciation,* also by Pontormo, at a right angle to the *Deposition.* The granite column in the piazza was erected in 1381 and marks a Christian cemetery. ⊠ *Piazza Santa Felicita, Via Guicciardini, Palazzo Pitti* ⊙ *Mon.–Sat. 9–noon and 3–6, Sun. 9–1.*

❷ **Santo Spirito.** The plain, unfinished facade gives nothing away, but the interior, although it appears chilly compared with later churches, is one of the most important examples of Renaissance architecture in Italy. Unfortunately, it's usually closed to the public except during Mass (Mon.–Sat. 9, Sun. 9, 10:30, and 6). You're welcome to attend the service, but if you go, be prepared to sit through the whole thing.

The interior is one of a pair designed in Florence by Filippo Brunelleschi in the early decades of the 15th century (the other is San Lorenzo). It was here that Brunelleschi supplied definitive solutions to the two major problems of interior Renaissance church design: how to build a cross-shaped interior using classical architectural elements borrowed from antiquity, and how to reflect in that interior the order and regularity that Renaissance scientists (among them Brunelleschi himself) were at the time discovering in the natural world around them.

The Boboli Gardens, located behind Palazzo Pitti, began to take shape in 1549, when the Pitti family sold the palace to Eleanor of Toledo, wife of Medici grand duke Cosimo I.

Brunelleschi's solution to the first problem was brilliantly simple: turn a Greek temple inside out. While ancient Greek temples were walled buildings surrounded by classical colonnades, Brunelleschi's churches were classical arcades surrounded by walled buildings. This brilliant architectural idea overthrew the previous era's religious taboo against pagan architecture once and for all, triumphantly claiming that architecture for Christian use.

Brunelleschi's solution to the second problem—making the entire interior orderly and regular—was mathematically precise: he designed the ground plan of the church so that all its parts were proportionally related. The transepts and nave have exactly the same width; the side aisles are precisely half as wide as the nave; the little chapels off the side aisles are exactly half as deep as the side aisles; the chancel and transepts are exactly one-eighth the depth of the nave; and so on, with dizzying exactitude. For Brunelleschi, such a design technique was a matter of passionate conviction. Like most theoreticians of his day, he believed that mathematical regularity and aesthetic beauty were flip sides of the same coin, that one was not possible without the other. In the **Santo Spirito refectory** (⌂ *Piazza Santo Spirito 29* ☎ *055/287043*), adjacent to the church, you can see Andrea Orcagna's highly damaged fresco of the Crucifixion. ⌂ *Piazza Santo Spirito* ☎ *055/210030* ✉ *Church free, refectory €2.20* ☺ *Church: open only during Mass. Refectory: Apr.–Sept., Tues.–Sat. 9–2; Oct.– Mar., Tues.–Sat. 9–1:30.*

> ### WORD OF MOUTH
>
> "My advice for Florence is to explore the city in early morning and nighttime walks. Go to the Oltrarno across the river. And walk the side streets—the crowds always tramp the same routes, and they are easy to escape—just take a couple of random turns down a pokey side street or two. It's amazing how very few tourists stray off the beaten path in this city." —Apres Londee

WHERE TO EAT

Florence's popularity with tourists means that, unfortunately, there's a higher percentage of mediocre restaurants here than you'll find in most Italian towns. Some restaurant owners cut corners and let standards slip, knowing that a customer today is unlikely to return tomorrow, regardless of the quality of the meal. So, if you're looking to eat well, it pays to do some research, starting with the recommendations here— we promise there's not a tourist trap in the bunch. Try to avoid places where waiters stand outside and invite you in, as well as those spots with little billboards outside showing pictures of their food. (Both practices are prevalent around San Lorenzo.)

Hours start at around 1 for lunch and 8 for dinner. Many of Florence's restaurants are small, so reservations are a must. You can sample such specialties as creamy *fegatini* (a chicken-liver spread) and *ribollita* (minestrone thickened with bread and beans and swirled with extra-virgin olive oil) in a bustling, convivial trattoria, where you share long wooden tables set with paper place mats, or in an upscale *ristorante* with linen tablecloths and napkins.

Those with a sense of culinary adventure should not miss the tripe sandwich, served from stands throughout town. This Florentine favorite comes with a fragrant *salsa verde* (green sauce) or a piquant red hot sauce—or both. Follow the Florentines' lead and take a break at an *enoteca* (wine bar) during the day and discover some excellent Chiantis and Super Tuscans from small producers who rarely export.

Use the coordinate (✛ B2) at the end of each listing to locate a site on the Where to Eat and Stay in Florence map.

WHAT IT COSTS IN EUROS					
	¢	$	$$	$$$	$$$$
AT DINNER	under €20	€20–€30	€30–€45	€45–€65	over €65

Prices are for a first course (*primo*), second course (*secondo*), and dessert (*dolce*).

THE DUOMO TO THE PONTE VECCHIO

$$
WINE BAR
✕ **Frescobaldi Wine Bar.** The Frescobaldi family has run a vineyard for more than 700 years, and this swanky establishment offers tasty and sumptuous fare to accompany the seriously fine wines. Warm terra-cotta-color walls with trompe l'oeil tapestries provide a soothing atmosphere. The menu is typically Tuscan, but turned up a notch or two: the *faraona in umido con l'uva* (stewed guinea fowl with grapes) comes with a side of feather-light mashed potatoes. Save room for dessert, as well as one of the dessert wines. A separate wine bar called Frescobaldino has a shorter menu. ⊠ *Via de' Magazzini 2-4/r, Piazza della Signoria* 🕾 *055/284724* ▭ *MC, V* ☉ *Closed Sun. No lunch Mon.* ✛ *E4.*

$$$
MODERN ITALIAN
Fodor's Choice
★
✕ **Ora d'Aria.** The name means "Hour of Air" and refers to the time of day when prisoners were let outside for fresh air—alluding to the fact that this gem was originally located across the street from what was once the old prison. In the kitchen, gifted young chef Marco Stabile turns out exquisite Tuscan classics as well as more fanciful dishes, which are as beautiful as they are delicious; intrepid diners will be vastly rewarded for ordering the tortellini *farciti con piccione* (stuffed with pigeon) if it's on the day's menu. Two tasting menus give Stabile even greater opportunity to shine, and the carefully culled wine list has something to please every palate. Do not miss his tiramisu espresso—something halfway between a dessert and a coffee. ⊠ *Via Georgefili 79/r, Piazza della Signoria* 🕾 *055/2001699* ▭ *AE, DC, MC, V* ☉ *Closed Sun. No lunch* ✛ *E4.*

SAN LORENZO AND BEYOND

¢
TUSCAN
✕ **da Nerbone.** The place has been around since 1872, and it's easy to see why: this tiny stall in the middle of the covered Mercato Centrale has been serving up food to Florentines who like their tripe. Tasty primi and secondi are available every day, but cognoscenti come for the *panino*

BEST BETS FOR FLORENCE DINING

With hundreds of restaurants to choose from, how will you decide where to eat? Fodor's writers and editors have selected their favorite restaurants by price, cuisine, and experience in the Best Bets lists below. In the first column, Fodor's Choice properties represent the "best of the best."

Fodor's Choice ★

Cibrèo, $$$$, p. 265
Ora d'Aria, $$$, p. 259
Mario, ¢, p. 261
Taverna del Bronzino, $$$, p. 261

Best by Price

¢

All'Antico Vinaio, p. 264
da Nerbone, p. 259
da Rocco, p. 265
La Casalinga, p. 267
Mario, p. 261

$

Cibrèo Trattoria, p. 265
Il Santo Bevitore, p. 267
Osteria Antica Mescita San Niccolò, p. 268

$$

Baldovino, p. 264
Frescobaldi Wine Bar, p. 259
Quattro Leoni, p. 268

$$$

Il Latini, p. 261
La Giostra, p. 266
Ora d'Aria, p. 259
Taverna del Bronzino, p. 261

$$$$

Cibrèo, p. 265

Best Experiences

FOR KIDS

Baldovino, $$, p. 264
Danny Rock, ¢, p. 265
Il Latini, $$$, p. 261

ROMANTIC

Enoteca Pinchiorri, $$$$, p. 265
Ora d'Aria, $$$, p. 259

BISTECCA FIORENTINA (TUSCAN STEAK)

Il Latini, $$$, p. 261
La Giostra, $$$, p. 266
Osteria de'Benci, $$, p. 266

OUTDOOR DINING

Fuori Porta, ¢, p. 267
Osteria de'Benci, $$, p. 266
Quattro Leoni, $$, p. 268

ALTA CUCINA (SOPHISTICATED CUISINE)

Enoteca Pinchiorri, $$$$, p. 265
Ora d'Aria, $$$, p. 259
Taverna del Bronzino, $$$, p. 261

CASALINGA (HOME COOKING)

La Casalinga, ¢, p. 267
Mario, ¢, p. 261

LUNCH SPOTS

Antico Noe, $$, p. 264
Benvenuto, $, p. 265
Cantinetta Antinori, $$$, p. 261
Frescobaldi Wine Bar, $$, p. 259

WINE LIST

Cantinetta Antinori, $$$, p. 261
Enoteca Pinchiorri, $$$$, p. 265
Fuori Porta, $, p. 267
Taverna del Bronzino, $$$, p. 261

con il lampredotto (tripe sandwich). Less adventurous sorts might want to sample the panino con il bollito (boiled beef sandwich). Ask that the bread be *bagnato* (briefly dipped in the tripe cooking liquid), and have both the salsa verde and *salsa piccante* (a spicy cayenne sauce) slathered on top. ⊠ *Mercato San Lorenzo* ☎ *055/219949* ▤ *No credit cards* ⊙ *Closed Sun. No dinner* ✛ *D1.*

¢ ✕ **Mario.** Florentines flock to this narrow family-run trattoria near San
TUSCAN Lorenzo to feast on Tuscan favorites served at simple tables under a
Fodor's Choice wooden ceiling dating from 1536. A distinct cafeteria feel and genuine
★ Florentine hospitality prevail: you'll be seated wherever there's room, which often means with strangers. Yes, there's a bit of extra oil in most dishes, which imparts calories as well as taste, but aren't you on vacation in Italy? Worth the splurge is *riso al ragù* (rice with ground beef and tomatoes). ⊠ *Via Rosina 2/r, corner of Piazza del Mercato Centrale, San Lorenzo* ☎ *055/218550* ◿ *Reservations not accepted* ▤ *No credit cards* ⊙ *Closed Sun. and Aug. No dinner* ✛ *E1.*

$$$ ✕ **Taverna del Bronzino.** Want to have a sophisticated meal in a 16th-
TUSCAN century Renaissance artist's studio? The former studio of Santi di Tito,
Fodor's Choice a student of Bronzino's, has a simple, formal decor, with white table-
★ cloths and place settings. The classic, dramatically presented Tuscan food is superb, and the solid, afforable wine list rounds out the menu. The service is outstanding. Reservations are advised, especially for eating at the wine cellar's only table. ⊠ *Via delle Ruote 25/r, San Marco* ☎ *055/495220* ▤ *AE, DC, MC, V* ⊙ *Closed Sun. and 3 wks in Aug.* ✛ *G1.*

SANTA MARIA NOVELLA TO THE ARNO

$$$ ✕ **Cantinetta Antinori.** After a morning of shopping on Via Tornabuoni,
ITALIAN stop for lunch in this 15th-century palazzo in the company of Florentine ladies (and men) who lunch and come to see and be seen. The panache of the food matches its clientele: expect treats such as *tramezzino con pane di campagna al tartufo* (country pâté with truffles served on bread) and the *insalata di gamberoni e gamberetti con carciofi freschi* (crayfish and prawn salad with shaved raw artichokes). ⊠ *Piazza Antinori 3, Santa Maria Novella* ☎ *055/292234* ▤ *AE, DC, MC, V* ⊙ *Closed weekends, 20 days in Aug., and Dec. 25–Jan. 6* ✛ *D3.*

$$$TUSCAN ✕ **Il Latini.** It may be the noisiest, most crowded trattoria in Florence, but it's also one of the most fun. The genial host, Torello ("little bull") Latini, presides over his four big dining rooms, and somehow it feels as if you're dining in his home. Ample portions of *ribollita* prepare the palate for the hearty meat dishes that follow. Both Florentines and tourists alike tuck into the *agnello fritto* (fried lamb) with aplomb. Though reservations are advised, there's always a wait anyway. ⊠ *Via dei Palchetti 6/r, Santa Maria Novella* ☎ *055/210916* ▤ *AE, DC, MC, V* ⊙ *Closed Mon. and 15 days at Christmas* ✛ *C3.*

$ ✕ **Obika.** Mozzarella takes center stage at this sleek eatery on Flor-
ITALIAN ence's swankiest street. The cheese, along with its culinary cousin *burrata* (a soft cheese filled with butter), arrives daily from southern Italy to become the centerpiece for various salads and pastas. Four different kinds of *rotoli* (rolled, stuffed mozzarella) are available; the one

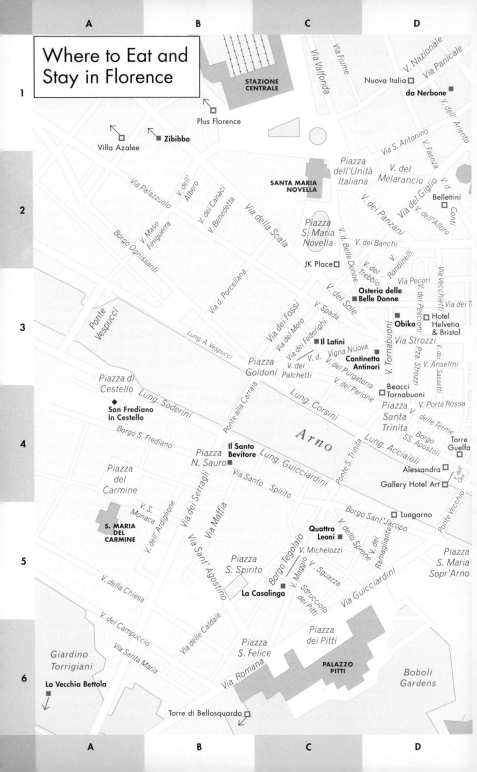

Where to Eat and Stay in Florence

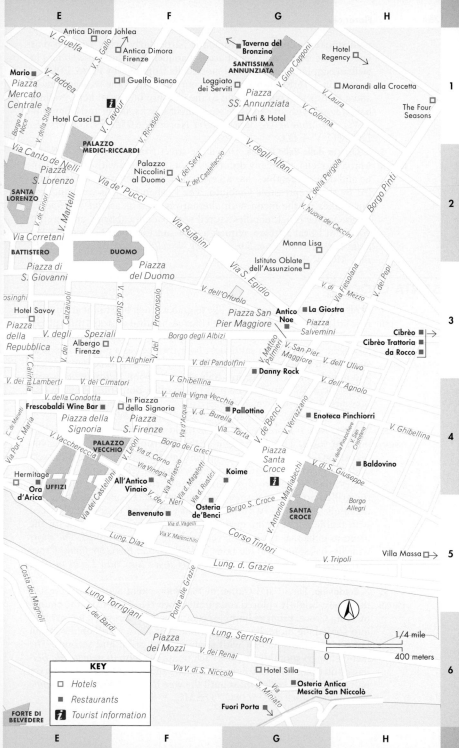

with smoked salmon and arugula is particularly tasty. You can pair your cheese with a number of accompaniments, including *caponata* (a Sicilian eggplant mélange) and mortadella from nearby Prato. Efficient service (in a 16th-century-palazzo courtyard when the weather's nice) and a well-priced wine list add to the pleasure of a meal here. Nightly happy hour, with an extensive selection of snacks, is fun and a bargain. ⊠ *Via Tornabuoni 16, Santa Maria Novella* ☎ *055/2773526* ▤ *AE, DC, MC, V* ✛ *D3.*

$ ✕ **Osteria delle Belle Donne.** Down the street from the church of Santa
TUSCAN   Maria Novella, this gaily decorated spot, festooned with ropes of garlic and other vegetables, has an ever-changing menu and stellar service led by the irrepressible Giacinto. The kitchen has Tuscan standards but shakes up the menu with alternatives such as *sedani con bacon, verza, e uova* (thick noodles sauced with bacon, cabbage, and egg). If you want to eat alfresco, request a table outside when booking. ⊠ *Via delle Belle Donne 16/r, Santa Maria Novella* ☎ *055/2382609* ▤ *AE, DC, MC, V* ✛ *D3.*

SANTA CROCE

¢   ✕ **All'Antico Vinaio.** Florentines like to grab a quick bite to eat at this nar-
DELI   row little sandwich shop near the Uffizi. A handful of stools offer places to perch while devouring one of their very fine sandwiches; most folks, however, simply grab a sandwich, pour themselves a glass of inexpensive wine in a paper cup (more serious wines can be poured into glasses), and mingle on the pedestrians-only street in front. If *porchetta* (a very rich, deliciously fatty roasted pork) is on offer, don't miss it. They also offer first-rate primi, which change daily. ⊠ *Via de' Neri 65, Santa Croce* ☎ *No phone* ▤ *No credit cards* ☉ *Closed Sun.* ✛ *F4.*

$$ ✕ **Antico Noe.** If Florence had diners (it doesn't), this would be the best
TUSCAN   diner in town. The short menu at the one-room eatery relies heavily on seasonal ingredients picked up daily at the market. Though the secondi are good, it's the antipasti and primi that really shine. The menu comes alive particularly during truffle and artichoke season (don't miss the grilled artichokes if they're on the menu). Locals rave about the tagliatelle *ai porcini* (with mushrooms); the fried eggs liberally laced with truffle might be the greatest truffle bargain in town. Ask for the menu in Italian, as the English version is much more limited. The short wine list has some great bargains. ⊠ *Volta di San Piero 6/r, Santa Croce* ☎ *055/2340838* ▤ *AE, DC, MC, V* ☉ *Closed Sun. and 2 wks in Aug.* ✛ *G3.*

$$ ✕ **Baldovino.** David and Catherine Gardner, expat Scots, have created
ITALIAN   this lively, brightly colored restaurant down the street from the church of Santa Croce. From its humble beginnings as a pizzeria, it has evolved into something more. It's a happy thing that pizza is still on the menu, but now it shares billing with sophisticated primi and secondi. The menu changes monthly and has such treats as *filetto di manzo alla Bernaise* (filet mignon with light béarnaise sauce). Baldovino also serves pasta dishes and grilled meat until the wee hours. ⊠ *Via San Giuseppe 22/r, Santa Croce* ☎ *055/241773* ▤ *MC, V* ✛ *H4.*

4

$ ✕ **Benvenuto.** At this Florentine institution, beloved for decades by locals
TUSCAN   and Anglophone Renaissance scholars alike, the service is ebullient, the
menu long (with often unwittingly humorous English typographical
errors), and the food simple, Tuscan, and tasty. The list of primi and
secondi is extensive, and there are daily specials as well. Don't miss the
scaloppine all Benvenuto (veal cutlets with porcini). ⊠ *Via della Mosca
16/r, at Via de' Neri, Santa Croce* ☎ *055/214833* ▭ *AE, DC, MC, V*
⊙ *Closed Sun.* ✛ *F5.*

$$$$ ✕ **Cibrèo.** The food at this upscale trattoria is fantastic, from the creamy
TUSCAN   crostini *di fegatini* (a savory chicken-liver spread) to the melt-in-your-
Fodor's Choice   mouth desserts. Many Florentines hail this as the city's best restaurant,
★   and Fodor's readers tend to agree—though some take issue with the
prices and complain of long waits for a table (even with a reservation).
If you thought you'd never try tripe—let alone like it—this is the place
to lay any doubts to rest: the *trippa in insalata* (cold tripe salad) with
parsley and garlic is an epiphany. The food is traditionally Tuscan,
impeccably served by a staff that's multilingual—which is a good thing,
because there are no written menus. ⊠ *Via A. del Verrocchio 8/r, Santa
Croce* ☎ *055/2341100* ⌕ *Reservations essential* ▭ *AE, DC, MC, V*
⊙ *Closed Sun. and Mon. and July 25–Sept. 5* ✛ *H3.*

$ ✕ **Cibrèo Trattoria.** This intimate little trattoria, known to locals as
TUSCAN   Cibreino, shares its kitchen with the famed Florentine culinary institution from which it gets its name. They share the same menu, too,
though Cibreino's is much shorter. Start with *il gelatina di pomodoro*
(tomato gelatin) liberally laced with basil, garlic, and a pinch of hot
pepper, and then sample the justifiably renowned *passato in zucca gialla*
(pureed yellow-pepper soup) before moving on to any of the succulent
second courses. Save room for dessert, as the pastry chef has a deft
hand with chocolate tarts. To avoid sometimes agonizingly long waits,
come early (7 PM) or late (after 9:30). ⊠ *Via dei Macci 118, Santa
Croce* ☎ *055/2341100* ⌕ *Reservations not accepted* ▭ *No credit cards*
⊙ *Closed Sun. and Mon. and July 25–Sept. 5* ✛ *H3.*

¢   ✕ **Danny Rock.** There's a bit of everything at this restaurant, which is
AMERICAN–   always hopping with Italians eager to eat well-made cheeseburgers and
CASUAL   fries or one of the many tasty crepes (served both sweet and savory).
☺   You can also find a basic plate of spaghetti as well as a respectable pizza
here. Interior decor isn't high on the list: you dine at a green metal table
with matching chairs. The young-at-heart feel might explain why the
main dining room has a big screen showing *Looney Tunes.* ⊠ *Via Pandolfini 13/r, Santa Croce* ☎ *055/2340307* ▭ *AE, DC, MC, V* ✛ *G3.*

¢   ✕ **da Rocco.** At one of Florence's biggest markets you can grab lunch
TUSCAN   to go, or you could cram yourself into one of the booths and pour
from the straw-cloaked flask (wine here is *da consumo,* which means
they charge you for how much you drink). Food is abundant, Tuscan, and fast; locals pack in. The menu changes daily, and the prices
are great. ⊠ *In Mercato Sant'Ambrogio, Piazza Ghiberti, Santa Croce*
☎ *No phone* ⌕ *Reservations not accepted* ▭ *No credit cards* ⊙ *Closed
Sun. No dinner* ✛ *H2.*

$$$$ ✕ **Enoteca Pinchiorri.** A sumptuous Renaissance palace with high frescoed
ITALIAN   ceilings and bouquets in silver vases provides the backdrop for this

restaurant, one of the most expensive in Italy. Some consider it one of the best, and others consider it a non-Italian rip-off, as the kitchen is presided over by a Frenchwoman with sophisticated, yet international-ist, leanings. Prices are high (think $100 for a plate of spaghetti) and portions are small; the vast holdings of the wine cellar (undoubtedly the best in Florence), as well as stellar service, dull the pain, however, when the bill is presented. ⊠ *Via Ghibellina 87, Santa Croce* 🕾 *055/242777* ⌂ *Reservations essential* ▭ *AE, MC, V* ⊗ *Closed Sun., Mon., and Aug. No lunch Tues. or Wed.* ✛ *G4.*

$–$$
JAPANESE

✕ **Koime.** If you're looking for a break from the ubiquitous ribollita, stop in at this eatery, which may be the only Japanese restaurant in the world to be housed in a 15th-century Renaissance palazzo. High, vaulted arches frame the Kaiten sushi conveyor belt. It's Japanese food, cafeteria style: selections, priced according to the color of the plate, make their way around a bar, where diners pick whatever they find appealing. Those seeking a more substantial meal head to the second floor, where Japanese barbecue is prepared at your table. The minimalist basement provides a subtle but dramatic backdrop for a well-prepared cocktail. ⊠ *Via de'Benci 41/r, Santa Croce* 🕾 *055/2008009* ▭ *AE, DC, MC, V* ✛ *G4.*

$$$
ITALIAN
★

✕ **La Giostra.** This clubby spot, whose name means "carousel" in Italian, was created by the late Prince Dimitri Kunz d'Asburgo Lorena, and is now expertly run by his handsome twin sons. In perfect English they will describe favorite dishes, such as the *taglierini con tartufo bianco,* a decadently rich pasta with white truffles. The constantly changing menu has terrific vegetarian and vegan options. For dessert, this might be the only show in town with a sublime tiramisu *and* a wonderfully gooey Sacher torte. ⊠ *Borgo Pinti 12/r, Santa Croce* 🕾 *055/241341* ▭ *AE, DC, MC, V* ✛ *G3.*

$$
ITALIAN

✕ **Osteria de'Benci.** A few minutes from Santa Croce, this charming oste-ria serves some of the most eclectic food in Florence. Try the spaghetti *degli eretici* (in tomato sauce with fresh herbs). The grilled meats are justifiably famous; the *carbonata* is a succulent piece of grilled beef served rare. When it's warm, you can dine outside with a view of the 13th-century tower belonging to the prestigious Alberti family. Right next door is Osteria de'Benci Caffè (¢–$), serving selections from the menu from 8 AM to midnight. ⊠ *Via de' Benci 11–13/r, Santa Croce* 🕾 *055/2344923* ▭ *AE, DC, MC, V* ⊗ *Closed Sun. and 2 wks in Aug.* ✛ *F5.*

$
TUSCAN

✕ **Pallottino.** With its tile floor, photograph-filled walls, and wooden tables, Pallottino is the quintessential Tuscan trattoria, with hearty, heartwarming classics such as *pappa al pomodoro* (bread and tomato soup) and *peposa alla toscana* (beef stew laced with black pepper). The menu changes frequently to reflect what's seasonal; the staff is friendly, as are the diners who often share a table and, eventually, conversation. They also do pizza here, as well as great lunch specials. ⊠ *Via Isola delle Stinche 1/r, Santa Croce* 🕾 *055/289573* ▭ *AE, DC, MC, V* ⊗ *Closed Mon. and 2–3 wks in Aug.* ✛ *G4.*

What Tripe!

While in Florence, those with a sense of culinary adventure should seek out a tripe sandwich, which is just about as revered by local gourmands as the bistecca alla fiorentina. In this case, however, the treasure comes on the cheap—sandwiches are sold from small stands found in the city center, topped with a fragrant green sauce or a piquant red hot sauce, or both. *Bagnato* means that the hard, crusty roll is first dipped in the tripe's cooking liquid; it's advisable to say *"sì"* when asked if that's how you like it. Sandwiches are usually taken with a glass of red wine poured from the tripe seller's *fiasco* (flask). If you find the tripe to your liking, you might also enjoy *lampredotto*, another, some say better, cut of stomach. For an exalted,

high-end tripe treat, try Fabio Picchi's cold tripe salad, served gratis as an *amuse-bouche* at the restaurant Cibrèo. It could make a convert of even the staunchest "I'd never try *that*" kind of eater.

Tripe carts are lunchtime favorites of Florentine working men—it's uncommon, but not unheard of, to see a woman at a tripe stand. Aficionados will argue which sandwich purveyor is best; here are three that frequently get mentioned: **La Trippaia** (⊠ *Via dell'Ariento, Santa Maria Novella* ☎ *No phone* ☺ *Closed Sun.*). **Il Trippaio** (⊠ *Via de' Macci at Borgo La Croce, Santa Croce* ☎ *No phone* ☺ *Closed Sun.*). **Nerbone** (⊠ *Inside the Mercato Centrale, Santa Maria Novella* ☎ *No phone* ☺ *Closed Sun.*).

4

THE OLTRARNO

¢–$
WINE BAR
✗ **Fuori Porta.** One of the oldest and best wine bars in Florence, this place serves cured meats and cheeses, as well as daily specials such as the sublime spaghetti *al curry*. *Crostini* and *crostoni*—grilled breads topped with a mélange of cheeses and meats—are the house specialty; the *verdure sott'olio* (vegetables with oil) are divine. All this can be enjoyed at rustic wooden tables, and outdoors when weather allows. One shortcoming is the staff, some of whom can be disinclined to explain the absolutely wonderful wine list. ⊠ *Via Monte alle Croci 10/r, San Niccolò* ☎ *055/2342483* ☰ *AE, MC, V* ✛ *G6.*

$
TUSCAN
✗ **Il Santo Bevitore.** Florentines and other lovers of good food flock to "The Holy Drinker" for tasty, well-priced dishes. Unpretentious white walls, dark-wood furniture, and paper placemats provide the simple decor; start with the exceptional vegetables *sott'olio* (marinated in olive oil) or the *terrina di fegatini* (a creamy chicken-liver spread) before sampling any of the divine pastas, such as the fragrant spaghetti with shrimp sauce. The extensive wine list is well priced, and the well-informed staff is happy to explain it. ⊠ *Via Santo Spirito 64/66r, Santo Spirito* ☎ *055/211264* ☰ *MC, V* ☺ *No lunch Sun.* ✛ *B4.*

¢
TUSCAN
✗ **La Casalinga.** *Casalinga* means "housewife," and this place has the nostalgic charm of a 1950s kitchen with Tuscan comfort food to match. If you eat *ribollita* anywhere in Florence, eat it here—it couldn't be more authentic. Mediocre paintings clutter the semipaneled walls, tables are set close together, and the place is usually jammed. The menu is long,

portions are plentiful, and service is prompt and friendly. For dessert, the lemon sorbet perfectly caps off the meal. ✉ *Via Michelozzi 9/r, Santo Spirito* ☎ *055/218624* ⊟ *AE, DC, MC, V* ☺ *Closed Sun., 1 wk at Christmas, and 3 wks in Aug.* ✛ *C5.*

$$ ✗ **La Vecchia Bettola.** The name doesn't exactly mean "old dive," but
TUSCAN it comes pretty close. This lively trattoria has been around only since 1979, but it feels as if it's been a whole lot longer. Tile floors and simple wood tables and chairs provide the interior decoration, such as it is. The recipes come from "wise grandmothers" and celebrate Tuscan food in its glorious simplicity. Here prosciutto is sliced with a knife, portions of grilled meat are tender and ample, service is friendly, and the wine list is well priced and good. This place is worth a taxi ride, even though it's just outside the centro storico. ✉ *Viale Vasco Pratolini, Oltrarno* ☎ *055/224158* ⊟ *No credit cards* ✛ *A6.*

$ ✗ **Osteria Antica Mescita San Niccolò.** It's always crowded, always good,
TUSCAN and always cheap. The osteria is next to the church of San Niccolò, and if you sit in the lower part you'll find yourself in what was once a chapel dating from the 11th century. The subtle but dramatic background is a nice complement to the food, which is simple Tuscan at its best. The *pollo con limone* is tasty pieces of chicken in a lemon-scented broth. In winter, try the *spezzatino di cinghiale con aromi* (wild boar stew with herbs). Reservations are advised. ✉ *Via San Niccolò 60/r, San Niccolò* ☎ *055/2342836* ⊟ *AE, MC, V* ☺ *Closed Sun. and Aug.* ✛ *G6.*

$$ ✗ **Quattro Leoni.** The eclectic staff at this trattoria in a small piazza is an
ITALIAN appropriate match for the diverse menu. In winter you can eat in one of two rooms with high ceilings, and in summer you can sit outside and admire the scenery. Traditional Tuscan favorites, such as *taglierini con porcini* (long, thin, flat pasta with porcini mushrooms), are on the menu, but so, too, are less typical dishes such as the earthy cabbage salad with avocado, pine nuts, and drops of *olio di tartufo* (truffle oil). Reservations are a good idea. ✉ *Piazza della Passera, Via dei Vellutini 1/r, Palazzo Pitti* ☎ *055/218562* ⊟ *AE, DC, MC, V* ☺ *No lunch Wed.* ✛ *C5.*

BEYOND THE CITY CENTER

$$$ ✗ **Zibibbo.** Benedetta Vitali, formerly of Florence's famed Cibrèo, has a
TUSCAN restaurant of her very own. It's a welcome addition to the sometimes-claustrophobic Florentine dining scene—particularly as you have to drive a few minutes out of town to get here. Off a quiet piazza, it has two intimate rooms with rustic, maroon-painted wood floors and a sloped ceiling. The *tagliatelle al sugo d'anatra* (wide pasta ribbons with duck sauce) are aromatic and flavorful, and *crocchette di fave con salsa di yogurt* (fava-bean croquettes with a lively yogurt sauce) are innovative and tasty. ✉ *Via di Terzollina 3/r, northwest of city center* ☎ *055/433383* ⊟ *AE, DC, MC, V* ☺ *Closed Sun.* ✛ *B1.*

CAFÉS

Cafés in Italy serve not only coffee concoctions and pastries but also drinks; some also serve light and inexpensive lunches. They open early in the morning and usually close around 8 PM.

The always-crowded **Caffè Giacosa/Roberto Cavalli** (⊠ *Via della Spada 10, near Santa Maria Novella* ☎ *055/2776328*), joined at the hip with the Florentine fashion designer's shop, is open for breakfast, lunch, tea, and cocktails—except on Sunday.

Gran Caffè (⊠ *Piazza San Marco 11/r* ☎ *055/215833*), down the street from the Accademia, is a perfect stop for a marvelous panino or sweet while raving about the majesty of Michelangelo's *David*.

Classy **Procacci** (⊠ *Via Tornabuoni 64/r, near Santa Maria Novella* ☎ *055/211656*) is a Florentine institution dating back to 1885; try one of the panini *tartufati* (a small roll with truffled butter) and swish it down with a glass of *prosecco* (a dry, sparkling white wine). It's closed Sunday.

Perhaps the best café for people-watching is **Rivoire** (⊠ *Piazza della Signoria, Via Vacchereccia 4/r* ☎ *055/214412*). Stellar service, light snacks, and terrific *aperitivi* (aperitifs) are the norm. Think twice, however, before ordering the more substantial fare, which is pricier than it should be.

GELATERIE AND PASTICCERIE

The convenient **Caffè delle Carrozze** (⊠ *Piazza del Pesce 3–5/r, near Piazza della Signoria* ☎ *055/2396810*) is around the corner from the Uffizi; their gelati, according to some, are the best in the historic center. **Dolci e Dolcezze** (⊠ *Piazza C. Beccaria 8/r, near Santa Croce* ☎ *055/2345458*), a *pasticceria* (bakery) in Borgo La Croce, probably has the prettiest and tastiest cakes, sweets, and tarts in town. It's closed Monday. **Gelateria Carabe** (⊠ *Via Ricasoli 60/r, San Marco* ☎ *055/289476*) specializes in Sicilian desserts (including cannoli). Its *granità* (granular, flavored ices), made only in summer, are tart and flavorful—perfect thirst quenchers.

Grom (⊠ *Via del Campanile, Duomo* ☎ *055/216158*) a stone's throw from the Duomo, is one of the best gelaterias in town. Flavors change frequently according to the season, so expect a fragrant gelato *di cannella* (cinnamon ice cream) in the winter and lively fresh fruit flavors in the summer. **Vestri** (⊠ *Borgo Albizi 11/r, near Santa Croce* ☎ *055/2340374*) is devoted to chocolate in all its guises, every day but Sunday. The small but sublime selection of chocolate-based gelati includes one with hot peppers. Most visitors consider **Vivoli** (⊠ *Via Isola delle Stinche 7/r, near Santa Croce* ☎ *055/292334*) the best gelateria around; Florentines find it highly overrated. It is closed Sunday.

SALUMERIE

Delicatessens and gourmet food shops (*salumerie*) specialize in cured meats and cheeses; they can be great places to assemble a picnic or purchase dinner. Most are closed Sunday.

The cheese collection at **Baroni** (⊠ *Mercato Central, enter at Via Signa, San Lorenzo* ☎ *055/289576*) may be the most comprehensive in Florence. They also have high-quality truffle products, vinegars, and other delicacies. 'ino (⊠ *Via dei Georgofili 3/r–7/r* ☎ *055/219208*) sells artisanal products such as olive oil, cheeses from all over Italy, top-notch chocolates, and boutique wines. It's right behind the Uffizi, making it a perfect place to grab a tasty sandwich and glass of wine before forging on to the next museum.

Looking for some cheddar cheese to pile in your panino? **Pegna** (⊠ *Via dello Studio 8, Duomo* ☎ *055/282701*) has been selling both Italian and non-Italian food since 1860. It's closed Saturday afternoon in July and August, Wednesday afternoon September through June, and Sunday year-round. **Perini** (⊠ *Mercato Centrale, enter at Via dell'Aretino, San Lorenzo* ☎ *055/2398306*), closed Sunday, sells prosciutto, mixed meats, sauces for pasta, and a wide assortment of antipasti. They're generous with their free samples.

WHERE TO STAY

No stranger to visitors, Florence is equipped with hotels for all budgets; for instance, you can find both budget and luxury hotels in the *centro storico* (historic center) and along the Arno. Florence has so many famous landmarks that it's not hard to find lodging with a panoramic view. The equivalent of the genteel *pensioni* of yesteryear still exist, though they are now officially classified as hotels. Generally small and intimate, they often have a quaint appeal that usually doesn't preclude modern plumbing.

Florence's importance not only as a tourist city but as a convention center and the site of the Pitti fashion collections guarantees a variety of accommodations. The high demand also means that, except in winter, reservations are a must. If you find yourself in Florence with no reservations, go to **Consorzio ITA** (⊠ *Stazione Centrale, Santa Maria Novella* ☎ *055/282893*). You must go there in person to make a booking.

Use the coordinate (✢ B2) at the end of each listing to locate a site on the Where to Eat and Stay in Florence map.

WHAT IT COSTS IN EUROS					
	¢	$	$$	$$$	$$$$
FOR TWO PEOPLE	under €75	€75–€125	€125–€200	€200–€300	over €300

Prices are for a standard double room in high season, including tax and service.

THE DUOMO TO THE ARNO

$ ⛫ **Albergo Firenze.** A block from the Duomo, this hotel is on one of the oldest piazzas in Florence. Though the reception area and hallways have all the charm of a college dormitory, the similarity ends upon entering the spotlessly clean rooms. A good number of triple and quadruple rooms make this a good choice for families. **Pros:** for the location, a great bargain. **Cons:** no-frills public areas. ✉ *Piazza Donati 1, Duomo* ☎ *055/214203* ⊕ *www.hotelfirenze-fi.it* ⤴ *58 rooms* ♿ *In-hotel: public Internet (fee), Wi-Fi (fee), parking (fee)* ⊟ *MC, V* ⦿*BP* ✛ *E3.*

$$ ⛫ **Hermitage.** A stone's throw from the Ponte Vecchio, this is a fine little hotel with an enviable location. All rooms are decorated with lively wallpaper; some have views of Palazzo Vecchio and others of the Arno. The rooftop terrace, where you can have breakfast or an aperitivo, is decked with flowers. The lobby suggests a friend's living room—its warm yellow walls are welcoming. Double glazing and air-conditioning help keep street noise at bay. **Pros:** views; friendly, English-speaking staff. **Cons:** short flight of stairs to reach elevator. ✉ *Vicolo Marzio 1, Piazza della Signoria* ☎ *055/287216* ⊕ *www.hermitagehotel.com* ⤴ *27 rooms, 1 suite* ♿ *In-room: safe. In-hotel: laundry service, public Wi-Fi, parking (fee), some pets allowed* ⊟ *MC, V* ⦿*BP* ✛ *E4.*

$$$$ ⛫ **Hotel Helvetia and Bristol.** Painstaking care has gone into making this
★   hotel one of the prettiest and most intimate in town. It has the extra plus of being in the center of the centro storico, making it a luxurious base from which to explore the city. From the cozy yet sophisticated lobby with its stone columns to the guest rooms decorated with prints, you might feel as if you're a guest in a sophisticated manor house. The restaurant serves sumptuous fare in a romantic setting. **Pros:** central location; superb staff. **Cons:** rooms facing the street get some noise. ✉ *Via dei Pescioni 2, Piazza della Repubblica* ☎ *055/26651* ⊕ *www. hbf.royaldemeure.com* ⤴ *54 rooms, 13 suites* ♿ *In-room: safe, refrigerator, VCR, Wi-Fi. In-hotel: restaurant, room service, bar, concierge, laundry service, parking (fee), some pets allowed* ⊟ *AE, DC, MC, V* ⦿*EP* ✛ *D3.*

$$$$ ⛫ **Hotel Savoy.** From the outside it looks very much like the turn-of-the-19th-century building that it is. Inside, sleek minimalism and up-to-the-minute amenities prevail. Sitting rooms have a funky edge, their cream-color walls dotted with contemporary prints. Muted colors dress the rooms, which have streamlined furniture and soaring ceilings; many have views of the Duomo's cupola or the Piazza della Repubblica. The deep marble tubs might be reason enough to stay here—but you'll also appreciate the efficient and courteous staff. **Pros:** location; trendy clientele (if that's your thing). **Cons:** smallish rooms; trendy clientele (if that's not your thing); breakfast ought to be included at these prices. ✉ *Piazza della Repubblica 7* ☎ *055/27351* ⊕ *www.roccofortehotels. com* ⤴ *88 rooms, 12 suites* ♿ *In-room: safe, refrigerator, VCR, dial-up, Wi-Fi. In-hotel: restaurant, room service, bar, concierge, children's programs (ages infant–12), laundry service, parking (fee)* ⊟ *AE, DC, MC, V* ⦿*EP* ✛ *E1.*

$$$
Fodor'sChoice
★

⊡ **In Piazza della Signoria.** Proprietors Alessandro and Sonia Pini want you to use their house—in this case, part of a 15th-century palazzo—as if it were your own. Such warm sentiments extend to the cozy feeling created in the rooms, all of which are uniquely decorated and lovingly furnished; some have damask curtains, others fanciful frescoes in the bathroom. **Pros:** marvelous staff; tasty breakfast with a view of Piazza della Signoria.

Cons: short flight of stairs to reach elevator. ⊠ *Via dei Magazzini 2, near Piazza della Signoria* ☎ *055/2399546* ⊕ *www.inpiazzadellasignoria. com* ⊲ *10 rooms, 3 apartments* ⌂ *In-room: safe, kitchen (some), refrigerator (some), Wi-Fi. In hotel: laundry service, public Internet, parking (fee)* ▭ *AE, DC, MC, V* ⦿*BP* ✛ *E4.*

$$$ ⊡ **Palazzo Niccolini al Duomo.** The graceful Marchesa Ginevra Niccolini di Camugliano refers to her lovingly restored hotel as her third child. She's taken her husband's family's palazzo (acquired by an ancestor in 1532) and turned it into a luxurious place that still manages to evoke a cozy, yet highly sophisticated, home. Rooms have high ceilings, damask drapes, and spacious, marble-floored bathrooms. Some have original 18th-century frescoes, others terrific views. The well-priced Dome Suite, with its remarkable view and hot tub, is worth a splurge, as the Duomo's so close you can practically touch it. An honor bar allows you to enjoy an after-dinner drink in a swank velvet-clad sitting room. **Pros:** steps away from the Duomo. **Cons:** street noise sometimes a problem. ⊠ *Via dei Servi 2* ☎ *055/282412* ⊕ *www.niccolinidomepalace.com* ⊲ *5 rooms, 5 suites* ⌂ *In-room: safe, refrigerator, Wi-Fi. In-hotel: public Internet, Wi-Fi, parking (fee)* ▭ *AE, DC, MC, V* ✛ *F2.*

SAN LORENZO AND BEYOND

$$ ⊡ **Antica Dimora Firenze.** Each room in the intimate *residenza* is painted a different pastel color—peach, rose, powder-blue. Simple furnishings and double-glazed windows ensure a peaceful night's sleep. You might ask for one of the rooms that has a small private terrace; if you contemplate a longer stay, one of their well-located apartments might suit. Coffee, tea, and fresh fruit, available all day in the sitting room, are on the house. **Pros:** ample DVD library; honor bar with Antinori wines. **Cons:** staff goes home at 8; no credit cards accepted. ⊠ *Via San Gallo 72, San Marco* ☎ *055/4627296* ⊕ *www.anticadimorafirenze.it* ⊲*6 rooms* ⌂ *In-room: safe, refrigerator, dial-up, Wi-Fi* ▭ *No credit cards* ⦿*BP* ✛ *E1.*

$$ ⊡ **Antica Dimora Johlea.** Lively color runs rampant at this small, cheerful hotel just minutes from San Marco. It's on the top floor of a 19th-century palazzo and has a charming flower-filled rooftop terrace where you can sip a glass of wine while taking in a view of Brunelleschi's cupola. Rooms have four-poster beds, colorful prints on the wall, and

sweeping curtains. Complimentary coffee, tea, and fruit are on hand all day in the comfortable sitting room. Single rooms are large by Italian standards—a boon if you're traveling alone. **Pros:** great staff; cheerful rooms; honor bar. **Cons:** staff goes home at 7; narrow staircase to get to roof terrace. ✉ *Via San Gallo 80, San Marco* ☎ *055/4633292* ⊕ *www. johanna.it* ⤴ *6 rooms* ⚭ *In-room: safe, DVD, Internet, Wi-Fi. In hotel: laundry service, Internet terminal, Wi-Fi, parking (paid)* ☰ *No credit cards* ⍩*BP* ⟡ *E1.*

$$ ⊞ **Arti & Hotel.** If Florence had town houses, this would be one: the entrance to the public room downstairs feels as if you're in someone's living room. Pale pastel walls, polished hardwood floors, and muted fabrics give rooms a simple, elegant look. Breakfast is taken on the top floor, and a small terrace provides city views. The highly capable staff is completely fluent in English. **Pros:** down the street from the Duomo. **Cons:** staff goes home at 11. ✉ *Via dei Servi 38/a, Santissima Annunziata* ☎ *055/2645307* ⊕ *www.hoteldellearti.it* ⤴ *9 rooms* ⚭ *In-room: refrigerator, Wi-Fi. In-hotel: laundry service, Wi-Fi, some pets allowed (fee)* ☰ *AE, DC, MC, V* ⍩*BP.*

$$ ⊞ **Bellettini.** You're in good hands at this small hotel run by Gina Naldini and Claudio, her husband. The top floor has two rooms with a view, and all the good-size guest rooms have Venetian or Tuscan provincial furnishings; bathrooms are bright and modern. Public rooms are simple but comfortable. A handful of triples and quadruples are available. An ample buffet breakfast includes tasty homemade cakes. **Pros:** excellent staff. **Cons:** two rooms have shared bath (but at significantly lower rates). ✉ *Via dei Conti 7, Santa Maria Novella* ☎ *055/213561* ⊕ *www. hotelbellettini.com* ⤴ *28 rooms, 26 with private bath* ⚭ *In-room: safe, refrigerator, Wi-Fi (some). In-hotel: bar, Wi-Fi, parking (fee), some pets allowed* ☰ *AE, DC, MC, V* ⍩*BP* ⟡ *D2.*

$$ ⊞ **Hotel Casci.** In this refurbished 14th-century palace, the home of Giacchino Rossini in 1851–55, the friendly Lombardi family runs a hotel with spotless rooms. Guest rooms are functional, and many of them open out onto various terraces (a view doesn't necessarily follow, however). It's on a very busy thoroughfare, but triple-glazed windows allow for a sound night's sleep. Many rooms easily accommodate an extra bed or two, and there are a number of triples and quads available. **Pros:** helpful staff; good option for families; English-language DVD collection with good selections for kids. **Cons:** bit of a college-dorm atmosphere; small elevator ✉ *Via Cavour 13, San Marco* ☎ *055/211686* ⊕ *www.hotelcasci.com* ⤴ *25 rooms* ⚭ *In-room: safe, refrigerator, DVD, Wi-Fi. In-hotel: laundry service, public Internet, parking (fee), some pets allowed* ☰ *AE, DC, MC, V* ⍩*BP* ⟡ *E1.*

$$–$$$ ⊞ **Il Guelfo Bianco.** The 15th-century building has all modern conveniences, but its Renaissance charm still shines. Rooms have high ceilings (some are coffered) and windows are triple-glazed. The Bargiacchi family has run the place for more than 20 years, and their collection of 20th-century art contrasts nicely with classic furnishings. Larger-than-usual single rooms have French-style beds and are a good choice for those traveling alone. Breakfast can be taken in a small outdoor garden when weather permits. Though the hotel is in the centro storico, it

4

still feels somewhat off the beaten path. **Pros:** stellar multilingual staff. **Cons:** rooms facing the street can be noisy. ⊠ *Via Cavour 29, San Marco* 🕿 *055/288330* ⊕ *www.ilguelfobianco.it* ⤶ *40 rooms* ⌂ *In-room: safe, refrigerator. In-hotel: concierge, laundry service, public Internet, parking (fee), some pets allowed* ⊟ *AE, DC, MC, V* ⦿| *BP* ⊹ *F1.*

$ 🖭 **Plus Florence.** The name is the only odd thing about this hostel, which has been in operation since 2008. Though it's certainly favored by the younger, backpacking set, it's also quite hospitable to those traveling in groups or with families. Spartan rooms, each with its own bath and shower, sleep up to eight people; plenty of doubles are on hand for those who want a little more privacy. The young, multilingual staff, on-site restaurant, and terrace bar make this a terrific option for those on a budget. **Pros:** bargain price; multilingual staff. **Cons:** feels like a college dorm; somewhat removed from the action. ⊠ *Via Santa Caterina d'Alessandria 15, San Marco* 🕿 *055/4628934* ⊕ *www.plusflorence. com* ⤶ *100 rooms* ⌂ *In-room: Wi-Fi. In hotel: restaurant, bar, pool, spa, laundry facilities, Internet terminal, Wi-Fi, parking (fee)* ⊟ *MC, V* ⦿| *EP* ⊹ *B1.*

SANTA MARIA NOVELLA TO THE ARNO

$–$$ 🖭 **Alessandra.** The location, a block from the Ponte Vecchio, and the clean, ample rooms make this a good choice. The building, known as the Palazzo Roselli del Turco, was designed in 1507 by Baccio d'Agnolo, a contemporary of Michelangelo's. Though little remains of the original design save for the high wood ceilings, there's still an aura of grandeur. Friendly hosts Anna and Andrea Gennarini speak fluent English. **Pros:** several rooms have views of the Arno; the spacious suite is a bargain. **Cons:** stairs to elevator; some rooms share bath. ⊠ *Borgo Santi Apostoli 17, Santa Maria Novella* 🕿 *055/283438* ⊕ *www.hotelalessandra.com* ⤶ *26 rooms, 19 with bath; 1 suite; 1 apartment* ⌂ *In-room: safe, refrigerator, dial-up, Wi-Fi. In-hotel: laundry service, parking (fee)* ⊟ *AE, MC, V* ☾ *Closed Dec. 10–26* ⦿| *BP* ⊹ *D4.*

$$ 🖭 **Beacci Tornabuoni.** Florentine pensioni don't get any classier than this. It has old-fashioned style and enough modern comfort to keep you happy, and it's in a 14th-century palazzo. The sitting room has a large fireplace, the terrace has a tremendous view of some major Florentine monuments, and the wallpapered rooms are inviting. On Monday, Wednesday, and Friday nights from May through October the dining room opens, serving Tuscan specialties. **Pros:** multilingual staff; flower-filled terrace. **Cons:** Fodor's readers advise to request rooms away from reception area, which can be noisy. ⊠ *Via Tornabuoni 3, Santa Maria Novella* 🕿 *055/212645* ⊕ *www.tornabuonihotels.com* ⤶ *28 rooms* ⌂ *In-room: refrigerator. In-hotel: restaurant, bar, laundry service, public Internet, parking (fee), some pets allowed* ⊟ *AE, DC, MC, V* ⦿| *BP* ⊹ *D4.*

$$$ 🖭 **Gallery Hotel Art.** High design resides at this art showcase near the Ponte Vecchio. The coolly understated public rooms have a revolving collection of photographs by artists like Helmut Newton adorning the walls; the reception area is subtly but dramatically lit. Rooms are sleek

and uncluttered and dressed mostly in neutrals. Luxe touches, such as leather headboards and kimono robes, abound. Both the bar and restaurant attract sophisticated, fashionable locals; brunch is served on weekends. **Pros:** cookies in the room; comfortable beds. **Cons:** sometimes elevator is slow. ✉ *Vicolo dell'Oro 5, Santa Maria Novella* ☎ *055/27263* ⊕ *www.lungarnohotels.com* ⤴ *65 rooms, 9 suites* ♿ *In-room: safe, refrigerator, Wi-Fi. In-hotel: restaurant, room service, bar, concierge, laundry service, parking (fee)* ▭ *AE, DC, MC, V* ❤|*BP* ✛ *D4.*

$$$$
Fodor's Choice
★

☺ **JK Place.** This sumptuously appointed boutique hotel has all the comforts of a luxe home away from home. A library serves as the reception room; buffet breakfast is laid out on a gleaming chestnut table in an interior atrium. Soothing earth tones prevail in the guest rooms, some of which have chandeliers, others canopied beds. A secluded rooftop terrace makes a perfect setting for an aperitivo, as do the ground-floor sitting rooms with their large, pillow-piled couches. The place is favored by young fashionistas, their entourages, and other beautiful people. **Pros:** intimate feel; stellar staff; free minibar; linen sheets; organic meals on room-service menu; Wi-Fi. **Cons:** breakfast at a shared table. ✉ *Piazza Santa Maria Novella 7* ☎ *055/2645181* ⊕ *www.jkplace.com* ⤴ *14 doubles, 6 suites* ♿ *In-room: safe, refrigerator, VCR, Wi-Fi. In-hotel: bar, concierge, laundry service, parking (fee), some pets allowed* ▭ *AE, DC, MC, V* ❤|*BP* ✛ *C3.*

$
☺ **Nuova Italia.** The genial English-speaking Viti family runs this hotel near the train station and well within walking distance of the sights. Its rooms are clean and simply furnished. Air-conditioning and triple-glazed windows ensure quiet nights. Some rooms can accommodate extra beds. **Pros:** reasonable rates. **Cons:** no elevator. ✉ *Via Faenza 26, Santa Maria Novella* ☎ *055/268430* ⊕ *www.hotelnuovaitalia.it* ⤴ *20 rooms* ♿ *In-room: Wi-Fi (some). In-hotel: no elevator, laundry service, public Wi-Fi, parking (fee), some pets allowed* ▭ *AE, MC, V* ⊗ *Closed Dec. 8–Dec. 26* ❤|*BP* ✛ *D1.*

$$
☺ **Torre Guelfa.** If you want a taste of medieval Florence, try this hotel hidden within a 13th-century tower. The Torre Guelfa once protected the wealthy Acciaiuoli family; now it's one of the best small hotels in the center of Florence. It's been run since 1995 by husband and wife Giancarlo and Sabina Avuri, who lend a personal touch. Guest rooms vary—some have canopied beds, some balconies. A simple breakfast is served in a serene glassed-in loggia. Those on a budget might consider one of the six less expensive rooms on the second floor, which are comparable to the rest of the rooms. **Pros:** rooftop terrace with tremendous views; wonderful staff; some family-friendly triple rooms. **Cons:** 72 steps to get to terrace; continental breakfast is available only at 8 AM. ✉ *Borgo Santi Apostoli 8, Santa Maria Novella* ☎ *055/2396338* ⊕ *www. hoteltorreguelfa.com* ⤴ *24 rooms, 2 suites* ♿ *In-room: safe (some), no TV (some). In-hotel: laundry service, Internet terminal (fee), Wi-Fi (fee), parking (fee), some pets allowed* ▭ *AE, MC, V* ❤|*BP* ✛ *D4.*

$$
☺ **Villa Azalee.** The 19th-century villa deftly recalls its previous incarnation as a private residence. It's been in the hands of the Brizzi family for more than 100 years, and they understandably take pride in the

4

prettiness of the place. Quilted, floral-print slipcovers dress the furniture; throw rugs pepper the floors. Many rooms have views of the hotel's garden, and some have private terraces. The hotel is five minutes on foot from the train station and steps from the Fortezza da Basso (site of the Pitti fashion shows). **Pros:** proximity to train station; two garden apartments are wheelchair accessible. **Cons:** feels a bit out of the way, despite being in city center. ⊠ *Viale Fratelli Rosselli 44, Santa Maria Novella* ☎ *055/214242* ⊕ *www.villa-azalee.it* ↗ *25 rooms* ⚐ *In-hotel: bar, bicycles, laundry service, Internet terminal, parking (fee), some pets allowed* ⊟ *AE, DC, MC, V* ⎪◯⎪ *BP* ⊹ *A1.*

THE OLTRARNO AND BEYOND

$$ ⊡ **Hotel Silla.** The entrance to this slightly off-the-beaten-path hotel is through a 15th-century courtyard lined with potted plants and sculpture-filled niches. The hotel, formerly a palazzo dating from the 15th century, is up a flight of stairs and has two floors. Rooms are simply furnished and walls are papered; some have views of Via de' Renai and the Arno, while others overlook a less traveled road. Breakfast may be taken in a room that preserves an Empire feel (including two chandeliers from the early 19th century); when it's warm, a large, sunny terrace is the perfect place to read or to write that postcard. **Pros:** a Fodor's reader raves, "It's in the middle of everything except the crowds." **Cons:** some readers complain of street noise and too-small rooms. ⊠ *Via de' Renai 5, San Niccolò* ☎ *055/2342888* ⊕ *www.hotelsilla.it* ↗ *35 rooms* ⚐ *In-room: safe, refrigerator, Wi-Fi. In-hotel: bar, concierge, laundry service, parking (fee), some pets allowed* ⊟ *AE, DC, MC, V* ⎪◯⎪ *BP* ⊹ *G6.*

$$$$ ⊡ **Lungarno.** Many rooms and suites here have private terraces that jut out right over the Arno, granting stunning views of the Palazzo Vecchio and the Lungarno. Four suites in a 13th-century tower preserve details like exposed stone walls and old archways, and look over a little square with a medieval tower covered in jasmine. The very chic interiors approximate breezily elegant homes, with lots of crisp, white fabrics with blue trim. A wall of windows and a sea of white couches make the lobby bar one of the most relaxing places in the city to stop for a drink. Inquire about the Lungarno Suites, across the river; they include kitchens, making them attractive if you're planning a longer stay. **Pros:** upscale without being stuffy. **Cons:** rooms without Arno views feel less special. ⊠ *Borgo San Jacopo 14, Lungarno Sud* ☎ *055/27261* ⊕ *www.lungarnohotels.com* ↗ *60 rooms, 13 suites* ⚐ *In-room: Wi-Fi. In-hotel: restaurant, bar, concierge, laundry service, parking (fee)* ⊟ *AE, DC, MC, V* ⎪◯⎪ *BP* ⊹ *D5.*

SANTA CROCE

$$$$ ⊡ **The Four Seasons.** Seven years of restoration have turned this 15th-century palazzo in Florence's center into a luxury hotel unlike any other in town. No place else can boast of an 11-acre garden dotted with centuries-old trees, a pool, and a state-of-the-art spa. A sweeping 16th-century courtyard with original frescoes leads to an elegant bar where Florentines enjoy aperitivi. No two guest rooms are alike; many have

original 17th-century frescoes, some face the garden, others quiet interior courtyards. Decorated in either yellow or green, they have large marble bathrooms with deep tubs and showers. If you crave heightened privacy, book yourself at the Conventino section of the hotel on the other side of the garden. **Pros:** a unique "city meets country" experience. **Cons:** not all staff members are as professional as they should be; expensive breakfast. ⊠ *Borgo Pinti 99e, Santa Croce* ☎ *055/26261* ⊕ *www.fourseasons.com/florence* ⇥ *117 rooms In-room: safe, refrigerator, DVD, Internet. In-hotel: 2 restaurants, room service, 2 bars, pool, gym, spa, bicycles, laundry service, Internet terminal, parking (paid)* ⊟ *AE, DC, MC, V* ⑪ *EP* ✛ *H1.*

$$$$ ⊡ **Hotel Regency.** The noise and crowds of Florence seem far from this stylish hotel in a residential district near the Sinagoga, though you're not more than 10 minutes from the Accademia and Michelangelo's *David*. Across the street is Piazza d'Azeglio, a small public park that somehow evokes 19th-century middle Europe. Rooms dressed in richly colored fabrics and antique-style furniture remain faithful to the hotel's 19th-century origins as a private mansion. The restaurant here is equally sophisticated. **Pros:** faces one of the few green parks in the center of Florence. **Cons:** a small flight of stairs takes you to reception. ⊠ *Piazza d'Azeglio 3, Santa Croce* ☎ *055/245247* ⊕ *www.regency-hotel. com* ⇥ *30 rooms, 4 suites* ⚮ *In-room: safe, refrigerator, Wi-Fi. In-hotel: restaurant, room service, bar, concierge, laundry service, parking (fee), some pets allowed, no-smoking rooms* ⊟ *AE, DC, MC, V* ⑪ *BP* ✛ *H1.*

$ ⊡ **Istituto Oblate dell'Assunzione.** Twelve nuns run this convent, which is minutes from the Duomo. Rooms are spotlessly clean and simple; some have views of the cupola, and others look out onto a carefully tended garden where you are welcome to relax. Several rooms have three and four beds, making them well suited for families. Curfew is at 11:30 PM. You can join Mass every morning at 7:30. For an additional three euros you can get a simple continental breakfast, and the nuns provide half or full pension for groups of 10 or more. None of the nuns speaks English, and they don't have a Web presence, so unless you speak Italian the best way to book is by fax. **Pros:** bargain price; great location; quiet rooms; garden. **Cons:** curfew; no credit cards. ⊠ *Borgo Pinti 15, Santa Croce* ☎ *055/2480582* ⧉ *055/2346291* ⇥ *28 rooms, 22 with bath* ⚮ *In-room: no phone, no TV. In-hotel: parking (fee)* ⊟ *No credit cards* ⑪ *EP* ✛ *G3.*

$$$$ ⊡ **Monna Lisa.** Housed in a 15th-century palazzo, this hotel retains some
★ of its wood-coffered ceilings from the 1500s, as well as its original staircase. Though some rooms are small, they are tasteful, and each is done in a different floral wallpaper. Some of the up-to-date bathrooms offer tubs as well as showers. The inviting public rooms, with gleaming terra-cotta floors and Oriental rugs, retain a 19th-century aura, and the pretty box-hedged garden offers a good place to unwind. Two annex buildings have elevators and lack the sometimes-challenging steps of the main hotel. **Pros:** lavish buffet breakfast; cheerful staff; garden. **Cons:** rooms in annex are much less charming than those in palazzo. ⊠ *Borgo Pinti 27, Santa Croce* ☎ *055/2479751* ⊕ *www.monnalisa.*

it ⌁ *45 rooms* ☖ *In-room: safe, refrigerator. In-hotel: bar, concierge, Internet terminal (fee), Wi-Fi, laundry service, parking (fee), some pets allowed* ⊟ *AE, DC, MC, V* ⦿| *BP* ⊹ *G3.*

$$ ⊞ **Morandi alla Crocetta.** You're made to feel like privileged friends of
★ the family at this charming and distinguished residence near Piazza Santissima Annunziata. The former convent is close to the sights but very quiet, and it's furnished comfortably in the classic style of a gracious Florentine home. One room retains original 17th-century fresco fragments, and two others have small private terraces. The Morandi is not only an exceptional hotel, but also a good value. It's very small, so book well in advance. **Pros:** interesting, offbeat location; terrific staff. **Cons:** extra charge for breakfast; two flights of stairs to reach reception and rooms. ⊠ *Via Laura 50, Santissima Annunziata* ☏ *055/2344747* ⊕ *www.hotelmorandi.it* ⌁ *10 rooms* ☖ *In-room: safe, refrigerator, Wi-Fi. In-hotel: no elevator, concierge, laundry service, parking (fee), some pets allowed* ⊟ *AE, DC, MC, V* ⦿| *EP* ⊹ *H1.*

OUTSIDE THE CITY

$$$ ⊞ **Torre di Bellosguardo.** *Bellosguardo* means "beautiful view"; given the view of Florence you get here, the name is fitting. The hotel, perched atop a hill minutes from the *viale*, is reached via a narrow road dotted with olive trees. Dante's friend Guido Calvacanti supposedly chose this serene spot for his country villa, but little remains from the early 14th century. The reception area, a former ballroom, has soaring ceilings with frescoes by Francavilla (1553–1615). Guest rooms, all with high ceilings, are simple and have heavy wooden furniture. Proprietor Signor Franchetti keeps a small menagerie on the grounds (including donkeys, rabbits, and chickens), and maintains a beautiful, peaceful garden, which guests have access to. **Pros:** great for escaping heat of the city in summer; a villa experience with the city just minutes away. **Cons:** a car is a necessity. ⊠ *Via Roti Michelozzi 2* ☏ *055/2298145* ⊕ *www. torrebellosguardo.com* ⌁ *9 rooms, 7 suites* ☖ *In-room: no a/c (some), refrigerator, no TV, Internet. In-hotel: bar, pool, concierge, laundry service, parking (no fee), some pets allowed* ⊟ *AE, MC, V* ⊹ *B6.*

$$$$ ⊞ **Villa La Massa.** You approach this tall and imposing villa, 15 minutes out of town, via a gravel drive lined with flowers. The public rooms, outfitted in Renaissance style in deep green, gold, and crimson, have an atmosphere of lush elegance. Guest rooms have high ceilings, some with frescoes, plush carpeting, and deep bathtubs. A pool and beautiful views of the Arno are bonuses. The superb Il Verocchio restaurant serves Tuscan classics using local seasonal ingredients; a pianist quietly plays old standards while you eat. A shuttle bus runs every hour to and from the center of Florence, but the place is so peaceful you might not want to bother. **Pros:** pleasing mix of city and country life; sumptuous buffet breakfast; views of the Tuscan hills; phenomenal staff. **Cons:** even with shuttle; a car is a necessity; not open year-round. ⊠ *Via della Massa 24, Candeli* ☏ *055/62611* ⊕ *www.villalamassa.com* ⌁ *19 rooms, 18 suites* ☖ *In-room: safe, refrigerator, Internet. In-hotel: restaurant, bar, pool, concierge, laundry service, public Internet, parking (fee), some pets allowed* ⊟ *AE, DC, MC, V* ☉ *Closed Dec.–Mar.* ⦿| *BP* ⊹ *H5.*

NIGHTLIFE AND THE ARTS

THE ARTS

MUSIC

The **Accademia Bartolomeo Cristofori** (⊠ *Via di Camaldoli 7/r, Santo Spirito/San Frediano* ☎ *055/221646* ⊕ *www.accademiacristofori.it*), also known as the Amici del Fortepiano (Friends of the Fortepiano), sponsors fortepiano concerts throughout the year. **Amici della Musica** (⊕ *www.amicimusica.fi.it*) organizes concerts at the **Teatro della Pergola** (*Box office* ⊠ *Via Alamanni 39, Lungarno North* ☎ *055/210804* ⊕ *www.teatrodellapergola.com*).

The **Maggio Musicale Fiorentino** (⊠ *Via Alamanni 39* ☎ *055/210804*), a series of internationally acclaimed concerts and recitals, is held in the **Teatro Comunale** (⊠ *Corso Italia 16, Lungarno North* ☎ *055/287222* ⊕ *www.maggiofiorentino.com*). Within Italy you can purchase tickets from late April through July directly at the box office or by phone at ☎ *055/2779350*. You can also buy them online. Other events—opera, ballet, and additional concerts—occur regularly throughout the year at different venues in town.

The **Orchestra da Camera Fiorentina** (⊠ *Via Monferrato 2, Piazza della Signoria* ☎ *055/783374* ⊕ *www.orcafi.it*) performs various concerts of classical music throughout the year at Orsanmichele, the grain market turned church.

The concert season of the **Orchestra della Toscana** (⊠ *Via Ghibellina 101, Santa Croce* ☎ *055/2340710* ⊕ *www.orchestradellatoscana.it*) runs from November to June.

NIGHTLIFE

Florentines are rather proud of their nightlife options. Most bars now have some sort of happy hour, which usually lasts for many hours and often has snacks that can substitute for a light dinner. (Check, though, that the buffet is free or comes with the price of a drink.) Clubs typically don't open until very late in the evening and don't get crowded until 1 or 2 in the morning. Though the cover charges can be steep, finding free passes around town is fairly easy.

BARS

One of the hottest spots in town is the bar at the Gallery Hotel Art, **Fusion Bar** (⊠ *Vicolo dell'Oro 13, Santa Maria Novella* ☎ *055/27266987*). **Kitsch** (⊠ *Via San Gallo 22/r, San Marco* ☎ *055/4620016*) has indoor and outdoor seating and a great list of wines by the glass. At aperitivo time €8 will buy you a truly tasty cocktail and give you access to the tremendous buffet—it's so good, you won't need dinner afterward. The oh-so-cool vibe at **La Dolce Vita** (⊠ *Piazza del Carmine 6/r, Santo Spirito* ☎ *055/284595* ⊕ *www.dolcevitaflorence.com*) attracts Florentines and the occasional visiting American movie star. **Rex** (⊠ *Via Fiesolana 23–25/r, Santa Croce* ☎ *055/2480331* ⊕ *www.rexcafe.it*) attracts a trendy, artsy clientele. **Sant'Ambrogio Caffè** (⊠ *Piazza Sant'Ambrogio*

7–8/r, Santa Croce ☎ 055/2477277) has outdoor summer seating with a view of an 11th-century church (Sant'Ambrogio) directly across the street.

Zoe (✉ Via de' Renai 11 3/r, San Niccolò ☎ 055/243111) calls itself a "caffetteria," and while coffee

may indeed be served (as well as terrific salads and burgers at lunchtime), elegant youngish Florentines flock here for the fine cocktails. Here's people-watching at its very best, done while listening to the latest CDs imported from England.

SHOPPING

Window-shopping in Florence is like visiting an enormous contemporary-art gallery. Many of today's greatest Italian artists are fashion designers, and most keep shops in Florence. Discerning shoppers may find bargains in the street markets. ■TIP→ Do not buy any knockoff goods from any of the hawkers plying their fake Prada (or any other high-end designer) on the streets. It's illegal, and fines are astronomical if the police happen to catch you. (The vendor doesn't pay the fine, you do.)

Shops are generally open 9 to 1 and 3:30 to 7:30 and are closed Sunday and Monday mornings most of the year. Summer (June to September) hours are usually 9 to 1 and 4 to 8, and some shops close Saturday afternoon instead of Monday morning. When looking for addresses, you'll see two color-coded numbering systems on each street. The red numbers are commercial addresses and are indicated, for example, as 31/r. The blue or black numbers are residential addresses. Most shops take major credit cards and ship purchases, but because of possible delays it's wise to take your purchases with you.

MARKETS

The **Mercato Centrale** (✉ Piazza del Mercato Centrale, San Lorenzo) is a huge indoor food market with a staggering selection of things edible. The clothing and leather-goods stalls of the **Mercato di San Lorenzo** in the streets next to the church of San Lorenzo have bargains for shoppers on a budget. It's possible to strike gold at the **Mercato di Sant'Ambrogio** (✉ Piazza Ghiberti, off Via dei Macci, Santa Croce), where clothing stalls abut the fruit and vegetables. Every Thursday morning from September through June the covered loggia in Piazza della Repubblica hosts a **Mercato dei Fiori** (flower market ✉ Piazza della Repubblica) ; it's awash in a lively riot of plants and flowers. If you're looking for cheery, inexpensive trinkets to take home, you might want to stop and roam through the stalls under the loggia of the **Mercato del Porcellino** (✉ Via Por Santa Maria at Via Porta Rossa, Piazza della Repubblica). You can find bargains at the **Piazza dei Ciompi flea market** (✉ Sant'Ambrogio, Santa Croce) Monday through Saturday and on the last Sunday of the month.

The bounty at Florence's Mercato Centrale

The second Sunday of every month brings the **Spirito flea market.** On the third Sunday of the month, vendors at the **Fierucola** organic fest sell such delectables as honeys, jams, spice mixes, and fresh vegetables.

SHOPPING DISTRICTS

Florence's most fashionable shops are concentrated in the center of town. The fanciest designer shops are mainly on **Via Tornabuoni** and **Via della Vigna Nuova.** The city's largest concentrations of antiques shops are on **Borgo Ognissanti** and the Oltrarno's **Via Maggio.** The **Ponte Vecchio** houses reputable but very expensive jewelry shops, as it has since the 16th century. The area near **Santa Croce** is the heart of the leather merchants' district.

SPECIALTY STORES

BOOKS AND PAPER

Alberto Cozzi (✉ *Via del Parione 35/r, Santa Maria Novella* ☎ *055/294968*) keeps an extensive line of Florentine papers and paper products. The artisans in the shop rebind and restore books and works on paper. One of Florence's oldest paper-goods stores, **Giulio Giannini e Figlio** (✉ *Piazza Pitti 37/r* ☎ *055/212621*) is *the* place to buy the marbleized stock, which comes in many shapes and sizes, from flat sheets to boxes and even pencils. Photograph albums, frames, diaries, and other objects ★ dressed in handmade paper can be purchased at **Il Torchio** (✉ *Via dei Bardi 17, San Niccolò* ☎ *055/2342862*). The stuff is high quality, and the prices lower than usual. **La Tartaruga** (✉ *Borgo Albizzi 60/r, Santa*

Croce ☎ *055/2340845*) sells brightly colored, recycled paper in lots of guises (such as calendars and stationery), as well as toys for children. **Libreria d'Arte Galleria Uffizi** (✉ *Piazzale degli Uffizi 6, near Palazzo Vecchio* ☎ *055/284508*) carries monographs on famous artists, some of whose work can be found in the Uffizi; it also carries scholarly works in both Italian and English.

Long one of Florence's best art-book shops, **Libreria Salimbeni** (✉ *Via Matteo Palmieri 14–16/r, Santa Croce* ☎ *055/2340905*) has an outstanding selection. **Pineider** (✉ *Piazza della Signoria 13/r, Piazza della Signoria* ☎ *055/284655*) has shops throughout the world, but the business began in Florence and still does all its printing here. Stationery and business cards are the mainstay, but the stores also sell fine leather desk accessories as well as a less stuffy, more lighthearted line of products.

CLOTHING

The usual fashion suspects—Prada, Gucci, Versace, to name but a few—all have shops in Florence.

Bernardo (✉ *Via Porta Rossa 87/r, Piazza della Repubblica* ☎ *055/283333*) specializes in men's trousers, cashmere sweaters, and shirts with details like mother-of-pearl buttons. **Cabó** (✉ *Via Porta Rossa 77–79/r, Piazza della Repubblica* ☎ *055/215774*) carries that sinuous Missoni knitwear. Trendy **Diesel** (✉ *Via dei Lamberti 13/r, Piazza della Signoria* ☎ *055/2399963*) started in Vicenza; its gear is on the "must-have" list of many self-respecting Italian teens.

The aristocratic Marchese di Barsento, **Emilio Pucci** (✉ *Via Tornabuoni 20–22/r, Santa Maria Novella* ☎ *055/2658082*), became an international name in the late 1950s when the stretch ski clothes he designed for himself caught on with the dolce vita crowd—his pseudopsychedelic prints and "palazzo pajamas" became all the rage. You can take home a custom-made suit or dress from **Giorgio Vannini** (✉ *Borgo Santi Apostoli 43/r, Santa Maria Novella* ☎ *055/293037*), who has a showroom for his prêt-à-porter designs.

The intrepid shopper might want to check out some other, lesser-known shops. At **L'essentiel** (✉ *Via del Corso 10/r, Piazza della Signoria* ☎ *055/294713*) Lara Caldieron has spun her club-going years into fashion that also works well on the street and in the office. **Maçel** (✉ *Via Guicciardini 128/r, Palazzo Pitti* ☎ *055/287355*) has collections by lesser-known Italian designers, many of whom use the same factories as the A-list. Florentine designer **Patrizia Pepe** (✉ *Piazza San Giovanni 12/r, Duomo* ☎ *055/2645056*) has body-conscious clothes perfect for all ages, especially for women with a tiny streak of rebelliousness. Members of the junior set desiring to look well clad, Florentine style, should consider stopping at **Piccolo Slam** (✉ *Via dei Neri 9–11/r, Santa Croce* ☎ *055/214504*).

Principe (✉ *Via del Sole 2, Santa Maria Novella* ☎ *055/292764*) is a Florentine institution with casual clothes for men, women, and children at far-from-casual prices. It also has a great housewares department. For cutting-edge fashion, the fun and funky window displays at **Spazio A** (✉ *Via Porta Rossa 109–115/r, Piazza della Repubblica* ☎ *055/212995*) merit a stop. The shop carries such well-known designers as Alberta Ferretti and Moschino, as well as lesser-known Italian, English, and French designers.

FRAGRANCES

Aromatherapy has been elevated to an art form at **Antica Officina del Farmacista Dr. Vranjes** (✉ *Borgo La Croce 44/r, Santa Croce* ☎ *055/241748* ✉ *Via San Gallo 63/r* ☎ *055/494537*). Dr. Vranjes makes scents for the body and for the house.

Lorenzo Villoresi (✉ *Via de'Bardi 14, Lungarno Sud* ☎ *055/2341187* ⊕ *www.lorenzovilloresi.com*) makes one-of-a-kind fragrances, which he develops after meeting with you. Such personalized attention does not come cheap.

The essence of a Florentine holiday is captured in the sachets of the **Officina Profumo Farmaceutica di Santa Maria Novella** (✉ *Via della Scala 16, Santa Maria Novella* ☎ *055/216276*), an art-nouveau emporium of herbal cosmetics and soaps that are made following centuries-old recipes created by Dominican friars.

JEWELRY

Angela Caputi (✉ *Borgo Santi Apostoli 44/46* ☎ *055/292993*) wows Florentine cognoscenti with her highly creative, often outsized plastic jewelry. A small, but equally creative, collection of women's clothing made of fine fabrics is also on offer. **Carlo Piccini** (✉ *Ponte Vecchio 31/r, Piazza della Signoria* ☎ *055/292030*) has been around for several generations, selling antique jewelry as well as making pieces to order; you can also get old jewelry reset here. **Cassetti** (✉ *Ponte Vecchio 54/r, Piazza della Signoria* ☎ *055/2396028*) combines precious and semiprecious stones and metals in contemporary settings. **Gatto Bianco** (✉ *Borgo Santi Apostoli 12/r, Santa Maria Novella* ☎ *055/282989*) has breathtakingly beautiful jewelry worked in semiprecious and precious stones; the feel is completely contemporary. **Oro Due** (✉ *Via Lambertesca 12/r, Piazza della Signoria* ☎ *055/292143*) sells gold jewelry the old-fashioned way: beauteous objects are priced according to the level of craftsmanship and the price of gold bullion that day. One of Florence's oldest jewelers, **Tiffany** (✉ *Via Tornabuoni 25/r, Santa Maria Novella* ☎ *055/215506*) has supplied Italian (and other) royalty with finely crafted gems for centuries. Its selection of antique-looking classics has been updated with a selection of contemporary silver.

LINENS AND FABRICS

Antico Setificio Fiorentino (✉ *Via L. Bartolini 4, Santo Spirito/San Frediano* ☎ *055/213861* ⊕ *www.anticsetificiofiorentino.com*) has been providing damasks and other fine fabrics for royalty and those who aspire to it since 1786. Visits by appointment are preferred. **Loretta Caponi** (✉ *Piazza Antinori 4/r, Santa Maria Novella* ☎ *055/213668*) is synonymous with Florentine embroidery, and the luxury lace, linens, and lingerie have earned the eponymous signora worldwide renown.

DID YOU KNOW?

Goldsmiths and jewelers have been selling their wares on the Ponte Vecchio since 1593.

OUTLETS

For bargains on Italian designer clothing, you need to leave the city. At **Barberino Designer Outlet** (⊠ *Via Meucci snc* ☎ *055/842161* ⊕ *www. mcarthurglen.it*) you'll find Prada, Pollini, Missoni, and Bruno Magli, among others. To get here, take the A1 to the Barberino di Mugello exit, and follow signs to the mall.

One-stop bargain shopping awaits at the **Mall** (⊠ *Via Europa 8* ☎ *055/8657775* ⊕ *www.themall.it*), where the stores sell goods by such names as Bottega Veneta, Giorgio Armani, Loro Piana, Sergio Rossi, and Yves St. Laurent. Cognoscenti drive 45 minutes or take the train to Montevarchi, and then taxi out of town to the **Prada Outlet** (⊠ *Levanella Spacceo, Estrada Statale 69, Montevarchi* ☎ *055/91911*).

SHOES AND LEATHER ACCESSORIES

The ultimate fine leathers are crafted into classic shapes at **Casadei** (⊠ *Via Tornabuoni 33/r, Santa Maria Novella* ⊕ *www.casadei.com* ☎ *055/287240*), winding up as women's shoes and bags. The classy **Ferragamo** (⊠ *Via Tornabuoni 2/r, Santa Maria Novella* ☎ *055/292123*), in a 13th-century palazzo, displays designer clothing and accessories, but elegant footwear still underlies the Ferragamo success. **Pollini** (⊠ *Via Calimala 12/r, Piazza della Repubblica* ☎ *055/214738*) has beautifully crafted shoes and leather accessories for those willing to pay that little bit extra.

Cellerini (⊠ *Via del Sole 37/r, Santa Maria Novella* ☎ *055/282533* ⊕ *www.cellerini.it*) is an institution in a city where it seems that just about everybody wears an expensive leather jacket. **Furla** (⊠ *Via Calzaiuoli 47/r, Piazza della Repubblica* ☎ *055/2382883*) makes beautiful leather bags and wallets in up-to-the-minute designs. **Giotti** (⊠ *Piazza Ognissanti 3–4/r, Lungarno Nord* ☎ *055/294265*) has a full line of leather goods, including clothing. **Il Bisonte** (⊠ *Via del Parione 31/r, off Via della Vigna Nuova, Santa Maria Novella* ☎ *055/215722* ⊕ *www. ilbisonte.net*) is known for its natural-looking leather goods, all stamped with the store's bison symbol. **Madova** (⊠ *Via Guicciardini 1/r, Palazzo Pitti* ☎ *055/2396526*) has high-quality leather gloves in a rainbow of colors and a choice of linings (silk, cashmere, and unlined). **Paolo Carandini** (⊠ *Borgo Allegri 73/r, Santa Croce* ☎ *055/245397*) crafts exquisite leather objects such as picture frames, jewelry boxes, and desk accessories.

A consortium of leatherworkers plies its trade at **Scuola del Cuoio** (⊠ *Piazza Santa Croce 16* ☎ *055/244533* ⊕ *www.leatherschool.com*), in the former dormitory of the convent of Santa Croce; high-quality, fairly priced jackets, belts, and purses are sold here.

SIDE TRIPS FROM FLORENCE

4

West of Florence, and easily accessible by car or train, is Pisa, the town known the world over for its great engineering mistake, the Leaning Tower. North of Pisa, and also a quick shot from Florence, is the relaxed, elegant town of Lucca, which feels like its own little world, surrounded by 16th-century ramparts that have been transformed into parklike promenades. Pisa's tower is definitely worth seeing—and there's more to see than just the tower—but ultimately Lucca has greater charms, making it a better choice if you're picking one for an overnight.

Farther west, a hop over the border from Tuscany into Liguria brings you to the Cinque Terre—five tiny, cliff-hugging coastal villages that have become one of Italy's most popular destinations. It's not impossible to visit the Cinque Terre on a day trip from Florence, but we don't recommend it; you'll spend about five hours on the train round-trip, or something close to that if you go by car. You're better off either overnighting in Lucca or Pisa and day-tripping from there, or (best of all) spending a night or two in the Cinque Terre itself.

LUCCA

Ramparts built in the 16th and 17th centuries enclose a charming town filled with churches (99 of them), terra-cotta-roof buildings, and narrow cobblestone streets, along which local ladies maneuver bikes to do their daily shopping. Here Caesar, Pompey, and Crassus agreed to rule Rome as a triumvirate in 60 BC. Lucca was later the first Tuscan town to accept Christianity, and it still has a mind of its own: when most of Tuscany was voting communist as a matter of course, Lucca's citizens rarely followed suit. The famous composer Giacomo Puccini (1858–1924) was born here; his work forms the nucleus of the summer Opera Theater and Music Festival, staged in open-air venues from mid-June through mid-July. The ramparts circling the center city are the perfect place to take a stroll, ride a bicycle, kick a ball, or just stand and look down upon Lucca.

GETTING HERE
You can reach Lucca easily by train from Florence; the historic center is a short walk from the station. If you're driving, take the A11/E76.

VISITOR INFORMATION
Lucca tourism office (✉ *Piazza Santa Maria 35* ☎ *0583/91991* ⊕ *www.lucca. turismo.toscana.it*).

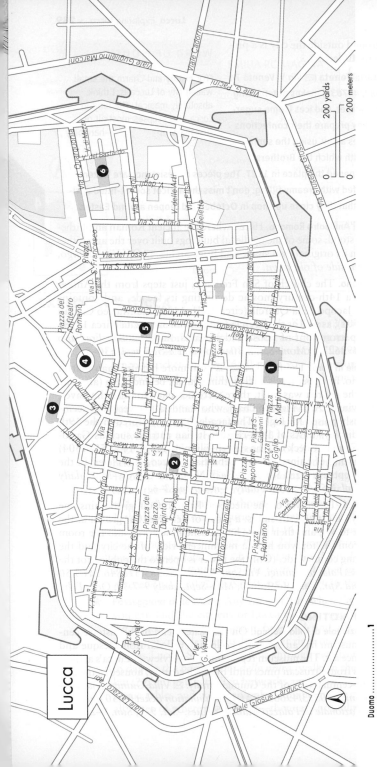

Lucca

WHERE TO EAT

$$ ✕**Buca di Sant'Antonio.** The staying power of Buca di Sant'Antonio—
TUSCAN   it's been around since 1782—is the result of superlative Tuscan food
★   brought to the table by waitstaff that doesn't miss a beat. The menu
includes the simple but blissful, like *tortelli lucchesi al sugo* (meat-
stuffed pasta with a tomato-and-meat sauce), and more daring dishes
such as roast *capretto* (kid) with herbs. A white-wall interior hung with
copper pots and brass musical instruments creates a classy but comfort-
able dining space. ⊠ *Via della Cervia 3* ☎ *0583/55881* ▤ *AE, DC, MC,
V* ⊘ *Closed Mon., 1 wk in Jan., and 1 wk in July. No dinner Sun.*

$$ ✕**i Santi.** This intimate little wine bar, just outside the Piazza
WINE BAR   dell'Anfiteatro, is the perfect place to have a light meal and a fine glass
of wine. The extensive wine list is strong on local varietals, as well as
on foreign (French) selections. The *carpaccio di manzo affumicato* (thin
slices of smoked beef served with celery and a young cheese) is a standout. Specials always include a pasta of the day. Great attention is given
to sourcing top-quality local, seasonal ingredients. ⊠ *Via dell'Anfiteatro
29/a* ☎ *0583/496124* ▤ *AE, DC, MC, V* ⊘ *Closed Wed.*

$–$$ ✕**Il Giglio.** Just off Piazza Napoleone, this restaurant has quiet, late-
TUSCAN   19th-century charm and classic cuisine. It's a place for all seasons, with
a big fireplace for chilly weather and an outdoor terrace in summer. If
mushrooms are in season, try the *tacchonni con funghi,* a homemade
pasta with mushrooms and a local herb called *nepitella.* A local favorite
during winter is the *coniglio con olive* (rabbit stew with olives). ⊠ *Piazza del Giglio 2* ☎ *0583/494508* ▤ *AE, DC, MC, V* ⊘ *Closed Wed.
and 15 days in Nov. No dinner Tues.*

$ ✕**Trattoria da Leo.** A few short turns away from the facade of San
ITALIAN   Michele, this noisy, informal, traditional trattoria delivers *cucina alla
casalinga* (home cooking) in the best sense. Try the typical minestra di
farro to start or just go straight to *secondi piatti* (entrées); in addition
to the usual roast meats, there's excellent chicken with olives and a
good cold dish of boiled meats served with a sauce of parsley and pine
nuts. Save some room for a dessert, such as the rich, sweet, fig-and-
walnut torte or the lemon sorbet brilliantly dotted with bits of sage,
which tastes almost like mint. ⊠ *Via Tegrimi 1, at corner of Via degli
Asili* ☎ *0583/492236* ▤ *No credit cards* ⊘ *No lunch Sun. Closed Sun.
Nov.–Mar.*

WHERE TO STAY

$$ ▥ **Albergo San Martino.** Down a narrow street facing a quiet, sun-sprin-
kled *piazzale* (small square) stands this small hotel. The brocade bed-
spreads are fresh and crisp, the proprietor friendly. Although around
the corner from the Duomo, the busy Corso Garibaldi, and the great
walls of Lucca, the inn, tucked away as it is, feels private—a place to
retreat to when you have seen all the church facades you can stand.
Two of the eight rooms are wheelchair accessible. In the cheerful apricot
breakfast room, filled with framed prints, you can get a more-than-solid
breakfast. A little terrace with wicker chairs provides a lovely place to
unwind. **Pros:** comfortable bed; great breakfast. **Cons:** breakfast costs

€10. ⊠ *Via della Dogana 9* ☎ *0583/469181* ⊕ *www.albergosanmartino. it* ⟿ *6 rooms, 2 suites* ♿ *In-room: refrigerator, Wi-Fi. In- hotel: bar, bicycles (fee), no elevator, laundry service, Wi-Fi* ⊟ *AE, DC, MC, V* ⦿ *EP.*

$$ ⦿ **Hotel Ilaria.** The former stables of the Villa Bottini have been transformed into a modern hotel within the historic center. A second-floor terrace, overlooking the villa, makes a comfortable place to relax, and there's a hot tub for the adventurous. Rooms are done in a warm wood veneer with blue-and-white fittings. The availability of free bicycles is a nice bonus in this bike-friendly city, and the sumptuous buffet breakfast could see you through to dinner. Residenza dell'Alba, the hotel's annex across the street, was originally part of a 14th-century church; now it's a luxe accommodation with in-room hot tubs. **Pros:** a Fodor's reader sums it up as a "nice, modern small hotel"; free bicycles. **Cons:** though in the city center, it's a little removed from main attractions. ⊠ *Via del Fosso 26* ☎ *0583/47615* 🖶 *0583/991961* ⊕ *www.hotelilaria.com* ⟿ *36 rooms, 5 suites* ♿ *In-room: safe, refrigerator, Wi-Fi. In-hotel: bar, bicycles, concierge, laundry service, Internet terminal, Wi-Fi, parking (no fee), some pets allowed (fee)* ⊟ *AE, DC, MC, V* ⦿ *BP.*

$$ ⦿ **Palazzo Alexander.** This small, elegant boutique hotel is on a quiet
★ side street a short walk from San Michele in Foro. The building, dating from the 12th century, has been restructured to create the ease common to Lucchesi nobility: timbered ceilings, warm yellow walls, and brocaded chairs adorn the public rooms, and the motif continues into the guest rooms, all of which have high ceilings and that same glorious damask. Top-floor suites have sweeping views of the town. One suite is on the mezzanine floor, but also has city views. **Pros:** intimate feel; gracious staff; bacon and eggs included in the buffet breakfast. **Cons:** some Fodor's readers complain of too-thin walls. ⊠ *Via S. Giustina 48* ☎ *0583/583571* 🖶 *0583/583610* ⊕ *www.palazzo-alexander.com* ⟿ *9 rooms, 3 suites, 1 apartment* ♿ *In-room: safe, refrigerator, Wi-Fi. In-hotel: bar, bicycles, concierge, laundry service, Internet terminal, Wi-Fi, parking (fee)* ⊟ *AE, DC, MC, V* ⦿ *BP.*

$ ⦿ **Piccolo Hotel Puccini.** Steps away from the busy square and church of San Michele, this little hotel is quiet and calm—and a great deal. Wallpaper, hardwood floors, and throw rugs are among the handsome decorations. Paolo, the genial manager, speaks fluent English and dispenses great touring advice. **Pros:** cheery, English-speaking staff. **Cons:** breakfast costs extra; some rooms are on the dark side. ⊠ *Via di Poggio 9* ☎ *0583/55421* 🖶 *0583/53487* ⊕ *www.hotelpuccini.com* ⟿ *14 rooms* ♿ *In-room: no a/c, safe. In-hotel: bar, laundry service, Wi-Fi, some pets allowed, no-smoking rooms* ⊟ *AE, MC, V* ⦿ *EP.*

NIGHTLIFE AND THE ARTS

The **Opera Theater and Music Festival of Lucca,** sponsored by Lucca's opera company and the school of music of the University of Cincinnati, runs from mid-June to mid-July; performances are staged in open-air venues.

Lucca's *centro storico* (including Piazza San Michele, shown here) was home to the composer Giacomo Puccini (1858–1924). His work is celebrated at Lucca's annual summer music festival.

Throughout summer there are jazz, pop, and rock concerts in conjunction with the **Estate Musicale Lucchese** music festival. The **Lucca Tourist Office** (⊠ *Piazza Santa Maria Verdi 35, San Michele* ☎ *0583/919931*) has schedule and ticket information for many local events, including the Opera Theater and Estate Musicale Lucchese festivals.

From September through April you can see operas, plays, and concerts staged at the **Teatro del Giglio** (⊠ *Piazza del Giglio, Duomo* ☎ *0583/46531* ⊕ *www.teatrodelgiglio.it*).

SPORTS AND THE OUTDOORS

A splendid bike ride may be had by circling the entire historic center along the top of the bastions—affording something of a bird's-eye view. **Poli Antonio Biciclette** (⊠ *Piazza Santa Maria 42* ☎ *0583/493787*) is an option for bicycle rental on the east side. Rentals cost about €12.50 for the day.

SHOPPING

Lucca's justly famed olive oils are available throughout the city (and exported around the world). Look for those made by Fattoria di Fubbiano and Fattoria Fabbri—two of the best. **Antica Bottega di Prospero** (⊠ *Via San Lucia 13* ☎ *No phone*) sells top-quality local products, including dried porcini mushrooms, olive oil, and wine.

Bargain hunters won't want to miss the **Benetton Stock Outlet** (⊠ *Via Mordini 17/19, Anfiteatro* ☎ *0583/464533*), with its brightly colored garments at reduced prices.

★ Chocoholics can get their fix at **Caniparoli** (⊠ *Via S. Paolino 96, San Donato* ☎ *0583/53456*). They are so serious about their sweets here that they do not make them from June through August because of the heat.

PISA

Most people think "Leaning Tower of" when they think of Pisa. Its position as one of Italy's most famous landmarks attracts hordes of day-trippers from around the world. But even if the building doesn't captivate you, Pisa has other treasures that make a visit worthwhile. Taken as a whole, the Campo dei Miracoli—the "Field of Miracles" where the Leaning Tower, the Duomo, the Camposanto, and the Baptistery are located—is one of the most dramatic and beautiful architectural complexes in Italy.

Pisa may have been inhabited as early as the Bronze Age. It was certainly populated by the Etruscans and, in turn, became part of the Roman Empire. In the early Middle Ages it flourished as an economic powerhouse—along with Amalfi, Genoa, and Venice, it was one of the maritime republics. The city's economic and political power ebbed in the early 15th century as it fell under the domination of Florence, though it enjoyed a brief resurgence under Cosimo I in the mid-16th century. Pisa endured heavy Allied bombing—miraculously, the Duomo and Leaning Tower, along with some other grand Romanesque structures, were spared, but the Camposanto sustained heavy damage.

GETTING HERE
About 84 km (52 mi) west of Florence, Pisa is a straight shot on the Fi-Pi-Li autostrada. By train it's an easy hour-long ride. The Pisa–Lucca train runs frequently and takes about 30 minutes.

VISITOR INFORMATION
Pisa tourism office (⊠ *Piazza Vittorio Emanuele II* ☎ *050/42291*).

EXPLORING PISA

Pisa, like many Italian cities, is best explored on foot, and most of what you'll want to see is within walking distance. The views along the Arno River are particularly grand and shouldn't be missed—there's a feeling of spaciousness that isn't found along the Arno in Florence.

As you set out, note that there are various combination-ticket options for sights on the Piazza del Duomo.

TOP ATTRACTIONS

❷ **Battistero.** This lovely Gothic baptistery, which stands across from the Duomo's facade, is best known for the pulpit carved by Nicola Pisano (circa 1220–84; father of Giovanni Pisano) in 1260. Ask one of the ticket takers if he'll sing for you inside; the acoustics are remarkable.

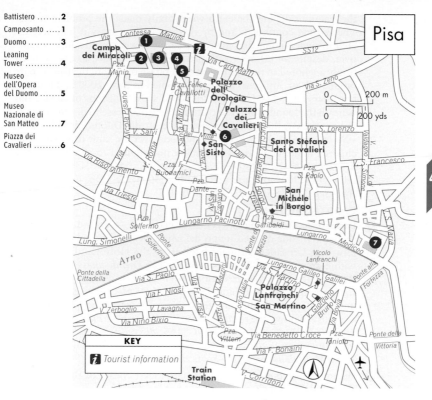

✉ *Piazza del Duomo* ☎ *050/835011* ⊕ *www.opapisa.it* 🎟 *€5, discounts available if bought in combination with tickets for other monuments* ⊘ *Nov.–Feb., daily 10–5; Mar., daily 9–6; Apr.–Sept., daily 8–8; Oct., daily 9–7.*

❸ Duomo. Pisa's cathedral brilliantly utilizes the horizontal marble-stripe motif (borrowed from Moorish architecture) that became common to Tuscan cathedrals. It is famous for the Romanesque panels on the transept door facing the tower that depict scenes from the life of Christ. The beautifully carved 14th-century pulpit is by Giovanni Pisano (son of Nicola). ✉ *Piazza del Duomo* ☎ *050835011* ⊕ *www.opapisa.it* 🎟 *€2, discounts available if bought in combination with tickets for other monuments* ⊘ *Nov.–Feb., daily 10–12:45 and 2–5; Mar., daily 10–6; Apr.–Sept., daily 10–8; Oct., daily 10–7.*

❹ Leaning Tower *(Torre Pendente).* Legend holds that Galileo conducted an experiment on the nature of gravity by dropping metal balls from the top of the 187-foot-high Leaning Tower of Pisa. Historians, however, say this legend has no basis in fact—which isn't quite to say that it's false. Work on this tower, built as a campanile (bell tower) for the Duomo, started in 1173: the lopsided settling began when construction reached the third story. The tower's architects attempted to compensate through such methods as making the remaining floors slightly taller on

Fodor'sChoice
★

the leaning side, but the extra weight only made the problem worse. The settling continued, and by the late 20th century it had accelerated to such a point that many feared the tower would simply topple over, despite all efforts to prop it up. The structure has since been firmly anchored to the earth. The final phase to restore the tower to its original tilt of 300 years ago was launched in early 2000 and finished two years later. The last phase removed some 100 tons of earth from beneath the foundation. Reservations, which are essential, can be made online or by calling the Museo dell'Opera del Duomo; it's also possible to arrive at the ticket office and book for the same day. Note that children under eight years of age are not allowed to climb. ⊠ *Piazza del Duomo* ☎ *050/835011* ⊕ *www.opapisa.it* ☜ *€17* ⊙ *Dec. and Jan., daily 10–4:30; Nov. and Feb., daily 9:30–5:30; Mar., daily 9–5:30; Apr.–Sept., daily 8:30–8; Oct., daily 9–7.*

WORTH NOTING

❶ **Camposanto.** According to legend, the cemetery—a walled structure on the western side of the Campo dei Miracoli—is filled with earth that returning Crusaders brought back from the Holy Land. Contained within are numerous frescoes, notably *The Drunkenness of Noah,* by Renaissance artist Benozzo Gozzoli (1422–97), presently under restoration; and the disturbing *Triumph of Death* (14th century; artist uncertain), whose subject matter shows what was on people's minds in a century that saw the ravages of the Black Death. ⊠ *Piazza del Duomo* ☎ *050/835011* ⊕ *www.opapisa.it* ☜ *€5, discounts available if bought in combination with tickets for other monuments* ⊙ *Nov.–Feb., daily 10–5; Mar., daily 9–6; Apr.–Sept., daily 8–8; Oct., daily 9–7.*

❺ **Museo dell'Opera del Duomo.** At the southeast corner of the sprawling Campo dei Miracoli, this museum holds a wealth of medieval sculptures and the ancient Roman sarcophagi that inspired Nicola Pisano's figures. ⊠ *Piazza del Duomo* ☎ *050/835011* ⊕ *www.opapisa.it* ☜ *€5, discounts available if bought in combination with tickets for other monuments* ⊙ *Nov.–Feb., daily 10–5; Mar., daily 9–6; Apr.–Sept., daily 8–8; Oct., daily 9–7.*

❼ **Museo Nazionale di San Matteo.** On the north bank of the Arno, this museum contains some incisive examples of local Romanesque and Gothic art. ⊠ *Lungarno Mediceo* ☎ *050/541865* ☜ *€5* ⊙ *Tues.–Sat. 9–7, holidays 9–2.*

❻ **Piazza dei Cavalieri.** The piazza, with its fine Renaissance **Palazzo dei Cavalieri, Palazzo dell'Orologio,** and Chiesa di **Santo Stefano dei Cavalieri,** was laid out by Giorgio Vasari in about 1560. The square was the seat of the Ordine dei Cavalieri di San Stefano (Order of the Knights of St. Stephen), a military and religious institution meant to defend the coast from possible invasion by the Turks. Also in this square is the prestigious **Scuola Normale Superiore,** founded by Napoléon in 1810 on the French model. Here graduate students pursue doctorates in literature, philosophy, mathematics, and science. In front of the school is a large statue of Ferdinando I de' Medici dating from 1596. On the extreme left is the tower where the hapless Ugolino della Gherardesca (died 1289) was imprisoned with his two sons and two grandsons; legend holds that he ate them. Dante immortalized him in Canto XXXIII of his *Inferno.* Duck into the **Church of Santo Stefano** (if you're lucky enough to find it open) and check out Bronzino's splendid *Nativity of Christ* (1564–65).

WHERE TO EAT

$-$$
ITALIAN
★

× **Beny.** Apricot walls hung with etchings of Pisa make this small, single-room restaurant warmly romantic. Husband and wife Damiano and Sandra Lazzerini have been running the place for two decades, and it shows in their obvious enthusiasm while talking about the menu and daily specials. Beny specializes in fish: its *ripieno di polpa di pesce a pan grattato con salsa di seppie e pomodoro* (fish-stuffed ravioli with tomato-octopus sauce) delights. Beny relies heavily on seasonal ingredients; Sandra works wonders with *tartufi estivi* (summer truffles), artichokes, and market fish of the day. ⊠ *Piazza Gambacorti 22* ☎ *050/25067* ⊟ *AE, DC, MC, V* ⊙ *Closed Sun. and 2 wks in mid-Aug. No lunch Sat.*

$
TUSCAN

× **La Pergoletta.** On an old town street named for its beautiful towers, this small, simple restaurant is in one such tower itself. There's also a shady garden for outdoor dining. Emma Forte, the proprietor and chef, cooks such Tuscan classics as *minestra di farro* (spelt soup) and choice interpretations of *grigliata* (grilled beef, veal, or lamb). Her sense of whimsy accounts for some of the non-Italian ingredients, such as ginger, that find their way into her dishes. Parents with small children may be pleased to find that there's a children's menu. ⊠ *Via delle Belle Torri 40* ☎ *050/542458* ⊟ *AE, DC, MC, V* ⊙ *Closed Mon. and 1 wk in Aug. No lunch Sat.*

$-$$
ITALIAN
★

× **Osteria dei Cavalieri.** This charming white-wall restaurant, a few steps from Piazza dei Cavalieri, is reason enough to come to Pisa. They can do it all here—serve up exquisitely grilled fish dishes, please vegetarians, and prepare *tagliata* (thin slivers of rare beef) for meat lovers. Three set menus, from the sea, garden, and earth, are available, or you can order à la carte. For dinner there's an early seating (around 7:30) and a later one (around 9); opt for the later one if you want time to linger over your meal. ⊠ *Via San Frediano 16* ☎ *050/580858* ⌂ *Reservations essential* ⊟ *AE, DC, MC, V* ⊙ *Closed Sun., 2 wks in Aug., and Dec. 29–Jan. 7. No lunch Sat.*

WHERE TO STAY

$$$$

⊞ **Hotel Relais dell'Orologio.** What used to be a private family palace opened as an intimate hotel in spring of 2003. Eighteenth-century antiques fill the rooms and public spaces; some rooms have stenciled walls and wood-beam ceilings. On the third floor sloped ceilings add romance. A large shared sitting room, complete with fireplace, provides a relaxing spot to read or sip a glass of wine. **Pros:** location—in the center of town, but on a quiet side street. **Cons:** breakfast costs extra. ⊠ *Via della Faggiola 12/14, off Campo dei Miracoli, Santa Maria* ☎ *050/830361* ⊟ *050/551869* ⊕ *www.hotelrelaisorologio.com* ⊷ *16 rooms, 5 suites* ⌂ *In-room: safe, refrigerator, Wi-Fi. In-hotel:*

4

restaurant, room service, bar, concierge, laundry service, Wi-Fi, parking (fee), some pets allowed ⊟ *AE, DC, MC, V* ⍐⍀*EP.*

$$ ⊡ **Royal Victoria.** In a pleasant palazzo facing the Arno, a 10-minute walk from the Campo dei Miracoli, this comfortably furnished hotel has been in the Piegaja family since 1837. That continuity may help explain why such notables as Charles Dickens and Charles Lindbergh enjoyed staying here. Antiques and reproductions are in the lobby and in some rooms, whose style ranges from the 1800s, complete with frescoes, to the 1920s. Ask for a room in the charming old tower. There's also a pretty rooftop garden where you can order cocktails. **Pros:** friendly staff; free use of a Lancia that seats five—a great vehicle for tooling around Pisa. **Cons:** rooms vary significantly in size; all are a little worn. ⊠ *Lungarno Pacinotti 12* 🕾 *050/940111* 🖷 *050/940180* ⊕ *www.royalvictoria. it* ⤳ *48 rooms, 40 with bath* ⚭ *In-room: no a/c (some), Wi-Fi. In-hotel: room service, bicycles, concierge, laundry service, Wi-Fi, parking (fee), some pets allowed* ⊟ *AE, DC, MC, V* ⍐⍀*BP.*

NIGHTLIFE AND THE ARTS

The **Luminaria** feast day on June 16 honors San Ranieri, the city's patron saint. Palaces along the Arno are illuminated with white lights, and there are plenty of fireworks; it's Pisa at its most beautiful.

Pisa has a lively performing arts scene, most of which happens at the 19th-century Teatro Verdi. Music and dance performances are presented from September through May. Contact **Fondazione Teatro di Pisa** (⊠ *Via Palestro 40, Lungarni* 🕾 *050/941111* ⊕ *www.teatrodipisa.pi.it*) for schedules and information.

THE CINQUE TERRE

FIVE REMOTE VILLAGES MAKE ONE MUST-SEE DESTINATION

"Charming" and "breath-taking" are adjectives that get a workout when you're traveling in Italy, but it's rare that both apply to a single location. The Cinque Terre is such a place, and this combination of characteristics goes a long way toward explaining its tremendous appeal.

The area is made up of five tiny villages (Cinque Terre literally means "Five Lands") clinging to the cliffs along a gorgeous stretch of the Ligurian coast. The terrain is so steep that for centuries footpaths were the only way to get from place to place. It just so happens that these paths provide beautiful views of the rocky coast tumbling into the sea, as well as access to secluded beaches and grottoes.

Backpackers "discovered" the Cinque Terre in the 1970s, and its popularity has been growing ever since. Despite summer crowds, much of the original appeal is intact. Each town has maintained its own distinct charm, and views from the trails in between are as breathtaking as ever.

Monterosso

Corniglia

Terracing around Corniglia

HIKING THE CINQUE TERRE

Monterosso—Vernazza Trail
The most demanding portion of the trail. Often narrow, with significant climbs and descents, particularly near Vernazza. Your labors are rewarded with the Trail No. 2's best views.

Mount Malpertuso

Mount Castello

Mount Gaginara

Le Stalle

Trail No 8a

Drignana

38

(Red Trail)

370

Madonna di Soviore

1hr 30min

Trail No 1

Trail No 89

51

Trail No 8

Santuario del Reggio

1hr

S. Bernardo

Trail No 8

Vernazza—Corniglia Trail
Ups and downs interspersed with olive groves and terraced vineyards.

Santuario Bernardino

1hr

Trail No 7

3 km/2 mi—1 hr 30 mm

Trail No 2 (Blue Trail)

3 km/2 mi—2 hrs

Vernazza

Guvano Beach

del Frate Island

Molinara Pt

Palma Pt

Monterosso al Mare

0   1 mi

0   1 km

FERRY TO LEVANTO

Monterosso
The most resort-like of the villages, with the largest beach.

Vernazza
Pretty and visitor-friendly. The best spot for lingering in a café and watching waves crash against the shore.

THE CLASSIC HIKE

Hiking is the most popular way to experience the Cinque Terre, and Trail No. 2, the Sentiero Azzurro (Blue Trail), is the most traveled path. To cover the entire trail is a full day: it's approximately 13 km (8 mi) in length, takes you to all five villages, and requires about five hours, not including stops, to complete. The best approach is to start at the eastern-

most town of Riomaggiore and warm up your legs on the easiest segment of the trail. As you work your way west, the hike gets progressively more demanding. For a less strenuous experience, you can choose to skip a leg or two and take the ferry (which provides its own beautiful views) or the inland train running between the towns instead.

Manarola

Along Trail No.2

Via dell'Amore

Corniglia– Manarola Trail
Runs through the hills near Manarola, descends to rocky beach near Corniglia.

Manarola–Riomaggiore Trail
Known as the Via dell'Amore (Lovers' Lane). A wide, paved, flat path with fine views.

KEY

··············· Major footpaths

- - - - - - Sanctuary footpaths

-------- Connecting footpaths

45min Hiking times

☨ Sanctuaries

No 1 (Red Trail)

Mount Capri

Mount Cuna

Trail No 6

Mount Galera

Mount Grosso

51

Trail No 7a

Trail No 6d

1hr 30min

Madonna della ☨ Salute

1hr

Volastra

Trail No 02

3 km/2 mi—1 hr
Trail No 2 (Blue Trail)

Spiaggione di Corniglia

51

Trail No 3

Madonna di Montenero
☨ 45min

370

370

Corniglia

del Luogo Pt

Manarola

Buonfiglio Pt

30min

Via dell' Amore

Riomaggiore

TO →
LA SPEZIA

Ligurian Sea

Trail No 2 (Blue Trail)

Torre Guardiola

C di M Nero

Corniglia
Perched on a cliff 500 ft. above the sea, reached by a switchback path (or by shuttle bus).

Manarola
The most photogenic of the villages, best seen from the cemetery a few minutes up the path toward Corniglia.

Riomaggiore
Cliff-clinging buildings are almost as striking as those in Manarola. Stairs to the left of the train station entrance cross over the tracks and lead to the trailhead.

BEYOND TRAIL NO.2

Trail No. 2 is just one of a network of trails crisscrossing the hills. If you're a dedicated hiker, spend a few nights and try some of the other routes. Trail No. 1, the Sentiero Rosso (Red Trail), climbs from Portovenere (east of Riomaggiore) and returns to the sea at Levanto (west of Monterosso al Mare). To hike its length takes from 9 to 12 hours; the ridge-top trail provides spectacular views from high above the villages, each of which can be reached via a steep path. Other shorter trails go from the villages up into the hills, some leading to religious sanctuaries. Trail No. 9, for example, starts from the old section of Monterosso and ends at the Madonna di Soviore Sanctuary.

FODOR'S FIRST PERSON

Angelo Benvenuto
Fisherman,
Monterosso al Mare

Angelo Benvenuto is a 10th-generation fisherman from Monterosso who organizes special boating excursions along the Cinque Terre in his *lampara* (wooden anchovy fishing boat).

Q: Although hiking the Cinque Terre has become a favorite with travelers, you and others maintain that the "way of life" in the Cinque Terre is really that of the sea....

A: For nearly one thousand years Monterosso has been a fishing village. We eat, live, and breathe the sea. In fact, when the barbarians invaded Italy during the middle ages, they did not come down to Monterosso because they were afraid of the sea. Because of this Monterosso as well as the other villages were protected and untouched. Everyday life is always connected to the sea.

Yet, the *sentiri* (trails) were also essential to our livelihood. They provided access to the elements we needed on land such as produce, animals, and of course wine! Now they are a source of entertainment and beauty for our visitors.

Q: How has the Cinque Terre changed over the past 20 years?

A: There are obviously more people visiting, but everyday life has remained the same. I still go out to fish for the majority of our meals, and my wife works in the garden to provide us with fresh vegetables, fruit, even eggs. It is this way for most of the Cinque Terre.

Of course, many of us have gone into the tourism business—hotels, restaurants, cafes. The tourists have brought us opportunity and some financial stability which is very good for us, for all of the villages.

Q: What is your perfect day in the Cinque Terre?

A: Take a hike up to the garden (located on the slopes above town) or maybe even to Vernazza to visit friends. Then after a nice fresh seafood lunch, glass of *Sciacchetra'* (local dessert wine) and a short *pisolino* (nap), I would then head out to sea on my lampara and enjoy the silence of the sea and the beautiful landscape, and catch some fish for dinner!

PRECAUTIONS

If you're hitting the trails, you'll want to carry water with you, wear sturdy shoes (hiking boots are best), and have a hat and sunscreen handy. ⚠ Check weather reports before you start out; especially in late fall and winter, thunderstorms can send townspeople running for cover and make the shelterless trails slippery and dangerous. Rain in October and November can cause landslides and close the trails. Note that the lesser-used trails aren't as well maintained as Trail No. 2. If you're undertaking the full Trail No. 1 hike, bring something to snack on as well as your water bottle.

ADMISSION

Entrance tickets for use of the trails are available at ticket booths located at the start of each section of Trail No. 2, and at information offices in the Levanto, Monterosso, Vernazza, Corniglia, Manarola, Riomaggiore, and La Spezia train stations.

A one-day pass costs €5, which includes a trail map and a general information leaflet. Information about local train and boat schedules is also available from the information offices.

Working Cinque Terre's vertical vineyards

GETTING HERE AND AROUND

The local train on the Genoa–La Spezia line stops at each of the Cinque Terre, and runs approximately every 30 minutes. Tickets for each leg of the journey (€1.30) are available at the five train stations. In Corniglia, the only one of the Cinque Terre that isn't at sea level, a shuttle service (€1) is provided for those who don't wish to climb (or descend) the hundred-or-so steps that link the train station with the cliff-top town.

Along the Cinque Terre coast two ferry lines operate. From June to September, Golfo Paradiso runs from Genoa and Camogli to Monterosso al Mare and Vernazza. The smaller, but more frequent, Golfo dei Poeti stops at each village from Lerici (east of Riomaggiore) to Monterosso, with the exception of Corniglia, four times a day. A one-day ticket costs €22.

WHEN TO GO

The ideal times to see the Cinque Terre are September and May, when the weather is mild and the summer tourist season isn't in full swing.

SWIMMING & BEACHES

Each town has something that passes for a beach, but there are only two options where you'll find both sand and decent swimming. The more accessible is in Monterosso, opposite the train station; it's equipped with chairs, umbrellas, and snack bars. The other is the secluded, swimwear-optional Guvano Beach, between Corniglia and Vernazza. To reach it from the Corniglia train station, bypass the steps leading up to the village, instead following signs to an abandoned train tunnel. Ring a bell at the tunnel's entrance, and the gate will automatically open; after a dimly lit 10-minute walk, you'll emerge at the beach. Both beaches have a nominal admission fee.

Monterosso al Mare

THE TOWNS

Riomaggiore

At the eastern end of the Cinque Terre, Riomaggiore is built into a river gorge (thus the name, which means "river major") and is easily accessible from La Spezia by train or car. It has a tiny harbor protected by large slabs of alabaster and marble, which serve as as tanning beds for sunbathers, as well as being the site of several outdoor cafes with fine views. According to legend, settlement of Riomaggiore dates far back to the 8th century, when Greek religious refugees came here to escape persecution by the Byzantine emperor.

Manarola

The enchanting pastel houses of Manarola spill down a steep hill overlooking a spectacular turquoise swimming cove and a bustling harbor. The whole town is built on black rock. Above the town, ancient terraces still protect abundant vineyards and olive trees. This village is the center of the wine and olive oil production of the region, and its streets are lined with shops selling local products.

Corniglia

The buildings, narrow lanes, and stairways of Corniglia are strung together amid vineyards high on the cliffs; on a clear day views of the entire coastal strip are excellent. The high perch and lack of harbor make this farming community the most remote of the Cinque Terre. On a pretty pastel square sits the 14th-century church of **San Pietro**. The rose window of marble imported from Carrara is impressive, particularly considering the work required to get it here. ⊠ *Main Sq.* ☎ *0187/3235582* ⊙ *Wed. 4–6, Sun. 10–noon.*

Vernazza

With its narrow streets and small squares, Vernazza is arguably the most charming of the five towns. Because it has the best access to the sea, it became wealthier than its neighbors—as evidenced by the elaborate arcades, loggias, and marblework. The village's pink, slate-roof houses and colorful squares contrast with the remains of the medieval fort and castle, including two towers, in the old town. The Romans first inhabited this rocky spit of land in the 1st century.

Today Vernazza has a fairly lively social scene. It's a great place to refuel with a hearty seafood lunch or linger in a café between links of the hike on Trail No. 2.

Monterosso al Mare

Beautiful beaches, rugged cliffs, crystal-clear turquoise waters, and plentiful small hotels and restaurants make Monterosso al Mare, the largest of the Cinque Terre villages (population 1,730), the busiest in midsummer. The village center bustles high on a hillside. Below, connected by stone steps, are the port and seaside promenade, where there are boats for hire. The medieval tower, Aurora, on the hills of the Cappuccini, separates the ancient part of the village from the more modern part. The village is encircled by hills covered with vineyards and olive groves, and by a forest of scrubby bushes and small trees.

Monterosso has the most festivals of the five villages, starting with the Lemon Feast on the Saturday preceding Ascension Sunday, followed by the Flower Festival of Corpus Christi, celebrated yearly on the second Sunday after Pentecost. During the afternoon, the streets and alleyways of the *centro storico* (historic center) are decorated with thousands of colorful flower petals set in beautiful designs that the evening procession passes over. Finally, the Salted Anchovy and Olive Oil Festival takes place each year during the second weekend of September.

Thursday, the **market** attracts mingled crowds of tourists and villagers from along the coast to shop for everything from pots and pans and underwear to fruits, vegetables, and fish. Often a few stands sell local art and crafts as well as olive oil and wine. ⊠ *Old town center* ☉ *Thurs. 8–1.*

The **Chiesa di San Francesco**, was built in the 12th century in the Ligurian Gothic style. Its distinctive black stripes and marble rose window make it one of the most photographed sites in the Cinque Terre. ⊠ *Piazza Garibaldi* ☏ *No phone* ✉ *Free* ☉ *Daily 9–1 and 4–7.*

Main Square, Vernazza

WHERE TO EAT AND STAY

From June through September, reservations are essential if you plan to stay in a hotel or B&B here. *Affitacamere* (rooms for rent in private homes) are a more modest alternative, often indicated by a simple sign on the front door. At agencies in Riomaggiore and Monterosso you can book officially licensed affitacamere. Rooms run the gamut; arrive early for a good selection.

Riomaggiore

$$–$$$ ✕ **La Lanterna.** Chalkboards in front of this small trattoria by the harbor list the day's selection of fresh fish; the set-up seems modest, but this is arguably the finest restaurant in the Cinque Terre. In winter, Chef Massimo teaches at the Culinary Academy in Switzerland; he always returns with new ideas for his menu. When available, *cozze ripiene* (stuffed mussels) shouldn't be missed. Other offerings may be a touch exotic, such sting ray with ligurian herbs. ⊠ *Via San Giacomo 10* ☎ *0187/920589* ▭ *AE, DC, MC, VC* ☻ *Closed Jan and 2 wks in Nov.*

Manarola

$$$ ▦ **La Torretta.** A welcome retreat after a day of exploring, this boutique accommodation has well-appointed rooms, most with sea views. The hotel has many nice touches such as a free aperitivo (aperitif) at sunset, a solarium, and iPod docking stations. **Pros:** head and shoulders above most accommodations in the area; lovely views. **Cons:** five- to ten-minute walk to the reception. ⊠ *Via Volto 20, 19017* ☎ *0187/920327* 🖶 *0187/920678* ⊕ *www.torrettas. com* 📑 *4 rooms, 5 suites* ♿ *In-room: a/c (some), safe, refrigerator, Wi-Fi. In-hotel: bar* ▭ *AE, DC, MC, V* ☻ *Closed Nov.–mid-Mar.* ¶◯ *BP.*

Corniglia

$–$$ ✕▦ **Cecio.** On the outskirts of Corniglia, many of the spotless rooms at the family-run Cecio have spectacular views of the town. The same memorable vista can be enjoyed from the hotel's restaurant, which serves inexpensive and well-prepared local seafood dishes. Try the delicious lasagna with pesto sauce as a first course. ⊠ *Via Serra 58, 19010, toward Vernazza* ☎ *0187/812043* 🖶 *0187/812138* 📑 *12 rooms* ♿ *Restaurant; no a/c, no room phones, no TV in some rooms* ▭ *DC, MC, V* ¶◯ *BP.*

Vernazza

$$$ ✕ **Bel Forte.** High above the sea in one of Vernazza's remaining stone towers is this unique restaurant serving typical Cinque Terre dishes. The prices are high, but it's worth it. People come from all over Liguria for Bel Forte's famous stuffed mussels and insalata di polpo (octopus salad). The setting is magnificent. ⊠ *Via Guidoni 42* ☎ *0187/812222* ▭ *AE, DC, MC, V* ☻ *Closed Tues. and Nov.–Easter.*

DID YOU KNOW?

Tiny Manarola is the best spot for purchasing the wine and olive oil produced in the Cinque Terre.

$$–$$$ ✕ **Gambero Rosso.** Relax on Vernazza's main square at this fine trattoria looking out at a church. Enjoy such delectable dishes as shrimp salad, vegetable torte, and squid-ink risotto. The creamy pesto, served atop spaghetti, is some of the best in the area. End your meal with Cinque Terre's own *sciacchetrà*, a dessert wine served with semisweet biscotti. Don't drink it out of the glass—dip the biscotti in the wine instead. ✉ *Piazza Marconi 7* ☎ *0187/812265* ▭ *AE, DC, MC, V* ⊙ *Closed Mon. Jan. and Feb.*

$$$ ✕🔲 **La Malà.** A cut above other lodging options in the Cinque Terre, this family-run B&B has only four rooms, and they fill up quickly. The rooms are small but well equipped, with flat screen TVs, a/c, marble showers, and comfortable bedding. Two of the rooms have sea views; the other two face the port of Vernazza. There's a shared terrace literally suspended over the Mediterranean. Book early! ✉ *Giovanni Battista 29, 19018* ☎ *334/2875718* ⊕ *www.lamala.it* ↪ *4 rooms* ⌂ *In-room: safe, refrigerator, satellite TV, hairdryer, tea & coffee maker.* ▭ *AE, DC, MC, V* ⊙ *Closed Jan. 10–Mar.*

Monterosso al Mare

★ **$$$** ✕ **Miky.** Specialties here are anything involving seafood. The *insalata di mare* (seafood salad), with squid and fish, is more than tasty; so are the grilled fish and any pasta with seafood. Miky has a beautiful little garden in the back, perfect for lunch on a sunny day. ✉ *Via Fegina 104* ☎ *0187/817608* ▭ *AE, DC, MC, V* ⊙ *Closed Nov. and Dec., and Tues. Sept.–July.*

$ ✕ **Enoteca Internazionale.** Located on the main street in centro, this wine bar offers a large variety of vintages, both local from further afield, plus delicious light fare; its umbrella-covered patio is a perfect spot to recuperate after a day of hiking. The owner, Susanna, is a certified sommelier who's always forthcoming with helpful suggestions on local wines. ✉ *Via Roma 62* ☎ *0187/817278* ▭ *AE, MC, V* ⊙ *Closed Tues., Jan–Mar.*

$$ ✕🔲 **Il Giardino Incantato.** This small B&B in the historic center of Monterosso oozes comfort and old-world charm. The building dates back to the 16th century and still maintains its wood beam ceiling and stone walls. Each room has been impeccably restored with modern amenities. Breakfast is served either in your room on request or in their lovely private garden under the lemon trees. The owner, Maria Pia, goes out of her way to make you feel at home and whips up a fabulous frittata for breakfast. ✉ *Via Mazzini 18, 19016* ☎ *0185/818315* ⊕ *www.ilgiardinoincantato.net* ↪ *3 rooms, 1 junior suite* ⌂ *In-room: safe, refrigerator, satellite TV, hairdryer, tea & coffee maker. In-hotel: private garden.* ▭ *AE, DC, MC.*

$$ 🔲 **Porto Roca.** The Cinque Terre's only "high-end" hotel is perched on the famous terraced cliffs, hovering over the magnificent sea below, and thankfully removed from the crowds. The hotel has an old-fashioned feel but the large balconies and panoramic views make it all worth it. There is also a nice restaurant serving very good Ligurian cuisine. Avoid the back rooms as they are dark and have no view. Pros: unobstructed sea views; tranquil position. Cons: some of the rooms could use updating; back-facing rooms can be a bit dark. ✉ *Via Volto 20, 19017* ☎ *0187/920327* 🖨 *0187/920678* ⊕ *www.torrettas.com* ↪ *4 rooms, 5 suites* ⌂ *In-room: a/c (some), safe, refrigerator, Wi-Fi. In-hotel: bar* ▭ *AE, DC, MC, V* ⊙ *Closed Nov.–mid-Mar.* ⦿❘ *BP.*

5

Between Florence and Venice

HIGHLIGHTS OF EMILIA-ROMAGNA
AND THE VENETO, PLUS MILAN

WORD OF MOUTH

"Verona is a wonderful walking town. We took many walks down
the upscale Via Mazzini to the Piazza Erbe, the heart of the city."
—basingstoke2

WELCOME TO EMILIA–ROMAGNA AND THE VENETO

TOP REASONS TO GO

★ **The signature foods of Emilia-Romagna:** This region's food—the *prosciutto crudo*, the Parmigiano-Reggiano, the balsamic vinegar, and perhaps above all, the pasta—alone makes the trip to Italy worthwhile.

★ **Mosaics that take your breath away:** The intricate tile creations in Ravenna's Mausuleo di Galla Placidia, in brilliantly well-preserved primary colors, depict pastoral scenes that transport you to another age.

★ **Villa Barbaro in Maser:** Master architect Palladio's graceful creation meets Veronese's splendid paintings in a one-time-only collaboration.

★ **Giotto's frescoes in the Capella degli Scrovegni:** At this chapel in Padua, Giotto's innovations in painting technique helped to launch the Renaissance.

★ **Opera in Verona's ancient arena:** Even if the music doesn't move you, the spectacle will.

1 Bologna. In Emilia–Romagna's cultural and intellectual center, rows of street arcades wind around ancient university buildings, grandiose towers—and some of the best restaurants in Italy.

2 Ferrara. This wonderfully characteristic medieval city north of Bologna is, among other things, home to the world's oldest wine bar, Osteria Al Brindisi, where they've been pouring since 1435.

3 Ravenna. It's worth a detour off the path between Florence and Venice to visit this well-preserved city with its remarkable mosaics— glittering treasures left from Byzantine rule.

4 Padua. Bustling with bicycles and lined with frescoes, Padua has long been a cultural center of northern Italy. It's home to Europe's second-oldest university (after the one in Bologna), and you can feel the youthful student energy everywhere.

Milan
Verona
Modena
Pavullo
Mar Ligure
Lucca
TOSCANA
Pisa
Empoli

0   20 mi
0   20 km

Ravenna

GETTING ORIENTED

Stretching between Florence and Venice, the region of Emilia-Romagna is Italy's bread basket. The flat expanses of farmland can't compete with the spectacular natural beauty of Tuscany and Umbria; the appeal instead lies in its prosperous, highly cultured midsize cities, where the locals seem to have mastered the art of living—and especially eating—well. The same holds true when you enter the Veneto region: lined up in a row to the west of Venice are three beautiful, artistically rich cities that compete for your attention.

5

5 Vicenza. The elegant art city of Vicenza, nestled on the green plain reaching inland from Venice's lagoon, is most noted for its palaces designed by the great 16th-century architect Andrea Palladio.

6 Verona. Shakespeare placed Romeo, Juliet, and a couple of gentlemen in Verona, one of the oldest, best-preserved, and most beautiful cities in Italy. Try to catch *Aida* at the gigantic Roman arena.

EMILIA–ROMAGNA AND THE VENETO PLANNER

Making the Most of Your Time

Each city in this chapter has at least one world-class sight that's reason enough to merit a visit, but once you've arrived, you're likely to be won over by the cities as a whole. Many travelers come to Italy to see Florence or Venice, only to fall in love with Bologna or Vicenza.

Bologna makes sense as a base in Emilia–Romagna—there's a lot to do in the city, and you can make easy day trips east to Ravenna and Ferrara.

In the Veneto, Padua, Vicenza, and Verona are all within day-trip distance of Venice. Or, if staying in Venice turns you off, you can make one of these cities your base and visit La Serenissima during the day.

Typical Travel Times	
Hours by Car/Train	
Florence–Venice	3:30/2:05
Florence–Bologna	1:30/1:00
Bologna–Ravenna	1:00/1:15
Venice–Bologna	2:15/1:25
Venice–Padua	1:15/0:30
Venice–Vicenza	1:30/0:45
Venice–Verona	2:00/1:30

Getting Around

The cities in these regions are connected by well-maintained highways and an efficient railway system. A car provides added freedom, but it's not essential, and it can be a headache. (See below.)

Going by Car: Italy's major north–south highway, A1, runs from Florence to Bologna, then makes a left and continues to Milan. From Bologna, A13 runs north through Ferrara to Padua. If you're driving from Florence to Venice and want to see the cities of the Veneto, continue on A1 past Bologna to A22 (just beyond Modena), which takes you north to Verona. From there A4 leads to Vicenza, Padua, and Venice.

Going by Train: There's frequent train service between the cities covered here. Travel times vary depending on the type of train: Eurostars are the fastest; avoid regional trains, which stop at every town along the line.

The Challenges of City Driving

When deciding whether to rent a car, keep in mind that driving in Italian cities is a trial: streets are difficult to navigate, congestion can be fierce, and drivers aren't known for their patience. In addition, Padua, Vicenza, and Verona sporadically limit car access—sometimes permitting only cars with plates ending in an even number on even days, odd on odd, or prohibiting cars altogether on weekends. There's no central source for such information; the best strategy is to check with your hotel. In Emilia–Romagna, Bologna's historic center is closed to cars during the day, and the center of Ravenna is closed to cars at all times.

Getting Here

Aeroporto Malpensa, 50 km (31 mi) northwest of Milan, is the major northern Italian hub for intercontinental flights and also sees substantial European and domestic traffic. Venice's **Aeroporto Marco Polo** also serves international destination, mainly from other European cities, though there are direct flights from New York's JFK.

There are regional airports in Bologna and Verona, and Milan has a secondary airport, Linate—all three can be reached on connecting flights from within Italy and from other European cities. If you fly into Malpensa but you don't plan to spend time in Milan, you can also continue your trip by train, using the Italian national rail system, **Ferrovie dello Stato** (☎ 892021 toll-free within Italy ⊕ www. trenitalia.com). Shuttle buses run three times an hour between Malpensa and Milan's main train station, Stazione Centrale; the trip takes about 75 minutes, depending on traffic. Note that the Malpensa Express Train, which takes 40 minutes, delivers you to Cadorna station, from which you have to take the metro or a taxi across town to reach Stazione Centrale.

Finding a Place to Stay

The hotels in these regions are run with uncommon efficiency; even the smallest and most remote places usually have high standards of quality and service. Many cater to the business traveler, but there are smaller, more intimate options as well. It's a trend for hotels to renovate and subsequently hike their prices, but good low-cost lodgings can still be found. Ask about weekend discounts, which are often available at business-oriented hotels. It's always smart to book in advance—the regions host many fairs and conventions that can fill up hotels even during low season.

WHAT IT COSTS IN EUROS

	¢	$	$$	$$$	$$$$
Restaurants	under €20	€20–€30	€30–€45	€45–€65	over €65
Hotels	under €75	€75–€125	€125–€200	€200–€300	over €300

Restaurant prices are for a first course (*primo*), second course (*secondo*), and dessert (*dolce*). Hotel prices are for two people in a standard double room in high season, including tax and service.

When to Go

The ideal times to visit are late spring and early summer (May and June) and in early fall (September and October). Summers tend to be hot and humid—though if you're an opera buff, it's worth tolerating the heat in order to see a performance at the Arena di Verona (where the season runs from July through September).

Winter is a good time to avoid travel to these regions: although the dense fog can be beautiful, it makes for bad driving conditions, and wet, bonechilling cold isn't unusual from November through March.

Planning Ahead

Three top sights in the region demand advance planning:

Reservations are required to see the Giotto frescoes in Padua's **Cappella degli Scrovegni**— though if there's space, you can "reserve" on the spot. On the outskirts of Vicenza, Palladio's **Villa La Rotonda** is open to the public only on Wednesday from mid-March through October. (Hours for visiting the grounds are less restrictive.) Another important Palladian villa, **Villa Barbaro** near Maser, is open from March through October on Tuesday, Saturday, and Sunday afternoons. For the rest of the year, it's open only on weekends.

5

EMILIA-ROMAGNA

Updated
by Patricia
Rucidlo

THE REGION OF EMILIA–ROMAGNA, made up predominantly of the Po River plain, doesn't have the drop-dead good looks that you'll find in many Italian landscapes. Instead, it wins your heart through your stomach. Many of Italy's signature food products come from here, including Parmigiano-Reggiano cheese (aka Parmesan), prosciutto di Parma, and balsamic vinegar. The pasta is considered Italy's finest—a reputation the region's chefs earn every day. But food isn't Emilia-Romagna's be-all and end-all. Attractive cities dot the map: Bologna is the principal cultural and intellectual center, with rows of street arcades winding through grandiose towers. The mosaics in Ravenna are glittering treasures left from the era of Byzantine rule, and Ferrara is a meticulously maintained medieval city with a youthful spirit.

BOLOGNA

Bologna, a city rich with cultural jewels, has long been one of the best-kept secrets in northern Italy. Tourists in the know can bask in the shadow of its leaning medieval towers, devour the city's wonderful food, and spend a little less money than elsewhere.

The charm of the *centro storico* (historical center), with its red-arcaded sidewalks and passageways, can be attributed to wise city counselors who, at the beginning of the 13th century, decreed that roads could not be built without *portici* (porticoes). Were these counselors to return to town eight centuries later, they would marvel at how little has changed.

The feeling of a university town permeates the air in Bologna. Its population is about 373,000, and it feels young and lively in a way that many other Italian cities do not. It also feels full of Italians in a way that many other towns, thronged with tourists, do not. Known as "Bologna the Fat" from as early as the Middle Ages, the town's agricultural prosperity led to a well-fed population, one that survives into the 21st century. Bolognese food is, arguably, the best in Italy. With its sublime food, lively spirit, and largely undiscovered art, Bologna is well worth a visit.

GETTING HERE

Frequent train service from Florence to Bologna makes getting here easy. Eurostar and Intercity trains run several times an hour, and take about an hour. Trains from Milan run as frequently, and take about 1¾ hours on the Eurostar, two hours on the Intercity, and just one hour on the high-speed Alta Velocità. The historic center is an easy and interesting walk from the station. If you're driving from Florence, take the A1, exiting onto the A14 and then catching the RA1 to Uscita 7–Bologna Centrale. The trip takes about an hour. From Milan, take the A1, exiting to the A14 as you near the city; from there, take the A13 and exit at Bologna, then follow the RA1 to Uscita 7–Bologna Centrale. The trip is just under three hours.

VISITOR INFORMATION

Bologna tourism offices (✉ *Aeroporto Guglielmo Marconi, Via Triumvirato 84* ✈ *10 km [6 mi] northwest of Bologna* ☎ *051/239660* ✉ *Stazione Centrale* ☎ *051/239660* ✉ *Piazza Maggiore 1* ☎ *051/239660* ⊕ *www.bolognaturismo.info*).

EXPLORING BOLOGNA

Piazza Maggiore and the adjacent Piazza del Nettuno are the historic centers of the city. Arranged around these two squares are the imposing Basilica di San Petronio, the massive Palazzo Comunale, the Palazzo del Podestà, the Palazzo Re Enzo, and the Fontana del Nettuno—one of the most visually harmonious groupings of public buildings in the country. From here, sights that aren't on one of the piazzas are but a short walk away, along delightful narrow cobbled streets or under the ubiquitous arcades that double as municipal umbrellas. Take at least a full day to explore Bologna; it's compact and lends itself to easy exploration, but there is plenty to see.

TOP ATTRACTIONS

2 Basilica di San Petronio. Construction on this cathedral began in 1390, and work is still in progress on this vast building some 600 years later. It's not finished yet, as you can see: the wings of the transept are missing and the facade is only partially decorated, lacking most of the marble facade originally intended to adorn it. The main doorway was carved in 1425 by the great Sienese master, Jacopo della Quercia. Above the center of the door is a Madonna and Child flanked by Saints Ambrose and Petronius, the city's patrons. Michelangelo, Giulio Romano, and Andrea Palladio (among others) submitted designs for the facade, which were all eventually rejected.

The interior of the basilica is huge: the Bolognesi had planned an even bigger church—you can still see the columns erected to support the larger church outside the east end—but had to tone down construction when the university seat was established next door in 1561. The **Museo di San Petronio** contains models showing how the church was originally intended to look. The most important art in the church is in the fourth chapel on the left; these frescoes by Giovanni di Modena date from 1410–15. ✉ *Piazza Maggiore* ☎ *051/225442* ☜ *Free* ☉ *Church: Apr.–Sept., daily 7:45–12:30 and 3:30–6; Oct.–Mar., daily 7:30–1 and 2:30–6. Museum: Weekdays 9:30–12:30 and 3–5:30, Sat. 9:30–12:30 and 3–4:30, Sun. 3–5:30.*

Fontana del Nettuno. Sculptor Giambologna's elaborate 1563–66 baroque fountain and monument to Neptune occupying Piazza Nettuno has been aptly nicknamed *Il Gigante* (The Giant). Its exuberantly sensual mermaids and undraped god of the sea drew fire when it was constructed, but not enough, apparently, to dissuade the populace from using the fountain as a public washing stall for centuries. ✉ *Piazza Nettuno, next to Palazzo Re Enzo, Piazza Maggiore area.*

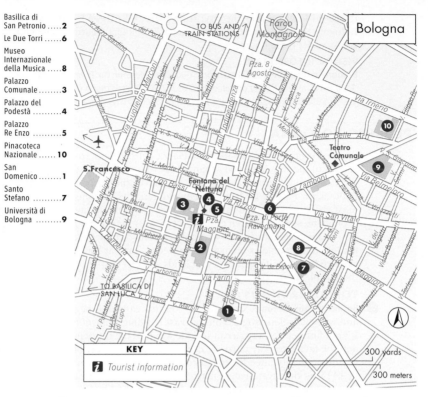

Bologna

KEY

ℹ *Tourist information*

6 **Le Due Torri.** Two landmark towers, mentioned by Dante in *The Inferno*,
★ stand side by side in the compact Piazza di Porta Ravegnana. Every
family of importance had a tower as a symbol of prestige and power,
and as a potential fortress; only 60 remain out of more than 200 that
once presided over the city. **Torre Garisenda** (from the late 11th century), which tilts 10 feet off perpendicular, was shortened to 165 feet
in the 1300s and is now closed to visitors. **Torre degli Asinelli** (circa
1109) is 320 feet tall and leans 7½ feet. If you're up to a serious physi-
cal challenge—and you're not claustrophobic—you may want to climb
the 500 narrow, wooden steps to get to the view over Bologna. ⊠ *Piazza di Porta Ravegnana, east of Piazza Maggiore* 🎟 €3 ⊙ *Torre degli
Asinelli: daily 9–5.*

7 **Santo Stefano.** This splendid and unusual basilica actually contains
☾ between four and seven connected churches (authorities differ). A 4th-
Fodor's Choice century temple dedicated to Isis was originally on this site, though much
★ of what you see dates from the 10th through the 12th century. The oldest
existing building is **Santi Vitale e Agricola,** parts of which date from the
5th century. The exquisite beehive-shape San Sepolcro contains a Nativity scene much loved by Bologna's children, who come at Christmastime
to pay their respects to the Christ Child. Just outside the church, which
probably dates from the 5th century with later alterations, is the **Cortile**

di Pilato (Pilate's Courtyard), named for the basin in the center. It's said that Pontius Pilate washed his hands in this basin after condemning Christ—despite the fact that it was probably crafted around the 8th century. Also in the building is a museum displaying various medieval religious works with a shop selling honey, shampoos, and jams made by the monks. ⊠ *Via Santo Stefano 24, Piazza Santo Stefano, University area* ☎ *051/223256* ⊙ *Daily 9–noon and 3:30–6.*

9 Università di Bologna. Take a stroll through the streets of the university area, a jumble of buildings, some dating as far back as the 15th century and most to the 17th and 18th. The neighborhood, as befits a college town, is full of bookshops, coffee bars, and inexpensive restaurants. None of them are particularly distinguished, but they're all characteristic of student life in the city. Try eating at the *mensa universitaria* (cafeteria) if you want to strike up a conversation with local students (most speak English). Political slogans and sentiments are scrawled on walls all around the university and tend to be ferociously leftist, sometimes juvenile, often entertaining. Among the university museums, the most interesting are the **Musei di Palazzo Poggi,** which display scientific instruments and paleontological, botanical, and university-related artifacts. ⊠ *Via Zamboni 33, University area* ☎ *051/2099610* ⊕ *www. museopalazzopoggi.unibo.it* ⊠ *Free* ⊙ *Tues.–Fri. 10–1 and 2–4, weekends 10:30–1:30 and 2:30–5:30.*

WORTH NOTING

8 Museo Internazionale della Musica. The music museum in the spectacular Palazzo Aldini Sanguinetti, with its 17th- and 18th-century frescoes, offers among its exhibits a 1606 harpsichord and a collection of beautiful musical manuscripts dating from the 1500s. ⊠ *Strada Maggiore 34, University area* ☎ *051/2757711* ⊕ *www.museomusicabologna.it* ⊠ *Free* ⊙ *Oct.–July, Tues.–Fri. 10–1, weekends 10–5.*

3 Palazzo Comunale. A mélange of building styles and constant modifications characterize this huge palace dating from the 13th to 15th century. When Bologna was an independent city-state, this was the seat of government, a function it still serves today. Over the door is a statue of Bologna-born Pope Gregory XIII (reigned 1572–85), most famous for reorganizing the calendar. There are good views from the upper stories of the palace. The first-floor **Sala Rossa** (Red Room) is open on advance request and during some exhibitions, while the **Sala del Consiglio Comunale** (City Council Hall) is open to the public for a few hours in the late morning. The old stock exchange, part of the Palazzo Comunale, which you enter from Piazza Nettuno, has been turned into a library, the **Sala Borsa** (⊕ *www.bibliotecasalaborsa.it*), which has an impressive interior courtyard. Within the palazzo there are also two museums. The **Collezioni Comunali d'Arte** exhibits paintings from the Middle Ages as well as some Renaissance works by Luca Signorelli (circa 1445–1523) and Tintoretto (1518–94). The **Museo Giorgio Morandi** (⊕ *www.museomorandi.it*) is dedicated to the 20th-century still-life artist Giorgio Morandi; in addition to his paintings, there's a re-creation of his studio and living space. Underground caves and the foundations of the old cathedral can be visited by appointment made through the tourist office. ⊠ *Piazza Maggiore 6* ☎ *051/203111 Palazzo,*

EMILIA-ROMAGNA THROUGH THE AGES

Ancient History. Emilia-Romagna owes its beginnings to a road. In 187 BC the Romans built the Via Aemilia, a long road running northwest from the Adriatic port of Rimini to the central garrison town of Piacenza, and it was along this central spine that the primary towns of the region developed.

Despite the unifying factor of what came to be known as the Via Emilia, the region has had a fragmented history. Its eastern part, roughly the area from Faenza to the coast, known as Romagna, first looked to the Byzantine east and then to Rome for art, political power, and, some say, national character. The western part, Emilia, from Bologna to Piacenza, looked more to the north with its practice of self-government and dissent.

Bologna was founded by the Etruscans and eventually came under the influence of the Roman Empire. The Romans established a garrison here, renaming the old Etruscan settlement Bononia. It was after the fall of Rome that the region began its fragmentation. Romagna, centered in Ravenna, was ruled from Constantinople. Ravenna eventually became the capital of the empire in the west in the 5th century, passing to papal control in the 8th century.

Even today, the city is still filled with reminders of two centuries of Byzantine rule.

Family Ties. The other cities of the region, from the Middle Ages on, became the fiefdoms of important noble families—the Este in Ferrara and Modena, the Pallavicini in Piacenza, and the Bentivoglio in Bologna. Today all these cities bear the marks of their noble patrons. When in the 16th century the papacy managed to exert its power over the entire region, some of these cities were divided among the papal families—hence the stamp of the Farnese family on Parma, Piacenza, and Ferrara.

A Leftward Tilt. Bologna and Emilia-Romagna have established a robust tradition of rebellion and dissent. The Italian socialist movement was born in the region, as was Benito Mussolini—in keeping with the political climate of his home state, he was a firebrand socialist during the early part of his career. Despite having Mussolini as a native son, Emilia-Romagna did not take to fascism: it was here that the antifascist resistance was born, and during World War II the region suffered terribly at the hands of the Fascists and the Nazis.

051/203526 Collezioni, 051/203332 Museo ▤ Free, except during special art exhibitions ☾ Sala del Consiglio Comunale: Tues.–Sat. 10–1. Sala Borsa: Mon. 2:30–8, Tues.–Fri. 10–8, Sat. 10–7. Collezioni and Museo: Tues.–Fri. 9–6:30, weekends 10–6:30.

❹ Palazzo del Podestà. This classic Renaissance palace facing the Basilica di San Petronio was erected in 1484, and attached to it is the soaring **Torre dell'Arengo.** The bells in the tower have rung whenever the city has celebrated, mourned, or called its citizens to arms. ⊠ *Piazza Nettuno, Piazza Maggiore area* ☎ *051/224500* ☾ *During exhibitions only.*

⑤ Palazzo Re Enzo. Built in 1244, this palace became home to King Enzo of Sardinia, who was imprisoned here in 1249 after he was captured during the fierce battle of Fossalta. He died here 23 years later in 1272. The palace has other macabre associations: common criminals received last rites in the tiny courtyard chapel before being executed in Piazza Maggiore. The courtyard is worth peeking into, but the palace merely houses government offices. ⊠ *Piazza Re Enzo, Piazza Maggiore area* ☎ *051/224500* ⊗ *During exhibitions only.*

⑩ Pinacoteca Nazionale. Bologna's principal art gallery contains many works by the immortals of Italian painting spanning the 13th to the 19th century. Its prize possession is the famous *Ecstasy of St. Cecilia* by Raphael (1483–1520). There's also a beautiful polyptych by Giotto (1267–1337), as well as *Madonna and Child with Saints Margaret, Jerome, and Petronio* by Parmigianino; note the rapt eye contact between St. Margaret and the Christ Child. ⊠ *Via delle Belle Arti 56, University area* ☎ *051/4209411* ⊕ *www.pinacotecabologna.it* ⊠ *€4* ⊗ *Tues.–Sun. 9–7.*

❶ San Domenico. The tomb of St. Dominic, who died here in 1221, is called the **Arca di San Domenico** and is found in this church in the sixth chapel on the right. Many artists participated in its decoration, notably Niccolò di Bari, who was so proud of his contribution that he changed his name to Niccolò dell'Arca to recall this famous work. The young Michelangelo (1475–1564) carved the angel on the right. In the right transept of the church is a tablet marking the last resting place of the hapless King Enzo, the Sardinian ruler imprisoned in the Palazzo Re Enzo. The attached museum contains religious relics. ⊠ *Piazza San Domenico 13, off Via Garibaldi, south of Piazza Maggiore* ☎ *051/6400411* ⊗ *Church: daily 8–12:30 and 3:30–6:30. Museum: weekdays 10–noon and 3:30–6, Sat. 9:30–noon and 3:30–5:30, Sun. 3:30–5:30.*

OFF THE BEATEN PATH

Basilica di San Luca. A spectacular one-hour walk (or 10-minute drive) leads uphill from Porta Saragozza to the Basilica di San Luca (follow Via Saragozza), an impressive church that has perched dramatically atop Monte della Guardia since 1160. The road is arcaded the entire way; you walk beneath 666 arches before arriving at the round basilica, which has a famous icon of the Madonna. But it's the sweeping views of the Emilian countryside and city from the 990-foot altitude that make the trip worthwhile—most of all in autumn, when the leaves of the hills on one side play off the blazing red rooftops of Bologna on the other. If you go by car (or, better yet, scooter), ask for directions at the church and take an unmarked route back through the hills, winding past rustic Emilian restaurants before reentering the city center through Porta San Mammolo (don't attempt this alternate route on foot—it's too far to walk). ⊠ *Via San Luca 36 3½ km (2 mi) southwest of Bologna* ☎ *051/6142339* ⊗ *Oct.–Feb., Mon.–Sat. 7–12:30 and 2:30–4:30, Sun. 7–5; Mar., Mon.–Sat. 7–12:30 and 2:30–6, Sun. 7–6; Apr.–Sept., Mon.–Sat. 7–12:30 and 2:30–7, Sun. 7–7.*

Museo del Patrimonio Industriale. Offering a refreshing change from art museums and churches, this museum's displays document the development of Bologna's industries and industrial technologies from the 16th to 21st century, including fascinating examples of antique machinery, scientific devices, and cars. ⊠ *Via della Beverara 123, northwest of city center* ☎ *051/6356611* ⊕ *www.comune.bologna.it/ patrimonioindustriale* ⊠ *Free* ☉ *Oct.–May, Tues.–Fri. 9–1, Sat. 9–1 and 3–6, Sun. 3–6; June–Sept., weekdays 9–1.*

WHERE TO EAT

$
EMILIAN
★
✕ **Da Cesari.** Just off Piazza Maggiore, this lovely, one-room restaurant has white tablecloths, dark wooden paneling, and wine bottle–lined walls. Genial host Paolino Cesari has been presiding over his restaurant since 1955, and both he and his staff go out of the way to make you feel at home. The food's terrific—if you're a lover of pork products, do try anything on the menu with *mora romagnola*. Paolino has direct contact with the people who raise this once nearly extinct type of porcine (referring to it as "my pig"). The meat is deep, highly flavorful, and makes divine salame, among other things. All the usual Bolognesi classics are here, as well as—in fall and winter—an inspired version of *scaloppa all Petroniano* (veal cutlet with prosciutto and fontina) that arrives at the table smothered in white truffles. ⊠ *Via de' Carbonesi 8, south of Piazza Maggiore* ☎ *051/237710* ⚱ *Reservations essential* ⊟ *AE, DC, MC, V* ☉ *Closed Sun., Aug., and 1 wk in Jan.*

$$
EMILIAN
✕ **Da Gianni a la Vecia Bulagna.** Locals simply call it "da Gianni," and they fill these two unadorned rooms at lunch and at dinner. Though the decor is plain and unremarkable, it doesn't much matter—this place is all about food. The usual starters such as a tasty tortellini in brodo are on hand, as are daily specials such as gnocchi made with pumpkin, then sauced with melted cheese. *Bollito misto* (mixed meats boiled in a rich broth) is a fine option here, and the cotechino *con purè di patate* (a deliciously oily sausage with mashed potatoes) elevated to sublimity by the accompanying salsa verde. ⊠ *Via Clavature 18, Piazza Maggiore area* ☎ *051/229434* ⚱ *Reservations essential* ⊟ *AE, DC, MC, V.*

¢
ITALIAN
✕ **Divinis.** Wine bottles line the walls on both floors of this spot, testimony to its commitment to serving fine wines (by the glass and by the bottle). Terrific food accompanies the oenophilic splendor. Cheese and cured meat plates are on offer, as are secondi, which frequently change. Special events, such as wine tastings and tango dancing, happen throughout the week. An added plus is Divinis's continuous opening hours, a rarity in Italy; you could have a coffee at 11 AM or a glass of wine well after midnight. ⊠ *Via Battibecco 4/c, Piazza Maggiore* ☎ *051/2961502* ⚱ *Reservations essential* ⊟ *AE, DC, MC, V* ☉ *Closed Sun.*

$$
EMILIAN
★
✕ **Drogheria della Rosa.** Chef Emanuele Addone, who presides over his intimate little restaurant, hits the food markets every day and buys what looks good. This brings a seasonality to his exceptional menu; he sauces his tortelli stuffed with *squacquerone* and *stracchino* (two creamy, fresh cow's-milk cheeses) with artichokes, zucchini flowers, or mushrooms, depending on the time of year. In order to do this place justice, you need to come with an appetite—you won't want to skip a course. Kick off the proceedings with a glass of prosecco and a plate of *affettati misti*

(mixed cured meats, a local specialty). Among the secondi, the tender *filetto al balsamico* (filet mignon with marvelous balsamic vinegar sauce on top) is exquisite. So is the wine list. ⊠ *Via Cartoleria 10, University area* ☎ *051/222529* ⊕ *www.drogheriadellarosa.it* ▭ *AE, DC, MC, V* ⊗ *Closed Sun.*

$ ✕**Godot Wine Bar.** It's beloved by locals and visitors alike, perhaps

WINE BAR because the kitchen stays open until midnight. The long wine list is full of temptations, and is particularly strong on lesser-known local estates. The ever-changing menu has flights of fancy such as *polenta fresco con salmi di cervo* (creamy polenta in a venison sauce), vegetarian and vegan options, and a killer tagliatelle al ragù. Save room for the desserts, as they're not your typical options—try the chocolate flan with Szechuan peppercorns. ⊠ *Via Cartoleria 12, University area* ☎ *051/226315* ▭ *AE, MC, V* ⊗ *Closed Sun. and 3 wks in Aug.*

¢ ✕**Tamburini.** Two small rooms inside, and kegs and bar stools outside

WINE BAR make up this lively, packed little wine bar. At lunchtime, office workers swarm at the "bistrot self service" with remarkably tasty primi and secondi. After lunch, it becomes a wine bar with a vast array of selections by the glass and the bottle. The overwhelming plate of affettati misti is crammed with top-quality local ham products and succulent cheeses (including, sometimes, a goat Brie). An adjacent salumeria offers many wonderful things to take away. ⊠ *Via Drapperie 1, Piazza Maggiore area* ☎ *051/234726* ▭ *AE, MC, V* ⊗ *No dinner.*

$ ✕**Trattoria del Rosso.** The decor's nothing to write home about, with glar-

EMILIAN ing yellow walls and the oddly placed ceramic plate, but the place teems

★ with locals. The mostly young crowd chows down on delicious basic regional fare at rock-bottom prices. The nimble staff bearing multiple plates sashay neatly between the closely spaced tables delivering such standards as *crescentine con salumi e squacquerone* (deep-fried flour puffs with cured meats and soft cheese) and tortellini in brodo. This is the kind of place where there's always a line of hungry people outside waiting to get in, but where they don't glare at you if you only order a plate of pasta. Another reason, perhaps, why it's a favorite of university students. ⊠ *Via Augusto Righi 30, University area* ☎ *051/236730* ▭ *AE, DC, MC, V* ⊗ *Closed Thurs.*

WHERE TO STAY

$ ▦ **Albergo Centrale.** It began life as a pensione in 1875, but subsequent restructurings have comfortably brought the Albergo Centrale into the 21st century. Innkeeper Werter Guizzardi has been tending this eminently affordable, highly comfortable place since 1987. Rooms are simply furnished and, if you book one of the rooms facing the inner courtyard without a view, really quiet. Bathrooms are large by Italian standards. A copious buffet breakfast includes all the usual suspects like breads, yogurt, and cheese, but also local specialties such as mortadella. The location cannot be beat, as this place is a stone's throw from Piazza Maggiore. ⊠ *Via della Zecca 2, Piazza Maggiore* ☎ *051/225114* ⊕ *www.albergocentralebologna.it* ↪ *31 rooms, 26 rooms with bath* ⚘ *In-room: a/c, safe, refrigerator, Wi-Fi. In hotel: Wi-Fi hotspot, parking (paid), some pets allowed* ▭ *AE, DC, MC, V.*

Continued on page 324

EATING AND DRINKING WELL IN EMILIA-ROMAGNA

Italians rarely agree about anything, but most would say that the best food in the country is in Emilia-Romagna. Tortellini, fettuccine, Parmesan cheese, and balsamic vinegar are just a few of the Italian delicacies born here.

One of the beauties of Emilia-Romagna is that its exceptional food can be had without breaking the bank. Many trattorias serve up classic dishes, mastered over the centuries, at reasonable prices. Cutting-edge restaurants and wine bars are often more expensive; their inventive menus are full of *fantasia*—reinterpretations of the classics. For the budget-conscious, Bologna is a university town and has great places for cheap eats.

Between meals, you can sustain yourself with the region's famous sandwich, the *piadina*. It's made with pita-thin bread, usually filled with prosciutto or mortadella, cheese, and vegetables. It's put under the grill and served hot, with the cheese oozing at the sides. These addictive sandwiches can be savored at sit-down places or ordered to go.

THE REAL RAGÙ

Emilia-Romagna's signature dish is *tagliatelle al ragù* (flat noodles with meat sauce), known as "spaghetti Bolognese" everywhere else. This primo is on every menu, and no two versions are the same. The sauce starts in a sauté pan with pancetta or *guanciale* (unsmoked bacon made from the jowls), butter, and minced onions. Purists use nothing but beef, but some add sausage, veal, or chicken. Regular ministrations of broth are added, and sometimes wine, milk, or cream. After a couple of hours of cooking, the ragù is ready to be joined with pasta and Parmesan and brought to the table.

PORK PRODUCTS

It's not just mortadella and cured pork products like prosciutto and *culatello* that Emilia-Romagnans go crazy for—they're wild about the whole hog.

You'll frequently find *cotechino* and *zampone,* both secondi (second courses), on menus; cotechino, photo below, is a savory, thick, fresh sausage served with lentils on New Year's Day (the combination is said to augur well for the new year) and with mashed potatoes year-round. Zampone, a stuffed pig's foot, is redolent of garlic, and is deliciously fatty.

BOLLITO MISTO

The name means "mixed boil," and they do it exceptionally well in this part of Italy. According to Emilia-Romagnans, it was invented here (its true origins are up for grabs, as other northern Italians, especially from Milan and the Piedmont, would argue this point). Chicken, beef, tongue, and zampone are tossed into a stockpot and boiled; they are then removed from the broth and served with a fragrant *salsa verde* (green sauce), made green by parsley and spiced with anchovies, garlic, and capers. This simple yet rich dish is usually served with mashed potatoes on the side, and savvy diners will mix some of the piquant salsa verde into the potatoes as well.

STUFFED PASTA

Among the many Emilian variations on stuffed pasta, *tortellini* (pictured at left), are the smallest. *Tortelli* (photo upper right), and *cappellacci* are larger pasta "pillows," about the size of a brussels sprout, but with the same basic form as tortellini; they're often filled with pumpkin or spinach and cheese.

Tortelloni are, in theory, even bigger, although their sizes vary. Stuffed pastas are generally served simply, with melted butter, sage, and (what else?) Parmigiano-Reggiano cheese, or (in the case of tortellini) *in brodo* (in beef or chicken broth), which brings out the subtle richness of the filling.

WINES

Emilia-Romagna's wines accompany the region's fine food rather than vying with it for accolades. The best known is Lambrusco, a sparkling red produced on the Po Plain that has some admirers and many detractors. It's praised for its tartness and condemned for the same quality. The region's best wines include Sangiovese di Romagna, somewhat similar to Chianti, from the Romagnan hills, and Barbera, from the Colli Piacetini and Apennine foothills. Castelluccio, Bonzara, Zerbina, Leone Conti, and Tre Monti are among the region's top producers—keep an eye out for their bottles.

5

$$$$ ☆ **Art Hotel Novecento.** This swank place, inspired by the 1930s Viennese
★   Secession movement, is in a remarkably serene cul-de-sac just minutes
from Piazza Maggiore. Clean lines and elegant restraint are the hallmarks of the rooms, the lobby, and even the elevators, and equally
svelte, well-dressed people like to stay here. It's well worth the extra
€10 or so to upgrade from a basic double, as the rooms are that much
bigger. The copious breakfast includes eggs, and every evening the bar
hosts a happy hour. **Pros:** spacious single rooms ideal for solo travelers; friendly, capable concierge service. **Cons:** some standard doubles
are small. ✉ *Piazza Galileo 4/3i, Piazza Maggiore area* ☎ *051/7457311*
⊕ *www.bolognarthotels.it/novecento* ⇆ *24 rooms, 1 suite* ♿ *In-room:
safe, Wi-Fi. In-hotel: bar, bicycles, laundry service, Internet terminal,
Wi-Fi hotspot, parking (paid), some pets allowed* ⊟ *AE, DC, MC, V*
⊠| *BP.*

$$$$ ☆ **Art Hotel Orologio.** The location can't be beat: it's right around the
corner from Piazza Maggiore, tucked in a quiet little side street. Reception is on the ground floor, and a flight of stairs takes you up to the
second floor to the elevator and the charming breakfast room. The
rooms are mostly painted yellow, with hardwood floors, and some have
tremendous views of 14th-century Palazzo Comunale just across the
way. A couple of rooms are ideally suited to families, as they're spacious
and have extra beds. Do note that this hotel frequently has discounted
prices and other offers. **Pros:** central location; great views. **Cons:** short
flight of steps to elevator. ✉ *Via IV Novembre 10, Piazza Maggiore
area* ☎ *051/7457411* ⊕ *www.bolognarthotels.it/orologio* ⇆ *26 rooms,
65 suites, 1 apartment* ♿ *In-room: safe, Wi-Fi. In-hotel: restaurant,
bicycles, Internet terminal, Wi-Fi hotspot, parking (paid), some pets
allowed* ⊟ *AE, DC, MC, V* ⊠| *BP.*

NIGHTLIFE AND THE ARTS

THE ARTS

Bologna's arts scene is one of the liveliest in Italy. Opera, ballet, rock concerts, and theatrical extravaganzas happen year-round, as do food festivals. The **Bologna tourism office** (☎ *051/239660* ⊕ *www.bolognaturismo.
info*) has information on performances and events.

FESTIVALS

The first weekend in October crowds celebrate the **Festa di San Petronio**
with bands, fireworks, and free mortadella sandwiches in Piazza Maggiore. Free movies are shown at the **Open-air Cinema** in the Arena Puccini, at Via Serlio near the train station, June–August. The tourist office
has the schedule.

MUSIC AND OPERA

The 18th-century **Teatro Comunale** (✉ *Largo Respighi 1, University area*
☎ *051/529958* ⊕ *www.tcbo.it*) presents concerts by Italian and international orchestras throughout the year, but is dominated by the highly
acclaimed opera performances November–May, so reserve seats well in
advance. The ticket office is open Tuesday–Saturday 11–6:30.

Cooking alla Bolognese

A fine way to truly appreciate the appeal of Bolognese food is to learn how to make it. Barbara Bertuzzi, author of the cookbook *Bolognese Cooking Heritage,* teaches classes at **La Vecchia Scuola Bolognese** (the Old Bolognese Cooking School). Her four-hour sessions focus on pasta making and are offered daily; they begin at 9:30 AM and continue to lunchtime, when you can eat the fruits of your labor. Evening courses are available, and Bertuzzi also offers lunches and dinners without the lessons. The school is near the Ospedale Maggiore—take Bus 19 from Via Rizzoli near Piazza Maggiore, or a €15 taxi ride from the centro storico. If you're the only aspiring chef in your party, the rest can join after the lesson for dinner at €35 each. ✉ *Via Malvasia 49* ☎ *051/6491576* ⊕ *www. lavecchiascuola.com* 🍴 *€70 per person, €90 with meal.*

If you prefer your cooking classes in a truly regal setting, you might want to try **La Tavola della Signoria,** held in the spectacular 17th-century rooms of the Palazzo Albergati (⊕ *www. palazzoalbergati.it*). These classes are offered only four or five times per month and are more expensive than some others, but they're also longer and more serious. Class starts at 8:30 AM and runs until 5:30 PM; you can choose between different modules, such as bread making, pasta making, desserts, and so on. For the true aficionados, two- and three-day fruit-and-vegetable courses are offered periodically. It's 10 km (6 mi) west of the city center; to get here take SS569, get off at the last Zona Predosa exit, and follow signs for the Palazzo Albergati. You can sign up online. ✉ *Via Masini 46* ☎ *051/6166542* ⊕ *www. tavoladellasignoria.it* 🍴 *€170–€200 per person for 1 day; up to €480 for 3 days.*

NIGHTLIFE

As a university town, Bologna has long been known for its busy nightlife. As early as 1300 it was said to have had 150 taverns. Most of the city's current 200-plus pubs and bars are frequented by Italian students, young adults, and international students, with the university district forming the hub. In addition to the university area, the pedestrians-only zone on Via del Pratello, lined with plenty of bars, is also a hopping night scene, as is Via delle Moline, with cutting-edge cafés and bars. A more-upmarket, low-key evening experience can be had at one of Bologna's many wine bars that are also restaurants. And then there are the hypertrendy bar-lounges that represent the newest of Bologna's many faces.

BARS

If you want a night out at a trendy spot, Bologna offers a lot to choose from.

Elegant **Bar Calice** (✉ *Via Clavature 13/a, at Via Marchesana, Piazza Maggiore area* ☎ *051/6569296*) runs an indoor-outdoor operation year-round (with heat lamps). It's extremely popular with thirtysomethings. A wine bar with romantic ambient lighting and a good draft beer selection, **Contavalli** (✉ *Via Belle Arti 2, University area* ☎ *051/235825*) is a great choice. At **Le Stanze** (✉ *Via del Borgo di San Pietro 1, University area* ☎ *051/228767* ⊕ *www.lestanzecafe.com* ◑ *Closed Mon., and July and Aug.*) you can sip an *aperitivo* or a late-night drink at a modern bar. The decor includes 17th-century frescoes in what was once the private chapel of Palazzo Bentivoglio. The adjoining cutting-edge restaurant serves Italian fusion cooking. Buca San Petronio, an arcaded tunnel street tucked near the Piazza Maggiore, has become quite the evening scene. The loud **Nu Bar Lounge** (✉ *Off Buca San Petronio, Via de' Musei 6, Piazza Maggiore area* ☎ *051/222532* ⊕ *www.nu-lounge. com*) draws a cocktail-loving crowd, who enjoy the free snacks that show up around 8 PM.

MUSIC VENUES

It's not hard to find drinks accompanied by live music in the city. With live music staged every night (€4.50 cover), **Cantina Bentivoglio** (✉ *Via Mascarella 4/b, University area* ☎ *051/265416*) is one of Bologna's most appealing nightspots. You can enjoy light meals and nibbles as well. **Osteria Buca delle Campane** (✉ *Via Benedetto XVI 4/a, University area* ☎ *051/220918*), an underground tavern in a 13th-century building, has good, inexpensive food and a lively after-dinner scene popular with locals, including students who come to listen to live music.

SHOPPING

CLOTHING

One of the most upscale malls in Italy, the **Galleria Cavour** (✉ *Piazza Cavour, south of Piazza Maggiore*) houses many of the fashion giants, including Gucci, Versace, and the jeweler and watchmaker Bulgari. If you don't feel like paying Galleria Cavour prices, **Castel Guelfo Outlet City** (✉ *Via del Commercio 20/a, Loc. Poggio Piccolo, Castel Guelfo* ☎ *0542/670765* ⊕ *www.thestileoutlets.com*) is about 20 minutes outside Bologna on the autostrada A14 toward Imola (take the Castel San Pietro Terme exit; 980 feet after the tollbooth, turn right onto Via San Carlo). It includes about 50 discounted stores, some from top designers such as Ferré. It's closed Monday morning.

WINE AND FOOD

Bologna is a good place to buy wine. Several shops have a bewilderingly large selection—to go straight to the top, ask the managers which wines have won the prestigious *Tre Bicchieri* (Three Glasses) award from Gambero Rosso's wine bible, *Vini d'Italia*.

Repeatedly recognized as one of the best wine stores in Italy, **Enoteca Italiana** (✉ *Via Marsala 2/b, north of Piazza Maggiore* ☎ *051/235989*) lives up to its reputation with shelves lined with excellent selections from all over Italy at reasonable prices. Their delicious sandwiches with wines by the glass also make a great light lunch. Friendly owners run the midsize, down-to-earth **Scaramagli** (✉ *Strada Maggiore 31/d, University area* ☎ *051/227132*) wine store. **La Baita** (✉ *Via Pescherie Vecchia 3/a, Piazza Maggiore area* ☎ *051/223940*) sells fresh tagliolini, tortellini, and other Bolognese pasta delicacies, as well as sublime food to take away. Their cheese counter teems with local cheeses of superlative quality.

If you favor sweets, head to **Le Dolcezze** (✉ *Via Murr 21i, Piazza Maggiore area* ☎ *051/444582*), a top local *pasticceria* (pastry shop) whose cakes are excellent, and whose *panettone,* the sweet bread produced only around the holiday season, is considered by some to be the best in town. **Roccati** (✉ *Via Clavature 17/a, Piazza Maggiore area* ☎ *051/261964* ⊕ *www.roccaticiocccolato.com*) has been crafting sculptural works of chocolate, as well as basic bonbons and simpler stuff since 1909. For fresh produce, meats, and other foods, head to **Via Oberdan** (✉ *Piazza Maggiore area*), the street just off Via dell'Indipendenza downtown. The **Mercato delle Erbe** (✉ *Via Ugo Bassi, Piazza Maggiore area* ☎ *051/230186*) is an equally bustling food market, open Monday through Wednesday, and Friday 7–1:15 and 5–7:30 (4:30–7:30 October–March), Thursday and Saturday 7–1:15. The **Mercato di Mezzo** (✉ *Via Peschiere Vecchie, Piazza Maggiore area*), which sells specialty foods, fruits, and vegetables, is an intense barrage of sights and smells. It's open Monday through Saturday 7–1 and 4:15–7:30, with the exception of Thursday afternoon, when it's closed.

5

RAVENNA

76 km (47 mi) east of Bologna, 93 km (58 mi) southeast of Ferrara.

A small, quiet, well-heeled city, Ravenna has brick palaces, cobbled streets, magnificent monuments, and spectacular Byzantine mosaics. The high point in the city's history occurred in the 5th century, when Pope Honorious moved his court here from Rome. Gothic kings Odoacer and Theodoric ruled the city until it was conquered by the Byzantines in AD 540. Ravenna then fell under the sway of Venice, and then, inevitably, the Papal States.

Because Ravenna spent much of its past looking to the East, its greatest art treasures show that influence. Churches and tombs with the most unassuming exteriors contain within them walls covered with sumptuous mosaics. These beautifully preserved Byzantine mosaics put great emphasis on nature, which you can see in the delicate rendering of sky, earth, and animals. Outside Ravenna, the town of Classe hides even more mosaic gems.

GETTING HERE

By car from Bologna, take the SP253 to the RA1, and then follow signs for the A14/E45 in the direction of Ancona. From here, follow signs for Ravenna, taking thc A14dir Ancona–Milano–Ravenna exit. Follow signs for the SS16/E55 to the center of Ravenna. It's a more-convoluted, but more interesting, drive from Ferrara: take the SS16 to the RA8 in the direction of Porto Garibaldi taking the Roma/Ravenna exit. Follow the SS309/E55 to the SS309dir/E55, taking the SS253 Bologna/Ancona exit. Follow the SS16/E55 into the center of Ravenna.

VISITOR INFORMATION

Ravenna tourism office (✉ *Via Salara 8* ☎ *0544/35404* ⊕ *www.turismo. ravenna.it*).

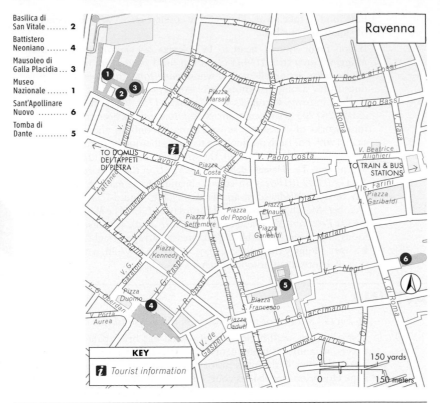

EXPLORING RAVENNA

A combination ticket (available at ticket offices of all included sights) admits you to four of Ravenna's important monuments: the Mausoleo di Galla Placidia, the Basilica di San Vitale, the Battistero Neoniano, and Sant'Apollinare Nuovo. Start out early in the morning to avoid lines (reservations are necessary for the Mausoleo and Basilica in May and June). A half day should suffice to walk the town alone; allow a half hour for the Mausoleo and the Basilica. Ticket offices often close 15 to 30 minutes before the sights themselves.

TOP ATTRACTIONS

② **Basilica di San Vitale.** The octagonal church of San Vitale was built in AD 547, after the Byzantines conquered the city, and its interior shows a strong Byzantine influence. In the area behind the altar are the most famous works in the church, depicting Emperor Justinian and his retinue on one wall, and his wife, Empress Theodora, with her retinue, on the opposite wall. Notice how the mosaics seamlessly wrap around the columns and curved arches on the upper sides of the altar area. Reservations are recommended from March through mid-June. ⊠ *Via San Vitale off Via Salara* ☎ *0544/541688 reservations, 800/303999 toll-free information* ⊕ *www.ravennamosaici.it* ▨ *Combination ticket*

€8.50 ⊗ *Nov.–Feb., daily 9:30–5; Mar. and Oct., daily 9–5:30; Apr.–Sept., daily 9–7.*

➍ **Battistero Neoniano.** The baptistery, next door to Ravenna's 18th-century cathedral, has one of the town's most important mosaics. It dates from the beginning of the 5th century AD, with work continuing through the century. In keeping with the building's role, the great mosaic in the dome shows the baptism of Christ, and beneath are the apostles. The lowest register of mosaics contains Christian symbols, the throne of God, and the cross. Note the naked figure kneeling next to Christ—he is the personification of the River Jordan. ⊠ *Via Battistero* ☎ *0544/541688 reservations, 800/303999 toll-free information* ⊕ *www.ravennamosaici.it* ✉ *Combination ticket €8.50* ⊗ *Nov.–Feb., daily 10–5; Mar. and Oct., daily 9:30–5:30; Apr.–Sept., daily 9–7.*

➌ **Mausoleo di Galla Placidia.** The little tomb and the great church stand side by side, but the tomb predates the Basilica di San Vitale by at least a hundred years. These two adjacent sights are decorated with the best-known, and most elaborate, mosaics in Ravenna. Galla Placidia was the sister of the Roman emperor Honorius, who moved the imperial capital to Ravenna in AD 402. She is said to have been beautiful and strong-willed, and to have taken an active part in the governing of the crumbling empire. This mausoleum, constructed in the mid-5th century, is her memorial.

Fodor's Choice
★

Viewed from the outside, it's a small, unassuming redbrick building; the exterior's seeming poverty of charm only serves to enhance by contrast the richness of the interior mosaics, in deep midnight blue and glittering gold. The tiny central dome is decorated with symbols of Christ, the evangelists, and striking gold stars. Over the door is a depiction of the Good Shepherd. Eight apostles are represented in groups of two on the four inner walls of the dome; the other four appear singly on the walls of the two transepts. Notice the small doves at their feet, drinking from the water of faith. Also in the tiny transepts are some delightful pairs of deer (representing souls), drinking from the fountain of resurrection. There are three sarcophagi in the tomb, none of which are believed to contain the remains of Galla Placidia. She died in Rome in AD 450, and there is no record of her body having been transported back to the place where she wished to lie. Reservations are required for the mausoleo from March through mid-June. ⊠ *Via San Vitale off Via Salara* ☎ *0544/541688 reservations, 800/303999 toll-free information* ⊕ *www.ravennamosaici.it* ✉ *€2 supplement in addition to obligatory €8.50 combination ticket Mar. 1–June 15* ⊗ *Nov.–Feb., Mon.–Sat. 9:30–5, Sun. 9:30–5:30; Mar. and Oct., Mon.–Sat. 9–5:30, Sun. 9–6; Apr.–Sept., daily 9–7.*

➏ **Sant'Apollinare Nuovo.** The mosaics displayed in this church date from the early 6th century, making them slightly older than those in San Vitale. Since the left side of the church was reserved for women, it's only fitting that the mosaics on that wall depict 22 virgins offering crowns to the Virgin Mary. On the right wall are 26 men carrying the crowns of martyrdom. They approach Christ, surrounded by angels. ⊠ *Via Roma at Via Guaccimanni* ☎ *0544/219518, 0544/541688 reservations,*

800/303999 toll-free information ⊕ *www.ravennamosaici.it* ✉ *Combination ticket €8.50* ⊙ *Nov.–Feb., daily 10–5; Mar. and Oct., daily 9:30–5:30; Apr.–Sept., daily 9–7.*

WORTH NOTING

Domus dei Tappeti di Pietra *(Ancient Home of the Stone Carpets).* This underground archaeological site was uncovered during the course of routine maintenance work in the 18th century church of Santa Eufemia by the city in 1993. Below

ground level (10 feet down) lie the remains of a Byzantine palace dating from the 5th and 6th centuries AD, in which a beautiful and well-preserved network of floor mosaics display themes that are fascinatingly un-Christian. ✉ *Via Barbiani, enter through Sant'Eufemia* ☎ *0544/32512* ⊕ *www.domusdeitappetidipietra.it* ✉ *€4* ⊙ *Sept.–June, daily 10–6:30; July and Aug., daily 10–6 and 9–11.*

① **Museo Nazionale.** The National Museum of Ravenna, next to the Church of San Vitale, contains artifacts from ancient Rome, Byzantine fabrics and carvings, and pieces of early Christian art. The collection is housed in a former monastery, and is well displayed and artfully lighted. ✉ *Via Fiandrini* ☎ *0544/543711* ✉ *€4* ⊙ *Tues.–Sun. 8:30–7:30.*

⑤ **Tomba di Dante.** The tomb of Dante is in a small neoclassical building next door to the large church of St. Francis. Exiled from his native Florence, the author of *The Divine Comedy* died here in 1321. The Florentines have been trying to reclaim their famous son for hundreds of years, but the Ravennans refuse to give him up, arguing that since Florence did not welcome Dante in life it does not deserve him in death. ✉ *Via Dante Alighieri 4 and 9* ☎ *0544/30252* ✉ *Free* ⊙ *Daily 9–noon and 2–5.*

OFF THE BEATEN PATH

Sant'Apollinare in Classe. This church, about 5 km (3 mi) southeast of Ravenna, is landlocked now, but when it was built it stood in the center of the busy shipping port known to the ancient Romans as Classis. The arch above and the area around the high altar are rich with mosaics. Those on the arch, older than the ones behind it, are considered superior. They show *Christ in Judgment* and the 12 lambs of Christianity leaving the cities of Jerusalem and Bethlehem. In the apse is the figure of Sant'Apollinare himself, a bishop of Ravenna, and above him is a magnificent *Transfiguration* against blazing green grass, animals in odd perspective, and flowers. ✉ *Via Romea Sud, Classe* ☎ *0544/473569* ✉ *€3* ⊙ *Daily 8:30–7.*

The mosaic of Empress Theodora in Ravenna's Basilica di San Vitale

WHERE TO EAT

$

NORTHERN
ITALIAN

✕ **Bella Venezia.** Graceful low archways lead into this attractive pink-and-white restaurant's two small, brightly lighted dining rooms. Try the beans with olive oil and *bottarga* (cured roe) or the owner's special risotto with butter, Parmesan, cured ham, mushrooms, and peas to start. For the second course, the *fegato alla Veneziana* (grilled liver with onions) is a good choice. The outdoor garden is quite pleasant in season. ✉ *Via IV Novembre 16* ☏ *0544/212746* ⊕ *www.bellavenezia.it* 🖃 *AE, DC, MC, V* ⊗ *Closed Sun. and 3 wks in Dec. and Jan.*

$

WINE BAR

★

✕ **Ca' de Ven.** A vaulted wine cellar in the heart of the old city, the Ca' de Ven is great for a hearty meal. You sit at long tables with other diners and feast on platters of delicious cold cuts, flat breads, and cold, heady white wine. The tortelli *di radicchio e pecorino* (stuffed with radicchio and sheep's milk cheese) makes the best first course. ✉ *Via C. Ricci 24* ☏ *0544/30163* 🖃 *AE, DC, MC, V* ⊗ *Closed Mon., 3 wks in Jan. and Feb., and 1st wk in June.*

¢

ITALIAN

✕ **La Gardèla.** The kitchen seems to operate with an otherworldly efficiency, making this bright, bustling downtown restaurant extremely popular with the local business crowd—especially at lunch (always a good sign). The place is best for classics like tagliatelle al ragù and Adriatic fish, such as *sardoncini* (tiny sardines, breaded and fried). ✉ *Via Ponte Marino 3* ☏ *0544/217147* 🖃 *AE, DC, MC, V* ⊗ *Closed Thurs. and 10 days in Jan.*

$ ✕ **Locanda del Melarancio.** This contemporary inn, in a late 16th-century
NORTHERN palazzo in the heart of the centro storico, has an osteria on the ground
ITALIAN floor, a restaurant on the second, and rooms on the third. Decor is
★ minimalist without being stark—contemporary art on the walls doesn't
detract from a warm, homey feeling. The menu changes daily; traditional ingredients are used to create inventive dishes. The tastily
innovative *gelato di Parmigiano* (Parmesan ice cream) is served with
prosciutto crudo and piadine, that Romagnolan specialty. *Formaggio
di fossa* (cheese aged in a cave) turns into *sformato* (an eggy flan) with
julienned salami, honey, and balsamic vinegar, while cappellacci in a
porcini-based sauce are filled with mascarpone and truffles. ✉ *Via Men-
tana 33* ☎ *0544/215258* ⊕ *www.locandadelmelarancio.it* ═ *AE, DC,
MC, V.*

WHERE TO STAY

$$ ⊞ **Hotel Bisanzio.** Steps from San Vitale and the Tomb of Galla Placidia,
this Best Western hotel is the most convenient lodging for mosaic enthu-
siasts. The exterior is drab, but rooms are comfortable and modern;
the lobby's Florentine lamps add a touch of style. Ask to be on the top
floor and you may get a view of the basilica. **Pros:** near the train station;
no-smoking rooms. **Cons:** part of a chain; popular with groups. ✉ *Via
Salara 30* ☎ *0544/217111* ⊕ *www.bisanziohotel.com* ➥ *38 rooms* ⅙ *In-
room: safe, Internet, Wi-Fi. In-hotel: room service, bar, laundry service,
Internet terminal, Wi-Fi hotspot, parking (paid), some pets allowed*
═ *AE, DC, MC, V* ⏍ *BP.*

$–$$ ⊞ **Sant'Andrea.** This simple B&B offers an absolutely prime location,
steps away from the Basilica di San Vitale. It's like staying in a well-
appointed house—rooms are big, bright, and clean, done up in primary
colors. The lobby is decked out with homey furniture, and breakfast
can be taken in the breakfast room or in the garden in good weather.
Bathrooms are spotless and modern. A suite costs only €30 extra and
can accommodate a family of four or five. **Pros:** children under 12 sleep
free; breakfast outdoors when it's warm; discounts for stays of three
nights or more. **Cons:** can get a little noisy; groups favor the place.
✉ *Via Carlo Cattaneo 33* ☎ *0544/215564* ⊕ *www.santandreahotel.
com* ➥ *10 rooms, 2 suites* ⅙ *In-room: safe. In-hotel: bar, parking (paid)*
═ *AE, DC, MC, V* ⏍ *BP.*

NIGHTLIFE AND THE ARTS

Friday nights from June to August bring **Mosaics by Night**, when the
Byzantine mosaic masterpieces in town are illuminated. The event is
also held on certain Tuesdays; to check, call the tourist office, which
also offers guided tours. The **Ravenna Festival** is a music festival held
every year in June and July. Orchestras from all over the world come
to perform in Ravenna's churches and theaters.

FERRARA

47 km (29 mi) northeast of Bologna, 74 km (46 mi) northwest of Ravenna.

When the legendary Ferrarese filmmaker Michelangelo Antonioni called his beloved hometown "a city that you can see only partly, while the rest disappears to be imagined," perhaps he was referring to the low-lying mist that rolls in off the Adriatic each winter and shrouds Ferrara's winding knot of medieval alleyways, turreted palaces, and ancient wine bars—once inhabited by the likes of Copernicus—in a ghostly fog. But perhaps Antonioni was also suggesting that Ferrara's striking beauty often conceals a dark and tortured past.

Though it was settled as early as the 6th century AD, Ferrara's history really begins with the arrival of the Este, who first made their appearance in the city in 1196. For more than three centuries the dynasty ruled with an iron fist; brother killed brother, son fought father, husband murdered wife. The majestic moated castle, now the architectural gem of the historic center, was originally built as a fortress to protect the ruthless Este dukes from their own citizens; deep within the castle the Este kept generations of political dissidents in dank cells. The greatest of the dukes, Ercole I (1433–1505), attempted to poison a nephew who challenged his power, and when that didn't work he beheaded him. Though the Jews were already well established in Ferrara as early at the 1380s, it is Ercole I who invited Sephardic Jews exiled from Spain to settle in Ferrara, thus giving form to one of the liveliest Jewish communities in Western Europe. The maze of twisting cobblestone streets in the ghetto witnessed the persecution of its Jews once Fascist Italy was officially at war with Nazi Germany in October 1943. This tragedy was documented in Giorgio Bassani's semiautobiographical book and Vittorio De Sica's film, *The Garden of the Finzi-Continis.*

Today you are likely to be charmed by Ferrara's prosperous air and meticulous cleanliness, its excellent restaurants and coffeehouses, and its lively wine bar scene. You'll find aficionados gathering outside any of the wine bars near the Duomo even on the foggiest of weekend evenings. Though Ferrara is a UNESCO World Heritage site, the city still draws amazingly few tourists—which only adds to its appeal.

GETTING HERE

Train service is frequent from Bologna (usually three trains per hour) and takes either a half hour or 45 minutes, depending upon which train type you take. It's a two-hour ride from Florence, and trains go just about every hour. The walk from the train station is easy but not particularly interesting. If you're driving from Bologna, take the RA1 out of town, take the A13 in the direction of Padova, and exit at Ferrara Nord. Follow the SP19 directly into the center of town. The trip should take about 45 minutes.

VISITOR INFORMATION

Ferrara tourism office (✉ *Estense* ☎ *0532/299303* ✉ *Piazza Municipale 11* ⊕ *www.ferrarainfo.com*).

EXPLORING FERRARA

If you plan to explore the city fully, consider buying a Card Musei ("museum card," €14) at the Palazzo dei Diamanti or at any of the museums around town; it grants admission to every museum, palace, and castle in Ferrara. The first Monday of the month is free at many museums.

TOP ATTRACTIONS

★ Massive **Castello Estense**, the former seat of Este power, dominates the center of town. The building was a suitable symbol for the ruling family: cold and menacing on the outside, lavishly decorated within. The public rooms are grand, but deep in the bowels of the castle are chilling dungeons where enemies of the state were held in wretched conditions— a function these quarters served as recently as 1943, when antifascist prisoners were detained there. In particular, the **Prisons of Don Giulio, Ugo, and Parisina** have some fascinating features, like 15th-century graffiti protesting the imprisonment of lovers Ugo and Parisina, who were beheaded in 1425 because Ugo's father, Niccolò III, didn't like the fact that his son was cavorting with Niccolò's wife.

The castle was established as a fortress in 1385, but work on its luxurious ducal quarters continued into the 16th century. Representative of Este grandeur are the **Sala dei Giochi**, extravagantly painted with athletic scenes, and the **Sala dell'Aurora**, decorated to show the times of the day. The tower, the terraces of the castle, and the hanging garden—once reserved for the private use of the duchesses—have fine views of the town and the surrounding countryside. You can cross the castle's moat, traverse its drawbridge, and wander through many of its arcaded passages at any time. Do note that the entrance price is substantially higher if there is a special exhibition on. ⊠ *Piazza Castello* ☎ *0532/299233* ⊕ *www.castelloestense.it* ⊠ *Castle €7, tower €1 extra* ☉ *Castle: Tues.–Sun. 9:30–5:30. Tower: Tues.–Sun. 10–4:45. Ticket office closes at 4:45.*

QUICK BITES **Caffetteria Castello** (⊠ *Largo Castello* ☎ *0532/299337* ☉ *Tues.–Sun. 9:30–5:30*) is spectacularly situated amid centuries of history. The second floor provides a great place to break for coffee while touring the castle, or to mingle with locals enjoying the lunchtime buffet. Right next door is a small book-and-gift shop.

★ The magnificent Gothic **Duomo**, a few steps from the Castello Estense, has a three-tier facade of slender arches and beautiful sculptures over the central door. Work began in 1135 and took more than 100 years to complete. The interior was completely remodeled in the 17th century. ⊠ *Piazza Cattedrale* ☎ *0532/207449* ☉ *Mon.–Sat. 7:30–noon and 3–6:30, Sun. 7:30–12:30 and 3:30–7:30.*

The collection of ornate religious objects in the **Museo Ebraico** *(Jewish Museum)* bears witness to the long history of the city's Jewish community. This history had its high points—1492, for example, when Ercole I invited the Jews to come over from Spain—and its lows, notably 1627, when Jews were enclosed within the **ghetto**, where they were forced to live until the advent of a united Italy in 1860. The triangular warren of narrow, cobbled streets that made up the ghetto originally extended as far as Corso Giovecca (originally Corso Giudecca, or Ghetto Street); when it was enclosed, the neighborhood was restricted to the area between Via Scienze, Via Contrari, and Via di San Romano. The museum, in the center of the ghetto, was once Ferrara's synagogue. All visits are led by a museum guide. ⊠ *Via Mazzini 95* ☏ *0532/210228* ⊕ *www.comune.fe.it/museoebraico* ⌨ *€4* ☺ *Tours: Weekdays at 10, 11, and noon.*

The **Palazzo dei Diamanti** *(Palace of Diamonds)* is so called because of the 12,600 small, pink-and-white marble pyramids ("diamonds") that stud the facade. The building was designed to be viewed in perspective—both faces at once—from diagonally across the street. Work began in the 1490s and finished around 1504. Today the palazzo contains the **Pinacoteca Nazionale,** which has an extensive art gallery and rotating exhibits. ⊠ *Corso Ercole I d'Este 19–21* ☏ *0532/244949* ⊕ *www.artecultura. fe.it* ⌨ *€4* ☺ *Tues. and Wed. and Fri.–Sun. 9–2, Thurs. 9–7.*

The oldest and most characteristic area of Ferrara is south of the Duomo, stretching between the Corso Giovecca and the city's ramparts. Here various members of the Este family built pleasure palaces, the most famous of which is the **Palazzo Schifanoia** *(schifanoia* means "carefree" or, literally, "fleeing boredom"). Begun in the late 14th century, the palace was remodeled between 1464 and 1469. The lavishly decorated interior, particularly the **Salone dei Mesi,** with an extravagant series of frescoes showing the months of the year and their mythological attributes, is well worth visiting. ⊠ *Via Scandiana 23* ☏ *0532/64178* ⊕ *www. artecultura.fe.it* ⌨ *€5* ☺ *Tues.–Sun. 9–6, call ahead to confirm.*

One of the streets most characteristic of Ferrara's past, the 2-km-long (1-mi-long) **Via delle Volte** is also one of the best-preserved medieval streets in Europe. The series of ancient *volte* (arches) along the narrow cobblestone alley once joined the merchants' houses on the south side of the street to their warehouses on the north side. The street ran parallel to the banks of the Po River, which was home to Ferrara's busy port.

WORTH NOTING

One of the loveliest of the Renaissance palaces along Ferrara's old streets is the charming **Casa Romei.** Built by the wealthy banker Giovanni Romei (1402–83), it is a vast structure with a graceful courtyard. Mid-15th-century frescoes decorate rooms on the ground floor; the *piano nobile* (main floor) contains detached frescoes from local churches as well as lesser-known Renaissance sculptures. The Sala delle Sibelle has a very large, 15th-century fireplace, and beautiful wood-coffered ceilings. ⊠ *Via Savonarola 30* ☏ *0532/234130* ⊕ *www.artecultura.fe.it* ⌨ *€3* ☺ *Tues.–Sun. 8:30–7:30.*

Some of the original decorations of the town's main church, the former church and cloister of San Romano, reside in the **Museo della Cattedrale,** which is across the piazza from the Duomo. Inside you'll find 22 codices commissioned 1477–1535, moving early 13th century sculpture by the Maestro dei Mesi, a mammoth oil on canvas by Cosmé Tura from 1469, and an exquisite Jacopo della Quercia *Madonna della*

Talking Politics

Emilia-Romagna might seem staid: city after city has immaculate streets filled with smartly dressed businessmen in impeccable shoes, covertly murmuring to each other through the winter fog over cups of coffee. But after dark, from Parma to Bologna, Piacenza to Ferrara, the middle managers are replaced on the streets by young, energetic would-be intellectuals, and the murmurs turn into impassioned political discussion—usually with a leftist slant—over jugs of table wine. If you enjoy this type of conversation, take time to stop for a drink after dinner in a student cafeteria, cozy café, or back-alley bar. Don't be afraid to join in—all ages are welcome, and divergent opinions, thoughtfully argued, are treated with respect. (Locals are usually happy to practice their English, which can often be quite good.) You'll experience another side of the region—a side that's important to understanding its culture and history.

Melograno. Though this sculpture dates 1403–1408, the playful expression on the Christ child seems very 21st century. ⊠ *Via San Romano 1* ☎ *0532/209988* ⊕ *www.comune.fe.it/musei-aa/schifanoia/catte.html* ☎ *€5* ⊙ *Tues.–Sun. 9–1 and 3–6.*

The grand but unfinished courtyard is the most interesting part of the luxurious **Palazzo di Ludovico il Moro**, a magnificent 15th-century dwelling built for Ludovico Sforza, husband of Beatrice d'Este. The palazzo contains the region's **Museo Archeologico**, a repository of relics of early man, Etruscans, and Romans found in the country surrounding the city. It's outside the city, near Palazzo Schifanoia, a half-hour walk from the Piazza Duomo. ⊠ *Via XX Settembre 124, near Palazzo Schifanoia* ☎ *0532/66299* ☎ *€4* ⊙ *Tues.–Sun. 9–2.*

On the busy Corso Giovecca is the **Palazzina di Marfisa d'Este**, a grandiose 16th-century palace that belonged to a great patron of the arts. It has painted ceilings, fine 16th-century furniture, and a garden containing a grotto and an outdoor theater. ⊠ *Corso Giovecca 170* ☎ *0532/207450* ⊕ *www.artecultura.fe.it* ☎ *€3* ⊙ *Tues.–Sun. 9–1 and 3–6.*

The courtyard of the peaceful **Palazzo del Paradiso** contains the tomb of the great writer Ariosto (1474–1533), author of the most popular work of literature of the Renaissance, the poem *Orlando Furioso*. The building now houses the city library, the **Biblioteca Ariostea** ⊠ *Via delle Scienze 17* ☎ *0532/418200* ☎ *Free* ⊙ *Weekdays 9–7:30, Sat. 9–1:30.*

WHERE TO EAT

$$$
MODERN ITALIAN
★

✕ **Il Don Giovanni.** Just down the street from Castello Estense, this warm and inviting restaurant is inside a lovely 17th-century palace and has but a handful of tables. Chef Pier Luigi Di Diego and partner Marco Merighi pay strict attention to what's seasonal, and the menu reflects this. Here tortellini is stuffed with guinea fowl and sauced with zabaione, Parmesan, and *prosciutto crocante* (fried prosciutto). Equally inventive is the delicate *tegame di pernice rossa ai frutti di bosco* (partridge in a fruit sauce), which delights the palate. Next door, the same proprietors run the less expensive, crowded, and trendy **La Borsa** wine bar, which has excellent cured meats, cheeses, lovely primi and secondi, as well as a fantastic wine-by-the-glass list. (The wine bar is open for lunch, but the restaurant is not.) ✉ *Corso Ercole I d'Este 1* ☎ *0532/243363* ⊕ *www.ildongiovanni.com* ⚒ *Reservations essential* ☰ *AE, DC, MC, V* ☼ *Closed Mon. No lunch.*

$$ ✗ **L'Oca Giuliva.** Food, service, and ambience unite in blissful harmony

EMILIAN at this casual yet elegant restaurant minutes from Piazza Repubblica.

Fodor's Choice Two small rooms in a 12th-century building provide the backdrop for

★ exquisitely prepared local foods. The chef has a deft hand with local specialties and executes them either in *tradizionale* (traditional) or *rivisitata* (updated) style. Particularly impressive are the primi, especially the *cappellacci di zucca al ragù* (pumpkin-stuffed pasta). It might be the best version in town. Meat-and-potatoes folk can opt for the *salama da sugo* (a salty, garlicky boiled sausage served over mashed potatoes), and adventurous sorts might try the *trancio di anguilla* (roasted eel) with polenta on the side. The amazing wine list is complemented by a terrific cheese plate. ✉ *Via Boccanale di Santo Stefano 38* ☎ *0532/207628* ☰ *AE, DC, MC, V* ☼ *Closed Mon. No lunch Tues.*

$ ✗ **Osteria al Brindisi.** Ferrara is a city of wine bars, beginning with this,

WINE BAR allegedly Europe's oldest, which opened in 1435. Copernicus drank here

★ while a student in the late 1400s, and the place still has a somewhat undergraduate aura; most of the staff and clientele are twentysomethings. Perfectly dusty wine bottles line the walls, and there are wooden booths in another small room for those who want to eat while they drink. A young staff pours terrific wines by the glass, and offers three different sauces (butter and sage, tomato, or ragù) with its *cappellacci di zucca*. Those in search of lighter fare might enjoy any of the salads or the grilled vegetable plate with melted pecorino. ✉ *Via degli Adelardi 11* ☎ *0532/209142* ☰ *AE, DC, MC, V* ☼ *Closed Mon.*

$$ ✗ **Quel Fantastico Giovedì.** It's worth taking a taxi to this off-the-beaten-

EMILIAN path eatery (you could walk, but it's hard to find), where locals seek out a sophisticated and tasty meal. Two small rooms, one white, the other with red accents, have linen tablecloths and jazz playing softly in the background. Chef Gabriele Romagnoli uses top-notch local ingredients to create gustatory taste sensations: his *sformatino di patate* more closely resembles a French gratin, but he sauces it with *salamina e Parmesan*, thus rendering it deliciously Ferraresi. Fish also figures prominently on the menu. The wine list is divine, and the service is top-notch. ✉ *Via Castelnuovo 9* ☎ *0532/760570* ⚒ *Reservations essential* ☰ *AE, DC, MC, V* ☼ *Closed Wed. No lunch Tues.*

WHERE TO STAY

$$ ⊞ **Duchessa Isabella.** An elegant 16th-century palace is now a luxurious hotel just slightly off the centro storico. Named after Isabella d'Este, a Renaissance woman of wealth and taste, it has lavish, opulent public rooms with high wood-coffered ceilings and damask drapes on the piano nobile. Rooms, in pastel colors of pink, yellow, or blue have a decidedly feminine touch, comfortable beds, and large bathrooms.

The terrific restaurant offers local specialties in swank surroundings; when it's warm, you can enjoy this tasty fare on a flower-filled terrace. **Pros:** lovely staff, garden; spared the noise from the centro storico. **Cons:** slightly removed from the centro storico. ⊠ *Via Palestra 68/70* ☎ *0532/202121* ⊕ *www.duchessaisabella.it* ➾ *21 rooms, 6 suites* ⚹ *In-room: a/c, safe, DVD, Internet, Wi-Fi. In hotel: restaurant, room service, bar, laundry service, Internet terminal, Wi-Fi hotspot, parking (free), some pets allowed* ═ *AE, DC, MC, V* ☉ *Closed Aug.*

$$ ▦ **Hotel Ripagrande.** The courtyards, vaulted brick lobby, and break-
★   fast room of this 15th-century noble's palazzo retain much of their lordly Renaissance flair. Rooms are decidedly more down-to-earth, but standard doubles and some of the enormous bi- and tri-level suites have faux-Persian rugs, tapestries, and cozy antique furniture; top-floor rooms and suites resemble a Colorado ski lodge, with terraces, and are roomy—especially good for families. Everything here, including the room service, is impeccable. The location is quiet but fairly convenient. **Pros:** beyond-helpful staff; good choice for families. **Cons:** staff goes home at midnight. ⊠ *Via Ripagrande 21* ☎ *0532/765250* ⊕ *www. ripagrandehotel.it* ➾ *20 rooms, 20 suites* ⚹ *In-room: safe, Wi-Fi. In-hotel: restaurant, room service, bar, laundry service, Internet terminal, Wi-Fi hotspot, parking (free), some pets allowed* ═ *AE, DC, MC, V* ℹ️ *BP.*

$ ▦ **Locanda Borgonuovo.** It began life as a 15th-century palazzo, was
★   transformed into a monastery in the 18th century, and is now a delightful bed-and-breakfast in the heart of town. The Orlandini family are the proprietors; they live on the floor above. Breakfast, in fact, is served in their living room, briefly transformed with linen tablecloths, into a breakfast room. Rooms have comfortable beds and flowers in the window boxes. When it's warmer, you can sit outside on a small terrace with a pergola. This place books up quickly, as many performers at the city's Teatro Comunale stay here. Both mother Adele and son Filippo are very hands-on, and are eager to help make your stay as wonderful as possible. Bicycles can be borrowed for free. **Pros:** phenomenal breakfast featuring local foods; Adele and Filippo. **Cons:** steep stairs to reception area and rooms; must reserve far in advance. ⊠ *Via Cairoli 29* ☎ *0532/211100* ⊕ *www.borgonuovo.com* ➾ *4 rooms, 2 apartments* ⚹ *In-room: safe, kitchen (some), Wi-Fi. In-hotel: restaurant, bicycles, Internet terminal, Wi-Fi hotspot, parking (free)* ═ *AE, MC, V* ℹ️ *BP.*

THE VENETO

Updated
by Bruce
Leimsidor

The green plains stretching west of Venice hold three of northern Italy's most appealing midsize cities: Padua, Vicenza, and Verona. Each has notable artistic treasures and an attractive historic center; Padua is famous for its Giotto frescoes, Vicenza for its Palladian villas, and Verona for its ancient arena. All three were once under the control of Venice, and one of the pleasures of exploring them is discovering the traces of Venetian influence—still evident in everything from food to architecture.

PADUA

A romantic warren of arcaded streets, Padua has long been one of the major cultural centers of northern Italy. It's home to Italy's second-oldest university, founded in 1222, which attracted such cultural icons as Dante (1265–1321), Petrarch (1304–74), and Galileo Galilei (1564–1642), thus earning the city the sobriquet *La Dotta* (The Learned). Padua's Basilica di Sant'Antonio, begun around 1238, is dedicated to Saint Anthony, and it attracts droves of pilgrims, especially on his feast day, June 13. Three great artists—Giotto (1266–1337), Donatello (circa 1386–1466), and Mantegna (1431–1506)—left significant works in Padua, with Giotto's Scrovegni Chapel one of the best-known, and most meticulously preserved, works of art in the country. Today, a cycle-happy student body—some 50,000 strong—flavors every aspect of local culture. Don't be surprised if you spot a *laurea* (graduation) ceremony marked by laurel leaves, mocking lullabies, and X-rated caricatures.

GETTING HERE

Many people visit Padua from Venice: the train trip between the cities is short, and regular bus service originates from Venice's Piazzale Roma. By car from Milan or Venice, Padua is on the Autostrada Torino–Trieste A4/E70. Take the San Carlo exit and follow Via Guido Reni to Via Tiziano Aspetti into town. From the south, take the Autostrada Bologna Padova A13 to its Padua terminus at Via Ballaglia. Regular bus service connects Venice's Marco Polo airport with downtown Padua.

Padua is a pedestrian's city. If you arrive by car, leave your vehicle in one of the parking lots on the outskirts, or at your hotel. Unlimited bus service is included with the Padova Card (€15, valid for 48 hours), which allows entry to all the city's principal sights. It is available at tourist information offices and at some museums and hotels.

VISITOR INFORMATION

Padua tourism office (✉ *Padova Railway Station* ☎ *049/8752077*✉ *Galleria Pedrocchi* ☎ *049/8767927* ⊕ *www.turismopadova.it*).

THE VENETIAN ARC, PAST AND PRESENT

Long before Venetians made their presence felt on the mainland in the 15th century, Ezzelino III da Romano (1194–1259), a larger-than-life scourge who was excommunicated by Pope Innocent IV, laid claim to Verona, Padua, and the surrounding lands and towns. After he was ousted, powerful families such as Padua's Carrara and Verona's della Scala (Scaligeri) vied throughout the 14th century to dominate these territories. With the rise of Venetian rule came a time of relative peace, when noble families from the lagoon and the mainland commissioned Palladio and other accomplished architects to design their palazzi and villas.

This rich legacy, superimposed upon medieval castles and fortifications, is central to the identities of present-day Padua, Vicenza, and Verona. The region remained under Venetian control until the Napoleonic invasion and the fall of the Venetian Republic in 1797. The Council of Vienna ceded it, along with Lombardy, to Austria in 1815. The region revolted against Austrian rule and joined the Italian Republic in 1866.

Friuli–Venezia Giulia has a diverse cultural history that's reflected in its architecture, language, and cuisine. It's been marched through, fought over, hymned by patriots, and romanticized by writers James Joyce, Rainer Maria Rilke, and Jan Morris. Trieste was also vividly depicted in the novels of the towering figure of early-20th-century Italian letters, Italo Svevo. The region has seen Fascists and Communists, Romans, Habsburgs, and Huns. It survived by forging sheltering alliances—Udine beneath the wings of San Marco (1420), Trieste choosing Duke Leopold of Austria (1382) over Venetian domination.

Some of World War I's fiercest fighting took place in Friuli–Venezia Giulia, where memorials and cemeteries commemorate hundreds of thousands who died before the arrival of Italian troops in 1918 finally liberated Trieste from Austrian rule. Trieste, along with the whole of Venezia Giulia, was annexed to Italy in 1920. During World War II, the Germans occupied the area and placed Trieste in an administrative zone along with parts of Slovenia. One of Italy's two concentration camps was near Trieste. After the war, during a period of cold war dispute, Trieste was governed by an allied military administration; it was officially reannexed to Italy in 1954, when Italy ceded the Istrian peninsula to the south to Yugoslavia. These arrangements, long de facto in effect, were ratified by Italy and Yugoslavia in 1975.

EXPLORING PADUA

TOP ATTRACTIONS

 Basilica di Sant'Antonio *(Basilica del Santo)*. Thousands of faithful make the pilgrimage here each year to pray at the tomb of Saint Anthony. The huge church, which combines elements of Byzantine, Romanesque, and Gothic styles, was probably begun around 1238, seven years after the death of the Portuguese-born saint. It was completed in 1310, with structural modifications added from the end of the 14th century into the mid-15th century. The imposing interior contains works by the

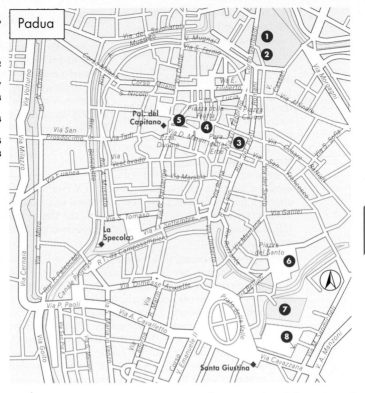

15th-century Florentine master Donatello. He sculpted the series of bronze reliefs illustrating the miracles of Saint Anthony, as well as the bronze statues of the Madonna and saints, on the high altar. But because of the site's popularity with pilgrims, masses are held in the basilica almost constantly, which makes it difficult to see these works. More accessible is the recently restored **Cappella del Santo** housing the tomb of the saint, which dates from the 16th century. Its walls are covered with impressive reliefs by various important Renaissance sculptors, including Jacopo Sansovino (1486–1570), the architect of the library in Venice's Piazza San Marco, and Tullio Lombardo (1455–1532), the greatest in a family of sculptors who decorated many churches in the area, among them Venice's Santa Maria dei Miracoli. In front of the church is an undisputed masterpiece of Italian Renaissance sculpture, Donatello's equestrian statue (1453) of the *condottiere* (mercenary general) Erasmo da Narni, known as Gattamelata. Inspired by the ancient statue of Marcus Aurelius in Rome's Campidoglio, it is the first in a series of Italian Renaissance monumental equestrian statues. ⊠ *Piazza del Santo* ☎ *049/8789722* ⊕ *www.santantonio.org* ☉ *Sept.–May, daily 6:20 AM–7 PM; June–Aug., daily 6:20 AM–7:45 PM.*

❶ **Cappella degli Scrovegni** *(The Arena Chapel).* This world-famous chapel and its frescoes were commissioned by Enrico Scrovegno to atone **Fodor's** Choice for the sins of his deceased father, Reginaldo, the usurer encountered **★**

by Dante in the Seventh Circle of the Inferno in his *Divine Comedy.* Giotto and his assistants decorated the interior from 1303 to 1305 with a universally acclaimed fresco cycle illustrating the lives of Mary and Jesus. The 38 panels are arranged in tiers and are to be read from left to right. The spatial depth, emotional intensity, and naturalism of these frescoes—note the use of blue sky instead of the conventional, depth-destroying gold background of

medieval painting—broke new ground in Western art. Opposite the altar is a *Last Judgment,* most likely designed and painted by Giotto's assistants, where Enrico offers his chapel to the Virgin, celebrating her role in human salvation—particularly appropriate, given the penitential purpose of the chapel.

Mandatory reservations, which should be made at least two days ahead online or by phone, are for a specific time and are nonrefundable. Reservations are necessary even if you have a Padova Card. In order to preserve the artwork, doors are opened only every 15 minutes. A maximum of 25 visitors at a time must spend 15 minutes in an acclimatization room before making a 15-minute (20-minute in winter) chapel visit. Punctuality is essential; it's best to arrive at the chapel before your reservation time. If you don't have a reservation, it's sometimes possible to buy your chapel admission on the spot—but you might have to wait a while until there's a group with an opening. You can see fresco details as part of a virtual tour at Musei Civici degli Eremitani. A good place to get some background before visiting the chapel is the multimedia room, which offers films and interactive computer presentations. ⊠ *Piazza Eremitani 8* ☎ *049/2010020 for reservations* ⊕ *www.cappelladegliscrovegni.it* ☎ *€12 includes Musei Civici, or €1 with Padova Card* ☉ *Early Nov.–early Mar. and mid-June–early Aug., daily 9–7; early Mar.–mid-June and early Aug.–early Nov., 9 AM–10 PM; entry by appointment only.*

4 Palazzo della Ragione. Also known as Il Salone, this spectacular arcaded
★ reception hall, which divides the Piazza delle Frutta from the Piazza delle Erbe, was built between 1303 and 1309, with later 15th-century additions. Giotto painted the original frescoes, which were destroyed in a fire in 1420. In the Middle Ages, as its name implies, the building housed Padua's law courts; today, its street-level arcades shelter shops and cafés. Art shows are often held upstairs in the frescoed **Salone,** at 85 feet high one of the largest and most architecturally pleasing halls in Italy. In the Salone there's an enormous wooden horse, crafted for a 15th-century public tournament, with a head and tail later remodeled to replicate the steed from Donatello's *Gattamelata.* In the piazza surrounding the building are Padua's colorful open-air fruit and vegetable markets. ⊠ *Piazza della Ragione* ☎ *049/8205006* ☎ *Salone €4*

or free with Padova Card ☉ *Feb.–Oct., Tues.–Sun. 9–7; Nov.–Jan., Tues.–Sun. 9–6.*

❺ **Piazza dei Signori.** Some fine examples of 15th- and 16th-century buildings line this square. On the west side, the **Palazzo del Capitanio** (facade constructed 1598–1605) has an impressive **Torre dell'Orologio,** with an astronomical clock dating from 1344 and a portal made by Falconetto in 1532 in the form of a Roman triumphal arch. The **Battistero del Duomo** (12th century, with frescoes by Giusto de Menabuoi, 1374–78) is just a few steps away.

❽ **Villa Pisani.** Extensive grounds with rare trees, ornamental fountains, and garden follies surround this extraordinary palace built in 1721 for the Venetian doge Alvise Pisani in Stra, 13 km (8 mi) southeast of Padua. Recalling Versailles more than a Veneto villa, it was one of the last and grandest of many stately residences constructed along the Brenta River from the 16th to 18th centuries by wealthy Venetians for their *villeggiatura*—vacation and escape from the midsummer humidity. Gianbattista Tiepolo's (1696–1770) spectacular frescoes on the ballroom ceiling alone are worth the visit. For a relaxing afternoon, explore the gorgeous park and maze. To get here from Venice, take bus 53 from Piazzale Roma. The villa is a five-minute walk from the bus stop in Stra. ✉ *Via Doge Pisani 7 Stra* ☎ *049/502074* 🔗 *Villa, maze, and park €7.50; maze and park only €4.50* ☉ *Apr.–Sept., Tues.–Sun. 9–8; villa and park only: Nov.–Mar., Tues.–Sun. 9–5; Oct., Tues.–Sun. 9–6. Last entry 1 hr before closing.*

WORTH NOTING

Chiesa degli Eremitani. This 13th-century church houses substantial fragments of Andrea Mantegna's frescoes (1448–50), damaged by allied bombing in World War II. Despite their fragmentary condition, Mantegna's still beautiful and historically important frescoes depicting the martyrdom of Saint James and Saint Christopher show the young artist's mastery of extremely complex problems of perspective. ✉ *Piazza degli Eremitani* ☎ *049/8756410* ☉ *Nov.–Mar., Mon.–Sat. 8:15–6:15, Sun. 10–1 and 4:15–7; Apr.–Oct., Mon.–Sat. 8:15–6:45, Sun. 10–1 and 4–7.*

❷ **Musei Civici degli Eremitani** *(Civic Museum).* What was formerly a monastery now houses works of Venetian masters, as well as fine collections of archaeological pieces and ancient coins. Notable are the Giotto Crucifix, which once hung in the Scrovegni Chapel, and the *Portrait of a Young Senator* by Giovanni Bellini (1430–1516). ✉ *Piazza Eremitani 10* ☎ *049/8204551* 🔗 *€10, €12 with Scrovegni Chapel, or free with Padova Card* ☉ *Tues.–Sun. 9–7.*

❼ **Orto Botanico** *(Botanical Garden).* The Venetian Republic ordered the creation of Padua's botanical garden in 1545 to supply the university with medicinal plants. You can stroll the arboretum and wander through hothouses and beds of plants that were first introduced to Italy in this late-Renaissance garden, which still maintains its original layout. A St. Peter's palm, planted in 1585, inspired Goethe to write his 1790 essay called "The Metamorphosis of Plants." ✉ *Via Orto Botanico 15*

5

🖼 *049/8272119* ⊕ *www.ortobotanico.unipd.it* 🎫 *€4, free with Padova Card* ☉ *Apr.–Oct., daily 9–1 and 3–7; Nov.–Mar., Mon.–Sat. 9–1.*

❸ **Palazzo del Bo'.** The University of Padua, founded in 1222, centers around this 16th-century palazzo with an 18th-century facade. It's named after the Osteria del Bo' (*bo'* means "ox"), an inn that once stood on the site. It's worth a visit to see the exquisite and perfectly proportioned anatomy theater (1594), the beautiful "Old Courtyard," and a hall with a lectern used by Galileo. You can enter only as part of a guided tour. Most guides speak English, but it is worth checking ahead by phone. ✉ *Via VIII Febbraio* 🖼 *049/8273044* ⊕ *www.unipd.it* 🎫 *€5* ☉ *Nov.–Feb., Mon., Wed., and Fri. at 3:15 and 4:15; Tues., Thurs., and Sat. at 10:15 and 11:15. Mar.–Oct., Mon., Wed., and Fri. at 3:15, 4:15, and 5:15; Tues., Thurs., and Sat. at 9:15, 10:15, and 11:15.*

WHERE TO EAT

$$$
MODERN ITALIAN

✗ **La Finestra.** Perhaps the trendiest restaurant in Padua, cozy yet elegant La Finestra richly deserves its reputation. The carefully prepared and creatively presented dishes may not always stick to the original recipes, but no one can contest that owners Carlo Vidali and Hélène Dao know what they're doing in the kitchen. Their version of the regional classic *pasta e fagioli,* for example, uses the most exquisite beans in the region, leaves out the pasta, and substitutes croutons and a dollop of foie gras. This is not grandma's bean soup, but it's heavenly. ✉ *Via dei Tadi 15* 🖼 *049/650313* ⊕ *www.ristorantefinestra.it* 🍽 *AE, MC, V* ☉ *Closed 2 wks in Aug. No lunch. Closed Sun. and Mon.*

$
WINE BAR
★

✗ **L'Anfora.** This mix between a traditional *bàcaro* (wine bar) and an *osteria* (tavernlike restaurant) is a local institution. Stand at the bar shoulder to shoulder with a cross section of Padovano society, from construction workers to professors, and let the friendly and knowledgeable proprietors help you choose a wine. The reasonably priced menu offers simple *casalinga* (home-cooked dishes), plus salads and a selection of cheeses. Portions are ample, and no one will look askance if you don't order the full meal. The place is packed with loyal regulars at lunchtime, so come early or expect a wait; if you come alone, you'll probably end up with a table of friends before you leave. ✉ *Via Soncin 13* 🖼 *049/656629* 🍽 *AE, V* ☉ *Closed Sun. (except in Dec.), 1 wk in Jan., and 1 wk in Aug.*

$$$$
MODERN ITALIAN

✗ **Le Calandre.** If you are willing to shell out €500 for a dinner for two, Le Calandre should definitely be on your itinerary. The quietly elegant restaurant is consistently judged by major restaurant critics as one of the two or three best restaurants in the country. The food, based on traditional Veneto recipes, is given a highly sophisticated and creative treatment. The traditional squid in its ink, for example, is served as a "cappuccino," in a glass with a crust of potato foam. The menu changes seasonally, and with owner-chef Massimiliano Alajmo's creative impulses. Alajmo considers food to be an art form, not nourishment, so be prepared for small portions. Make reservations well in advance. Le Calandre is in the village of Sarmeola di Rubano, a few kilometers west of Padua and easily reached by taxi. ✉ *Via Liguria 1*

Sarmeola di Rubano ☎ *049/630303* ⊕ *www.calandre.com* ⌖ *Reservations essential* ▭ *MC, V* ⊘ *Closed Sun. and Mon., late Dec.–early Jan., mid-Aug.–early Sept.*

$$$ ✕ **Nerodiseppia.** Behind the Basilica di San Antonio, Nerodiseppia has a
ITALIAN cool atmosphere and unadorned decor. Don't be put off, as this is one of the finest fish restaurants in a region noted for its seafood. Patrizia and Eugenia Rubin, its friendly Padovane owners, serve up carefully but simply prepared dishes using the freshest fish from the catch of the day. The reasonably priced menu varies according to the season and what local fishermen brought in that day. In the fall, locals flock here to try the *moeche,* baby soft-shell crabs dipped in eggs and flour and fried to a crispy, golden brown. The weekday set lunch, ranging from €16.50 to €18, is one of the city's gastronomic bargains. ⊠ *Via San Francesco 161* ☎ *049/8364049* ⊕ *www.ristorantenerodiseppia.it* ▭ *DC, MC, V* ⊘ *Closed Sun. and Mon., Dec. 26–Jan. 7 and in Aug.*

$$ ✕ **Osteria Dal Capo.** A friendly trattoria in the heart of what used to be
VENETIAN Padua's Jewish ghetto, Osteria Dal Capo serves almost exclusively tra-
★ ditional Veneto dishes and does so with refinement and care. The liver and onions is extraordinarily tender. Even the accompanying polenta is grilled to perfection—slightly crisp on the outside and moist on the inside. And the desserts are nothing to scoff at, either. Word is out among locals about this hidden gem, and the tiny place fills up quickly, so reservations are necessary. ⊠ *Via degli Oblizzi 2* ☎ *049/663105* ⌖ *Reservations essential* ▭ *AE, DC, MC, V* ⊘ *Closed Sun., 2 wks in early Jan., and 3 wks in Aug. No lunch Mon.*

5

WHERE TO STAY

$ ⬚ **Al Fagiano.** This delightfully funky budget hotel sits near Basilica di Sant'Antonio, and some rooms have views of the church's spires and cupolas. The interior includes sponge-painted walls, brush-painted chandeliers, and an elevator where self-proclaimed artists can add graffiti to their heart's content. An amiable staff and relatively central location make Al Fagiano pleasant and convenient. Breakfast is available for €6. **Pros:** large rooms; relaxed atmosphere; convenient location. **Cons:** no room service or help with baggage; some find the eclectic decor a bit much. ⊠ *Via Locatelli 45* ☎ *049/8750073* ⊕ *www.alfagiano.com* ↝ *40 rooms* ⌂ *In room: a/c, Wi-Fi (some). In-hotel: room service, bar, Wi-Fi hotspot, some pets allowed* ▭ *AE, DC, MC, V* ⊚⊢ *EP.*

$$ ⬚ **Majestic Toscanelli.** Close to the Piazza delle Erbe, this is easily the best-
★ located hotel in the city. The charming entrance, with potted evergreens flanking the steps, sets the tone in this pleasant lodging. The cozy bedrooms are furnished in different styles from Louis XV to French Empire. Your welcoming hosts offer discounts to seniors, AAA members, and those carrying Fodor's guidebooks. **Pros:** excellent location; attentive staff; pleasant and warm atmosphere. **Cons:** rooms, while ample, are not large; little natural light and few views; some street noise at night, especially on weekends; hefty parking fee. ⊠ *Via dell'Arco 2, near Piazza delle Erbe* ☎ *049/663244* ⊕ *www.toscanelli.com* ↝ *26 rooms, 6 suites* ⌂ *In-room: safe (some), refrigerator, Internet, Wi-Fi. In-hotel:*

Continued on page 348

EATING AND DRINKING WELL IN VENETIAN ARC

With the decisive seasonal changes of the Venetian Arc, it's little wonder that many restaurants shun printed menus. Elements from field and forest define much of the region's cuisine, including white asparagus, wild herbs, chestnuts, radicchio, and mushrooms.

Restaurants of the Venetian Arc tend to cling to tradition, not only in the food they serve but how they serve it. This means that from 3 in the afternoon until 8 in the evening most places are closed tight (though you can pick up a snack at a bar during these hours), and on Sunday afternoon restaurants are packed with Italian families and friends indulging in a weekly ritual of lunching out.

Meals are still a sacred ritual for most Italians, so don't be surprised if you get disapproving looks when you gobble down a sandwich or a slice of pizza while seated on the church steps or a park bench. In many places it is actually illegal to do so. If you want to fit in with the locals, eat while standing at the bar and they may not even notice that you are a tourist.

THE BEST IN BEANS

Pasta e fagioli, a thick bean soup with pasta, served slightly warm or at room temperature, is made all over Italy. Folks in Veneto, though, take a special pride in their version. It features particularly fine beans that are grown around the village of Lamon, near Belluno.

Even when bought in the Veneto, the beans from Lamon cost more than double the next most expensive variety, but their rich and delicate taste is considered to be well worth the added expense. You never knew bean soup could taste so good.

PASTA, RISOTTO, POLENTA

For *primi* (first courses), the Veneto dines on *bigoli* (thick whole-wheat pasta) generally served with an anchovy-onion sauce, and risotto—saturated with red wine in Verona and prosecco in Conegliano. Polenta is everywhere, varying from a stiff porridge topped with Gorgonzola or stew, to a patty grilled alongside meat or fish, as in the photo below.

FISH

The catch of the day is always a good bet, whether sweet and succulent Adriatic shellfish, sea bream, bass, or John Dory, or freshwater fish from Lake Garda near Verona. But be sure to note whether the fish is wild or farmed—the taste, texture, and price difference are considerable.

A staple in the Veneto is *baccalà*, dried salt cod, soaked in water or milk, and then prepared in a different way in each city. In Vicenza, *baccalà alla vicentina*, pictured at left, is cooked with onions, milk, and cheese, and is generally served with polenta. Locals consider it as central to their city's identity as Palladio.

MEAT

Inland, meat prevails: pork and veal are standards, while goose, duck, and guinea fowl are common poultry options. Lamb is best in spring, when it's young and delicate. In Friuli–Venezia Giulia, menus show the influences of Austria-

Hungary: you may find deer and hare on the menu, as well as Eastern European–style goulash. Throughout the Veneto an unusual treat is *nervetti*—cubes of gelatin from a cow's knee with onions, parsley, oil, and lemon.

RADICCHIO DI TREVISO

In fall and winter be sure to try the radicchio di Treviso, pictured above, a red endive grown near that town but popular all over the region. It's best in a stew with chicken or veal, in a risotto, or just grilled or baked with a drizzle of olive oil and perhaps a bit of taleggio cheese from neighboring Lombardy.

WINE

Wine is excellent here: the Veneto produces more D.O.C. (Denominazione di Origine Controllata) wines than any other region in Italy. Amarone, the region's crowning achievement, is a robust and powerful red with an alcohol content as high as 16%. Valpolicella and Bardolino are other notable appellations.

The best of the whites are Soave, sparkling prosecco, and pinot bianco (pinot blanc). In Friuli–Venezia Giulia, the local wines par excellence are Tocai Friulano, a dry, lively white made from Tocai grapes that has attained international stature, and piccolit, perhaps Italy's most highly prized dessert wine.

restaurant, bar, Internet terminal, parking (paid), some pets allowed ⊟ AE, DC, MC, V ⫟◯❙ BP.

$$ ⊞ **Methis.** The strikingly modern
★ Methis takes its name from the Greek word for style and spirit. Four floors of sleekly designed guest rooms reflect the elements: gentle earth tones, fiery red, watery cool blue, and airy white in the top-floor suites. Rooms have Japanese-style tubs, and four are equipped for guests with disabilities. The lobby has one lounge and a quieter reading room. There's a pleasant view from the front rooms, which face the canal. **Pros:** attractive rooms; helpful and attentive staff; pleasant little extras like umbrellas. **Cons:** A 15-minute walk from major sights and restaurants; public spaces are cold and uninviting. ✉ *Riviera Paleocapa 70* ☎ *049/8725555* ⊕ *www.methishotel.com* ⫞ *52 rooms, 7 suites* ⟁ *In-room: safe, refrigerator, Wi-Fi. In-hotel: bar, gym, Internet terminal, parking (free)* ⊟ *AE, DC, MC, V* ⫟◯❙ *BP.*

> ### COCKTAIL HOUR ON PADUA'S PIAZZAS
>
> One of Padua's greatest traditions is the outdoor en-masse consumption of aperitifs: *spritz* (a mix of Aperol or Campari, soda water, and wine), prosecco (sparkling wine), or wine. It all happens in the Piazza delle Erbe and Piazza delle Frutta. Several bars there provide drinks in plastic cups, so you can take them outside and mingle among the crowds. The ritual, practiced primarily by students, begins at 6 PM or so, at which hour you can also pick up a snack from one of the outdoor vendors. On weekends, the open-air revelry continues into the wee hours.

CAFÉS AND WINE BARS

No visit to Padua is complete without a trip to **Caffè Pedrocchi** (✉ *Piazzetta Pedrocchi* ☎ *049/8781231* ⊕ *www.caffepedrocchi.it*). You can still sit here, as the French writer Stendahl did shortly after the café was established in 1831, and observe a good slice of Veneto life, especially, as he noted, the elegant ladies sipping their coffee. The massive café, built in a style reflecting the fashion set by Napoléon's expeditions in Egypt, has long been central to the city's social life. It also serves lunch and dinner, and is proud of its innovative menu. Open 9 AM to midnight daily from mid-June to mid-September; hours for the rest of the year are Sunday to Wednesday 9 to 9, Thursday to Saturday 9 AM to midnight.

Hostaria Ai Do Archi (✉ *Via Nazario Sauro 23* ☎ *049/652335*) is the most popular Padovano version of the *bàcari* that are so typical of the Veneto: wine bars where people sip wine, sample local treats, and talk politics. The Ai Do Archi is as famous for its impressive platters of sliced meats as it is for its selections of wine. Besides attracting students and locals, it is also a meeting place for many of Padova's reggae fans.

VICENZA

Vicenza bears the distinctive signature of the 16th-century architect Andrea Palladio, whose name has been given to the "Palladian" style of architecture. He effectively emphasized the principles of order and harmony in the classical style of architecture established by Renaissance architects such as Brunelleschi, Alberti, and Sansovino. He used these principles and classical motifs not only for public buildings but also for private dwellings. His elegant villas and palaces were influential in propagating classical architecture in Europe, especially Britain, and later in America—most notably at Thomas Jefferson's Monticello.

In the mid-16th century Palladio was commissioned to rebuild much of Vicenza, which had been greatly damaged during wars waged against Venice by the League of Cambrai, an alliance of the papacy, France, the Holy Roman Empire, and several neighboring city-states. He made his name with the basilica, begun in 1549 in the heart of Vicenza, and then embarked on a series of lordly buildings, all of which adhere to the same classicism and principles of harmony.

GETTING HERE

Vicenza is midway between Padua and Verona, and several trains leave from both cities every hour. By car, take the Autostrada Brescia–Padova/Torino–Trieste A4/E70 to SP247 North directly into Vicenza.

VISITOR INFORMATION

Vicenza tourism office (✉ *Piazza Giacomo Matteotti 12* ☎ *0444/320854* ⊕ *www.vicenzae.org*).

EXPLORING VICENZA

Many of Palladio's works are near the Venetian Gothic and baroque palaces that line Corso Palladio, an elegant shopping thoroughfare where Vicenza's status as one of Italy's wealthiest cities is evident. Part of this wealth stems from Vicenza's being a world center for gold jewelry.

TOP ATTRACTIONS

❷ **Teatro Olimpico.** Palladio's last, and perhaps most spectacular work, was completed after his death by Vincenzo Scamozzi (1552–1616). Based closely on the model of ancient Roman theaters, it represents an important development in theater and stage design and is noteworthy for its acoustics and the cunning use of perspective in Scamozzi's permanent backdrop. The anterooms are frescoed with images of important figures in Venetian history. ✉ *Piazza Matteotti* ☎ *0444/222800* 💶 *€8 includes admission to Palazzo Chiericati* ☉ *Sept.–June, Tues.–Sun. 9–5; July and Aug., Tues.–Sun. 9–7; times may vary depending on performance schedule.*

Fodor's Choice
★

❹ **Villa della Rotonda (Villa Almerico Capra).** This beautiful Palladian villa, commissioned in 1556 as a suburban residence for Paolo Almerico, is undoubtedly the purest expression of Palladio's architectural theory and aesthetic. Although it seems more of a pavilion showplace, it was in fact commissioned as a residence, and as such demonstrates the priority Palladio gave to architectural symbolism of celestial harmony

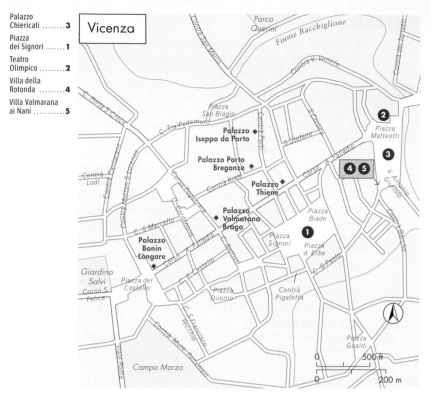

over practical considerations. It's more a villa-temple than a house to live in, and in this respect, it goes beyond the rational utilitarianism of Renaissance architecture. Although a visit to the interior of the building may be difficult to schedule (it's still privately owned), it is well worth the effort in order to get an idea of how the people who commissioned the residence actually lived. Viewing the exterior and the grounds is a must for any visit to Vicenza. The villa is a 20-minute walk from town or a short ride on the No. 8 bus from Piazza Roma. ⊠ *Via della Rotonda* 🕾 *0444/321793* 🖃 *€10 grounds and interior, €5 grounds only* ☉ *Grounds: Tues.–Sun. 10–noon and 2:30–6 (5 PM closing mid-Nov.– mid-Mar.); interior: Mar.–Nov., Wed. 10–noon and 2:30–6.*

5 **Villa Valmarana ai Nani.** Inside this 17th- to 18th-century country house, named for the statues of dwarfs adorning the garden, is a series of frescoes executed in 1757 by Gianbattista Tiepolo depicting scenes from *The Illiad,* Tasso's *Gerusalemme Liberata,* and Ariosto's *Orlando Furioso.* They include his *Sacrifice of Iphigenia,* unanimously acclaimed by critics as a major masterpiece of 18th-century painting. The neighboring *foresteria* (farmworkers' dormitory) is also part of the museum; it contains frescoes showing 18th-century life at its most charming, and scenes of chinoiserie popular in the 18th century, by Tiepolo's son Giandomenico (1727–1804). The garden dwarves are probably taken from

Continued on page 356

PALLADIO COUNTRY

Wealthy 16th-century patrons commissioned Andrea Palladio to design villas that would reflect their sense of cultivation and status. Using a classical vocabulary of columns, arches, and domes, he gave them a series of masterpieces in the towns and hills of the Veneto that exemplify the neo-Platonic ideals of harmony and proportion. Palladio's creations are the perfect expression of how a learned 16th century man saw himself and his world, and as you stroll through them today, their serene beauty is as powerful as ever. Listen closely and you might even hear that celestial harmony, the music of the spheres, that so moved Palladio and his patrons.

TOWN & COUNTRY

Although the villa, or "country residence," was still a relatively new phenomenon in the 16th century, it quickly became all the rage once the great lords of Venice turned their eyes from the sea toward the fertile plains of the Veneto. They were forced to do this once their trade routes had faltered when Ottoman Turks conquered Constantinople in 1456 and Columbus opened a path to the riches of America in 1492. In no time, canals were built, farms were laid out, and the fashion for *villeggiatura*—the attraction of idyllic country retreats for the nobility—became a favored lifestyle. As a means of escaping an overheated Rome,

villas had been the original brainchild of the ancient emperors and it was no accident that the Venetian lords wished to emulate this palatial style of country residence. Palladio's method of evaluating the standards, and standbys, of ancient Roman life through the eye of the Italian Renaissance, combined with Palladio's innate sense of proportion and symmetry, became the lasting foundation of his art. In turn, Palladio threw out the jambalaya of styles prevalent in Venetian architecture—Oriental, Gothic, and Renaissance—for the pure, noble lines found in the buildings of the Caesars.

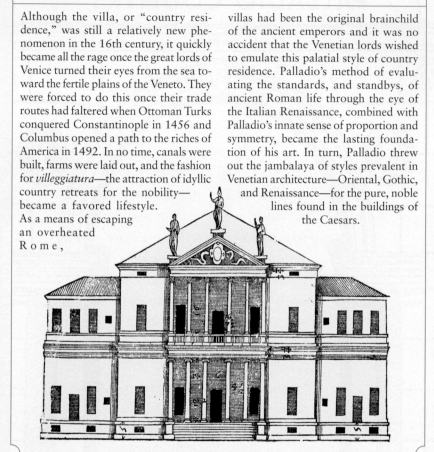

PALLADIO, STAR ARCHITECT

Andrea Palladio (1508–1580)

"Face dark, eyes fiery. Dress rich. His appearance that of a genius." So was Palladio described by his wealthy mentor, Count Trissino. Trissino encouraged the young student to trade in his birth name, Andrea di Pietro della Gondola, for the elegant Palladio. He did, and it proved a wise move indeed. Born in Padua in 1508, Andrea moved to nearby Vicenza in 1524 and was quickly taken up by the city's power elite. He experienced a profound revelation on his first

THE OLD BECOMES NEW

La Malcontenta

Studying ancient Rome with the eyes of an explorer, Palladio employed a style that linked old with new—but often did so in unexpected ways. Just take a look at Villa Foscari, nicknamed **"La Malcontenta"** (Mira, 041/5470012, www. lamalcontenta.com €8. Open May–Oct., Tues. and Sat. 9–noon; from Venice, take an ACTV bus from Piazzale Roma to Mira or opt for a boat ride up on the Burchiello). Shaded by weeping willows and mirrored by the Brenta Canal, "The Sad Lady" was built for Nicolò and Alvise Foscari and is the quintessence of Palladian poetry. Inspired by the grandeur of Roman public buildings, Palladio applied the ancient motif of a temple facade to a domestic dwelling, topped off by a pediment, a construct most associated with religious structures. Inside, he used the technique of vaulting seen in ancient Roman baths, with giant windows and immense white walls ready-made for the colorful frescoes painted by Zelotti. No one knows for certain the origin of the villa's nickname—some say it came from a Venetian owner's wife who was exiled there due to her scandalous behavior. Regardless of the name, it's hard today to associate such a beautiful, graceful villa with anything but harmony and contentment.

trip, in 1541, to Rome, where he sensed the harmony of the ancient ruins and saw the elements of classicism that were working their way into contemporary architecture. This experience led to his spectacular conversion of the Vicenza's Palazzo della Ragione (1545) into a basilica recalling the great meeting halls of antiquity. In years to come, after relocating to Venice, he created some memorable churches, such as S. Giorgio Maggiore (1564). Despite these varied projects, Palladio's unassailable position as one of the world's greatest architects is tied to the countryside villas, which he spread across the Veneto plains like a firmament of stars. Nothing else in the Veneto illuminates more clearly the idyllic beauty of the region than these elegant residences, their stonework now nicely mellowed and suntanned after five centuries.

VICENZA, CITY OF PALLADIO

Palazzo della Ragione

La Rotonda

To see Palladio's pageant of palaces, head for Vicenza. His **Palazzo della Ragione**, or "Basilica," marks the city's heart, the Piazza dei Signori. This building rocketed young Palladio from an unknown to an architectural star. Across the way is his redbrick **Loggia dei Capitaniato.**

One block past the Loggia is Vicenza's main street, appropriately named Corso Andrea Palladio. Just off this street is the Contrà Porti, where you'll find the **Palazzo Barbaran da Porto** (1570) at No. 11, with its fabulously rich facade erupting with Ionic and Corinthian pillars. Today, this is the Centro Internazionale di Studi di Architettura Andrea Palladio (0444/323014, www.cisapalladio. org), a study center which mounts impressive temporary exhibitions. A few steps away, on the Contrà San Gaetano Thiene, is the Palazzo Thiene (1542-58), designed by Giulio Romano and completed by Palladio.

Doubling back to Contrà Porti 21, you find the **Palazzo Iseppo da Porto** (1544), the first palazzo where you can see the neoclassical effects of young Palladio's trip to Rome. Following the Contrà Reale, you come to Corso Fogazzaro 16 and the **Palazzo Valmarana Braga** (1565). Its gigantic pilasters were a first for domestic architecture.

Returning to the Corso Palladio, head left to the opposite end of the Corso, about five blocks, to the Piazza Mattoti and **Palazzo Chiericati** (1550). This was practically a suburban area in the 16th century, and for the palazzo Palladio combined elements of urban and rural design. The pedestal raising the building and the steps leading to the entrance—unknown in urban palaces— were to protect from floods and to keep cows from wandering in the front door. (For opening times and details, see the main text).

Across the Corso Palladio is Palladio's last and one of his most spectacular works, the **Teatro Olimpico** (1580). By careful study of ancient ruins and architectural texts, he reconstructed a Roman theater with archaeological precision. Palladio died before it was completed, but he left clear plans for the project. (For opening times and details, see the main text.)

Although it's on the outskirts of town, the **Villa Almerico Capra**, better known as **La Rotonda** (1566), is an indispensable part of any visit to Vicenza. It's the iconic Palladian building, the purest expression of his aesthetic. (For opening times, details, and a discussion of the villa, see the main text.)

A MAGNIFICENT COLLABORATION

Villa Barbaro

At the **Villa Barbaro** (1554) near the town of Maser in the province of Treviso, 48 km (30 miles) northeast of Vicenza, you can see the results of a one-time collaboration between two of the greatest artists of their age.

Palladio was the architect, and Paolo Veronese decorated the interior with an amazing cycle of trompe l'oeil frescoes—walls dissolve into landscapes, and illusions of courtiers and servants enter rooms and smile down from balustrades.

Legend has it a feud developed between Palladio and Veronese, with Palladio feeling the illusionistic frescoes detracted from his architecture; but there is prac-

tically nothing to support the idea of such a rift.

It's also noteworthy that Palladio for the first time connected the two lateral granaries to the main villa. This was a working farm, and Palladio thus created an architectural unity by connecting with graceful arcades the working parts of the estate to the living quarters, bringing together the Renaissance dichotomy of the active and the contemplative life. *Via Cornuda 7, Maser, 0432/923004 www. villadimaser.it, €5 Open April- October Tues. and weekends 3-6; Nov.- March, weekends 2:30- 5, or by reservation; Closed 24 Dec.- 6 Jan.*

5

IN FOCUS PALLADIO COUNTRY

ALONG THE BRENTA CANAL

During the 16th century the Brenta was transformed into a landlocked version of Venice's Grand Canal with the building of nearly 50 waterside villas. Back then, boating parties viewed them in *"burchielli"*—beautiful boats. Today, the Burchiello excursion boat (Via Orlandini 3, Padua, 049/8206910, www.ilburchiello. it) makes full- and half-day tours along the Brenta, from March to November, departing from Padua on Wednesday, Friday, and Sunday and from Venice on Tuesday, Thursday, and Saturday; tickets are €40–€71 and can also be bought at American Express at Salizzada San Moisè in Venice. You visit three houses, including the Villas Pisani and Foscari, with a lunchtime break in Oriago. Another canal excursion is run by the Battelli del Brenta (www.battellidel brenta.it). Note that most houses are on the left side coming from Venice, or the right from Padua.

designs by Giandomenico. You can reach the villa on foot by following the same path that leads to Palladio's Villa della Rotonda. ⊠ *Via dei Nani 2/8* ☏ *0444/321803* ⌨ *€8* ⊘ *Mid-Mar.–Oct., Tues.–Sun. 10–noon and 3–6; Nov.–mid-Mar., weekends 10–noon and 2–4:30.*

WORTH NOTING

❸ **Palazzo Chiericati.** This imposing Palladian palazzo (1550) would be worthy of a visit even if it didn't house Vicenza's **Museo Civico**. Because of the ample space surrounding the building site, Palladio combined here elements of an urban palazzo with those he used in his country villas. The museum's important Venetian collection includes significant paintings by Cima, Tiepolo, Piazzetta, and Tintoretto, but its main attraction is an extensive collection of highly interesting and rarely found painters from the Vicenza area, such as Jacopo Bassano (1515–92) and the eccentric and innovative Francesco Maffei (1605–60), whose work foreshadowed important currents of Venetian painting of subsequent generations. ⊠ *Piazza Matteotti* ☏ *0444/325071* ⌨ *€8 includes admission to Teatro Olimpico* ⊘ *Sept.–June, Tues.–Sun. 9–5; July and Aug., Tues.–Sun. 9–5.*

❶ **Piazza dei Signori.** At the heart of Vicenza sits this square, which contains the **Palazzo della Ragione** (1549), commonly known as Palladio's basilica, a courthouse, and public meeting hall (the original Roman meaning of the term *basilica*). The previously almost-unknown Palladio made his name by successfully modernizing the medieval building, grafting a graceful two-story exterior loggia onto the existing Gothic structure. Take a look also at the **Loggia del Capitaniato,** opposite, which Palladio designed but never completed. The palazzo and the loggia are open to the public only when there's an exhibition; ask at the tourist office.

WHERE TO EAT

$$
NORTHERN
ITALIAN
⨉ **Antico Ristorante agli Schioppi.** When they want to eat well, Vicenza's natives generally travel to the adjoining countryside—Antico Ristorante agli Schioppi is one of the few in the city frequented by Vicentino families and businessmen. Veneto country-style decor, with enormous murals, matches simple, well-prepared regional cuisine at this family-run restaurant. The risotto, delicately flavored with wild mushrooms and zucchini flowers, is creamy and—a rarity in restaurant risottos—beautifully textured. This is also an excellent place to try *baccalà*, a cod dish that is a Vicenza specialty. ⊠ *Contrà Piazza del Castello 26* ☏ *0444/543701* ⊕ *www.ristoranteaglischioppi.com* ▭ *AE, DC, MC, V* ⊘ *Closed Sun., last wk of July–mid-Aug., and Jan. 1–6. No dinner Sat.*

¢
PIZZERIA
⨉ **Da Vittorio.** It has little in the way of atmosphere or decor, but Vicentini flock to this small eatery for what is perhaps the best pizza north of Naples. There's an incredible array of toppings, from the traditional to the exotic (mangoes), but the pies are all so authentic that they will make you think you are sitting by the Bay of Naples. The service is friendly and efficient. This is a great place to stop for lunch if you're walking to Palladio's Rotonda or the Villa Valmarana. ⊠ *Borgo Berga 52* ☏ *0444/525059* ▭ *No credit cards* ⊘ *Closed Tues.*

$
NORTHERN
ITALIAN
★

✕**Ponte delle Bele.** Vicenza lies at the foot of the Alps, and many residents spend at least a part of summer in the mountains to escape the heat. Alpine cuisine has been incorporated into the local culture and can be enjoyed at this popular and friendly Veneto trattoria. The house specialty, *stinco di maiale al forno* (roast port shank), is wonderfully fragrant with herbs and aromatic vegetables. Also try such game as venison with blueberries or guinea fowl roasted with white grapes. The rather kitschy decor doesn't detract from the good, hearty food. ⊠ *Contrà Ponte delle Bele 5* ☎ *0444/320647* ⊕ *www.pontedellebele.it* ⊟ *AE, DC, MC, V* ☻ *Closed Sun. and 2 wks in mid-Aug.*

¢
ITALIAN

✕**Righetti.** For a city of its size, Vicenza has few distinguished restaurants. That's why many people gravitate to this popular cafeteria, which serves classic dishes without putting a dent in your wallet. There's frequently a hearty soup such as *orzo e fagioli* (barley and bean) on the menu. The classic *baccalà alla vicentina*, a cod dish, is a great reason to stop by on Friday. ⊠ *Piazza Duomo 3* ☎ *0444/543135* ⊟ *No credit cards* ☻ *Closed weekends, 1st wk in Jan., and Aug.*

5

WHERE TO STAY

During annual gold fairs in January, May, and September, it may be quite difficult to find lodging. Be sure to reserve well in advance and expect to pay higher rates.

$$

🛏 **Campo Marzio.** A five-minute walk from the railway station, this comfortable hotel is right in front of the city walls. You can borrow a bicycle to explore the town. Rooms are ample and furnished in a pleasant modern style, but don't expect anything spectacular or romantic. This is the only full-service hotel in Vicenza, so it fills up quickly during the gold fairs—when rates nearly double. **Pros:** central location; more amenities than its competitors; set back from the street, so it's quiet and bright. **Cons:** public spaces are uninspiring; incredibly expensive during fairs. ⊠ *Viale Roma 21* ☎ *0444/5457000* ⊕ *www.hotelcampomarzio.com* ➫ *36 rooms* ᴥ *In-room: safe, refrigerator, Internet, Wi-Fi. In-hotel: bar, parking (free), some pets allowed* ⊟ *AE, DC, MC, V* �ⓘ *BP.*

$
★

🛏 **Due Mori.** Authentic turn-of-the-20th-century antiques fill the rooms at this 1883 hotel, one of the oldest in the city. Regulars favor the place because the high ceilings in the main building make it feel light and airy. This comfortable hotel, just off the Piazza dei Signori, has a great location. It's also a true bargain—rates stay the same throughout the year, with no high-season price hikes. Breakfast is available for €5. **Pros:** tastefully furnished rooms; friendly staff; central location. **Cons:** no air-conditioning (although ceiling fans minimize the need for it); no one to help with baggage. ⊠ *Contrà Do Rode 24* ☎ *0444/321886* ⊕ *www.hotelduemori.com* ➫ *53 rooms* ᴥ *In-room: no a/c, no TV, Wi-Fi (some). In-hotel: bar, parking (free), some pets allowed* ⊟ *MC, V* ☻ *Closed 1st 2 wks of Aug. and 2 wks in late Dec.* �ⓘ *EP.*

VERONA

On the banks of the fast-flowing River Adige, 60 km (37 mi) west of Vicenza, enchanting Verona has timeless monuments, a picturesque town center, and a romantic reputation as the setting of Shakespeare's *Romeo and Juliet*. With its lively Venetian air and proximity to Lake Garda, it attracts hordes of tourists, especially Germans and Austrians. Tourism peaks during summer's renowned season of open-air opera in the arena and during spring's **Vinitaly** (⊠ *Fiera di Verona, Viale del Lavoro 8* ☎ *045/8298170* ⊕ *www.vinitaly.com*), one of the world's most important wine expos. For five days you can sample the wines of more than 3,000 wineries from dozens of countries.

Verona grew to power and prosperity within the Roman Empire as a result of its key commercial and military position in northern Italy. With its Roman arena, theater, and city gates, it has the most significant monuments of Roman antiquity north of Rome. After the fall of the empire, the city continued to flourish under the guidance of barbarian kings such as Theodoric, Alboin, Pepin, and Berenger I, reaching its cultural and artistic peak in the 13th and 14th centuries under the della Scala (Scaligero) dynasty. (Look for the *scala*, or ladder, emblem all over town.) In 1404 Verona traded its independence for security and placed itself under the control of Venice. (The other recurring architectural motif is the lion of Saint Mark, a symbol of Venetian rule.)

GETTING HERE

Verona is midway between Venice and Milan. It is served by a small airport, Aeroporto Valerio Catullo, which accommodates domestic and European flights; however, many travelers still prefer to fly into Venice or Milan and drive or take the train to Verona. Several trains per hour depart from any point on the Milan–Venice line. By car, from the east or west, take the Autostrada Trieste–Torino A4/E70 to the SS12 and follow it north into town. From the north or south, take the Autostrada del Brennero A22/E45 to the SR11 East (initially, called the Strada Bresciana) directly into town.

VISITOR INFORMATION

Verona tourism office (⊠ *Piazza Brà* ☎ *045/8068680* ⊠ *Porta Nuova railway station* ☎ *045/8000861* ⊕ *www.tourism.verona.it*).

EXPLORING VERONA

If you're going to visit more than one or two sights, it's worthwhile to purchase a VeronaCard, available at museums, churches, and tobacconists for €10 (one day) or €15 (three days). It buys a single admission to most of the city's significant museums and churches, plus you can ride free on city buses. If you are mostly interested in churches, a €5 Chiese Vive Card is sold at Verona's major houses of worship and gains you entry to the Duomo, San Fermo Maggiore, San Zeno Maggiore, Sant'Anastasia, and San Lorenzo. Do note that Verona's churches strictly enforce their dress code: no sleeveless shirts, shorts, or short skirts.

TOP ATTRACTIONS

☝ **Ancient City Gates/Triumphal Arch.** In addition to its famous arena and Roman theater, two of ancient Verona's city gates and a beautiful triumphal arch have survived from antiquity. These graceful and elegant portals give us an idea of the high aesthetic standards of ancient Verona. The oldest, the Porta dei Leoni (on Via Leoni, just a few steps from Piazza delle Erbe), dates from the 1st century BC, but its original earth-and-brick structure was sheathed in local marble during early Imperial times. The Porta dei Borsari (at the beginning of Corso Porta Borsari, just a few steps from the opposite side of Piazza della Erbe), as its elegant decoration suggests, was the main entrance to ancient Verona, and, in its present state, dates from the 1st century AD. Continuing down Corso Cavour, which starts on the other (front) side of Porta dei Borsari, you can find the beautiful Arco dei Gavi, which is simpler and less imposing, but certainly more graceful, than the triumphal arches in Rome. It was built in the 1st century AD by the architect Lucius Vitruvius Cerdo to celebrate the accomplishments of the patrician Gavia family. It was highly esteemed by several Renaissance architects, including Palladio.

Fodor's Choice
★

5

❸ **Arena di Verona.** Only Rome's Colosseum and Capua's arena would dwarf this amphitheater. Though four arches are all that remain of the arena's outer arcade, the main structure is complete. It dates from the early Imperial age, and was used for gymnastic competitions, choreographed sacrificial rites, and games involving hunts, fights, battles, and wild animals. Unlike at Rome's Colosseum, there is no evidence that Christians were ever put to death here. Today you can visit the arena year-round; in summer, you can join up to 16,000 people packing the stands for one of Verona's spectacular opera productions. Even those who aren't crazy about opera can sit in the stands and enjoy Italians enjoying themselves—including, at times, singing along with their favorite hits. ⊠ *Arena di Verona, Piazza Brà 5* ☎ *045/8003204* ⊕ *www.arena.it* ⊠ *€5, free with Chiese Vive and VeronaCard, €1 1st Sun. of month* ☉ *Mon. 1:30–7:30, Tues.–Sun. 8:30–7:30 (8–3:30 on performance days); last entry 45 mins before closing.*

☝
Fodor's Choice
★

❷ **Castelvecchio** *(Old Castle).* This crenellated, russet brick building with massive walls, towers, turrets, and a vast courtyard was built for Cangrande II della Scala in 1354. It presides over a street lined with attractive old buildings and palaces of the nobility. Only by going inside the **Museo di Castelvecchio** can you really appreciate this massive castle complex with its vaulted halls. You also get a look at a significant collection of Venetian art, medieval weapons, and jewelry. The interior of the castle was restored and redesigned as a museum between 1958 and 1975 by one of the most important architects of the 20th century, Carlo Scarpa. Behind the castle is the Ponte Scaligero (1355), which spans the River Adige. ⊠ *Corso Castelvecchio 2* ☎ *045/8062611* ⊠ *€6, free with Chiese Vive and VeronaCard, free 1st Sun. of month* ☉ *Mon. 1:45–7:30, Tues.–Sun. 8:30–7:30. Last entry 6:45.*

❼ **Duomo.** The present church was begun in the 12th century in the Romanesque style; its later additions are mostly Gothic. On pilasters guarding the main entrance are 12th-century carvings thought

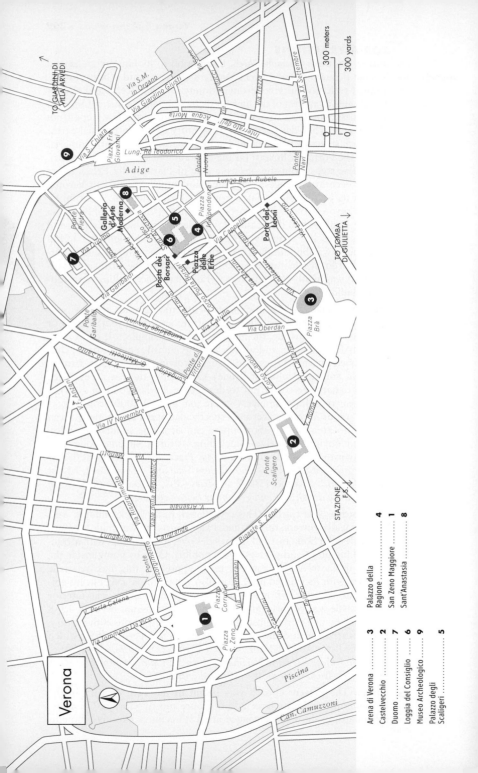

Verona

Arena di Verona **3**	Palazzo della
Castelvecchio **2**	Ragione **4**
Duomo **7**	San Zeno Maggiore **1**
Loggia del Consiglio **6**	Sant'Anastasia **8**
Museo Archeologico **9**	
Palazzo degli	
Scaligeri **5**	

300 meters

300 yards

TO GIARDINO DI
VILLA ARVEDI

Via S.M.
in Organo

Via Giardino Giusti

Interrato dell' Acqua Morta

Via Trezza

Via XX Settembre

Via S. Chiara

Piazza Fra'
Giovanni

Lung. Re Teodorico

Adige

Ponte
Pietra

Galleria
d'Arte
Moderna

Ponte
Nuovo

Lungo Bart. Rubele

Ponte
Navi

Via Tubano

Via Garibaldi

Via Cappello

Porta dei
Leoni

TO TOMBA
DI GIULIETTA

Porta dei
Borsari

Piazza
delle
Erbe

Piazza
Indipendenza

Lungadige Campagnola

Via Cattaneo

Via Oberdan

Piazza
Brà

Via Mattuelli

V. Patto Santo

Via Anzani

V. F.

Via IV Novembre

Lungadige Re Teodorico

Via Risorgimento

Viale della Repubblica

Lungadige

Ponte
Garibaldi

Ponte d.
Vittoria

Corso Cavour

Corso Porta Nuova

Via Roma

STAZIONE
F.S.

Ponte
Scaligero

V. Arsenale

Via Manzoni

Via Barbarani

Rigaste S. Zeno

Ponte
Risorgimento

Candriano

Porta Catena

Via Tommaso Da Vico

Piazza
Corrubio

Via S. Zeno

Piazza
S. Zeno

Piscina

Can. Camuzzoni

to represent Oliver and Roland, two of Charlemagne's knights and heroes of several medieval epic poems. Inside, Titian's *Assumption* (1532) graces the first chapel on the left. ⊠ *Via Duomo* ☏ *045/592813* ⊕ *www.chieseverona.it* ◩ *€2.50, free with Chiese Vive and VeronaCard* ◔ *Nov.–Feb., Tues.–Sat. 10–1 and 1:30–4, Sun. 10–5; Mar.–Oct., Mon.–Sat. 10–5:30, Sun. 1:30–5:30.*

Piazza delle Erbe. Frescoed buildings surround this medieval square, on a site where a Roman forum once bustled. During the week it's still bustling, as vendors hawk produce and trinkets. Relax at one of the cafés and take in the chaos.

➊ ★ San Zeno Maggiore. San Zeno is one of Italy's finest Romanesque churches. The rose window by the 13th-century sculptor Brioloto represents a wheel of fortune, with six of the spokes formed by statues depicting the rising and falling fortunes of mankind. The 12th-century porch is the work of Maestro Niccolò. Eighteen 12th-century marble reliefs flanking the porch by Niccolò and Maestro Guglielmo depict scenes from the Old and New Testaments and scenes from the legend of Theodoric. The bronze doors are from the 11th and 12th centuries; some were probably imported from Saxony and some are from Veronese workshops. They combine allegorical representations with scenes from the lives of saints. Inside, look for the 12th-century statue of San Zeno to the left of the main altar. In modern times it has been dubbed the "Laughing San Zeno" because of a misinterpretation of its conventional Romanesque grin. A justly famous *Madonna and Saints* triptych by Andrea Mantegna (1431–1506) hangs over the main altar, and a peaceful cloister (1120–38) lies to the left of the nave. The detached bell tower was begun in 1045, before the construction of much of the present church, and finished in 1173. ⊠ *Piazza San Zeno* ☏ *045/592813* ⊕ *www.chieseverona.it* ◩ *€2.50, free with Chiese Vive and VeronaCard* ◔ *Nov.–Feb., Tues.–Sat. 10–1 and 1:30–4, Sun. 1–5; Mar.–Oct., Mon.– Sat. 8:30–6, Sun. 1–6.*

➑ Sant'Anastasia. Verona's largest church, begun in 1290 but consecrated in 1471, is a fine example of Gothic brickwork and has a grand doorway with elaborately carved biblical scenes. The main reason for visiting this church, however, is *St. George and the Princess* (1434, but perhaps earlier) by Pisanello (1377–1455) above the Pellegrini Chapel off the main altar. As you come in, look also for the *gobbi* (hunchbacks) supporting holy-water stoups. ⊠ *Vicolo Sotto Riva 4* ☏ *045/592813* ⊕ *www.chieseverona.it* ◩ *€2.50, free with Chiese Vive and VeronaCard* ◔ *Nov.–Feb., Tues.–Sat. 10–1 and 1:30–4, Sun. 1–5; Mar.–Oct., Mon.–Sat. 9–6, Sun. 1–6.*

WORTH NOTING

➏ Loggia del Consiglio. This graceful structure on the north flank of the Piazza dei Signori was finished in 1492 and built to house city council meetings. Although the city was already under Venetian rule, Verona still had a certain degree of autonomy, which was expressed by the splendor of the loggia. Very strangely for a Renaissance building of this quality, its architect remains unknown, but it is undoubtedly the finest surviving example of late-15th-century architecture in Verona. ⊠ *Piazza dei Signori* ◔ *Closed to the public.*

⑨ Museo Archeologico and Teatro Romano. Housed in what was a 15th-century monastery, the museum's collections were formed largely out of the donated collections of Veronese citizens proud of their city's classical past. Though there are few blockbusters here, there are some very noteworthy pieces (especially among the bronzes), and it is interesting to see what cultured Veronese from the 17th to 19th century collected. The museum sits high above the Teatro Romano, ancient Verona's theater, dating from the 1st century AD. ⊠ *Rigaste del Redentore 2* ☏ *045/8000360* ☐ *€4.50, free 1st Sun. of month or with Chiese Vive and VeronaCard* ☺ *Mon. 1:30–7:30, Tues.–Sun. 8:30–7:30. Last entry 6:45.*

⑤ Palazzo degli Scaligeri (Palazzo di Cangrande). The della Scalas ruled Verona from this stronghold built at the end of the 13th century by Cangrande I. At that time Verona controlled the mainland Veneto as far as Treviso and Lombardy to Mantua and Brescia. The portal facing the Piazza dei Signori was added in 1533 by the accomplished Renaissance architect Michele Sanmicheli. You have to admire the palazzo from the outside, as it's not open to the public. ⊠ *Piazza dei Signori.*

④ Palazzo della Ragione. An elegant pink marble staircase leads up from the *mercato vecchio* (old market) courtyard to the magistrates' chambers in the 12th-century palace, built at the intersection of the main streets of the ancient Roman city. The building is now used for art exhibitions. You can get the highest view in town from atop the attached 270-foot-tall **Torre dei Lamberti,** which attained its present height through a modification in 1452. ⊠ *Piazza dei Signori* ☏ *045/8032726* ☐ *€2, free with Chiese Vive and VeronaCard* ☺ *Mon. 1:30–7:30, Tues.–Sun. 8:30–7:30. Last entry 6:45.*

WHERE TO EAT

$
NORTHERN
ITALIAN
★

✕ Antica Osteria al Duomo. This friendly side-street eatery, lined with old wood paneling and decked out with musical instruments, serves Veronese food to a Veronese crowd; they come to quaff the local wine (€1 to €3 per glass) to savor excellent versions of local dishes like *bigoli con sugo di asino* (thick whole-wheat spaghetti with sauce made from donkey meat) and *pastisada con polenta* (horse-meat stew with polenta). Don't be put off by the dishes featuring unconventional meats; they're tender and delicious, and this is probably the best place in town to sample them. First-rate Veronese home cooking comes at very reasonable prices here and is served by helpful, efficient staff. This is a popular place, so arrive early. Reservations are not possible on weekends. ⊠ *Via Duomo 7/a* ☏ *045/8004505* ☐ *AE, MC, V* ☺ *Closed Sun. (except in Dec. and during wine fair).*

$$$$
NORTHERN
ITALIAN

✕ Dodici Apostoli. In a city where many high-end restaurants tend toward nouvelle cuisine, this highly esteemed restaurant is an exceptional place to enjoy classic dishes made with elegant variations on traditional recipes. Near Piazza delle Erbe, it stands on the foundations of a Roman temple. Specialties include gnocchi *di zucca e ricotta* (with squash and ricotta cheese) and *vitello alla Lessinia* (veal with mushrooms, cheese, and truffles). ⊠ *Vicolo Corticella San Marco 3* ☏ *045/596999*

⊕ *www.12apostoli.it* ═ *AE, DC, MC, V* ⊘ *Closed Mon., Jan. 1–10, and June 15–30. No dinner Sun.*

$$$$
MODERN ITALIAN

✕ **Il Desco.** *Cucina dell'anima,* meaning food of the soul, is how Chef Elia Rizzo describes his cuisine. True to Italian culinary traditions, his technique preserves natural flavors through quick cooking and limiting the number of ingredients. But there is little tradition in the inventive and even daring way in which he combines those few ingredients in dishes such as duck breast with grappa, grapes, and eggplant puree, or beef cheeks with goose liver and caramelized pears. For a gastronomic adventure, order the tasting menu (€130), which includes appetizers, two first courses, two second courses, and dessert. The decor is elegant, if overdone, with tapestries, paintings, and an impressive 16th-century lacunar ceiling. The service is efficient, if not exactly friendly. ⊠ *Via Dietro San Sebastiano 7* ☎ *045/595358* ⚱ *Reservations essential* ═ *AE, DC, MC, V* ⊘ *Closed Sun. and Mon., Dec. 25–Jan. 10, and 1st 2 wks in June. No lunch Mon. in July, Aug., and Dec.*

$$$$
MODERN ITALIAN
★

✕ **Ostaria La Fontanina.** Veronese go to La Fontanina to enjoy a sumptuous meal under vine-covered balconies on a quiet street in one of the oldest sections of town. The Tapparini family takes great pride in the kitchen's modern versions of traditional dishes. Particularly successful is the risotto made with Verona's famed sweet wine, riciotto di Soave, accompanied with a slice of foie gras. There are also such standards as *risotto al Amarone* made with Verona's treasured red wine, *patissada* (horse-meat stew) with polenta, and, of course, an excellent version of assorted baccalà preparations. There are several reasonably priced set menus. ⊠ *Portichiette fontanelle S. Stefano 3, Verona* ☎ *045/045/913305* ⊕ *www.ristorantelafontanina.com* ⚱ *Reservations essential* ═ *AE, DC, MC, V* ⊘ *Closed Sun., 1 wk in Jan., and 2 wks in Aug. No lunch Mon.*

WHERE TO STAY

Book hotels months in advance for spring's Vinitaly, usually the second week in April, and for opera season. Verona hotels are also very busy during the January, May, and September gold fairs in neighboring Vicenza. Hotels jack up prices considerably during trade fairs and the opera season.

$$–$$$
★

▥ **Hotel Accademia.** The columns and arches of Hotel Accademia's stately facade are a good indication of what you can discover inside: an elegant, full-service historic hotel in the center of old Verona. Despite the location, the traditionally furnished rooms are reasonably quiet. The staff is friendly and helpful. The buffet breakfast, included in the rate, is sumptuous. **Pros:** central location; old-world charm; up-to-date services. **Cons:** expensive parking; few standard rooms. ⊠ *Via Scala 12* ☎ *045/596 222* ⊕ *www.accademiavr.it* ⤺ *93 rooms* ⚿ *In-room: safe, refrigerator, Wi-Fi. In-hotel: restaurant, bars, parking (paid)* ═ *AE, DC, MC, V* ⑩ *BP.*

$$$

▥ **Hotel Victoria.** Busy business executives and tourists demanding a bit of pampering frequent this full-service hotel located near the Piazza delle Erbe. The Victoria offers a modern, sleek entryway and traditionally decorated, comfortable rooms. As is the case with many Verona hotels, lower rates are available depending on the season. Standard rooms are attractive and well proportioned, but the "superior" rooms (€335) are really quite lavish (some have hydromassage showers). **Pros:** quiet and tasteful rooms; central location; good business center. **Cons:** no views; expensive parking; staff not particularly helpful. ⊠ *Via Adua 8* ☎ *045/5905664* ⊕ *www.hotelvictoria.it* ⟿ *66 rooms* ⅏ *In-room: safe, refrigerator, Wi-Fi. In-hotel: bar, gym, laundry service, parking (paid)* ▤ *AE, DC, MC, V* ⍩ *EP.*

$ ⛫ **Torcolo.** At this budget hotel you can count on a warm welcome from the owners and the courteous, helpful service; pleasant rooms decorated tastefully with late-19th-century furniture; and a central location close to Piazza Brà. Breakfast, which costs an extra €8 to €15, is quite generous and is served on the front terrace in summer. Note that during opera season and during the wine fair, the price for a double jumps to €155 (though breakfast is included). **Pros:** tastefully decorated rooms; staff gives reliable advice. **Cons:** some street noise; no help with baggage; pricey parking. ⊠ *Vicolo Listone 3* ☎ *045/8007512* ⊕ *www.hoteltorcolo.it* ⟿ *19 rooms* ⅏ *In-room: safe, refrigerator. In-hotel: bar, parking (paid), some pets allowed* ▤ *AE, DC, MC, V* ⍉ *Closed Dec. 21–27 and 2 wks in Jan. and Feb.* ⍩ *EP.*

OPERA

Fodor'sChoice ★ Milan's La Scala, Venice's La Fenice, and Parma's Teatro Regio offer performances more likely to satisfy serious opera fans, but none offers a greater spectacle than the **Arena di Verona** (*Box office* ⊠ *Via Dietro Anfiteatro 6/b* ☎ *045/8005151* ⊕ *www.arena.it* ⟿ *Tickets start at €22* ⍉ *Box office Sept.–June 20, weekdays 9–noon and 3:15–5:45, Sat. 9–noon; June 21–Aug., daily noon–9*). During its summer season (July–September) audiences of as many as 16,000 sit on the original stone terraces or in modern cushioned stalls. The best operas are the big, splashy ones, like *Aïda*, which demand huge choruses, lots of color and movement, and, if possible, camels, horses, or elephants. Order tickets by phone or online: if you book a spot on the cheaper terraces, be sure to take or rent a cushion—four hours on a 2,000-year-old stone bench can be an ordeal. Sometimes you can even hear the opera from Piazza Brà cafés.

MILAN

Updated by
Nan McElroy

Milan isn't between Florence and Venice, but as a major transport center, with Italy's biggest international airport, it may well be your point of entry into the country. It's also Italy's business hub, serving as the capital of commerce, finance, fashion, and media. Leonardo Da Vinci's *Last Supper* and other great works of art are here, as well as a spectacular Gothic Duomo, the finest of its kind. Milan even reigns supreme where it really counts (in the minds of many Italians), routinely trouncing the rest of the nation with its two premier soccer teams.

And yet, Milan hasn't won the battle for hearts and minds. Most tourists prefer Tuscany's hills and Venice's canals to Milan's hectic efficiency and wealthy indifference, and it's no surprise that in a country of medieval hilltop villages and skilled artisans, a city of grand boulevards and global corporations leaves visitors asking the real Italy to please stand up. They're right, of course. Milan is more European than Italian, a new buckle on an old boot, and although its old city can stand cobblestone for cobblestone against the best of them, seekers of Roman ruins and fairy-tale towns may pass. But Milan's secrets reveal themselves slowly to those who look. A side street conceals a garden complete with flamingos (Via dei Cappuccini, just off Corso Venezia), and a renowned 20th-century art collection hides modestly behind an unspectacular facade a block from Corso Buenos Aires (the Museo Boschi-di Stefano). Visitors lured by the world-class shopping will appreciate Milan's European sophistication while discovering unexpected facets of a country they may have thought they knew.

Virtually every invader in European history—Gaul, Roman, Goth, Longobard, and Frank—as well as a long series of rulers from France, Spain, and Austria, took a turn at ruling the city. After being completely sacked by the Goths in AD 539 and by the Holy Roman Empire under Frederick Barbarossa in 1157, Milan became one of the first independent city-states of the Renaissance. Its heyday of self-rule proved comparatively brief. From 1277 until 1500 it was ruled by the Visconti and subsequently the Sforza dynasties. These families were known, justly or not, for a peculiarly aristocratic mixture of refinement, classical learning, and cruelty, and much of the surviving grandeur of Gothic and Renaissance art and architecture is their doing. Be on the lookout in your wanderings for the Visconti family emblem—a viper, its jaws straining wide, devouring a child.

VISITOR INFORMATION

The **tourism office** (✉ *Piazza Duomo 19/A, Piazza Duomo* ☎ *02/77404343* ⊕ *www.visitamilano.it* ☉ *Mon.–Sat. 8:45–1 and 2–6, Sun. 9–1 and 2–5*) in Piazza Duomo is the perfect place to begin your visit. It's accessible by elevator and down a deco stairway under the arches on the north side of Piazza Duomo; you can also enter from the Galleria in front of the Park Hyatt hotel. There are excellent maps, booklets with museum descriptions and itineraries on a variety of themes, and a selection of brochures about smaller museums and cultural initiatives. Pick up a copy of the English-language *Hello Milano* (ask, if it is not on display, or see ⊕ *www.hellomilano.it*), a monthly publication with a day-to-day schedule of events of interest to visitors and a comprehensive map. The Autostradale bus operator, sightseeing companies, and a few theaters have desks in the tourism office where you can buy tickets.

THE DUOMO AND POINTS NORTH

Milan's main streets radiate out from the massive Duomo, a late-Gothic cathedral that was started in 1386. Leading north is the handsome Galleria Vittorio Emanuele, an enclosed walkway that takes you to the world-famous opera house known as La Scala. Beyond are the winding streets of the elegant Brera neighborhood, once the city's bohemian quarter. Here you'll find many art galleries, as well as the academy of fine arts. Heading northeast from La Scala is Via Manzoni, which leads to the *Quadrilatero della moda,* or fashion district. Its streets are lined with elegant window displays from the world's most celebrated designers—the Italians taking the lead, of course.

Leading northeast from the Duomo is Corso Vittorio Emanuele. Locals and visitors stroll along this pedestrians-only street, looking at the shop windows, buying ice cream, or stopping for a coffee at one of the sidewalk cafés. Northwest of the Duomo is Via Dante, at the top of which is the imposing outline of the Castello Sforzesco.

TOP ATTRACTIONS

⑧ ★ Castello Sforzesco. For the serious student of Renaissance military engineering, the Castello must be something of a travesty, so often has it been remodeled or rebuilt since it was begun in 1450 by the *condottiere* (hired mercenary) who founded the city's second dynastic family, Francesco Sforza, fourth duke of Milan. Though today "mercenary" has a pejorative ring, during the Renaissance all Italy's great soldier-heroes were professionals hired by the cities and principalities that they served. Of them—and there were thousands—Francesco Sforza (1401–66) is considered one of the greatest, most honest, and most organized. It is said he could remember the names not only of all his men but of their horses as well. His rule signaled the enlightened age of the Renaissance but preceded the next foreign rule by a scant 50 years. The castle's crypts and battlements, including a tunnel that emerges well into the Parco Sempione behind, can be visited with privately reserved guides from **Ad Artem** (☎ *02/6596937* ☯ *Weekdays 9–1 and 2–4* ⊕ *www. adartem.it* or **Opera d'Arte** (☎ *02/45487400* ⊕ *www.operadartemilano. it/turismo-eng.html* ☯ *Weekdays 9–noon and 2–5*).

Since the turn of the 20th century, the Castello has been the depository of several city-owned collections of Egyptian and other antiquities, musical instruments, arms and armor, decorative arts and textiles, prints and photographs (on consultation), paintings, and sculpture. Highlights include the **Sala delle Asse,** a frescoed room still sometimes attributed to Leonardo da Vinci (1452–1519), which, at the time of writing, is closed for restoration (scheduled to reopen sometime before 2015). Michelangelo's unfinished *Rondanini Pietà* is believed to be his last work—an astounding achievement for a man nearly 90, and a moving coda to his life. The *pinacoteca* (picture gallery) features paintings from medieval times to the 18th century, including 230 works by

Antonello da Messina, Canaletto, Andrea Mantegna, and Bernardo Bellotto. The **Museo dei Mobili** (furniture museum), which illustrates the development of Italian furniture from the Middle Ages to current design, includes a delightful collection of Renaissance treasure chests of exotic woods with tiny drawers and miniature architectural details. A single ticket purchased in the office in an inner courtyard admits visitors to these separate installations, which are dispersed around the castle's two immense courtyards. ✉ *Piazza Castello, Brera* ☎ *02/88463700* ⊕ *www.milanocastello.it* 🎫 *€3, free Fri. 2–5* ◷ *Castle: Apr.–Oct, daily. 7–7; Nov.–Mar., daily 7–6. Museums: Tues.–Sun. 9–5:30; last entry at 5* Ⓜ *Cairoli; Tram 1, 3, 4, 7, 12, 14, 27.*

❶ Duomo. This intricate Gothic structure has been fascinating and exas-
★ perating visitors and conquerors alike since it was begun by Galeazzo Visconti III (1351–1402), first duke of Milan, in 1386. Consecrated in the 15th or 16th century, it was not completed until just before the coronation of Napoléon as king of Italy in 1809. Whether you concur with travel writer H.V. Morton's 1964 assessment that the cathedral is "one of the mightiest Gothic buildings ever created," there is no deny-ing that for sheer size and complexity it is unrivaled. It is the second-largest church in the world—the largest being St. Peter's in Rome. The capacity is reckoned to be 40,000. Usually it is empty, a sanctuary from the frenetic pace of life outside and the perfect place for solitary contemplation.

The building is adorned with 135 marble spires and 2,245 marble stat-ues. The oldest part is the apse. Its three colossal bays of curving and counter-curved tracery, especially the bay adorning the exterior of the stained-glass windows, should not be missed. At the end of the southern transept down the right aisle lies the **tomb of Gian Giacomo Medici**. The tomb owes some of its design to Michelangelo but was executed by Leone Leoni (1509–90) and is generally considered to be his mas-terpiece; it dates from the 1560s. Directly ahead is the Duomo's most famous sculpture, the gruesome but anatomically instructive figure of San Bartolomeo (St. Bartholomew), whose glorious martyrdom con-sisted of being flayed alive. It is usually said the saint stands "holding" his skin, but this is not quite accurate. It would appear more that he is luxuriating in it, much as a 1950s matron might have shown off a new fur stole.

As you enter the apse to admire those splendid windows, glance at the sacristy doors to the right and left of the altar. The lunette on the right dates from 1393 and was decorated by Hans von Fernach. The one on the left also dates from the 14th century and is ascribed jointly to Giacomo da Campione and Giovanni dei Grassi. Don't miss the view from the Duomo's roof; walk out the left (north) transept to the stairs and elevator. Sadly, air pollution drastically reduces the view on all but the rarest days. As you stand among the forest of marble pinnacles, remember that virtually every inch of this gargantuan edi-fice, including the roof itself, is decorated with precious white marble dragged from quarries near Lake Maggiore by Duke Visconti's team along road laid fresh for the purpose and through the newly dredged canals. Audio guides can be rented inside the Duomo from March to

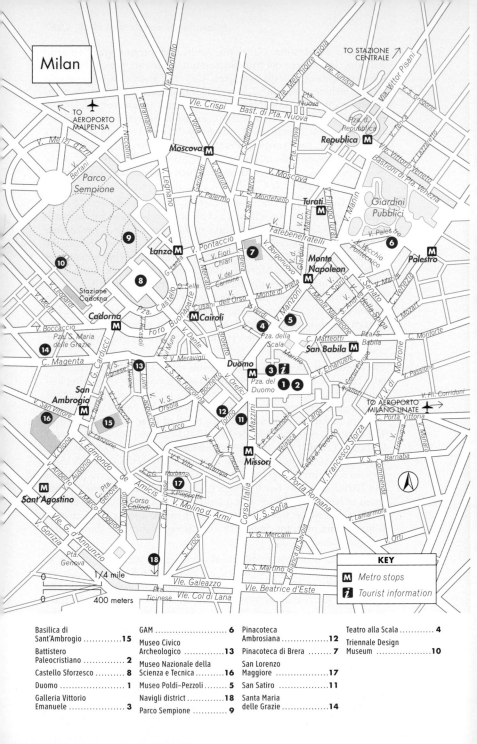

Milan

TO AEROPORTO MALPENSA

Parco Sempione

Moscova Ⓜ

TO STAZIONE CENTRALE

Pza. Nuova

Bast. di Pta. Nuova

Republica Ⓜ

Pza. d. Repubblica

Turati Ⓜ

Giardini Pubblici

Lanza Ⓜ

Chiari

Monte Napoleon

6

Palestro Ⓜ

9

10

7

8

Stazione Cadorna

Cadorna Ⓜ

Ⓜ Cairoli

4

5

Pza. della Scala

San Babila Ⓜ

14

13

Duomo

Ⓜ

3 **i**

1 **2**

Pza. del Duomo

TO AEROPORTO MILANO LINATE

San Ambrogio Ⓜ

16

15

12

11

Missori Ⓜ

17

Sant'Agostino Ⓜ

18

1/4 mile

400 meters

December and at Duomo Point in Piazza Duomo (just behind the cathedral) all year long. Exhibits at the **Museo del Duomo** shed light on the cathedral's history and include some of the treasures removed from the exterior for preservation purposes. At this writing, the museum is closed for restoration with no estimated date for completion. ⊠ *Piazza del Duomo* ☎ *02/72023375* ⊕ *www.duomomilano.it/ground1024_en.html* ▨ *Stairs to roof €5, elevator €8* ⊘ *Mar.–Oct., daily 9–5:45; Nov.–Feb., daily 9–4:45; May–Sept. hrs lengthen as the days do, the latest being 9 PM* Ⓜ *Duomo.*

③ ★ Galleria Vittorio Emanuele. This spectacular, late-19th-century glass-topped, belle epoque, barrel-vaulted tunnel is essentially one of the planet's earliest and most select shopping malls. Like its suburban American cousins, the Galleria Vittorio Emanuele fulfills numerous social functions. This is the city's heart, midway between the Duomo and La Scala. It teems with life, inviting people-watching from the tables that spill from the bars and restaurants, where you can enjoy an overpriced coffee. Books, records, clothing, food, pens, pipes, hats, and jewelry are all for sale. Known as Milan's "parlor," the Galleria is often viewed as a barometer of the city's well-being. By the 1990s, the quality of the stores (with the exception of the Prada flagship) and restaurants was uninspired. The city government, which owns the Galleria, and merchants' groups evicted some longtime tenants who had enjoyed anomalously low rents, in favor of Gucci, Tod's, and Louis Vuitton. The historic, if somewhat overpriced and inconsistent, Savini restaurant hosts the beautiful and powerful of the city, just across from McDonald's. Like the cathedral, the Galleria is cruciform in shape. Even in poor weather the great glass dome above the octagonal center is a splendid sight. Look up! The paintings at the base of the dome represent Europe, Asia, Africa, and America. Those at the entrance arch are devoted to science, industry, art, and agriculture. And the floor mosaics are a vastly underrated source of pleasure, even if they are not to be taken too seriously. Be sure to follow tradition and spin your heels once or twice on the more "delicate" parts of the bull beneath your feet in the northern apse; the Milanese believe it brings good luck. ⊠ *Piazza del Duomo* Ⓜ *Duomo.*

QUICK BITES

One thing has remained constant in the Galleria: the **Caffè Zucca,** known by the Milanese as **Camparino.** Its inlaid counter, mosaics, and wrought-iron fixtures have been welcoming tired shoppers since 1867. Enjoy a Campari or Zucca *aperitivo* (aperitif) as well as the entire range of Italian coffees, served either in the Galleria or in an elegant upstairs room where lunch is also served (⊕ *www.caffemiani.it).*

⑤ Museo Poldi-Pezzoli. This exceptional museum, opened in 1881, was once a private residence and collection, and contains not only pedigreed paintings but also porcelain, textiles, and a cabinet with scenes from Dante's life. The gem is undoubtedly the *Portrait of a Lady* by Antonio Pollaiuolo (1431–98), one of the city's most prized treasures and the source of the museum's logo. The collection also includes masterpieces by Botticelli (1445–1510), Andrea Mantegna (1431–1506),

Milan's spire-studded Duomo is the second-largest church in the world.

Giovanni Bellini (1430–1516), and Fra Filippo Lippi (1406–69). Private guided tours are available by reservation. ⊠ *Via Manzoni 12, Brera* ☎ *02/794889* ⊕ *www.museopoldipezzoli.it* 🎫 *€8* ⏱ *Wed.–Mon. 10–6* Ⓜ *Montenapoleone.*

❾ **Parco Sempione.** Originally the gardens and parade ground of the Castello Sforzesco, this open space was reorganized during the Napoleonic era, when the arena on its northeast side was constructed, and then turned into a park during the building boom at the end of the 19th century. It is still the lungs of the city's fashionable western neighborhoods, and the **Aquarium** (⊠ *Viale Gadio 2* ☎ *02/878459* ⊕ *www. acquariocivicomilano.eu* 🎫 *Free* ⏱ *Tues.–Sun. 9–1 and 2–5:30)* still attracts Milan's schoolchildren. The park became a bit of a design showcase in 1933 with the construction of the Triennale *(see below)*. The Fiat café offers outdoor dining in summer along with a view of De Chirico's sculpture-filled fountain *Bagni Misteriosi (Mysterious Baths)*.

Even if a walk in the park is not appealing, it is worth visiting to see the **Torre Branca** (⊠ *Parco Sempione* ☎ *02/3314120* 🎫 *€4* ⏱ *Irregular, seasonal hrs; check at www.branca.it/torre/dati.asp)*. Designed by architect Gio Ponti, who was behind so many of the projects that made Milan the design capital that it is, this steel tower rises 330 feet over the Triennale. Take the elevator up to get a nice view of the city, then have a drink at the glitzy Just Cavalli Café (Monday–Saturday, 8 PM-2 AM) at its base. *Parco Sempione* ⊠ *Piazza Castello, Brera* ⏱ *Nov.–Feb., daily 6:30–8; Mar., Apr., and June–Oct., daily 6:30–9; May, daily 6:30–10* Ⓜ *Cadorna; Bus 61.*

GETTING AROUND MILAN

The city center is compact and walkable; trolleys and trams make it even more accessible, and the efficient Metropolitana (subway) and buses provide access to locations farther afield. Driving in Milan is difficult and parking miserable, so a car is a liability. In addition, drivers within the second ring of streets (the *bastioni*) must hold an Ecopass. (Ask your hotel about getting a pass.)

BY PUBLIC TRANSIT

A standard public transit ticket costs €1 and is valid for a 75-minute trip on a subway, bus, or tram. An all-inclusive subway, bus, and tram pass costs €3 for 24 hours or €5.50 for 48 hours. Individual tickets and passes can be purchased from news vendors and tobacconists, and at ticket counters and ticket machines at larger stops. Another option is a *carnet* (€9.20), good for 10 tram or subway rides. Once you have your ticket or pass, either stamp it or insert it into slots in station turnstiles or on poles inside trolleys and buses. (The electronic tickets will not function if bent or demagnetized. If you have a problem, contact a station manager, who can usually issue a new ticket.) Trains run from 6 AM to 12:20 AM (1:30 AM on Saturday). From 8 PM to 2 AM, **Radiobus** (☎ *02/48034803* ⊕ *www.atm-mi.it/en*) will pick you up and drop you off anywhere in Milan for a €1.50 supplement to a transit pass. Advance booking is required. For more information, check the Web site of **ATM** (*Azienda Trasporti Milanesi* ⊕ *www.atm-mi.it/en*) or visit information offices at the Duomo, Stazione Cadorna, Stazione Centrale, and Loreto stops.

BY TAXI

Taxi fares in Milan are higher than in American cities. A short ride will run about €15. Taxis wait at stands, or you can call one of the city's taxi companies—**Amicotaxi** (☎ *02/4000*), **Autoradiotaxi** (☎ *02/8585*), **Radiotaxi** (☎ *02/6969*), or **Taxiblu** (☎ *02/4040*). Dispatchers may speak some English; they'll ask for the phone number you're calling from, and they'll tell you the number of your taxi and how long it will take to arrive. If you're in a restaurant or bar, ask the staff to call a cab for you. It's not customary to hail taxis in the street, but drivers do sometimes stop. For car service, contact **Autonoleggio Pini** (☎ *02/29400555* ⊕ *www.pini.it* or *www.limousine. eu*). English-speaking drivers are available.

BY BICYCLE

The innovative BikeMI (⊕ *www. bikemi.com*) makes hop-on, drop-off bicycles available at designated spots around the city. There are more than 100 stations, and more than 300 stations are planned. Weekly and daily rates for tourists are available. Buy your subscription online; the site has a map showing stations and availability.

TOURS

A refurbished 1920s tramcar operates a hop-on/hop-off tour of the city. Tickets (€20) are valid all day and can be purchased on board. Departures are at 11 and 1 (also at 3, April–October) from Piazza Castello. The organization **A Friend in Milan** (⊕ *www.friendinmilan.co.uk*) conducts walking tours, including a visit to *The Last Supper,* day trips to the lakes, and shopping tours.

5

❼ Pinacoteca di Brera *(Brera Gallery).*
★ The collection here is star-studded
even by Italian standards. The
entrance hall (Room I) displays
20th-century sculpture and painting, including Carlo Carrà's (1881–
1966) confident, stylish response
to the schools of cubism and sur-
realism. The museum has nearly 40
other rooms, arranged in chronological order—pace yourself.

The somber, moving *Cristo Morto* (*Dead Christ*) by Mantegna dominates Room VI, with its sparse palette of umber and its foreshortened
perspective. Mantegna's shocking, almost surgical precision—in the
rendering of Christ's wounds, the face propped up on a pillow, the
day's growth of beard—tells of an all-too-human agony. It is one of
Renaissance painting's most quietly wondrous achievements, finding an
unsuspected middle ground between the excesses of conventional gore
and beauty in representing the Passion's saddest moment.

Room XXIV offers two additional highlights of the gallery. Raphael's
(1483–1520) *Sposalizio della Vergine,* with its mathematical composition and precise, alternating colors, portrays the betrothal of Mary
and Joseph (who, though older than the other men gathered, wins her
hand when the rod he is holding miraculously blossoms). *La Vergine
con il Bambino e Santi* (*Madonna with Child and Saints*), by Piero della
Francesca (1420–92), is an altarpiece commissioned by Federico da
Montefeltro (shown kneeling, in full armor, before the Virgin); it was
intended for a church to house the duke's tomb. The ostrich egg hanging
from the apse, depending on whom you ask, either commemorates the
miracle of his fertility—Federico's wife died months after giving birth
to a long-awaited male heir—or alludes to his appeal for posthumous
mercy, the egg symbolizing the saving power of grace. ⊠ *Via Brera 28,
Piazza Duomo* ☎ *02/92800361* ⊕ *www.brera.beniculturali.it* ⊠ *€10,
higher during special exhibitions* ⊙ *Tues.–Sun. 8:30–7:15; last admission 45 mins before closing* Ⓜ *Montenapoleone.*

❹ Teatro alla Scala. You need know nothing of opera to sense that, like
Carnegie Hall, La Scala is closer to a cathedral than an auditorium.
Here Verdi established his reputation and Maria Callas sang her way
into opera lore. It looms as a symbol—both for the performer who
dreams of singing here and for the opera buff who knows every note
of *Rigoletto* by heart. Audiences are notoriously demanding and are
apt to jeer performers who do not measure up. The opera house was
closed after destruction by Allied bombs in 1943, and reopened at a
performance led by Arturo Toscanini in 1946.

If you are lucky enough to be here during the opera season, which runs
from December to June, do whatever is necessary to attend. Tickets go
on sale two months before the first performance and are usually sold
out the same day. Hearing opera sung in the magical setting of La Scala
is an unparalleled experience.

At **Museo Teatrale alla Scala** you can admire an extensive collection of librettos, paintings of the famous names of Italian opera, posters, costumes, antique instruments, and design sketches for the theater. It is also possible to take a look at the theater, which was completely restored in 2004. Special exhibitions reflect current productions. ⊠ *Piazza della Scala; museum Largo Ghiringhelli 1* ☎ *02/72003744 theater, 02/88797473 museum* ⊕ *www.teatroallascala.org* ▣ *Museum €5* ☉ *Museum daily 9–12:30 and 1:30–5:30; last entry ½ hr prior to closing.*

⓵⓪ Triennale Design Museum. After decades of false starts and controversy, Milan's Triennale is a museum that honors Italy's design talent, as well as offering a regular series of exhibitions on design from around the world. Originally the home of triennial decorative arts shows, a spectacular bridge entrance leads to a permanent collection, an exhibition space, and a stylish café (whose seating is an encyclopedia of design icons). The Triennale also manages the museum-studio of designer Achille Castiglione in nearby Piazza Castello. ⊠ *Via Alemagna 6, Parco Sempione* ☎ *02/724341* ⊕ *www.triennaledesignmuseum.com* ▣ *€8* ☉ *Tues., Wed., and weekends 10:30–8:30; Thurs., Fri. 10:30–11; last entrance 1 hr before closing.*

WORTH NOTING

② Battistero Paleocristiano. Beneath the Duomo's piazza lies this baptistery ruin dating from the 4th century. Although opinion remains divided, it is widely believed to be where Ambrose, Milan's first bishop and patron saint, baptized Augustine. Tickets are available at the kiosk inside the cathedral. ⊠ *Piazza del Duomo, enter through Duomo* ☎ *02/72023375* ▣ *€4* ☉ *Daily 9:30–5:15* Ⓜ *Duomo.*

Casa-Museo Boschi di Stefano *(Boschi di Stefano House and Museum).* To most people, Italian art means Renaissance art. But the 20th century in Italy was a productive—if less well-known—era. Just a block behind the Corso Buenos Aires shopping area, the Casa-Museo Boschi di Stefano is a tribute to the enlightened private collectors who replaced popes and nobles as Italian patrons. An apartment on the second floor of a stunning art deco building designed by Milan architect Portaluppi houses this private collection, which was donated to the city of Milan in 2003. Its walls are lined with the works of postwar greats, such as Fontana, De Chirico, and Morandi. Along with the art, the museum holds distinctive postwar furniture and stunning Murano glass chandeliers. ⊠ *Via Jan 15, Corso Buenos Aires* ☎ *02/20240568* ⊕ *www.fondazioneboschidistefano.it* ▣ *Free* ☉ *Tues.–Sun. 10–6 Mon.; last entry at 5:30.*

⑥ ★ GAM: Galleria d'Arte Moderna/Villa Reale. One of the city's most beautiful buildings, this museum is an outstanding example of neoclassical architecture, it was built between 1790 and 1796 as a residence for a member of the Belgioioso family. It later became known as the Villa Reale (royal) when it was donated to Napoléon, who lived here briefly with Empress Josephine. Its origins as residence are reflected in the elegance of its proportions and its private garden behind.

Likewise, the collection of paintings is domestic rather than monumental. There are many portraits, as well as collections of miniatures on porcelain. Unusual for an Italian museum, this collection derives from private donations from Milan's hereditary and commercial aristocracies. On display are the collection left by prominent painter and sculptor Marino Marini and the immense *Quarto Stato (Fourth Estate)*, which is at the top of the grand staircase. Completed in 1901 by Pellizza da Volpedo, this painting of striking workers is an icon of 20th-century Italian art and labor history, and as such it has been satirized almost as much as the *Mona Lisa*. This museum is a unique glimpse of the splendors hiding behind Milan's discreet and often stern facades. ⊠ *Via Palestro 16* ☎ *02/76340809* ⊕ *www.gam-milano.com* 🎟 *Free* ⊙ *Daily 9:30–1 and 2–4:30* Ⓜ *Palestro.*

Ⓒ The **Giardini Pubblici** *(Public Gardens)*, across Via Palestro from the Villa Reale, were laid out by Giuseppe Piermarini, architect of La Scala, in 1770. They were designed as public pleasure gardens, and today they still are popular with families who live in the city center. Generations of Milanese have taken pony rides and gone on the miniature train and merry-go-round. The park also contains a small planetarium and the **Museo Civico di Storia Naturale.** *Municipal Natural History Museum* ⊠ *Corso Venezia 55* ☎ *02/88463337* ⊕ *www.assodidatticomuseale.it* 🎟 *€5* ⊙ *Weekdays 9:30–1 and 2–4, weekends 9:30–1 and 2–5:30.*

> **QUICK BITES**
>
> If your energy is flagging after shopping or chasing children around the park, try some of Milan's best cappuccino and pastry at Dolce In (⊠ *Via Turati 2/3* ☎ *02/6572523* ⊕ *www.massimodolcein.com* ⊙ *Tues.–Sun. 7 AM–8 PM*), which is equally close to Via della Spiga and the Giardini Pubblici. It's famous for its pastry and also serves sandwiches and hot and cold dishes at lunch. On Sunday morning, classic-car enthusiasts meet informally here, parking their handsome machines out front while they have coffee.

SOUTH AND WEST OF THE DUOMO

If the part of the city to the north of the Duomo is dominated by its shops, the section to the south is famous for its works of art. The most famous is *Il Cenacolo*—known in English as *The Last Supper*. If you have time for nothing else, make sure you see this masterwork, which has now been definitively restored, after many, many years of work. Reservations will be needed to see this fresco, housed in the refectory of Santa Maria delle Grazie. Make these at least three weeks before you depart for Italy, so you can plan the rest of your time in Milan.

There are other gems as well. Via Torino, the ancient road for Turin, leads to a half-hidden treasure: Bramante's Renaissance masterpiece, the church of San Satiro. At the intersection of Via San Vittore and Via Carducci is the medieval Basilica di Sant'Ambrogio, named for Milan's patron saint. Another lovely church southeast of Sant'Ambrogio along Via de Amicis is San Lorenzo Maggiore. It's also known as San Lorenzo alle Colonne because of the 16 columns running across the facade.

TOP ATTRACTIONS

 Basilica di Sant'Ambrogio *(Basilica of Saint Ambrose).* Noted for its medieval architecture, the church was consecrated by Milan's bishop, Saint Ambrose (one of the original Doctors of the Catholic Church), in AD 387. Saint Ambroeus, as he is known in Milanese dialect, is the city's patron saint, and his remains—dressed in elegant religious robes, a miter, and gloves—can be viewed inside a glass case in the crypt below the altar. Until the construction of the more imposing Duomo, this was Milan's most important church. Much restored and reworked over the centuries (the gold-and-gem-encrusted altar dates from the 9th century), Sant'Ambrogio still preserves its Romanesque characteristics (5th-century mosaics may be seen for €2). The church is often closed for weddings on Saturday. ⊠ *Piazza Sant'Ambrogio 15, Corso Magenta* ☎ *02/86450895* ⊕ *www.santambrogio-basilica.it* ☉ *Mon.–Sat. 7:30 AM–12:30 PM and 2:30–7, Sun. 7:30 AM–1 PM and 3–8* Ⓜ *Sant'Ambrogio.*

5

QUICK BITES

A bit overcrowded at night, when teenagers virtually block the sidewalk and traffic, the Bar Magenta (⊠ *Via Carducci 13, at Corso Magenta, Sant'Ambrogio* ☎ *02/8053808* Ⓜ *Sant'Ambrogio*) **can be a good stop en route during the day. Beyond coffee at all hours, lunch, and beer, the real attraction is its mix of old and new, trendy and aristocratic—a quintessentially Milanese ambience. It celebrated its 100th birthday in 2007 and is open weekdays 8 AM–2 AM and weekends 9 AM–2 AM. There's free Wi-Fi.**

⑫ **Pinacoteca Ambrosiana.** Cardinal Federico Borromeo, one of Milan's native saints, founded this picture gallery in 1618 with the addition of his personal art collection to a bequest of books to Italy's first public library. More recent renovations have reunited the core works of the collection, including such treasures as Caravaggio's *Basket of Fruit* and Raphael's monumental preparatory drawing (known as a "cartoon") for *The School of Athens,* which hangs in the Vatican. Heavy on Lombard artists, there are also paintings by Leonardo, Botticelli, Luini, Titian, and Jan Brueghel. Previous renovations done in the 1930s with their mosaics and stained-glass windows are worth a look, as are other odd items, including 18th-century scientific instruments and gloves worn by Napoléon at Waterloo. Access to the library, the Biblioteca Ambrosiana, is limited to researchers who apply for entrance tickets. ⊠ *Piazza Pio XI 2, near Duomo* ☎ *02/806921* ⊕ *www.ambrosiana.it* ☜ *€15 or €20, depending on type of visit* ☉ *Tues.–Sun. 9–7* Ⓜ *Duomo.*

⑰ **San Lorenzo Maggiore alle Colonne.** Sixteen ancient Roman columns line the front of this sanctuary; 4th-century paleo-Christian mosaics survive in the Cappella di Sant'Aquilino (Chapel of Saint Aquilinus). ⊠ *Corso di Porta Ticinese 39* ☎ *02/89404129* ⊕ *www.sanlorenzomaggiore.com* ☜ *Mosaics €2* ☉ *Daily 7:30–12:30 and 2:30–6.*

⑪ **San Satiro.** Just a few steps from the Duomo, this architectural gem
★ was first built in 876 and later perfected by Bramante (1444–1514), demonstrating his command of proportion and perspective, keynotes of Renaissance architecture. Bramante tricks the eye with a famous optical illusion that makes a small interior seem extraordinarily spacious and

airy, while accommodating a beloved 13th-century fresco. ✉ *Via Torino 9, near Duomo* ☏ *02/874683*☉ *Weekdays 7:30–11:30 and 3:30–6:30, Sat. 3:30–7, Sun. 10–noon and 3:30–7* Ⓜ *Duomo.*

⓮ **Santa Maria delle Grazie.** Leonardo da Vinci's *The Last Supper,* housed in
★ the church and former Dominican monastery of Santa Maria delle Grazie, has had an almost unbelievable history of bad luck and neglect—its near destruction in an American bombing raid in August 1943 was only the latest chapter in a series of misadventures, including, if one 19th-century source is to be believed, being whitewashed over by monks. Well-meant but disastrous attempts at restoration have done little to rectify the problem of the work's placement: it was executed on a wall unusually vulnerable to climatic dampness. Yet Leonardo chose to work slowly and patiently in oil pigments—which demand dry plaster—instead of proceeding hastily on wet plaster according to the conventional fresco technique. Novelist Aldous Huxley (1894–1963) called it "the saddest work of art in the world." After years of restorers' patiently shifting from one square centimeter to another, Leonardo's masterpiece is free of the shroud of scaffolding—and centuries of retouching, grime, and dust. Astonishing clarity and luminosity have been regained.

Despite Leonardo's carefully preserved preparatory sketches in which the apostles are clearly labeled by name, there still remains some small debate about a few identities in the final arrangement. But there can be no mistaking Judas, small and dark, his hand calmly reaching forward to the bread, isolated from the terrible confusion that has taken the hearts of the others. One critic, Frederick Hartt, offers an elegantly terse explanation for why the composition works: it combines "dramatic confusion" with "mathematical order." Certainly, the amazingly skillful and unobtrusive repetition of threes—in the windows, in the grouping of the figures, and in their placement—adds a mystical aspect to what at first seems simply the perfect observation of spontaneous human gesture.

Reservations are required to view the work. Viewings are in 15-minute, timed slots, and visitors must arrive 15 minutes before their assigned time in order not to lose their slot. Reservations can be made via phone (☏ *02/92800360*) or online (🌐 *www.cenacolovinciano.net*); it is worthwhile to make a call because tickets are set aside for phone reservations. Call at least three weeks before if you want a Saturday slot, two weeks for a weekday slot. The telephone reservation office is open 9 AM to 6 PM weekdays and 9 AM to 2 PM on Saturday. Operators do speak English, though not fluently, and to reach one you must wait for the Italian introduction to finish and then press "2." However, you can sometimes get tickets from one day to the next. Some city bus tours include a visit in their regular circuit, which may be a good option. Guided tours in English are available for €3.50 and require a reservation.

The painting was executed in what was the order's refectory, which is now referred to as the **Cenacolo Vinciano.** Take a moment to visit Santa Maria delle Grazie itself. It's a handsome, completely restored church, with a fine dome, which Bramante added along with a cloister about the time that Leonardo was commissioned to paint *The Last Supper*. If you're wondering how two such giants came to be employed decorating and remodeling the refectory and church of a comparatively modest religious order, and not, say, the Duomo, the answer lies in the ambitious but largely unrealized plan to turn Santa Maria delle Grazie into a magnificent Sforza family mausoleum. Though Ludovico il Moro Sforza (1452–1508), seventh duke of Milan, was but one generation away from the founding of the Sforza dynasty, he was its last ruler. Two years after Leonardo finished *The Last Supper*, Ludovico was defeated by Louis XII and spent the remaining eight years of his life in a French dungeon. ⊠ *Piazza Santa Maria delle Grazie 2, off Corso Magenta, Sant'Ambrogio* ☎ *02/89421146* ⊕ *www.cenacolovinciano.net* ⊠ *Last Supper, €6.50 plus €1.50 reservation fee; church free* ☉ *Last Supper, weekdays 9–6, Sat. 9–2; church weekdays 7–noon and 3–7, Sun. 7:30– 12:15 and 3:30–9* Ⓜ *Cadorna, Tram 16.*

WORTH NOTING

⓭ Museo Civico Archeologico *(Municipal Archaeological Museum)*. Appropriately situated in the heart of Roman Milan, this museum's garden encloses the polygonal Ansperto tower, which was once part of the Roman walls. Housed in a former monastery, this museum has some everyday utensils, jewelry, an important silver plate from the last days of paganism, and several fine examples of mosaic pavement. ⊠ *Corso Magenta 15, Sant'Ambrogio* ☎ *02/86450011* ⊠ *€2* ☉ *Tues.–Sun. 9–1 and 2–5:30* Ⓜ *Cadorna.*

⓰ Museo Nazionale della Scienza e Tecnica *(National Museum of Science and Technology)*. This converted cloister is best known for the collection of models based on Leonardo da Vinci's sketches (although these are not captioned in English, the labeling in many other exhibits is bilingual). On the ground level—in the hallway between the courtyards—is a room featuring interactive, moving models of the famous *vita aerea* (aerial screw) and *ala battente* (beating wing), thought to be forerunners of the modern helicopter and airplane, respectively. The museum also houses a varied collection of industrial artifacts including trains, a celebrated Italian-built submarine, and several reconstructed workshops including a watchmaker's, a lute maker's, and an antique pharmacy. Displays also illustrate papermaking and metal founding, which were fundamental to Milan's—and the world's—economic growth. There's a bookshop and a bar. The 16th-century church in the same piazza is **San Vittore al Corpo** (☉ *Sat.–Tues. and Thurs. 3–5:45*), which has one of the most beautiful interiors in Milan. ⊠ *Via San Vittore 21, Sant'Ambrogio* ☎ *02/485551* ⊕ *www.museoscienza.org* ⊠ *€8* ☉ *Wed.–Fri. 9:30–5, weekends 9:30– 6:30* Ⓜ *Conciliazione; Tram 16, Bus 50, 58, 94.*

⓲ Navigli District. In medieval times, a network of *navigli*, or canals, crisscrossed the city. Almost all have been covered over, but two—Naviglio Grande and Naviglio Pavese—are still navigable. Once a down-at-theheels neighborhood, the Navigli district has undergone some gentrification over the last 20 years. Humble workshops have been replaced by boutiques, art galleries, cafés, bars, and restaurants. The Navigli at night is about as close as you will get to more-southern-style Italian street life in Milan. On weekend nights, it is difficult to walk (and impossible to park, although an underground parking area has been under construction for years) among the youthful crowds thronging the narrow streets along the canals. Check out the antiques fair on the last Sunday of the month. ⊠ *South of Corso Porta Ticinese, Porta Genova* Ⓜ *Porta Genova; Trams 2, 3, 9, 15, 29, 30.*

WHERE TO EAT

CINQUE GIORNATE

$$$
ITALIAN

✕ **Da Giacomo.** The fashion and publishing crowd, as well as international bankers and businessmen, favor this Tuscan/Ligurian restaurant. The emphasis is on fish; even the warm slice of pizza served while you study the menu has seafood in it. The specialty, *gnocchi Da Giacomo,* has a savory seafood-and-tomato sauce. Service is friendly and efficient; the wine list broad; and the dessert cart, with tarte tatin and Sicilian *cassata* (a concoction of sponge cake, ricotta, and candied fruit), rich and varied. With its tile floor and bank of fresh seafood, it has a refined neighborhood-bistro style. ⊠ *Via P. Sottocorno 6, entrance in Via Cellini, Cinque Giornate* ☎ *02/76023313* ⊕ *www.ristorantedagiacomo.it* ⌕ *Reservations essential* ▤ *AE, DC, MC, V* ☉ *Closed Christmas wk and last 2 wks of Aug.* Ⓜ *Tram 9, 12, 27, 29, 30. Bus 54, 60.*

DUOMO

$$$$
MODERN ITALIAN
★

✕ **Cracco.** To international epicures, Carlo Cracco is on a similar plane as innovators Heston Blumenthal and Ferran Adrià. The tasting menus are a good way to savor many of the delicate inventions of Cracco's creative talent, though an à la carte menu is available. Delightful appetizers and desserts vary seasonally, but may include the scampi cream with freshwater shrimp, the disk of "caramelized Russian salad," and the mango cream with mint gelatin. Specialties include Milanese classics revisited—Cracco's take on saffron risotto and breaded veal cutlet should not be missed. The elegant dining room favors cool earth tones and clean lines. ⊠ *Via Victor Hugo 4, Duomo* ☎ *02/876774* ⊕ *www.ristorantecracco.it* ⌕ *Reservations essential* ▤ *AE, MC, V* ☉ *Sept.–June: closed Sun., no lunch Sat.; July and 1 wk of Aug.: closed weekends; closed 10 days in early Jan. and 2 wks in Aug.* Ⓜ *Duomo.*

$$$–$$$$
MODERN ITALIAN
★

✕ **Don Carlos.** One of the few restaurants open after La Scala lets out, Don Carlos, in the Grand Hotel et de Milan, is nothing like its indecisive operatic namesake (whose betrothed was stolen by his father). Flavors are bold, their presentation precise and full of flair: calamari stuffed with cod lies on a bed of potato puree, and broiled red mullet floats on a lacy layer of crispy leeks. Walls are blanketed with sketches of the theater, and the low-key opera recordings are every bit as well chosen as the wine list, setting the perfect stage for discreet business negotiation or, better yet, refined romance. A gourmet menu costs €85 for six courses (two-person minimum), excluding wine. ⊠ *Grand Hotel et de Milan, Via Manzoni 29, Duomo* ☎ *02/723141* ⊕ *www.ristorantedoncarlos. it* ⌕ *Reservations essential* ▤ *AE, DC, MC, V* ☉ *No lunch* Ⓜ *Montenapoleone; Tram 1, 2.*

$
PIZZA

✕ **La Bruschetta.** This tiny, bustling first-class pizzeria near the Duomo serves specialties from Tuscany and other parts of Italy. The wood oven is in full view, so you can see your pizza cooking in front of you. Aside from the pizza, the menu is essentially Tuscan. Try the seasonal specialties: in summer, the *panzanella,* a salad with toasted bread; and in winter, the *ribollita,* a dense soup of vegetables, cabbage, and bread. The *tagliata,* thin slices of grilled Tuscan beef garnished with rosemary and peppercorns or arugula, is another specialty. Reservations are essential on weekends, when two sittings of diners are squeezed in between the cinema showtimes. ⊠ *Piazza Beccaria 12, Duomo* ☎ *02/8692494* ⌕ *Reservations essential* ═ *AE, MC, V* ⊙ *Closed Mon., 3 wks in Aug., and late Dec.–early Jan.* Ⓜ *Duomo.*

GARIBALDI

$–$$ ✕ **Osteria Vecchi Sapori.** Simple but savory fare and a menu that varies
PIZZA, MEDITER- weekly characterize one osteria with two locations run by two broth-
RANEAN ers, Paolo and Roberto. Specialties include their truffle tagliolini, and primi of stuffed pasta like gorgonzola-filled fiocchetti, or pear and parmigiano-filled ravioli with a saffron butter sauce. Their extensive, meat-rich second-course dishes are paired with creamy polenta *taragna* (made with corn meal and buckwheat flour) or their handcut fried potatoes. The dessert menu changes daily with in-house cakes, tiramisu, and *crostate* (tarts or pies) reflecting traditional tastes and seasonal availability. Great when you're eating late, they're open til 1 A.M. ⊠ *Via Carmagnola, 3, Garbaldi* ☎ *02/6686148* ⊕ *www.vecchisapori.it* ⌕ *Reservations essential* ═ *AE, DC, MC, V* Ⓜ *Garibaldi, Zara.*

$–$$ ✕ **Pizzeria La Fabbrica.** This lively pizzeria has two wood-burning ovens
PIZZA going full-steam every day of the week. Skip the appetizers and go straight to the pizza. Pizzas vary from traditional *(quattro stagioni)* to vegetable-based (with leeks and gorgonzola) to in-house specialties like the *tartufona* (with truffles). The menu also offers pasta like *pici* with Tuscan sausage and main *(secondi)* dishes. Save room for a worthy dessert like the *torta caprese al cioccolato* or tiramisu—though after pizza, you might want to share. The Fabbrica is spacious enough to handle groups; seek out a seat in the spacious garden area when the weather's fine. ⊠ *Viale Pasubio 2, Garbaldi* ☎ *02/6552271* ⊕ *www.lafabbricapizzeria.it* ═ *AE, DC, MC, V* ⊙ *No lunch* Ⓜ *Garibaldi.*

LORETO

$–$$ ✕ **Da Abele.** If you love risotto, then make a beeline for this neighbor-
MILANESE hood trattoria. The superb risotto dishes change with the season, and
★ there may be just two or three on the menu at any time. It is tempting to try them all. The setting is relaxed, the service informal, the prices strikingly reasonable. Outside the touristy center of town but quite convenient by subway, this trattoria is invariably packed with locals. ⊠ *Via Temperanza 5, Loreto* ☎ *02/2613855* ═ *AE, DC, MC, V* ⊙ *Closed Mon., Aug., and Dec. 22–Jan. 7. No lunch* Ⓜ *Pasteur.*

PORTA VENEZIA

$$$$ ✕ **Joia.** At this haute-cuisine vegetarian restaurant near Piazza della
VEGETARIAN Repubblica, delicious dishes are artistically prepared by chef Pietro Leemann. Vegetarians, who often get short shrift in Italy, will marvel at the variety of culinary traditions—Asian and European—and artistry offered here. The ever-changing menu offers dishes in unusual

formats: tiny glasses of creamed cabbage with ginger, spheres of crunchy vegetables that roll across the plate. Fish also makes an appearance. Joia's restful dining room has been refurbished, another room added, and its kitchen enlarged. The fixed-price lunch "box" is a good value (€17 and €35), but be sure to reserve ahead. Multicourse menus in the evening range from €50 to €100, excluding wine. ⊠ *Via Panfilo Castaldi 18, Porta Venezia* ☎ *02/29522124* ⊕ *www.joia.it* ⊟ *AE, DC, MC, V* ⊘ *Closed Sun., 3 wks in Aug., and Dec. 25–Jan. 7. No lunch Sat.* Ⓜ *Repubblica; Tram 1, 5, 11, 29, 30.*

¢   ✕ **Pizza OK.** Pizza is almost the only item on the menu at this popular
PIZZA   spot near Corso Buenos Aires in the Porta Venezia area. The pizza is extra thin and good, and possibilities for toppings seem endless. A good choice for families, this dining experience will be easy on your pocketbook. A second location is on Via San Sio 9 in Corso Vercelli. ⊠ *Via Lambro 15, Porta Venezia* ☎ *02/29401272* ⊟ *No credit cards* ⊘ *Closed Aug. and Dec. 24–Jan. 7. No lunch Sun.* Ⓜ *Porta Venezia.*

PROCACCINI

$$ ✕ **Trattoria Montina.** Twin brothers Maurizio and Roberto Montina have
MILANESE   turned this restaurant into a local favorite. Don't be fooled by the
Fodor's Choice   "trattoria" name. The sage-green paneling makes it airy and cozy on a
★   gray Milan day. Chef Roberto creates exquisite modern Italian dishes such as warmed risotto with merlot and taleggio cheese, while Maurizio chats with guests, regulars, and local families. Milan's famous *cotoletta* (breaded veal cutlet) is light and tasty. Try fish or the *frittura impazzita,* a wild-and-crazy mix of delicately fried seafood. There's a fine selection of sweets on the dessert cart. ⊠ *Via Procaccini 54, Procaccini* ☎ *02/3490498* ⊟ *AE, DC, MC, V* ⊘ *Closed Sun., Aug., and Dec. 25–Jan. 7. No lunch Mon.* Ⓜ *Tram 1, 19, 29, 33.*

QUADRILATERO

¢   ✕ **Bar Tempio.** This wine bar, not far from Giardini Pubblici and the
WINE BAR   shops of the Quadrilatero, was once so unprepossessing that it didn't have a name—but it turned out some of Milan's best panini. It's been renovated and given a name, but the same artist is still making the sandwiches. This is a lunch-only establishment, and you might have to wait your turn, as panini are made to order from a list (not in English, so ask for a translation or bring your phrase book). They feature cured ham, *cipolle* (onions), and various cheeses (including easily recognizable Brie). ⊠ *Piazza Cavour 5, enter from Via Turati where you see the "T" sign, Quadrilatero* ☎ *02/6551946* ⊟ *No credit cards* ⊘ *Closed Sun. No dinner* Ⓜ *Turati; Tram 1, 2; Bus 94, 61.*

$$ ✕ **Paper Moon.** Hidden behind Via Montenapoleone and thus handy
ITALIAN   to the restaurant-scarce Quadrilatero, Paper Moon is a cross between a neighborhood restaurant and a celebrity hangout. Clients include families from this well-heeled area, professionals, football players, and television stars. What the menu lacks in originality it makes up for in reliable consistency—pizza and cotoletta, to name just two. Like any Italian restaurant, it's not child-friendly in an American sense—no high chairs or children's menu—but children will find food they like. It's open

until 12:30 A.M. ⊠ *Via Bagutta 1, Quadrilatero* ☎ *02/76022297* ▭ *MC, V* ⊘ *Closed Sun., 2 wks in Aug., and Dec. 25–Jan. 2* Ⓜ *San Babila.*

SANT'AMBROGIO

$ ✕**Taverna Morigi.** This dusky, wood-panel wine bar near the stock
WINE BAR exchange is the perfect spot to enjoy a glass of wine with cheese and
cold cuts. At lunch, pasta dishes and select entrées are available; pasta is
the only hot dish served in the evening. Platters of cheese and cold cuts
are always available; if you're coming for a meal, a reservation is a good
idea. ⊠ *Via Morigi 8, Sant'Ambrogio* ☎ *02/80582007* ▭ *AE, DC, MC,
V* ⊘ *Closed Sun. Dec. 25–Jan. 7 and Aug. No lunch Sat.* Ⓜ *Cairoli.*

BEYOND CITY CENTER

$$$$ ✕**Antica Osteria del Ponte.** Rich, imaginative seasonal cuisine composed
ITALIAN according to the inspired whims of chef Ezio Santin is reason enough
Fodor's Choice to make your way 20 km (12 mi) southwest of Milan to one of Italy's
★ finest restaurants. The setting is a traditional country inn, where a wood
fire warms the rustic interior in winter. The menu changes regularly; in
fall, wild porcini mushrooms are among the favored ingredients. Various fixed menus (€55 at lunch and €85 at dinner) offer broad samplings
of antipasti, primi, and meat or fish; some include appropriate wine
selections, too. ⊠ *Piazza G. Negri 9, Beyond City Center, Cassinetta
di Lugagnano* ✛ *3 km (2 mi) north of Abbiategrasso* ☎ *02/9420034*
⊕ *www.anticaosteriadelponte.it* ⌕ *Reservations essential* ▭ *AE, MC, V*
⊘ *Closed Sun. and Mon., Dec. 25–1st wk of Jan., and Aug.*

WHERE TO STAY

DUOMO

$$–$$$ 🏨**Ariston.** This hotel claims it is designed around "bio-architectural"
principles. Rooms are decorated in simple, minimalist style, and breakfast offers a selection of organic, unprocessed foods. The location is
close to the lively Porta Ticinese shops and restaurants and the young
people's fashion mecca, Via Torino. Although a longish walk from the
nearest subway stop, the Duomo, it is well served by tram. **Pros:** good
location; parking available. **Cons:** simple rooms. ⊠ *Largo Carrobbio 2,
Duomo* ☎ *02/72000556* ⊕ *www.aristonhotel.com* ⇌ *52 rooms* ⌂ *In-
room: Wi-Fi. In-hotel: room service, bar, bicycles, laundry service, Internet terminal, Wi-Fi hotspot, parking (paid), some pets allowed* ▭ *AE,
DC, MC, V* ⦵ *BP* Ⓜ *Duomo; Tram 2, 14.*

$$–$$$ 🏨**Hotel Gran Duca di York.** This small hotel has spare but classically
elegant and efficient rooms—four with private terraces. Built around
a courtyard, the 1890s building was originally a seminary and still
belongs to a religious institution. With an ideal location a few steps west
of the Duomo, it offers exceptional value for Milan and is managed by
the same family that owns the Spadari. **Pros:** central; airy; well priced.
Cons: rooms are simple. ⊠ *Via Moneta 1/a, Duomo* ☎ *02/874863*
⊕ *www.ducadiyork.com* ⇌ *33 rooms* ⌂ *In-room: Wi-Fi. In-hotel: room
service, bar, laundry service, Internet terminal, Wi-Fi hotspot, parking
(paid)* ▭ *AE, MC, V* ⊘ *Closed Aug.* ⦵ *EP* Ⓜ *Cordusio.*

$$$ ⊡ **Hotel Spadari al Duomo.** That this hotel is owned by an architect's family shows in the details, including architect-designed furniture and a fine collection of contemporary art. The owner's idea of creating a hotel/gallery extends to the guest rooms, where paintings by young Milanese artists are on rotating display. For all the artistic accents, this is still a comfortable, homey hotel, with an inviting frescoed breakfast room and many rooms with private terraces. Personal touches, such as a collection of short stories on the turned-down beds, abound. **Pros:** feedback on Fodors.com: "excellent breakfast, perfect location, and, above all, staff that seems to care about your having a wonderful experience." **Cons:** it's a splurge. ⊠ *Via Spadari 11, Duomo* 🕾 *02/72002371* ⊕ *www. spadarihotel.com* ⤴ *40 rooms, 3 suites* ♿ *In-room: Internet, Wi-Fi. In-hotel: bar, Internet terminal, Wi-Fi (free), parking (paid)* ⊟ *AE, DC, MC, V* ⸾◯⸿ *BP* Ⓜ *Duomo.*

$$$ ⊡ **UNA Maison Milano.** An understated entrance leads the visitor into what seems more like a sophisticated, upscale residence than a hotel—which is precisely the feeling the designers of Maison were striving for. This faithfully restored palazzo dates from the early 1900s; inside, spaciousness is accentuated with soft white interior, muted fabrics and marbles, and clean, contemporary lines. Massive mirrors that don't hang, they lean; baths are almost as spacious as the living area. Two sets of windows separate you from any eventual street noise, and your personal butler will make sure your every need is met. Single-price (not per person) breakfast is served in your room. **Pros:** the warmth of a residence and luxury of a design hotel. **Cons:** breakfast not included. ⊠ *Via Mazzini 4, Duomo* 🕾 *02/85605* ⊕ *www.unahotels.it* ⤴ *13 rooms, 6 jr. suites, 5 suites, penthouse.* ♿ *In-room: safe, refrigerator, Internet, Wi-Fi. In-hotel: bar, Internet terminal, Wi-Fi (free)* ⊟ *AE, DC, MC, V* ⸾◯⸿ *BP* Ⓜ *Duomo.*

PIAZZA REPUBBLICA

$ ⊡ **Hotel Casa Mia Milan.** Easy to reach from the central train station (a few blocks away) and easy on the budget, this tiny hotel, up a flight of stairs, is family-run. Rooms are simple and clean with individual (small) baths, renovated in 2009. Although not in the center of things, it's two short blocks from transport center Piazza Repubblica (tram and metro lines), which also hosts the doyenne of Milan's palace hotels, the Principe di Savoia. **Pros:** clean; good value. **Cons:** not the nicest neighborhood in Milan. ⊠ *Viale Vittorio Veneto 30, Piazza Repubblica* 🕾 *02/6575249* ⊕ *www.casamiahotel.it* ⤴ *15 rooms* ♿ *In-hotel: room service, bar, laundry service, Internet terminal, Wi-Fi hotspot, parking (paid)* ⊟ *AE, DC, MC, V* ⸾◯⸿ *BP* Ⓜ *Repubblica.*

PORTA NUOVA

$$$$ ⊡ **Principe di Savoia.** Milan's grande dame has all the trappings of
★ an exquisite traditional hotel: lavish mirrors, drapes, and carpets, and Milan's largest guest rooms, outfitted with eclectic fin de siècle furnishings. Forty-eight Deluxe Mosaic rooms (named for the glass mosaic panels in their ample bathrooms) are even larger, and the three-bedroom Presidential Suite features its own marble pool. The Winter Garden bar is an elegant aperitivo spot, and the Acanto restaurant

has garden seating. Lighter food is served in the Lobby Lounge. **Pros:** probably the most serious spa/health club (considered chic by Milanese) in town. **Cons:** overblown luxury in a not-very-central or attractive neighborhood; close enough to the train station to attract pickpockets. ⊠ *Piazza della Repubblica 17, Porta Nuova* ☎ *02/62301* ⊕ *www. hotelprincipedisavoia.com* ⤳ *269 rooms, 132 suites* ♿ *In-room: safe, DVD, Wi-Fi. In-hotel: 2 restaurants, room service, bar, pool, gym, spa, laundry service, Internet terminal, parking (paid), some pets allowed* ▭ *AE, DC, MC, V* ⃥⃝⃒ *EP* Ⓜ *Repubblica.*

QUADRILATERO

$$$$ ⌦ **Four Seasons.** The Four Seasons has been cited more than once by the Italian press as the country's best city hotel—perhaps because once you're inside, the feeling is anything but urban. Built in the 15th century as a convent, the hotel surrounds a colonnaded cloister, and some rooms have balconies looking onto a glassed-in courtyard. Parts of the original frescoes can still be seen in the lobby and lounge. Everything about the place is Four Seasons (high) style. The Theater restaurant has some of Milan's best hotel dining provided by chef Sergio Mei. There is a Sunday brunch that is well worth the €80 charge. Ask about the "Chocolate Room" when it is time for dessert. **Pros:** beautiful setting that feels like Tuscany rather than central Milan. **Cons:** expensive. ⊠ *Via Gesù 6–8, Quadrilatero* ☎ *02/7708167* ⊕ *www.fourseasons.com* ⤳ *77 rooms, 41 suites* ♿ *In-room: safe, DVD, Internet, Wi-Fi. In-hotel: 2 restaurants, room service, bar, gym, spa, laundry service, parking (paid)* ▭ *AE, DC, MC, V* ⃥⃝⃒ *EP* Ⓜ *Montenapoleone.*

SANT'AMBROGIO

$$–$$$ ⌦ **Antica Locanda Leonardo.** Only a block from the church that houses *The Last Supper* and in one of Milan's most desired and historic neighborhoods with elegant shops and bars, this hotel has been family-run for more than 100 years. Half the rooms face a courtyard and the others a back garden. Many have balconies, and one ground-floor room has a private garden with table and chairs. The hotel has a relaxed feel, and the owners who live in the building are helpful. They have a special relationship with a car service that offers moderate-price airport pickups and tours to nearby factory outlets. **Pros:** very quiet and homey; breakfast is ample. **Cons:** more like a bed-and-breakfast than a hotel. ⊠ *Corso Magenta 78, Sant'Ambrogio* ☎ *02/463317* ⊕ *www. anticalocandaleonardo.com* ⤳ *20 rooms* ♿ *In-room: Wi-Fi. In-hotel: bar, laundry service* ▭ *AE, DC, MC, V* ⊗ *Closed Dec. 31–Jan. 7 and 3 wks in Aug.* ⃥⃝⃒ *BP* Ⓜ *Sant'Ambrogio.*

SCALA

$$$$ ⌦ **Grand Hotel et de Milan.** Only blocks from La Scala, this hotel, which opened in 1863, is sometimes called the Hotel Verdi because the composer lived here for 27 years. His apartment, complete with his desk, is now the Presidential Suite. It's everything you hope for in a traditional European hotel; dignified but not stuffy, elegant but not ostentatious. Moss-green and persimmon velvet enliven the 19th-century look without sacrificing dignity and luxury. The Don Carlos restaurant is one of Milan's best. **Pros:** traditional and elegant; great location. **Cons:**

though well equipped, fitness center is small. ⊠ *Via Manzoni 29, Scala* ☎ *02/723141* ⊕ *www.grandhoteletdemilan.it* 🖘 *83 rooms, 12 suites* ♿ *In-room: Wi-Fi. In-hotel: restaurant, room service, bar, gym, laundry service, Internet terminal, parking (paid), no-smoking rooms, some pets allowed* ⊟ *AE, DC, MC, V* 🍴 *EP* Ⓜ *Montenapoleone.*

$$$$
Fodor's Choice
★

🔲 **Park Hyatt Milan.** Extensive use of warm travertine stone creates a sophisticated, yet inviting and tranquil backdrop for the Park Hyatt. Modern art embellishing the suites and the 30-ft-high glass-domed "Cupola." Rooms are spacious and opulent, with walk-in closets and bathrooms featuring double sinks, octagonal glass-enclosed rain showers, and separate soaking tubs; rooftop suites have terraces with city views. The hotel seems determined to spoil its demanding clientele with a seemingly endless number of amenities. **Pros:** central, contemporary, refined. **Cons:** not particularly intimate. ⊠ *Via Manzoni 29, Scala* ☎ *02/88211234* ⊕ *milan.park.hyatt.com* 🖘 *83 rooms, 29 suites* ♿ *In-room: Wi-Fi. In-hotel: restaurant, room service, bar, gym, spa, laundry service, bicycles, parking (paid), some pets allowed* ⊟ *AE, DC, MC, V* 🍴 *EP* Ⓜ *Montenapoleone.*

VIA SANTA SOFIA

$ 🔲 **Hotel Canada.** An attentive, just-completed renovation features wood flooring, thorough soundproofing, and contemporary furnishings that maximize space and bring in light. Flat-panel screens up to 32 inches bring in six Sky channels; Wi-Fi is available in every room, including the corner suite with outside terrace. **Pros:** services and decor make it a good value for business or pleasure. **Cons:** although trams and buses are handy, it's a short walk to the nearest metro stop. ⊠ *Via San Sofia 16, Via San Sofia* ☎ *02/58304844* ⊕ *www. canadahotel.it* 🖘 *37 rooms* ♿ *In-room: safe, Wi-Fi (paid). In-hotel: room service, bar, Internet terminal, Wi-Fi (free), parking (paid)* ⊟ *AE, DC, MC, V* 🍴 *BP* Ⓜ *Repubblica.*

NIGHTLIFE AND THE ARTS

THE ARTS

For events likely to be of interest to non-Italian speakers, see *Hello Milano* (⊕ *www.hellomilano.it*), a monthly magazine available at the tourist office in Piazza Duomo, or *The American* (⊕ *www.theamerican-mag.com*), which is available at international bookstores and newsstands, and which has a thorough cultural calendar. The tourist office publishes the monthly *Milano Mese*, which also includes some listings in English.

MUSIC

The modern **Auditorium di Milano** (⊠ *Largo Gustav Mahler [Corso San Gottardo, at Via Torricelli], Conchetta* ☎ *02/83389201 [also 02 and 03]* ⊕ *www.laverdi.org*), known for its excellent acoustics, is home to the **Orchestra Verdi,** founded by Milan-born conductor Richard Chailly. The season, which runs from September to June, includes many top international performers and rotating guest conductors.

The two halls belonging to the **Conservatorio** (⊠ *Via del Conservatorio 12, Duomo* ☎ *02/7621101* ⊕ *www.consmilano.it* Ⓜ *San Babila*) host some of the leading names in classical music. Series are organized by several organizations, including the venerable chamber music society, the **Società del Quartetto** (⊕ *www.quartettomilano.it*).

The **Teatro Dal Verme** (⊠ *Via San Giovanni sul Muro 2, Castello* ☎ *02/87905201* ⊕ *www.dalverme.org* Ⓜ *Cairoli*) stages frequent classical music concerts from October to May.

OPERA

Milan's hallowed **Teatro alla Scala** (⊠ *Piazza della Scala* ☎ *02/72003744* ⊕ *www.teatroallascala.org* ◷ *Daily 9–noon* Ⓜ *Duomo*) underwent a complete renovation from 2002 to 2004, with everything refreshed, refurbished, or replaced except the building's exterior walls. Special attention was paid to the acoustics, which have always been excellent. The season runs from December 7, the feast day of Milan patron Saint Ambrose, through June. Plan well in advance, as tickets sell out quickly. For tickets, visit the **Biglietteria Centrale** (⊠ *Galleria del Sagrato, Piazza Del Duomo* ◷ *Daily noon–6* Ⓜ *Duomo*), which is in the Duomo subway station. To pick up tickets for performances from two hours prior until 15 minutes after the start of a performance, go to the box office at the theater, which is around the corner in Via Filodrammatici 2. Although you might not get seats for the more popular operas with big stars, it is worth trying; ballets are easier. The theater is closed from the end of July through August and on national and local holidays.

NIGHTLIFE

BARS

Milan has a bar somewhere to suit any style; those in the better hotels are respectably chic and popular meeting places for Milanese as well as tourists. **Blue Note** (⊠ *Via Borsieri 37, Garibaldi* ☎ *02/69016888* ⊕ *www.bluenotemilano.com*), the first European branch of the famous New York nightclub, features regular performances by some of the most famous names in jazz, as well as blues and rock concerts. Dinner is available, and there's a popular jazz brunch on Sunday. It's closed Monday. **Brellin Caffè** (⊠ *Vicolo Lavandai at Alzaia Naviglio Grande* ☎ *02/58101351*) in the arty Navigli district has live music and serves late-night snacks. **Cafè Trussardi** (⊠ *Piazza della Scala 5, Duomo* ☎ *02/80688295* ⊕ *www.trussardi.it*) has an enormous plasma screen that keeps hip barflies entertained with video art. Open throughout the day, it's a great place for coffee. In Brera, check out the **Giamaica** (⊠ *Via Brera 32* ☎ *02/876723* ⊕ *www.jamaicabar.it*), a traditional hangout for students from the nearby Brera art school. On summer

---

"LET'S GO TO THE COLUMNS"

Andiamo al Le Colonne in Milanese youthspeak means to meet up at the sober Roman columns in front of the Basilica San Lorenzo Maggiore. Attracted by the bars and shops along Corso di Porta Ticinese, the young spill out on the street to chat and drink. Neighbors may complain about the noise and confusion, but students and nighthawks find it indispensable for socializing at all hours. It's a street—no closing time.

5

'Appy Hour

The *aperitivo*, or prelunch or predinner drink, is part of life everywhere in Italy, and each town has its own rites and favorite drinks. Milan bar owners came up with something to fit their city's fast pace and work-oriented culture. They enriched the nibbles from olives, nuts, and chips into full finger (and often fork) buffets serving cubes of pizza and cheese, fried vegetables, rice salad, sushi, and even pasta, and they baptized it 'Appy Hour—with the first "h" dropped and the second one pronounced. For a fixed fee per drink (around €8), you can fill yourself up—don't be rude; remember Italian standards are moderate—on hors d'oeuvres and make a meal of it.

There are 'Appy Hours and *aperitivi* for all tastes and in all neighborhoods. Changes happen fast, but these are reliable: **Arthé** (✉ *Via Pisacane 57* ☎ *02/29528353*) is a chic *enoteca* (wine bar) with fresh and fried vegetables and pasta. The **Capo Verde** (✉ *Via Leoncavallo 16* ☎ *02/26820430*) is in a greenhouse/nursery and is especially popular for after-dinner drinks. **G Lounge** (✉ *Via Larga 8* ☎ *02/8053042*) has rotating DJs and quality music. The elegant **Hotel Sheraton Diana Majestic** (✉ *Viale Piave 42* ☎ *02/20582081*) attracts a young professional crowd in good weather to its beautiful garden, which gets yearly thematic transformations. In the Brera neighborhood, the highly rated enoteca **'N Ombra de Vin** (✉ *Via S. Marco 2* ☎ *02/6599650* ⊕ *www. nombradevin.it*) serves wine by the glass and, in addition to the plates of sausage and cheese nibbles, has light food and not-so-light desserts. Check out the impressive vaulted basement where the bottled wine and spirits are sold. **Peck** (✉ *Via Cesare Cantù 3* ☎ *02/8693017* ⊕ *www.peck.it*), the Milan gastronomical shrine near the Duomo, also has a bar that serves up traditional—and excellent—pizza pieces, olives, and toasted nuts in a refined setting.

nights this neighborhood pulses with life; street vendors and fortune-tellers jostle for space alongside the outdoor tables. For an evening of live music—predominantly rock to jazz—head to perennial favorite **Le Scimmie** (✉ *Via Ascanio Sforza 49, Navigli* ☎ *02/89402874* ⊕ *www. scimmie.it*). It features international stars, some of whom jet in to play here, while others, including Ronnie Jones, are longtime residents in Milan. Dinner is an option. The bar of the **Sheraton Diana Majestic** (✉ *Viale Piave 42* ☎ *02/20581*), which has a splendid garden, is a prime meeting place for young professionals and the fashion people from the showrooms of the Porta Venezia neighborhood. For a break from the traditional, check out ultratrendy **SHU** (✉ *Via Molino delle Armi, Ticinese* ☎ *02/58315720*), whose gleaming interior looks like a cross between *Star Trek* and Cocteau's *Beauty and the Beast*.

NIGHTCLUBS

For nightclubs, note that the cover charges can change depending on the day of the week. **Magazzini Generali** (✉ *Via Pietrasanta 14, Porta Vigentina* ☎ *02/5393948* ⊕ *www.magazzinigenerali.it*), in what was an abandoned warehouse, is a fun, futuristic venue for dancing and concerts. The €20 cover charge includes a drink. Its venerable age notwithstanding, **Plastic** (✉ *Viale Umbria 120* ☎ *02/733996* ⊕ *www. thisisplastic.com*), closed Monday through Wednesday and some Thursdays, is still considered Milan's most transgressive, avant-garde, and fun club, complete with drag-queen shows. The action starts late, even by Italian standards—don't bother going before midnight. Cover is €15 to €20.

Rolling Stone (✉ *Corso XXII Marzo 32, Porta Vittoria* ☎ *02/733172* ⊕ *www.rollingstone.it* ☽ *Closed Mon.–Wed.*) has been Milan's temple of rock since 1982, hosting the best of foreign and local talent. It reopened with a new sound system and renewed commitment to rock and roll in 2007. Check the Web site for the concert schedule. The €14 cover includes a drink. To its regular discotheque fare, **Tocqueville** (✉ *Via Alexis de Tocqueville, Corso Como* ☎ *02/29002973* ☽ *Closed Mon.*) has added two nights per week of live music, featuring young and emerging talent. The cover at this ever-popular Milan club is €10–€13.

SHOPPING

The heart of Milan's shopping reputation is the **Quadrilatero della moda** district north of the Duomo. Here the world's leading designers compete for shoppers' attention, showing off their ultrastylish clothes in stores that are works of high style themselves. You won't find any bargains, but regardless of whether you're making a purchase, the area is a great place for window-shopping and people-watching. But fashion is not limited to one neighborhood, and there is a huge and exciting selection of clothing that is affordable, well made, and often more interesting than what is offered by the international luxury brands with shops in the Quadrilatero.

Wander around the **Brera** to find smaller shops with some appealing offerings from lesser-known names that cater to the well-schooled taste of this upscale neighborhood. The densest concentration is along Via Brera, Via Solferino, and Corso Garibaldi. For inexpensive and trendy clothes—for the under-25 set—stroll **Via Torino**, which begins in Piazza Duomo. Stay away on Saturday afternoon if you don't like crowds. Milan has several shopping streets that serve nearby residential concentrations. In the Porta Venezia area, visit **Corso Buenos Aires**, which runs northeast from the Giardini Pubblici. The wide and busy street is lined with affordable shops. It has the highest concentration of clothing stores in Europe, so be prepared to give up halfway. Avoid Saturday after 3 PM, when it seems the entire city is here looking for bargains. Near the Corso Magenta area, walk a few blocks beyond *The Last Supper* to **Corso Vercelli**, where you will find everything from a branch of the Coin department store to the quintessentially Milanese **Gemelli** (✉ *Corso Vercelli 16* ☎ *02/48004689* ⊕ *www.gemelli.it*).

QUICK BITES

Pasticceria Biffi (✉ *Corso Magenta 87* ☎ *02/48006702*) is a Milan institution and the official pastry shop of this traditionally wealthy neighborhood. Have a coffee or a rich hot chocolate in its paneled room before facing the crowds in Corso Vercelli.

Continued on page 392

THE FASHIONISTA'S MILAN

Opera buffs and lovers of Leonardo's *Last Supper,* skip ahead to the next section. No one else should be dismayed to learn that clothing is Milan's greatest cultural achievement. The city is one of the fashion capitals of the world and home base for practically every top Italian designer. The same way art aficionados walk the streets of Florence in a state of bliss, the style-conscious come here to be enraptured.

It all happens in the *quadrilatero della moda,* Milan's toniest shopping district, located just north of the Duomo. Along the cobblestone streets, Armani, Prada, and their fellow *stilisti* sell the latest designs from flagship stores that are as much museums of chic as retail establishments. Any purchase here qualifies as a splurge, but you can have fun without spending a euro—just browse, window-

FLORENCE HAS THE *DAVID.*

ROME HAS THE PANTHEON.

MILAN HAS THE CLOTHES.

shop, and people-watch. Not into fashion? Think of the experience as art, design, and theater all rolled into one. If you wouldn't visit Florence without seeing the Uffizi, you shouldn't visit Milan without seeing the quadrilatero.

On these pages we give a selective, street-by-street list of stores in the area. Hours are from around 10 in the morning until 7 at night, Monday through Saturday.

VIA DELLA SPIGA
(east to west)

Dolce & Gabbana
(No. 2)
☎ 02/795747
www.dolcegabbana.it
women's accessories

Gio Moretti (No. 4)
☎ 02/76003186
women's and men's
clothes: many labels,
as well as books,
CDs, flowers, and an
art gallery

Bulgari Italia (No. 6)
☎ 02/777001
www.bulgari.com
jewelry, fragrances,
accessories

Boutique Ferré
(No. 6)
☎ 02/783050
www.gianfrancoferre.
com
women's, men's, and
children's sportswear

Malo (No. 7)
☎ 02/76016109
www.malo.it
everything cashmere

cross Via Sant'Andrea

Fay (No. 15)
☎ 02/76017597
www.fay.it
women's and men's
clothes, accessories: a
flagship store, designed
by Philip Johnson

Prada (No. 18)
☎ 02/76394336
www.prada.com
accessories

Giorgio Armani (No. 19)
☎ 02/783511
www.giorgioarmani.com
accessories

Tod's (No. 22)
☎ 02/76002423
www.tods.com
shoes and handbags:
the Tod's flagship store

Dolce & Gabbana (No. 26)
☎ 02 76001155
www.dolcegabbana.it
women's clothes, in a
baroque setting

Moschino (No. 30)
☎ 02/76004320
www.moschino.it
women's, men's, and
children's clothes: Chic
and Cheap, so they say

✔ Just Cavalli (No. 30)
☎ 02/76390893
www.robertocavalli.net
women's and men's
clothes, plus a café
serving big salads
and carpaccio. It's
the offspring of the
Just Cavalli Café
in Parco Sempione, one
of the hottest places in
town for drinks (with or
without dinner).

Roberto Cavalli
(No. 42)
☎ 02/76020900
www.robertocavalli.net
women's and men's
clothes, accessories:
3,200 square feet of
Roberto Cavalli

I Pinco Pallino (No.
42) ☎ 02/781931
www.ipincopallino.it
extravagant children's
clothing

Marni (No. 50)
☎ 02/76317327
www.marni.com
women's clothes

VIA MONTENAPO-LEONE
(east to west)

Fratelli Rossetti
(No. 1)
☎ 02/76021650
www.rossetti.it
shoes

Giorgio Armani
(No. 2)
☎ 02/76390068
www.giorgioarmani.com
women's and men's clothes

Salvatore Ferragamo Donna
(No. 3)
☎ 02/76000054
www.ferragamo.com
women's clothes, shoes, accessories

Bottega Veneta
(No. 5)
☎ 02/76024495
www.bottegaveneta.com
leather goods: signature woven-

leather bags

Etro (No. 5)
☎ 02/76005049
www.etro.it
women's and men's clothes, leather goods, accessories

Gucci (No. 5/7)
☎ 02/771271
www.gucci.com
women's and men's clothes

Prada (No. 6)
☎ 02/76020273
www.prada.com
men's clothes

Prada (No. 8)
☎ 02/7771771
www.prada.com
women's clothes and accessories

Agnona (No. 21)
☎ 02/76316530
www.agnona.com
women's clothes: Ermenegildo excellence for women

Ermenegildo Zegna
(No. 27A)
☎ 02/76006437
www.zegna.com.
men's clothes, in the finest fabrics

Versace in
Via Montenapoleone

cross Via Sant'Andrea

Armani Junior (in galleria) (No. 10)
☎ 02/783196
www.giorgioarmani.com
children's clothes: for the under-14 fashionista

FASHION SHOPPING, ACCESSORIZED

Milan's most ambitious shops don't just want to clothe you— they want to trim your hair, clean your pores, and put a cocktail in your hand. Some "stores with more" in and around the quadrilatero are indicated by a ✔.

Versace (No. 11)
☎ 02/76008528
www.versace.com
everything Versace, except Versus and children's clothes

Corneliani (No. 12)
☎ 02/777361
www.corneliani.com
men's clothes: bespoke tailoring excellence

5

REFUELING

If you want refreshments and aren't charmed by the quadrilatero's in-store cafés, try traditional **Cova** (Via Montenapoleone 8, ☎ 02/76000578) or more mod **Sant'Ambroeus** (Corso Matteotti 7, ☎ 02/76000540). Both serve coffee, aperitifs, and snacks in an ambience of starched tablecloths and chandeliers.

Cova's courtyard café

When the hurly-burly's done, head for the **Bulgari Hotel** (Via Fratelli Gabba 7b, ☎ 02/8058051), west of Via Manzoni, for a quiet (if pricey) drink, In summer, the bar extends into a beautiful, mature garden over an acre in size.

Aspesi (No. 13)
☎ 02/76022478
www.aspesi.it
low-key local design genius

Lorenzi (No. 9)
☎ 02/76022848
www.glorenzi.com
unique Milan—cutlery, razors, gifts

Valentino (No. 20)
corner Via Santo Spirito
☎ 02/76020285
www.valentino.it
women's clothes: elegant designs for special occasions

Salvatore Ferragamo Uomo (No. 20/4)
☎ 02/76006660
www.ferragamo.com
men's clothing and accessories

Loro Piana (No. 27c)
☎ 02/7772901
www.loropiana.it
women's and men's clothes, accessories: cashmere everything

VIA SAN PIETRO ALL'ORTO
(east to west)

Belfe-Postcard (No. 7)
☎ 02/781023
www.belfe.it
chic sport and skiwear

Pomellato (No. 17)
☎ 02/76006086
www.pomellato.it
classic Milan—style jewelry

Jimmy Choo (No. 17)
☎ 02/45481770
www.jimmychoo.com
women's and men's shoes

CORSO VENEZIA
(south to north)

Prada Linea Rossa (No. 3)
☎ 02/76001426
www.prada.com
Prada's sports line for men and women

D&G (No. 7)
☎ 02/76004095
www.dolcegabbana.it
swimwear, underwear, accessories: Dolce & Gabbana's younger line

Armani Collezioni (No. 9)
☎ 02/76390068
men's and women's clothing and accessories

✔ **Dolce & Gabbana** (No. 15)
☎ 02/76028485
www.dolcegabbana.it
Men's clothes, sold in a four-story, early 19th-century patrician home. An added feature is the Martini Bar, which also serves light lunches.

VIA VERRI
(south to north)

cross Via Bigli

D&G in Via della Spiga

Etro Profumi
corner Via Bigli
☎ 02/76005450
www.etro.it
fragrances

VIA SANT'ANDREA
(south to north)

✔ **Trussardi** (No. 5)
☎ 02/76020380
www.trussardi.com
Women's and men's clothes. The nearby flagship store (Piazza della Scala 5) includes the Trussardi Marino alla Scala Café
(☎ 02/80688242), a fashion-forward bar done in stone, steel, slate, and glass. For a more substantial lunch, and views of Teatro alla Scala, head upstairs to the Marino alla Scala Ristorante
(☎ 02/80688201), which serves creative Mediterranean cuisine.

Missoni (angolo via Bagutta)
☎ 02/76003555

BARGAIN-HUNTING AT THE OUTLETS

Milan may be Italy's richest city, but that doesn't mean all its well-dressed residents can afford to shop at the boutiques of the quadrilatero. Many pick up their designer clothes at outlet stores, where prices can be reduced by 50 percent or more.

Salvagente (Via Bronzetti 16 ☎ 02/76110328, www.salvagentemilano.it) is the top outlet for designer apparel and accessories from both large are small houses. There's a small men's department. To get there, take the 60 bus, which runs from the Duomo to the Stazione Centrale, to the intersection of Bronzetti and Archimede. Look for the green iron gate with the bronze sign, between the hairdressers and an apartment building. No credit cards.

DMagazine Outlet (Via Montenapoleone 26 ☎ 02/76006027, www.dmagazine.it) has bargains in the

women's and men's clothing

Banner (No. 8/A)
☎ 02/76004609
women's and men's clothes: a multibrand boutique

Moschino (No. 12)
☎ 02/76000832
www.moschino.it
women's clothes: world-renowned window displays

✔ **Gianfranco Ferré** (No. 15)
☎ 02/794864
www.gianfrancoferre.com
Everything Ferré, plus a spa providing facials, Jacuzzis, steam baths, and mud treatments. Reservations are essential (☎ 02/76017526), preferably a week in advance.

Miu Miu (No. 21)
☎ 02/76001799
www.prada.com
Prada's younger line

Armani in Via Manzoni

VIA MANZONI (south to north)

Valextra (No. 3)
☎ 02/99786000
www.valextra.it
glamorous bags and luggage

✔ **Armani Megastore** (No. 31)
☎ 02/72318600
www.giorgioarmani.com
The quadrilatero's most conspicuous shopping complex. Along with many Armani fashions, you'll find a florist, a bookstore, a chocolate shop (offering Armani pralines), the Armani

CORSO COMO
✔ **10 Corso Como**
☎ 02/29000727
www.10corsocomo.com
Outside the quadrilatero, but it's a must see for fashion addicts. The bazaar-like 13,000-square-foot complex includes women's and men's boutiques, a bar and restaurant, a bookstore, a record shop, and an art gallery specializing in photography. You can even spend the night (if you can manage to get a reservation) at Milan's most exclusive B&B, Three Rooms (☎ 02/626163). The furnishings are a modern design-lover's dream.

Prada store in the Galleria

Caffè, and Nobu (of the upscale Japanese restaurant chain). The Armani Casa furniture collection is next door at number 37.

GALLERIA VITTORIO EMANUELE

(not technically part of the quadrilatero, but nearby)

✔ **Gucci**
☎ 02/8597991
www.gucci.com

Gucci accessories, plus the world's first Gucci café. Sit outside behind the elegant boxwood hedge and watch the world go by.

Prada (No. 63-65)
☎ 02/876979
www.prada.com
the original store: look for the murals downstairs.

Louis Vuitton
☎ 02/72147011
www.vuitton.com
accessories, women's and men's shoes, watches

Tod's
☎ 02/877997
www.tods.com
women's and men's shoes, leather goods, accessories

Borsalino (No. 92
☎ 02/804337
www.borsalino.com
hats

Galleria Vittorio Emanuele

midst of the quadrilatero. Names on sale include Armani, Cavalli, Gucci, and Prada.

DT-Intrend (Galleria San Carlo 6 ☎ 02/76000829) sells last year's Max Mara, Max & Co, Sportmax, Marella, Penny Black, and Marina Rinaldi. It's just 300 meters from the Max Mara store located on Corso Vittorio Emanuele at the corner of Galleria de Cristoforis.

At the **10 CorsoComo** outlet (Via Tazzoli 3 ☎ 02/29015130, www.10corsocomo.com) you can find clothes, shoes, bags, and accessories. It's open Fri.–Sun. 11–7.

Fans of **Marni** who have a little time on their hands will want to check out the outlet (Via Tajani 1 ☎ 02/70009735 or 02/71040332, www.marni.com). Take the 61 bus to the terminus at Largo Murani, from which it's about 200 meters on foot.

Giorgio Armani has an outlet, but it's way out of town—off the A3, most of the way to Como. The address is Strada Provinciale per Bregnano 13, in the town of Vertemate (☎ 031 887373, www.giorgioarmani.com).

Milan's Furniture Fair

During the Salone del Mobile, Milan's furniture fair, in early April, the city is a scene—there are showroom openings, cocktail parties, and product launches, and design types dressed in black and wearing funny glasses fill the sidewalks and bars.

Except for a few free days, the Salone del Mobile is for professionals only. But you can still participate. Newspapers such as *Corriere della Sera* usually run an English supplement, and special design-week freebies list public events. Major players such as bathroom and kitchen specialist Boffi (Via Solferino 11) and Capellini (Via Santa Cecilia, 4) launch new products in their stores. Warning: Do not visit if you have not planned ahead. Hotel rooms and restaurant seating are impossible to find. See ⊕ *www. fieramilano.it* for dates.

MARKETS

Weekly open markets selling fruits and vegetables—and a great deal more—are still a regular sight in Milan. Many also sell clothing and shoes. Monday- and Thursday-morning markets in **Mercato di Via S. Marco** (✉ *Brera*) cater to the wealthy residents of this central neighborhood. In addition to food stands where you can get cheese, roast chicken, and dried beans and fruits, there are several clothing and shoe stalls that are important stops for some of Milan's most elegant women. Check out the knitwear at Valentino, about midway down on the street side. Muscle in on the students from the prestigious high school nearby who rush here for the french fries and potato croquettes at the chicken stand at the Via Montebello end.

Bargains in designer apparel can be found at the huge **Mercato Papiniano** (✉ *Porta Genova*) on Saturday and Tuesday from about 9 to 1. The stalls to look for are at the Piazza Sant'Agostino end of the market. It's very crowded and demanding—watch out for pickpockets.

Venice

WORD OF MOUTH

"My favorite memory of Venice is just walking the little alleyways in the evening. . . . We happened upon a little bar, ordered a couple glasses of wine, and sat outside on the steps of the bridge nearby. As the evening went on, the bar became pretty full of locals, all joining us on the bridge to relax."

—sherhatfield

WELCOME TO VENICE

TOP REASONS TO GO

★ **Basilica di San Marco:** Whether its opulence seduces you or overwhelms you, it's a sight to behold.

★ **Santa Maria Gloriosa dei Frari:** With "glorious" architecture *and* art, this church competes with San Marco for top billing.

★ **Gallerie dell'Accademia:** The world's best collection of Venetian paintings is on display at this world-class museum.

★ **Cruising the Grand Canal:** Whether seen by gondola or by water bus, Venice's Main Street is like no other in the world.

★ **Snacking at a bàcaro:** The best way to sample tasty Venetian tidbits is to head for one the city's many sociable wine bars.

1 **The Grand Canal.** Venice's major thoroughfare is lined with grand palazzi that once housed the city's most prosperous and prominent families.

2 **San Marco.** The streets of one of Italy's most affluent neighborhoods are lined with fashion boutiques, art galleries, and grand hotels. Its Piazza San Marco—which Napoléon called "the world's most beautiful drawing room"—is the heart of Venice and the location of the Basilica di San Marco and the Palazzo Ducale.

3 **Dorsoduro.** This elegant residential area is home to the Santa Maria della Salute, the Gallerie dell'Accademia, and the Peggy Guggenheim Collection. The Zattere promenade is one of the best spots to stroll with a gelato or linger at an outdoor café.

4 **Santa Croce and San Polo.** These bustling *sestieri* (districts) are both residential and commercial, with all sorts of shops and artisan studios, several major sights, and the Rialto fish and produce markets.

5 Cannaregio. Brimming with residential Venetian life, this sestiere provides some of the sunniest open-air canal-side walks in town. The Fondamenta della Misericordia is a nightlife center, and the Jewish Ghetto has a fascinating history and tradition all its own.

6 Castello. Along with Cannaregio, this area is home to most of the locals. With its gardens, park, and narrow, winding walkways, it's the sestiere least influenced by Venice's tourist culture—except when the Biennale art festival is on.

GETTING ORIENTED

Seen from the window of an airplane, central Venice looks like a fish laid out on a blue platter. The train station at the western end is the fish's eye, and the Castello *sestiere* (district) is the tail. In all, the "fish" consists of six sestieri—Cannaregio, Santa Croce, San Polo, Dorsoduro, San Marco, and Castello. More sedate outer islands float around them—San Giorgio Maggiore and the Giudecca just to the south, beyond them the Lido, the barrier island; to the north, Murano, Burano, and Torcello.

6

(map of central Venice)

4 km

Fond. d.

THE JEWISH GHETTO

Misericordia

5

CANNAREGIO

Grande

Canal

1

Canal Grande

Ca' d'Oro

SANTA CROCE

4

SAN POLO

anta Maria
a dei Frari

2

SAN MARCO

Piazza
San Marco

Basilica di
San Marco

6

CASTELLO

Palazzo Ducale

Canal Grande

Gallerie dell'
Accademia

Peggy
Guggenheim
Collection

3

Santa Maria
della Salute

DORSODURO

Zattere
Promenade

G
MA

IUDECCA

VENICE PLANNER

Festivals to Build a Trip Around

Venice's most famous festival is **Carnevale**, drawing revelers from all over the world. For 10 days leading up to Ash Wednesday, it takes over the city—think Mardi Gras meets Casanova.

The prestigious **Biennale** is a century-old international contemporary art festival held in late summer and early fall of odd-number years. It has spawned other festivals, including the **Biennale Danza**, **Biennale Musica**, and, most famously, **Biennale Cinema**, also known as the Venice Film Festival, held yearly at the end of August.

The **Festa della Redentore** (Feast of the Redeemer), on the third Sunday in July, is the biggest celebration of the year among locals, concluding Saturday evening when boats carry revelers out onto the Bacino San Marco to await the late-night fireworks display.

There are three main annual contests of Venetian rowing: the **Regata delle Bafane**, on January 6; **Vogalonga** (long row), on a Sunday in May, in which any boat can participate; and the splendidly costumed **Regata Storica**, on the first Sunday in September.

Making the Most of Your Time

The classic introduction to Venice is a ride on *vaporetto* (water bus) Line 1 or 2 from Piazzale Roma or the train station all the way down the Grand Canal. If you've just arrived and have luggage in tow, you'll need to weigh the merits of taking this trip right away versus first getting settled at your hotel. (Crucial factors: your mood, the lines, the bulk of your bags, your hotel's location.)

Seeing Piazza San Marco and the surrounding sights can fill a day, but if you're going to be around awhile, consider holding off on your visit here—the crowds can be overwhelming, especially when you're fresh off the boat. Instead, spend your first morning at Santa Maria Gloriosa dei Frari and the Scuola Grande di San Rocco, then wander through the Dorsoduro sestiere, choosing among visits to Ca' Rezzonico, the Gallerie dell'Accademia, the Peggy Guggenheim Collection, and Santa Maria della Salute—all A-list attractions. End the afternoon with a gelato-fueled stroll along the Zattere boardwalk. Then, tackle San Marco on Day 2.

Alternative sights to mix and match, depending on your interests: the Rialto fish and produce markets; Madonna dell'Orto, Ca d'Oro, and the Jewish Ghetto in Cannaregio; Santa Maria dei Miracoli, the Querini-Stampalia, and Santi Giovanni e Paolo in Castello; and, across the water from Piazza San Marco, the island of San Giorgio Maggiore. A day on the outer islands of Murano, Burano, and Torcello is good for a change of pace, but choose one or two: all three are too much for one day.

Tourist Offices

The multilingual staff of the **Venice tourism office** (☎ 041/5298711 ⊕ www.turismovenezia.it) can provide directions and up-to-the-minute information. Its free, quarterly *Show and Events Calendar* lists current happenings and venue hours. Tourist office branches are at Marco Polo Airport; the Venezia Santa Lucia train station; Garage Comunale, on Piazzale Roma; at Piazza San Marco near Museo Correr at the southwest corner; the Venice Pavilion (including a Venice-centered bookstore), on the *riva (canal-front street)* between the San Marco vaporetto stop and the Royal Gardens; and on the Lido at the main vaporetto stop. The train-station branch is open daily 8–6:30; other branches generally open at 9:30.

Passes and Discounts

Avoid lines and save money by booking services and venue entry online with **Venice Connected** (⊕ veniceconnected.com). The service was introduced in 2009 and continues to evolve. Currently, you must book at least seven days in advance; discounts depend on arrival dates. For example, during the "medium/low" season, a weeklong vaporetto transit pass is €37.50 instead of €50. Venice Connected guarantees the lowest prices on parking, public transit passes, toilet service, museum passes, Wi-Fi access, and airport transfers. Venice Connected may replace the **VENICEcard** (☎ 041/2424 ⊕ www.hellovenezia.com), a pass that provides more comprehensive discounted access to sights and transportation.

Sixteen of Venice's most significant churches are part of the **Chorus Foundation** (☎ 041/2750462 ⊕ www.chorusvenezia.org) umbrella group, which coordinates their administration, hours, and admission fees. Churches in the group are open to visitors all day except Sunday morning. Single church entry costs €3; you have a year to visit all 16 with the €10 Chorus Pass. Family and student discounts are also available. Get a pass at any church or online.

The Museum Pass (€18) from **Musei Civici** (☎ 041/2715911 ⊕ www.museicivicivenezia.it) includes one-time entry to 12 Venice museums. The Museums of San Marco Pass Plus (€13; April–October) is good for the museums on the Piazza, plus another civic museum of your choice. The Museums of San Marco Pass (€12; November–March) is good only for the Piazza's museums. All these passes are discounted at VeniceConnected.com.

Venetian Vocabulary

Venetians use their own terms to describe their unique city. In fact, the Venetian language predates Italian; if you have an ear for Italian, you'll notice a distinct difference. Here are a few key words:

sestiere: One of six neighborhoods in central Venice.

rio: A small canal.

riva: A street running along a canal where a boat can dock.

fondamenta: A street with buildings on one side and a rio on the other.

calle: A passage or walkway with buildings (as opposed to a canal) on either side.

campo: A square—what elsewhere in Italy is called a piazza. (The only piazza in Venice is Piazza San Marco.)

bàcaro: A traditional wine bar.

cicchetto (pronounced chee-kay-toh): A snack served at a bàcaro—roughly the Venetian equivalent of tapas.

ombra: A small glass of wine served at a bàcaro.

GETTING HERE AND AROUND

Getting Here by Car

Venice is in the middle of the lagoon at the end of SR11, just off the east–west A4 autostrada. Cars are nonexistent in Venice; if possible, to avoid parking fees, return your rental car when you arrive.

A word of warning: don't be waylaid by illegal touts, often wearing fake uniforms, who may try to flag you down and offer to arrange parking and hotels; drive on to one of the established parking garages. Consider reserving a space in advance. The **Autorimessa Comunale** (☎ 041/2727211 ⊕ www.asmvenezia.it) costs €24 for 24 hours, less if you book with Venice Connected (⊕ www.veniceconnected.com). The private **Garage San Marco** (☎ 041/5232213 ⊕ www. garagesanmarco.it) costs €24 for up to 12 hours and €30 for 12 to 24 hours with online reservations. On its own island, **Tronchetto** (☎ 041/5207555) charges €21 for 6 to 24 hours. Watch for its signs coming over the bridge—you'll turn right just before you reach Piazzale Roma.

Many hotels and the Casinò have guest discounts with San Marco or Tronchetto garages; get a voucher when you check in at your hotel and present it when you pay the garage.

Getting Here by Air

Venice's **Aeroporto Marco Polo** (☎ 041/2609260 ⊕ www. veniceairport.it) is 10 km (6 mi) north of the city on the mainland. It's served by domestic and international flights, including connections from 21 European cities, plus direct flights from New York's JFK.

Water transfer: From Marco Polo terminal it's a well-marked, mostly covered seven-minute walk to the dock where public and private transportation departs for Venice's historic center. **Alilaguna** (☎ 041/2401701 ⊕ www. alilaguna.it) has regular ferry service from predawn until nearly midnight. The charge is €13, including bags, and it takes about 1½ hours to reach the landing near Piazza San Marco. Depending on the line, there may be stops at Fondamente Nove, Murano, Lido, the Cannaregio Canal, and the Rialto. For €25 you can take the one-hour Oro line direct to San Marco. A *motoscafo* (water taxi) carries up to four people and four bags to the city center in a sleek powerboat—with a base cost of €95 for the 25-minute trip. Each additional person, bag, and stop costs extra; it's essential to agree on a fare before boarding.

Land transfer: Blue buses run by **ATVO** (☎ 0421/383672 ⊕ www.atvo.it) make a less-scenic but quicker (20-minute) and cheaper (€3) trip from the airport to Piazzale Roma, from where you can get a vaporetto to the stop nearest your hotel. Tickets are sold from machines and at the airport booth in Ground Transportation (open daily 9–7:30), and on the bus when tickets are otherwise unavailable. A land taxi to Piazzale Roma costs about €35.

Getting Here by Train

Venice has rail connections with every major city in Italy and Europe. Note that Venice's train station is **Venezia Santa Lucia**, not to be confused with Venezia-Mestre, which is the mainland stop prior to arriving in the historic center. Some trains do not continue beyond the Mestre station; in such cases you can catch the next Venice-bound train. Get a €1 ticket from the newsstand on the platform and validate it (in the yellow time-stamp machine) to avoid a fine.

Getting Around by Vaporetto

Venice's primary public transportation is the vaporetto (water bus). The **ACTV** (☎ 041/2424 ⊕ www.hellovenezia. com) operates *vaporetti* on routes throughout the city. Beginning at 11 PM there is limited night service. Although most landings are well marked, the system takes some getting used to; check before boarding to make sure the boat is going in your desired direction. Line 1 is the Grand Canal local, making all stops and continuing via San Marco to the Lido. The trip takes about 35 minutes from Ferrovia to San Marco. Line 2 travels up the Grand Canal (with fewer stops), down the Giudecca Canal to San Zaccaria, and back again (continuing to Lido in summer).

A single ticket for all lines costs €6.50, and is good for 60 minutes one-way. A better option is a Travel Pass: €16 for 12 hours, €18 for 24 hours, €33 for 72 hours, and €50 for a week of unlimited travel. Travelers ages 14–29 can opt for the €4 Rolling Venice card (available from the Hello-Venezia booth at principal vaporetto stops), which allows 72 hours of travel for €18. A ticket to take the vaporetto one stop across the Grand Canal is €2. ■TIP➔ The best discounts are available in advance through VeniceConnected.com.

Line information is posted at each landing, and complete timetables for all lines are available at ACTV ticket booths, at most major stops, and are free for download at Hello-Venezia.com. ■TIP➔ If you board without a valid ticket, ask immediately to buy one onboard to avoid the possibility of a €35 fine. (Pleading ignorance will not spare you.) The law says you must buy tickets for bags more than 28 inches long (the charge is waved if you have a Travel Pass), but this is generally enforced only for very bulky bags.

Getting Around by Traghetto

Many tourists are unaware of these two-man gondola ferries that cross the Grand Canal at or near most gondola stations. At €0.50, they're the cheapest and shortest gondola ride in Venice—and can also save a lot of walking. Look for TRAGHETTO signs and hand your fare to the gondolier when you board; they're marked on many maps. Stand up in these gondolas, straddling the width to keep your balance, unless the gondolier tells you otherwise.

Getting Around by Water Taxi

A *motoscafo* (water taxi) isn't cheap: you'll spend about €60 for a short trip in town, €75 to the Lido, and €90 per hour to visit the outer islands. The fare system is convoluted, with luggage handling, waiting time, early or late hours, and even ordering a taxi from your hotel adding expense. Always agree on the price before departing.

Getting Around by Gondola

An enchanting diversion rather than a practical way to get around, *un giro in gondola* is a round-trip ride. Some consider these trips tourist traps; others wouldn't miss them. To make the most of it, request to go through more-remote side canals, where you'll get an intimate glimpse of the city that can't be seen any other way.

San Marco is loaded with gondola stations, so the waters are crowded with gondolas. Instead, try the San Tomà or Santa Sofia (near Ca' d'Oro) station. The price of a 40-minute ride is supposed to be €80 for up to six passengers, increasing to €100 between 7:30 PM and 8 AM. (Never pay a per-person rate.) Agree on cost and duration of the ride beforehand, and make it clear you want to see the more serene areas of the city. Feel free to bring prosecco—your gondolier may even supply glasses.

EATING AND DRINKING WELL IN VENICE

The catchword in Venetian restaurants is fish, often at its tastiest when it looks like nothing you've seen before. How do you learn about the catch of the day? A visit to the Rialto's *pescheria* (fish market) is more instructive than any book. Never be afraid to ask a restaurant's recommendation, either: it's what a local would do.

Dining options in Venice range from the ultra high-end, where jackets and ties are a must, to the very casual. Once staunchly traditional, many restaurants have renovated their menus along with their dining rooms, creating dishes that blend classic Venetian elements with ingredients far less common to the lagoon environs. Mid-range restaurants are often more willing to make the break, offering innovative options while keeping dishes like *sarde in saor* and *fegato alla veneziana* (calves' liver and onions) available as mainstays. The best places are often small and have limited seating, so be sure to reserve ahead.

GOING BÀCARO

You can sample regional wines and scrumptious *cicchetti* (bite-size snacks) in *bàcari* (traditional wine bars), a great Venetian tradition. For centuries, locals have gathered at these neighborhood spots to chat over a glass of *sfuso* (wine on tap) or the ubiquitous spritz: an iridescent red cocktail of white wine, seltzer, and either Aperol, Select, or Bitter liqueur. *Crostini* (toast with toppings) and *polpette* (meat, fish, or vegetable croquettes) are popular cicchetti, as are small sandwiches, seafood salads, *baccalà mantecato* (cod creamed with olive oil), and toothpick-speared items such as roasted peppers, marinated artichokes, and mozzarella balls.

SEAFOOD

Venetian cuisine is based on seafood. *Granseola* (crab), *moeche* (soft-shell crab), and *seppie* or *seppioline* (cuttlefish) are all prominently featured. Trademark dishes include *sarde in saor* (panfried sardines with olive oil, vinegar, onions, pine nuts, and raisins, photo right), *la frittura* (tempuralike fried fish), and *baccalà mantecato* (creamed cod).

When prepared whole, fish is usually priced by the *etto* (100 grams, about 4 ounces) and can be expensive; but once you try it that way, you'll never want filleted fish again.

RISOTTO, PASTA, POLENTA

As a first course, Venetians favor the creamy rice dish risotto *al onda* ("undulating," as opposed to firm), prepared with vegetables or shellfish. Pasta is accompanied by seafood sauces, too: *pasticcio di pesce* is pasta baked with fish, usually *baccalà* (salt cod), and *bigoli* is a strictly local pasta shaped like short, thick spaghetti, usually served *in salsa* (an anchovy sauce), or with *nero di seppia* (squid-ink sauce).

A classic first course is *pasta e fagioli* (bean soup with pasta). Polenta (creamy cornmeal) is another staple; it's often served with *fegato alla veneziana* (calves' liver and onions).

VEGETABLES

The larger islands of the lagoon are legendary for their fine vegetables, such as

the Sant'Erasmo *castraure* artichokes that herald spring. Just a few stalls at the Rialto Market sell local crops, but most feature high-quality produce from the surrounding regions. Spring treats are fat white asparagus, and artichoke bottoms (*fondi*), usually sautéed with olive oil, parsley, and garlic. From December to March, the prized red *radicchio di Treviso* is grilled, used in salads, and added to risotto. Fall brings small wild mushrooms called *chiodini*, and *zucca barucca,* a bumpy squash often used in soups or stuffed into ravioli.

TIRAMISU

Tiramisu, *pictured below,* is the most popular dessert in town. Each restaurant follows its own tiramisu creed: some add sweet liqueur to the coffee; some stir whipped cream or crème anglaise into the mascarpone and egg-yolk filling; some scatter bits of bitter chocolate on top instead of cocoa.

WINES

Regional wines go far beyond the famous Amarone, and include some crisp whites like Malvasia, Ribolla Gialla and Tocai, the rounder Garganega (Soave) and bubbly prosecco. Reds can match well with the regional cuisine: try Cabernet Franc, Corvina (Valpolicella, Bardolino), Marzemino, Lagrein, Refosco, Raboso, or Teroldego Rotaliano. Confused? Head to a bàcaro for some expert guidance.

6

Updated by
Nan McElroy

IT'S CALLED LA SERENISSIMA, "THE MOST SERENE," a reference to the majesty, wisdom, and monstrous power of this city that was for centuries the unrivaled leader in trade between Europe and the Orient, and the bulwark of Christendom against the tides of Turkish expansion. "Most serene" could also describe the way lovers of this miraculous city feel when they see it, imperturbably bobbing on its calm blue lagoon.

Built entirely on water by men who defied the sea, Venice is unlike any other town. No matter how often you've seen it in movies or on TV, the real thing is more dreamlike than you could ever imagine—forget the Las Vegas imitation. Its landmarks, the Basilica di San Marco and the Palazzo Ducale, hardly seem Italian: delightfully idiosyncratic, they are exotic mixes of Byzantine, Gothic, and Renaissance styles. Shimmering sunlight and silvery mist soften every perspective here; it's easy to understand how the city became renowned in the Renaissance for its artists' rendering of color. It's full of secrets, inexpressibly romantic, and at times given over entirely to pleasure.

You'll see Venetians going about their daily affairs in *vaporetti* (water buses), aboard the *traghetti* (traditional gondola ferries) that carry them across the Grand Canal, in the *campi* (squares), and along the *calli* (narrow streets). They are nothing if not skilled—and remarkably tolerant—in dealing with the veritable armies of tourists from all over the world who fill the city's streets for most of the year.

PIAZZA SAN MARCO

One of the world's most evocative squares, Piazza San Marco (Saint Mark's Square) is the heart of Venice, a vast open space bordered by an orderly procession of arcades marching toward the fairy-tale cupolas and marble lacework of the Basilica di San Marco. It's perpetually packed by day with people and fluttering pigeons (the latter in smaller numbers of late). At night it can be magical, especially in winter, when mists swirl around the lampposts and the campanile.

If you face the basilica from in front of the Correr Museum, you'll notice that rather than being a strict rectangle, this square opens wider at the basilica end, creating the illusion that it's even larger than it is. On your left, the long, arcaded building is the Procuratie Vecchie, built in the early 16th century as offices and residences for the powerful procurators (magistrates).

On your right is the Procuratie Nuove, built half a century later in a more grandiose, classical style. It was originally planned by Venice's great Renaissance architect, Jacopo Sansovino (1486–1570), to carry on the look of his Libreria Sansoviniana (Sansovinian Library), but he died before construction on the Nuove had begun. Vincenzo Scamozzi (circa 1552–1616), a neoclassicist pupil of Andrea Palladio (1508–80), completed the design and construction. Still later, the Procuratie Nuove was modified by architect Baldassare Longhena (1598–1682), one of Venice's baroque masters.

When Napoléon (1769–1821) entered Venice with his troops in 1797, he called Piazza San Marco "the world's most beautiful drawing

Continued on page 410

CRUISING THE GRAND CANAL

THE BEST INTRODUCTION TO VENICE IS A TRIP DOWN MAIN STREET

Venice's Grand Canal is one of the world's great thoroughfares. It winds its way in the shape of a backward "S" from Ferrovia (the train station) to Piazza San Marco, passing 200 palazzos born of a culture obsessed with opulence and fantasy. There's a theatrical quality to a boat ride on the canal: it's as if each pink- or gold-tinted facade is trying to steal your attention from its rival across the way.

The palaces were built from the 12th to 18th centuries by the city's richest families. A handful are still private residences, but many have been converted to other uses, including museums, hotels, government offices, university buildings, a post office, a casino, and even a television station.

It's romantic to see the canal from a gondola, but the next best thing, at a fraction of the cost, is to take the Line 1 *vaporetto* (water bus) from Ferrovia to San Marco. The ride costs €6 and takes about 35 minutes. Invest in a Travel Card (€15 buys 24 hours of unlimited passage) and you can spend the better part of a day hopping on and off at the vaporetto's 16 stops, visiting the sights along the banks.

Either way, keep your eyes open for the highlights listed here; the major sites also have fuller descriptions later in this chapter.

FROM FERROVIA TO RIALTO

Palazzo Labia
On September 3, 1951, during the Venice Film Festival, the Palazzo Labia hosted what's been dubbed "the party of the century." The Aga Khan, Winston Churchill, Orson Welles, and Salvador Dalí were among those who donned 18th-century costume and danced in the Tiepolo-frescoed ballroom.

Santa Maria di Nazareth

Ponte di Scalzi

R. DI BIASIO

Stazione Ferrovia Santa Lucia

FERROVIA

SANTA CROCE

As you head out from Ferrovia, the baroque church immediately to your left is **Santa Maria di Nazareth**. Its shoeless friars earned it the nickname Chiesa degli Scalzi (Church of the Barefoot).

One of the four bridges over the Grand Canal is the **Ponte di Scalzi**. The original version was built of iron in 1858; the existing stone bridge dates from 1934.

After passing beneath the Ponte di Scalzi, ahead to the left you'll spy **Palazzo Labia**, one of the most imposing buildings in Venice, looming over the bell tower of the church of San Geremia.

A hundred yards or so further along on the left bank, the uncompleted façade of the church of **San Marcuola** gives you an idea of what's behind the marble decorations of similar 18th-century churches in Venice.

Across the canal, flanked by two *torricelle* (side wings in the shape of small towers) and a triangular *merlatura* (crenellation), is the **Fondaco dei Turchi,** one of the oldest Byzantine palaces in Venice; it's now a natural history museum. Next comes the plain brick **Depositi del Megio**, a 15th-century granary—note the lion marking it as Serenissima property—and beyond it the obelisk-topped **Ca' Belloni-Battagia**. Both are upstaged by the **Palazzo Vendramin-Calergi** on the opposite bank: this Renaissance gem was built in the 1480s, at a time when late-Gothic was still the prevailing style. A gilded banner identifies the palazzo as site of Venice's casino.

Palazzo Vendramin-Calergi
The German composer Richard Wagner died in Palazzo Vendramin-Calergi in 1883, soon after the success of his opera Parsifal. His room has been preserved—you can visit it on Saturday mornings by appointment.

CANNAREGGIO

Church of San Marcuola

GHETTO

S. MARCUOLA

Ca' Belloni-Battagia

S. STAE

Ca' Pesaro

Ca' d'Oro
Ca' d'Oro means "house of gold." but the gold is long gone—the gilding that once accentuated the marble carvings of the facade has worn away over time.

Fondaco dei Turchi

Depositi del Megio

San Stae Church

CA' D'ORO

SAN POLO

Ca' Corner della Regina

Pescheria
The pescheria has been in operation for over 1,000 years. Stop by in the morning to see the exotic fish for sale—one of which may wind up on your dinner plate. Produce stalls fill the adjacent *fondamenta*, and butchers and cheesemongers occupy the surrounding shops.

Rialto Mercato

Fondaco dei Tedeschi

Ca' dei Camerlenghi

RIALTO

SAN MARCO

The white, whimsically baroque church of **San Stae** on the right bank is distinguished by a host of marble saints on its facade. Further along the bank is another baroque showpiece, **Ca' Pesaro**, followed by the tall, balconied **Ca' Corner della Regina**. Next up on the left is the flamboyant pink-and-white **Ca' d'Oro**, arguably the finest example of Venetian Gothic design.

Across from Ca' d'Oro is the loggia-like, neo-Gothic **pescheria**, Venice's fish market, where boats dock in the morning to deliver their catch.

The canal narrows as you approach the impressive Rialto Bridge. To the left, just before the bridge, is the **Fondaco dei Tedesch**i. This was once the busiest trading center of the republic—German, Austrian, and Hungarian merchants kept warehouses and offices here; today it's the city's main post office. Across the canal stands

the curiously angled **Ca' dei Camerlenghi**. Built in 1525 to accommodate the State Treasury, it had a jail for tax evaders on the ground floor.

FROM RIALTO TO THE PONTE DELL' ACCADEMIA

SAN POLO

Ca' Foscari
Positioned at one of the busiest junctures along the Grand Canal, Ca' Foscari was recently restored after suffering severe foundation damage as a result of the relentless wake from passing boats.

Ponte di Rialto

▲ **RIALTO**

Palazzo Barzizza

Ca' Loredan

S. SILVESTRO ▲

Ca' Farsetti

Palazzo Pisani Moretta

Ca' Grimani

S. ANGELO ▲

Ca' Corner-Spinelli
If Ca' Corner-Spinelli has a familiar look, that's because it became a prototype for later Grand Canal buildings—and because its architect, Mauro Codussi, himself copied the windows from Palazzo Vendramin-Calergi.

TOMA ▲

Ca' Garzoni

Palazzo Grassi

Palazzo Falier
Palazzo Falier is said to have been the home of Doge Martin Fallier, who was beheaded for treason in 1355.

SAN MARCO

Ca' Rezzonico

REZZONICO ▲

ACCADEMIA ▲

Gallerie dell'Accademia

DORSODURO

Until the 19th century, the shop-lined **Ponte di Rialto** was the only bridge across the Grand Canal.

Rialto is the only point along the Grand Canal where buildings don't have their primary entrances directly on the water, a consequence of the two spacious *rive* (waterside paths) once used for unloading two Venetian staples: coal and wine. On your left along Riva del Carbon stand **Ca' Loredan** and **Ca' Farsetti**, 13th-century Byzantine palaces that today make up Venice's city hall. Just past the San Silvestro vaporetto landing on Riva del Vin is the 12th- and 13th-century facade of **Palazzo Barzizza**, an elegant example of Veneto-Byzantine architecture that managed to survive a complete renovation in the 17th century. Across the water, the sternly Renaissance **Ca' Grimani** has an intimidating presence that seems appropriate for today's Court of Appeals. At the Sant'Angelo landing, the vaporetto passes close to another massive Renaissance palazzo, **Ca' Corner-Spinelli**.

Back on the right bank, in a salmon color that seems to vary with the time of day, is elegant **Palazzo Pisani Moretta**, with twin water entrances. To your left, four-storied **Ca' Garzoni**, part of the Universita di Venezia Ca' Foscari, stands beside the San Toma *traghetto* (gondola ferry), which has operated since 1354. The boat makes a sharp turn and, on the right, passes one of the city's tallest Gothic palaces, **Ca' Foscari**.

The vaporetto passes baroque **Ca' Rezzonico** so closely that you get to look inside one of the most fabulous entrances along the canal. Opposite stands the Grand Canal's youngest palace, **Palazzo Grassi**, commissioned in 1749. Just beyond Grassi and Campo San Samuele, the first house past the garden was once Titian's studio. It's followed by **Palazzo Falier**, identifiable by its twin loggias (windowed porches).

Approaching the canal's fourth and final bridge, the vaporetto stops at a former church and monastery complex that houses the world-renowned **Gallerie dell'Accademia**.

The wooden pilings on which Venice was built (you can see them at the bases of the buildings along the Grand Canal) have gradually hardened into mineral form.

ARCHITECTURAL STYLES ALONG THE GRAND CANAL

BYZANTINE: 12th and 13th centuries. **Distinguishing characteristics:** high, rounded arches, relief panels, multicolored marble. **Examples:** Fondaco dei Turchi, Ca' Loredan, Ca' Farsetti, Palazzo Barzizza (and, off the canal, Basilica di San Marco).

GOTHIC: 14th and 15th centuries. **Distinguishing characteristics:** Pointed arches, high ceilings, and many windows. **Examples:** Ca' d'Oro, Ca' Foscari, Ca' Franchetti, Palazzo Falier (and, off the canal, Palazzo Ducale).

RENAISSANCE: 16th century. **Distinguishing characteristics:** classically influenced emphasis on order, achieved through symmetry and balanced proportions. **Examples:** Palazzo Vendramin-Calergi, Ca' Grimani, Ca' Corner-Spinelli, Ca' dei Camerlenghi (and, off the canal, Libreria Sansoviniana on Piazza San Marco and the church of San Giorgio Maggiore).

BAROQUE: 17th century. **Distinguishing characteristics:** Renaissance order wedded with a more dynamic style, achieved through curving lines and complex decoration. **Examples:** churches of Santa Maria di Nazareth and San Stae, Ca' Pesaro, Ca' Rezzonico (and, off the canal, the church of Santa Maria della Salute).

FROM THE PONTE DELL'ACCADEMIA TO SAN ZACCARIA

Ca' Franchetti
Until the late 19th century, Ca' Franchetti was a *squero* (gondola workshop). A few active *squeri* remain, though none are on the Grand Canal. The most easily spotted is Squero di San Trovaso, in Dorsoduro on a small canal near the Zattere boat landing.

Ca' Barbaro
Monet, Henry James, and Cole Porter are among the guests who have stayed at Ca' Barbaro. Porter later lived aboard a boat in Giudecca Canal.

SAN MARCO

Ponte dell' Accademia

Casetta Rossa

Ca' Pisani-Gritti

ACCADEMIA

S. M. DEL GIGLIO

DORSODURO

SALUTE

Ca' Barbarigo

Palazzo Venier dei Leoni
When she was in residence at Palazzo Venier dei Leoni, Peggy Guggenheim kept her private gondola parked at the door and left her dogs standing guard (in place of Venetian lions).

Palazzo Salviati

S. Maria della Salute

Ca' Dario
However tilted Dario might be, it has outlasted its many owners, who seem plagued by misfortune. They include the Italian industrialist Raul Gardini, whose 1992 suicide followed charges of corruption and an unsuccessful bid to win the America's Cup.

The wooden **Ponte dell' Accademia**, like the Eiffel Tower (with which it shares a certain structural grace), wasn't intended to be permanent. Erected in 1933 as a quick replacement for a rusting iron bridge built by the Austrian military in 1854, it was so well liked by Venetians that they kept it. (A perfect replica, with steel bracing, was installed 1986.)

You're only three stops from the end of the Grand Canal, but this last stretch is packed with sights. The lovely **Ca' Franchetti**, with a central balcony made in the style of Palazzo Ducale's loggia, dates from the late Gothic period, but its gardens are no older than the cedar tree standing at their center.

Ca' Barbaro, next door to Ca' Franchetti, was the residence of the illustrious family who rebuilt the church of Santa Maria del Giglio.

Farther along on the left bank, a garden, vibrant with flowers in summer, surrounds **Casetta Rossa** (small red house) as if it were the centerpiece of its bouquet. Across the canal, bright 19th-century mosaics on **Ca' Barbarigo** give you some idea how the frescoed facades of many Venetian palaces must have looked in their heyday. A few doors down are the lush gardens within the walls of the unfinished **Palazzo Venier dei Leoni**, which holds the **Peggy Guggenheim Collection** of contemporary art.

Basilica di S. Marco

S A N
Z A C C A R I A

C A S T

Palazzo Ducale

PIAZZA
SAN MARCO

S. ZACCARIA

VALLARESSO

Punta della Dogana

The Grand Canal is 2½ miles long, has an average depth of 9 feet, and is 76 yards wide at its broadest point and 40 yards at its narrowest.

ute

SAN GIORGIO
MAGGIORE

Lovely, leaning **Ca' Dario** on the right bank is notable for its colorful marble facade.

Past the landing of Santa Maria del Giglio stands the 15th-century **Ca' Pisani-Gritti**, now the Gritti Palace Hotel. On the other bank, narrow **Palazzo Salviati**, with its 20th-century mosaic facade, was among the last glass factories to operate within the Venice city center. At this point the cupola of **Santa Maria della Salute** dominates the scene, but spare a glance for picturesque Rio di San Gregorio and what remains of its Gothic abbey. At **Punta della Dogana** on the tip of Dorsoduro, note the former customhouse, topped by Palla della Fortuna—a golden ball and a weather vane depicting Fortune. At the Vallaresso vaporetto stop you've left the Grand Canal, but stay on board for a view of the **Palazzo Ducale**, with **Basilica di San Marco** behind it, then disembark at San Zaccaria.

room"—and promptly gave orders to redecorate it. His architects demolished a 16th-century church with a Sansovino facade in order to build the Ala Napoleonica (Napoleonic Wing), or Fabbrica Nuova (New Building), which linked the two 16th-century *procuratie* (procurators' offices) and effectively enclosed the Piazza.

Piazzetta San Marco is the "little square" leading from Piazza San Marco to the waters of Bacino San Marco (Saint Mark's Basin); its *molo* (landing) once served as the grand entrance to the Republic. Two distinguished columns tower above the waterfront. One is topped by the winged lion, a traditional emblem of Saint Mark that became the symbol of Venice itself; the other supports Saint Theodore, the city's first patron, along with his dragon. (A third column fell off its barge and ended up in the bacino before it could be placed alongside the others.) Though the towers are a glorious vision today, the Republic traditionally executed convicts between them.

TIMING

It takes a full day to take in everything on the piazza thoroughly, so if time is limited you'll have to prioritize. Plan on 1½ hours for the basilica and its Pala d'Oro, Galleria, and Museo di San Marco. You'll want at least 2 hours to appreciate the Palazzo Ducale. If you choose to take in the piazza itself from a café table with an orchestra, keep in mind there'll be an additional charge for the music.

TOP ATTRACTIONS

❶ Basilica di San Marco. An opulent synthesis of Byzantine and Romanesque styles, Venice's gem is laid out in a Greek-cross floor plan and topped with five plump domes. It didn't become the cathedral of Venice until 1807, but its original role as the *Chiesa Ducale* (the doge's private chapel) gave it immense power and wealth. The original church was built in 828 to house the body of Saint Mark the Evangelist. His remains, filched from Alexandria by the doge's agents, were supposedly hidden in a barrel under layers of pickled pork to sneak them past Muslim guards. The escapade is depicted in the 13th-century mosaic above the door farthest left of the front entrance, one of the earliest mosaics on the heavily decorated facade; look closely to see the church as it appeared at that time.

A 976 fire destroyed most of the original church. It was rebuilt and reopened in 1094, and for centuries it would serve as a symbol of Venetian wealth and power, endowed with all the riches admirals and merchants could carry off from the Orient, to the point where it earned the nickname "Chiesa d'Oro" (Golden Church). The four bronze horses that prance and snort over the doorway are copies of sculptures that victorious Venetians took from Constantinople in 1204 after the fourth crusade (the originals are upstairs in the Museo di San Marco). The rich, colorful exterior decorations, including the numerous different marble columns, all came from the same source. Look for a medallion of red porphyry in the floor of the porch inside the main door. It marks the spot where, in 1177, Doge Sebastiano Ziani orchestrated the reconciliation between Barbarossa—the Holy Roman emperor—and Pope

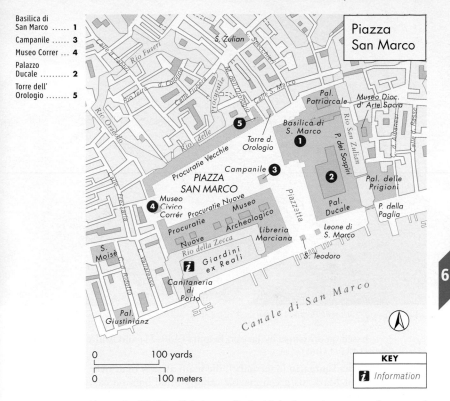

Alexander III. Dim lighting, galleries high above the naves—they served as the *matroneum* (women's gallery)—the *iconostasis* (altar screen), and the single massive Byzantine chandelier all seem to wed Christianity with the Orient, giving San Marco its exotic blend of majesty and mystery.

The basilica is famous for its 43,055 square feet of mosaics, which run from floor to ceiling thanks to an innovative roof of brick vaulting. Many of the original windows were filled in to make room for even more artwork. At midday, when the interior is fully illuminated, the mosaics truly come alive, the shimmer of their tiny gold tiles becoming nothing short of magical. The earliest mosaics are from the 11th and 12th centuries, and the last were added in the early 1700s. One of the most recent is the *Last Judgment*, believed to have been designed by Tintoretto (1518–94), on the arch between the porch and the nave. Inside the main entrance, turn right on the porch to see the Book of Genesis depicted on the ceiling. Ahead through a glass door, 13th-century mosaics depict Saint Mark's life in the **Cappella Zen** (Zen Chapel). The **Cappella della Madonna di Nicopeia,** in the left transept, holds the altar icon that many consider Venice's most powerful protector. In nearby **Cappella della Madonna dei Mascoli,** the life of the Virgin Mary is depicted in fine 15th-century mosaics that are believed to be

The Golden Mosaics of the Basilica di San Marco

based on drawings by Jacopo Bellini (1400–71) and Andrea Mantegna (1431–1506).

In the **Santuario** (Sanctuary), the main altar is built over the tomb of Saint Mark, its green marble canopy lifted high on carved alabaster columns. Perhaps even more impressive is the **Pala d'Oro**, a dazzling gilt silver screen encrusted with 1,927 precious gems and 255 enameled panels. Originally commissioned (976–978) in Constantinople by Doge Orseolo I, it was enlarged and embellished over four centuries by master craftsmen and wealthy merchants. The bronze door leading from the sanctuary into the sacristy is by Jacopo Sansovino. In the top left corner the artist included a self-portrait, and above that, he pictured friend and fellow artist Titian (1485–1576). The **Tesoro** (Treasury), entered from the right transept, contains many treasures carried home from conquests abroad.

Climb the steep stairway to the **Galleria** and the **Museo di San Marco** for the best overview of the basilica's interior. From here you can step outdoors for a sweeping panorama of Piazza San Marco and out over the lagoon to San Giorgio. The displays focus mainly on the types of mosaic and how they have been restored over the years. But the highlight is a close-up view of the original gilt bronze horses that were once on the outer gallery. The four were most probably cast in Rome and taken to Constantinople, where the Venetians pillaged them after sacking that city. When Napoléon sacked Venice in 1797, he took them to Paris. They were returned after the fall of the French Empire, but came home "blind"—their big ruby eyes had been sold.

Be aware that guards at the basilica door turn away anyone with bare shoulders, midriff, or knees: no shorts, short skirts, or tank tops are allowed. Volunteers offer free, guided tours in English from April to October—look for the calendar to the right of the center entrance, or get more info by calling the phone number below. ■**TIP➜** To skip the line at the Basilica entrance, reserve your arrival—at no extra cost—on the Basilica Web site. ⊠ *Piazza San Marco, San Marco 328* ☎ *041/2708311 basilica, 041/2413817 (10–noon weekdays) tour info* ⊕ *www.basilicasanmarco. it* 🕮 *Basilica free, Tesoro €2, Santuario and Pala d'Oro €1.50, Galleria and Museo di San Marco €3* ☉ *May–Sept., Mon.–Sat. 9:45–5, Sun. 2–5; Oct.–Apr., Mon.–Sat. 9:45–5, Sun. 2–4. Last entry 1 hr before closing* Ⓥ *Vallaresso/San Zaccaria.*

➋ **Palazzo Ducale** *(Doge's Palace).* Rising above the Piazzetta San Marco, ★ this Gothic-Renaissance fantasia of pink-and-white marble is a majestic expression of the prosperity and power attained during Venice's most glorious period. Some architectural purists find the building top-heavy—its hulking upper floors rest upon a graceful ground-floor colonnade—but the design is what gives the palace its distinctive identity; it's hard to imagine it any other way. Always much more than a residence, the palace was Venice's White House, Senate, torture chamber, and prison rolled into one.

Though a fortress for the doge stood on this spot in the early 9th century, the building you see today was begun in the 12th century, and, like the basilica next door, was continually remodeled over the centuries. Near the basilica you'll see the ornately Gothic **Porta della Carta** (Gate of the Paper), where official decrees were traditionally posted, but you enter under the portico facing the water. You'll find yourself in an immense courtyard with the **Scala dei Giganti** (Stairway of the Giants) directly ahead, guarded by Sansovino's huge statues of Mars and Neptune. Though ordinary mortals must use the central interior staircase, its upper flight is the lavishly gilded **Scala d'Oro** (Golden Staircase), also by Sansovino. It may seem odd that you have to climb so many steps to reach the government's main council rooms and reception halls, but imagine how this extraordinary climb must have impressed, and perhaps intimidated, foreign emissaries.

The palace's sumptuous chambers have walls and ceilings covered with works by Venice's greatest artists. Visit the **Anticollegio,** a waiting room outside the Collegio's chamber, where you can see the *Rape of Europa* by Veronese (1528–88) and Tintoretto's *Bacchus and Ariadne Crowned by Venus.* Veronese also painted the ceiling of the adjacent **Sala del Collegio.** The ceiling of the **Sala del Senato** (Senate Chamber), featuring *The Triumph of Venice* by Tintoretto, is magnificent, but it's dwarfed by his masterpiece *Paradise* in the **Sala del Maggiore Consiglio** (Great Council Hall). A vast work commissioned for a vast hall, this dark, dynamic piece is the world's largest oil painting (23 by 75 feet). The room's carved gilt ceiling is breathtaking, especially with Veronese's majestic *Apotheosis of Venice* filling one of the center panels. Around the upper walls, study the portraits of the first 76 doges, and you'll notice one picture is missing near the left corner of the wall opposite *Paradise.* A black painted curtain, rather than a portrait, marks Doge

Palazzo Ducale, the massive palace that was Venice's seat of power

Marin Falier's fall from grace; he was beheaded for treason in 1355, which the Latin inscription bluntly explains.

A narrow canal separates the palace's east side from the cramped cell blocks of the **Prigioni Nuove** (New Prisons). High above the water arches the enclosed marble **Ponte dei Sospiri** (Bridge of Sighs), which earned its name from the sighs of those being led to their fate. Look out its windows to see the last earthly view these prisoners beheld.

■**TIP→** Reserve your spot for the palazzo's popular Secret Itineraries tour well in advance. You'll visit the doge's private apartments, through hidden passageways to the interrogation (torture) chambers, and into the rooftop *piombi* (lead) prison, named for its lead roofing. Venetian-born writer and libertine Giacomo Casanova (1725–98), along with an accomplice, managed to escape from the piombi in 1756, the only men ever to do so.

✉ *Piazzetta San Marco* ☎ *041/2715911, 041/5209070 Secret Itineraries tour* ⊕ *www.museiciviciveneziani.it* ⌨ *Museums of San Marco pass €12 (Nov.–Mar.) or €13 (Apr.–Oct.), Musei Civici pass €18, Secret Itineraries tour €18* ⊙ *Apr.–Oct., daily 9–7; Nov.–Mar., daily 9–5. Last entry 1 hr before closing* Ⓥ *San Zaccaria, Vallaresso.*

■ QUICK BITES

Caffè Florian (☎ *041/5205641*), in the Piazza's Procuratie Nuove, has served coffee to the likes of Casanova, Charles Dickens, and Marcel Proust. It's Venice's oldest café, continuously in business since 1720 (though you'll find it closed Wednesday in winter). Counter seating is less expensive than taking a table, especially when there's live music. In the Procuratie Vecchie, **Caffè Quadri** (☎ *041/5289299*) exudes almost as much history as Florian across the way, and is similarly pricey. It was shunned by 19th-century Venetians when the occupying Austrians made it their gathering place. In winter it closes on Monday.

WORTH NOTING

❸ Campanile. Venice's famous brick bell tower (325 feet tall, plus the angel) had been standing nearly 1,000 years when in 1902, practically without warning, it collapsed, taking with it Jacopo Sansovino's 16th-century marble loggia at the base (the largest original bell, called the Marangona, remains). The crushed loggia was promptly restored, and the new tower, rebuilt to the old plan, reopened in 1912. In the 15th century, clerics found guilty of immoral behavior were suspended in wooden cages from the tower, some forced to subsist on bread and water for as long as a year, others left to starve. The stunning view from the tower on a clear day includes the Lido, the lagoon, and the mainland as far as the Alps, but, strangely enough, none of the myriad canals that snake through the city. ⊠ *Piazza San Marco* 🕾 *041/5224064* 🖻 *€8* 🕙 *Easter–June, Oct., and Nov., daily 9–7; July–Sept., daily 9–9; Nov.–Easter, daily 9–3:45. Last entry 1 hr before closing* Ⓥ *Vallaresso/ San Zaccaria.*

❹ Museo Correr. Exhibits in this museum of Venetian art and history range from the absurdly high-soled shoes worn by 16th-century Venetian ladies (who walked with the aid of a servant) to the huge *Grande Pianta Prospettica* by Jacopo de' Barbari (circa 1440–1515), which details in carved wood every nook and cranny of 16th-century Venice. The city's proud naval history is evoked in several rooms through highly descriptive paintings and numerous maritime objects, including ships' cannons and some surprisingly large iron mast-top navigation lights. The Correr has a room devoted entirely to antique games, and its second-floor **Quadreria** (Picture Gallery) has works by Venetian, Greek, and Flemish painters. The Correr exhibition rooms lead directly into the **Museo Archeologico** and the **Stanza del Sansovino,** the only part of the **Biblioteca Nazionale Marciana** open to visitors. ⊠ *Piazza San Marco, Ala Napoleonica (opposite the basilica)* 🕾 *041/2405211* ⊕ *www.museiciviciveneziani.it* 🖻 *Museums of San Marco pass €12 (Nov.–Mar.) or €13 (Apr.–Oct.), Musei Civici pass €18* 🕙 *Apr.–Oct., daily 9–7; Nov.–Mar., daily 9–5. Last entry 1 hr before closing* Ⓥ *Vallaresso, San Zaccaria.*

❺ Torre dell'Orologio. Five hundred years ago, when this enameled clock was built, twin Moor figures would strike the hour, and three wise men with an angel would walk out and bow to the Virgin Mary on Epiphany (January 6) and during Ascension Week (40 days after Easter). An inscription on the tower reads HORAS NON NUMERO NISI SERENAS ("I only count happy hours"). After years of painstaking work, the clock tower has been reassembled and returned to its former glory. Visits in English are offered daily and must be booked in advance at the Museo Correr or online. ⊠ *North side of Piazza San Marco at the Merceria* 🕾 *041/5209070* ⊕ *www.museiciviciveneziani.it* 🖻 *€12* 🕙 *Tours in Eng-*

6

VENICE THROUGH THE AGES

Up from the Muck. Venice was founded in the 5th century when the Veneti, inhabitants of the mainland region roughly corresponding to today's Veneto, fled their homes to escape invading Lombards. The unlikely city, built atop wooden posts driven into the marshes, would evolve into a maritime republic lasting over a thousand years. After liberating the Adriatic from marauding pirates, its early fortunes grew as a result of its active role in the Crusades, beginning in 1095 and culminating in the Venetian-led sacking of Constantinople in 1204. The defeat of rival Genoa in the Battle of Chioggia (1380) established Venice as the dominant sea power in Europe.

Early Democracy. As early as the 7th century, Venice was governed by a participatory democracy, with a ruler, the doge, elected to a lifetime term. Beginning in the 12th century, the doge's power was increasingly subsumed by a growing number of councils, commissions, and magistrates. In 1268 a complicated procedure for the doge's election was established to prevent nepotism, but by that point power rested foremost with the Great Council, which at times numbered as many as 2,000 members.

Laws were passed by the Senate, a group of 200 elected from the Great Council; executive powers belonged to the College, a committee of 25. In 1310 the Council of Ten was formed to protect state security. When circumstances dictated, the doge could expedite decision making by consulting only the Council of Ten. To avoid too great a concentration of power, these 10 served only one year and belonged to different families.

A Long Decline. Venice reached its height of power in the 15th and 16th centuries, during which time its domain included all of the Veneto region and part of Lombardy. But beginning in the 16th century, the tide turned. The Ottoman Empire blocked Venice's Mediterranean trade routes, and newly emerging sea powers such as Britain and the Netherlands ended Venice's monopoly by opening oceanic trading routes. The Republic underwent a slow decline. When Napoléon arrived in 1797, he took the city without a fight, eventually delivering it to the Austrians, who ruled until 1848. In that tumultuous year throughout Europe, the Venetians rebelled, an act that would ultimately lead to their joining the Italian Republic in 1866.

Art Stars. In the 13th through 15th centuries the influence of Gothic architecture resulted in palaces in the florid Gothic style, for which the city is famous. Renaissance sensibilities arrived comparatively late. Early Venetian Renaissance artists—Carpaccio, Giorgione, and the Bellini brothers, Giovanni and Gentile—were active in the late 15th and early 16th centuries. Along with the stars of the next generation—Veronese, Titian, and Tintoretto—they played a key role in the development of Western art, and their best work remains in the city.

Like its dwindling fortunes, Venice's art and culture underwent a prolonged decline, leaving only the splendid monuments to recall a fabled past. The 18th-century paintings of Canaletto and Tiepolo were a glorious swan song.

CLOSE UP

Wading Through the Acqua Alta

There are two ways to get anywhere in Venice: walking and by water. Occasionally you walk *through* water, when falling barometers, southeasterly winds, and even a full moon may exacerbate normally higher fall and spring tides. The result is *acqua alta*—flooding in the lowest parts of town, especially Piazza San Marco, and lasting a few hours until the tide recedes.

Venetians handle the high waters with aplomb, donning waders and erecting temporary walkways, but they're well aware of the damage caused by the flooding and the threat it poses to their city. The Moses Project, underwater gates that would close off the lagoon when high tides threaten, is still in progress. The expensive works have altered the lagoon-scape, and still represent a much-debated response to an emotionally charged problem, particularly after the historic tide in December 2008. How to protect Venice from high tides—as well as high use and lagoon-altering wave action caused by powerboats—are among the city's most contentious issues.

lish Mon.–Wed. at 10 and 11; Thurs.–Sun. at 2 and 3 Ⓥ *Vallaresso/ San Zaccaria.*

DORSODURO

The sestiere Dorsoduro (named for its "hard back" solid clay foundation) is across the Grand Canal to the south of San Marco. It is a place of monumental churches, meandering canals, modern art galleries, the city's finest art museums, and a promenade called the Zattere, where on sunny days you'll swear half the city is out for a *passeggiata,* or stroll. The eastern tip of the peninsula, the Punta della Dogana, was once the city's customs point; it became accessible to the public in 2009 when the old customs house was reopened as a contemporary art museum. At the western end of the sestiere is the Stazione Marittima, where in summer cruise ships line the dock. Midway between these two points, just off the Zattere, is the Squero di San Trovaso, where gondolas have been built and repaired for centuries.

Dorsoduro is also home to the Gallerie dell'Accademia, which has an unparalleled collection of Venetian painting, and gloriously restored Ca' Rezzonico, which houses the Museo del Settecento Veneziano. Another of its landmark sites, the Peggy Guggenheim Collection, has a fine selection of 20th-century art.

TIMING

The Gallerie dell'Accademia demands a few hours, but if time is short an audio guide can help you cover the highlights in about an hour. Give yourself at least 1½ hours for the Guggenheim Collection. Ca' Rezzonico deserves at least a couple of hours.

TOP ATTRACTIONS

❸ **Ca' Rezzonico.** Designed by Baldassare Longhena in the 17th century,
★ this palace was completed nearly 100 years later by Giorgio Massari
and became the last home of English poet Robert Browning (1812–
89). Stand on the bridge by the Grand Canal entrance to spot the
plaque with Browning's poetic excerpt, "*Open my heart and you will
see graved inside of it, Italy . . .*" on the left side of the palace. Eliza-
beth Taylor and Richard Burton danced in the baroque ballroom in the
1960s. Today Ca' Rezzonico is the home of the **Museo del Settecento**
(Museum of Venice in the 1700s). Its main floor successfully retains the
feel of a magnificent Venetian palazzo, packed with period furniture
and tapestries in gilded salons: note the four Tiepolo ceiling frescoes.
Upper floors contain hundreds of paintings, most from Venetian schools
of artists. There's even a restored apothecary, complete with powders
and potions. Even if you don't visit the whole museum, stop in to see
the gondola with the once-common sheltering *felze (cover)* in the foyer.
✉ *Fondamenta Rezzonico, Dorsoduro 3136* ☎ *041/2410100* ⊕ *www.
museiciviciveneziani.it* 🎟 *€6.50, Musei Civici pass €18* ⊙ *Apr.–Oct.,
Wed.–Mon. 10–6; Nov.–Mar., Wed.–Mon. 10–5. Last entry 1 hr before
closing* Ⓥ *Ca' Rezzonico.*

❼ **Gallerie dell'Accademia.** Napoléon founded these galleries in 1807 on
★ the site of a religious complex he'd suppressed, and what he initiated
now amounts to the world's most extraordinary collection of Venetian art. Jacopo Bellini is considered the father of the Venetian Renaissance, and in Room 2 you can compare his *Madonna and Child with
Saints* with such later works as *Madonna of the Orange Tree* by Cima
da Conegliano (circa 1459–1517) and *Ten Thousand Martyrs of Mt.
Ararat* by Vittore Carpaccio (circa 1455–1525). Jacopo's son Giovanni
(circa 1430–1516) draws your eye not with his subjects but with his
rich color. Rooms 4 and 5 are full of his Madonnas; note the contrast between the young Madonna and child and the neighboring older
Madonna after the crucifixion—you'll see the colors of dawn and dusk
in Venice. Room 5 contains *Tempest* by Giorgione (1477–1510), a work
that was revolutionary in its time and has continued to intrigue viewers
and critics over the centuries. It depicts a storm approaching as a nude
woman nurses her child and a soldier looks on. The overall atmosphere
that Giorgione creates is as important as any of his figures.

In Room 10, *Feast in the House of Levi,* commissioned as a Last Supper,
got Veronese dragged before the Inquisition over its depiction of dogs,
jesters, and German (therefore Protestant) soldiers. The artist saved his
neck by simply changing the title, so that the painting represented a
different biblical feast. Titian's *Presentation of the Virgin* (Room 24) is
the collection's only work originally created for the building in which it
hangs. Don't miss rooms 20 and 21, with views of 15th- and 16th-cen-
tury Venice by Carpaccio and Gentile Bellini (1429–1507), Giovanni's
brother—you'll see how little the city has changed.

Booking tickets in advance isn't essential but helps during busy seasons
and costs only an additional €1. Booking is necessary to see the **Quadreria,** where additional works cover every inch of a wide hallway. A

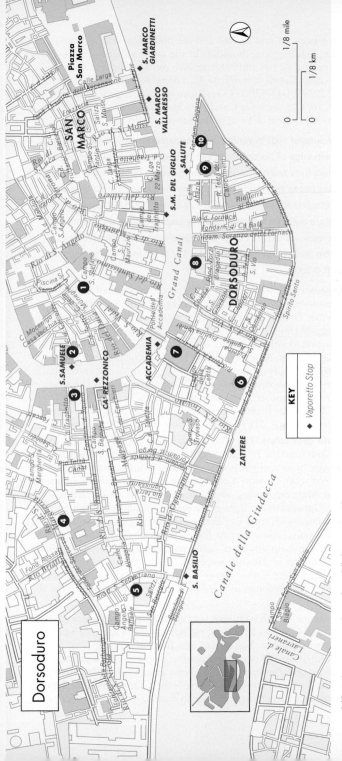

Dorsoduro

KEY

♦ Vaporetto Stop

free map names art and artists, and the bookshop sells a more-informative English-language booklet. In the main galleries, a €4 audio guide saves reading but adds little to each room's excellent annotation. ⊠ *Campo della Carità, just off the Accademia Bridge, Dorsoduro 1050* ☎ *041/5222247, 041/5200345 reservations* ⊕ *www.gallerieaccademia. org* ☑ *€6.50, €11 includes Ca' d'Oro and Museo Orientale* ☉ *Tues.– Sun. 8:15–7:15, Mon. 8:15–2* Ⓥ *Accademia.*

▌ QUICK
BITES

There's no sunnier spot in Venice than Fondamenta delle Zattere, along the southern edge of Dorsoduro. It's the city's gigantic public terrace, with bustling bars and gelato shops; come here to stroll, read in the open air, and play hooky from sightseeing. Enjoy the Zattere's most decadent treat at **Gelateria Nico** (⊠ *Dorsoduro 922* ☎ *041/5225293*)—their famous *gianduiotto,* a nutty slab of chocolate ice cream floating on a cloud of whipped cream—and relax on the big, welcoming deck. Saunter up to **El Chioschetto** (⊠ *Dorsoduro 1406* ☎ *041/5225293*) for a fine sandwich or *bibita* (soft drink).

❽ **Peggy Guggenheim Collection.** A small but choice selection of 20th-century
Ⓒ painting and sculpture is on display at this gallery in the heiress Guggenheim's former Grand Canal home. Through wealth and social connections, Guggenheim (1898–1979) became a serious art patron, and her collection here in Palazzo Venier dei Leoni includes works by Picasso, Kandinsky, Pollock, Motherwell, and Ernst (at one time her husband). The museum serves beverages, snacks, and light meals in its refreshingly shady, artistically sophisticated garden. On Sunday at 3 PM, the museum offers a free tour and art workshop for children 12 and under. ⊠ *Fondamenta Venier dei Leoni, Dorsoduro 701* ☎ *041/2405411* ⊕ *www. guggenheim-venice.it* ☑ *€10* ☉ *Wed.–Mon. 10–6* Ⓥ *Accademia.*

❾ **Santa Maria della Salute.** The view of La Salute (as this church is commonly called) from the Riva degli Schiavoni at sunset or from the Accademia Bridge by moonlight is unforgettable. Baldassare Longhena was 32 years old when he won a competition to design a shrine honoring the Virgin Mary for saving Venice from a plague that killed 47,000 residents. Outside, this simple white octagon is adorned with a colossal cupola lined with snail-like buttresses and a Palladian-style facade; inside are a polychrome marble floor and six chapels. The Byzantine icon above the main altar has been venerated as the Madonna della Salute (Madonna of Health) since 1670, when Francesco Morosini brought it here from Crete. Above it is a sculpture showing Venice on her knees to the Madonna as she drives the wretched plague from the city.

Do not leave the church without a visit to the **Sacrestia Maggiore,** which contains a dozen works by Titian, including his *San Marco Enthroned with Saints* altarpiece. You'll also see Tintoretto's *The Wedding at Canaan,* and on special occasions the altar displays a 15th-century tapestry depicting the Pentecost. For the Festa della Salute, held November 21, a votive bridge is constructed across the Grand Canal, and locals make pilgrimages here to light candles in thanksgiving for another year's health. ⊠ *Punta della Dogana, Dorsoduro* ☎ *041/2743928* ⌂ *Church free, sacristy €2* ☉ *Apr.–Sept., daily 9–noon and 3–6:30; Oct.–Mar., daily 9–noon and 3–5:30* Ⓥ *Salute.*

Filled with cafés, restaurants, and university students, **Campo Santa Margherita** also has produce vendors, pizza by the slice, and benches where you can sit and eat. For more than a portable munch, bask in the sunshine at popular **Il Caffè** (⊠ *Dorsoduro 2963* ☎ *041/5287998*), commonly called **Caffè Rossa** for its bright red exterior. It's open past midnight, serving drinks and light refreshment every day except Sunday. If you fancy some of the best homemade gelato in the city, stop by **Il Doge** (⊠ *Dorsoduro 3058* ☎ *041/5244049*), *fatta in casa* (homemade) for more than 25 years.

WORTH NOTING

❶ Campo Santo Stefano. In Venice's most prestigious residential neighborhood, you'll find one of the city's busiest crossroads just over the Accademia Bridge; it's hard to believe this square once hosted bullfights, with bulls or oxen tied to a stake and baited by dogs. For centuries the *campo* was grass except for a stone avenue called the *liston*. It was so popular for strolling that in Venetian dialect *"andare al liston"* still means "to go for a walk." A sunny meeting spot popular with Venetians and visitors alike, the campo also hosts outdoor fairs during Christmas and Carnevale seasons. Check out the 14th-century **Chiesa di Santo Stefano** and its ship's-keel roof, created by shipbuilders. You'll see works by Tintoretto and the tipsiest bell tower in town—best appreciated from nearby Campo San Angelo. The church belongs to the Chorus Foundation (Discounts and Deals at the beginning of the chapter). ⊠ *Campo Santo Stefano, San Marco* ☎ *041/2750462 Chorus Foundation* ⊕ *www. chorusvenezia.org* ⌂ *€3, Chorus Pass €10* ☉ *Mon.–Sat. 10–5, Sun. 1–5* Ⓥ *Accademia.*

❻ Gesuati. When the Dominicans took over the church of Santa Maria della Visitazione from the suppressed order of Gesuati laymen in 1668, Giorgio Massari was commissioned to build this structure. It has a score of works by Giambattista Tiepolo (1696–1770), Giambattista Piazzetta (1683–1754), and Sebastiano Ricci (1659–1734). ⊠ *Zattere, Dorsoduro* ☎ *041/2750462* ⊕ *www.chorusvenezia.org* ⌂ *€3, Chorus Pass €10* ☉ *Mon.–Sat. 10–5, Sun. 1–5* Ⓥ *Zattere.*

❷ Palazzo Grassi. This 18th-century palazzo would be worth a visit even without the art it houses. Once owned by auto magnate Giovanni Agnelli, the palace was bought by French businessman François Pinaut in 2005 to house his collection of modern and contemporary art. Pinaut brought in Japanese architect Tadao Ando to restore the interior. Check online for a schedule of temporary exhibitions. ⊠ *Campo San Samuele, San Marco* ☎ *041/5231680* ⊕ *www.palazzograssi.it* ⌂ *€15, €20 includes the Punta della Dogana* ☉ *Daily 9–6* Ⓥ *San Samuele.*

❿ Punta della Dogana. The François Pinault Foundation had Japanese architect Tadao Ando restore this former customs house, now home to works from Pinault's collection of contemporary art. The streaming light, polished surfaces, and clean lines of Ando's renovation contrast beautifully with the brick, massive columns, and sturdy beams of the original Dogana design. Even if you don't visit the museum, saunter down to the *punta* (point) for a unique view of the Venetian basin. Check online for a schedule of temporary exhibitions. ⊠ *Punta della Dogana, Dorsoduro* ☎ *041/5231680* ⊕ *www.palazzograssi.it* 🎟 *€15, €20 includes the Palazzo Grassi* ⊘ *Wed.–Mon. 10–7. Last entry 1 hr before closing at 6. Closed Dec. 24–Jan. 1* Ⓥ *Salute.*

⑤ San Sebastiano. Paolo Veronese (1528–88) established his reputation while still in his twenties with the frescoes at this, his parish church, and for decades he continued to embellish them with amazing trompe l'oeil scenes. Don't miss his altarpiece *Madonna in Glory with Saints.* Veronese is buried beneath his bust near the organ. ⊠ *Campo San Sebastiano, Dorsoduro* ☎ *041/2750462* ⊕ *www.chorusvenezia.org* 🎟 *€3, Chorus Pass €10* ⊘ *Mon.–Sat. 10–5, Sun. 1–5* Ⓥ *San Basilio.*

④ Scuola Grande dei Carmini. When the order of Santa Maria del Carmelo commissioned Baldassare Longhena to build Scuola Grande dei Carmini in the late 1600s, their brotherhood of 75,000 members was the largest in Venice and one of the wealthiest. Little expense was spared in the decorating of stuccoed ceilings and carved ebony paneling, and the artwork was choice, even before 1739, when Tiepolo painted the **Sala Capitolare.** In what many consider his best work, Tiepolo's nine great canvases vividly transform some rather unpromising religious themes into flamboyant displays of color and movement. ⊠ *Campo dei Carmini, Dorsoduro 2617* ☎ *041/5289420* 🎟 *€5* ⊘ *Daily 10–5* Ⓥ *Ca' Rezzonico.*

SAN POLO AND SANTA CROCE

The two smallest of Venice's six sestieri, San Polo and Santa Croce were named after their main churches, though the Chiesa di Santa Croce was demolished in 1810. The city's most famous bridge, the Ponte di Rialto, unites sestiere San Marco (east) with San Polo (west). The Rialto Bridge takes its name from Rivoaltus, the high ground on which it was built.

San Polo has two other major sites, Santa Maria Gloriosa dei Frari and the Scuola Grande di San Rocco, as well as some worthwhile but lesser-known churches.

Shops abound in the area surrounding the Rialto Bridge. On the San Marco side you'll find fashions, on the San Polo side, food. Chiesa di San Giacometto, where you see the first fruit vendors as you come off the bridge on the San Polo side, was probably built in the 11th and 12th centuries, about the time the surrounding market came into being. Public announcements were traditionally read in the church's campo; its 24-hour clock, though lovely, has rarely worked.

TIMING

To do the area justice requires at least half a day. If you want to take part in the food shopping, come early to beat the crowds. Bear in mind that a *metà* (half) kilo is about a pound and one *etto* is 100 grams, or about 3.5 ounces. The campo of San Giacomo dell'Orio, west of the

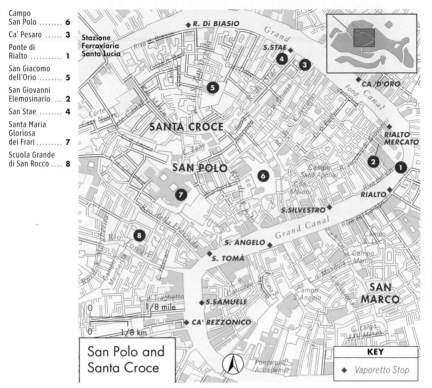

San Polo and
Santa Croce

KEY

◆ *Vaporetto Stop*

6

main thoroughfare that takes you from the Ponte di Rialto to Santa
Maria Gloriosa dei Frari, is a peaceful place for a drink and a rest. The
museums of Ca' Pesaro are a time commitment—you'll want at least
two hours to see them both.

TOP ATTRACTIONS

❶ Ponte di Rialto *(Rialto Bridge).* The competition to design a stone bridge
across the Grand Canal (replacing earlier wooden versions) attracted
the late-16th-century's best architects, including Michelangelo, Palladio,
and Sansovino, but the job went to the less famous but appropriately
named Antonio da Ponte (1512–95). His pragmatic design featured
shop space and was high enough for galleys to pass beneath; it kept
decoration and cost to a minimum at a time when the Republic's coffers
were low due to continual wars against the Turks and the opening of
oceanic trade routes. Along the railing you'll enjoy one of the city's most
famous views: the Grand Canal vibrant with boat traffic. Ⓥ *Rialto.*

❼ Santa Maria Gloriosa dei Frari. This immense Gothic church of russet-
color brick, completed in the 1400s after more than a century of work,
is deliberately austere, befitting the Franciscan brothers' insistence on
spirituality and poverty. However, I Frari (as it's known locally) contains
some of the most brilliant paintings in any Venetian church. Visit the

Touring Venice

If you want some expert guidance around Venice, you may opt for private tours, semiprivate tours, or large group tours. Any may include a boat tour as a portion of a longer walking tour. For private tours, make sure to choose an authorized guide.

PRIVATE TOURS
Walks Inside Venice (⊕ *www. walksinsidevenice.com*) offers a host of particularly creative private tours from historic to artistic to gastronomic. Luisella Romeo of **See Venice** (⊕ *www.seevenice.it*) is a delightful guide capable of bringing to life even the most convoluted aspects of Venice's art and history. **A Guide in Venice** (⊕ *www.aguideinvenice.com*) offers a wide variety of innovative, entertaining, and informative themed tours for groups of up to 10 people. **Venice Events** (✉ *Frezzaria, San Marco 1827* ☎ *041/5239979* ⊕ *www. tours-venice-italy.com*) offers a daily, 10-person-max canal tour, along with many other group and private tour options.

SEMIPRIVATE TOURS
Venice Cultural Tours (⊕ *venice-cultural-tours.com*) is a group of

collaborating guides who offer regularly scheduled, semiprivate group tours with a maximum of only eight participants, making a nice alternative to more costly private tours.

LARGE GROUP TOURS
Visit any **Venice tourism office** (☎ *041/5298711* ⊕ *www. turismovenezia.it*) to book walking tours of the San Marco area (€38), which ends with a glassblowing demonstration daily (no Sunday tour in winter). From April to October there's also an afternoon walking tour that ends with a gondola ride (€40), and a daily serenaded gondola ride (€40). Other options can be purchased at local travel agencies. Check the tourist office or Web site for scheduled offerings. The **Cooperativa Guide Turistiche Autorizzate** (✉ *San Marco 750, near San Zulian* ☎ *041/5209038* ⊕ *www.guidevenezia.it*) has a list of more than 100 licensed guides. Two-hour tours with an English-speaking guide start at €133 for up to 30 people. Agree on a total price before you begin, as there can be additional administrative and pickup fees. Guides are of variable quality.

sacristy first, to see Giovanni Bellini's 1488 triptych *Madonna and Child with Saints* in all its mellow luminosity, painted for precisely this spot. The Corner Chapel on the other side of the chancel is graced by Bartolomeo Vivarini's (1415–84) 1474 altarpiece *St. Mark Enthroned and Saints John the Baptist, Jerome, Peter, and Nicholas,* of similar exquisite detail and color. There is also a fine sculpture of Saint John the Baptist here by Jacopo Sansovino. You can see the rapid development of Venetian Renaissance painting by contrasting Bellini and Vivarini with the heroic energy of Titian's *Assumption,* over the main altar, painted only 30 years later. Unveiled in 1518, this work was not initially accepted by the church, precisely because of the innovative style and bright colors, especially Titian's trademark red, which would make it famous.

Titian's beautiful *Madonna di Ca' Pesaro,* in the left aisle, was modeled after his wife, who died in childbirth. The painting took almost 10 years to complete, and in it Titian totally disregarded the conventions of his time by moving the Virgin out of center frame and making the saints active participants. On the same side of the church, look at the spooky, pyramid-shape monument to the sculptor Antonio Canova (1757–1822). Across the nave is a neoclassical 19th-century monument to Titian, executed by two of Canova's pupils. ⊠ *Campo dei Frari, San Polo* ☎ *041/2728618, 041/2750462 Chorus Foundation* ⊕ *www. chorusvenezia.org* ⊠ *€3, Chorus Pass €10* ⊙ *Mon.–Sat. 9–6, Sun. 1–6* Ⓥ *San Tomà.*

On a narrow passage between the Frari and San Rocco, Gelateria Millevoglie (⊠ *Salizzada San Rocco, San Polo 3033* ☎ 041/5244667) has pizza slices, calzones, and gelato so popular it backs up traffic. It's closed December and January, but it's open seven days a week—10 AM to midnight in summer and until 9 PM October–March. Just off Campo San Tomà is the decadent Vizio Virtù (⊠ *Calle Campaniel, San Polo 3033* ☎ 041/2750149 ⊕ *www.viziovirtu.com*). If it's too cold for a gelato, have a hot chocolate (that's *pure* hot chocolate—undiluted by milk) to go, or choose from a selection of gourmet chocolate creations.

❽ Scuola Grande di San Rocco. Saint Rocco's popularity stemmed from his miraculous recovery from the plague and his care for fellow sufferers. Throughout the plague-filled Middle Ages, followers and donations abounded, and this elegant example of Venetian Renaissance architecture was the result. Although it is bold and dramatic outside, its contents are even more stunning—a series of more than 60 paintings by Tintoretto. In 1564 Tintoretto edged out competition for a commission to decorate a ceiling by submitting not a sketch, but a finished work, which he moreover offered free of charge. *Moses Striking Water from the Rock, The Brazen Serpent,* and *The Fall of Manna* represent three afflictions—thirst, disease, and hunger—that San Rocco and later his brotherhood sought to relieve. ⊠ *Campo San Rocco, San Polo 3052* ☎ *041/5234864* ⊕ *www.scuolagrandesanrocco.it* ⊠ *€7 (includes audio guide)* ⊙ *Daily 9:30–5:30. Last entry ½ hr before closing* Ⓥ *San Tomà.*

Just over the bridge in front of the Frari church is **Caffè dei Frari** (⊠ *Fondamenta dei Frari, San Polo* ☎ 041/5241877), where you'll find a delightful assortment of sandwiches and snacks. Established in 1870, it's one of the last Venetian tearooms with its original decor. **Pasticceria Tonolo** (⊠ *Calle Crosera, Dorsoduro 3764* ☎ 041/5237209) has been fattening up Venetians since 1886. During Carnevale it's still the best place in town for *fritelle,* fried doughnuts (traditional raisin or cream-filled); during acqua alta flooding, the staff dons rubber boots and keeps working. The place is closed Monday, and there's no seating anytime.

CLOSE UP

Venice's Scuola Days

An institution you'll inevitably encounter from Venice's glory days is the *scuola* (plural *scuole*). These weren't schools, as the word today translates, but an important network of institutions established by different social groups—enclaves of foreigners, tradesmen, followers of a particular saint, and parishioners.

For the most part secular despite their devotional activities, the scuole concentrated on charitable work, either helping their own membership or assisting the city's neediest citizens.

The tradesmen's and servants' scuole formed social security nets for elderly and disabled members. Wealthier scuole assisted orphans or provided dowries so poor girls could marry. By 1500 there were more than 200 major and minor scuole in Venice, some of which contributed substantially to arts and crafts guilds. The Republic encouraged their existence—the scuole kept strict records of the names and professions of contributors to the brotherhood, which helped when it came time to collect taxes.

WORTH NOTING

❻ Campo San Polo. Only Piazza San Marco is larger than this square, where not even the pigeons manage to look cozy, and the echo of children's voices bouncing off the surrounding palaces makes the space seem even more cavernous. Campo San Polo once hosted bull races, fairs, military parades, and packed markets, and now especially comes alive on summer nights, when it's home to the city's outdoor cinema. The **Chiesa di San Polo** has been restored so many times that little remains of the original 9th-century church, and sadly, 19th-century alterations were so costly that the friars sold off many great paintings to pay bills. Though Giambattista Tiepolo is represented here, his work is outdone by 16 paintings by his son Giandomenico (1727–1804), including the *Stations of the Cross* in the oratory to the left of the entrance. The younger Tiepolo also created a series of expressive and theatrical renderings of the saints. Look for altarpieces by Tintoretto and Veronese that managed to escape auction. San Polo's bell tower remained unchanged through the centuries—don't miss the two lions guarding it, playing with a disembodied human head and a serpent. ⊠ *Campo San Polo* ☎ *041/2750462 Chorus Foundation* ⊕ *www.chorusvenezia. org* 🖾 *€3, Chorus Pass €10* ⊙ *Mon.–Sat. 10–5, Sun. 1–5* Ⓥ *San Silvestro/San Tomà.*

❸ Ca' Pesaro. Baldassare Longhena's grand baroque palace is the beautifully restored home of two impressive collections. The **Galleria Internazionale d'Arte Moderna** has works by 19th- and 20th-century artists such as Klimt, Kandinsky, Matisse, and Miró. It also has a collection of representative works from Venice's Biennale art show that amounts to a panorama of 20th-century art. The **Museo Orientale** has a small but striking collection of Oriental porcelains, musical instruments, arms, and armor. ⊠ *San Stae, Santa Croce 2076* ☎ *041/721127 Galleria, 041/5241173 Museo Orientale* ⊕ *www.museicivicivenetiani.it* 🖾 *€7* *includes both museums, Museums of San Marco Plus Pass €13 (Apr.–Oct.), Musei Civici pass €18 ⊙ Apr.–Oct., daily 10–6; Nov.–Mar., daily 10–5. Last entry 1 hr before closing* ⓥ *San Stae.*

⑤ San Giacomo dell'Orio. It was named after a laurel tree *(orio)*, and today trees give character to this square. Add benches and a fountain (with a drinking bowl for dogs), and the pleasant, oddly shaped campo becomes a welcoming place for friendly conversation, picnics, and neighborhood kids at play. Legend has it the **Chiesa di San Giacomo dell'Orio** was founded in the 9th century on an island still populated by wolves. The current church dates from 1225; its short unmatched Byzantine columns survived renovation during the Renaissance, and the church never lost the feel of an ancient temple sheltering beneath its 15th-century ship's-keel roof. In the sanctuary, large marble crosses are surrounded by a bevy of small medieval Madonnas. The altarpiece is *Madonna with Child and Saints* (1546) by Lorenzo Lotto (1480–1556), and the sacristies contain works by Palma il Giovane (circa 1544–1628). ✉ *Campo San Giacomo dell'Orio, Santa Croce* ☎ *041/2750462 Chorus Foundation* ⊕ *www.chorusvenezia.org* 💰*€3, Chorus Pass €10* ⊙ *Mon.–Sat. 10–5, Sun. 1–5* ⓥ *San Stae.*

② San Giovanni Elemosinario. Storefronts make up the facade, and the altars were built by market guilds—poulterers, messengers, and fodder merchants—at this church intimately bound to the Rialto Market. It's as rich inside as it is simple outside. During San Giovanni Elemosinario's restoration, workers stumbled upon a frescoed cupola by Pordenone (1484–1539) that had been painted over centuries earlier. Don't miss Titian's *St. John the Almsgiver* and Pordenone's *Sts. Catherine, Sebastian, and Roch*, which in 2002 were returned after 30 years by the Gallerie dell'Accademia, a rare move for an Italian museum. ✉ *Rialto Ruga Vecchia San Giovanni, Santa Croce* ☎ *041/2750462 Chorus Foundation* ⊕ *www.chorusvenezia.org* 💰*€3, Chorus Pass €10* ⊙ *Mon.–Sat. 10–5. Last entry 4:45* ⓥ *San Silvestro/Rialto.*

④ San Stae. The most renowned Venetian painters and sculptors of the early 18th century—known as the Moderns—decorated this church with the legacy left by Doge Alvise Mocenigo II, who's buried in the center aisle. A broad sampling of these masters includes works by Tiepolo, Ricci, Piazzetta, and Lazzarini. ✉ *Campo San Stae, Santa Croce* ☎ *041/2750462 Chorus Foundation* ⊕ *www.chorusvenezia.org* 💰*€3, Chorus Pass €10* ⊙ *Mon.–Sat. 9–5* ⓥ *San Stae.*

CASTELLO AND CANNAREGIO

Twice the size of tiny San Polo and Santa Croce, Castello and Cannaregio combined spread east to west from one end of Venice to the other. From working-class shipbuilding neighborhoods to the world's first ghetto, here you see a cross section of city life that's always existed beyond the palace walls. There are churches that could make a Renaissance pope jealous and one of the Grand Canal's prettiest palaces, Ca' d'Oro, as well as detour options for leaving the crowds behind.

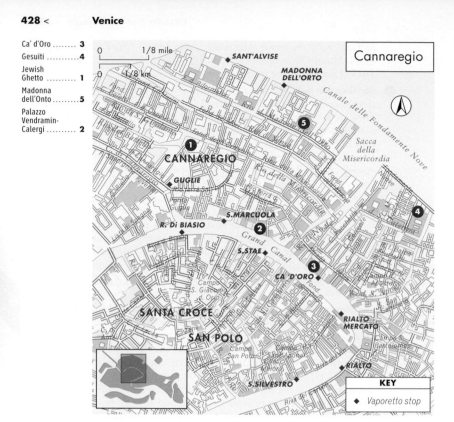

TIMING

Visiting both sestieri involves a couple of hours of walking, even if you never enter a building, and there are few chances to hop a boat and save your legs. Some sights have restricted hours, making it virtually impossible to see everything even in a full day. Your best bet is to choose a few sights as priorities, time your tour around their open hours, and then drop in at whatever others happen to be open as you're passing by. If you're touring on Friday, keep in mind that synagogues close at sunset.

TOP ATTRACTIONS

Arsenale. The Venetian Republic never could have thrived without the Arsenale shipyard. Today it belongs to the Italian Navy and isn't regularly open to the public, but it opens for the Biennale and for Venice's festival of traditional boats, **Mare Maggio** (⊕ *www.maremaggio.it*), held every May, and has begun to renovate the enormous former ship-building spaces for commercial use. If you're here during those times, don't miss the chance for a look inside, even entering from the back via a northern-side walkway leading from the Ospedale vaporetto stop.

The Arsenale is said to have been founded in 1104 on twin islands. The immense facility that evolved was given the old Venetian dialect name *arzanà*, borrowed from the Arabic *darsina'a,* meaning "workshop." At times it employed as many as 16,000 *arsenalotti,* workers who were among the most respected shipbuilders in the world. (Dante immortalized these sweating men armed with pitch and boiling tar in his *Inferno*.) Their diligence was confirmed time and again—whether building 100 ships in 60 days to battle the Turks in Cyprus (1597) or completing one perfectly armed warship—start to finish—while King Henry III of France attended a banquet.

The Arsenale's impressive Renaissance **gateway** (1460) is guarded by four lions, war booty of Francesco Morosini, who took the Peloponnese from the Turks in 1687. The 10-foot-tall lion on the left stood sentinel more than 2,000 years ago near Athens, and experts say its mysterious inscription is runic "graffiti" left by Viking mercenaries hired to suppress 11th-century revolts in Piraeus. If you look at the winged lion above the doorway, you'll notice that the Gospel at his paws is open but lacks the customary *Pax* inscription; praying for peace perhaps seemed inappropriate above a factory that manufactured weapons. ⊠ *Campo dell'Arsenale, Castello* Ⓥ *Arsenale.*

6

❸ **Ca' d'Oro.** This exquisite Venetian Gothic palace was once literally
★ a "Golden House," when its marble traceries and ornaments were embellished with pure gold. Created in 1434 by the enamored patrician Marino Contarini for his wife, Ca' d'Oro became a love offering a second time when a 19th-century Russian prince gave it to Maria Taglioni, a celebrated classical dancer who collected palaces along the Grand Canal. The last proprietor, perhaps more taken with Venice than with any of his lovers, left Ca' d'Oro to the city, after having had it carefully restored and filled with antiquities, sculptures, and paintings that today make up the **Galleria Franchetti.** Besides Andrea Mantegna's celebrated *St. Sebastian* and other first-rate Venetian works, the Galleria Franchetti contains the type of fresco that once adorned the exteriors of Venetian buildings (commissioned by those who could not afford a marble facade). One such detached fresco displayed here was made by a young Titian for the (now grayish-white) facade of the Fondaco dei Tedeschi, now the main post office. ⊠ *Calle Ca' d'Oro, Cannaregio 3933* ☎ *041/5238790* ⊕ *www.cadoro.org* 🎟 *€5, plus €1 to reserve; €11 includes Gallerie dell'Accademia and Museo Orientale* ⊙ *Tues.–Sun. 8:15–7, Mon. 8:15–2. Last entry ½ hr before closing* Ⓥ *Ca' d'Oro.*

❶ **Jewish Ghetto.** The neighborhood that gave the world the word *ghetto* is today a quiet warren of backstreets that is still home to Jewish institutions, a kosher restaurant, a rabbinical school, and five synagogues. Though Jews may have arrived earlier, the first synagogues weren't built and a cemetery wasn't founded until the Askenazim, or Eastern European Jews, came in the late 1300s. Dwindling coffers may have prompted the Republic to sell temporary visas to Jews, but over the centuries they were alternately tolerated and expelled. The Rialto commercial district, as vividly recounted in Shakespeare's *The Merchant of Venice,* depended on Jewish merchants and moneylenders for trade, and to help cover ever-increasing war expenses.

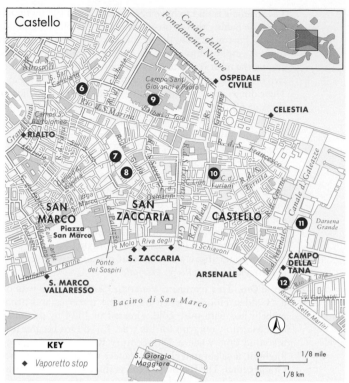

In 1516 relentless local opposition forced the Senate to confine Jews to an island in Cannaregio, named for its *geto* (foundry), which produced cannons. Gates at the entrance were locked at night, and boats patrolled the surrounding canals. The German accents of early residents changed the soft *g* sound of "geto" (pronounced *zheto*) into the hard *g* in "ghetto." Jews were allowed only to lend money at low interest, operate pawnshops controlled by the government, trade in textiles, or practice medicine. Jewish doctors were highly respected and could leave the ghetto at any hour when on duty. Though ostracized, Jews were nonetheless safe in Venice, and in the 16th century the community grew considerably, with refugees from the Near East, southern and central Italy, Spain, and Portugal. The ghetto was allowed to expand twice, but it still had the city's densest population and consequently ended up with the city's tallest buildings (nine stories); notice the slanting apartment blocks on Campo del Ghetto Nuovo. Although the gates were pulled down after Napoléon's 1797 arrival, the Jews realized full freedom only in the late 19th century with the founding of the Italian state. On the eve of World War II there were about 1,500 Jews left in the ghetto: 247 were deported by the Nazis; 8 returned.

The area has Europe's highest density of Renaissance-era synagogues, and visiting them is a unique cross-cultural experience. Though each is marked by the tastes of its individual builders, Venetian influence is evident throughout. Women's galleries resemble those of theaters from the same era, and some synagogues were decorated by artisans who were simultaneously active in local churches.

The small but well-arranged **Museo Ebraico** highlights centuries of Jewish culture with splendid silver Hanukkah lamps and Torahs, and handwritten, beautifully decorated wedding contracts in Hebrew. Hourly tours (on the half hour) of the ghetto in Italian and English leave from the museum. ⊠ *Campo del Ghetto Nuovo, Cannaregio 2902/b* ☎ *041/715359* ⊕ *www.museoebraico.it* ⬛ *Museum €3; guided tour, museum, and synagogues €8.50* ⊙ *June–Sept., Sun.–Fri. 10–7; Oct.–May, Sun.–Fri. 10–6. Tours hourly starting at 10:30* Ⓥ *San Marcuola/Guglie.*

You might complete your circuit of Jewish Venice with a visit to the **Antico Cimitero Ebraico** *(Ancient Jewish Cemetery)* on the Lido, full of fascinating old tombstones half hidden by ivy and grass. The earliest grave dates from 1389; the cemetery remained in use until the late 18th century. ⊠ *Via Cipro at San Nicolo, Lido* ☎ *041/715359* ⬛ *€8.50* ⊙ *Tours Apr.–Oct., Sun. at 2:30, by appointment other days; call to reserve* Ⓥ *Lido/San Nicolo.*

❺ **Madonna dell'Orto.** Though squatly Romanesque and sporting a later pre-Renaissance doorway, Madonna dell'Orto remains one of the most typical Gothic churches in Venice. Tintoretto lived nearby, and this, his parish church, contains some of his most powerful work. Lining the chancel are two huge (45 feet by 20 feet) canvases, *Adoration of the Golden Calf* and *Last Judgment.* In glowing contrast to this awesome spectacle is Tintoretto's *Presentation of the Virgin at the Temple* and the simple chapel where Tintoretto and his children, Marietta and Domenico, are buried. Paintings by Domenico, Cima da Conegliano, Palma il Giovane, Palma il Vecchio, and Tiziano also hang in the church. A chapel displays a photographic reproduction of a precious *Madonna with Child* by Giovanni Bellini. The original was stolen one night in 1993. ⊠ *Campo della Madonna dell'Orto, Cannaregio* ☎ *041/2750462 Chorus Foundation* ⊕ *www.chorusvenezia.org* ⬛ *€3, Chorus Pass €10* ⊙ *Mon.–Sat. 10–5, Sun. 1–5* Ⓥ *Orto.*

❻ **Santa Maria dei Miracoli.** Tiny yet perfectly proportioned, this early-Renaissance gem is sheathed in marble and decorated inside with exquisite
★ marble reliefs. Architect Pietro Lombardo (circa 1435–1515) miraculously compressed the building into its confined space, then created the illusion of greater size by varying the color of the exterior, adding extra pilasters on the building's canal side, and offsetting the arcade windows to make the arches appear deeper. The church was built in the 1480s to house *I Miracoli,* an image of the Virgin Mary that is said to perform miracles—look for it on the high altar. ⊠ *Campo Santa Maria Nova, Cannaregio* ☎ *041/2750462 Chorus Foundation* ⊕ *www.chorusvenezia. org* ⬛ *€3, Chorus Pass €10* ⊙ *Mon.–Sat. 10–5* Ⓥ *Rialto.*

❾ **Santi Giovanni e Paolo.** This massive Dominican church, commonly called
★ San Zanipolo, contains a wealth of art. The 15th-century stained-glass window near the side entrance is breathtaking for its brilliant colors

6

and beautiful figures, made from drawings by Bartolomeo Vivarini and Gerolamo Mocetto (circa 1458–1531). The second official church of the Republic after San Marco, San Zanipolo is the Venetian equivalent of London's Westminster Abbey, with a great number of important people, including 25 doges, buried here. Artistic highlights include an outstanding polyptych by Giovanni Bellini (right aisle, second altar), Alvise Vivarini's *Christ Carrying the Cross* (sacristy), and Lorenzo Lotto's *Charity of St. Antonino* (right transept). Don't miss the *Cappella del Rosario* (Rosary Chapel), off the left transept, built in the 16th century to commemorate the 1571 victory of Lepanto, in western Greece, when Venice led a combined European fleet to defeat the Turkish Navy. The chapel was devastated by a fire in 1867 and restored in the early years of the 20th century with works from other churches, among them the sumptuous Veronese ceiling paintings. However quick your visit, don't miss the Pietro Mocenigo tomb to the right of the main entrance, a monument built by the ubiquitous Pietro Lombardo and his sons. ⊠ *Campo dei Santi Giovanni e Paolo, Castello* ☎ *041/5235913* ⌚*€2.50* ☉ *Daily 7:30–6:30, subject to change* Ⓥ *Fondamente Nove/Rialto.*

QUICK BITES

To satisfy your sweet tooth, head for Campo Santa Marina and the family-owned and -operated **Didovich Pastry Shop** (⊠ *Campo Santa Marina, Castello* ☎ *041/5230017*). It's a local favorite, especially for Carnevale-time *fritelle* (fried doughnuts). There is limited seating inside, but in the warmer months you can sit outside. **Un Mondo di Vino** (⊠ *Salizzada San Cancian, Cannaregio* ☎ *041/5211093*), below Campo Santa Maria Nova on Calle San Canciano, is a friendly place to recharge with a *cicchetto* (snack) or two and some wine. Closed Sunday.

WORTH NOTING

❹ **Gesuiti.** Extravagantly baroque, this 18th-century church completely abandons classical Renaissance straight lines in favor of flowing, twisting forms. Its interior walls resemble brocade drapery, and only touching them will convince skeptics that rather than paint, the green-and-white walls are inlaid marble. Over the first altar on the left, the *Martyrdom of St. Lawrence* is a dramatic example of Titian's feeling for light and movement. ⊠ *Campo dei Gesuiti, Cannaregio* ☎ *041/5286579* ☉ *Daily 10–noon and 4–6* Ⓥ *Fondamente Nove.*

⓬ **Museo Storico Navale** *(Museum of Naval History).* The boat collection here includes scale models such as the doges' ceremonial *Bucintoro,* and full-size boats such as Peggy Guggenheim's private gondola complete with romantic *felze* (cabin). There's a range of old galley and military pieces, and also a large collection of seashells. ⊠ *Campo San Biagio, Castello 2148* ☎ *041/2441399* ⊕ *www.marina.difesa.it/venezia/museo. asp* ⌚*€1.55* ☉ *Weekdays 8:45–1:30, Sat. 8:45–1* Ⓥ *Arsenale.*

❷ **Palazzo Vendramin-Calergi.** This Renaissance classic with an imposing carved frieze is the work of Mauro Codussi (1440–1504). You can see some of its interior by dropping into the **Casinò di Venezia.** Fans of

Richard Wagner (1813–83) might enjoy visiting the **Sala di Wagner,** the room (separate from the casino) in which the composer died. Though rather plain, it's loaded with music memorabilia. To visit the Sala call the dedicated tour line by noon the day before a scheduled tour, or book a private tour. ⊠ *Cannaregio 2040* ☏ *041/5297111, 338/4164174 Sala di Wagner tours* ⊕ *www.casinovenezia.it* ▣ *Casinò €10, Sala di Wagner tour €5 suggested donation* ⊙ *Casinò Sun.–Thurs. 3:30* PM–2:30 AM, *Fri. and Sat. 3:30* PM–3 AM; *slot machines open daily at 3* PM. *Sala di Wagner tours Tues. and Sat. at 10:30, Thurs. at 2:30 (call until noon the day before to reserve)* Ⓥ *San Marcuola.*

⑧ **Querini-Stampalia.** The art collection at this Renaissance palace includes Giovanni Bellini's *Presentation in the Temple* and Sebastiano Ricci's triptych *Dawn, Afternoon, and Evening.* Portraits of newlyweds Francesco Querini and Paola Priuli were left unfinished on the death of Giacomo Palma il Vecchio (1480–1528); note the groom's hand and the bride's dress. Original 18th-century furniture and stuccowork are a fitting background for Pietro Longhi's portraits. Nearly 70 works by Gabriele Bella (1730–99) capture scenes of Venetian street life; downstairs is a café. ⊠ *Campo Santa Maria Formosa, Castello 5252* ☏ *041/2711411* ⊕ *www.querinistampalia.it* ▣ *€8* ⊙ *Tues.–Sat. 10–8, Sun. 10–7. Last entry 1 hr before closing* Ⓥ *San Zaccaria.*

⑦ **Santa Maria Formosa.** Guided by his vision of a beautiful Madonna, 7th-century Saint Magno is said to have followed a small white cloud and built a church where it settled. Gracefully white, the marble building you see today dates from 1492, built by Mauro Codussi on an older foundation. The interior is a blend of Renaissance decoration, a Byzantine cupola, barrel vaults, and narrow-columned screens. Of interest are two fine paintings: *Our Lady of Mercy* by Bartolomeo Vivarini and *Santa Barbara* by Palma il Vecchio. The surrounding square bustles with sidewalk cafés and a produce market on weekday mornings. ⊠ *Campo Santa Maria Formosa, Castello* ☏ *041/2750462 Chorus Foundation* ⊕ *www.chorusvenezia.org* ▣ *€3, Chorus Pass €10* ⊙ *Mon.–Sat. 10–5* Ⓥ *Rialto.*

⑩ **Scuola di San Giorgio degli Schiavoni.** Founded in 1451 by the Dalmatian community, this small scuola was, and still is, a social and cultural center for migrants from what is now Croatia. It's dominated by one of Italy's most beautiful rooms, lavishly yet harmoniously decorated with the *teleri* (large canvases) of Vittore Carpaccio. A lifelong Venice resident, Carpaccio painted legendary and religious figures against backgrounds of Venetian architecture. Here he focused on saints especially venerated in Dalmatia: Saints George, Tryphone, and Jerome. He combined observation with fantasy, a sense of warm color with a sense of humor (don't miss the priests fleeing Saint Jerome's lion, or the body parts in the dragon's lair). ⊠ *Calle dei Furlani, Castello 3259/A* ☏ *041/5228828* ▣ *€4* ⊙ *Tues.–Sat. 9:15–1 and 2:45–6, Sun. 10–12:30. Last entry 1 hr before closing* Ⓥ *Arsenale/San Zaccaria.*

6

DID YOU KNOW?

Venice is a city of 200 canals and not a single roadway. Here, boats take the place of family cars, and all commercial deliveries—from produce to appliances—are made by water.

Let's Get Lost

Getting around Venice presents some unusual problems: the city's layout has few straight lines; house numbering seems nonsensical; and the six *sestieri* (districts) of San Marco, Cannaregio, Castello, Dorsoduro, Santa Croce, and San Polo all duplicate each other's street names. The numerous vaporetto lines can be bewildering, and often the only option for getting where you want to go is to walk. Yellow signs, posted on many busy corners, point toward the major landmarks—San Marco, Rialto, Accademia, and so forth—but don't count on finding such markers once you're deep into residential neighborhoods. Even buying a good map at a newsstand—the kind showing all street names and

vaporetto routes—won't necessarily keep you from getting lost.

Fortunately, as long as you maintain your patience, getting lost in Venice can be a pleasure. For one thing, being lost is a sign that you've escaped the tourist throngs. And although you might not find the Titian masterpiece you'd set out to see, instead you could wind up coming across an ageless bàcaro or a quirky shop that turns out to be the highlight of your afternoon. Opportunities for such serendipity abound. Keep in mind that the city is nothing if not self-contained: sooner or later, perhaps with the help of a patient native, you can rest assured you'll regain your bearings.

SAN GIORGIO MAGGIORE AND THE GIUDECCA

Beckoning travelers across Saint Mark's Basin, sparkling white through the mist, is the island of San Giorgio Maggiore, separated by a small channel from the Giudecca. A tall brick campanile on that distant bank perfectly complements the Campanile of San Marco. Beneath it looms the stately dome of one of Venice's greatest churches, San Giorgio Maggiore, the creation of Andrea Palladio.

You can reach San Giorgio Maggiore via vaporetto Line 2 from San Zaccaria. The next three stops on the line take you to the Giudecca. The island's past may be shrouded in mystery, but today it's about as down to earth as you can get and one of the city's few remaining neighborhoods that feels truly Venetian.

TIMING

A half-day should be plenty of time to visit the area. Allow about a half hour to see each of the churches and an hour or two to look around the Giudecca.

TOP ATTRACTIONS

Giudecca. The island's name is something of a mystery. It may come from a possible 14th-century Jewish settlement, or because 9th-century nobles condemned to *giudicato* (exile) were sent here. It became a pleasure garden for wealthy Venetians during the Republic's long and luxurious decline, but today, like Cannaregio, it's largely working class. The Giudecca provides spectacular views of Venice and is becoming increasingly gentrified. While here, visit the **Santissimo Redentore** church, designed by Palladio and built to commemorate a plague. The third weekend in July, it's the site of the Venetians' favorite festival, Redentore, featuring boats, fireworks, and outdoor feasting. Thanks to several bridges, you can walk the entire length of the Giudecca's promenade, relaxing at one of several restaurants or just taking in the lively atmosphere. Accommodations run the gamut from youth hostels to the city's most exclusive hotel, Cipriani. ☒ *Fondamenta San Giacomo, Giudecca* ☎ *041/2750462 Chorus Foundation* ⊕ *www.chorusvenezia.org* ☒ *€3, Chorus Pass €10* ⊙ *Mon.–Sat. 10–5* Ⓥ *Redentore.*

> **WORD OF MOUTH**
>
> "Be sure to wander off the beaten path and get yourself lost in the endless mazes of canals, streets, alleys. Every turn will reveal a new discovery for the intrepid photographer." —bg_collier

San Giorgio Maggiore. There's been a church on this island since the 8th century, with a Benedictine monastery added in the 10th century (closed to the public). Today's refreshingly airy and simply decorated church of brick and white marble was begun in 1566 by Palladio and displays his architectural hallmarks of mathematical harmony and classical influence. *The Last Supper* and the *Gathering of Manna*, two of Tintoretto's later works, line the chancel. To the right of the entrance hangs *The Adoration of the Shepherds* by Jacopo Bassano (1517–92); his affection for his foothills home, Bassano del Grappa, is evident in the bucolic subjects and terra-firma colors he chooses. The monks are happy to show Carpaccio's *St. George and the Dragon,* hanging in a private room, if they have time. The campanile is so tall that it was struck by lightning in 1993; in any direction it offers some of the finest views in town. ☒ *Isola di San Giorgio Maggiore* ☎ *041/5227827* ☒ *Church free, campanile €3* ⊙ *Daily 9–12:30 and 2:30–6* Ⓥ *San Giorgio.*

ISLANDS OF THE LAGOON

The perfect vacation from your Venetian vacation is an escape to Murano, Burano, and sleepy Torcello, the islands of the northern lagoon. Torcello offers ancient mosaics, greenery, breathing space, and picnic opportunities (remember to pack lunch). Burano is an island of fishing traditions and houses painted in a riot of colors—blue, yellow, pink, ocher, and dark red. Visitors still love to shop here for "Venetian" lace, even though the vast majority of it is machine-made in Taiwan; visit the island's Museo di Merletto (Lace Museum) to discover the undeniable difference between the two.

Murano is renowned for its glass, plenty of which you can find in Venice itself. It's also notorious for high-pressure sales on factory tours, even those organized by top hotels. Vaporetto connections to Murano aren't difficult, and for the price of a boat ticket (included in any vaporetto pass), you'll buy your freedom and more time to explore. The Murano "guides" herding new arrivals follow a rotation so that factories take turns giving tours, but you can avoid the hustle by just walking away. ■ **TIP→** Refuse the "free" taxi to Murano: it only means that should you choose to buy (and you will be strongly encouraged), your taxi fare and commission will be included in the price you pay.

TIMING

Hitting all the sights on all the islands takes a busy, full day. If you limit yourself to Murano and San Michele, you can easily explore for an ample half day; the same goes for Burano and Torcello. In summer, the express vaporetto Line 5 will take you to Murano from San Zaccaria (the Jolanda landing) in 25 minutes; otherwise, local Line 41 makes a 45-minute trip from San Zaccaria every 20 minutes, circling the east end of Venice, stopping at Fondamente Nove and San Michele island cemetery on the way. To see glassblowing, get off at Colonna; the Museo stop will put you near the Museo del Vetro.

Line LN goes from Fondamente Nove direct to Murano and Burano every 30 minutes (Torcello is a five-minute ferry from there); the full trip takes 45 minutes each way. To get to Burano and Torcello from Murano, pick up Line LN at the Faro stop (Murano's lighthouse).

TOP ATTRACTIONS

❸ ★ **Burano.** Cheerfully painted houses line the canals of this quiet village where lace-making rescued a faltering fishing-based economy centuries ago. As you walk the 100 yards from the dock to Piazza Galuppi, the main square, you pass stall after stall of lace vendors. These good-natured ladies won't press you with a hard sell, but don't expect precise product information or great bargains—authentic, handmade Burano lace costs $1,000 to $2,000 for a 10-inch doily.

The **Museo del Merletto** (Lace Museum) lets you marvel at the intricacies of Burano's lace making. At this writing, the museum is closed for renovations, with plans to reopen by the end of 2010. The museum will likely continue to host a "sewing circle" of sorts, where on most weekdays you can watch local women carrying on the lace-making tradition. They may have authentic pieces for sale privately. ⊠ *Piazza Galuppi 187* ☎ *041/730034* ✉ *€4.50, Museums of San Marco Plus Pass €13 (Apr.–Oct.), Musei Civici pass €18* ☺ *Apr.–Oct., daily 10–5; Nov.–Mar., daily 10–4* Ⓥ *Burano.*

❷ ☺ **Murano.** As in Venice, bridges here link a number of small islands, which are dotted with houses that once were workmen's cottages. In the 13th century the Republic, concerned about fire hazard and anxious to maintain control of its artisans' expertise, moved its glassworks to Murano, and today you can visit the factories and watch glass being made. Many of them line the Fondamenta dei Vetrai, the canal-side walkway leading from the Colonna vaporetto landing.

Before you reach Murano's Grand Canal (a little more than 800 feet from the landing), you'll pass **Chiesa di San Pietro Martire**. Reconstructed in the 16th century, it houses Giovanni Bellini's Madonna and Child and Veronese's St. Jerome. ⊠ *Fondamenta dei Vetrai* ☎ *041/739704* ☺ *Weekdays 9–6, Sat. 2–6, Sun. 11:30–5* Ⓥ *Colonna.*

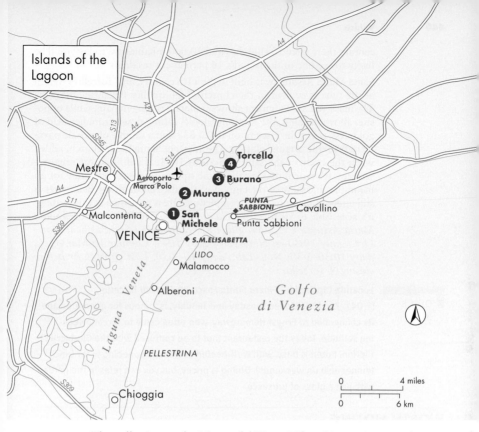

The collection at the **Museo del Vetro** (*Glass Museum*) ranges from priceless antiques to only slightly less expensive modern pieces. You can see an exhibition on the history of glass, along with a chance to review authentic Venetian styles, patterns, and works by the most famous glassmakers, all free of sales pressure. Don't miss the famous Barovier wedding cup (1470–80). ⊠ *Fondamenta Giustinian 8* ☎ *041/739586* ⊕ *www.museicivicivenezia ni.it* ☞ *€6.50, Museums of San Marco Plus Pass €13 (Apr.–Oct.), Musei Civici pass €18* ☉ *Apr.–Oct., Thurs.–Tues. 10–6; Nov.–Mar., Thurs.–Tues. 10–5. Last entry 1 hr before closing* Ⓥ *Museo.*

The **Basilica dei Santi Maria e Donato,** just past the glass museum, is among the first churches founded by the lagoon's original inhabitants. The elaborate mosaic pavement includes the date 1140; its ship's-keel roof and Veneto-Byzantine columns add to the semblance of an ancient temple. ⊠ *Fondamenta Giustinian* ☎ *041/739056* ☉ *Mon.–Sat. 8–6, Sun. 2–6* Ⓥ *Museo.*

❹ ★ **Torcello.** In their flight from barbarians 1,500 years ago, the first Venetians landed here, prospering even after many left to found the city of Venice. As malaria took its toll and the island's wool manufacturing was priced out of the market, Torcello became a ghost town. In the 16th century there were 10 churches and 20,000 inhabitants; today you'll be lucky to see one of the island's 16 permanent residents.

Santa Maria Assunta was built in the 11th century, and Torcello's wealth at the time is evident in the church's high-quality Byzantine mosaics. The massive Last Judgment shows sinners writhing in pain, while opposite, above the altar, the Madonna looks calmly down from her field of gold. Ask to see the inscription dated 639 and a sample of mosaic pavement from the original church. The adjacent **Santa Fosca** church, added when the body of the saint arrived in 1011, is still used for religious services. It's worth making the climb up the adjacent campanile for an incomparable view of the lagoon wetlands. Although the bell tower is still undergoing renovation (completion date is unknown at this writing) it's accessible to visitors. ⊠ *Isola di Torcello* ☎ *041/2960630* 🖃 *Santa Maria Assunta €5, audio guide €1, campanile €5* ⊙ *Basilica: Mar.–Oct., daily 10:30–6; Nov.–Feb., daily 10–5. Campanile: Mar.–Oct., daily 10:30–5:30; Nov.–Feb., daily 10–4:30. Last entry ½ hr before closing* Ⓥ *Torcello.*

QUICK
BITES

Locanda Cipriani (⊠ *Piazza Santa Fosca 29, Isola di Torcello* ☎ *041/730150*), closed Tuesday and January, is famous for good food and its connection to Ernest Hemingway, who often came to Torcello seeking solitude. Today the restaurant (not to be confused with the Giudecca's Cipriani hotel) is busy, with well-heeled customers speeding in for lunch (dinner also on weekends). Dining is pricey, but you can relax in the garden with just a glass of prosecco.

WORTH NOTING

❶ San Michele. Tiny, cypress-lined San Michele is home to the pretty **San Michele in Isola** Renaissance church—and to some of Venice's most illustrious deceased—and nothing else. The church was designed by Codussi; the graves include those of poet Ezra Pound (1885–1972), impresario and art critic Sergey Diaghilev (1872–1929), and composer Igor Stravinsky (1882–1971). Surrounded by the living sounds of Venice's lagoon, this would seem the perfect final resting place. However, these days newcomers are exhumed after 10 years and transferred to a less grandiose location. ⊠ *Isola di San Michele* ☎ *041/7292811* ⊙ *Apr.–Sept., daily 7:30–6; Oct.–Mar., daily 7:30–4* Ⓥ *Cimitero.*

WHERE TO EAT

There's no getting around the fact that Venice has more than its share of overpriced, mediocre eateries that prey on tourists. Avoid places with cajoling waiters standing outside, and beware of restaurants that don't display their prices. At the other end of the spectrum, showy *menu turistico* (tourist menu) boards make offerings clear in a dozen languages, but for the same 15 to 20 euros you'd spend at such places you could do better at a bàcaro (the local version of a wine bar) making a meal of *cicchetti* (traditional, bite-size bar snacks). Note that reservations are usually only needed for dinner.

Use the coordinate (✛ B2) at the end of each listing to locate a site on the Where to Eat and Stay in Venice map.

WHAT IT COSTS IN EUROS					
	¢	$	$$	$$$	$$$$
AT DINNER	under €20	€20–€30	€30–€45	€45–€65	over €65

Prices are for a first course (*primo*), second course (*secondo*), and dessert (*dolce*).

CANNAREGIO

$$$

VENETIAN

✗ **Al Fontego dei Pescatori.** Having had a stall at the Rialto fish market for more than 25 years, and being the president of the area fishmongers association for 10, proprietor "Lolo" knows his fish. The seafood served here might just be the freshest in Venice. Antipasti include Orologio, a "clock" of raw selections; Poker, four different *tartars* of seafood and fresh fruit; and succulent grilled *capelunghe* (razor clams). The pasta is served al dente and risotto *al onda* (undulating, as opposed to firm). Chef Massimo prepares entrées simply but always with a twist, such as *branzino* (sea bass) topped with its own crispy skin or a frizzle of zucchini. The wine list includes excellent regional choices that pair well with fish. There's meat for non–fish eaters, too. The dining rooms are spacious and the garden is enchanting in temperate weather. ⊠ *Calle Priuli, Cannaregio 3711* ☎ *041/5200538* ▭ *MC, V* ☉ *Closed Mon., 3 wks in Jan., 2 wks in Aug. No lunch in July and Aug.* Ⓥ *Ca' d'Oro* ✛ *D2.*

$$

ITALIAN

✗ **Algiubagiò.** A waterfront table is still relatively affordable at lunchtime here on Venice's northern Fondamente Nove, where you can gaze out toward San Michele and Murano—on a clear day you can even see the Dolomites. Algiubagiò has a dual personality: pizzas and big salads at lunch; at dinner, creative *primi* (first courses) like ravioli stuffed with *pecorino di fossa* (a hard sheep's-milk cheese) are followed by elegant *secondi* (second courses) such as Angus fillets with vodka and Gorgonzola. The young, friendly staff also serves ice cream, drinks, and sandwiches all day. A lunch table here is worth the walk for the view; the price rises considerably at dinner. ⊠ *Fondamente Nove, Cannaregio 5039* ☎ *041/5236084* ⊕ *www.algiubagio.net* ⌦ *Reservations essential*- ▭ *MC, V* Ⓥ *Fondamente Nove* ✛ *E2.*

$–$$

VENETIAN

✗ **Anice Stellato.** Off the main concourse, on one of the most romantic *fondamente* (canal-side streets) of Cannaregio, this family-run bàcaro-trattoria is the place to stop for fairly priced, satisfying fare, though service can feel indifferent. The space has plenty of character: narrow columns rise from the colorful tile floor, dividing the room into cozy sections. Venetian classics are enriched with such offerings as *carpacci di pesce* (thin slices of raw tuna, swordfish, or salmon dressed with olive oil and fragrant herbs), tagliatelle with king prawns and zucchini flowers, and several tasty fish stews. They also serve several meat dishes,

BEST BETS FOR VENICE DINING

With hundreds of restaurants to choose from, how will you decide where to eat? Fodor's writers and editors have selected their favorite restaurants by price and experience in the Best Bets lists below. In the first column, Fodor's Choice properties represent the "best of the best."

Fodor's Choice ★

Al Paradiso, $$$, p. 449

Antiche Carampane, $$$, p. 449

La Zucca, $, p. 450

Osteria Orto dei Mori, $$, p. 443

Vini da Gigio, $$, p. 444

By Price

¢

Cantinone Già Schiavi, p. 445

$

Al Prosecco, p. 450

Antico Panificio, p. 450

Botteghe di Promessi Sposi, p. 443

La Cantina, p. 443

La Zucca, p. 450

Muro Pizzeria con Cucina, p. 451

Ostaria al Garanghelo, p. 450

$$

Anice Stellato, p. 441

La Bitta, p. 448

Osteria Orto dei Mori, p. 443

Vini da Gigio, p. 444

$$$

Al Fontego dei Pescatori, p. 441

Al Paradiso, p. 449

Antiche Carampane, p. 449

$$$$

De Pisis, p. 448

Fiaschetteria Toscana, p. 443

Il Ridotto, p. 445

Best by Experience

OUTDOOR DINING

Al Fontego dei Pescatori, $$$, p. 441

Algiubagiò, $$, p. 441

La Cantina, $, p. 443

Muro Pizzeria con Cucina, $, p. 451

Osteria Orto dei Mori, $$, p. 443

Ristorante Riviera, $$$, p. 448

ROMANTIC

Al Fontego dei Pescatori, $$$, p. 441

Al Paradiso, $$$, p. 449

Anice Stellato, $$, p. 441

De Pisis, $$$$, p. 448

Osteria Orto dei Mori, $$, p. 443

Ristorante Riviera, $$$, p. 448

GOOD FOR KIDS

Ai Tosi Grandi, ¢, p. 444

Antico Panificio, $, p. 450

Ostaria al Garanghelo, $, p. 450

IF YOU DON'T WANT FISH

La Bitta, $$, p. 448

La Zucca, $, p. 450

Muro Pizzeria con Cucina, $, p. 451

Vini da Gigio, $$, p. 444

GREAT VIEWS

Algiubagiò, $$, p. 441

De Pisis, $$$$, p. 448

Ristorante Riviera, $$$, p. 448

EXCEPTIONAL WINE LIST

Antiche Carampane, $$$, p. 449

La Cantina, $, p. 443

Osteria Orto dei Mori, $$, p. 443

Ristoteca Oniga, $$, p. 448

Vini da Gigio, $$, p. 444

GOOD FOR LUNCH

Al Prosecco, $, p. 450

El Rèfolo, $, p. 444

La Cantina, $, p. 443

La Zucca, $, p. 450

Muro Pizzeria con Cucina, $, p. 451

Ostaria al Garanghelo, $, p. 450

CUCINA ALTA (SOPHISTICATED CUISINE)

De Pisis, $$$$, p. 448

Il Ridotto, $$$$, p. 445

CASALINGA (HOME COOKING)

Ai Tosi Grandi, ¢, p. 444

Antico Panificio, $, p. 450

Ostaria al Garanghelo, $, p. 450

including a tender beef fillet stewed in Barolo wine with potatoes. Book early to grab one of the outdoor waterside tables on summer evenings. ⊠ *Fondamenta de la Sensa, Cannaregio 3272* ☎ *041/720744* ▤ *MC, V* ⊗ *Closed Mon. and Tues., 1 wk in Feb., and 3 wks in Aug.* Ⓥ *San Alvise/San Marcuola* ✛ *C1.*

$–$$
VENETIAN

✕ **Botteghe di Promessi Sposi.** The former Promessi Sposi eatery was rejuvenated when three *fioi* (guys) with decades of restaurant experience joined forces to open this restaurant. Claudio mans the kitchen, while Nicola and Cristiano will serve you either an *ombra* (small glass of wine) and cicchetto at the *banco* (counter), or a delightful meal in the dining room or the intimate courtyard. A season-centered menu includes standards like Venetian calves' liver and grilled *canestrelli* (tiny Venetian scallops) along with more adventurous creations, like homemade ravioli stuffed with *rapi rossi* (red turnip) and topped with the Sardinian ricotta *salata* (a firm, medium-aged ricotta), or a steak tartar served with bean sprouts and spoonfuls of capers, paprika, mustard, and minced red onions. It's the best of many worlds: a comfy trattoria where there's something for everyone. ⊠ *Calle de l'Oca (just off Campo Santi Apostoli), Cannaregio 4367* ☎ *041/2412747* ⌖ *Reservations essential* ▤ *No credit cards* ⊗ *Closed Wed.* Ⓥ *Ca' d'Oro* ✛ *E2.*

$$$$
ITALIAN

✕ **Fiaschetteria Toscana.** Contrary to what the name suggests, there's nothing Tuscan about this restaurant's menu. It was formerly a Tuscan wine and oil storehouse, and it's worth a visit for its cheerful and courteous service, fine *cucina* (cooking), and noteworthy cellar. The owners, Albino and Mariuccia Busatto, make their presence felt as they walk among the well-appointed tables, opening special bottles of wine and discussing the menu. Gastronomic highlights include a light *tagliolini neri al ragù di astice* (thin spaghetti served with squid ink and mixed with a delicate lobster sauce), and zabaglione. ⊠ *Campo San Giovanni Crisostomo, Cannaregio 5719* ☎ *041/5285281* ⌖ *Reservations essential* ⊕ *www.fiaschetteriatoscana.it* ▤ *AE, DC, MC, V* ⊗ *Closed Tues. and 4 wks in July and Aug. No lunch Wed.* Ⓥ *Rialto* ✛ *E3.*

$
VENETIAN

✕ **La Cantina.** With its understated facade, you'd never guess that La Cantina offered anything more than a nice sandwich and an acceptable pinot grigio. Perhaps if you spotted the fresh raw oysters, a whole tuna patiently waiting to be filleted, or the sign for today's *zuppa di lenticchie* (lentil soup), you might begin to understand how satisfying a meal here might be. Co-owner and chef Francesco chooses from only the choicest meats and cheeses, the freshest vegetables, seasonings, and fish to create his inspired meals. There's effectively no menu: tell co-owner Andrea or wine expert Giovanni your preferences and your budget, then sit back and wait to be satisfied. One caveat: Service can be slow on busier evenings, especially after 8 PM. ⊠ *Campo San Felice, Cannaregio 3689* ☎ *041/5228258* ⌖ *Reservations essential* ▤ *AE, MC, V* ⊗ *Closed Sun. and Mon.* Ⓥ *Ca' d'Oro* ✛ *D2.*

$$
ITALIAN
Fodor's Choice
★

✕ **Osteria Orto dei Mori.** "Pure pleasure" might be the best way to describe the dining experience here: from the fanciful, tasteful interior decor, to romantic candlelit tables dotting the Campo dei Mori, to the inspired *cucina*. The attentive expertise of chef and co-owner Lorenzo is evident in every dish: try the *fagotti*, bundles of beef marinated in Chianti with goat cheese, or a seafood version with prawns, zucchini, and ricotta. Risotto with scampi and savory *fenferli* mushrooms won't disappoint, nor will the signature parchment-baked monkfish. Co-owner Micael has artfully constructed the wine list—ask about periodic tastings. The osteria is just under the nose of the campo's corner statue. ⊠ *Campo dei Mori, Fondamenta dei Mori, Cannaregio 3386* ☎ *041/5235544* ☰ *AE, DC, MC, V* ⊘ *Closed Tues.* Ⓥ *Orto, Ca d'Oro, San Marcuola* ⊕ *D1.*

¢   ✕ **Tiziano.** A staggering array of *tramezzini* (sandwiches) line the display
CAFÉ   cases at this *tavola calda* (roughly the Italian equivalent of a cafeteria); inexpensive salad plates and daily pasta specials are also served. It's a handy place for a quick detour and snack at very modest prices. Vegetarians delight in Tiziano's version of the classic Italian toast, in this case a grilled-cheese sandwich with eggplant slices and roasted zucchini. ⊠ *Salizzada San Giovanni Crisostomo, Cannaregio 5747* ☎ *041/5235544* ☰ *No credit cards* Ⓥ *Rialto* ⊕ *E3.*

$$ ✕ **Vini da Gigio.** Paolo and Laura, a brother-sister team, run this refined
VENETIAN   trattoria as if they've invited you to dinner in their home, while keeping
Fodor's Choice   the service professional. Deservedly popular with Venetians and visitors
★   alike, it's one of the best values in the city. Indulge in homemade pastas such as rigatoni with duck sauce and arugula-stuffed ravioli. Fish is well represented—try the sesame-encrusted tuna—but the meat dishes steal the show. The *anatra* (duck) is a flavorful fricassee; the steak with red-pepper sauce and the *tagliata di agnello* (sautéed lamb fillet with a light, crusty coating) are both superb, and you'll never enjoy a better *fegato alla veneziana* (Venetian-style liver with onions). It's a shame to order the house wine here: just let Paolo know your budget and he'll choose for you from his more than 3,000 labels. ⊠ *Fondamenta San Felice, Cannaregio 3628/A* ☎ *041/5285140* ⊕ *www.vinidagigio.com* ⬧ *Reservations essential* ☰ *MC, V* ⊘ *Closed Mon. and Tues., 2 wks in Jan., and 3 wks in Aug.* Ⓥ *Ca' d'Oro* ⊕ *D2.*

CASTELLO

¢   ✕ **Ai Tosi Grandi.** Even if you're not staying in Castello Basso, it's worth-
ITALIAN   while to make your way to either of the Tosi eateries for a satisfying meal. The word *tosi* refers to the youthful, energetic servers, contrasting with stuffy, grumpy waiters you might encounter elsewhere. The Grandi's seating includes an expansive garden that on a summer evening will be brimming with families, people on dates, the tosi, and other diners, all of whom will seem to know each other. But, you'll not feel left out, and could enjoy some of the best pizza in Venice, and arguably beyond. Venetian favorites are served alongside more imaginative fare, at prices even a local would classify as reasonable. **Ai Tosi Piccoli** is a smaller, more typical trattoria, exuding the same relaxed, residential ambience on a more intimate scale, just down the calle at Seco Marina 738. ⊠ *Seco Marina 985/A, Castello* ☎ *041/5234182 Grandi, 041/5237102 Piccoli* ☰ *MC, V* ⊘ *Closed Mon.* Ⓥ *Giardini* ⊕ *H5.*

$ ✕ **El Rèfolo.** This hip hangout is named after a play by turn-of-the-20th-
WINE BAR   century emancipated lady Amalia Rosselli—look for the framed title page inside. El Rèfolo (The Breeze, in Venetian) is a contemporary cantina in an otherwise very Venetian neighborhood, and is more for

lunch, *un aperitivo* (an aperitif), or supper than formal dinner. Owner Massimiliano pairs great wines with select meats, savory cheese, and seasonal vegetable combos. In temperate weather, this niche-size *enoteca*'s exuberance effervesces out onto the city's broadest street. It's open every day but Sunday from 9:30 AM to 12:30 AM. ⊠ *Via Garibaldi 1580, Castello* ☎ *No phone* ═ *MC, V* ⊘ *Closed Sun., hrs limited in winter* Ⓥ *Arsenale* ✢ *H5.*

$$$$
VENETIAN

✕ **Il Ridotto.** Longtime restaurateur Gianni Bonaccorsi of nearby Aciugheta fame has succeeded in opening a locale that is the pure expression of the best he has to offer. Ridotto, "reduced" in Italian, may refer to the size of this tiny, gracious restaurant. The dimensions allow Gianni to spoil you, should you manage to snag one of the five tables (easier at lunch). The artful menu is revised daily, a luxury only such a personalized restaurant can afford; you may find fettucine with Piedmont Fassona beef ragout or scampi with crustacean sauce, and, for dessert, pistachio flan. The tasting menu never fails to impress. Have Gianni choose a wine for you from his excellent cantina. ⊠ *Campo SS Filippo e Giacomo, Castello 4509* ☎ *041/5208280* ⌂ *Reservations essential* ═ *AE, DC, MC, V* ⊘ *Closed Wed. No lunch Thurs.* Ⓥ *San Zaccaria* ✢ *F4.*

DORSODURO

$$
VENETIAN

✕ **Ai 4 Feri.** The paper tablecloths and cozy, laid-back ambience are part of this small restaurant's charm. The menu varies according to what's fresh that day; imaginative combinations of ingredients in the primi— herring and sweet peppers, salmon and radicchio, giant shrimp and broccoli with pumpkin gnocchi—are the norm. A meal here followed by after-dinner gelato at Il Doge or drinks in Campo Santa Margherita, a five-minute walk away, makes for a lovely evening. The kitchen is open until 10:30 PM. ⊠ *Calle Lunga San Barnaba, Dorsoduro 2754/A* ☎ *041/5206978* ═ *No credit cards* ⊘ *Closed Sun. and 2 wks in June* Ⓥ *Ca' Rezzonico* ✢ *B5.*

$$$
SOUTHERN
ITALIAN

✕ **Avogaria.** In terms of both food and architecture, ultrafashionable Avogaria lends modern flavor to the Venice restaurant scene. The clean, elegant design of the dining room and garden leaves no doubt that here, you're in the Venice of the present. The cuisine is from the Puglia region in the heel of Italy's boot; highlights among the primi include *orecchiette* (small, round pasta) with turnip tops, and zucchini *involtini* (roll-ups) made with soft, fresh *stracciatella* cheese. Pugliese cooking, like Venetian, reveres fresh seafood, and you can taste this sensibility in the slow-cooked, sesame-encrusted tuna steak. ⊠ *Calle Avogaria, Dorsoduro 1629* ☎ *041/2960491* ⌂ *Reservations essential* ═ *AE, DC, MC, V* ⊘ *Closed Tues.* Ⓥ *San Basilio* ✢ *B5.*

¢
WINE BAR

✕ **Cantinone Già Schiavi.** This beautiful 19th-century *bàcaro* opposite the *squero* (gondola repair shop) of San Trovaso has original furnishings and one of the best wine selections in town—the walls are covered floor to ceiling by bottles for purchase. Cicchetti here are some of the most inventive in Venice: try the crostini-style layers of bread, smoked swordfish, and slivers of raw zucchini, or pungent slices of parmigiano, fig, and toast. They also have a creamy version of *baccalà mantecato*

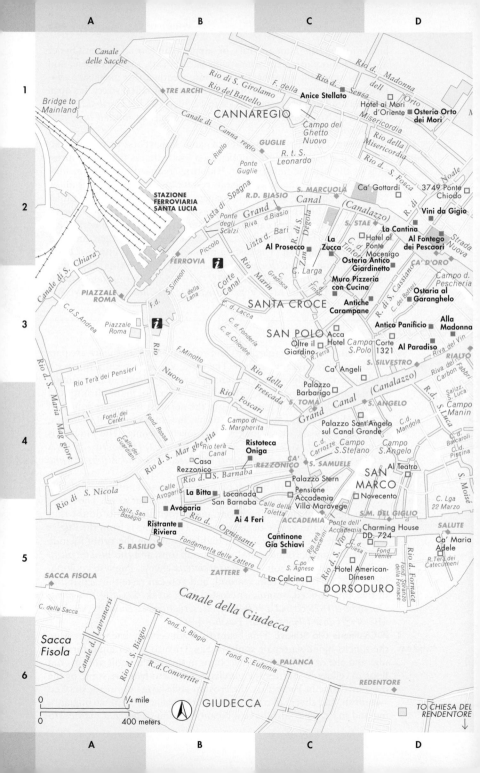

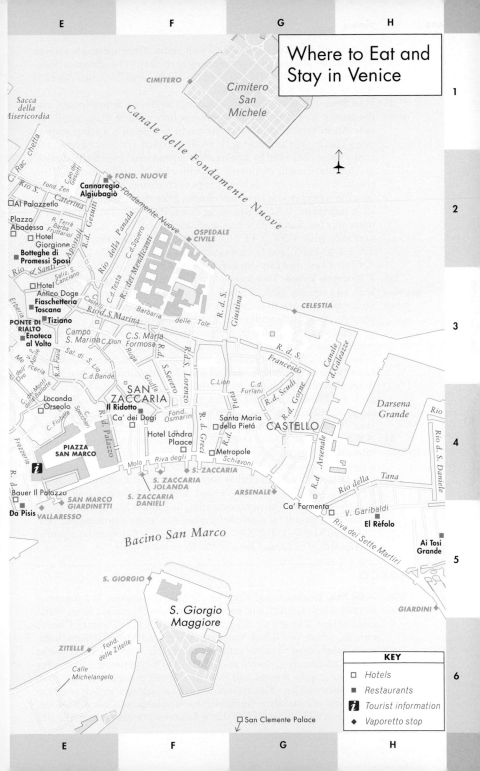

Where to Eat and Stay in Venice

E F G H

1

Sacca della Misericordia

CIMITERO
Cimitero San Michele

Canale delle Fondamente Nuove

FOND. NUOVE

Cannaregio Algiubagiò

Fond. Zen
C.po dei Gesuiti

2

□Al Palazzetto

Plazzo Abadessa

□ **Hotel Giorgione**

R. Terrà Barba Fruttariol

Botteghe di Promessi Sposi

Rio d'Santi

Rio della Panada

Fondamente Nuove

OSPEDALE CIVILE

□Hotel Antico Doge

Fiaschetteria Toscana

PONTE DI RIALTO

Tiziano

Enoteca al Volto

Campo S. Marina

Rio d.S.Marina

CELESTIA

3

C.S. Maria Formosa

R.d.S. Lorenzo

R. d. S.

Giustina

R. d. S. Francesco

Canale d.Galeazze

Sal. di S. Lio

C.d.Bande

Ruga Giuffa

S.Severo

C.Lion

C.d. Furlani

R.d. Scudi

Darsena Grande

Rio

4

SAN ZACCARIA

Il Ridotto

Ca' dei Dogi

Hotel Londra Plaace

Fond. Osmarin

R.d. Greci

Pietà

Santa Maria della Pietà

Metropole

Riva degli Schiavoni

CASTELLO

R.d. Gorne

R.d. Arsenale

Rio d. S. Daniele

PIAZZA SAN MARCO

Molo

S. ZACCARIA JOLANDA

S.-ZACCARIA

ARSENALE

Rio della Tana

Ca' Formenta

V. Garibaldi

El Rèfolo

Ai Tosi Grande

5

Bauer Il Palazzo

SAN MARCO GIARDINETTI

S. ZACCARIA DANIELI

Da Pisis

VALLARESSO

Bacino San Marco

Riva dei Sette Martiri

GIARDINI

S. GIORGIO

S. Giorgio Maggiore

ZITELLE

Fond. delle Zitelle

Calle Michelangelo

□San Clemente Palace

6

E F G H

(cod creamed with olive oil) spiced with herbs. There are nearly a dozen open bottles of wine for experimenting at the bar. ⊠ *Fondamenta Nani, Dorsoduro 992* ☎ *041/5230034* 🚍 *No credit cards* ⊗ *Closed 2 wks in Aug.* Ⓥ *Zattere/Accademia* ✛ *C5.*

$$ ✕ **La Bitta.** The decor is more discreet, the dining hours longer, and
ITALIAN the service friendlier and more efficient here than in many small restaurants in Venice—and the creative non-fish menu is a temptation at every course. You can start with a light salad of Treviso radicchio and crispy bacon, followed by smoked-beef carpaccio or *gnocchetti ubriachi al Montasio* (small, marinated gnocchi with Montasio cheese). Then choose a *secondo* such as lamb chops with thyme, *anatra in pevarada* (duck in a pepper sauce), or Irish Angus fillet steak. Secondi are served with vegetables, which helps bring down the price. The restaurant is open only for dinner, but serves much earlier and later than most, continuously from 6:30 to 11. ⊠ *Calle Lunga San Barnaba, Dorsoduro 2753/A* ☎ *041/5230531* ✍ *Reservations essential* 🚍 *No credit cards* ⊗ *Closed Sun. and July. No lunch* Ⓥ *Ca' Rezzonico* ✛ *B4.*

$$$ ✕ **Ristorante Riviera.** Two lovely dining rooms and a canal-side terrace
NORTHERN with an exquisite view, combined with truly inspired cuisine, make a
ITALIAN visit to Riviera one to remember. Chef Monica Scarpa brings her creative touch to both traditional and contemporary dishes. Fish lovers will enjoy the tuna tartare, seafood risotto, or a mixed-fish platter, while carnivores can dig into prosciutto with figs and pecorino cheese followed by a plate of succulent lamb chops with blueberry sauce. Host Luca excels at selecting the perfect wine for any combination of foods. A simple but appealing children's menu is offered. ⊠ *Zattere, Dorsoduro 1473* ☎ *041/5227621* ⊕ *www.ristoranteriviera.it* ✍ *Reservations essential* 🚍 *MC, V* ⊗ *Closed Mon. and 4 wks in Jan. and Feb. No lunch Wed.* Ⓥ *San Basilio* ✛ *B5.*

$$ ✕ **Ristoteca Oniga.** Marino Oniga and his wife, Annika, successfully com-
VENETIAN bine classic Venetian elements in an out-of-the-ordinary way, adding a touch of personality and imagination to both creation and presentation. Delectably roasted duck is only one of the meat alternatives to the fresh fish; the wine list is ample, and Annika's desserts are all *fatti in casa* (homemade). The outdoor seating in Campo San Barnaba makes a charming setting for a delightful meal. ⊠ *Campo San Barnaba, Dorsoduro 2852* ☎ *041/0997534* ⊕ *www.oniga.it* ✍ *Reservations essential* 🚍 *AE, MC, V* ⊗ *Closed Tues.* Ⓥ *Ca' Rezzonico* ✛ *B4.*

SAN MARCO

$$$$ ✕ **De Pisis.** Romance and elegance pervade the interior and luminous
MODERN ITALIAN terrace, whose Grand Canal panorama includes the radiant Santa Maria della Salute. The service is impeccable, as is Chef Giovanni Ciresa's cuisine, where you'll find Venetian, Asian, and Mediterranean influences synthesized to create inspired, delectable works of art. If you're feeling adventurous, do try one of the chef's experimental dishes for which he is quite famous and let your sommelier suggest a wine from their masterful list. This formal restaurant attracts well-dressed clientele and is certainly a fine choice for a splurge. ⊠ *Calle San Moise, San Marco 1459* ☎ *041/5207022* ✍ *Reservations essential* 🚍 *AE, DC,*

MC, V Ⓥ *Valaresso/Santa Maria del Giglio* ✢ *E5.*

$$ **✗Enoteca al Volto.** A short walk
WINE BAR from the Rialto Bridge, this bar has been around since 1936; the fine cicchetti and primi have a lot to do with its staying power. Two small, dark rooms with a ceiling plastered with wine labels provide a classic backdrop for simple fare. The place prides itself on its considerable wine list of both Italian and foreign vintages, as you might reckon from the decoration. If you stick to *panini* (sandwiches) and a cicchetto or two, you'll eat well for relatively little. If you opt for one of the primi of the day, the price category goes up a notch. ✉ *Calle Cavalli, San Marco 4081* ☎ *041/5228945* ⊕ *www.alvoltoenoteca.it* ⌕ *Reservations essential* ▭ *No credit cards* ☾ *Closed Sun.* Ⓥ *Rialto* ✢ *E3.*

SAN POLO

6

$$$ **✗Al Paradiso.** In a small dining room made warm and cozy by its pleas-
MODERN ITALIAN ing and unpretentious decor, proprietor Giordano makes all diners feel
Fodor's Choice like honored guests. Pappardelle "al Paradiso" takes pasta with sea-
★ food sauce to new heights, while risotto with shrimp, champagne, and grapefruit puts a delectable twist on a traditional dish. The inspired and original array of entrées includes meat and fish selections such as a salmon with honey and balsamic vinegar in a stunning presentation. Desserts include a perfect panna cotta. ✉ *Calle del Paradiso, San Polo 767* ☎ *041/5234910* ⌕ *Reservations essential* ▭ *AE, MC, V* ☾ *Closed Mon. and 3 wks in Jan. and Feb.* Ⓥ *San Silvestro* ✢ *D3.*

$$$ **✗Alla Madonna.** Locals relax at Alla Madonna, which prides itself on
VENETIAN the freshness, abundance, and caliber of their fish. In business since 1954 (Rado Fluvio still runs the place), it is a classic in service, atmosphere, and cuisine. The quality of *la materia prima* (the principal ingredients) is of paramount importance here, and impeccable preparation ensures its characteristics are always accentuated, never overwhelmed. Get your server's recommendation for the day. There are a variety of meat dishes, a fine wine list, and space for groups. It's a popular spot, so expect a lively and bustling atmosphere. ✉ *Calle della Madonna, San Polo 594* ☎ *041/5223824* ⊕ *www.ristoranteallamadonna.com* ⌕ *Reservations essential* ▭ *AE, MC, V* ☾ *Closed Sun., Jan., and 2 wks in Aug.* Ⓥ *San Silvestro* ✢ *D3.*

$$$ **✗Antiche Carampane.** Since its appearance in the first of Donna Leon's
VENETIAN Inspector Brunetti mysteries, Piera Bortoluzzi Librai's trattoria has lost
Fodor's Choice none of its charm but gained considerably in elegance. You'll find all
★ the classic Venetian fish dishes ranging from a mixed seafood antipasto to fish soups, pasta, and perfectly grilled fish. Updated plates such as seafood and fruit salads for starters and entrées like turbot with citrus sauce also delight diners. Chocolate mousse, panna cotta, and sweet wine with biscotti make delectable desserts. Francesco, the son of

Franco and Piera, whose family recipes elevate many of the classics, is responsible for some of the new presentations. ⊠ *Rio Terà della Carampane, San Polo 1911* ☎ *041/5240165* ⊕ *www.antichecarampane.com* ♨ *Reservations essential* ▭ *AE, MC, V* ⊘ *Closed Sun. and Mon., 10 days in Jan., and 3 wks in July and Aug.* Ⓥ *San Silvestro* ✛ *D3.*

$
ITALIAN
✕ **Antico Panificio.** Tasty, economical fare in a friendly atmosphere *senza pretesa* (without pretense) can be a tall order in Venice, but the Antico Panificio succeeds in offering just that: traditional, satisfying dishes, from pizza in every form conceivable to pasta with meat sauce, to a grilled pork chop or fillet of sole—all at a handy location just down from the Rialto. It's apparent from the mix of locals and travelers chattering away that the Panificio is no secret, so arrive on the early side for lunch, and be sure to reserve in the evening. Service can be a bit slow when the place is full, so it's best not to come here in a rush. ⊠ *Campiello del Sole, San Polo 945/A–B* ☎ *041/2770967* ▭ *AE, MC, V* ⊘ *Closed Tues.* Ⓥ *San Silvestro* ✛ *D3.*

$
ITALIAN
★
✕ **Ostaria al Garanghelo.** Superior quality, competitive prices, and great ambience mean this place is often packed with Venetians, especially for lunch and an after-work *ombra* (glass of wine) and *cicchetti* (snack). Chef Renato takes full advantage of the fresh ingredients from the Rialto Market, a few steps away, bakes his own bread daily, and prefers cooking many dishes *al vapore* (steamed). The spicy *fagioli al uciletto* (literally "bird-style beans," prepared with a light marinara sauce) has an unusual name and Tuscan origins; it's a perfect companion to a plate of fresh pasta. Don't confuse this restaurant with one of the same name in Via Garibaldi. ⊠ *Calle dei Boteri, San Polo 1570* ☎ *041/721721* ▭ *MC, V* ⊘ *Closed Sun.* Ⓥ *Rialto* ✛ *D3.*

SANTA CROCE

$
WINE BAR
✕ **Al Prosecco.** Locals stream into this friendly wine bar, down a "spritz" (a combination of white wine, Campari or Aperol, and seltzer water), and continue on their way. Al Prosecco is the perfect place to explore wines from the region—or from anywhere in the county for that matter. They accompany a carefully chosen selection of meats, cheeses, and other food from small, artisanal producers, used in tasty panini like the *porchetta romane verdure* (roast pork with greens). Proprietors Davide and Stefano preside over a young and friendly staff who reel off the day's specials with ease. There are a few tables in the intimate back room, and when the weather coorperates you can sit outdoors on the lively campo, watching the Venetian world go by. It's open 9 to 9, and later if the mood strikes. ⊠ *Campo San Giacomo dell'Orio, Santa Croce 1503* ☎ *041/5240222* ⊕ *www.alprosecco.com* ▭ *No credit cards* ⊘ *Closed Sun.* Ⓥ *San Stae* ✛ *C2.*

$
ITALIAN
Fodor's Choice
★
✕ **La Zucca.** The simple place settings, lattice-wood walls, canal window, and mélange of languages make this place feel as much like a typical vegetarian restaurant as you could expect to find in Venice. Though the menu does have superb meat dishes such as the *piccata di pollo ai caperi e limone con riso* (sliced chicken with capers and lemon served with rice), more attention is paid to dishes from the garden: try the radicchio *di Treviso con funghi e scaglie di Montasio* (with mushrooms and

shavings of Montasio cheese) or the *finocchi piccanti con olive* (fennel in a spicy tomato-olive sauce). ⊠ *Calle del Tintor, Santa Croce 1762* 🕾 *041/5241570* ⚓ *Reservations essential* ⊟ *AE, DC, MC, V* ⊗ *Closed Sun. and 1 wk in Dec.* Ⓥ *San Stae* ✛ *C2.*

$ ✕ **Muro Pizzeria con Cucina.** Don't let the moniker *pizzeria con cucina* fool
ITALIAN you: Muro offers a varied menu using high-quality ingredients, taking its cue from its more refined sister restaurant, Muro Rialto, upstairs. Select from excellent Venetian fare and pizza in classic and innovative forms—try the *arrotolata amoretesoro* (a rolled pizza) with *bresaola* (thinly sliced salt-cured beef), *scamorza* (mozzarella-like cow's-milk cheese), and radicchio. Chef Francesco adds dimension to the menu with classic Italian and ethnic selections, along with the *piatti unici*, a single course fancifully combining elements of first and second courses. A wide selection of beer is on tap. ⊠ *Campiello dello Spezier, Santa Croce 2048* 🕾 *041/5241628* ⊕ *www. murovenezia.com* ⚓ *Reservations essential* ⊟ *MC, V* ⊗ *Closed Tues.* Ⓥ *San Stae* ✛ *C3.*

$$$ ✕ **Osteria Antico Giardinetto.** The name refers to the intimate, open-air
ITALIAN garden where co-owner Larisa will welcome you warmly, once you've wound your way from the Rialto or San Stae down the narrow calle to this romantic locale. (There's an indoor dining room as well, but the garden is covered and heated in winter.) Larisa's husband, Virgilio, mans the cucina, where he prepares such dishes as sea bass in salt crust and a grilled fish platter. Be sure to try the homemade gnocchi or pasta—perhaps the *tagliolini* with scallops and artichokes. You'll also find some fine meat options here. Desserts, like the chocolate mousse or crème caramel are *fatto in casa* (homemade) as well. The wine list features excellent regional selections. ⊠ *Calle dei Morti, Santa Croce 2953* 🕾 *041/722882* ⊕ *www.anticogiardinetto.it* ⊟ *MC, V* ⊗ *Closed Mon., and Jan. 4–31* Ⓥ *San Stae* ✛ *D2.*

WHERE TO STAY

Many of Venice's hotels are in renovated palaces, but space is at a premium—and comes for a price—and rooms may feel cramped by American standards. The most-exclusive hotels are indeed palatial, although they may well have some small, dowdy rooms, so it's best to verify ahead of time that yours isn't one of them. Smaller hotels may not have lounge areas, and because of preservation laws, some are not permitted to install elevators, so if these features are essential, ask ahead of time. Although the city has no cars, it does have boats plying the canals and pedestrians chattering in the streets sometimes late into the night (most likely along principal thoroughfares, in San Marco and near the Rialto), so ask for a quiet room if you're concerned about noise.

Many travelers assume a hotel near Piazza San Marco will give them the most convenient location, but keep in mind that Venice is scaled to humans (on foot) rather than automobiles; it's difficult to find a location that's *not* convenient to most of the city. Areas away from San Marco may also offer the benefit of being less overrun by day-trippers.

It is essential to have detailed directions to your hotel when you arrive. Arm yourself with not only a clear map and postal address (e.g.,

Dorsoduro 825), but the actual street name (e.g., Fondamenta San Trovaso) and the nearest campo.

You can compare Venice hotels from A to Z at **Venezia.net** (⊕ *www. venezia.net*) ; it furnishes links to hotels' official Web sites. The Web site of **Venezia Sì** (☎ *199/173309 in Italy, 39/0415222264 from abroad* ⊙ *Mon.–Sat. 9 AM–11 PM* ⊕ *www.veneziasi.it*) lists most hotels in town (with some photographs), and they offer a free reservation service over the phone. It's the public relations arm of AVA (Venetian Hoteliers Association) and has booths where you can make same-day reservations at Piazzale Roma (☎ *041/5231397* ⊙ *Daily 9 AM–10 PM*), Santa Lucia train station (☎ *041/715288 or 041/715016* ⊙ *Daily 8 AM–9 PM*), and Marco Polo Airport (☎ *041/5415133* ⊙ *Daily 9 AM–10 PM*). Be aware that if you arrive in the afternoon without a reservation, pickings will be slim and you may be unable to find a room at all.

Use the coordinate (✛ B2) at the end of each listing to locate a site on the Where to Eat and Stay in Venice map.

PRICES

Venetian hotels cater to all tastes and come in a variety of price ranges. Rates are about 20% higher than in Rome and Milan but can be reduced by as much as half off-season, from November to March (excluding Christmas, New Year's, and Carnevale), and likely in August as well.

WHAT IT COSTS IN EUROS				
¢	$	$$	$$$	$$$$
HOTELS under €75	€75–€125	€125–€200	€200–€300	over €300

Prices are for a standard double room in high season.

CANNAREGIO

$$ ⊞ **3749 Ponte Chiodo.** This cheery, homey bed-and-breakfast takes its
★ name from the bridge leading to its entrance (one of only two left in the lagoon without hand railings). Attentively appointed rooms with geranium-filled window boxes overlook either the bridge and expansive canals below or the spacious enclosed garden. It's a family-owned operation, and service is accommodating and friendly; you can get lots of suggestions for dining and sightseeing. The private garden and patio are perfect for a relaxing breakfast or scribbling postcards. Some bathrooms are smallish, but overall it's an excellent value. The location is also handy to the Ca' d'Oro vaporetto. **Pros:** highly attentive service; warm, relaxed atmosphere; private garden; canal views. **Cons:** no elevator could be a problem for some. ⊠ *Calle Racchetta, Cannaregio 3749* ☎ *041/2413935* ⊕ *www.pontechiodo.it* ↰ *6 rooms* ⌂ *In-room: no phone, safe, refrigerator, Wi-Fi. In-hotel: room service, bar, Wi-Fi, Internet terminal* ☰ *MC, V* ⅩⅠ *BP* Ⓥ *Ca' d'Oro* ✛ *D2.*

$–$$ ⊞ **Al Palazzetto.** Understated yet gracious Venetian decor, original
★ open-beam ceilings and terrazzo flooring, spotless marble baths, and friendly, attentive service are the hallmarks of this intimate, family-owned *locanda* (inn). Rooms overlooking the canals are the best in

terms of size as well as view. The spacious common salon overlooks a side canal, Rio San Sofia. The location is tranquil, but still handy to the Ca' d'Oro stop, the traghetto across to the Rialto Market, and the San Marco area. Al Palazzetto is good for groups, as there are triple and quad rooms; some are connecting. Spring for the attic suite if it's available. **Pros:** standout service; owner on-site; canal views from some rooms; free Wi-Fi. **Cons:** not for amenity seekers or lovers of ultramodern decor. ⊠ *Calle delle Vele, Cannaregio 4057* ☎ *041/2750897* ⊕ *www.guesthouse.it* ⤴ *6 rooms, 1 suite* ⚤ *In-room: safe, refrigerator, Internet, Wi-Fi. In-hotel: Wi-Fi, laundry facilities* ⊟ *AE, DC, MC, V* ⦿⦿ *BP* ☑ *Ca' d'Oro* ⊹ *E2.*

$$–$$$$ ⊡ **Ca' Gottardi.** Ca' Gottardi is part of a new generation of small hotels
★ that mix traditional Venetian style with contemporary design. The clean white-marble entrance leading up to the luminous *piano nobile* (main floor) of the 15th-century palace gracefully contrasts with the opulent Murano chandeliers and rich wall brocades in the guest rooms. Some rooms have canal views, bathrooms are large and modern, and a rich breakfast is served in a bright salon that overlooks a wide canal. The location, just off the Grand Canal near the Ca' d'Oro and a variety of good eateries, is another plus. Confirm the type of room (suite or standard, with or without a view) and its situation (in the annex or the main hotel) when booking. **Pros:** great location; mix of old and new styles; canal views. **Cons:** no outdoor garden or terrace; annex rooms are generally smaller. ⊠ *Strada Nova, Cannaregio 2283* ☎ *041/2759333* ⊕ *www.cagottardi.com* ⤴ *23 rooms, 2 junior suites, 3 suites* ⚤ *In-room: safe, refrigerator, Internet, Wi-Fi. In-hotel: bar* ⊟ *DC, MC, V* ⦿⦿ *BP* ☑ *Ca' d'Oro* ⊹ *D2.*

$$–$$$ ⊡ **Hotel ai Mori d'Oriente.** The theme here, reflected in the decor, is Venice's connection with the exotic East. Some rooms and suites overlook the expansive canal along the Fondamenta della Sensa, one of the bright, broad byways typical of the upper Cannaregio district. In good weather, you can also take breakfast or a Venetian Spritz cocktail at a sunny table along the canal. Though the atmosphere harkens back to Venice's past, facilities and amenities are everything you'd expect from a 21st-century establishment, and the staff is accommodating. Ask about the type and location of room you're reserving when booking. Rooms overlooking the canal are especially pleasant. **Pros:** modern construction; nice for families; large number of rooms makes it a good last-minute option. **Cons:** a bit remote from the Piazza; fee for Wi-Fi. ⊠ *Fondamenta della Sensa, Cannaregio 3319* ☎ *041/711001* ⊕ *www.morihotel.com* ⤴ *58 rooms, 2 suites* ⚤ *In-room: safe, refrigerator, DVD, Internet, Wi-Fi. In-hotel: room service, bar, laundry facilities, laundry service, Internet terminal, Wi-Fi, some pets allowed* ⊟ *AE, DC, MC, V* ⦿⦿ *BP* ☑ *San Marcuola/Madonna dell'Orto* ⊹ *D1.*

$$$–$$$$ ⊡ **Hotel Antico Doge.** Once the home of Doge Marino Falier, this palazzo has been modernized in an elegant Venetian style, with a wealth of textiles and some fine original furnishings. Some rooms have *baldacchini* (canopied beds) and views; all have fabric walls and hardwood floors. The location, on the main thoroughfare from the station to San Marco, is handy but can stay quite lively well into the night, especially

6

during festivals. An ample buffet breakfast is served in a room with a frescoed ceiling and a Murano chandelier. **Pros:** convenient to the Rialto. **Cons:** on a busy street; no outdoor garden or terrace; fee for Wi-Fi. ⊠ *Campo Santi Apostoli, Cannaregio 5643* ☏ *041/2411570* ⊕ *www.anticodoge.com* 🖙 *10 rooms, 9 junior suites, 1 suite* ⚃ *In-room: safe, Internet, Wi-Fi, In-hotel: room service, bar, laundry service, Wi-Fi, Internet terminal* ⊟ *MC, V* ⊚| *BP* Ⓥ *Ca' d'Oro/Rialto* ✢ *E3.*

WORD OF MOUTH

"I don't think you can select a 'wrong place' to stay in Venice. Each district or sestiere is unique. All are safe and delightful to be in."   —Mormor

$$$ 🏨 **Hotel Giorgione.** Family owned and operated, this quietly elegant hotel charms guests with its original terrazzo flooring, gracious courtyard and marble fountain, and billiard salon. The staff is professional and helpful, and the location is convenient for exploring in any direction. Rooms are decorated with traditional Venetian fabric and furniture, are comfortably appointed, and have either rooftop or courtyard views. Room sizes vary considerably, so book early and ask about the size and view. Seasonal refreshments are offered each afternoon. **Pros:** family run; unique ambience; elegant garden. **Cons:** no canal views. ⊠ *Off Campo Santi Apostoli, Cannaregio 4587* ☏ *041/5225810* ⊕ *www. hotelgiorgione.com* 🖙 *76 rooms* ⚃ *In-room: safe, refrigerator, Internet. In-hotel: bar, laundry service, Internet terminal* ⊟ *AE, DC, MC, V* ⊚| *BP* Ⓥ *Ca' d'Oro/Fondamente Nove* ✢ *E2.*

$$$–$$$$ 🏨 **Palazzo Abadessa.** At this elegant late-16th-century palazzo, you can
★   experience gracious hospitality and a luxurious atmosphere in keeping with Venice's patrician heritage. You'll feel like nobility yourself as you ascend the majestic staircase and enter the expansive piano nobile, which overlooks a side canal. Unusually spacious rooms are well appointed with antique furniture, frescoed ceilings, and fine silk fabrics. The location is remote enough to escape the San Marco throngs while still within striking distance of all of the major sights, and there's a private dock for taxi arrival. In summer, breakfast is served in a walled garden complete with sculptures and marble benches. Wi-Fi (free) is being added in 2010; call to make sure it's available. **Pros:** a unique, historic lodging; spacious rooms and garden; superb guest service. **Cons:** not the best choice for families with young children, who may have difficulty dodging the antique accessories. ⊠ *Calle Priuli off Strada Nova, Cannaregio 4011* ☏ *041/2413784* ⊕ *www.abadessa.com* 🖙 *8 rooms, 5 suites* ⚃ *In-room: safe, refrigerator, Wi-Fi. In-hotel: room service, bar, Wi-Fi hotspot, laundry service, Internet terminal, some pets allowed* ⊟ *AE, DC, MC, V* ⊚| *BP* Ⓥ *Ca' d'Oro* ✢ *E2.*

CASTELLO

$$$ 🏨 **Ca' Formenta.** In a residential rather than tourist area of Venice, Ca' Formenta offers high-quality services in a thoroughly removed 15th-century building. Front rooms have a wonderful view of the lagoon. The 15-minute stroll along the waterfront between Piazzo San Marco and the hotel is through a genuinely "local" part of the city, with plenty of cafés

and restaurants. One of the rear rooms has direct access to a pleasant rooftop terrace with tables. **Pros:** Castello area still feels like authentic Venice; convenient to the Piazza, the Lido, and the north lagoon islands. **Cons:** not as convenient to San Polo or upper Dorsoduro. ⊠ *Via Garibaldi, Castello 1650* ☎ *041/5285494* ⊕ *www.hotelcaformenta.it* ⚲ *12 rooms, 2 junior suites* ⚙ *In-room: safe, refrigerator, Internet, Wi-Fi (some). In-hotel: room service, bar, laundry service, Wi-Fi hotspot, some pets allowed* ⊟ *AE, DC, MC, V* ⦿ *BP* ⓥ *Arsenale/Giardini* ✛ *G5.*

$$$$ ⊞ **Hotel Londra Palace.** A wall of windows makes this the hotel of choice for soaking up extraordinary, sweeping views of the lagoon and the island of San Giorgio. The downstairs restaurant is all glass, light, and water views, and the superior rooms and junior suites offer the same spectacle. The vista must have been pleasing to Tchaikovsky, who wrote his Fourth Symphony here in 1877. Neoclassical public rooms, with splashes of blue-and-green glass suggesting the sea, play nicely off guest rooms, which have fine fabric, damask drapes, Biedermeier furniture, and Venetian glass. The staff is top-notch, as are the restaurant and the bar. **Pros:** superlative views; professional service. **Cons:** area is one of the most touristy in Venice, and the Riva's liveliness can extend late into the evening. ⊠ *Riva degli Schiavoni, Castello 4171* ☎ *041/5200533* ⊕ *www. londrapalace.com* ⚲ *36 rooms, 17 suites* ⚙ *In-room: safe, refrigerator, Internet, Wi-Fi. In-hotel: restaurant, room service, bars, laundry service, Internet terminal* ⊟ *AE, DC, MC, V* ⦿ *BP* ⓥ *San Zaccaria* ✛ *D2.*

$$$$ ⊞ **Metropole.** Eccentrics, eclectics, and fans of Antonio Vivaldi (who
Fodor's Choice taught music here) love the Metropole, a labyrinth of intimate, opu-
★ lent spaces featuring exotic Eastern influences and jammed with cabinets displaying collections of ivory-adorned cigarette cases, antique corkscrews, beaded bags, and more. The owner, a lifelong collector of unusual objects, fills common areas and the sumptuously appointed guest rooms with endless antiques. The best rooms are up on the roof, where there are also two spacious rooftop terraces. Only six of the standard double rooms offer lagoon views. Suites feature sparkling mosaic sunken baths, Fortuny fabrics, and other notable architectural details. Their Met restaurant has one of Venice's most acclaimed chefs, Corado Fasolato. **Pros:** owner has exquisite taste and collections; hotel harkens back to a gracious Venice of times past. **Cons:** one of the most densely touristed locations in the city. ⊠ *Riva degli Schiavoni, Castello 4149* ☎ *041/5205044* ⊕ *www.hotelmetropole.com* ⚲ *67 rooms, 13 junior suites, 9 suites* ⚙ *In-room: safe, refrigerator, Internet. In-hotel: restaurant, room service, bar, laundry service, Wi-Fi hotspot, some pets allowed* ⊟ *AE, DC, MC, V* ⦿ *BP* ⓥ *San Zaccaria* ✛ *F4.*

$ ⊞ **Santa Maria della Pietà.** Though this *casa per ferie* (vacation house) is more spartan than sumptuous, there's more light and space here than in many of Venice's four-star lodgings. The hotel, which occupies the upper floors of two historic palaces, has large windows, restored Venetian terrazzo floors, and a huge rooftop terrace with a coffee shop, bar, and unobstructed lagoon views. On top of these advantages, it's well situated—just 100 yards from the main waterfront and about a 10-minute walk from Saint Mark's. The shared bathrooms are plentiful, spacious, and scrupulously clean. Some rooms have en-suite baths, and

6

family rooms with up to six beds are available. **Pros:** space, light, and views at a bargain price. **Cons:** not luxurious; few amenities. ✉ *Calle della Pietà, Castello 3701* ☎ *041/2443639* ⊕ *www.pietavenezia.org/ casaferie.htm* ⇌ *15 rooms* ♿ *In-room: no phone, no TV. In-hotel: bar* ▭ *No credit cards* ⅋ *BP* Ⓥ *Arsenale/San Zaccaria* ⚓ *F4.*

DORSODURO

$$$$ 🏨 **Ca' Maria Adele.** One of Venice's most elegant small hotels is a mix of classic style—terrazzo floors, dramatic Murano chandeliers, antique furnishings—and touches of the contemporary, found in the African-wood reception area and breakfast room. Five dramatic "concept rooms" take on themes from Venetian history; the Doge's Room is draped in deep-red brocades, while the Oriental Room is inspired by the travels of Marco Polo. Ca' Maria Adele's location is a tranquil yet convenient spot near the church of Santa Maria della Salute. **Pros:** quiet and romantic; imaginative contemporary decor; free Wi-Fi. **Cons:** more-formal atmosphere may not suit young children. ✉ *Campo Santa Maria della Salute, Dorsoduro 111* ☎ *041/5203078* ⊕ *www.camariaadele. it* ⇌ *12 rooms, 4 suites* ♿ *In-room: safe, refrigerator, Wi-Fi. In-hotel: room service, bar, laundry service, Wi-Fi hotspot, some pets allowed* ▭ *AE, DC, MC, V* ⅋ *BP* Ⓥ *Salute* ⚓ *D5.*

$$ 🏨 **Casa Rezzonico.** Rooms here are the rarest occurrence in Venice: an
Fodor's Choice excellent value. A sunny fondamenta and canal front the hotel entrance;
★ a private garden beckons you to enjoy the inner courtyard for breakfast or after a long day of sightseeing. Rooms vary in size but are pleasant and comfortable, with traditional furnishings that compliment the Venetian terrazzo or parquet flooring and overlook either the garden or the canal. Young owners Matteo and Mattia are attentive and helpful, and the location is convenient for exploring the sights from the Rialto to the Salute. **Pros:** a garden for relaxing; canal views at a reasonable rate; lively campo nearby; great for families. **Cons:** must reserve well in advance. ✉ *Fondamenta Gherardini, Dorsoduro 2813* ☎ *041/2770653* ⊕ *www.casarezzonico.it* ⇌ *6 rooms* ♿ *In-room: safe, Internet, Wi-Fi. In-hotel: room service, Wi-Fi hotspot* ▭ *AE, MC, V* ⅋ *BP* Ⓥ *Ca' Rezzonico* ⚓ *B4.*

$$$$ 🏨 **Charming House DD 724.** This ultramodern boutique hotel abandons all things traditionally Venetian, opting instead to create the air of a stylish residence. With impeccable, minimalist decor, Charming House has a contemporary, warmly romantic, and occasionally even dramatic atmosphere. Some rooms overlook small canals and side calli; apartment options with kitchenettes are available. The location is convenient to the Guggenheim, Accademia, Zattere, and San Marco. Art borrowed from neighboring museums is on display in common areas. The Web site lists additional locations with similar ambience in Castello. **Pros:** unique decor; variety of lodging options. **Cons:** not traditional Venetian style. ✉ *Ramo da Mula off Campo San Vio, Dorsoduro 724* ☎ *041/2770262* ⊕ *www.thecharminghouse.com* ⇌ *5 rooms, 2 junior suites, 2 suites* ♿ *In-room: safe, refrigerator (some), Wi-Fi. In-hotel: room service, laundry service, Internet terminal, some pets allowed* ▭ *AE, DC, MC, V* ⅋ *BP* Ⓥ *Accademia* ⚓ *D5.*

$$$–$$$$ ⊡ **Hotel American–Dinesen.** This quiet, family-run hotel has a yellow stucco facade typical of Venetian houses. A hall decorated with reproduction antiques and Oriental rugs leads to a breakfast room reminiscent of a theater foyer, with red velvet chairs and gilt wall lamps. Guest rooms are spacious and tastefully furnished in sage-green and delicate pink fabrics with lacquered Venetian-style furniture throughout. Some front rooms have terraces with canal views. Although the four-story building has no elevator, you'll have assistance with your luggage, if needed. The exceptional service will help you feel at home. Three adjacent apartments are also available. **Pros:** high degree of personal service; on a bright, quiet, exceptionally picturesque canal; free Wi-Fi. **Cons:** no elevator. ⊠ *San Vio, Dorsoduro 628* ☎ *041/5204733* ⊕ *www. hotelamerican.com* ⇩ *28 rooms, 2 suites* ⌂ *In-room: safe, refrigerator, Wi-Fi. In-hotel: room service, bar, laundry service, Wi-Fi hotspot, some pets allowed* ⊟ *AE, MC, V* Ⓨ⍉⎮ *BP* ☑ *Accademia/Salute* ⊹ *C5.*

$$–$$$ ⊡ **La Calcina.** In 1877, *Stones of Venice* author John Ruskin lodged at
★ the eclectic La Calcina, which sits in an enviable position along the sunny Zattere, and has front rooms offering heady vistas across the expansive Giudecca Canal. You can sunbathe on the *altana* (wooden roof terrace) or enjoy an afternoon tea in one of the lounge's reading corners with flickering candlelight and barely perceptible classical music. A stone staircase leads to the rooms upstairs, which have parquet floors, original art deco furniture, and firm beds. Besides full meals at lunch and dinner, the Piscina bar and restaurant offers drinks and fresh snacks all day in the elegant dining room or on the waterside terrace. A variety of apartments is also available. One single room does not have a private bath. **Pros:** rare rooftop altana; panoramic views from some rooms. **Cons:** quite eclectic; not for travelers who want contemporary surroundings; no elevator. ⊠ *Dorsoduro 780* ☎ *041/5206466* ⊕ *www. lacalcina.com* ⇩ *27 rooms, 26 with bath; 5 suites* ⌂ *In-room: safe, refrigerator, Internet, Wi-Fi. In-hotel: restaurant, room service, bar, laundry service* ⊟ *AE, DC, MC, V* Ⓨ⍉⎮ *BP* ☑ *Zattere* ⊹ *C5.*

$$ ⊡ **Locanda San Barnaba.** This family-run establishment, housed in a
★ 16th-century palazzo, is handily located just off the Ca' Rezzonico vaporetto stop. The arches in the garden walls peek through to the side canal, and there's a rooftop terrace for viewing Venetian sunsets. There's no elevator, but the staff will happily assist with your luggage and ground-level rooms are available. The two Superior rooms have original 18th-century frescoes, and one of the junior suites has two small balconies and is exceptionally luminous, but all the rooms are spacious and attractive. **Pros:** outdoor space; a variety of room options; excellent value. **Cons:** no elevator. ⊠ *Calle del Traghetto, Dorsoduro 2785–2786* ☎ *041/2411233* ⊕ *www.locanda-sanbarnaba.com* ⇩ *11 rooms, 2 junior suites* ⌂ *In-room: safe, Internet. In-hotel: room service, bar* ⊟ *AE, DC, MC, V* Ⓨ⍉⎮ *BP* ☑ *Ca' Rezzonico* ⊹ *C4.*

$$$–$$$$ ⊡ **Palazzo Stern.** The gracious terrace that eases onto the Grand Canal
★ is almost reason alone to stay here. An opulent refurbishment of this early-15th-century neo-Gothic palace, carried out by the Stern family in the early 20th century, incorporated marble-columned arches, terrazzo floors, frescoed ceilings, mosaics, and a majestic carved staircase (copied

6

from the Ca' d'Oro). It's also one of a limited number of palaces in the city that have not one, but two exposed sides decorated, one facing the Canal Grand, the other Rio Malpaga. Inside, some rooms have tufted walls, parquet flooring, and 42-inch, flat-screen TVs. From the rooftop terrace—which has a Jacuzzi—you get a classic Venetian view: over the city's roofs to the Campanile, and even to the Dolomites on a clear day. Lodgings range from standard rooms to junior suites to an eclectic attic suite. **Pros:** excellent service; lovely views from many rooms; modern renovation retains historic ambience. **Cons:** no in-house restaurant (at this writing). ⊠ *Calle del Traghetto, Dorsoduro 2792* ☎ *041/2770869* ⊕ *www.palazzostern.com* ↩ *21 rooms, 3 suites* ♿ *In-room: safe, refrigerator, Wi-Fi. In-hotel: room service, bar, laundry service* ═ *AE, MC, V* ⦿*EP* Ⓥ *Ca' Rezzonico* ✤ *C4.*

$$–$$$ 🔝 **Pensione Accademia Villa Maravege.** Aptly nicknamed "Villa of the Wonders," this patrician retreat once served as the Russian embassy and was the fictional residence of Katharine Hepburn's character in the film *Summertime.* Outside, a garden awaits just beyond an iron gate, complete with a mini Palladian-style villa, flower beds, stone cupids, and verdant trees—all rarities in Venice. The hotel is on a peaceful promontory where two side canals converge with the Grand Canal. The conservative rooms are outfitted with Venetian-style antiques and fine tapestry. Book well in advance. **Pros:** a historic, classic Venetian property. **Cons:** formal setting with antiques not well suited to children; fee for Wi-Fi. ⊠ *Fondamenta Bollani, Dorsoduro 1058* ☎ *041/5210188* ⊕ *www.pensioneaccademia.it* ↩ *27 rooms, 2 suites* ♿ *In-room: safe, Internet, Wi-Fi. In-hotel: bar, laundry service, Wi-Fi hotspot* ═ *AE, DC, MC, V* ⦿*BP* Ⓥ *Accademia* ✤ *C4.*

LAGOON

$$$$ 🔝 **San Clemente Palace.** If you prefer wide-open spaces to the intimacy of Venice, this is your hotel. This massive complex occupies an entire island, about 15 minutes from Piazza San Marco by (free) shuttle launch, with acres of parkland, a swimming pool, tennis courts, a wellness center, and four restaurants. The 19th-century buildings are on the site of a 12th-century monastery, of which only the chapel remains. They form a large quadrangle and contain spacious, modern rooms. The view back to Venice, with the Dolomites behind on a clear day, is stunning. You get all the five-star comforts here: it even has three holes of golf. **Pros:** true five-star service and amenities. **Cons:** quite remote. ⊠ *Isola di San Clemente 1* ☎ *041/2445001* ⊕ *www.sanclemente.thi.it* ↩ *107 rooms, 96 suites* ♿ *In-room: safe, refrigerator, Internet, Wi-Fi. In-hotel: 4 restaurants, bar, golf course, tennis courts, pool, gym, spa, laundry service, some pets allowed* ═ *AE, DC, MC, V* ⦿*BP* ✤ *G6.*

SAN MARCO

$$ 🔝 **Al Teatro.** Behind the Fenice Theater, just off the Maria Callas Bridge, this small B&B is the renovated home of owners Fabio and Eleonora—in fact, it's where Eleanora was born. There are three spacious, comfortable, and conscientiously appointed rooms with private

baths, each overlooking a gondola-filled canal; the largest r̄
a broad balcony. An ample breakfast (served at a common table,
exceptional service make Al Teatro an excellent value and a relaxi
choice in the sometimes-frenetic San Marco atmosphere. Book well in
advance. **Pros:** airy rooms; convenient San Marco location; good for
families. **Cons:** the intimacy of a three-room B&B is not for everyone.
⊠ *Fondamenta della Fenice, San Marco 2554* ☎ *041/5204271* ⊕ *www.
bedandbreakfastalteatro.com* ⇦ *3 rooms* ⌂ *In-room: safe, refrigerator,
Wi-Fi. In-hotel: room service, Internet terminal, Wi-Fi hotspot* ⊟ *AE,
MC, V* ⏘ *BP* Ⓥ *Santa Maria del Giglio* ✚ *D4.*

$$$$ 🛈 **Bauer Il Palazzo.** This is the ultimate word in luxury, Venetian-style.
★ Surroundings are spacious yet intimate, with high ceilings, tufted walls
of Bevilacqua and Rubelli fabrics, Murano glass, marble bathrooms,
and damask drapes; no two rooms decorated the same. Many rooms
have sweeping views over the Grand Canal and beyond. Breakfast is
served on Venice's highest rooftop terrace, appropriately named Il Settimo Cielo (Seventh Heaven). The highly lauded De Pisis restaurant
overlooks the Grand Canal. The outdoor hot tub, also on the rooftop,
offers views of La Serenissima that will leave you breathless, and personable, professional staff will accommodate your every whim. **Pros:**
pampering service, high-end luxury. **Cons:** in one of the busiest areas
of the city. ⊠ *Campo San Moisè, San Marco 1413/d* ☎ *041/5207022*
⊕ *www.ilpalazzovenezia.com* ⇦ *44 rooms, 38 suites* ⌂ *In-room: safe,
refrigerator, DVD, Wi-Fi. In-hotel: restaurant, room service, bars, gym,
laundry service, Internet terminal, some pets allowed* ⊟ *AE, DC, MC,
V* ⏘ *EP* Ⓥ *San Marco/Vallaresso* ✚ *E4.*

$$ 🛈 **Ca' dei Dogi.** Amid the crush of mediocre hotels around Piazza San
Marco, this delightful choice, in a 15th-century palace and in a quiet
courtyard secluded from the melee, stands out. The thoughtful, personal
touches added by owners Stefano and Susanna are evident everywhere,
from the six individually decorated rooms (some with private terraces),
to the carefully chosen contemporary furniture, to classic Venetian ele-
ments such as wall tapestries and mosaic tiles. Service is highly personal:
guests are often welcomed by one of the owners. There's a courtyard
where you can enjoy breakfast or an evening interlude, and one attic
apartment is available. **Pros:** terraces with views of the Doge's Palace.
Cons: rooms are not expansive; few amenities; nearby dining selection
is limited. ⊠ *Corte Santa Scolastica, Castello 4242* ☎ *041/2413751*
⊕ *www.cadeidogi.it* ⇦ *6 rooms* ⌂ *In-room: safe, Internet, Wi-Fi. In-
hotel: room service, Internet terminal, some pets allowed* ⊟ *AE, DC,
MC, V* ⏘ *BP* Ⓥ *San Zaccaria* ✚ *F4.*

$$$ 🛈 **Locanda Orseolo.** This cozy, elegant hotel offers a welcome respite
Fodor's Choice from the throngs churning around Piazza San Marco. Family owned,
★ it has an attentive staff and comfortable, well-appointed rooms. Classic Venetian designs are given a Carnevale theme, with each room's
decor dedicated to one of the traditional masks. The relaxed atmosphere
pervades at breakfast, where it's common to get engrossed in conversation with the other guests. **Pros:** intimate and romantic; extraordinarily
friendly staff; Wi-Fi is free. **Cons:** in the one of the busiest and most
commercial areas of the city. ⊠ *Corte Zorzi, off Campo San Gallo, San*

6

ɔ 1083 ☎ 041/5204827 ⊕ *www.locandaorseolo.com* ↪ *12 rooms* ⸱room: safe, refrigerator, Wi-Fi. In-hotel: room service, laundry ⸱ies, laundry service, Internet terminal, Wi-Fi hotspot ▭ AE, DC, V ⊙ Closed Jan. ⦅❍⦆BP Ⓥ Rialto/Vallaresso ✛ E4.*

vecento. This small, family-run hotel is on a quiet street a 10-min-⸱alk from the Piazza San Marco. Inspired by the style of Mariano ᵣₒᵣᵤₙy, the early-1900s Spanish artist and fashion designer who made Venice his home, the intimate rooms are a surprisingly elegant mélange of multiethnic and exotic furnishings. The Mediterranean, Indian, and Venetian fabrics, silverware, chandeliers, and furniture create a sensual turn-of-the-20th-century atmosphere. In fine weather, breakfast is served in the inner courtyard. **Pros:** intimate, romantic atmosphere; free Wi-Fi. **Cons:** a bit of a walk to vaporetto stop. ✉ *Calle del Dose, Campo San Maurizio, San Marco 2683/84* ☎ *041/2413765* ⊕ *www.novecento. biz* ↪ *9 rooms* ⚸ *In-room: safe, refrigerator, Internet, Wi-Fi. In-hotel: bar, laundry service, Internet terminal, Wi-Fi hotspot, some pets allowed* ▭ *AE, DC, MC, V* ⦅❍⦆*BP* Ⓥ *Santa Maria del Giglio* ✛ *C4.*

$$$$ ⦅⚏⦆**Palazzo Sant'Angelo sul Canal Grande.** There's a distinguished yet comfortable feel to this elegant palazzo, which is large enough to deliver expected facilities and services but small enough to pamper its guests. Rooms have tapestry-adorned walls and Carrara and Alpine marble in the bath; those facing the Grand Canal have balconies that practically bring the canal to you. Common areas include an entrance hall with original Palladian flooring, a bright front lounge, and an intimate bar that puts the canal almost at arm's length. Ask ahead for a room with a view. **Pros:** convenient to vaporetto stop. **Cons:** some rooms have no special view; fee for Wi-Fi. ✉ *Campo Sant'Angelo, San Marco 3488* ☎ *041/2411452* ⊕ *www.palazzosantangelo.com* ↪ *14 rooms* ⚸ *In-room: safe, refrigerator, Internet, Wi-Fi. In-hotel: bar, laundry service, Wi-Fi hotspot, some pets allowed* ▭ *AE, DC, MC, V* ⦅❍⦆*EP* Ⓥ *Sant'Angelo* ✛ *C4.*

SAN POLO

$$ ⦅⚏⦆**Acca Hotel.** This small, newish hotel is one of Venice's better moderately priced options, with bright, well-appointed rooms and simple but attentive service. Furnishings are updated, traditional, and comfortable; suites have tufted walls and Jacuzzis. There's no staff on hand in the evening, but you get your own key. The location is good, and breakfast is served in the courtyard, weather permitting. **Pros:** lots of amenities; modern construction; an excellent value. **Cons:** no canal views; no night porter. ✉ *Calle Pezzana, San Polo 2160* ☎ *041/2440126* ⊕ *www. accahotel.com* ↪ *8 rooms, 1 suite* ⚸ *In-room: safe, refrigerator, Wi-Fi. In-hotel: laundry service, Internet terminal, Wi-Fi hotspot* ▭ *MC, V* ⦅❍⦆*BP* Ⓥ *San Silvestro* ✛ *C3.*

$$ ⦅⚏⦆**Ca' Angeli.** The heirs of a Venetian architect have transformed his former residence, on the third and top floors of a palace along the Grand Canal, into an elegant B&B. It retains the classic style instilled by the former owner—most of the furniture was his, including an 18th-century briar-wood bureau, and there's a private library accessible to guests. The five rooms and two suites have views of either the Grand Canal or a side canal—or in the case of the smallish room 6, rooftops from a terrace twice the size of the room. A rich breakfast, including select cheeses and meats from local producers, is served in a salon overlooking the Grand Canal. There's also an attic apartment option. **Pros:** historic residence with Grand Canal views; helpful staff. **Cons:** a bit of a walk from the vaporetto stop; credit cards accepted only for stays of two or more nights. ✉ *Calle del Traghetto della Madoneta, San Polo 1434* 🖃 *041/5232480* ⊕ *www.caangeli.it* ⇆ *5 rooms, 1 junior suite, 1 suite, 1 apartment* ⚭ *In-room: safe, refrigerator, Wi-Fi. In-hotel: Wi-Fi hotspot* ▤ *MC, V* ⧀*BP* ☑ *San Silvestro* ✛ *C3.*

$$ 🏨 **Corte 1321.** If you're looking for something more up-to-date than the 18th-century-style decor that predominates in Venetian hotels, try Corte 1321, which is nestled away off the main drag. It has friendly, personal service; spacious, carefully renovated rooms with sparkling baths and "ethnic-chic" decor; and an intimate garden. Unwind here after a long day of exploring, perhaps sharing discoveries of the day with other guests. Corte 1321's owner is an American of Italian descent. **Pros:** lively, eclectic atmosphere great for meeting other guests. **Cons:** no canal views. ✉ *Campiello Ca' Bernardi, San Polo 1321* 🖃 *041/5224923* ⊕ *www.corte1321.com* ⇆ *4 rooms, 1 mini-apartment* ⚭ *In-room: safe, Internet, Wi-Fi. In-hotel: bar, laundry service, Internet terminal, Wi-Fi hotspot* ▤ *MC, V* ⊘ *Closed Jan.* ⧀*BP* ☑ *San Silvestro* ✛ *D3.*

$$–$$$ 🏨 **Oltre il Giardino–Casaifrari.** It's easy to overlook—and it can be a challenge to find—this secluded palazzo, sheltered behind a brick wall just over the bridge from the Frari church. Especially in high season, the eight-room hotel with airy, individually decorated rooms and an expansive garden is an oasis of peace. The prevalent white-and-pastel color scheme (in fact, each room is named for its predominant hue) and elegant, understated decor contribute to a relaxed, high-country ambience not found anywhere else in the city. Antiques complement the contemporary but unimposing furnishings. The house was once the residence of Alma Mahler, widow of composer Gustav Mahler and a fascinating woman in her own right; it still conveys her style and charm today. The owner's service and professional attention is as conscientious as the renovation. **Pros:** a peaceful, gracious, and convenient setting. **Cons:** no Grand Canal views. ✉ *San Polo 2542* 🖃 *041/2750015* ⊕ *www.oltreilgiardino-venezia.com* ⇆ *4 rooms, 4 suites* ⚭ *In-room: safe, refrigerator, Internet, Wi-Fi. In-hotel: room service, bar, Internet terminal, some pets allowed* ▤ *AE, DC, MC, V* ⧀*BP* ☑ *San Tomà* ✛ *C3.*

$$$$ 🏨 **Palazzo Barbarigo.** It is not unusual to find an opulent hotel along the Grand Canal; it is unusual to discover black marble, matte lacquer, indirect lighting, and decidedly art deco contours ensconced in a 16th-century Venetian palace. Massive mirrors soar floor to ceiling to accent the spaciousness, and the minimalist decor draws your attention to every detail. Each of the 18 rooms, whether suite or standard, feels like a refuge; all have Grand Canal or side-canal views and 42-inch flat-panel TVs. The expansive, ultrachic bar runs the length of the soaring piano nobile to a balcony above the canal, just large enough for a table and two chairs. There's a front water entrance; a narrow calle leads you in

6

from the back, right past the entrance to the Palazzo Pisani Moretta. **Pros:** small; lavish; an uncommon ambience. **Cons:** no outdoor terrace. ⊠ *San Polo 3765* ☎ *041/74072* ⊕ *www.palazzobarbarigo.it* ⇗ *8 rooms, 6 junior suites* ⚭ *In-room: safe, refrigerator, Internet, Wi-Fi. In-hotel: bar, laundry service* ⊟ *AE, DC, MC, V* ❢❁❢ *BP* Ⓥ *San Tomà* ⊹ *C4.*

SANTA CROCE

$$ ☎ **Hotel al Ponte Mocenigo.** A columned courtyard welcomes you to this elegant, charming palazzo, former home of the Santa Croce branch of the Mocenigo family (which has a few doges in its past). The meticulously renovated interior has an updated 18th-century Venetian feel, incorporating a number of distinctive architectural elements such as open-beam ceilings, fireplaces transformed into writing nooks, and Murano chandeliers. The courtyard offers an ideal ambience for breakfast or an aperitivo, and there's a Turkish sauna for unwinding after a day of seeing sights. The hotel is located on a side canal convenient to any number of sights, eateries, and shops. **Pros:** enchanting courtyard; water access; friendly staff; free Wi-Fi. **Cons:** rooms do not overlook a canal (although the courtyard and foyer do). ⊠ *Fondamento de Rimpeto a Ca' Mocenigo, Santa Croce 2063* ☎ *041/5244797* ⊕ *www. alpontemocenigo.com* ⇗ *10 rooms, 1 junior suite* ⚭ *In-room: safe, refrigerator, Wi-Fi. In-hotel: room service, bar, Internet terminal, Wi-Fi hotspot* ⊟ *AE, DC, MC, V* ❢❁❢ *BP* Ⓥ *San Stae* ⊹ *C2.*

NIGHTLIFE AND THE ARTS

THE ARTS

A Guest in Venice, an online portal and a monthly bilingual booklet free at most hotels, is an up-to-date guide to Venice happenings. It also includes information about pharmacies, vaporetto and bus lines, and the main trains and flights. Visit ⊕ *www.aguestinvenice.com* for a preview of musical, artistic, and sporting events. *Venezia News* (VENews), available at newsstands, has similar information but also includes in-depth articles about noteworthy events. The tourist office publishes a handy, free quarterly *Calendar* in Italian and English, listing daily events and current museum and venue hours. *Venezia da Vivere* is a seasonal guide listing nightspots and live music. Several Venice Web sites allow you to scan the cultural horizon before you arrive; try ⊕ *www. turismovenezia.it, www.veneziasi.it, www.veniceonline.it,* and *www. venicebanana.com.* And don't ignore the posters you'll see plastered on the walls as you walk—they're often the most up-to-date information you can find.

CARNEVALE

The first historical evidence of *Carnevale* (Carnival) in Venice dates from 1097, and for centuries the city marked the days preceding *quaresima* (Lent) with abundant feasting and wild celebrations. The word *carnevale* is derived from the words for meat (*carne*) and to remove (*levare*), as eating meat was prohibited during Lent. Venice earned its international reputation as the "city of Carnevale" in the 18th century, when partying would begin right after Epiphany (January 6) and the city seemed to be one continuous decadent masquerade. With the Republic's fall in 1797, the city lost a great deal of its vitality, and the tradition of Carnevale celebrations was abandoned.

It was revived in the 1970s when residents began taking to the calli and campi in their own impromptu celebrations. It didn't take long for the tourist industry to embrace the revival as a means to stimulate business during low season. The efforts were successful. Each year over the 10- to 12-day Carnevale period (ending on the Tuesday before Ash Wednesday) more than a half million people attend concerts, theater and street performances, masquerade balls, historical processions, fashion shows, and contests. Since 2008, Carnevale has been organized by the **Consorzio Venezia Marketing & Eventi** (✉ *Dorsoduro 948* ☎ *041/2412988* ⊕ *www.carnevale.venezia.it*). *A Guest in Venice* is also a complete guide to public and private Carnevale festivities. Stop by the **tourist office** (☎ *041/5298711* ⊕ *www.turismovenezia.it*) or Venice Pavilion for information, but be aware they can be mobbed. If you're not planning on joining in the revelry, you'd be wise to choose another time to visit Venice. Crowds clog the streets (which become one-way, with police directing foot traffic), bridges are designated "no-stopping" zones to avoid gridlock, and prices skyrocket.

FESTIVALS

The **Biennale** (⊕ *www.labiennale.org*) cultural institution organizes events year-round, including the **Venice Film Festival,** which begins the last week of August. **La Biennale di Venezia,** an international exhibition of contemporary art, is held in odd-numbered years, usually from mid-June to early November, at the Giardini della Biennale, and in the impressive Arsenale. On the third weekend of July, the **Festa del Redentore** *(Feast of the Redeemer)* commemorates the end of a 16th-century plague that killed about 47,000 city residents. Just as doges have done annually for centuries, you, too, can make a pilgrimage across the temporary bridge connecting the Zattere to the Giudecca. Venetians take to the water to watch fireworks at midnight, but if you can't find a boat, the Giudecca is the best place to be. Young people traditionally greet sunrise on the Lido beach while their elders attend church.

MUSIC

The vast majority of music you'll hear is classical, with Venice's famed composer, Vivaldi, frequently featured. Churches, palazzi, and scuole *grandi* host a broad variety of concerts and even opera, as do the Ca' Rezzonico and Querini-Stampalia museums. To find out what's on, stop by the tourist pavilion, or look in the tourist office's *Shows and Events Calendar* and in *A Guest in Venice* (⊕ *www.aguestinvenice.com*). You can book at the tourist office, any travel agency, the venue itself, or online with Music in Venice (⊕ *musicinvenice.com*).

HelloVenezia (☎ *041/2424* ⊕ *www.hellovenezia.com* ☉ *Daily 8–8*) has information about events at the Fenice, the Malibran, and a variety of other venues. Check their online calendar and purchase your tickets

on the Web site or through any booking service. Scan the posters and notices on the streets to spot free concerts offered by local choral groups and music schools.

OPERA

Teatro La Fenice (⊠ *Campo San Fantin, San Marco* ☎ *041/786511* ⊕ *www.teatrolafenice.it*), one of Italy's oldest opera houses, has witnessed many memorable premieres, including the 1853 first-night flop of Verdi's *La Traviata*. It's also had its share of disasters, including not one but two fires, the most recent being deliberately set in January 1996. It was impeccably and luxuriously restored, and reopened to great fanfare in 2004. Visit the HelloVenezia Web site (⇨ *above*) for a schedule of performances and to buy tickets. HelloVenezia also handles tickets for the smaller, enchanting **Teatro Malibran** (⊠ *Campo San Fantin, Cannaregio* ☎ *041/786511* ⊕ *www.teatrolafenice.it*).

NIGHTLIFE

Piazza San Marco is a popular meeting place in nice weather, when the cafés stay open late and all seem to be competing to offer the best live music. The younger crowd, Venetians and visitors alike, tends to gravitate toward the area around Rialto Bridge, with Campi San Bartolomeo and San Luca on one side and Campo Rialto Nuovo on the other. Especially popular with university students are the bars along Cannaregio's Fondamenta della Misericordia and around Campo Santa Margherita and San Pantalon. Pick up a booklet of *2Night* or visit ⊕ *www.2night. it* for nightlife listings and reviews.

BARS AND CLUBS

Venice Jazz Club (⊠ *Fondamenta del Squero, Dorsoduro 3102* ☎ *041/5232056 or 340/1504985* ⊕ *venicejazzclub.com* ✉ €*25*) is a throwback to the old "listening rooms." The live jazz you'll hear ranges from the contemporary to tributes to past jazz legends; there are often special guests. Entrance includes a selection of cold meats served prior to the nightly set. You may also reserve online at www. musicinvenice.com.

Bácaro Jazz (⊠ *Across from Rialto post office* ☎ *041/5285249*) has (not live) music and meals until 2 AM, and its gregarious staff is unlikely to let you feel lonely. Nothing special by day, **Bar Torino** (⊠ *Campo San Luca* ☎ *041/5223914*) is one of Venice's liveliest nightspots, open late and spilling out onto the campo in summer.

The patio in front of **L'Olandese Volante** (⊠ *Campo San Lio near Rialto* ☎ *041/5289349*) is a popular, central, relaxing hangout; how late depends on the crowd.

Hidden in plain sight behind the plate-glass windows of a Mondadori bookstore, the simply named **Bàcaro** (⊠ *Piscina Frezzeria, San Marco 1345* ☎ *041/2960687*) adds a much-needed dash of modern to the antiquities surrounding Piazza San Marco. The circular bar is more crowded and lively than the restaurant upstairs, and serves strong cocktails until 2 AM.

6

The **Martini Scala Club** (⊠ *Campo San Fantin, San Marco 1983* ☎ *041/5224121*), the Antico Martini restaurant's elegant bar, has live dance music from 10 PM to 3:30 AM. Full meals are served until 2 AM.

One of the hippest bars for the late-night, chill-out crowd, **Centrale** (⊠ *Piscina Frezzeria, San Marco 1659/B* ☎ *041/2960664*) is in a former movie theater—and the crowd does look more Hollywood than Venice. Excellent mojitos and other mixed drinks, black-leather couches, and dim lighting strike a loungey note, and the DJ keeps the beats cool.

Campo Santa Margherita is a student hangout all day and into the night. Try **Orange** (⊠ *Campo Santa Margherita, Dorsoduro 3054/A* ☎ *041/5234740*) for sandwiches, drinks, and soccer games on a massive screen. Bohemian **Il Caffè** (⊠ *Campo Santa Margherita, Dorsoduro 2963* ☎ *041/5287998*), also known as Caffè Rosso for its red exterior, is especially popular in nice weather.

SHOPPING

Alluring shops abound in Venice. You'll find countless vendors of trademark Venetian wares such as glass and lace; the authenticity of some goods can be suspect, but they're often pleasing to the eye regardless of their place of origin. For more-sophisticated tastes (and deeper pockets), there are jewelers, antiques dealers, and high-fashion boutiques on a par with those in Italy's larger cities but often maintaining a uniquely Venetian flair. There are also some interesting craft and art studios, where you can find high-quality one-of-a-kind articles, from handmade shoes to decorative lamps and mirrors.

If you pass a shop that interests you, make sure to mark your map or collect their business card so you'll be sure to find it again in the maze of tiny streets. Regular store hours are usually 9 to 12:30 and 3:30 or 4 to 7:30; some stores close Saturday afternoons or Monday mornings. Food shops are open 8 to 1 and 5 to 7:30, and may close Wednesday afternoon and all day Sunday. Many tourist-oriented shops are open all day, every day. Some shops close for both a summer and a winter vacation.

FOOD MARKETS

Smaller fresh markets dot the city, but the morning open-air fruit-and-vegetable market at **Rialto** offers animated local color and commerce. On Tuesday through Saturday mornings the **fish market** (adjacent to the Rialto produce market) will amaze you with an impressive lesson in ichthyology; it's fun to count the number of species you've never seen before. You can also find a lively food market weekday mornings on **Via Garibaldi** in the Castello district, in the San Leonardo area in Cannaregio, and in Campo San Margherita in Dorsoduro.

SHOPPING DISTRICTS

The **San Marco** area is full of shops and couture boutiques such as Armani, Missoni, Valentino, Fendi, and Versace. **Le Mercerie**, the Frezzeria, Calle dei Fabbri, and Calle Larga XXII Marzo, all leading from Piazza San Marco, are some of Venice's busiest shopping streets. Other good shopping areas surround Calle del Teatro and Campi San Salvador, Manin, San Fantin, and San Bartolomeo. You can find somewhat less expensive, more varied and imaginative shops between the Rialto Bridge and San Polo and in Santa Croce, and art galleries in Dorsoduro from the Salute to the Accademia.

SPECIALTY STORES

ART GLASS

The glass of Murano is Venice's number-one product, and you'll be confronted by mind-boggling displays of traditional and contemporary glassware, too much of it kitsch. Traditional Venetian glass is hot, blown glass, not lead crystal; it comes in myriad forms including the classic ornate goblets and chandeliers, to beads, vases, sculpture, and more. To make a smart purchase, take your time and be selective. You can learn a great deal without sales pressure at the Museo del Vetro on Murano; unfortunately you'll likely find the least-attractive glass where public demonstrations are offered. Although prices in Venice and on Murano are comparable, shops in Venice with wares from various glassworks may charge slightly less. ■ TIP→ A "free" taxi to Murano always comes with sales pressure. Take the vaporetto that's included in your transit pass, and if you prefer, a private guide who specializes in the subject but has no affinity to any specific furnace.

Domus (✉ *Fondamenta dei Vetrai, Murano 82* ☎ *041/739215*) has a selection of smaller objects and jewelry from the best glassworks.

For chic, contemporary glassware, Carlo Moretti is a good choice; his designs are on display at **L'Isola** (✉ *Campo San Moisè, San Marco 1468* ☎ *041/5231973* ⊕ *www.carlomoretti.com*).

Go to Michel Paciello's **Paropàmiso** (✉ *Frezzeria, San Marco 1701* ☎ *041/5227120*) for stunning Venetian glass beads and traditional jewelry from all over the world.

Pauly & C (✉ *Piazza San Marco 73 and 77, San Marco* ☎ *041/5235484 or 041/2770279* ⊕ *www.pauly.it*), established in 1866, features a truly impressive selection of authentic Murano art glass (both traditional and contemporary styles) by the most accomplished masters—and at better prices than on the island. The showroom at No. 73 houses the more traditional collection; at No. 77 you can find works by artists and designers.

Venini (✉ *Piazzetta dei Leoncini 314, San Marco* ☎ *041/5224045* ⊕ *www.venini.com*) has been an institution since the 1930s, attracting some of the foremost names in glass design. Visit their Web site to see a series of glass artisans in action. For a more refined experience and to see some of their best offerings, visit the **Venini Showroom** (✉ *Fondamenta Vetrai 47, Murano* ☎ *041/2737211*).

LACE AND FABRICS

The best of Burano's renowned lace-making tradition is rarely represented by the examples you'll see on display. However, at **Il Merletto** (✉ *Sotoportego del Cavalletto under the Procuratie Vecchie, Piazza San Marco 95* ☎ *041/5208406*), you can ask for the authentic, handmade lace safeguarded in drawers behind the counter. This is the only place in Venice connected with the students of the Scuola del Merletto in Burano, who, officially, do not sell to the public. Hours of operation are daily 10 to 5.

Jesurum (✉ *Via Belloto 30, Mestre* ☎ *041/713300* ⊕ *www.jesurum.it*) has been the name for fine linen and Burano lace designs for bed, bath, and table since 1870. Go to **Lorenzo Rubelli** (✉ *Palazzo Corner Spinelli, San Marco 3877* ☎ *041/5236110* ⊕ *www.rubelli.com*) for the same brocades, damasks, and cut velvets used by the world's most prestigious decorators. **Venetia Studium** (✉ *Calle Larga XXII Marzo, San Marco 2403* ☎ *041/5229281*✉ *Calle Larga XXII Marzo, San Marco 723* ☎ *041/5229859* ⊕ *www.venetiastudium.com*) sells silk scarves, bags, and cushion covers, as well as the famous Fortuny lamps.

MASKS

Guerrino Lovato, proprietor of **Mondonovo** (✉ *Rio Terà Canal, Dorsoduro 3063* ☎ *041/5287344* ⊕ *www.mondonovomaschere.it*) is one of the most respected mask makers in town. He was called on to oversee reconstruction of reliefs and sculptures in Teatro La Fenice after it burned to the ground in 1996.

GETTING HERE AND AROUND

▌ AIR TRAVEL

Air travel to Italy is frequent and virtually problem-free, except for airport- or airline-related union strikes that may cause delays. Although most nonstop flights are to Rome and Milan, many travelers find it more convenient to connect through a European hub to Florence, Pisa, Venice, Bologna, or another smaller airport. The airport in Venice also caters to international carriers.

Flying time to Milan or Rome is approximately 8–8½ hours from New York, 10–11 hours from Chicago, and 11½ hours from Los Angeles.

Labor strikes are frequent and can affect not only air travel but also local transit that serves airports (private transit is not affected by strikes, however). Confirm flights within Italy the day before travel. Your airline will have information about strikes directly affecting its flight schedule. If you are taking a train to the airport, check with the local tourist agency or rail station about upcoming strikes. Be aware it's not unusual for strikes to be canceled at the last minute.

Airline Security Issues Transportation Security Administration (⊕ *www.tsa.gov*) has answers for almost every question that might come up.

Contact A helpful Web site for information (location, phone numbers, local transportation, etc.) about all the airports in Italy is ⊕ *www. travel-library.com*.

AIRPORTS

The major gateways to Italy include Rome's Aeroporto Leonardo da Vinci (FCO), better known as Fiumicino, and Milan's Aeroporto Malpensa (MPX). Most flights to Venice, Florence, and Pisa make connections at Fiumicino and Malpensa or another European airport hub. You can take the FS airport train to Rome's Termini station or an express motorcoach

to Milan's central train station (Centrale), and catch a train to any other location in Italy. It will take about 30 minutes to get from Fiumicino to Roma Termini, about an hour to Milano Centrale.

Many carriers fly into the smaller airports. Venice is served by Aeroporto Marco Polo (VCE), Naples by Aeroporto Capodichino (NAP), and Palermo by Aeroporto Punta Raisi (PMO). Florence is serviced by Aeroporto A. Vespucci (FLR), which is also called Peretola, and by Aeroporto Galileo Galilei (PSA), which is about 2 km (1 mi) outside the center of Pisa and about one hour from Florence. The train to Florence stops within 100 feet of the entrance to the Pisa airport terminal. Bologna's airport (BLQ) is a 20-minute direct Aerobus-ride away from Bologna Centrale, which is about 40 minutes from Florence by train.

Italy's major airports are not known for being new, fun, or efficient. They have been ramping up security measures, which include random baggage inspection and bomb-detection dogs. All the airports have restaurants and snack bars, and there is Wi-Fi Internet access. Each airport has at least one nearby hotel. In the case of Florence, Pisa, and Bologna, the city centers are only a 15-minute taxi or bus ride away—so if you encounter a long delay, spend it in town.

When you take a connecting flight from a European airline hub (Frankfurt or Paris, for example) to a local Italian airport (Florence or Venice), be aware that your luggage might not make it onto the second plane with you. The airlines' lost-luggage service is efficient, however, and your delayed luggage is usually delivered to your hotel or holiday rental within 12 to 24 hours.

Airport Information Aeroporto A. Vespucci *(FLR, also called Peretola⊹ 6 km [4 mi] north-west of Florence* ☎ *055/3061300* ⊕ *www. aeroporto.firenze.it).* **Aeroporto di Venezia**

(VCE, also called Marco Polo ✈ 6 km [4 mi] north of Venice ☎ 041/2609260 ⊕ www.veniceairport.it). **Aeroporto Galileo Galilei** (PSA ✈ 2 km [1 mi] south of Pisa, 80 km [50 mi] west of Florence ☎ 050/849300 ⊕ www.pisa-airport.com). **Aeroporto di Bologna** (BLQ, also called Guglielmo Marconi ✈ 6 km [4 mi] northwest of Bologna ☎ 051/6479615 ⊕ www.bologna-airport.it). **Aeroporto Malpensa** (MPX✈ 45 km [28 mi] north of Milan ☎ 02/74852200 ⊕ www.sea-aeroportimilano.it). **Aeroporto Leonardo da Vinci** (FCO, also called Fiumicino✈ 35 km [20 mi] southwest of Rome ☎ 06/65951 ⊕ www.adr.it). **Naples International Airport** (NAP, also called Capodichino ✈ 7 km [4 mi] northeast of Naples ☎ 081/7896111 ⊕ www.naples-airport.com). **Palermo International Airport** (PMO, also called Punta Raisi ✈ 32 km [19 mi] northwest of Palermo ☎ 091/7020272 ⊕ www.gesap.it).

FLIGHTS

On flights from the United States, Alitalia and Delta Air Lines serve Rome, Milan, Pisa, and Venice. The major international hubs in Italy, Milan, and Rome are also served by Continental Airlines and American Airlines, and US Airways serves Rome. From April through October, the Italy-based Meridiana EuroFly has non-stop flights from New York to Naples and Palermo.

Alitalia and British Airways have direct flights from London to Milan, Venice, Rome, and 10 other locations in Italy. Smaller, no-frills airlines also provide service between Great Britain and Italy. EasyJet connects Gatwick with Milan, Venice, Rome, and Bologna. British Midland connects Heathrow and Milan (Linate), Naples, and Venice. Ryanair, departing from London's Stansted airport, flies to Milan, Rome, Pisa, and Venice. Meridiana has flights between Gatwick and Olbia on Sardinia in summer, and flights to Rome and Florence throughout the year.

Tickets for flights within Italy, on Alitalia and small carriers, such as EuroFly, Meridiana, and Air One, cost less when purchased from agents within Italy. Tickets are frequently sold at discounted prices, so check the cost of flights, even one-way, as an alternative to train travel.

Airline Contacts Alitalia (☎ 800/223–5730 in U.S., 06/2222 in Rome, 800/650055 elsewhere in Italy ⊕ www.alitalia.it). **American Airlines** (☎ 800/433–7300, 02/69682464 in Milan ⊕ www.aa.com). **British Airways** (☎ 800/247–9297 in U.S., 119/712266 in Italy ⊕ www.britishairways.com). **British Midland** (☎ 0807/6070–555 for U.K. reservations, 1332/64–8181 callers outside U.K. ⊕ www.flybmi.com). **Continental Airlines** (☎ 800/523–3273 for U.S. reservations, 800/231–0856 for international reservations, 02/69633256 in Milan, 800/555580000 elsewhere in Italy ⊕ www.continental.com). **Delta Air Lines** (☎ 800/221–1212 for U.S. reservations, 800/241–4141 for international reservations, 848/780376 in Italy ⊕ www.delta.com). **EasyJet** (☎ 0905/821–0905 in U.K., 899/234589 in Italy ⊕ www.easyjet.com). **Northwest Airlines** (☎ 800/225–2525 ⊕ www.nwa.com). **Ryanair** (☎ 08701/24–60000 in U.K., 899/678910 in Italy ⊕ www.ryanair.com). **United Airlines** (☎ 800/864–8331 for U.S. reservations, 800/538–2929 for international reservations ⊕ www.united.com). **US Airways** (☎ 800/428–4322 for U.S. reservations, 800/622–1015 for international reservations, 848/8813177 in Italy ⊕ www.usairways.com).

Domestic Carriers Air One (☎ 06/48880069 in Rome, 800/650055 elsewhere in Italy ⊕ www.flyairone.it). **Meridiana EuroFly** (☎ 866/387–6359 in U.S., 892928 in Italy. ⊕ www.euroflyusa.com).

▌ BUS TRAVEL

Italy's regional bus network, often operated by private companies with motorcoach fleets, is extensive, although not as attractive an option as in other European countries, partly due to convenient train travel. Schedules are often drawn up with commuters and students in mind and may be sketchy on weekends. Regional bus companies often provide the only means (not including car travel) of getting to out-of-the-way places. Even when this isn't the case, buses can be faster and more direct than local trains, so it's a good idea to compare bus and train schedules. SITA operates throughout Italy; Lazzi Euro-lines operates in Tuscany and central Italy. Dolomiti Bus serves the Dolomites.

All major cities in Italy have urban bus service. It's inexpensive, and tickets may be purchased in blocks or as passes. Buses can become jammed during busy travel periods and rush hours.

Smoking is not permitted, and both public and private buses offer only one class of service. Cleanliness and comfort levels are high on private motorcoaches, which have plenty of legroom and comfortable seats, but no toilets. Private bus lines usually have a ticket office in town or allow you to pay when you board. When traveling on city buses, you must buy your ticket from a machine, newsstand, or tobacco shop and stamp it on board (although some city buses have ticket machines on board).

Bus Information ATAC (✉ *Rome* ☎ *800/431784 or 06/46952027* ⊕ *www.atac. roma.it [no English version]*). **ATAF** (✉ *Stazi-one Centrale di Santa Maria Novella, Florence* ☎ *800/424500* ⊕ *www.ataf.net*). **DolomitiBus** (✉ *Via Col da Ren 14, Belluno* ☎ *0437/217111* ⊕ *www.dolomitibus.it*). **Lazzi Eurolines** (✉ *Via Mercadante 2, Florence* ☎ *055/363041* ⊕ *www.lazzi.it*). **SITA** (✉ *Via Santa Caterina da Siena 17/r, Florence* ☎ *055/47821* ⊕ *www. sitabus.it*).

▌ CAR TRAVEL

Italy has an extensive network of *auto-strade* (toll highways), complemented by equally well-maintained but free *super-strade* (expressways). Save the ticket you are issued at an autostrada entrance, as you need it to exit; on some shorter auto-strade, you pay the toll when you enter. Viacards, on sale for €25 and up at many autostrada locations, allow you to pay for tolls in advance, exiting at special lanes

where you simply slip the card into a designated slot.

An *uscita* is an "exit." A *raccordo annulare* is a ring road surrounding a city, while a *tangenziale* bypasses a city entirely. *Strade regionale* and *strade provinciale* (regional and provincial highways, denoted by *S, SS, SR,* or *SP* numbers) may be two-lane roads, as are all secondary roads; directions and turnoffs aren't always clearly marked.

GASOLINE

Gas stations are along the main highways. Those on autostrade are open 24 hours. Otherwise, gas stations generally are open Monday–Saturday 7–7, with a break at lunchtime. At self-service gas stations the pumps are operated by a central machine for payment, which doesn't take credit cards; it accepts only bills in denominations of 5, 10, 20, and 50 euros, and does not give change. Those with attendants accept cash and credit cards. It's not customary to tip the attendant.

At this writing, gasoline (*benzina*) costs about €1.33 per liter and is available in unleaded (*verde*) and superunleaded (*super*). Many rental cars in Italy use diesel (*gasolio*), which costs about €1.18 per liter (ask about the fuel type for your rental car before you leave the agency).

PARKING

Parking is at a premium in most towns, especially in the *centri storici* (historic centers). Fines for parking violations are high, and towing is common. Don't think about tearing up a ticket, as car-rental companies can use your credit card to be reimbursed for any fines you incur. It's a good idea to park in a designated (and preferably attended) lot. And don't leave valuables in your car, as thieves often target rental cars.

In congested cities, indoor parking costs €25–€30 for 12–24 hours; outdoor parking costs about €10–€20. Parking in an area signposted *zona disco* (disk zone) is allowed for short periods (from 30 minutes to two hours or more—the time is posted); if you don't have a cardboard disk (check in the glove box of your rental car) to show what time you parked, you can use a piece of paper. In most metropolitan areas you can find the curbside *parcometro:* once you insert change, it prints a ticket that you then leave on your dashboard.

RENTALS

Fiats, Fords, and Alfa Romeos in a variety of sizes are the most typical rental cars. Note that most Italian cars have standard transmission, so if you need to rent an automatic, be specific when you reserve the car. Significantly higher rates will apply.

Most American chains have affiliates in Italy, but the rates are usually lower if you book a car before you leave home. A company's rates are the standard throughout the country: rates are the same for airport and city pickup; airport offices are open later. An auto broker such as AutoEurope.com can allow you to compare rates among companies while guaranteeing lowest rates.

Most rental companies will not rent to someone under age 21 and also refuse to rent any car larger than an economy or subcompact car to anyone under age 23, and, further, require customers under age 23 to pay by credit card. Additional drivers must be identified in the contract and must qualify with the age limits. There is likely a supplementary daily fee for additional drivers. Upon rental, all companies require credit cards as a warranty; to rent bigger cars (2,000 cc or more), you must often show two credit cards. There are no special restrictions on senior citizen drivers. Book car seats, required for children under age three, in advance (the cost is generally about €36 for the duration of the rental).

Hiring a car with a driver can come in handy, particularly if you plan to do some wine tasting or drive along the Amalfi Coast. Search online (the travel forums at fodors.com are a good resource) or ask at your hotel for recommended drivers. Drivers are paid by the day, and are usually rewarded with a tip of about 15% upon completion of the journey.

All rental agencies operating in Italy require that you buy a collision-damage waiver (CDW) and a theft-protection policy, but those costs will already be included in the rates you are quoted. Be aware that coverage may be denied if the named driver on the rental contract is not the driver at the time of the incident. In Sicily there are some roads for which rental agencies deny coverage; ask in advance if you plan to travel in remote regions. Also ask your rental company about other included coverage when you reserve the car and/or pick it up.

ROAD CONDITIONS

Autostrade are well maintained, as are most interregional highways. Most autostrade have two lanes in both directions; the left lane is used only for passing. Italians drive fast and are impatient with those who don't, so tailgating (and flashing with bright beams to signal an intent to pass) is the norm if you dawdle in the left lane; the only way to avoid it is to stay to the right.

The condition of provincial (county) roads varies, but road maintenance at this level is generally good in Italy. In many small hill towns the streets are winding and extremely narrow; consider parking at the edge of town and exploring on foot.

Driving on the back roads of Italy isn't difficult as long as you're on the alert for bicycles and passing cars. In addition, street and road signs are often missing or placed in awkward spots, so a good map or GPS, and lots of patience are essential.

Be aware that some maps may not use the *SR* or *SP* (*strade regionale* and *strade provinciale*) highway designations, which took the place of the old *SS* designations in 2004. They may use the old *SS* designation or no numbering at all.

ROADSIDE EMERGENCIES

Automobile Club Italiano offers 24-hour road service; English-speaking operators are available. Your rental-car company may also have an emergency tow service with a toll-free call; keep that number handy. Be prepared to report which road you're on, the *verso* (direction) you're headed, and your *targa* (license plate number). Also, in an emergency, call the police (113).

When you're on the road, always carry a good road map and a flashlight; a cell phone is highly recommended. There are also emergency phones on the autostrade and superstrade; to locate them, look on the pavement for painted arrows and the term "SOS."

Emergency Services Automobile Club Italiano (*ACI* ☎ *803/116 emergency service* ⊕ *www.aci.it*).

RULES OF THE ROAD

Driving is on the right. Speed limits are 130 kph (80 mph) on autostrade, reduced to 110 kph (70 mph) when it rains, 90 kph (55 mph) on state and provincial roads, unless otherwise marked. In towns, the speed limit is 50 kph (30 mph), which may drop as low as 10 kph (6 mph) near schools, hospitals, and other designated areas. Note that right turns on red lights are forbidden. Headlights are required to be on while driving on all roads (large or small) outside municipalities. You must wear seat belts and strap young children into car seats at all times. Using hand-held mobile phones while driving is illegal; fines can exceed €100. In most Italian towns the use of the horn is forbidden in many areas; a large sign, *zona di silenzio*, indicates a no-honking zone.

In Italy you must be 18 years old to drive a car. A U.S. driver's license is acceptable to rent a car, but by law Italy requires non-Europeans also to carry an International Driver's Permit (IDP), which essentially translates your license into Italian (and a dozen other languages). In practice, it depends on the police officer who pulls you over whether you will be penalized for not carrying the IDP. Obtaining an IDP is simple and costs only $15; check the AAA Web site for more information.

The blood-alcohol content limit for driving is 0.5 gr (stricter than U.S. limits) with fines up to €5,000 for surpassing the limit and the possibility of six months' imprisonment. Although enforcement of laws varies depending on the region, fines for speeding are uniformly stiff: 10 kph over the speed limit can warrant a fine of up to €500; greater than 10 kph, and your license could be taken away from you. The police have the power to levy on-the-spot fines.

▌ TRAIN TRAVEL

In Italy, traveling by train is simple and efficient. Service between major cities is frequent, and trains usually arrive on schedule. The fastest trains on the Ferrovie dello Stato (FS), the Italian State Railways, are the **Eurostar** express trains, and the fastest Eurostar lines are designated as **Alta Velocità;** they run between all major cities from Venice, Milan, and Turin down through Florence and Rome to Naples. Seat reservations are mandatory on all Eurostar trains. You will be assigned a specific seat in a specific coach; to avoid having to squeeze through narrow aisles, board only at your designated coach (the number on your ticket matches the one near the door of each coach). Reservations are also required for the next-fastest, and less-frequent **Intercity (IC)** trains, tickets for which are about half the price of Eurostar. If you miss your reserved train, go to the ticket counter within the hour and you will be able to move your reservation to a later train (check these rules at booking).

Reservations are available but not required on **Interregionale** trains, which are slower and make more stops, and are less expensive still. **Regionale** and **Espresso** trains make the most stops and are the most economical; many serve commuters. There are refreshments on long-distance trains, purchased from a mobile cart or a dining car, but not on the commuter trains.

All but commuter trains have first and second classes. On local trains a first-class fare ensures you a little more space and a likely emptier coach. On long-distance trains you also get wider seats (three across as opposed to four) and a bit more legroom, but the difference is minimal. At peak travel times, a first-class fare may be worth the additional cost as the coaches may be less crowded. In Italian, *prima classe* is first class; second is *seconda classe*.

Many cities—Milan, Turin, Genoa, Naples, Florence, Rome, and even Verona included—have more than one train station, **so be sure you get off at the right place.** When buying train tickets be particularly aware that in Rome and Florence some trains do not stop at all of the cities' train stations and may not stop at the main, central station. This is a common occurrence with regional and some Intercity trains. When scheduling train travel on the Internet or through a travel agent, be sure to request to arrive at the station closest to your destination in Rome and Florence.

Except for Pisa, Milan, and Rome, none of the major cities have trains that go directly to the airports, but there are always commuter (frequently direct) bus lines connecting train stations and airports.

You can pay for your train tickets in cash or with a major credit card such as MasterCard, Visa, American Express, and Diners Club at travel agencies, and at the train station ticket counters and automatic ticketing machines. If you would like to board a train and do not have a ticket, seek out the conductor prior to boarding; he or she will tell you if you may board and what the surcharge will be (usually €8). If you board a train without a ticket you will be fined €50 plus the price of the ticket. Trains can be crowded, so it's always a good idea to make a reservation

when that's possible. You can review schedules at the FS Web site and reserve seats up to three months in advance at the train station or at an Italian travel agency displaying the FS emblem. You will need to reserve seats even if you are using a rail pass.

Even though it's not required for high-speed travel, for other trains **you must validate your ticket before boarding** by punching it at a yellow box in the waiting area of smaller train stations or at the end of the track in larger stations. If you forget, tell the conductor immediately to avoid a hefty fine.

Train strikes of various kinds are common, so it's a good idea to make sure your train is running. During a strike, minimum service is guaranteed, but what exactly that service consists of is difficult to predict.

Traveling by night can be a good deal (if somewhat of an adventure), as you will pass a night without having to have a hotel room. More comfortable trains run on the longer routes (Sicily–Rome, Sicily–Milan, Sicily–Venice, Rome–Turin, Lecce–Milan); ask for the good-value T3 (three single beds), Intercity Notte, and Carrozza Comfort. The Vagone Letto Excelsior has private bathrooms and single-, double-, or twin-bed suites.

Information FS–Trenitalia (☎ 892021 *in Italy* ⊕ *www.trenitalia.com*).

TRAIN PASSES

Rail passes may offer the possibility to save on train travel. Compare rail pass cost with actual fares to determine whether you truly save, as fares can vary considerably. Generally, the more often you plan to travel long distances on high-speed trains, the more likely a rail pass would make sense.

A Eurail Italy Pass allows a certain number of travel days within Italy over the course of two months. Three to 10 days of travel cost from $277 to $510 (first class) or $225 to $413 (second class). If you're in a group of from two to five people, consider the discounted **Eurail Italy Pass Saver**: a pass for three to ten travel days costs from $236 to $434 (first class) or $192 to $351 (second class); children's passes are further discounted. **Eurail Italy Youth** (for those under 26) is second-class only and costs from $183 to $337 for one to 10 days of travel.

Italy is one of 17 countries that accept the Eurail Pass, which allows unlimited first- and second-class travel. If you plan to rack up the miles, get a Global Eurail Pass. The Eurail Select Pass allows for travel in three to five contiguous countries. In addition to standard Eurail Passes, there are the Eurail Youth Pass (for those under 26), the Eurail Flexipass (which allows a certain number of travel days within a set period), the Eurail Saver (which gives a discount for two or more people traveling together), and the Eurail Drive Pass (which combines travel by train and rental car).

All passes must be purchased before you leave for Europe. Keep in mind that even with a rail pass, you still need to reserve seats on the trains you plan to take.

Contacts Rail Europe (📠 *800/622-8600* ⊕ *www.raileurope.com*). **Europe on Rail** (📠 *866/858-6854* ⊕ *www.europeonrail.com*). **RailPass** (📠 *877/724-5727* ⊕ *www.railpass.com*).

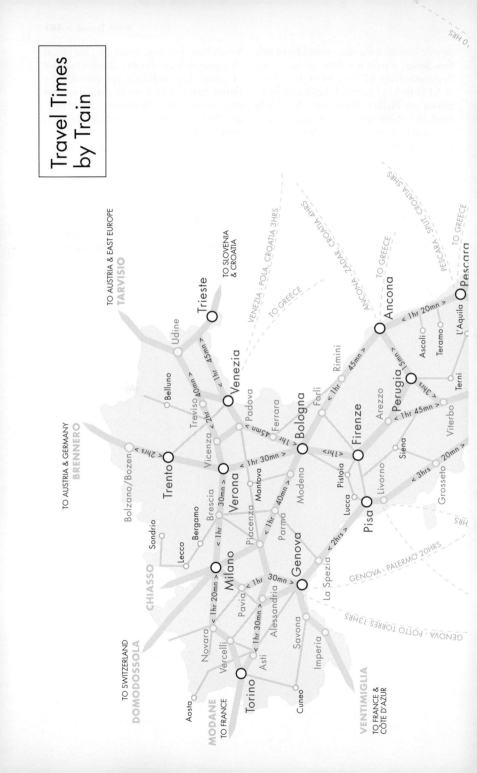

Travel Times
by Train

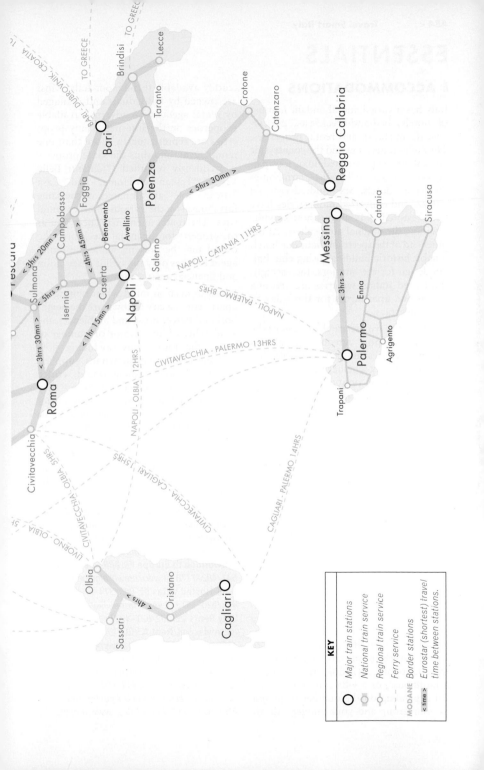

ESSENTIALS

▪ ACCOMMODATIONS

Italy has a varied and abundant number of hotels, bed-and-breakfasts, *agriturismi* (farm stays), and rental properties. Throughout the cities and the countryside you can find sophisticated, luxurious palaces and villas as well as rustic farmhouses and small hotels. Six-hundred-year-old palazzi and converted monasteries have been restored as luxurious hotels, while retaining the original atmosphere. At the other end of the spectrum, boutique hotels inhabit historic buildings using chic Italian design for the interiors. Increasingly, the famed Italian wineries are creating rooms and apartments for three-day to weeklong stays.

The lodgings we list are the cream of the crop in each price category. We always list the facilities that are available, but we don't specify whether they cost extra; when pricing accommodations, always ask what's included and what costs extra. Properties are assigned price categories based on the range between their least and most expensive standard double room at high season (excluding holidays).

Hotels with the designation **BP** (for Breakfast Plan) at the end of their listing include breakfast in their rate; offerings can vary from coffee and a roll to an elaborate buffet. Those designated **EP** (European Plan) have no meals included; **MAP** (Modified American Plan) means you get breakfast and dinner; **FAP** (Full American Plan) includes all meals.

APARTMENT AND HOUSE RENTALS

More and more travelers are turning away from the three-countries-in-two-weeks style of touring and choosing to spend a week in one city or a month in the countryside. Renting an apartment, a farmhouse, or a villa can be economical depending on the number of people in your group and your budget. All are readily available throughout Italy. Most are owned by individuals and managed by rental agents who advertise available properties on the Internet. Many properties are represented by more than one rental agent, and thus the same property is frequently renamed ("Chianti Bella Vista," "Tuscan Sun Home," and "Casa Toscana Sole" are all names of the same farmhouse) on the various Internet rental sites. The rental agent may meet you at the property for the initial check-in or the owner may be present, while the rental agent handles only the online reservation and financial arrangements.

Issues to keep in mind when renting an apartment in a city or town are the neighborhood (street noise and ambience), the availability of an elevator or number of stairs, the furnishings (including pots and pans and linens), what's supplied on arrival (dishwashing liquid, coffee or tea), and the cost of utilities (are they included in the rental rate?). Inquiries about countryside properties should also include how isolated the property is. (Do you have to drive 45 minutes to reach the nearest town?) If you're arriving too late in the day to grocery shop, request that provisions for the next day's breakfast be supplied.

Contacts At Home Abroad (☏ 212/421–9165 ⊕ www.athomeabroadinc.com). **Barclay International Group** (☏ 800/845–6636 or 516/364–0064 ⊕ www.barclayweb.com). **Drawbridge to Europe** (☏ 888/268–1148 or 541/482–7778 ⊕ www.drawbridgetoeurope.com). **Hosted Villas** (☏ 800/374–6637 or 416/920–1873 ⊕ www.hostedvillas.com). **Italy Rents** (☏ 202/821–4273 ⊕ www.italyrents.com). **Rent A Villa** (☏ 877/250–4366 or 206/417–3444 ⊕ www.rentavilla.com). **Suzanne B. Cohen & Associates** (☏ 207/622–0743⊕ www.villaeurope.com). **Tuscan House** (☏ 800/844–6939 ⊕ www.tuscanhouse.com). **Villas & Apartments Abroad** (☏ 212/213–6435 ⊕ www.vaanyc.

com). **Villas International** (☎ 800/221–2260 or 415/499–9490 ⊕ www.villasintl.com). **Villas of Distinction** (☎ 800/289–0900 ⊕ www.villasofdistinction.com). **Wimco** (☎ 866/850–6140 ⊕ www.wimco.com).

CONVENTS AND MONASTERIES

Throughout Italy, tourists can find reasonably priced lodging at convents, monasteries, and religious houses. Religious orders usually charge from €30 to €60 per person per night for rooms that are clean, comfortable, and convenient. Many have private bathrooms; spacious lounge areas and secluded gardens or terraces are standard features. A continental breakfast ordinarily comes with the room, but be sure to ask. Sometimes, for an extra fee, family-style lunches and dinners are available.

Be aware of three issues when considering a convent or monastery stay: most have a curfew of 11 PM or midnight; you need to book in advance, because they fill up quickly; and your best means of booking is usually e-mail or fax—the person answering the phone may not speak English.

Contact Hospites.it (⊕ www.hospites.it) has listings of convents throughout Italy.

FARM HOLIDAYS AND AGRITOURISM

Rural accommodations in the *agriturismo* (agricultural tourism) category are increasingly popular with both Italians and visitors to Italy; you stay on a working farm or vineyard. Accommodations vary in size and range from luxury apartments, farmhouses, and villas to basic facilities. Agriturist has compiled *Agriturism,* which is available only in Italian, but includes more than 1,600 farms in Italy; pictures and the use of international symbols to describe facilities make the guide a good tool. Local APT tourist offices also have information.

Information Agriturismo.net ⊕ www.agriturismo.net). **Agriturist** (☎ 06/6852342

⊕ www.agriturist.it). **Italy Tourist: Farm Holiday** (⊕ www.italytourist.it).

HOME EXCHANGES

With a direct home exchange you stay in someone else's home while they stay in yours. Some outfits also deal with vacation homes, so you're not actually staying in someone's full-time residence, just their vacant weekend place.

Italians have historically not been as enthusiastic about home exchanges as others have been; however, there are many great villas and apartments in Italy owned by foreigners, such as Americans, who use the home-exchange services.

Exchange Clubs Home Exchange.com (☎ 800/877–8723 ⊕ www.homeexchange.com); membership is $9.95 monthly or $15.95 for three months. **HomeLink International** (☎ 800/638–3841 ⊕ www.homelink.org); $115 for one year, $118 for two. Additional listings, $18 each. **Intervac U.S.** (☎ 800/756–4663 ⊕ www.intervacus.com); $99 for one-year membership.

HOSTELS

Hostels offer bare-bones lodging at low, low prices—often in shared dorm rooms with shared baths—to people of all ages, though the primary market is young travelers, especially students (some have an upper age limit, in fact). Most hostels serve breakfast; dinner and/or shared cooking facilities may also be available. In some hostels you aren't allowed to be in your room during the day, and there may be a curfew at night. Nevertheless, hostels provide a sense of community, with public rooms where travelers often gather to share stories. Many hostels are affiliated with Hostelling International (HI), an umbrella group of hostel associations with some 4,500 member properties in more than 70 countries. Other hostels are independent and may be nothing more than a really cheap hotel.

Membership in any HI association, open to travelers of all ages, allows you to stay in HI-affiliated hostels at member rates.

One-year membership is about $28 for adults; hostels charge about $20–$40 per night. Members have priority if the hostel is full; they're also eligible for discounts around the world, even on rail and bus travel in some countries.

Hostels in Italy run the gamut from low-end hotels to beautiful villas. In Florence, the campground and hostel near Piazzale Michelangelo has a better view of the city than any luxury hotel in town.

Information HiHostels (☎ +44 0 1707 324170 ⊕ www.hihostels.com). **Hostelling International—USA** (☎ 301/495–1240 national office; check online for phone number of office in your state ⊕ www.hiusa.org). **Hostel World** (⊕ www.hostelworld.com). **Hostelz** (⊕ www.hostelz.com).

▌ COMMUNICATIONS

INTERNET

Getting online in Italian cities isn't difficult: public Internet stations and Internet cafés, some open 24 hours, are common. Prices differ from place to place, so spend some time to find the best deal. Chains like Internet Train can be handy if you're moving about the country, as you can simply prepay your time, and then use the nearest location to connect without staff intervention. You can even use your own laptop if you prefer.

Wi-Fi hot spots can be found in lodgings from high-end hotels to B&Bs, major airports and train stations, cafés, and shopping centers, but are rarely free.

Broadband and Wi-Fi connections are becoming increasingly common in lodging. Some hotels have in-room modem lines, but, as with phones, using the hotel's line is relatively expensive. Always check modem rates before plugging in. You may need a plug adapter for your computer for the European-style electric socket (a converter will likely not be necessary). If you are traveling with a laptop, carry a spare battery and an adapter. Never plug your computer into any socket before asking about surge protection. IBM sells a tiny modem tester that plugs into a telephone jack to check whether the line is safe to use.

Contact Jiwire (⊕ www.jiwire.com) has a fairly complete, comprehensive list of Italian Wi-Fi locations, including maps. **Internet Cafes in Italy** (⊕ cafe.ecs.net) has an extensive list of Italian Internet cafés.

PHONES

The good news is that you can now make a direct-dial telephone call from virtually any point on Earth. The bad news? You can't always do so cheaply. Calling from a hotel is almost always the most expensive option; hotels usually add huge surcharges to all calls, particularly international ones. Calling cards can keep costs to a minimum, but only if you purchase them locally. And then there are mobile phones; as expensive as mobile phone calls can be, they are still usually a much cheaper option than calling from your hotel. With a little effort, you can manage to reduce the call expense, though.

CALL ITALY FROM ABROAD

When calling Italy from North America, dial 011 (which gets you an international line), followed by Italy's country code, 39, and the phone number, including any leading 0. Note that Italian cell numbers have 10 digits and always begin with a 3; Italian landline numbers will contain from 4 to 10 digits, and will always begin with a 0. So for example, when calling Rome, whose numbers begin with 06, you dial 011 + 39 + 06 + phone number; for a cell phone, dial 011 + 39 + cell number.

CALLING WITHIN ITALY

With the advent of mobile phones, public pay phones are becoming increasingly scarce, although they can be found at train and subway stations, main post offices, and in some bars. In rural areas, town squares usually have a pay phone. Pay phones require a *scheda telefonica* (phone card ⇨ *below*).

For all calls within Italy, whether local or long-distance, you'll dial the entire phone

LOCAL DO'S AND TABOOS

GREETINGS

Upon meeting and leave-taking, both friends and strangers wish each other good day or good evening (*buongiorno, buonasera*); *ciao* isn't used between strangers. Italians who are friends greet each other with a kiss, usually first on the left cheek, then on the right. When you meet a new person, shake hands.

SIGHTSEEING

Italy is full of churches, and many of them contain significant works of art. They are also places of worship, however, so be sure to dress appropriately.

Shorts, tank tops, and sleeveless garments are taboo in most churches throughout the country. In summer carry a sweater or other item of clothing to wrap around your bare shoulders to avoid being denied entrance.

You should never bring food into a church, and do not sip from your water bottle while inside. If you have a cell phone, turn it off before entering. Ask if photographs are allowed; never use flash. And never enter a church when a service is in progress, especially if it is a private affair such as a wedding or baptism.

OUT ON THE TOWN

Table manners in Italy are formal; rarely do Italians share food from their plates. In a restaurant, be formal and polite with your waiter—no calling across the room for attention.

When you've finished your meal and are ready to go, ask for the check (*il conto*); unless it's well past closing time, no waiter will put a bill on your table until you've requested it.

Italians do not have a culture of sipping cocktails or chugging pitchers of beer. Wine, beer, and other alcoholic drinks are almost always consumed as part of a meal. Public drunkenness is abhorred.

Smoking has been banned in all public establishments, much like in the United States.

Flowers, chocolates, or a bottle of wine are appropriate hostess gifts when invited to dinner at the home of an Italian.

DOING BUSINESS

Showing up on time for business appointments is the norm and expected in Italy. There are more business lunches than business dinners, and even business lunches aren't common, as Italians view mealtimes as periods of pleasure and relaxation.

Business cards are used throughout Italy, and business attire is the norm for both men and women. To be on the safe side, it is best not to use first names or a familiar form of address until invited to do so.

Business gifts are not the norm, but if one is given it is usually small and symbolic of your home location or type of business.

LANGUAGE

One of the best ways to connect with Italians is to learn a little of the local language. You need not strive for fluency; just mastering a few basic words and terms is bound to make interactions more rewarding.

"Please" is *per favore,* "thank you" is *grazie,* "you're welcome" is *prego,* and "excuse me" is *scusi.*

In larger cities such as Venice, Rome, and Florence, language is not a big problem. Most hotels have English speakers at their reception desks, and if not, they can always find someone who speaks at least a little English. You may have trouble communicating in the countryside, but a phrase book and expressive gestures will go a long way. A phrase book and language-tape set can help get you started before you go. *Fodor's Italian for Travelers* (available at bookstores everywhere) is excellent.

number that starts with 0, or 3 for cell phone numbers. Rates from landlines vary according to the time of day; it's cheaper to call before 9 AM and after 7 or 8 PM; calling a cell phone will cost significantly more. Italy uses the prefix "800" for toll-free or "green" numbers.

MAKING INTERNATIONAL CALLS

Because of the high rates charged by most hotels for long-distance and international calls, you're better off making such calls from public phones or your mobile phone (⇨ *below*), using an international calling card (⇨ *below*). If you prefer to use the hotel phone to make an international call, you can still save money by using an international calling card.

Although not advised because of the exorbitant cost, you can place international calls or collect calls through an operator by dialing 170. Rates to the United States are lowest on Sunday around the clock and between 10 PM and 8 AM (Italian time) on weekdays and Saturday. You can also place a direct call to the United States using your U.S. phone calling-card number. You automatically reach a U.S. operator and thereby avoid all language difficulties.

The country code for the United States and Canada is 1 (dial 00 + 1 + area code and number).

Access Codes AT&T Direct (☎ 800/172–444). **MCI WorldPhone** (☎ 800/905–825). **Sprint International Access** (☎ 800/172–405).

CALLING CARDS

Prepaid *schede telefoniche* (phone cards) are available throughout Italy and are best for calls within the country. Cards in different denominations are sold at post offices, newsstands, tobacco shops, and some bars. When using with pay phones, tear off the corner of the card and insert it into the phone's slot. When you dial, the card's value appears in a display window. After you hang up, the card is returned (so don't walk off without it).

International calling cards are different; you call a toll-free number from any

phone, entering the code found on the back of the card followed by the destination number. The best card for calling North America and elsewhere in Europe is the Europa card, which comes in two denominations, €5 for 180 minutes and €10 for 360 minutes, available at tobacco shops. Just ask for a card for calling the United States (or the country you prefer).

MOBILE PHONES

If you have a multiband phone (Europe and North America use different calling frequencies) and your service provider uses the world-standard GSM network (as do T-Mobile, AT&T, and Verizon), you can probably use your own phone and provider abroad. Roaming fees can be steep, however: 99¢ a minute is considered reasonable. And overseas you normally pay the toll charges for incoming calls. It's almost always cheaper to send a text message than to make a call, since text messages have a low set fee (often less than 15¢).

To further reduce calling expenses, consider buying an Italian SIM card (making sure your service provider first unlocks your phone for use with a different SIM) and a prepaid service plan once at your destination. You then have a local number and can make calls at local rates (which also means you pay only for calls made, not received).

■**TIP→** If you travel internationally frequently, save one of your old mobile phones (ask your cell phone company to unlock it for you) or buy an unlocked, multiband phone online; take it with you as a travel phone, buying a new SIM card with pay-as-you-go service in each destination.

The cost of cell phones is dropping; you can purchase a dual band (Europe only) cell phone with a prepaid call credit (no monthly service plan) in Italy for less than €50, then top off the credit as you go if necessary. This plan will not allow you to call the United States, but using an international calling card with the cell phone solves that problem in an inexpensive manner. Most medium-to-large towns have stores dedicated to selling cell phones. The purchase of a multiband phone means it will also function once you return home; European phones are not "locked" to their provider's SIM (which is also why they cost more). You will need to present your passport to purchase any SIM card.

Rental cell phones are available online prior to departure (⇨ *below*) and in Italy in cities and larger towns. Many Internet cafés offer them, but shop around for the best deal. Most rental contracts require a refundable deposit that covers the cost of the cell phone (€75–€150) and then set up a monthly service plan that is automatically charged to your credit card. Frequently, rental cell phones will be triple band with a plan that allows you to call North America. Be sure to check the rate schedule to avoid a nasty surprise when you receive your credit-card bill two or three months later. Often the prepaid option will be the more cost-effective one.

■TIP➜ Beware of cell phone (and PDA) thieves. Keep your phone or PDA in a secure pocket or purse. Do not lay it on the bar when you stop for an espresso. Do not zip it into the outside pocket of your backpack in crowded cities. Do not leave it in your hotel room. If you are using a phone with a monthly service plan, notify your provider immediately if it is lost or stolen.

Contacts Cellular Abroad (☎ 800/287–5072 ⊕ *www.cellularabroad.com*) rents and sells GMS phones and sells SIM cards that work in many countries. **Mobal** (☎ 888/888–9162 ⊕ *www.mobal.com*) rents mobiles and sells GSM phones (starting at $49) that will operate in 140 countries. Per-call rates vary throughout the world. **Planet Fone** (☎ 888/988–4777 ⊕ *www.planetfone.com*) rents cell phones, but the per-minute rates are expensive.

■ CUSTOMS AND DUTIES

You're always allowed to bring goods of a certain value back home without having to pay any duty or import tax. But there's a limit on the amount of tobacco and liquor you can bring back duty-free, and some countries have separate limits for perfumes; for exact figures, check with your customs department. The values of so-called duty-free goods are included in these amounts. When you shop abroad, save all your receipts, as customs inspectors may ask to see them as well as the items you purchased. If the total value of your goods is more than the duty-free limit, you'll have to pay a tax (most often a flat percentage) on the value of everything beyond that limit.

Travelers from the United States should experience little difficulty clearing customs at any airport in Italy.

Italy requires documentation of the background of all antiques and antiquities before the item is taken out of the country. Under Italian law, all antiquities found on Italian soil are considered state property, and there are other restrictions on antique artwork. Even if purchased from a business in Italy, legal ownership of such artifacts may be in question if brought into the United States. Therefore, although they do not necessarily confer ownership, documents such as export permits and receipts are required when importing such items into the United States.

For returning to the United States, clearing customs is sometimes more difficult. U.S. residents are normally entitled to a duty-free exemption of $800 on items accompanying them. Although there is no problem with aged cheese (vacuum-sealed works best), you cannot bring back any of that delicious prosciutto or salami or any other meat product. Fresh mushrooms, truffles, or fresh fruits and vegetables are also forbidden. There are also restrictions on the amount of alcohol allowed in duty-free. Generally, you are allowed to bring in one liter of wine, beer, or other alcohol without paying a customs duty.

Information in Italy Dogana Sezione Viaggiatori (☎ 06/65954343 ⊕ www. agenziadogane.it). **Ministero delle Finanze, Direzione Centrale dei Servizi Doganali, Divisione I** (☎ 06/50242117 ⊕ www.finanze.it).

U.S. Information U.S. Customs and Border Protection (⊕ www.cbp.gov).

▌ EATING OUT

Italian cuisine is still largely regional. Ask what the local specialties are: by all means, have spaghetti *alla carbonara* (with bacon and egg) in Rome, pizza in Rome or Naples, *bistecca alla fiorentina* (steak) in Florence, *cinghiale* (wild boar) in Tuscany, truffles in Piedmont, and risotto *alla milanese* in Milan. Although most restaurants in Italy serve traditional local cuisine, you can find Asian and Middle Eastern alternatives in Rome, Venice, and other cities.

The restaurants we list are the cream of the crop in each price category.

MEALS AND MEALTIMES

What's the difference between a ristorante and a trattoria? Can you order food at an *enoteca* (wine bar)? Can you go to a restaurant just for a snack, or order just a salad at a pizzeria? The following definitions should help.

Not too long ago, *ristoranti* tended to be more elegant and expensive than trattorias and *osterie*, which serve traditional, home-style fare in an atmosphere to match. But the distinction has blurred considerably, and an osteria in the center of town might be far fancier (and pricier) than a ristorante across the street. In any sit-down establishment, be it a ristorante, osteria, or trattoria, you are generally expected to order at least a two-course meal, such as: a *primo* (first course) and a *secondo* (main course) or a *contorno* (vegetable side dish); an *antipasto* (starter) followed by either a primo or secondo; or a secondo and a *dolce* (dessert).

In an enoteca (wine bar) or pizzeria it's common to order just one dish. An enoteca menu is often limited to a selection of cheese, cured meats, salads, and desserts, but if there's a kitchen you can also find soups, pastas, and main courses. The typical pizzeria fare includes *affettati misti* (a selection of cured pork), simple salads, various kinds of bruschetta, *crostini* (similar to bruschetta, with a variety of toppings) and, in Rome, *fritti* (deep-fried finger food) such as *olive ascolane* (green olives with a meat stuffing) and *supplì* (rice balls stuffed with mozzarella).

The handiest and least expensive places for a quick snack between sights are probably bars, cafés, and pizza *al taglio* (by the slice) spots. Pizza al taglio shops are easy to negotiate but few have seats. They sell pizza by weight: just point out which kind you want and how much.

Bars in Italy resemble what we think of as cafés, and are primarily places to get a coffee and a bite to eat, rather than drinking establishments. Most bars have a selection of *panini* (sandwiches) warmed up on the griddle (*piastra*) and *tramezzini* (sandwiches made of untoasted white bread triangles). In larger cities, bars also serve vegetable and fruit salads, cold pasta dishes, and gelato. Most bars offer beer and a variety of alcohol as well as wines by the glass (sometimes good but more often mediocre). A café is like a bar but usually with more tables. Pizza at a café should be avoided—it's usually heated in a microwave.

If you place your order at the counter, ask if you can sit down: some places charge for table service (especially in tourist centers); others do not. In self-service bars and cafés it's good manners to clean your table before you leave. Note that in some places (such as train stations and stops along the highway) you first pay a cashier, then show your *scontrino* (receipt) at the counter to place your order. Menus are posted outside most restaurants (in English in tourist areas); if not, you might step inside and ask to take a look at the menu (but don't ask for a table unless you intend to stay). Italians take their food as it is listed on the menu, seldom if ever making special requests such as "dressing on the side" or "hold the olive oil." If you have special dietary needs, however, make them known; they can usually be accommodated. Although mineral water makes its way to almost every table, you can order a carafe of tap water (*acqua di rubinetto* or *acqua semplice*) instead, but keep in mind that such water can be highly chlorinated.

Wiping your bowl clean with a (small) piece of bread is usually considered a sign of appreciation, not bad manners. Spaghetti should be eaten with a fork only, although a little help from a spoon won't horrify locals the way cutting spaghetti into little pieces might. Order your caffè (Italians drink cappuccino only in the morning) after dessert, not with it. Don't ask for a doggy bag.

Breakfast (*la colazione*) is usually served from 7 to 10:30, lunch (*il pranzo*) from 12:30 to 2:30, dinner (*la cena*) from 7:30 to 10; outside those hours, best head for a bar. Peak times are usually 1:30 for lunch and 9 for dinner. *Enoteche* and *bàcari* (wine bars) are open also in the morning and late afternoon for a snack at the counter. Most pizzerias open at 8 PM and close around midnight—later in summer and on weekends. Most bars and cafés are open from 7 AM until 8 or 9 PM; a few stay open until midnight.

Unless otherwise noted, the restaurants listed in this guide are open daily for lunch and dinner.

PAYING

Most restaurants have a cover charge per person, usually listed at the top of the check as *coperto* or *pane e coperto*. It should be a modest charge (€1–€2.50 per person) except at the most expensive restaurants. Whenever in doubt, ask before you order to avoid unpleasant discussions later. It is customary to leave a small tip (around 10%) in appreciation of good service. If *servizio* is included at the bottom of the check, no tip is necessary. Tips are always given in cash.

The price of fish dishes is often given by weight (before cooking), so the price you see on the menu is for 100 grams of fish, not for the whole dish. (An average fish portion is about 350 grams.) In Tuscany, *bistecca alla fiorentina* (Florentine steak) is also often priced by weight (€4 for 100 grams or €40 for 1 kilogram [2.2 pounds]).

Major credit cards are widely accepted in Italy, though cash is always preferred. More restaurants take Visa and MasterCard than American Express.

When you leave a dining establishment, take your meal bill or receipt with you; although not a common experience, the Italian finance (tax) police can approach you within 100 yards of the establishment at which you've eaten and ask for a receipt. If you don't have one, they can fine you and will fine the business owner for not providing the receipt. The measure is intended to prevent tax evasion; it's not necessary to show receipts when leaving Italy.

RESERVATIONS AND DRESS

Regardless of where you are, it's a good idea to make a reservation. We only mention them specifically when reservations are essential (there's no other way you'll ever get a table) or when they are not accepted. For popular restaurants, book as far ahead as you can (often 30 days), and reconfirm as soon as you arrive. (Large parties should always call ahead to check the reservations policy.) If you change your mind, be sure to cancel, even at the last minute.

We mention dress only when men are required to wear a jacket or a jacket and tie. But unless they're dining outside or at an oceanfront resort, Italian men never wear shorts or running shoes in a restaurant. The same applies to women: no casual shorts, running shoes, or plastic sandals when going out to dinner. Shorts are acceptable in pizzerias and cafés.

WINES, BEER, AND SPIRITS

The grape has been cultivated in Italy since the time of the Etruscans, and Italians justifiably take pride in their local vintages. Though almost every region produces good-quality wine, Tuscany, Piedmont, the Veneto, Puglia, Calabria, and Sicily are some of the more renowned areas. Wine in Italy is less expensive than almost anywhere else, so it's often affordable to order a bottle of wine at a restaurant rather than to stick with the house wine (which, nevertheless, is sometimes quite good). Many bars have their own *aperitivo della casa* (house aperitif); Italians are imaginative with their mixed drinks, so you may want to try one.

You can purchase beer, wine, and spirits in any bar, grocery store, or enoteca, any day of the week, any time of the day. Italian and German beer is readily available, but it can be more expensive than wine.

There's no minimum drinking age in Italy. Italian children begin drinking wine mixed with water at mealtimes when they are teens (or thereabouts). Italians are rarely seen drunk in public, and public drinking, except in a bar or eating establishment, isn't considered acceptable behavior. Bars usually close by 9 PM; hotel and restaurant bars stay open until midnight. Brewpubs and discos serve until about 2 AM.

▌ELECTRICITY

The electrical current in Italy is 220 volts, 50 cycles alternating current (AC); wall outlets take Continental-type plugs, with two or three round prongs.

Consider the purchase of a universal adapter, which has several types of plugs in one lightweight, compact unit, available at travel specialty stores and online. You can pick up plug adapters in Italy in any electric supply store for about €2 each. You'll likely not need a converter, however; most portable devices are dual voltage (i.e., they operate equally well on

110 and 220 volts), so require only an adapter; just check label specifications and manufacturer instructions to be sure. Don't use 110-volt outlets marked FOR SHAVERS ONLY for high-wattage appliances such as hair dryers.

Contacts Steve Kropla's Help for World Travelers (⊕ *www.kropla.com*) has information on electrical and telephone plugs around the world. **Walkabout Travel Gear** (⊕ *www. walkabouttravelgear.com*) has a good coverage of electricity under "adapters."

▌EMERGENCIES

No matter where you are in Italy, you can dial 113 in case of emergency: the call will be directed to the local police. Not all 113 operators speak English, so you may want to ask a local person to place the call. Asking the operator for *"pronto soccorso"* (first aid and also the emergency room of a hospital) should get you an *ambulanza* (ambulance). If you just need a doctor, ask for *"un medico."*

Italy has the *carabinieri* (national police force, their emergency number is 112 from anywhere in Italy) as well as the *polizia* (local police force). Both are armed and have the power to arrest and investigate crimes. Always report the loss of your passport to the police as well as to your embassy. When reporting a crime, you'll be asked to fill out *una denuncia* (official report); keep a copy for your insurance company. You should also contact the police any time you have a car accident of any sort.

Local traffic officers, known as *vigili*, are responsible for, among other things, giving out parking tickets. They wear white (in summer) or black uniforms. Should you find yourself involved in a minor car accident in town, contact the vigili.

Pharmacies are generally open weekdays 8:30–1 and 4–8, and Saturday 9–1. Local pharmacies rotate covering the off-hours in shifts: on the door of every pharmacy is a list of which pharmacies in the vicinity will be open late.

Foreign Embassies U.S. Consulate Florence (✉ *Via Lungarno Vespucci 38, Florence* ☎ *055/266951*). **U.S. Consulate Milan** (✉ *Via Principe Amedeo 2/10, Milan* ☎ *02/290351*). **U.S. Consulate Naples** (✉ *Piazza della Repubblica, Naples* ☎ *081/5838111*). **U.S. Embassy** (✉ *Via Veneto 119/A, Rome* ☎ *06/46741* ⊕ *www.usembassy.it*).

General Emergency Contacts Emergencies (☎ *113*). **National police** (☎ *112*).

▮ HOURS OF OPERATION

Religious and civic holidays are frequent in Italy. Depending on the holiday's local importance, businesses may close for the day. Businesses do not close Friday or Monday when the holiday falls on the weekend.

Banks are open weekdays 8:30–1:30 and for one or two hours in the afternoon, depending on the bank. Most post offices are open Monday–Saturday 9–12:30; central post offices are open 9–6:30 weekdays, 9–12:30 or 9–6:30 on Saturday. On the last day of the month all post offices close at midday.

Most churches are open from early morning until noon or 12:30, when they close for three hours or more; they open again in the afternoon, closing at about 6 PM. A few major churches, such as St. Peter's in Rome and San Marco in Venice, remain open all day. Walking around during services is discouraged. Many museums are closed one day a week, often Monday. During low season, museums often close early; during high season, many stay open until late at night.

Pharmacies are generally open weekdays 8:30–1 and 4–8, and Saturday 9–1. Local pharmacies rotate covering the off-hours in shifts: on the door of every pharmacy is a list of which pharmacies in the vicinity will be open late or available in emergency.

Most shops are open Monday–Saturday 9–1 and 3:30 or 4–7:30. Clothing shops are generally closed Monday mornings. Barbers and hairdressers, with some exceptions, are closed Sunday and Monday. Some bookstores and fashion and tourist-oriented shops in places such as Rome and Venice are open all day, as well as Sunday. Large chain supermarkets such as Standa, COOP, and Esselunga do not close for lunch and are usually open Sunday; smaller *alimentari* (delicatessens) and other food shops are usually closed one evening during the week (it varies according to the town) and are almost always closed Sunday.

HOLIDAYS

Traveling through Italy in August can be an odd experience. Although there are some deals to be had, the heat can be oppressive, and much of the population is on vacation. Most cities are deserted (except for foreign tourists) and many restaurants and shops are closed. The National holidays in 2011 include January 1 (New Year's Day); January 6 (Epiphany); April 24 and April 25 (Easter Sunday and Monday); April 25 (Liberation Day); May 1 (Labor Day or May Day); June 2 (Festival of the Republic); August 15 (Ferragosto); November 1 (All Saints' Day); December 8 (Immaculate Conception); and December 25 and 26 (Christmas Day and the feast of Saint Stephen).

In addition, feast days of patron saints are observed locally. Many businesses and shops may be closed in Florence, Genoa, and Turin on June 24 (Saint John the Baptist); in Rome on June 29 (Saints Peter and Paul); in Palermo on July 15 (Santa Rosalia); in Naples on September 19 (San Gennaro); in Bologna on October 4 (San Petronio); in Trieste on November 3 (San Giusto); and in Milan on December 7 (Saint Ambrose). Venice's feast of Saint Mark is April 25, the same as Liberation Day, so the Madonna della Salute on November 21 makes up for the lost holiday.

▮ MAIL

The Italian mail system has a bad reputation but has become noticeably more efficient in recent times with some privatization. Allow from 7 to 15 days for mail to get to the United States. Receiving mail in Italy, especially packages, can take weeks, usually due to customs (not postal) delays.

Most post offices are open Monday–Saturday 9–12:30; central post offices are open weekdays 9–6:30, Saturday 9–12:30 (some until 6:30). On the last day of the month, post offices close at midday. You can buy stamps at tobacco shops as well as post offices.

Posta Prioritaria (for regular letters and packages) is the name for standard postage. It guarantees delivery within Italy in three to five business days and abroad in five to six working days. The more expensive express delivery, *Postacelere* (for larger letters and packages), guarantees one-day delivery to most places in Italy and three- to five-day delivery abroad. The postal service has no control over customs, however, which makes international delivery estimates meaningless.

Mail sent as Posta Prioritaria to the United States costs €0.85 for up to 20 grams, €1.50 for 21–50 grams, and €1.85 for 51–100 grams. Mail sent as Postacelere to the United States costs €43–€50 for up to 500 grams.

Other package services to check are Quick Pack Europe, for delivery within Europe; and EMS Express Mail Service, a global three- to five-day service for letters and packages that can be less expensive than Postacelere.

Two-day mail is generally available during the week in all major cities and at popular resorts via UPS and Federal Express. Service is reliable; a Federal Express letter to the United States costs about €35. If your hotel can't assist you, try an Internet café, many of which also offer two-day mail services using major carriers.

SHIPPING PACKAGES

You can ship parcels only via air, which takes about two weeks. If you have purchased antiques, ceramics, or other objects, ask if the vendor will do the shipping for you; in most cases this is a possibility, and preferable, because they have experience with these kinds of shipments. If so, ask if the article will be insured against breakage. When shipping a package out of Italy, it is virtually impossible to find an overnight delivery option—the fastest delivery time is 48 to 72 hours, though this will not include any time your shipment might spend in customs.

▮ MONEY

Prices vary from region to region and are substantially lower in the country than in the cities. Of Italy's major cities, Venice and Milan are by far the most expensive. Resorts such as Portofino and Cortina d'Ampezzo cater to wealthy people and charge top prices. Good values can be had in the scenic Trentino–Alto Adige region of the Dolomites and in Umbria and the Marches. With a few exceptions, southern Italy and Sicily also offer bargains for those who do their homework before they leave home.

Prices throughout this guide are given for adults. Substantially reduced fees are almost always available for children, students, and senior citizens from the EU; citizens of non-EU countries rarely get discounts, but be sure to inquire before you purchase your tickets because this situation is constantly changing.

▮**TIP→** Banks never have every foreign currency on hand, and it may take as long as a week to order. If you're planning to exchange funds before leaving home, don't wait until the last minute.

ATMS AND BANKS

An ATM (*bancomat* in Italian) is the easiest way to get euros in Italy. There are numerous ATMs in large cities and small towns, as well as in airports and train stations. They are not common in places such as grocery stores. Be sure to **memorize your PIN in numbers,** as ATM keypads in Italy don't usually display letters. Check with your bank to confirm that you have an international PIN (*codice segreto*) that will be recognized in the countries you are visiting, to find out your maximum daily withdrawal allowance, and to learn what your bank's fee is for withdrawing money.

■**TIP→** Be aware that PINs beginning with a 0 (zero) tend to be rejected in Italy.

Your own bank may charge a fee for using ATMs abroad or charge for the cost of conversion from euros to dollars. Nevertheless, you can usually get a better rate of exchange at an ATM than you will at a currency-exchange office or even when changing money inside a bank with a teller. Extracting funds as you need them is a safer option than carrying around a large amount of cash. Finally, it's a good idea to obtain more than one card that can be used for cash withdrawal, in case something happens to your main one.

CREDIT CARDS

Throughout this guide, the following abbreviations are used: **AE,** American Express; **DC,** Diners Club; **MC,** Master-Card; and **V,** Visa.

It's a good idea to **inform your credit-card company before you travel,** especially if you're going abroad and don't travel internationally often. Otherwise, the credit-card company might put a hold on your card owing to unusual activity—not a good thing halfway through your trip. Record all your credit-card numbers—as well as the phone numbers to call if your cards are lost or stolen—in a safe place, so you're prepared should something go wrong. MasterCard and Visa have general numbers you can call (collect if you're abroad) if your card is lost, but you're better off calling the number of your issuing bank, because MasterCard and Visa generally just transfer you to your bank; your bank's number is usually printed on your card.

Although it's usually cheaper (and safer) to use a credit card abroad for large purchases (so you can cancel payments or be reimbursed if there's a problem), note that some credit-card companies *and* the banks that issue them add substantial percentages to all foreign transactions, whether they're in a foreign currency or not. Check on these fees before leaving home, so there won't be any surprises when you get the bill. Because of the exorbitant fees, avoid using your credit card for ATM withdrawals or cash advances (use a debit or cash card instead).

■**TIP→** Before you charge something, ask the merchant whether or not he or she plans to do a dynamic currency conversion (DCC). In such a transaction the credit-card processor (shop, restaurant, or hotel, not Visa or MasterCard) converts the currency and charges you in dollars. In most cases you'll pay the merchant a 3% fee for this service in addition to any credit-card company and issuing-bank foreign-transaction surcharges.

Dynamic currency conversion programs are becoming increasingly widespread. Merchants who participate in them are supposed to ask whether you want to be charged in dollars or the local currency, but they don't always do so. And even if they do offer you a choice, they may well avoid mentioning the additional surcharges. The good news is that you *do* have a choice. And if this practice really gets your goat, you can avoid it entirely thanks to American Express; with its cards, DCC simply isn't an option.

MasterCard and Visa are preferred by Italian merchants, but American Express is usually accepted in popular tourist destinations. Credit cards aren't accepted everywhere, though; if you want to pay with a credit card in a small shop, hotel, or restaurant, it's a good idea to make your intentions known early on.

Reporting Lost Cards American Express (☎ 800/268–9824 in U.S., 336/393–1111 collect from abroad ⊕ www.americanexpress.com.

com). **Diners Club** (☎ 800/234-6377 in U.S., 303/799-1504 collect from abroad ⊕ www. dinersclub.com). **MasterCard** (☎ 800/627-8372 in U.S., 636/722-7111 collect from abroad ⊕ www.mastercard.com). **Visa** (☎ 800/847-2911 in U.S., 410/581-9994 collect from abroad, 800/819014 in Italy ⊕ www. visa.com).

CURRENCY AND EXCHANGE

The euro is the main unit of currency in Italy, as well as in 12 other European countries. Under the euro system there are 100 *centesimi* (cents) to the euro. There are coins valued at 1, 2, 5, 10, 20, and 50 centesimi as well as 1 and 2 euros. There are seven notes: 5, 10, 20, 50, 100, 200, and 500 euros.

At this writing, 1 euro was worth about 1.41 U.S. dollars.

Post offices exchange currency at good rates, but you will rarely find an employee who speaks English, so be prepared. (Writing your request can help in these cases.)

■**TIP→** Even if a currency-exchange booth has a sign promising no commission, rest assured that there's some kind of huge, hidden fee. You're almost always better off getting foreign currency at an ATM or exchanging money at a bank.

▌PASSPORTS AND VISAS

U.S. citizens need only a valid passport to enter Italy for stays of up to 90 days.

PASSPORTS

Although somewhat costly, a U.S. passport is relatively simple to obtain and is valid for 10 years. You must apply in person if you're getting a passport for the first time; if your previous passport was lost, stolen, or damaged; or if your previous passport has expired and was issued more than 15 years ago or when you were under 16. All children under 18 must appear in person to apply for or renew a passport. Both parents must accompany any child under 14 (or send a notarized statement with their permission) and provide proof of their relationship to the child.

There are 13 regional passport offices, as well as 7,000 passport acceptance facilities in post offices, public libraries, and other governmental offices. If you're renewing a passport, you can do so by mail. Forms are available at passport acceptance facilities and online.

The cost to apply for a new passport is $100 for adults, $85 for children under 16; renewals are $75. Allow six weeks for processing, both for first-time passports and renewals. For an expediting fee of $60 you can reduce this time to about two weeks. If your trip is less than two weeks away, you can get a passport even more rapidly by going to a passport office with the necessary documentation. Private expediters can get things done in as little as 48 hours, but charge hefty fees for their services.

■**TIP→** Before your trip, make two copies of your passport's data page (one for someone at home and another for you to carry separately). Or scan the page and e-mail it to someone at home and/or yourself.

VISAS

When staying for 90 days or less, U.S. citizens are not required to obtain a visa prior to traveling to Italy. If you plan to travel or live in Italy or the European Union for longer than 90 days, you must acquire a valid visa from the Italian consulate serving your state *before you leave the United States*. Plan ahead because the process of obtaining a visa will take at least 30 days, and the Italian government does not accept visa applications submitted by visa expediters.

U.S. Passport Information U.S. Department of State (☎ 877/487-2778 ⊕ www.travel.state. gov/passport).

U.S. Passport Expediters A. Briggs Passport & Visa Expeditors (☎ 800/806-0581 or 202/338-0111 ⊕ www.abriggs.com). **American Passport Express** (☎ 800/455-5166 ⊕ www.americanpassport.com). **Passport Express** (☎ 800/362-8196 ⊕ www. passportexpress.com). **Travel Document Systems** (☎ 800/874-5100 or 202/638-3800 *[additional offices in New York and San Francisco]* ⊕ *www.traveldocs.com).* **Travel the World Visas** (☎ *866/886–8472 or 202/223–8822* ⊕ *www.world-visa.com).*

▍TAXES

A 10% V.A.T. (value-added tax) is included in the rate at all hotels except those at the upper end of the range.

No tax is added to the bill in restaurants. A service charge of approximately 10%–15% is often added to your check; in some cases a service charge is included in the prices.

The V.A.T. is 20% on clothing, wine, and luxury goods. On consumer goods it's already included in the amount shown on the price tag (look for the phrase "IVA inclusa"), whereas on services it may not be; feel free to confirm. Because you are not a European citizen, if your purchases in a single transaction total more than €155, you may be entitled to a refund of the V.A.T.

When making a purchase, ask whether the merchant gives refunds—not all stores do, nor are they required to. If they do, they'll help you fill out the V.A.T. refund form, which you'll submit to a company that will issue you the refund in the form of cash, check, or credit-card adjustment.

As you leave the country (or, if you're visiting several European Union countries, on leaving the EU), present your merchandise and the form to customs officials, who will stamp it. After you're through passport control, take the stamped form to a refund-service counter for an on-the-spot refund (the quickest and easiest option). You may also mail it to the address on the form (or on the envelope with it) after you arrive home, but processing time can be long, especially if you request a credit-card adjustment. Note that in larger cities the cash refund can be obtained at in-town offices prior to departure; just ask the merchant or check the envelope for local office addresses.

Global Refund is the largest V.A.T.-refund service with 225,000 affiliated stores and more than 700 refund counters at major airports and border crossings. Its refund form, called a Tax Free Check, is the most common across the European continent. Premier Tax Free is another company that represents more than 70,000 merchants worldwide. Look for their logos in store windows.

V.A.T. Refunds Global Refund (☎ *800/566–9828* ⊕ *www.globalrefund.com).* **Premier Tax Free** (☎ *905/542–1710* ⊕ *www.premiertaxfree. com).*

▍TIME

Italy is in the Central European Time Zone (CET). From March to October it institutes Daylight Saving Time. Italy is 6 hours ahead of U.S. Eastern Standard Time, 1 hour ahead of Great Britain, 10 hours behind Sydney, and 12 hours behind Auckland. Like the rest of Europe, Italy uses the 24-hour (or "military") clock, which means that after noon you continue counting forward: 13:00 is 1 PM, 23:30 is 11:30 PM.

▍TIPPING

In restaurants a service charge of 10% to 15% may appear on your check. If so, it's not necessary to leave an additional tip. If service is not included, leave a tip of up to 10%. Always leave your tip in cash, even if there's a line item on your credit-card slip for a tip (otherwise the server will never see it). Tip checkroom attendants €1 per person and restroom attendants €0.50 (more in expensive hotels and restaurants). In major cities, tip €0.50 or more for table service in cafés. At a hotel bar, tip €1 and up for a round or two of drinks.

Italians rarely tip taxi drivers, which is not to say that you shouldn't. A euro or two is appreciated, particularly if the driver helps with luggage. Service-station attendants are tipped only for special services; give them €1 for checking your tires. Railway and airport porters charge a fixed rate per bag. Tip an additional €0.25 per person, more if the porter is helpful. Give a barber €1–€1.50 and a hairdresser's assistant €1.50–€4 for a shampoo or cut, depending on the type of establishment.

On sightseeing tours, tip guides about €1.50 per person for a half-day group tour, more if they are especially knowledgeable. In monasteries and other sights where admission is free, a contribution (€0.50–€1) is expected.

In hotels, give the *portiere* (concierge) about 10% of the bill for services, or €2.50–€5 for help with dinner reservations and such. Leave the chambermaid about €0.75 per day, or about €4.50–€5 a week in a moderately priced hotel; tip a minimum of €1 for valet or room service. In an expensive hotel, double these amounts; tip doormen €0.50 for calling a cab and €1.50 for carrying bags to the check-in desk and bellhops €1.50–€2.50 for carrying your bags to the room.

∎ TOURS

Guided tours are a good option when you don't want to do it all yourself. You travel along with a group (sometimes large, sometimes small), stay in prebooked hotels, eat with your fellow travelers (the cost of meals may or may not be included in the price of your tour), and follow a schedule. Not all guided tours are an if-it's-Tuesday-this-must-be-Belgium experience, however. A knowledgeable guide can take you places that you might never discover on your own, and you may be pushed to see more than you would have otherwise. Tours aren't for everyone, but they can be just the thing for trips to places where making travel arrangements is difficult or time-consuming, particularly when you don't speak the language.

Whenever you book a guided tour, find out what's included and what isn't. A "land-only" tour includes all your travel (by bus, in most cases) in the destination, but not necessarily your flights to and from or even within it. Also, in most cases prices in tour brochures don't include fees and taxes. You'll also want to review how much free as opposed to organized time you'll have, and see if that meets with your personal preferences. Remember, too, that you'll be expected to tip your guide (in cash) at the end of the tour.

Even when planning independent travel, keep in mind that every province and city in Italy has tour guides licensed by the government. Some are eminently qualified in relevant fields such as architecture and art history and are a pleasure to spend time with; others have simply managed to pass the test and have weaker interpersonal skills. Lots of private guides have Web sites: check online and in travel forums for recommendations. Best to book before you leave home, especially for popular destinations. Tourist offices and hotel concierges can also provide the names of knowledgeable local guides and the rates for certain services. When hiring on the spot, ask about their background and qualifications and make sure you can understand each other. Tipping is always appreciated, but never obligatory, for local guides.

Recommended Generalists Abercrombie & Kent (☎ 800/554–7016 ⊕ *www.abercrombiekent.com*). **CIE Tours International** (☎ 800/243–8687 +353 1/703 0888, in Ireland ⊕ *www.cietours.com*). **Maupin Tour** (☎ 800/255–4266 ⊕ *www.maupintour.com*). **Perillo Tours** (☎ 800/431–1515 ⊕ *www.perillotours.com*). **Travcoa** (☎ 800/992–2005 ⊕ *www.travcoa.com*).

Biking and Hiking Tour Contacts Backroads (☎ 800/462–2848 ⊕ *www.backroads.com*). **Butterfield & Robinson** (☎ 866/551–9090 ⊕ *www.butterfield.com*). **Ciclismo Classico** (☎ 800/866–7314 ⊕ *www.ciclismoclassico.com*). **Genius Loci Travel** (☎ +39 089 791 896 ⊕ *www.genius-loci.it*). **Italian Connection** (☎ 800/462–7911 ⊕ *www.italian-connection.com*).

Culinary Tour Contact Epiculinary (🖥 888/380–9010 ⊕ www.epiculinary.com).

Golf Tour Contact Rosso Soave (🖥 +39 055/2305210 ⊕ www.rossosoave.com/ GolfETuscany.html).

Volunteer Programs Elderhostel (🖥 800/454–5768 ⊕ www.elderhostel.com).

Wine Tour Contacts Cellar Tours (🖥 310 928 7559 ⊕ www.cellartours.com). **Food & Wine Trails** (🖥 800/367–5348 ⊕ www. foodandwinetrails.com).

▌ TRIP INSURANCE

Comprehensive trip insurance is valuable if you're booking an expensive or complicated trip (particularly to an isolated region) or if you're booking far in advance. Comprehensive policies typically cover trip cancellation and interruption, letting you cancel or cut your trip short because of illness, or, in some cases, acts of terrorism in your destination. Such policies usually also cover evacuation and medical care. (For trips abroad you should have at least medical and medical evacuation coverage. With a few exceptions, Medicare does not provide coverage abroad, nor does regular health insurance.) Some also cover you for trip delays because of bad weather or mechanical problems as well as for lost or delayed luggage.

Another type of coverage to consider is financial default—that is, when your trip is disrupted because a tour operator, airline, or cruise line goes out of business. Generally you must buy this when you book your trip or shortly thereafter, and it's available to you only if your operator isn't on a list of excluded companies.

Many travel insurance policies have exclusions for preexisting conditions as a cause for cancellation. Most companies waive those exclusions, however, if you take out your policy within a short period (which varies by company) after the first payment toward your trip.

Always read the fine print of your policy to make sure that you're covered for the risks that most concern you. Compare several policies to be sure you're getting the best price and range of coverage available.

Insurance Comparison Info Insure My Trip (🖥 800/487–4722 ⊕ www.insuremytrip.com). **Square Mouth** (🖥 800/240–0369 or 727/564–9203 ⊕ www.squaremouth.com).

Comprehensive Insurers Access America (🖥 800/284–8300 ⊕ www.accessamerica.com). **CSA Travel Protection** (🖥 800/711–1197 ⊕ www.csatravelprotection.com). **HTH Worldwide** (🖥 610/254–8700 ⊕ www.hthworldwide. com). **Travel Guard** (🖥 800/826–4919 ⊕ www.travelguard.com). **Travelex Insurance** (🖥 800/228–9792 ⊕ www.travelexinsurance.com). **Travel Insured International** (🖥 800/243–3174 ⊕ www.travelinsured.com).

INDEX

PHOTO CREDITS

1, Paul D'Innocenzo. 2-3, PCL/Alamy. 5, Javier Larrea/age fotostock. Chapter 1: Experience Italy: 8-9, SIME s.a.s/eStock Photo. 12, Ant Clausen/Shutterstock. 14, Albo/Shutterstock. 15 (left), Antonio Petrone/Shutterstock. 15 (right), vario images GmbH & Co.KG/Alamy. 16 (left), Ronald Sumners/Shutterstock. 16 (top center), Victoria German/Shutterstock. 16 (top right), Knud Nielsen/Shutterstock. 16 (bottom right), pxlar8/Shutterstock. 17 (top center), Thomas M Perkins/Shutterstock. 17 (top right), Ivonne Wierink/Shutterstock. 17 (bottom right), Rostislav Glinsky/Shutterstock. 18, italianestro/Shutterstock. 19 (left), Thomas M Perkins/Shutterstock. 19 (right), Yanta/Shutterstock. 20, Eric Gevaert/Shutterstock. 21, Stefano Cellai/age fotostock. 24, Peter Clark/Shutterstock. 25 (left), Olav Wildermann/Shutterstock. 25 (right), Steven Lee/Shutterstock. 27, Gina Sanders/Shutterstock. 28, Robert Harding Picture Library Ltd/Alamy. Chapter 2: Rome: 29, Angelo Campus. 30 (top) and 31, Paul D'Innocenzo. 30 (bottom), Angelo Campus. 32 and 35, Angelo Campus. 36 and 37 (bottom), Jono Pandolfi. 37 (top), Angelo Campus. 41 (left), Justin D. Paola. 41 (right), Edis Jurcys/age fotostock. 42-43 (bottom), Justin D. Paola. 43 (top left), Joe Viesti/viestiphoto.com. 43 (top right), Joe Viesti/viestiphoto.com. 44-45 (bottom), Justin D. Paola. 45 (top left), Rome Tourist Board. 45 (top right), Atlantide S.N.C./age fotostock. 47 (left), Chie Ushio. 47 (right), Joe Viesti/viestiphoto.com. 49 (left), Chie Ushio. 49 (right), Corbis. 59, Anthony Majanlahti. 70, Paul D'Innocenzo. 72-73 (top), SuperStock. 74, Russell Mountford/age fotostock. 76-79, Dave Drapak. 91, Art Kowalsky/Alamy. 101, Russell Mountford/age fotostock. 114 (top left), Hassler Roma. 114 (top right), Hotel Scalinata. 114 (center left), Hotel Eden. 114 (center right), Relais Le Clarisse. 114 (bottom left), Dominique Bollinger. 114 (bottom right), Yes Hotel. 125, Alvaro Leiva/age fotostock. Chapter 3: Between Rome & Florence: 131, Atlantide S.N.C./age fotostock. 132, Tommaso di Girolamo. 133 (top), Walter Bibikow/age fotostock. 133 (bottom), Danilo Donadon/age fotostock. 134, Atlantide S.N.C./age fotostock. 135, CuboImages srl/Alamy. 136, Andre Jenny/Alamy. 144, B&Y Photography/Alamy. 145 (top), MEHMET OZCAN/iStockphoto. 145 (bottom), Doco Dalfiano/age fotostock. 149, Joe Viesti/Viestiphoto.com. 157, Atlantide S.N.C./age fotostock. 158, Picture Finders/age fotostock. 159 (all), Fototeca ENIT. 160-161, Tommaso di Girolamo/age fotostock. 162, Atlantide S.N.C./age fotostock. 166, Duncan Campbell/iStockphoto. 170, David Noton Photography/Alamy. 176, Javier Larrea/age fotostock. 176 (inset), Photodisc. 178 (top and middle), Vittorio Sciosia/viestiphoto.com. 178 (bottom), Bruno Morandi/age fotostock. 182, Bon Appetit/Alamy. 183 (top), Marco Scataglini/age fotostock. 183 (bottom), Nico Tondini/age fotostock. 193, Photodisc. 201 (left), Black Rooster Consortium. 201 (top right), Cephas Picture Library/Alamy. 201 (middle right), Adriano Bacchella/viestiphoto.com. 201 (bottom right), Cephas Picture Library/Alamy. 202 (right), Cephas Picture Library/Alamy. 203 (top left), Chuck Pefley/Alamy. 203 (top right), Jon Arnold Images/Alamy. 204 (top left), CuboImages srl/Alamy. 204 (middle right), Cephas Picture Library/Alamy. 204 (bottom), Black Rooster Consortium. 206 (left), Steve Dunwell/age fotostock. 206 (top right), IML Image Group Ltd/Alamy. 206 (bottom right), www.stradavinonobile.it. 207, Guven Guner/Alamy. Chapter 4: Florence: 209, alysta/Shutterstock. 210 (top), Ronald Sumners/Shutterstock. 210 (bottom), PhotoDisc. 211, Bertrand Collet/Shutterstock. 212, Luciano Mortula/Shutterstock. 213, Planet Art. 215, Timur Kulgarin/Shutterstock. 216, CuboImages srl/Alamy. 217 (top), Paolo Gallo/Alamy. 217 (bottom), Sue Wilson/Alamy. 226–27, Wojtek Buss/age fotostock. 229 (top), eye35.com/Alamy. 229 (inset), Alfio Giannotti/viestiphoto.com. 229 (bottom), Rough Guides/Alamy. 230 (top left), Mary Evans Picture Library/Alamy. 230 (top right), Library of Congress Prints and Photographs Division (LC-USZ62-10534). 230 (bottom), Bruno Morandi/age fotostock. 232, Wojtek Buss/age fotostock. 247 (left and right), Classic Vision/age fotostock. 247 (center), SuperStock/age fotostock. 248 (left), Chie Ushio. 248 (right), Planet Art. 249 (top), Classic Vision/age fotostock. 249 (center),

NOTES

NOTES

NOTES

ABOUT OUR WRITERS

Hailing from Washington, D.C., Lynda Albertson relocated to Italy in 2003. From her base in Rome she writes articles on food, wine, and travel. Her book *The Misadventures of an Italian Girl in Italy* was published in the United Kingdom in 2010. The updater of our Rome shopping section, Lynda has an uncanny knowledge of where to purchase absolute necessities, from truffle oil to that perfect Piranesi print.

After her first Italian coffee and her first Italian *bacio* in 1999, Nicole Arriaga headed to the Eternal City to work on her master's degree at Rome's La Sapienza University, write for *The American*, and work for American Study Abroad. She updated the Rome introduction and Where to Stay sections.

After completing his master's degree in art history, Peter Blackman, updater of the Tuscany section, settled permanently in Italy in 1986. Since then he's worked as a biking and walking tour guide. When he's not leading a trip, you'll find Peter at home in Florence.

Martin Wilmot Bennett's extensive background in Italian art and civilization made him a natural to update the Rome Exploring section. A major contributor to *Fodor's Rome* and a graduate of Cambridge University, he teaches at Rome's University of Tor Vergata.

Rome-based Erica Firpo writes for an array of publications, including *National Geographic Traveler and The American. She has written* a series of restaurant guides that includes *Rome Little Black Book,* and she tracks life in modern Rome in her blog, www.moscerina.com. For this book she updated the Nightlife and Arts section of the Rome chapter.

Dana Klitzberg trained in top restaurant kitchens in New York and Rome and is owner of Blu Aubergine (*www.bluaubergine.com*), through which she caters, instructs, and writes about food. She updated the Where to Eat section of the Rome chapter.

Bruce Leimsidor studied Renaissance literature and art history at Swarthmore College and Princeton University, and in addition to his scholarly works, he has published articles on political and social issues in the *International Herald Tribune* and the *Frankfurter Allgemeine Zeitung.* He lives in Venice, where he teaches at the university, works for the municipality, collects 17th- and 18th-century drawings, and is rumored to make the best *pasta e fagioli* in town. He updated the Veneto section.

Nan McElroy is the author of the palm-size, purely practical *Italy: Instructions for Use.* (The series also includes France and Greece.) She traveled throughout Italy before relocating to Venice in 2004, where she writes *www.livingveniceblog. com* and publishes the Vap Map downloadable vaporetto guide. Nan is also an AIS sommelier who conducts wine tastings and an avid practitioner of the *voga alla veneta*—traditional Venetian rowing. She updated the Venice chapter and the Milan section.

Florence and Emilia–Romagna updater Patricia Rucidlo holds master's degrees in Italian Renaissance history and art history, and after a year of arduous study earned her license to be a tour guide in Florence. When she's not extolling the virtues of a Pontormo masterpiece or angrily defending the Medici, she's leading tours and catering private dinner parties.

Jonathan Willcocks, a Brit by birth with degrees in French and English literature from the Sorbonne, teaches language, literature, and translation at the university in Perugia. He updated the Umbria coverage.